Approaches to the Study
of Politics

Approaches to the Study of Politics

BERNARD SUSSER

Bar Ilan University
Ramat Gan, Israel

Macmillan Publishing Company
New York

Maxwell Macmillan Canada
Toronto

Editor: Bruce Nichols
Production Supervisor: Publication Services
Production Manager: Aliza Greenblatt
Cover Designer: Jane Edelstein
This book was set in Aster and Electra by Publication Services
and was printed and bound by Arcata Graphics.

Macmillan Publishing Company
866 Third Avenue, New York, New York 10022

Maxwell Macmillan Canada, Inc.
1200 Eglinton Avenue East
Suite 200
Don Mills, Ontario M3C 3M1

Library of Congress Cataloging-in-Publication Data
Susser, Bernard, 1942-
    Approaches to the study of politics / Bernard Susser.
        p. cm.
    Includes bibliographical references and index.
    ISBN 0-02-418710-0
    1. Political science.   I. Title.
JA71.S85   1992
    320–dc20   91-691
                                                            CIP

To My Son Yair
With Love

PREFACE

Like individuals, academic disciplines have biographies. They take faltering first steps, mature, have crises, make fresh starts, suffer disappointments—in some cases they even die. At any given point in this odyssey of development, what they are is what they have become over time. And understanding what they have become is impossible without understanding what they have been.

Political science has a particularly rich past. It reaches back at least to the time of Plato and Aristotle. Subsequent to the classical era, the study of political matters formed a central part of the medieval curriculum, and it retained this centrality—with the inevitable ups and downs that overtake all human pursuits—into the modern era. When we embark on an exploration of how politics is studied at the end of the twentieth century, we are, therefore, in the position of heirs who have come into a lavish inheritance.

Other courses, particularly those that address the history of political thought, deal with the discipline's main concerns prior to the twentieth century. But the chronicle of contemporary political science, particularly its development since World War II, constitutes one of the most turbulent and fascinating chapters in its long history. It is a period marked by high hopes and revolutionary change, a period that has witnessed a broadening of the discipline's subject matter and a striking reorientation in its methods and techniques. But it is also a period characterized by deep rifts and heated battles. The most basic questions regarding what political science should be and what political scientists should be doing were fiercely, sometimes venomously, debated. And the debate, although somewhat muted by the passing years and the onset of fatigue, will, no doubt, continue into the future.

As it is now studied in thousands of universities worldwide, political science is not the same discipline that answered to that name a few decades ago. The very courses that are taught in political science departments have changed substantially. Had you studied political science, say, in the 1920s or 1930s, it is unlikely that courses in political sociology or political psychology would have been offered. Nor would you have been likely to find course offerings in research methods and statistics. Courses in modernization and development, in African or Asian politics, would have been missing as well. It is even doubtful that a contemporary staple such as comparative politics would have been listed in a 1920 syllabus. Instead, you would have found titles such as "Public Law and Government" and histories galore of diplomacy and political institutions.

It is the object of this text to provide an introduction to post–World War II schools of political science. While most courses in politics study this or that political reality, here prior and more basic questions are addressed, such as (1) how should the study of politics proceed? (2) what are the dominant characteristics of politics and which approaches are relevant to them? (3) how do approaches to the study of politics relate to the central issues raised by the philosophy of science? and (4) what have each of the examined approaches contributed to the knowledge that political science seeks?

I have aimed this text* at courses on the scope and methods of political science or on approaches to political analysis, or at introductory courses for political science majors. It traces the development of postwar political science through an examination of its main schools, research programs, and professional methods. Each approach to the study of politics is analyzed in a general, orienting essay designed to give a broad overview of the subject. This essay is followed by key, classic readings that aim to provide a firsthand sense of the approach under study. A short bibliography of relevant literature closes each section.

No student majoring in political science today can make sense of the literature without understanding the key methodological contributions of its most influential practitioners. Nor can today's students ignore the debates over behavioralism, structure-functionalism, or rational choice theory. Hopefully, the introductory essays combined with the readings will help guide students on a fascinating intellectual journey.

---

*Much of this book is based on a written course prepared for the Open University of Israel.

CONTENTS

INTRODUCTION

From classical times until the dawning of the modern era, the study of politics was overwhelmingly philosophical in character. It was understood to be a normative and ethical discipline, a practical branch of moral philosophy. By way of illustration, premodern political study was far more interested in the question "what is justice?" than in the quite different query "what do different societies perceive to be just?" or "how important are considerations of justice, as opposed to consideration of interest, in formulating public policy?" Like much of premodern thought, it had little interest in empirical questions or empirical investigation; its concerns and style were markedly speculative and cerebral. The staples with which it concerned itself included issues such as the nature of the best state, the proper relation between spiritual and mundane human goals, the ultimate objects of political life, the nature of man as a political creature, and the implications of human nature for a suitable ordering of the state. In the words of the British political philosopher Michael Oakeshott, it was concerned with the relation between "politics and eternity."

To be sure, there have always been those who broke ranks with the prevailing ethos. Aristotle and Machiavelli, for example, are notable for their careful studies of the actual political process. Nevertheless, it was not until the fairly recent past that the horizon of political study expanded, on a significant scale, beyond the limits of the philosophical. One important element of this extension was due to the growth, during the last three centuries, of legal-constitutional and historical schools of thought in Europe. These approaches added the richness of juridical and developmental perspectives to the philosophical tradition of political inquiry. States were studied in terms of their "public law," their constitutional charters, and their formal structures. Their institutional evolution, the precedents and antecedents that accounted for a state's unique historical development, also underwent serious probing.

These changes, however, are relatively small when compared to the massive transformation that the study of politics has undergone in the twentieth century, particularly its second half. Under the influence of the scientific revolution and particularly in the light of its spectacular successes in the natural sciences, social scientists began to dream of their own breakthrough, of their own Newton who would liberate them from the thrall of imprecision and inconclusiveness. Rumblings of this aspiration were already audible in the early nineteenth century (in the work of Auguste Comte, for example), but it was not until the mid-twentieth century that the project of empirically and scientifically reconstructing the social sciences began in earnest.

Four decades later, this project is not exactly dead, but it is certainly tarnished. The Newton-awaiters have dwindled to a small band of increasingly marginal stalwarts. Although the study of politics will surely never be the same again, it also seems unlikely ever to lose its more tentative, contextual, value-based character. Perhaps the most important change in the discipline of political science over the past two decades—even if it is a subtle and not particularly dramatic one—has been the growing recognition that this departure from the natural sciences is not altogether a bad thing.

Whatever will be the eventual outcome of political science's scientific aspirations, the academic energy it unleashed was monumental. New approaches luxuriated, fresh avenues of inquiry were explored, and novel methods and techniques proliferated. In the short span of some twenty years, from 1950 to 1970, most approaches to the study of politics that are still with us today received their definitive formulation. Systems analysis, functionalism, cybernetic theories, game theories, economic theories, psychological approaches, and so on, all belong to this prolific period. The passing years have been kinder to some than to others, but for the most part these approaches have enjoyed a noteworthy resilience. There is therefore something of a retrospective character—a focus on the 1950s and 1960s—that inevitably attaches itself to the study of contemporary approaches to political science.

Certainly nothing in the above discussion is meant to suggest that since those fertile years the study of politics has stood still (a laughable thought). It is intended only to alert the reader to what is an important historical phenomenon, a clustering of creativity that dominates the intellectual horizon. Since those fruitful times, approaches have been developed, perfected, criticized, and abandoned. But with a few notable exceptions—such as "the return of the state" theorists and their "corporatist" allies—new approaches have failed to make significant inroads. *

Wherever possible, alongside a description of the "classic" formulation of an approach (usually belonging to the 1950s and 1960s), I have attempted to note some of the directions that it has subsequently taken. The criticisms that have been leveled against it, as well as the prospects for its future, are also explored. For whatever the date of their birth, these approaches are hardly history; they remain the basic tools that today's political scientists utilize in practicing their craft.

---

*Sociobiology has been thought too eccentric, insufficiently crystallized, and too far from the mainstream to become central to political analysis.

CHAPTER ONE

FROM BURGESS TO BEHAVIORALISM AND BEYOND

Early one morning in June 1880, a telegram awakened Professor John W. Burgess of Columbia University. It notified him that the trustees of Columbia College had ratified his plan to set up a School of Political Science. It was to be the first organized program in the United States for the training of scholars in politics.

In all fairness it should be remarked that a quasi-juristic discipline called *Staatswissenschaft* had long existed in German universities. Indeed, even during the Middle Ages the study of philosophic works on politics was quite common. But Burgess and Columbia had something different in mind. As opposed to political science as a traditional law-centered field or as a branch of didactic philosophy, the program instituted at Columbia promised to be quite revolutionary. It featured such unusual requirements as courses in statistics, geography, and economics and was based on the very antitraditional proposition that—as Burgess put it—politics should be studied by the very same method that "has been found so productive in the domain of Natural Science."[1]

To be sure, the program was a far cry from what is taught today in the Political Science department at Columbia—or for that matter in any of the thousands of departments worldwide bearing that name—but it is the closest thing to a historical beginning for modern political science. Quantitatively speaking (at the very least), Burgess's program can be counted a stunning success. Today the profession of political science teems with activity; it has well-organized and highly specialized subdisciplines, scores of journals, thousands of books and monographs published annually, and a veritable army of professional fellow travelers. Suffice it to say that no self-respecting university could consider being without its own tribe of political scientists.

Because our main concern here is not with history per se, we shall not follow the checkered course of political science during the period of more than a century that has elapsed since Burgess received his epochal telegram. Instead, we shall begin our analysis by racing ahead some seven and a half decades to the mid-1950s, when another revolutionary transformation was remaking the discipline. By focusing carefully on the intellectual fault lines that divided the professional community in the post–World War II years into rival and sometimes quite hostile camps, we will be in a good position to understand, on the one hand, the kind

3

of discipline into which political science had developed up to that point and, on the other, where substantial groups of dissatisfied practitioners wanted it to go. It will also allow us to make sense of some of the perennial issues that have periodically convulsed political science as a profession, issues that remain alive and relevant as the discipline enters the last decade of the twentieth century.

The rumblings of discontent could be heard in the early years of the century, and they continued a quasi-underground existence in the twenties and thirties. Writers such as Arthur F. Bentley, Charles Merriam, and Harold Lasswell, each in his own way, expressed disaffection with the kind of research that was prevalent within the political science community. Although their critiques derived from very different intellectual quarters, there was a common flavor to them all: they objected to a certain formalist, derivative, and obscure character that marred research into politics.

What was being studied, they complained, was not the actual rough-and-tumble public process in which individuals and groups struggle to achieve their ends in the cauldron of public life, but rather an anemic mixture of law, philosophy, and history. The study of power, which ought to have been recognized as the heart of the political process, was replaced by the study of the formal constitutional prerogatives accorded to this or that office. The interest groups that created the typical momentum of political give-and-take were given short shrift and once again the formal institutions of government were endlessly described and compared. The psychological motives, both individual and collective, that underpin the process of politics and create its manifest character were ignored in favor of speculative disquisitions on "virtue" and "justice" or learned descriptions recounting the historical evolution of laws, institutions, and ideas.

For despite the American attempt to break free of the legalist and theoretical way in which political life was studied in European academia, a great many of these traits persisted in dominating the discipline. Probably not least among the reasons for this tenacity was that it was entirely unclear what could be substituted for these time-honored approaches; that is, no one could say what a political science that was neither historical nor legal nor yet philosophical, would actually look like.

The answer to this question began to emerge just prior to World War II. New tools and novel methodological possibilities that had developed independently of political science became available for political research. Public opinion polling and survey research developed promisingly — encouraged especially by the need to organize and control the millions of men under arms. Mathematical statistics made impressive advances, and computer technology took its first faltering steps. The legacy of logical positivism together with the teachings of Max Weber, both so crucial for the growth of a scientific approach to politics, arrived in the

New World along with a host of émigré scholars who had fled war-torn Europe. Just as the world political arena expanded to include the newly emerging countries of (what has subsequently been called) the Third World—countries for which the narrowly institutional, legal, descriptive, Western-centered methods of traditional political science were singularly inappropriate—developments in the neighboring disciplines of anthropology and sociology rendered non-Western political systems intriguingly within our scholarly reach.

Although the new currents in political science did not all flow in a single direction or with similar intensity, the name "behavioralism"[2] became affixed to these novel approaches, lumping them all together as if they were a unit. In fact, at least two broad movements came under the behavioral rubric. The first aimed at transforming political studies into a veritable science. In the spirit of Burgess's call many decades earlier, his latter-day disciples urged students of politics to adopt natural scientific methods. They rejected the traditional approaches based on what they saw as inconclusive and prescientific speculation. If political science did not apply the rigorous methods of science, one behavioralist remarked, it might as well take up permanent cohabitation with literary criticism.[3]

The second current gave the movement its name. Politics, this school claimed, was not primarily about such formal structures as institutions, constitutions, and legislation. Its proper subject was the actual behavior of people in public life, whether this behavior took place within formal political structures or not. Political behavior was a dynamic struggle for public power that included a wide and extremely diverse series of phenomena, many of which were only obliquely related to institutions of governance narrowly conceived. It included, for example, the socialization of children into a political culture, the relationship between all manner of social characteristics (such as income, age, sex, education, and ethnicity) and political perceptions, the actual dynamics (not merely the prescribed manner) in which political decisions are made, the organization of groups to further their political interests, the relationship between political elites and the mass of citizens, and so on. There was, in short, far more to "politics" than its prebehavioral practitioners had imagined.[4]

Normally, the "scientific" and the "behavioral" elements challenging traditional political science acted as loyal allies. In the characteristic credos of the new political science that appeared regularly at the time, the two elements tended to be inextricably integrated. And yet it is not difficult to see—at least with the aid of retrospection—that they are quite distinct in their respective programs. It is possible, for example, to accept the need for a more dynamically behavioral, as opposed to a static and descriptive, political science while harboring serious reservations about the desirability or indeed the feasibility of a study of politics modeled on the natural sciences. Suffice it to say that in the postbehavioral era this erstwhile alliance between the two strands of behavioral revolution did not always remain intact.

It is a dangerous business to summarize the main tenets of a complex intellectual development like behavioralism, and hence a word of caution is in place. Invariably, such synopses err in being excessively orderly, clear-sighted, and single-voiced. Reducing the behavioral credo to a short checklist will not do justice to the great variety of viewpoints that prevail within the movement. Doubtless, some very central behavioral practitioners will object to this or that item as unrepresentative of their views. And, of course, they will be right. For example, some behavioralists understand the predictive capacity of political science as critical; for others it is a more questionable prospect (see item 1 below). Some would entirely banish research informed by value preferences; for others, values have a certain conditional legitimacy (see item 4 below). Indeed, whether value-freedom is possible and mandatory or whether it is only a call to researchers to do their very best to avoid bias is also a point of contention (see item 5 below). Still, whatever the pitfalls, it is imperative to present a number of broadly formulated elements that have tended to repeat themselves in the various treatments the subject has received.

1. The study of politics should aim at becoming a science capable of explanation and prediction. Such a political science is possible and within our reach even if its actual achievement must necessarily be a long-term goal. The rigorous search for regularities in political behavior is essential to the systematic development of political knowledge.
2. Political scientists must focus on phenomena that are empirically accessible—that is, phenomena that can be observed, charted, and measured. If individual and group behaviors lend themselves readily to this kind of study, institutions resist it. Institutions, to be properly analyzed, need to be understood as the sum total of the actions of the individuals and groups that constitute them.
3. The requirement that research be rigorous involves the need for the quantification of findings. Only such precise, mathematically stated findings can enable us to discover relations and regularities in political life.
4. Values cannot be established scientifically and are beyond the scope of legitimate research. No more than the natural sciences does political science have any proper concern with ethical questions. The "great issues" with which the political philosophers deal are therefore outside the ken of political science.
5. Political scientists should pursue their research without intruding their own value predilections. By following proper technique, by self-consciously criticizing their own procedures and analyses, they can progress toward the goal of eliminating those idiosyncratic elements that distort the objectivity of research. Although a great many behav-

ioralists would admit that absolute value-freedom is an unattainable goal, it remains for them the guiding principle of research.
6. Human behavior is a fluid whole and not easily compartmentalized. Political behavior is but a single form of behavior that we distinguish from other kindred forms of activity only by drawing conventional rather than essential boundaries. Consequently, political science should draw upon the techniques and skills that neighboring fields have developed; that is to say, it should strive toward a more interdisciplinary character.

On a more philosophic level, behavioralism adopted a number of critical propositions in regard to the nature of science. First, it rejected the argument—raised by a wide array of critics from traditionalists to Marxists—that the social sciences are unique in their methodological requirements and that they involve tools, cognitive skills, and practical operations different from those that are mandated by the natural sciences. There was only one way of doing science, they insisted, and asking for special indulgences in regard to the science of human behavior meant, in effect, denying its scientific status. This position is often referred to as "the methodological unity of the sciences."

Allied to this proposition is a second contention that goes under the title of "methodological individualism." Science, it is argued, has no place within it for "essences" or "wholes," that is, for those quasi-real entities that claim to combine the many concrete and accessible elements of sense experience into totalities that hover beyond our empirical reach. Reality can be apprehended only in its particularity, in its actual and specific manifestations. Those mystifications that refuse to translate themselves back into concrete experiences, that insist on being more than the sum of their constituent elements, decline thereby to submit to the rigorous discipline of science and render themselves outside the pale of scientifically verifiable discourse.

Those, for example, who contend that "society" entails more than the sum of its individual human parts, those for whom "the state" means more than government and its constituent organs, and those who speak of an essential "national character" without recognizing that this means no more than many individuals with individual characters, are guilty of a mystification typical of prescientific thought. In this connection, behavioralists like to recall a visitor to Oxford University who, after having been shown the libraries, the various colleges, the playing fields, the lecture halls, and the pubs, said to his host: "I have seen the libraries, colleges, fields, halls, and pubs, but where is Oxford University?"

By the early 1960s, behavioralism was no longer a minority voice fighting against an entrenched orthodoxy. According to Robert Dahl, one of the leading articulators of the new behavioral approach, it was already a successful revolution that could be spoken of in the past tense. It had succeeded in winning the sympathy of a young and enthusiastic cadre of scholars, and it was now in the process of creating the agenda for political science. Indeed, he boldly prophesied that behavioralism would grow to be so familiar and noncontroversial that it would become invisible as a special approach. Behavioralism, he believed,

> will gradually disappear. By this I mean only that it will slowly decay as a distinctive mood and outlook. For it will become, and in fact already is becoming, incorporated into the main body of the discipline. The behavioral mood will not disappear because it has failed. It will disappear rather because it has succeeded. As a separate, somewhat sectarian, slightly factional outlook it will be the first victim of its own triumph.[5]

The descriptive part of Dahl's assertions is indisputable. Behavioralism had become a major—many would say *the* major—approach within the political science community. On the other hand, his prediction that behavioralism would gradually become so unexceptionable as to be taken for granted is a much more complex issue to address—even though we are armed with the wisdom of hindsight. It is a question to which we will need to return at a later stage of our account.

What is certain, however, is that not long after Dahl made his glowing predictions about the future of behavioralism, its fortunes took a sharp turn for the worse. It became the object of severe criticism, criticism that for sheer quantity and intensity had no precedent in American academia. For this was not the decorous kind of criticism that normally attends any methodological innovation, but criticism with an unruly, often strident political edge to it. The environment out of which these impassioned criticisms emerged was fired by the student revolt, the Vietnam War resistance, and the black militancy of the 1960s. The intellectual ferment of those turbulent times penetrated deep into the political science community, created a set of research and value priorities that were difficult to reconcile with the behavioralist world view, and placed an indelible stamp on a generation of scholars who today constitute the mid-life backbone of the discipline.[6]

Criticisms of the behavioral outlook came from many different quarters, not all of them compatible, and we shall address many of them in the course of this introductory essay. Still, it can be said of virtually all the different forms of critique that there was a certain moral élan, a crusading, high-principled intensity that gave them their typical character. Probably most representative of this genre of critique is Christian Bay's essay, "Politics and Pseudopolitics: A Critical Evaluation of Some Behavioral Literature."[7]

Bay's primary objection to behavioralism is, in essence, quite simple: it asks the wrong questions. Or, perhaps more cautiously stated, Bay asserts that while behavioralism asks some legitimate questions, it ignores the most important of all questions. Behavioralists wish to purchase rigor, Bay complains, "at the price of excluding much of the meat and spirit of politics." Dahl, for example, speaks of "politics" as referring to "patterns of human relations that involve, to a significant extent, power, rule or authority." Insofar as it goes, this description cannot be faulted. It fails, however, in what it does not include: the *purpose* of political activity. Beyond referring to power, Bay states, politics should "refer to some conception of human welfare or the public good."

Not only do the behavioralists limit the scope of their inquiry exclusively to observable behavior—ignoring thereby the underlying moral purposes and human visions that animate political life—they also impoverish the criteria by which to judge empirical research itself. For if we exclude the empirically inaccessible standards that orient political activity toward human goals, how are we to judge whether our research has tackled significant or trivial issues? If politics shuns the realm of normative concerns and focuses exclusively on what is actually done in the context of power relationships, do we not, Bay asks accusingly, "disclaim all political significance to our work"?

While behavioralists are adept at dealing with policy questions in terms of cost, economy, alternatives, and so on, they refuse the challenge of assessing the goals to which the costs, economies, and alternatives are directed. They deal with a formal rationality of means, while declining to confront the substantive rationality of ends. They describe the needs that groups and individuals actually pursue, without addressing the authentic human needs that *ought* to lie at the basis of political activity. They consistently refuse, as a matter of methodological principle, to reflect on the political preferences and ideals that underlie all that they study, preferring instead to keep their eyes glued to the present, the immediate, and the accessible.

Ironically, Bay continues, their neglect of normative analysis does not prevent their work from being exploited for normative purposes. Even if behavioral political scientists struggle valiantly to leave their own value commitments outside their research, the real and present danger is that they will "unwittingly become the tool of other people's commitments." Their work, Bay admonishes in the spirit of the 1960s, may well "serve the irrational purposes of genteel bigotry in domestic policies or of paranoid jingoism and reckless gambling with our chances of survival in foreign policies." Because their research is ostensibly done in a value vacuum, the values of others—normally the dominant values of the society—will rush in to fill the void.

But this value vacuum in which behavioral research is said to be conducted is by no means hermetically sealed. Bay represented a large constituency of skeptics when he contended that values insinuate their way into research willy-nilly. By "natural and uninvestigated processes," the prevailing professional and social values percolate imperceptibly into all that is done. What emerges then is not a neutral political science, but one unaware of the value preferences that underlie its activities. By not directly confronting the normative assumptions of all political activity, behavioralists suffer the gamut of maladies all at once. First, despite protestations to the contrary, their work is based on values. Second, because they refuse to treat normative issues self-consciously, these issues surface only elusively and episodically, without system or order. Lastly, being fugitive presences, normative commitments are inevitably poor and banal, little more than ad hoc, inarticulate, and unexplored claims.

Bay believes that this ad hoc inarticulateness is most clearly present when behavioralists need to square their commitment to liberal democracy with their claims to value freedom. The result is a typical, even predictable, confusion. They write as if they want it both ways: "to be rigorously value-neutral and at the same time be impeccable champions of conventional pluralist democracy." They write positively about democracy as the most satisfactory of political arrangements, but never in so many words. They allow themselves to make normative judgments, but only when they are reasonably indeterminate and oblique. They affirm Western democracy with all necessary indirection, but fail to articulate or justify the value principles upon which this judgment is based.

Bay concludes his essay with a plea for a "humane" political science that unashamedly places the fulfillment of human needs at its center. Other critics, less overtly hortatory in their approach, have examined behavioralism's research commitments and found an underlying network of interrelated political preferences and ethical assumptions that, when pieced together, add up to a substantial world view. As Bay indicated (although only in a general way), the behavioral persuasion had a striking affinity to liberal-pluralist-individualist-democratic values, particularly as they were prevalent in the Anglo-American states.

Behavioralism's commitments to "methodological individualism" and "value-freedom," it was argued, involved considerably more than technical research directives. They led to certain clear substantive consequences of a "political" kind. Pluralism, for example, was the not-so-surprising result of a commitment to methodological individualism. If the world can be apprehended only in its specific manifestations, there is, of course, no sense in speaking of a "general structure of power" that broadly underlies political life. This is only a loose, mystified, and prescientific manner of avoiding rigorous, quantitative research. Science can only speak of specific individuals in specific roles making specific decisions; to go beyond the concrete and the specific was to enter a muddleheaded domain of elusively vague and scientifically nondemonstrable propositions.

But if the lens of behavioral analysis reveals a world with atomistic characteristics—that is, if it breaks down all wholes into their constituent parts—should we be surprised that the behavioralists regularly find a multiplicity of factors at work, a plurality of groups competing, an irreducible diversity of decisions that never add up to a social "totality." Focusing on specific decisions in specific contexts closes off the option that the "meaning" of the social process may lie in its integral wholeness, in its total structure. Research that begins with the assumption that such "wholes" are vacuous and slipshod notions has made a methodological commitment with political consequences. And, as was regularly pointed out—invariably linked to charges of bad faith—these consequences are entirely compatible with the very similar assumptions made by liberal pluralism.

Value freedom in political science was also alleged to have more than a merely technical scientific standing. Critics of behavioralism charged that it carried along with it an underlying conservative bias* in regard to both the kind of political thinking it sanctioned and the kind of political activity it encouraged. Behavioralism, with its narrowly empirical outlook, so it was argued, undermines our critical senses and dulls our moral imagination.

What is at stake is encapsulated in Dahl's stark description of the practical import of value freedom: "The empirical political scientist is concerned with what is, not with what ought to be." Thinking beyond the confines of the immediate and the actual to some more satisfactory reality violates the nonnormative bent of scientific research and precipitates the author into the less-than-enviable world of science fiction. If a theory fails to describe a reality accurately, it is always the theory that is at fault and not the reality—even if the theory describes the reality as it ought to be while the reality has strayed from the ideal through corruption or weakness.

In a sense, reality as it happens to be sets the outer limits to the behavioral imagination. Critical standards that derive from independent sources, that set the given into the context of the possible, that appreciate what *is* as contingent upon our will and design, have little place in a world constructed to behavioralist specifications. Reality-bound, noncritical research, whether it deliberately sets out to do so or not, is option-denying research. In the end, it underwrites the political world as it exists by denying the legitimacy of constructing alternatives to it.[8]

In this light, we are justified in asking—if only parenthetically and without pausing to attempt an exhaustive answer—an intriguing theoretical question. Are methodological commitments related solely to technical research procedures, or is there an important sense in which the method determines the matter? Does the choice of a method decisively affect the matter that is under study? Can we speak of method as a mere key that opens the door to the phenomenal world without substantially affecting what is perceived or concluded? Or, given what we have said to this point, perhaps this view reveals itself as naive and misleading. Might it be true that a method describes the world to which it is appropriate in the same way that a key is designed to open only certain locks? In other words, are methodological loyalties ever *only* methodological loyalties?

---

*In fairness, it should be noted that behavioralists, as individuals, do not fit into a single ideological category. They have ranged from neoconservatives to social democrats. It is the inherently conservative upshot of the behavioral position, rather than the ideological convictions of this or that behavioralist, that is being criticized.

Let it be said that a growing consensus rejects the proposition that methods are merely honest brokers that lead us to the truth. It has become broadly accepted that methods are rarely, if ever, merely methods, that is, technical means of proceeding. They inevitably imply commitments about reality itself: how it is to be perceived, what perceptions are worthy of the title "knowledge," which research projects merit pursuing, and so on.

A great deal of effort by a wide spectrum of non- and antibehavioralists has gone into revealing the political commitments to which the behavioral method subscribed. It was charged, for example, that behavioralists tended to justify the patent inequalities of American society by emphasizing their positive contribution to democracy and to political stability. Various behavioral studies found that the privileged were more likely to participate in politics and to support democratic norms than the lower orders of society. By contrast, the poor, the poorly educated, and the uninformed were shown to have deep-seated authoritarian tendencies and to be only indifferently committed to democracy. The conclusion that many behavioralists reached on the basis of these findings is curious: because the elites are more likely to support democratic values, the inordinate power they wield is not undesirable. Moreover, if the lower classes are insufficiently open-minded, tolerant, and pragmatic to fit into the norms of American democracy, is it an entirely bad thing that they are apathetic to political life, that they do not turn out in great numbers to vote, and that they do not make insistent demands on the political system? Should we not take some comfort in the fact that those who are least likely to support the democratic process are also those who are least likely to be involved in it? Just so, argued the behavioral champions of "mass apathy." The causes of moderation, gradualism, compromise, tolerance, and the like were well served by leaving political leadership to those who are most likely to exercise it wisely and within the constraints imposed by democracy.[9]

Apart from the obviously conservative nature of these ideas, it is interesting to speculate on their affinity with the behavioral commitment to value freedom explored above. Theories of democracy current in the classical age of liberalism envisaged an informed and active citizenry that assessed issues carefully and arrived at their political decisions on the basis of full and free public discussions of the issues. Empirical findings laid this appealing portrait of democracy to a well-deserved rest. Ignorance, irrationality, indifference, often even shocking political illiteracy were found to be the common coin of mass political attitudes.[10]

These indisputable findings can be approached in one of two ways. It can be said, on the one hand, that since classical theory failed to describe the democratic reality accurately, it is mistaken and needs to be packed up and thrown out much as modern science ejected the anachronous beliefs in alchemy and astrology. After clearing away the erroneous debris of the past, a new theory that fashions itself to the precise contours of real democratic practice needs to be designed. Democracy needs to be reinterpreted in the light of what actually transpires in the political arena. A theory has failed and a new theory consonant with the facts needs to be formulated.

Broadly speaking, this was the behavioral strategy.[11] Democracy had proved itself incompatible with the high-minded aspirations that its classical theorists had entertained, and hence a new understanding that suited the uninspiring reality was necessary. If democracy did not rest on a concerned and informed populace, it was not democracy that was at fault, but rather the theory that described it. If it rested on the apathy of the masses and the preponderant participation of the privileged and well-placed, democratic theory had to reflect this imbalance without casting nostalgic glances on what might have been.

The second alternative, which the antibehavioralists defended, did not, of course, dispute the findings that described the sorry state of participatory democracy. What they did, instead, was to insist that the dreary reality of democracy was not the only standard by which to judge it. What democracy, in fact, *is* could not be analyzed outside the context of what it might be and what it ought to be. Dahl's structures notwithstanding, political scientists could not be concerned only with what is and not with what ought to be. In the human sciences such a narrow and self-limiting approach was guilty of reification[12] and tantamount to the abdication of moral responsibility.

Moreover, the accumulated factual data upon which the behavioralists rested their case was capable of another and far more dynamic interpretation. Rather than extrapolating with matter-of-fact casualness from popular apathy to the real nature of democracy, one could turn the tables and make the antithetical argument. Since high educational attainments and privileged economic standing correlate with support for democratic norms, true democracy entails including wider and wider groups of citizens into the circles of the economically established and well educated. Poverty apparently forces a single-minded concern with far more pressing issues than foreign policy or pending budgetary legislation. That the well-heeled are also the well-informed is hardly an indication that democracy depends on inequality. On the contrary, it is a stirring challenge to the authentic democrat to eradicate the blight of political boorishness and jingoism by eradicating the conditions upon which they rest—rather than an invitation to incorporate the pathology into democracy's definition.

If both interpretations are true to the findings, the fact that the behavioralists chose the static to the dynamic understanding is highly revealing—at least to their adversaries. Behavioralists chose to view the apathy and inequality turned up by research not as contingent upon certain social circumstances or as a reality that calls out for correction, but as part of the definition of democracy itself. Since democracy can be nothing but what it is in fact, to define democracy is only to reflect its current state. Something basic has gotten lost here, the antibehavioralists declare; empirical and ethical-political judgments have imperceptibly blended into an indissoluble unit.

Rejecting concern with the ideal as nonscientific therefore appears to have a direct impact on our interpretive judgments. Opponents of behavioralism complain that what gets lost in the shuffle is not merely a careful examination of the ideal but also—and no less significantly—a dynamic and critical appreciation of the facts. The "facts" of social life are never merely facts; they are invariably related to human will and to human choices. And as such they are indissociable from human ideals.

NOTES

1. See Albert Somit and Joseph Tanenhaus, *The Development of American Political Science: From Burgess to Behavioralism* (Boston, Allyn and Bacon, 1967), pp. 11–48.
2. Strictly speaking, *behavioralism* needs to be distinguished from the earlier term *behaviorism*, which refers to the stimulus-response school in psychology. In practice, the terms are often used interchangeably.
3. Robert Dahl, "Political Theory: Truth and Consequences," *World Politics*, 12 (1960), p. 98.
4. A typical portrait of the traditional approach as it appeared to a middle-of-the-road critic in the mid-1950s is contained in Roy C. Macridis's "Major Characteristics of the Traditional Approach" in *The Study of Comparative Politics*, pp. 7–14. See below pp. 16–26.
5. Robert Dahl, "The Behavioral Approach in Political Science: Epitaph for a Monument to a Successful Revolution," *American Political Science Review*, 55 (1961), p. 770. See below, pp. 27–46.
6. One interesting account of the intellectual and psychological underpinnings of the 1960s phenomenon is Theodore Roszak, *The Making of a Counter Culture* (Garden City, NJ, Anchor Books, 1969).
7. *American Political Science Review*, 59, 1 (March 1965), pp. 39–51. See below, pp. 51–75.
8. These points are elaborated in Bernard Susser, "The Behavioral Ideology: A Review and a Retrospect," *Political Studies*, XXII, 3 (1974). See below, pp. 76–100.
9. For a critical study of behavioralism, see David Ricci, *The Tragedy of Political Science: Politics, Scholarship and Democracy* (New Haven, Yale University Press, 1984).
10. The most famous and controversial of these studies was Philip Converse's pioneering essay, "The Nature of Belief in Mass Publics," in David Apter, ed., *Ideology and Discontent* (New York, Free Press, 1964).
11. See, for example, H. A. McClosky, "Consensus and Ideology in American Politics," *American Political Science Review*, 58 (1964), pp. 361–382.
12. *Reification* is a term extensively used in social theory, especially in Marxist-related discourse. It means treating a humanly created reality as if it were a fact of nature or relating to a product of human will and design—that could perhaps be willed and designed otherwise—as if it were a "thing" beyond

our power to influence. Another meaning the term has assumed is, ironically, closer to the behavioral point of view. In this sense, to reify is to treat an abstract concept as if it were a thing—for example, to speak of the "state" as if it had some inherent character apart from the various elements of which it is constituted.

SUGGESTIONS FOR FURTHER READING

De Sola Pool, I., ed. *Contemporary Political Science: Toward Empirical Theory* (New York, McGraw-Hill, 1967).

Graham, G. J., and G. W. Carey, *The Post-Behavioral Era: Perspectives on Political Science* (New York, David McKay, 1972).

Ricci, D. *The Tragedy of Political Science: Politics, Scholarship and Democracy* (New Haven, Yale University Press, 1984).

Shapiro, M. J. *Language and Political Understanding: The Politics of Discursive Practices* (New Haven, Yale University Press, 1981), pp. 1–25.

Taylor, C. "Neutrality in Political Science." in C. Taylor, *Philosophy and the Human Sciences: Philosophical Papers 2* (Cambridge, Cambridge University Press, 1985), pp. 58–90.

Roy C. Macridis

Major Characteristics of the Traditional Approach

1   A brief account of the characteristics of the traditional approach and emphasis in the comparative study of government will reveal the source of the current dissatisfaction and will point to the need for reorientation. Comparative study has thus far been comparative in name only. It has been part of what may loosely be called the study of foreign governments, in which the governmental structures and the formal organization of state institutions were treated in a descriptive, historical, or legalistic manner. Primary emphasis has been placed on written documents like constitutions and the legal prescriptions for the allocation of political power. Finally, studies of foreign governments were largely addressed to the Western European democracies or to the political systems of Western Europe, Great Britain, and the Dominions.

2   It may be worthwhile to discuss briefly each of these characteristics of the traditional approach.

Essentially Noncomparative

3   The vast majority of publications in the field of comparative government deal either with one country or with parallel descriptions of the institutions of a number of countries. The majority of texts illustrate this approach. The student is led through the constitutional foundations, the organization of political power, and a description of the ways in which such powers are exercised. In each case "problem areas" are discussed with reference to the country's institutional structure. The right of dissolution is often cited to explain political instability in France, and, conversely, political stability in England is discussed with reference to the prerogatives of the Crown, with particular emphasis, of course, on the Prime Minister's power of dissolution. The interest of the student is concentrated primarily on an analysis of the structure of the state, the location of sovereignty, the electoral provisions, and the distribution of the electorate into political parties whose ideologies and programs are described. This approach will be found in any standard text and in a number of monographs which aspire to be more comparative in character.[1]

From *The Study of Comparative Politics* (New York, Random House, 1955), pp. 7–14. Reprinted by permission.

Essentially Descriptive

It may well be argued that description of the formal polit- 4
ical institutions is vital for the understanding of the political
process and that as such it leads to comparative study. If so,
we hardly ever have any comparison between the particular
institutions described. A reading, for instance, of one of the
best texts, *Governments of Continental Europe*, edited by James
T. Shotwell, will reveal that as we pass from France to Italy,
Switzerland, Germany, and the U.S.S.R. there is no common
thread, no criterion of why these particular countries were
selected and no examination of the factors that account for
similarities and differences. The same generally applies to
Frederick Ogg's and Harold Zink's *Modern Foreign Governments*, and to Fritz M. Marx's *Foreign Governments*. In a somewhat different fashion John Ranney's and Gwendolen Carter's
Major Foreign Powers has the virtue of addressing itself to only
four political systems and of discussing them with reference to
some basic problem areas, but again the connecting link and
the criterion of selection are missing. Another pioneer book in
the field, Daniel Witt's *Comparative Political Institutions,* abandons the country-by-country approach in favor of categories
within which comparison is more feasible, but the author is
satisfied to include under such categories as "The Citizen and
the Government" and "The Electoral Process" separate descriptions of the institutions of individual countries, and fails to
make explicit comparisons.

It should be clearly understood here that these remarks are 5
not meant to reflect on the scholarly quality of the books cited,
nor to disparage the descriptive approach. They are meant
merely to point out that these books are limited primarily to
political morphology or what might also be called political
anatomy. They describe various political institutions generally without attempting to compare them; what comparison *is*
made is limited exclusively to the identification of differences
between types or systems, such as federal versus unitary system or parliamentary versus presidential system or the more
elusive differences between democratic and totalitarian systems.

There are two typical approaches in the descriptive study of 6
political institutions. The first is *historical* and the second is
legalistic. The historical approach centers on the study of the
origins and growth of certain institutions. We trace the origins of the British parliamentary system to Magna Carta and
study its development through successive historical stages. It

is assumed that parallel historical accounts of the evolution of the French parliament or the German representative assemblies will indicate similarities and differences. The approach followed is almost identical with that used by the historian. There is no effort to evolve an analytical scheme within which an antecedent factor is related in terms other than chronological to a particular event or development.[2]

7   The second most prevalent approach is what we might call the legalistic approach. Here the student is exposed primarily to the study of the "powers" of the various branches of government and of their relationships with reference to the existing constitutional and legal prescriptions. This is almost exclusively the study of what can be done or what cannot be done by various governmental agencies with reference to legal and constitutional provisions. Again, this approach, like its historical counterpart with which it often goes hand in hand, describes the political system in a very narrow frame. It does not seek the forces that shape the legal forms, nor does it attempt to establish the causal relationships that account for the variety in constitutional prescriptions from one system to another or from one period to another. A typical illustration of this approach are two recent studies on post–World War II constitutional developments in Western Europe: Arnold Zurcher's *Constitutionalism and Constitutional Trends Since World War II,* and Mirkine Guetzevitch's *Les Constitutions Europeènnes.* To a great extent Ivor Jennings's works on the British Cabinet and the British Parliament rely on the legalistic approach with particular emphasis on the search for precedents that "explain" the powers of various governmental organs.

8   The combination of the historical and the legalistic approaches is found in the great majority of books published on foreign systems that purport to be comparative. Despite the fact that they give us a cameralike picture of the development and the relationships of the various political organs in a system, and point to parallel historical development, they do not attempt to devise a general frame of reference in which we can get broad hypotheses about the development and operation of institutions.

Essentially Parochial

9   The great number of studies on foreign political systems has been addressed to the examination of Western European institutions. Accessibility of the countries studied, relative ease

of overcoming language barriers, and the availability of official documents and other source materials, as well as cultural affinities, account for this fact. France, Great Britain, Germany, Switzerland, and to a lesser extent the Scandinavian countries and the British Dominions have been the countries to which writing and research has been directed and which are being included in the various comparative government courses in the greater number of American universities. Again, however, no systematic effort has been made to identify the similarities and the differences among these countries except in purely descriptive terms. No effort has been made to define in analytical terms the categories that constitute an "area" of study. True, most authors seem to identify these countries in terms of a common historical and cultural background and they often pay lip service to some other common traits, such as their advanced economic systems, parliamentary institutions, and democracy. What is meant by "advanced" economic systems, however, and, more specifically, what is the relationship between political institutions and the existing economic system? We often find the statement that Germany did not develop a democratic ideology and parliamentary institutions because capitalism developed "late," but no effort is being made to test the validity of such a generalization comparatively—for, after all, capitalism developed "late" in the United States and in some of the British Dominions. Often statements about the existence of a common ideology are made without attempting to define what is "common" and how ideology is related to political institutions.³

There is no doubt that references to social and economic 10 configurations, political ideologies, and institutions that can be found in texts should be interrelated into a system that would make comparative analyses of these Western European countries possible. No such effort, however, with the exception of Carl Friedrich's *Constitutional Government and Democracy*, has been made, and even Professor Friedrich is concerned only with the interplay between ideology and institutions. There is no systematic synthesis of the various "characteristics" or "traits" of different political systems. Yet without such a conceptualization no variables can be identified and compared, and as a result no truly comparative analyses of the Western governmental systems have been made by political scientists.

Some notable exceptions, in addition to Professor Friedrich's 11 and Professor Herman Finer's books, are Michels's book on *Political Parties*⁴ and the recent comparative analysis of the structure and the organization of political parties and the relationship between structure and ideology by Professor Maurice Duverger.[5] Another good illustration of a more sophisticated study is a current essay on the French political system by François Goguel[6] in which he points out that political, economic, and social instability in France is due to the uneven development of various regions in the country, thus suggesting a relationship between political stability and uniformity of economic development within a country.

12   Concentration on Western systems cannot be exclusively attributed to some of the considerations suggested above. An even more important factor was the belief at one time shared by many political scientists that democracy was the "normal" and durable form of government and that it was destined to spread throughout the world. In fact, "comparative study" would embrace more political systems only as they developed democratic institutions. James Bryce put this in very succinct terms:

> The time seems to have arrived when the actualities of democratic government in its diverse forms, should be investigated, and when the conditions most favorable to its success should receive more attention than students, as distinguished from politicians, have been bestowing upon them.[7]

13   It was natural that such a point of view should limit comparative study to the democratic systems and that it would call for the study of other systems only for the purpose of identifying democratic institutions and forms. As we shall see, such a preoccupation distorted the analysis and study of non-Western systems by centering upon patterns and institutions that were familiar to the Western observer, such as constitutions and legislatures, but whose relevance to the political processes of non-Western countries was only incidental.

Essentially Static

14   In general the traditional approach has ignored the dynamic factors that account for growth and change. It has concentrated on what we have called political anatomy. After the evolutionary premises of some of the original works in the nineteenth century were abandoned, students of political institutions apparently lost all interest in the formulation of other theories in the light of which change could be comparatively studied.

15   The question of sovereignty and its location occupied students of politics for a long time; the study of constitutional

structures became a favorite pastime, though no particular effort was made to evaluate the effectiveness of constitutional forms in achieving posited goals or to analyze the conditions underlying the success or failure of constitutionalism. The parallel development of administration was noted, but again its growth was studied with reference to a constitutional setting, as Dicey's work amply illustrates.[8] The growth of political parties was studied, but aside from descriptions of their legal status little consideration was given by political scientists to the radical transformation parties were to bring about in the organization of political power. Henry Maine's and William Lecky's[9] bold hypotheses about the impact on democracy of the development of party government and of the extension of the franchise were abandoned in the light of contrary evidence and were never replaced with new ones. Indeed, Walter Bagehot's[10] analysis of the British Cabinet remained standard until the turn of the century, though the word "party" rarely appears in it, and Dicey's formal statement of the limitations of parliamentary sovereignty were considered for a long time to be the most definitive formulation of the problem.[11] The British people, it was pointed out by Dicey, constituting the "political sovereign" body limited the "legal sovereignty" of the Parliament and such limitation was institutionalized through the courts. Federalism and its development in the various dominions was also discussed with reference to the legal organization of power and to its relationship with the concept of sovereignty. In all cases the studies made were a dissection of the distribution of the powers in terms of their legal setting and left out of the picture altogether the problem of change and the study of those factors—political or other—that account for change.

Essentially Monographic

The most important studies of foreign systems, aside from basic texts, have taken the form of monographs that have concentrated on the study of the political institutions of one system or on the discussion of a particular institution in one system. Works such as those by John Marriot, Arthur K. Keith, Joseph Barthelemy, James Bryce, Ivor Jennings, Harold Laski, A. V. Dicey, Frank Goodnow, W. A. Robson, Abbott L. Lowells, Woodrow Wilson,[12] and many others were addressed generally to only one country or to a particular institutional development within one country. The American presidency, the British parliamentary system, the congressional form of government were presented in studies in which the particular institutional forms were placed in the context of the whole tradition and legal system of the country involved. Sometimes such monographs represented great advances over the legalistic approach because they brought into the open nonpolitical factors and institutions or attempted to deal analytically with some of the problems facing the democratic systems. They had a focal point and the description of the institutions was always related to a common theme or was undertaken in the light of a common political problem, such as the relationship between executive and legislature, the growth of administrative law and the institutions of administration, the relationship between national characteristics and political ideology, and the like. The relationships established between political and nonpolitical factors, however, hardly attain a systematic formulation that can be used for comparative study, i.e., for identifying variables and attempting to account for them. Nor is the suggestion ever explicitly made that the particular way in which a problem is studied or certain institutional developments discussed is applicable to parallel phenomena in other countries.

The Problem Approach in the Traditional Literature

17   A number of studies dealing with problem areas have employed the traditional approach. Examples are studies of the relationship between democracy and economic planning; of representation and the growth of administrative agencies with new economic and social functions; of the decay of bicameralism; or of the efforts of representative assemblies to reconcile the social and economic conflicts arising in democratic societies between the two world wars.

18   Such studies have usually been confined to the institutional framework of the country involved. Analyses of policy-orientation have not gone beyond the examination of reforms of the formal institutional structure, as in studies of the reorganization of the House of Lords, the development of functional representative assemblies, the establishment of economic federalism, the delegation of legislative powers to the executive, the association of professional groups in policy-making, the integration rather than separation of policy-making organs, and, finally, measures to combat the growth of antidemocratic parties within democratic systems. The study of such problems has paved the way, however, for the abandonment of the traditional formal categories, for these problems cannot be ex-

amined in that restricting frame. They call for the development of a more precise analysis of human behavior and of the relationship between political institutions and social and economic factors. They call for an approach in which politics is conceived as a process that cannot be understood without reference to the contextual factors of a political system.

The Area Focus

Only recently has the study of foreign systems been cast in 19 a frame that carries more promise for comparative analysis. Partly as the result of the war and the need to acquire better knowledge about certain geographic areas, and partly as the result of the intensive and more systematic study by sociologists and anthropologists of human behavior in various non-Western countries, political scientists have become involved in interdisciplinary studies of "areas." An area is a cluster of countries which, because of certain policy preoccupations, geographic propinquity, or common problems and theoretic interests, can be studied as a unit. The political and economic systems, languages, history, culture, and psychology are jointly explored by representatives of various disciplines in universities and government departments. Area studies have developed rapidly in the United States in the last fifteen years. Every big university now has a number of such programs ranging from Western Europe to the Middle East and Africa.[13]

On its face the so-called area programs provide what many 20 students of comparative government consider to be the best laboratory for comparative analysis. For it has been assumed that an area is a cluster of countries in which there is enough cultural uniformity to make the comparative study of political institutional variables between them possible. Furthermore, it has also been assumed that the interdisciplinary approach provides for a more sophisticated and systematic analysis in which the investigator or group of investigators can gain a "total" picture of the system and subsequently be able to dissect it and compare its component elements.

The interdisciplinary approach has suggested some impor- 21 tant organizational concepts on the basis of which data could be gathered, variables identified, and comparative study undertaken. Most important among them have been the concepts of *culture* and *personality*. The former stresses the particular traits that constitute the configuration of a culture.[14] Culture-traits or culture-patterns can be identified and compared with each other. Yet in most cases comparison here, even among anthropologists, has assumed primarily the character of pointing out differences rather than explaining them. The *personality* concept on the other hand, by pointing out various personality traits or patterns, provides an instrument for the study of motivational aspects and their variations from one culture to another.[15]

22   It is difficult to assess the contributions of the area approach to the comparative study of politics. Very often, instead of suggesting a systematic analytical frame within which political scientists might attempt intracultural comparisons, the area approach has degenerated into either a descriptive analysis of institutional political structures within the given areas or merely produced monographs in which certain problems were studied with more sophistication with reference to one country. Such books as Robert Scalapino's *Democracy and the Party Movement in Pre-War Japan,* Barrington Moore's *Soviet Politics, the Dilemma of Power,* Alex Inkeles's *Public Opinion in the Soviet Union,* George Blanksten's *Peron's Argentina,* and Merle Fainsod's *How Russia Is Ruled* are the best representative works in area studies, but their excellence lies not so much in their systematic orientation or in the development of analytical concepts for comparison but rather in the sophistication with which the authors relate the political process in the system discussed to the ideological, cultural, and social contextual elements. Institutions are no longer described as if they had a reality which is taken for granted but rather as functioning entities operating within a given context. The descriptive approach gained as a result a richness and flavor which could not be found in the traditional legalistic and historical approach.

23   But in general, the area approach with its interdisciplinary orientation has failed to provide us with a systematic frame for comparative analysis. For, after all, the very definition of an area is subject to methodological questions with which many of the area specialists never grapple. An area is not a concrete reality as has often been asserted or taken for granted on the basis of considerations of policy or expediency. It is, or rather ought to be, an analytical concept which subsumes certain categories for the compilation of data, provides for certain uniformities which suggest a control situation of the laboratory type within which variables can be studied. Area programs, however, have not attained this level of systematic orientation and as a result their contributions to comparative analysis has been limited. They have enriched our awareness of cultures

and institutions in which the political forms vary greatly from the Western forms and they have been suggestive, at least to the political scientist, of the need to broaden his horizon and include in his study of formal institutions many of the informal processes of a system.

Notes

1. See for instance some of the best texts: James T. Shotwell (ed.): *Governments of Continental Europe*, New York, The Macmillan Co., 1950; Taylor Cole (ed.): *European Political Systems*, New York, Alfred A. Knopf, Inc., 1953; Gwendolen Carter, John Ranney and John Hertz: *Major Foreign Powers*, New York, Harcourt, Brace and Co., 1952; Frederic Ogg and Harold Zink: *Modern Foreign Governments*, New York, The Macmillan Co., 1953.
2. Some of the best illustrations of this approach are David Thomson: *Democracy in France*, New York, Oxford University Press, 1952; A. Soulier: *L'Instabilité Ministerielle*, Paris, Sirey, 1939; François Goguel: *La Politique des Partis sous la Troisiéme République*, Paris, Aux Editions du Seuil, 1946.
3. T. D. Weldon: *The Vocabulary of Politics*, London, Pelican, 1953.
4. Herman Finer: *The Theory and Practice of Modern Government*, New York, Henry Holt and Co., 1949; Robert Michels: *Political Parties: A Sociological Study of the Oligarchic Tendencies of Modern Democracies*, New York, Heart's International Library Co., 1915.
5. Maurice Duverger: *Les Partis Politiques*, Paris, Colin, 1951; and the excellent review articles of Samuel H. Beer: "Les Partis Politiques," *The Western Political Quarterly* 6: 512–17 (Sept. 1953) and Sigmund Neumann: "Toward a Theory of Political Parties," *World Politics* 6:549–63 (July 1954).
6. François Goguel: "Political Instability in France," *Foreign Affairs* 33: 111–22 (Oct. 1954).
7. James Bryce: *Modern Democracies*, New York, The Macmillan Co., 1921, Vol. I, p.4.
8. A. V. Dicey: *The Law of the Constitution*, New York, The Macmillan Co., 1902.
9. Henry Maine: *Popular Government*, London, T. Murray, 1890, and William Lecky: *Democracy and Liberty*, London, Longmans, Green and Co., 1896.
10. Walter, Bagehot: *The English Constitution*, London, Oxford University Press, 1936.
11. Dicey, *op. cit.*
12. See John Marriott: *English Political Institutions.* Oxford, The Clarendon Press, 1910, *The Mechanics of the Modern State*, Oxford, The Clarendon Press, 1927, *Second Chambers*, Oxford, The Clarendon Press, 1910; Abbot L. Lowell: *The Government of England*, New York, The Macmillan Co., 1908, *Governments and Parties in Continental Europe*, Boston and New York, Houghton Mifflin and Co., 1897, *Greater European Governments*, Cambridge, Harvard

University Press, 1918; Joseph Barthelemy: *Le Role du Puvoir Executif dans les republiques modernes*, Paris, Giard et Briere, 1906, *Le Gouvernment de la France*, Paris, Payot, 1925; Woodrow Wilson: *Congressional Government*, Boston and New York, Houghton Mifflin and Co., 1913, *Congressional Government in the United States*, New York, Columbia University Press, 1913; Arthur B. Keith: *The British Cabinet System* (2nd ed.), London, Stevens and Sons, Ltd., 1952; Frank Goodnow: *Comparative Administrative Law*, New York and London, G. P. Putnam's Sons, 1893, *Politics and Administration*, New York, The Macmillan Co., 1900; W. A. Robson: *Justice and Administrative Law* (2nd ed.), London, Stevens and Sons, Ltd., 1947; Ivor Jennings; *Cabinet Government*, New York, The Macmillan Co., 1936 *Parliament*, New York, The Macmillan Co., 1940; James Bryce: *Modern Democracies*, New York, The Macmillan Co., 1921.

13. W. C. Bennet: *Area Studies in American Universities*, New York, Social Science Research Council, 1951.

14. Ruth Benedict: *Patterns of Culture*, Boston and New York, Houghton Mifflin and Co., 1934; Melville Herskovits: *Man and His Works*, New York, Alfred A. Knopf, Inc., 1951 Clyde Kluckhohn: *The Mirror for Man*, New York, Whittlesey House, 1949.

15. Some of the most illustrative works are: Theodore Adorno and others: *The Authoritarian Personality*, New York, Harper & Brothers, 1950; Gabriel Almond: *The Appeal of Communism*, Princeton, Princeton University Press, 1954; David Levy: *New Fields of Psychiatry*, New York, W. W. Norton & Company, Inc., 1947. See also the excellent review article by Raymond Bauer: "The Psycho-Cultural Approach to Soviet Studies," *World Politics* 7:119–32 (Oct. 1954).

Robert A. Dahl

The Behavioral Approach in Political Science: Epitaph for a Monument to a Successful Protest

Perhaps the most striking characteristic of the "behavioral 1 approach" in political science is the ambiguity of the term itself, and of its synonym "political behavior." The behavioral approach, in fact, is rather like the Loch Ness monster: one can say with considerable confidence what it is not, but it is difficult to say what it *is*. Judging from newspaper reports that appear from time to time, particularly just before the summer tourist season, I judge that the monster of Loch Ness is not Moby Dick, nor my daughter's goldfish that disappeared down the drain some ten years ago, nor even a misplaced American eight heading for the Henley Regatta. In the same spirit, I judge that the behavioral approach is not that of the speculative philosopher, the historian, the legalist, or the moralist. What, then, is it? Indeed, does it actually exist?

I

Although I do not profess to know of the full history of the 2 behavioral approach, a little investigation reveals that confusing and even contradictory interpretations have marked its appearance from the beginning. The first sightings in the roily waters of political science of the phenomenon variously called political behavioral approach, or behavioral(ist) research, evidently occurred in the 1920s. The term "political behavior," it seems, was used by American political scientists from the First World War onward.[1] The honor of first adopting the term as a book title seems to belong, however, not to a political scientist but to the American journalist Frank Kent, who published a book in 1928 entitled *Political Behavior, The Heretofore Unwritten Laws, Customs, and Principles of Politics as Practised in the United States*.[2] To Kent, the study of political behavior meant the cynical "realism" of the tough-minded newspaperman who reports the way things "really" happen and not the way they're supposed to happen. This meaning, I may say, is often implied

From *American Political Science Review*, 55 (1961), pp. 763–772. Reprinted by permission.

even today. However, Herbert Tingsten rescued the term for political science in 1937 by publishing his path-breaking *Political Behavior: Studies in Election Statistics*. Despite the fact that Tingsten was a Swede, and his work dealt with European elections, the term became increasingly identified with American political science.

3   The rapid flowering of the behavioral approach in the United States no doubt depended on the existence of some key attitudes and predispositions generated in the American culture— pragmatism, fact mindedness, confidence in science, and the like.[3] But there were also at least six specific, interrelated, quite powerful stimuli.

4   One was Charles E. Merriam. In his presidential address to the American Political Science Association in 1925, Merriam said:

> Some day we may take another angle of approach *than the formal, as other sciences do,* and begin to look at *political behavior* as one of the essential objects of inquiry.[4]

5   During the next decade under Merriam's leadership at the University of Chicago, the Department of Political Science was the center of what would later have been called the behavioral approach. A number of the political scientists who subsequently were widely regarded as leaders in introducing that approach into American political science were faculty members or graduate students there: for example, Harold Lasswell as a faculty member and V. O. Key, Jr., David Truman, Herbert Simon, and Gabriel Almond, all graduate students in Merriam's department before the Second World War. Chicago was not the only place where the new mood of scientific empiricism was strong. At Cornell University, for example, G. E. G. Catlin was expounding similar views.[5] But the collective impact of "the Chicago school" as it was sometimes called, was greater than that of a single scholar.

6   A second force was the arrival in the United States in the 1930s of a considerable number of European scholars, particularly German refugees, who brought with them a sociological approach to politics that strongly reflected the specific influence of Max Weber and the general influence of European sociology. American political science had always been strongly influenced by Europeans. Not only have Americans often interpreted their own political institutions most clearly with the aid of sympathetic foreigners like de Tocqueville, Bryce, and Brogan, but American scholars have owed specific debts to

European scholarship. The first American university chair in political science (actually in History and Political Science), established in 1858 at Columbia, was occupied by the liberal German refugee Francis Lieber. In the second half of the nineteenth century, many of the leading academic advocates of a "science of politics" sought to profit from the methods and teachings in some of the leading European universities.[6]

In the 1930s, there was once again an abrupt revival of European influences as the life of American universities was enriched by the great influx of refugee scholars. 7

A number of these scholars who came to occupy leading positions in departments of sociology and political science insisted on the relevance of sociological and even psychological theories for an understanding of politics. They drew attention to the importance of Marx, Durkheim, Freud, Pareto, Mosca, Weber, Michels and others. Although some of them might later reject the behavioral approach precisely because they felt it was too narrow, men like Franz Neumann, Sigmund Neumann, Paul Lazarsfeld, Hans Speier, Hans Gerth, Reinhard Bendix and many others exerted, both directly and indirectly, a profound influence on political research in the United States. Political sociology began to flourish. Political scientists discovered that their sociological colleagues were moving with speed and skill into areas they had long regarded as their own. 8

The Second World War also stimulated the development of the behavioral approach in the United States, for a great many American political scientists temporarily vacated their ivory towers and came to grips with day-to-day political and administrative realities in Washington and elsewhere: a whole generation of American political science later drew on these experiences. The confrontation of theory and reality provoked, in most of the men who performed their stint in Washington or elsewhere, a strong sense of the inadequacies of the conventional approaches of political science for describing reality, much less for predicting in any given situation what was likely to happen. 9

Possibly an even bigger impetus—not unrelated to the effects of the War—was provided by the Social Science Research Council, which has had an unostentatious but cumulatively enormous impact on American social science. A leading spirit in the Council for the past two decades has been a distinguished political scientist, E. Pendleton Herring. His own work before he assumed the presidency of the Council in 1948 reflected a concern for realism, for breaking the bonds of research confined entirely to the library, and for individual and group influences on politics and administration. In the mid- 10

1940s Herring was instrumental in creating an SSRC committee on political behavior. The Annual Report of the SSRC for
1944–45 indicated that the Council had reached a

> ...decision to explore the feasibility of developing a new ap-
> proach to *the study of political behavior.* Focused upon *the be-
> havior of individuals* in political situations, this approach calls
> for examination of the political relationship of men—as citizens,
> administrators, and legislators—by disciplines which can throw
> light on the problems involved, with the object of *formulating
> and testing hypotheses,* concerning *uniformities of behavior* in
> different institutional settings. (Emphasis added.)

11   In 1945 the Council established a Committee on Political Behavior, with Herring as the chairman. The three other
members[7] were also well known political scientists with a definite concern about the state of conventional political science.
In 1949, the Council, together with the University of Michigan's Department of Political Science and its Institute for Social Research held a week's conference on Research on Political Behavior at Ann Arbor. The topics covered help to provide
an implicit definition of the term: papers were presented on
regional politics, the possible contributions of related social
sciences (*e.g.,* George P. Murdoch, the anthropologist, discussed
the "Possibility of the General Social Science of Government"),
voting behavior, political attitudes, groups, and methodological problems.[8]

12   Near the end of 1949, a new SSRC Committee on Political
Behavior was appointed, with V. O. Key, Jr., as the chairman.
In 1950, this committee succinctly defined its task: "The committee is concerned with the *development of theory* and *improvement in methods* which are needed if *social science research* on
the *political process* is to be more effective."[9] This committee
has been an active stimulant in the growth of the behavioral
approach down to the present time; indeed, in recent years
(under the chairmanship of David Truman) the committee has
also awarded research grants.

13   The fifth factor was the rapid growth of the "survey" method
as a tool available for the study of political choices and attitudes, and specifically of the behavior of voters. Where Tingsten had necessarily relied on aggregate voting statistics, the
survey method provided direct access to the characteristics
and behavior of individuals: an advantage that anyone who
has ever labored with aggregate data is quick to recognize.
As survey methods became more and more "scientific," par-

ticularly under the auspices of the Survey Research Center of the University of Michigan and the Bureau of Applied Social Research at Columbia, political scientists found their presumed monopoly of skills in the scholarly interpretation of voting and elections rudely destroyed by sociologists and social psychologists who in a series of path-breaking studies of presidential elections began to convert the analysis of voting from impressionistic—even when it was brilliant—history or insightful journalism to a more pedestrian but occasionally more impressive and convincing empirical science. To political scientists dissatisfied with the conventional methods and manners of the discipline, the new voting studies offered encouragement. For in spite of obvious defects, the voting studies seemed to provide ground for the hope that if political scientists could only master the tools employed in the other social sciences—survey methods and statistical analysis, for example—they might be able to go beyond plausible generalities and proceed to test hypotheses about how people in fact do behave in making political choices.

A sixth factor that needs to be mentioned is the influence of those uniquely American institutions, the great philanthropic foundations—especially Carnegie, Rockefeller, and more recently Ford—which because of their enormous financial contributions to scholarly research, and the inevitable selection among competing proposals that these entail, exert a considerable effect on the scholarly community. The relationship between foundation policy and current trends in academic research is too complex for facile generalities. Perhaps the simplest accurate statement is that the relationship is to a very high degree reciprocal: the staffs of the foundations are highly sensitive to the views of distinguished scholars, on whom they rely heavily for advice, and at the same time because even foundation resources are scarce, the policies of foundation staffs and trustees must inevitably encourage or facilitate some lines of research more than others. If the foundations had been hostile to the behavioral approach, there can be no doubt that it would have had very rough sledding indeed. For characteristically, behavioral research costs a good deal more than is needed by the single scholar in the library—and sometimes, as with the studies of voting in presidential elections, behavioral research is enormously expensive.

In the period after the Second World War, however, the foundations—reflecting important trends within the social sciences themselves, stimulated by the factors I have already mentioned—tended to view interdisciplinary and behavioral studies with sympathy. The Rockefeller Foundation, for example, had helped finance the pioneering panel study by Lazarsfeld, Berelson, and Gaudet of voting in the 1940 presidential election in Erie County, Ohio, and it has also, almost single-handedly, financed the costly election studies of the Survey Research Center at the University of Michigan. In the newest and richest foundation, Ford, the short-lived Behavioral Sciences Program probably increased the use and acceptability of the notion of behavioral sciences as something both more behavioral and more scientific than the social sciences (I confess the distinction still remains cloudy to me despite the earnest attempts of a number of behavioral scientists to set me straight). The most durable offshoot of the Behavioral Sciences Program at Ford is the Center for Advanced Study in the Behavioral Sciences at Palo Alto. Although the Center has often construed its domain in most catholic fashion—the "fellows" in any given year may include mathematicians, philosophers, historians, or even a novelist—in its early years the political scientists who were fellows there tended to be discontented with traditional approaches, inclined toward a more rigorously empirical and scientific study of politics, and deeply interested in learning wherever possible from the other social sciences.

16   All these factors, and doubtless others, came to fruition in the decade of the 1950s. The behavioral approach grew from the deviant and unpopular views of a minor sect into a major influence. Many of the radicals of the 1930s (professionally speaking) had, within two decades, become established leaders in American political science.

17   Today, many American departments of political science (including my own) offer undergraduate or graduate courses in Political Behavior. Indeed, in at least one institution (the University of Michigan) Political Behavior is not only a course but a field of graduate study parallel with such conventional fields as political theory, public administration, and the like—and recently buttressed, I note enviously, with some fat fellowships.

18   The presidency of the American Political Science Association furnishes a convenient symbol of the change. From 1927, when Merriam was elected president, until 1950, none of the presidents was prominently identified as an advocate of the behavioral approach. The election of Peter Odegard in 1950 might be regarded as the turning point. Since that time, the presidency has been occupied by one of Merriam's most brilliant and intellectually unconventional students, Harold Lasswell, and by three of the four members of the first SSRC Committee on Political Behavior.

Thus the revolutionary sectarians have found themselves, 19
perhaps more rapidly than they thought possible, becoming
members of the Establishment.

II

I have not, however, answered the nagging question I set out 20
to answer, though perhaps I have furnished some materials
from which an answer might be derived. What *is* the behavioral approach in political science?

Historically speaking, the behavioral approach was a protest 21
movement within political science. Through usage by partisans, partly as an epithet, terms like political behavior and
the behavioral approach came to be associated with a number
of political scientists, mainly Americans, who shared a strong
sense of dissatisfaction with the achievements of conventional
political science, particularly through historical, philosophical, and the descriptive-institutional approaches, and a belief that additional methods and approaches either existed or
could be developed that would help to provide political science
with empirical propositions and theories of a systematic sort,
tested by closer, more direct and more rigorously controlled
observations of political events.

At a minimum, then, those who were sometimes called "Be- 22
haviorists" or "Behavioralists" shared a mood: a mood of skepticism about the current intellectual attainments of political
science, a mood of sympathy toward "scientific" modes of investigation and analysis, a mood of optimism about the possibilities of improving the study of politics.

Was—or is—the behavioral approach ever anything more 23
than this mood? Are there perhaps definite beliefs, assumptions, methods or topics that can be identified as constituting
political behavior or the behavioral approach?

There are, so far as I can tell, three different answers to this 24
question among those who employ the term carefully. The first
answer is an unequivocal yes. Political behavior is said to refer
to the study of *individuals* rather than larger political units.
This emphasis is clear in the 1944–45 SSRC report (which I
quoted earlier) that foreshadowed the creation of the Political
Behavior Committee. This was also how David Easton defined
the term in his searching analysis and criticism of American
political science published in 1953.[10] In this sense, Tingsten,
Lasswell, and studies of voting behavior are prime examples
of the behavioral approach.

25   The second answer is an unequivocal no. In his recent *Political Science: A Philosophical Analysis* (1960), Vernon Van Dyke
remarks: "Though stipulative definitions of *political behavior*
are sometimes advanced, as when a course or a book is given
this title, none of them has gained general currency."[11] Probably the most eloquent and resounding "No!" was supplied three
years ago by an editorial in *PROD*, a journal that some American political scientists—and many of its readers—probably
regarded as the authentic spokesman for the newest currents
among the *avant garde* of political behavior. As an alumnus
both of Merriam's Chicago department and the SSRC Committee on Political Behavior, the editor of PROD, Alfred de Grazia,
could be presumed to speak with authority. He denied that the
term referred to a subject matter, an interdisciplinary focus,
quantification, any specific effort at new methods, behaviorist psychology, "realism" as opposed to "idealism," empiricism
in contrast with deductive systems, or voting behavior—or, in
fact, to anything more than political science as something that
some people might like it to be. He proposed that the term be
dropped.[12]

26   The third view is perhaps no more than an elaboration of the
mood I mentioned a moment ago. In this view the behavioral
approach is an attempt to improve our understanding of politics by seeking to explain the empirical aspects of political life
by means of methods, theories, and criteria of proof that are
acceptable according to the canons, conventions, and assumptions of modern empirical science. In this sense, "a behavioral
approach," as one writer recently observed, "is distinguished
predominantly by the nature of the purpose it is designed to
serve. The purpose is scientific...."[13]

27   If we consider the behavioral approach in political science
as simply an attempt to make the empirical component of the
discipline more scientific, as that term is generally understood
in the empirical sciences, much of the history that I have referred to falls into place. In a wise, judicious, and until very
recently neglected essay entitled "The Implications of Political
Behavior Research," David Truman, writing in 1951, set out
the fruits of a seminar on political behavior research held at
the University of Chicago in the summer of 1951. I think it is
not misleading to say that the views Truman set forth in 1951
have been shared in the years since then by the members of
the Committees on Political Behavior.

> Roughly defined, [he wrote] the term political behavior compre-
> hends those actions and interactions of men and groups which
> are involved in the process of governing.... At the maximum this

conception brings under the rubric of political behavior any human activities which can be said to be a part of governing.

Properly speaking, political behavior is not a "field" of social science; it is not even a "field" of political science.

... Political behavior is not and should not be a specialty, for it represents rather an orientation or a point of view which aims at *stating all the phenomena of government in terms of the observed and observable behavior of men.* To treat it as a "field" coordinate with (and presumably isolated from) public law, state and local government, international relations, and so on, would be to defeat its major aim. That aim includes an eventual reworking and extension of most of the conventional "fields" of political science....

The developments underlying the current interest in political behavior imply two basic requirements for adequate research. In the first place, research must be systematic.... This means that research must grow out of a precise statement of hypotheses and a rigorous ordering of evidence.... In the second place, research in political behavior must place primary emphasis upon empirical methods.... Crude empiricism, unguided by adequate theory, is almost certain to be sterile. Equally fruitless is speculation which is not or cannot be put to empirical test.

... *The ultimate goal of the student of political behavior is the development of a science of the political process....* [14]

Truman called attention to the advantages of drawing on the other social sciences and cautioned against indiscriminate borrowings. He argued that the "political behavior orientation... necessarily aims at being quantitative wherever possible. But ... the student of political behavior... deals with the political institution and he is obliged to perform his task in *quantitative terms if he can and in qualitative terms if he must.*" (Emphasis added). He agreed that "inquiry into how men *ought* to act is not a concern of research in political behavior" but insisted on the importance of studying values as "obviously important determinants of men's behavior." 28

Moreover, in political behavior research, as in the natural sciences, the values of the investigator are important in the selection of the objects and lines of inquiry....A major reason for any inquiry into political behavior is to discover uniformities, and through discovering them to be better able to indicate the consequences of such patterns and of public policy, existing or proposed, for the maintenance or development of a preferred system of political values.

29   Truman denied that "the political behavior orientation implies a rejection of historical knowledge...Historical knowledge is likely to be an essential supplement to contemporary
observation of political behavior." Finally, while suggesting
that the conventional graduate training of political scientists
needed to be supplemented and modified, Truman emphatically opposed the notion that the behavioral approach required
"the elimination of...traditional training."

> Any new departure in an established discipline must build upon
> the accomplishments of the past. Although much of the existing
> literature of politics may be impressionistic, it is extensive and
> rich in insights. Without a command of the significant portions
> of that literature, behavioral research...is likely to be naive and
> unproductive....Many attempts made by persons not familiar
> with the unsystematized facts [have been] substantively naive
> even when they may have been methodologically sound.

30   I have cited Truman's views at length for several reasons: because I wholeheartedly agree with them; because they were expressed a decade ago when the advocates of the behavioral approach were still searching for acceptance and self-definition;
because they have been neglected; and because I believe that if
the partisans and critics of "political behavior" and "the behavioral approach" had read them, understood them, and accepted
them as a proper statement of objectives, much of the irrelevant, fruitless, and ill-informed debate over the behavioral approach over the past decade need never have occurred—or at
any rate might have been conducted on a rather higher level
of intellectual sophistication.

III

31   Thus the "behavioral approach" might better be called the
"behavioral mood" or perhaps even the "scientific outlook."
32   Yet to explain the behavioral approach as nothing more or
less than an emphasis on the term "science" in the phrase
"political science" leaves unanswered whatever questions may
be raised as to the present or potential achievements of this
mood of protest, skepticism, reform, and optimism. Fortunately, there is an element of self-correction in intellectual life.
The attempt to increase the scientific competence of political
studies will inevitably be judged by results. And the judges
of the next generation will share the skepticism of the past.

If closer attention to methodological niceties, to problems of observation and verification, to the task of giving operational meaning to political concepts, to quantification and testing, to eliminating unproductive intervening variables, to sources of data, hypotheses, and theory in the other social sciences; if all of these activities do not yield explanations of some important aspects of politics that are more thoroughly verified, less open to methodological objections, richer in implications for further explanation, and more useful in meeting the perennial problems of political life than the explanations they are intended to replace; if, in short, the results of a scientific outlook do not measure up to the standards that serious students of politics have always attempted to apply, then we may confidently expect that the attempt to build an empirical science of politics will lose all the impetus in the next generation that it gained in the last.

The representatives of the "scientific outlook" are, it seems 33 to me, right in saying that it is a little early to appraise the results. We shall need another generation of work before we can put the products of this new mood and outlook in political science in perspective. Nonetheless, I believe it may be useful to make a tentative if deliberately incomplete assessment.

The oldest and best example of the modern scientific outlook 34 at work is to be found in studies of voting behavior using survey methods. These begin with *The People's Choice,*[15] a study of the 1940 presidential election first published in 1944, and end—for the moment at least—with the magnificent study of the 1956 election entitled *The American Voter.*[16] It is no exaggeration to say that in less than two decades this series of studies has significantly altered and greatly deepened our understanding of what in some ways is the most distinctive action for a citizen of a democracy—deciding how to vote, or indeed whether to vote at all, in a competitive national election. Each study has profited from the last; and as broadly trained political scientists have begun to work on these studies together with sociologists and social psychologists, the contributions of the studies to our understanding of politics—rather than of individual psychology—have greatly increased. On many topics where only a generation ago we had not much beyond impressionistic evidence, today we can speak with some confidence.

Although in a field as ambiguous and rich in contradic- 35 tory hypotheses as political science, it is nearly always possible to regard a finding as merely confirming the obvious, in fact a number of the findings point in rather unexpected directions: *e.g.,* that "independent" voters tend to be less in-

terested, involved, or informed than partisan voters;[17] that
socio-economic "class" whether objectively or subjectively defined is not a factor of constant weight in American presidential elections but a variable subject to great swings; and that
only a microscopic proportion of American voters can be said
to bring any ideological perspectives, even loosely defined, to
bear on their decisions. Where once one might have asserted
these propositions or their contraries with equal plausibility,
the evidence of the voting studies tends to pile up in a single
direction. Moreover—and this is perhaps the most important
point of all—these studies are cumulative. The early studies
were highly incomplete and in many ways unsatisfactory. They
were subject to a good deal of criticism, and properly so. Even
the latest ones will not escape unharmed. Yet it seems to me
there has been a steady and obvious improvement in quality,
range, and depth.

36   The voting studies may have provided an indirect stimulus
to the "scientific outlook" because of a psychological effect. It
seems to be beyond much doubt that some political scientists,
particularly younger ones, compared the yield produced by
the methods used in the studies on voting with the normal
yield of conventional methods and arrived at the inference—
which is probably false—that the application of comparable
new methods elsewhere could produce a comparative gain in
results.

37   A closely related topic on which the scientific outlook, has,
in my view, produced some useful and reliable results of great
importance to an understanding of politics is in the general domain of political participation. A listing of some of the chapter
headings in Robert E. Lane's *Political Life* (1959) indicates the
sort of question on which our knowledge is very much better
off than it was only a few years ago: "Who Takes Part in Elections and What Do They Do?," "Who Tries to Influence Public
officials and How Do They Do It?," "Political Discussion: Who
Listens to What? Who Talks to Whom?," "Why Lower-Status
People Participate Less than Upper-Status People," "The Way
of the Ethnic in Politics," etc.

38   Since I am not responsible for a complete inventory, I shall
limit myself to mentioning one more subject where the behavioral mood has clearly made itself felt. This is in understanding the psychological characteristics of *homo politi-
cus:* attitudes, beliefs, predispositions, personality factors. The
range of "behavioral" scholars and research in this area is very
great, though the researchers and the research may not always
bear the professional label "political science." A few scattered

names, titles, and topics will indicate what I have in mind: Lasswell, the great American pioneer in this area; Cantril; Lane; McClosky; Adorno, et al. *The Authoritarian Personality;* Almond, *The Appeals of Communism;* Stouffer, *Communism, Conformity and Civil Liberties;* and Lipset, "Working Class Authoritarianism" in *Political Man.* The fact that these scholars bear various professional labels—sociologist, psychologist, political scientist—and that it is not easy to read from the professional or departmental label of the author to the character of the work itself may be regarded by some political scientists as an appalling sign of disintegration in the distinctive properties of political science, but it is also a sign of the extent to which a concern by "behavioral scientists" with similar problems now tends to transcend (though not to eliminate entirely) differences in professional origins.

IV

What of the yield in other matters that have always been 39 of concern to students of political life? There are a number of important aspects of political studies where the behavioral mood has had, is having, or probably soon will have an impact, but where we must reserve judgment for the time being simply because the results are too scanty.

A good example is the analysis of political *systems*. The most 40 distinctive products of the behavioral mood so far have dealt with *individuals*—individuals who vote, participate in politics in other ways, or express certain attitudes or beliefs. But an individual is not a political system, and analysis of individual preferences cannot fully explain collective decisions, for in addition we need to understand the mechanisms by which individual decisions are aggregated and combined into collective decisions. We cannot move from a study of the attitudes of a random sample of American citizens to a reasonably full explanation of, say, presidential nominations or the persistent problems of policy coordination in the United States.

Yet one classic concern of students of politics has been the 41 analysis of *systems* of individuals and groups. Although the impact of the scientific outlook on the study of political systems is still unclear, there are some interesting straws in the wind. In *Union Democracy*, Lipset, Trow and Coleman brought the behavioral mood and the intellectual resources of three highly trained social scientists to bear on the task of explaining how it is that a legitimate two-party system is maintained, as it is

not in other American trade unions, in the International Ty-
pographyers' Union. Recently a number of political scientists
have followed sociologists into the study of local communities as systems of influence or decision-making.[18] Deutsch
reflects the behavioral mood in his study of international political systems.[19] A number of other studies are in process that
may help us formulate some new, or if not new then more persuasive, answers to some ancient questions.[20] But until more
evidence is in, anyone who does not believe he knows *a priori*
the outcome of this present expression of the scholar's age-old
quest for knowledge will perhaps be pardoned if he reserves
judgment and awaits the future with skepticism—mixed, depending on his prejudices, with hope or dread.

V

42   Where will the behavioral mood, considered as a movement
of protest, go from here? I think it will gradually disappear.
By this I mean only that it will slowly decay as a distinctive
mood and outlook. For it will become, and in fact already is
becoming, incorporated into the main body of the discipline.
The behavioral mood will not disappear, then, because it has
failed. It will disappear rather because it has succeeded. As a
separate, somewhat sectarian, slightly factional outlook it will
be the first victim of its own triumph.

43   Lest I be misunderstood in what I am about to say, let me
make clear that the present and probable future benefits of the
behavioral revolt to political studies seem to me to outweigh
by far any disadvantages. In retrospect, the "behavioral" revolt
in political science was, if anything, excessively delayed. Moreover, had that revolt not taken place, political science would
have become increasingly alienated, I believe, from the other
social sciences. One consequence of the behavioral protest has
been to restore some unity within the social sciences by bringing political studies into closer affiliation with theories, methods, findings, and outlooks in modern psychology, sociology,
anthropology and economics.

44   But if the behavioral revolt in political science has helped to
restore some unities, it has shattered others; and the fragments
probably cannot ever again be united exactly along the old
lines. There are, so to speak, five fragments in search of a unity.
These are: empirical political science, standards of evaluation,
history, general theory and speculation.

45   The empirical political scientist is concerned with what *is*,
as he says, not with what *ought* to be. Hence he finds it difficult

and uncongenial to assume the historic burden of the political philosopher who attempted to determine, prescribe, elaborate, and employ ethical standards—values, to use the fashionable term—in appraising political acts and political systems. The behaviorally minded student of politics is prepared to *describe* values as empirical data; but, *qua* "scientist" he seeks to avoid prescription or inquiry into the grounds on which judgments of value can properly be made. To whom, then, are we to turn for guidance on intricate questions of political appraisal and evaluation? Today, probably no single professional group is qualified to speak with wisdom on all important political alternatives.

It may be said that this is the task of the political philoso- 46 pher. But the problem of the political philosopher who wishes to engage in political evaluation in a sophisticated way is rendered ever more formidable by the products of the behavioral mood. An act of political evaluation cannot be performed in a sterile medium free from contamination by brute facts. Surely no one today, for example, can intelligently consider the relative merits of different political systems, or different arrangements within a particular political system, unless he knows what there is to be known about how these systems or arrangements work, what is required to make them work, and what effects they have on participants. No doubt the specialist who "knows the facts"—whether as physicist, physician, or political scientist—sometimes displays great naïveté on matters of policy. Still, the impatience of the empirical political scientist with the political philosopher who insists upon the importance of "values" arises in part from a feeling that the political philosopher who engages in political evaluation rarely completes all his homework. The topic of "consensus" as a condition for democracy is a case in point; when the political philosopher deals with this question, it seems to me that he typically makes a number of assumptions and assertions of an empirical sort without systematic attention to existing empirical data, or the possibility of gaining better empirical data.[21] Obviously some division of labor will always be necessary in a field as broad as the study of politics, but clearly the field needs more people who do not regard rapid shifts of mood—I mean from the behavioral to the philosophical—as a symptom of severe schizophrenia.

Second, in his concern for analyzing what *is*, the behavioral 47 political scientist has found it difficult to make systematic use of what *has been:* i.e., with history. In a trivial sense, of course, all knowledge of fact is historical; but I am speaking here of the history of the historian. Despite disclaimers and intentions to the contrary, there seems to me little room for doubt that the actual content of almost all the studies that reflect the behavioral mood is a-historical in character. Yet the scientific shortcomings of an a-historical theory in political science are manifest, and political scientists with "behavioral" predispositions are among the first to admit them. As the authors of *The American Voter* remark:

> In somewhat severe language, theory may be characterized as a generalized statement of the inter-relationships of a set of variables. In these terms, historical description may be said, to be a statement of the values assumed by these variables through time....
>
> If theory can guide historical descriptions, the historical context of most research on human behavior places clear limitations of the development of theory. In evolving and testing his theoretical hypotheses the social scientist usually must depend on what he is permitted to observe by the progress of history.... It is evident that *variables of great importance in human affairs may exhibit little or no change in a given historical period*. As a result, the investigator whose work falls in this period *may not see the significance of these variables* and may fail to incorporate them in his theoretical statements. And even if he does perceive their importance, the *absence of variation will prevent a proper test of hypotheses* that state the relation of these factors to other variables of his theory (pp. 8–10, emphasis added).

48   There are, I think, a number of nodes around which a unity between behavioral political studies and history may be expected to grow. Because it is unreasonable to suppose that anything like the whole field of history will lend itself successfully to the behavioral approach, both historians and political scientists might profitably look for targets-of-opportunity on which the weapons forged by modern social science can be brought to bear. In this respect the work of the American historian, Lee Benson, seems to me particularly promising. By the application of rather elementary methods, which the historian has not been prone to employ, including very simple statistical analysis, Benson has shown how the explanations of five eminent American historians of four different presidential elections are dubious, if not, in fact, downright absurd.[22] The sociologist, S. M. Lipset, has also contributed a new interpretation of the 1860 election, based upon his analysis of Southern voting patterns in the presidential election of that year and in referenda on secession a few months later.[23] Benson has also turned his atten-

tion both to Charles A. Beard's famous interpretation—which Beard called an economic interpretation—of the creation and adoption of the American Constitution, and to the latter-day critics of Beard's somewhat loosely stated theory; he demonstrates convincingly, at least to me, some of the gains that can arise from a greater methodological sophistication on matters of causation, correlation, and use of quantitative data than is customary among professional historians.[24]

In addition to these targets-of-opportunity that occur here 49 and there in historical studies, a problem that obviously needs the joint attention of historian and "behavioral" political scientist is the matter of political change. To the extent that the political scientist is interested in gaining a better understanding of political change—as, say, in the developing countries, to cite an example of pressing importance—he will have to work with theories that can only be fully tested against historical data. Unfortunately, the a-theoretical or even anti-theoretical biases of many historians often make their works a storehouse of data so vast as to be almost unmanageable for the theorist. Rather than demand that every theorist should have to become his own historian, it may be more feasible to demand that more historians should become theorists, or at any rate familiar with the most relevant issues, problems, and methods of the modern social sciences.

I have already implied the third unity that needs to be estab- 50 lished, namely a unity between empirical political studies and a concern for general theory. The scientific outlook in political science can easily produce a dangerous and dysfunctional humility: the humility of the social scientist who may be quite confident of his findings on small matters and dubious that he can have anything at all to say on larger questions. The danger, of course, is that the quest for empirical data can turn into an absorbing search for mere trivialities unless it is guided by some sense of the difference between an explanation that would not matter much even if could be shown to be valid by the most advanced methods now available, and one that would matter a great deal if it should turn out to be a little more or a little less plausible than before, even if it still remained in some considerable doubt. So far, I think, the impact of the scientific outlook has been to stimulate caution rather than boldness in searching for broad explanatory theories. The political scientist who mixes skepticism with methodological rigor is all too painfully aware of the inadequacies of any theory that goes much beyond the immediate data at hand. Yet it seems clear that unless the study of politics generates and is guided by broad, bold, even if highly vulnerable general theories, it is headed for the ultimate disaster of triviality.

51   Finally, I should like to suggest that empirical political science had better find a place for speculation. It is a grave though easy error for students of politics impressed by the achievements of the natural sciences to imitate all their methods save the most critical one: the use of the imagination. Problems of method and a proper concern for what would be regarded as an acceptable test of an empirical hypothesis have quite properly moved out of the wings to a more central position on the great stage of political science. Yet surely it is imagination that has generally marked the intelligence of the great scientist, and speculation—often-times foolish speculation, it turned out later—has generally preceded great advances in scientific theory. It is only fair to add, however, that the speculation of a Galileo, a Kepler, a Newton, or an Einstein, was informed and controlled by a deep understanding of the hard empirical facts as they were known at the time: Kepler's speculations always had to confront the tables of Tycho Brahe.

52   There is every reason to think that unities can be forged anew. After all, as the names of Socrates, Aristotle, Machiavelli, Hobbes, and Tocqueville remind us, from time to time in the past the study of politics has been altered, permanently, by a fresh infusion of the spirit of empirical inquiry—by, that is to say, the scientific outlook.

Notes

  1. David Easton, *The Political System* (1953), p. 203.
  2. Kent's earlier book, *The Great Game of Politics* (1924), made no pretence of being systematic and continued to be widely read by students of American politics, but within a few years *Political Behavior* fell into an obscurity from which it has never recovered.
  3. *Cf.* Bernard Crick, *The American Science of Politics, Its Origins and Conditions* (London, 1959).
  4. "Progress in Political Research," *American Political Science Review*, Vol. 20 (February, 1926), p. 7, quoted in David B. Truman, "The Implications of Political Behavior Research," *Items* (Social Science Research Council, December, 1951), p. 37. Emphasis added.
  5. See Catlin's *Science and Methods of Politics* (1927). Another early example of the behavioral approach was Stuart Rice, *Quantitative Methods in Politics* (1928). Rice had received his Ph.D. at Columbia University.
  6. *Cf.* Bernard Crick, *op. cit.,* pp. 21–31. Crick notes that "The Fifth Volume of the Johns Hopkins University *Studies in Historical and Political Science* published a long study, edited by Andrew D. White, 'European Schools of History and Politics' (December,

1887). It reprinted his Johns Hopkins address on 'Education in Political Science' together with reports on 'what we can learn from' each major European country." Fn. 1, p. 27.

7. Herbert Emmerich, Charles S. Hyneman, and V. O. Key, Jr.

8. Alexander Heard, "Research on Political Behavior: Report of a Conference," *Items* (Social Science Research Council, December, 1949), pp. 41–44.

9. Social Science Research Council, *Items* (June, 1950), p. 20. (Emphasis added.)

10. "To precisely what kind of research does the concept of political behavior refer? It is clear that this term indicates that the research worker wishes to look at participants in the political system as individuals who have the emotions, prejudices, and predispositions of human beings as we know them in our daily lives.... Behavioral research...has therefore sought to elevate the actual human being to the center of attention. Its premise is that the traditionalists have been reifying institutions, virtually looking at them as entities apart from their component individuals.... Research workers often use the terms...to indicate that they are studying the political process by looking at the relation of it to the motivations, personalities, or feelings of the participants as individual human beings." David Easton, *The Political System* (1953), pp. 201–205.

11. As we shall see, Van Dyke distinguishes the term "behavioral approach" from "political behavior."

12. "What is Political Behavior?," *PROD*, July, 1958.

13. *Ibid.*, p. 159.

14. Social Science Research Council, *Items* (December, 1951), pp. 37–39. (Emphasis added.)

15. Paul F. Lazarsfeld, Bernard Berelson, and Hazel Gaudet, *The People's Choice* (New York, 1944).

16. Angus Campbell, Philip Converse, Donald Stokes, and Warren Miller, *The American Voter* (New York, 1960), a study extended and refined by the same authors in "Stability and Change in 1960: A Reinstating Election," *American Political Science Review*, Vol. 55 (1961), pp. 269–280.

17. A finding, incidentally, that may have to be revised in turn. A recent re-analysis of the data of the voting studies, completed after this paper was prepared, has turned up new evidence for the active, interested independent voter. William Flanigan, *Partisanship and Campaign Participation* (Ph.D. dissertation. Yale University Library, 1961).

18. *Cf.* Janowitz, ed., *Community Political Systems* (1961); Edward Banfield, *Political Influence* (1961); and the English study by Birch and his colleagues at the University of Manchester, *Small Town Politics* (1959).

19. *E.g.*, in his *Nationalism and Social Communication* (1953). See also his recent article with the economist Alexander Eckstein, "National Industrialization and the Declining Share of the International Economic Sector, 1890–1959," *World Politics* (January,

1961), pp. 267–299; and his "Social Mobilization and Political Development," *American Political Science Review*, Vol. 55 (September, 1961), pp. 493–514.

20. For an interesting example of an application of the behavioral mood to comparative policies, see Stein Rokkan and Henry Valen, "Parties, Elections and Political Behavior in the Northern Countries: A Review of Recent Research," *Politische Forschung* (1960). Probably the most ambitious attempt to apply survey methods to comparative politics is represented by a study of political socialization and political values in five nations, conducted by Gabriel A. Almond [not yet completed at the time of this writing].

21. In 1942, in *The New Belief in the Common Man*, C. J. Friedrich challenged the prevailing generalizations about the need for consensus (ch. 5). However, his challenge seems to have met with little response until 1960, when Prothro and Grigg reported the results of an empirical study of consensus on "democratic" propositions in Ann Arbor, Michigan and Tallahassee, Florida. See their "Fundamental Principles of Democracy," *Journal of Politics* (May, 1960), pp. 276–294.

22. The historians and the elections were: Arthur Schlesinger, Jr., on the election of 1824, Samuel E. Morison and Henry S. Commager on the election of 1860, Allan Nevins on the election of 1884, and William Diamond on the election of 1896. See his "Research Problems in American Political Historiography," in Komarovsky, ed., *Common Frontiers of the Social Sciences* (1957).

23. "The Emergence of the One-Party South—the Election of 1860," in *Political Man* (1960).

24. Lee Benson, *Turner and Beard, American Historical Writing Reconsidered* (1960).

David Easton

The Current Meaning of Behavioralism

What is the nature of [the] assumptions and objectives, the 1
intellectual foundation stones on which [behavioralism] has
been constructed? No single way of characterizing them is satisfactory to everyone, but the following itemized list provides
a reasonably accurate and exhaustive account of them.

1. *Regularities.* There are discoverable uniformities in political behavior. These can be expressed in generalizations or
theories with explanatory and predictive value.

2. *Verification.* The validity of such generalizations must
be testable, in principle, by reference to relevant behavior.

3. *Techniques.* Means for acquiring and interpreting data
cannot be taken for granted. They are problematic and need
to be examined self-consciously, refined, and validated so that
rigorous means can be found for observing, recording, and analyzing behavior.

4. *Quantification.* Precision in the recording of data and
the statement of findings requires measurement and quantification, not for their own sake, but only where possible, relevant, and meaningful in the light of other objectives.

5. *Values.* Ethical evaluation and empirical explanation
involve two different kinds of propositions that, for the sake of
clarity, should be kept analytically distinct. However, a student
of political behavior is not prohibited from asserting propositions of either kind separately or in combination as long as he
does not mistake one for the other.

6. *Systematization.* Research ought to be systematic, that
is, theory and research are to be seen as closely intertwined
parts of a coherent and orderly body of knowledge. Research
untutored by theory may prove trivial, and theory unsupport-
able by data, futile.

7. *Pure science.* The application of knowledge is as much
a part of the scientific enterprise as theoretical understanding.
But the understanding and explanation of political behavior
logically precede and provide the basis for efforts to utilize
political knowledge in the solution of urgent practical problems of society.

From David Easton, "The Current Meaning of Behavioralism," in James C. Charlesworth,
ed. *Contemporary Political Analysis* (New York, The Free Press, 1967). Reprinted by
permission.

8. *Integration.* Because the social sciences deal with the whole human situation, political research can ignore the findings of other disciplines only at the peril of weakening the validity and undermining the generality of its own results. Recognition of this interrelationship will help to bring political science back to its status of earlier centuries and return it to the main fold of the social sciences.

David Easton
Tenets of Post-Behavioralism

New as post-behavioralism is, the tenets of its faith have 1
already emerged clearly enough to be identifiable. They form
what could be called a Credo of Relevance. I would describe
the tenets of this post-behavioral credo as follows:

1. Substance must precede technique. If one *must* be sacrificed for the other—and this need not always be so—it is more
important to be relevant and meaningful for contemporary urgent social problems than to be sophisticated in the tools of
investigation. For the aphorism of science that it is better to
be wrong than vague, post-behavioralism would substitute a
new dictum, that it is better to be vague than non-relevantly
precise.

2. Behavioral science conceals an ideology of empirical
conservatism. To confine oneself exclusively to the description
and analysis of facts is to hamper the understanding of these
same facts in their broadest context. As a result empirical political science must lend its support to the maintenance of the
very factual conditions it explores. It unwittingly purveys an
ideology of social conservatism tempered by modest incremental change.

3. Behavioral research must lose touch with reality. The
heart of behavioral inquiry is abstraction and analysis and
this serves to conceal the brute realities of politics. The task
of post-behavioralism is to break the barriers of silence that
behavioral language necessarily has created and to help political science reach out to the real needs of mankind in a time
of crisis.

4. Research about and constructive development of values
are inextinguishable parts of the study of politics. Science cannot be and never has been evaluatively neutral despite protestations to the contrary. Hence to understand the limits of our
knowledge we need to be aware of the value premises on which
it stands and the alternatives for which this knowledge could
be used.

5. Members of a learned discipline bear the responsibilities of all intellectuals. The intellectuals' historical role has
been and must be to protect the humane values of civilization. This is their unique task and obligation. Without this they
become mere technicians, mechanics for tinkering with society.

From *American Political Science Review*, 63 (1969), p. 1052. Reprinted by permission.

They thereby abandon the special privileges they have come to claim for themselves in academia, such as freedom of inquiry and a quasi-extraterritorial protection from the onslaughts of society.

6. To know is to bear the responsibility for acting and to act is to engage in reshaping society. The intellectual as scientist bears the special obligations to put his knowledge to work. Contemplative science was a product of the nineteenth century when a broader moral agreement was shared. Action science of necessity reflects the contemporary conflict in society over ideals and this must permeate and color the whole research enterprise itself.

7. If the intellectual has the obligation to implement his knowledge, those organizations composed of intellectuals—the professional associations—and the universities themselves, cannot stand apart from the struggles of the day. Politicization of the professions is inescapable as well as desirable.

*Christian Bay**

Politics and Pseudopolitics:
A Critical Evaluation of
Some Behavioral Literature

A curious state of affairs has developed within the academic 1
discipline that bravely calls itself Political Science—the discipline that in a much-quoted phrase has been called "a device, invented by university teachers, for avoiding that dangerous subject politics, without achieving science."[1] A growing and now indeed a predominant proportion of leading American political scientists, the behavioralists, have become determined to achieve science. Yet in the process many of them remain open to the charge of strenuously avoiding that dangerous subject, politics.

Consider a recent essay on the behavioral persuasion in pol- 2
itics. The conclusion stresses the purpose of political inquiry: "The Goal is Man." There is to be a commitment to some humane purpose after all. But what kind of man? A democratic kind of man, a just man, or perhaps a power-seeking man? The answer follows: "These are philosophical questions better left to the philosophers."[2] Behavioral students of politics should, as scientists, engage in no value judgments concerning the kind of man or society their researches ought to serve. This is the general inference to be drawn, not only from this particular essay, but from much of the contemporary literature on political behavior.

As Heinz Eulau, the author, points out in the same essay, 3
the area of behavioral political science includes a particular domain called policy science, in which empirical inquiry is geared to explicitly stated goal formulations; within *this* domain "political science, as all science, should be put in the service of whatever goals men pursue in politics." *Any* goals? Not quite; in this context Eulau points out that the choice of what goals to serve is a matter of personal ethics, and incidentally reminds us that behavioral research can be readily utilized also for purposes conflicting with the original ones.

* I am indebted to my friend Herbert H. Hyman, who has been generous with advice for improvements on an earlier draft. It should not be inferred that he is in agreement with opinions expressed in this paper, or that he might not once again find much to criticize in it. At a later stage I have received helpful suggestions also from Sidney Verba and Andrew Hacker.

From *American Political Science Review*, 59 (1965), pp. 39–51. Reprinted by permission.

"In this sense, at least, science is value-free. I don't think the scientist can escape this dilemma of having his work misused without giving up his calling." And the author concludes with these words: "Only if he places himself at the service of those whose values he disagrees with does he commit intellectual treason."

4   In these pages I am concerned with sins less serious than intellectual treason; perhaps intellectual indolence is a more accurate term. My argument will be that much of the current work on political behavior generally fails to articulate its very real value biases, and that the political impact of this supposedly neutral literature is generally conservative and in a special sense anti-political. In conclusion I propose to develop a perspective on political inquiry that would relate it more meaningfully to problems of human needs and values; in that context I will suggest some important but neglected problems lending themselves to empirical research.

5   I am not about to argue that our investments in political behavior research have been too large; on the contrary, we need much more work in this area. But my principal concern is to argue for a more pressing need: an intellectually more defensible and a politically more responsible theoretical framework for guiding and interpreting our empirical work; a theory that would give more meaning to our research, even at the expense of reducing its conceptual and operational neatness.

I

6   It is necessary first to clarify some basic terms in which my concern is stated.

7   The prevailing concepts of "politics" in the literature under consideration are surely an important source of the difficulty. Definitions gravitate toward the most conspicuous *facts* and shy away from all reference to more norm-laden and less easily measurable aspects of social life. For the sake of brevity, let us consider only the most recent formulation by one of the unquestionably most influential political scientists of the present generation: "A political system is any persistent pattern of human relationships that involves, to a significant extent, power, rule, or authority."[3] My objection is not primarily to the extension of the reference of "political" to private as well as to public associations, and even to clans and families as well; rather, it is to the absence of any reference to a public purpose. Research work on power, rule, or authority can contribute significantly to our political knowledge, even if the data come from contexts

not ordinarily thought of as political. But its significance must be gauged in relation to some criteria; until these are articulated and justified, or at any rate chosen, we can only intuit whether our researches on, say, power behavior are tackling significant or trivial issues.

"Politics" should refer to power, but the term should also re- 8
fer to some conception of human welfare or the public good. The achievement of Plato and Aristotle is in part a result of their starting out by asking some of the right questions; above all, what is politics *for*? Their limitations were logical and methodological or, if you prefer, conceptual: they had not learned to distinguish between verifiable *descriptive* statements, statements of *normative* positions, and (empirically empty and normatively neutral) *analytical* statements, including definitions and other equations.

Once these distinctions had been developed, a process that 9
began with David Hume, it became easy and fashionable to expose fallacies in Plato and Aristotle; but instead of attacking the ancient and perennial problems of politics with our new and sharper conceptual tools, recent generations of political scientists appear to have sought safety in seeking to exclude the normative realm altogether from the scope of their scientific inquiry. "Politics" has consequently been defined in a simple institutional or behavioral manner, unrelated to normative conceptions of any sort. Ironically, most modern behavioralists are back with the Greeks again in their assumption that political inquiry can be pursued by much the same methods as natural science inquiry; they have adjusted to David Hume and the modern logical positivists by the neat advice of definitions that limit the scope of their inquiry to observable behavior.

This surely is a stance of premature closure. The alternative 10
proposed here is to insist on the need for a political theory that deals with *basic human needs* as well as overt desires and other observable aspects of behavior. The task of improving concepts and methods toward establishing a stricter science of politics is formidable; but let us avoid establishing an orthodoxy that would have the whole profession contract for a fainthearted purchase of rigor at the price of excluding much of the meat and spirit of politics.

As a modest and fragmentary beginning toward a more 11
appropriate theory, let me suggest a distinction between "politics" and "pseudopolitics." I would define as *political* all activity aimed at improving or protecting conditions for the satisfaction of human needs and demands in a given society or community, according to some universalistic scheme

of priorities, implicit or explicit.[4] *Pseudopolitical* in this paper refers to activity that resembles political activity but is
exclusively concerned with either the alleviation of personal
neuroses or with promoting private or private interest-group
advantage, deterred by no articulate or disinterested conception of what would be just or fair to other groups.

12   Pseudopolitics is the counterfeit of politics. The relative
prevalence of the counterfeit variety of democratic politics presumably depends on many ascertainable factors, including a
society's degree of commercialization and the degree of socioeconomic mobility (or the size of the stakes in the competitive
struggle); on the other hand, the proportion of pseudo-political
activity would correlate negatively with the amount of psychological security, the amount of social welfare-type security, and
the amount of political education effectively taught.

13   For present purposes it is not necessary to demonstrate in detail how the distinction between politics in the narrower sense
and pseudopolitics can be made operationally useful. Suffice it
to say that only a saint is pure from the taint of pseudopolitics
and that hardly any pseudopolitician would be *wholly* without
concern for the public welfare; mixed motives, in proportions
varying from one person to the next and from one situation
to the next, pervade all actions. It is a difficult but surely not
an impossible task to develop indices for assessing the relative
prevalence of political versus pseudopolitical incentives in voters and other political actors; the only essential prerequisite is
to decide that the task must be tackled.

14   Without attempting to make this kind of distinction, untidy
as it may at first appear to many a behavioralist, I don't see
how we can begin to approach a condition of tidiness in our
discussions of the *political significance* of research, or of the
political responsibility of political scientists. But what should
we mean by these two highly eulogistic terms; might we not
be better advised to shun them altogether? The bulk of this
paper seeks to demonstrate some sorry consequences of the
latter course. We cannot avoid the realm of normative issues
unless we really wish to disclaim all political significance for
our work. Probably very few in our profession would adopt
this position.

15   Although explicit cognizance of normative assumptions in
his theoretical frame of reference is likely to entail some inconvenience for the researcher, he will by no means be blocked
from continuing much of his present work. It should be clear
that all competent research on pseudopolitical behavior illumi-
nates political behavior as well, as the relative presence of one
signals the relative absence of the other. In the real world the

two aspects of behavior always coexist. My quarrel is not with research on pseudopolitics *per se,* but with the way findings are usually reported and interpreted. I object to the tendency in much of the behavior literature to deal with the pseudopolitical aspects of behavior almost exclusively, and to imply that the prevalence of pseudopolitics is and always will be the natural or even the desirable state of affairs in a democracy. Consequently, I object also to the absence of interest in research that could reveal some of the determinants of the relative prevalence of pseudopolitical behavior on our political arena, by which we might learn more about how we may advance toward a more strictly political consciousness, in the sense of concern for the public interest and for the future, in our population.

Now, how should we define political significance and political responsibility? In my conceptual world the two terms are tied together; I would judge degrees of political significance of research studies in the same way that I would judge degrees of political responsibility of political scientists (in the role of theorist-researcher, as distinct from the role of citizen). A research report is politically significant to the extent that it contributes to the kinds of knowledge most needed by politically responsible political scientists. 16

"Political responsibility" in this paper refers to the extent to which the social scientist observes the canons of rationality on two levels, which I shall call formal and substantive.[5] Formal rationality refers to the familiar notion of clarifying the objectives first and then paying heed to the best available knowledge when seeking ways and means to implement them. Competent behavioral research in political science is highly rational in this formal sense; this is what the extensive work in theory and methodology is *for.* 17

The lack of political responsibility that I ascribe to much political behavior literature relates to the other level of rationality, the substantive level, which involves articulate attention to questions of fundamental commitment in social and political research literature. Problems of human welfare (including justice, liberty, security, etc.), the objects of political research and of politics, can be adequately studied, and dealt with, only if their *ought*-side is investigated as carefully as their *is*-side. Ought-side inquiry must pertain to wants (or desires or, if insisted on, demands) as well as needs. Political communication must be analysed carefully so that we may learn what aspects of *wants* are most salient and could be frustrated only at the cost of resentment, alienation, or upheaval. Yet, only analysis of data on wants in terms of a theory of *needs* will permit us 18

to evaluate wants and aspects of wants with a view to longer-term consequences of their relative satisfaction or frustration.
19   There will be more to say about wants and needs in the concluding section. At this point it should only be added that the student of politics, once he has adopted a conception of human needs, should proceed from there to make explicit his inferences about political objectives and his choice of commitments with the utmost care. If this kind of inquiry is neglected, as it certainly is in the political science curricula in most of our universities, the danger is that the political scientist unwittingly becomes the tool of other people's commitments. And *theirs* may be even less responsibly arrived at; conceivably, the expertise of the political scientist may come to serve the irrational purposes of genteel bigotry in domestic policies or of paranoid jingoism and reckless gambling with our chances of survival in foreign policies. If advice-giving social scientists don't feel called on to invest their best intellectual energies in studying the ultimate ends of our national policies, it is unlikely that anyone else of influence will; most active politicians have, after all, more immediately pressing worries, and these are anyway the kinds of concerns they are best trained to handle.
20   Intellectual treason, to return to Eulau's phrase, is probably a remote hazard in our profession. For, rather than placing himself in the service "of those whose values he disagrees with," the political scientist usually will by natural, uninvestigated processes come to agree with the prevailing values of his profession, of the major foundations and of his government, at least on the more basic public policy objectives and assumptions. His training and career incentives focus on formal rationality. It is fortunate that many social scientists for other reasons tend to be humane and liberal individuals. We will be far better off, however, if we can make it respectable or even mandatory for many more of our researchers to be guided in their choice of theory and problems by their own articulated values, instead of acting willy-nilly on the supposedly neutral values impressed on them by the conventional wisdom of their profession.

II

21   In the contemporary political science literature it is by no means unusual to see the articulation of political norms begin and end with a commitment to "democracy" in some unspecified sense. Fifteen years ago a respected political scientist

suggested a more critical orientation: "The democratic myth is that the people are inherently wise and just, and that they are the real rulers of the republic. These propositions do have meaning; but if they become, as they do even among scholars, matters of faith, then scientific progress has been sacrificed in the interest of a morally satisfying demagogy."[6] This advice has not been generally heeded. Even today many political scientists are writing as if democracy unquestionably is a good thing, from which unquestionably good things will flow, while at the same time they profess a disinterest in settling value issues. "The only cure for the ills of democracy is more democracy," is still the implicit slogan of quite a few social scientists, who seem unaware of even the *conceptual* difficulties involved in developing generally useful criteria, let alone a rationale, for "more democracy." To put it bluntly, it appears that a good number of otherwise able political scientists confuse a vaguely stated conventional "democratism"[7] with scientific objectivity.

That behavioral research not explicitly related to problems 22 of democracy tends to be vague in its implications for normative democratic theory is perhaps to be expected. It is paradoxical that some of the leading behavioral writers *on democracy* continue to write as if they want to have it both ways: to be rigorously value-neutral and at the same time be impeccable champions of conventional pluralist democracy. To straddle on a sharp issue would not be comfortable; if we want to write as good democrats and as logical positivists, too, it is perhaps necessary to be obtuse on issues like "why democracy?" or "what is democracy for?" and, indeed, "what is democracy?"

For a first example, take the late V. O. Key's most recent 23 book on *Public Opinion and American Democracy*.[8] Here we are presented with an admirably organized survey of what is now known of the characteristics of contemporary public opinion and of the extent of its bearing on American governmental decision processes. Yet for all these facts about public opinion, there is hardly a hint of their implications, in the author's judgment, for any of the relevant normative issues of democracy; what little is said on this score is uninformative indeed. For example, the point is made toward the end that political deviants "play a critical role in the preservation of the vitality of a democratic order as they urge alterations and modifications better to achieve the aspirations of men. Hence the fundamental significance of freedom of speech and agitation" (p. 555). There is no elaboration of this point, which one might take to be an important issue, considering the book's title and general subject. And there is no other discussion of what purpose all this political knowledge should serve. Is it the "preservation of the vitality of a democratic order" as far as we can articulate the criteria for the best possible government, or for trends in the best direction? What does "vitality" mean here, and what aspects of our democracy are most in need of it? Is free speech valuable solely as a means to this rather obscurely conceived end?

24   Or take the volume on *Voting*, by a team of top-notch political sociologists.[9] One of the book's two themes, we are told (p. x) is the social problem of how political preferences are formed, while the "confrontation of democratic theory with democratic practice is the second implied theme that runs throughout the book." There is much about certain kinds of practices, yes; but democratic theory is limited to a few examples of "impossible" demands of "traditional normative theory" on the role of the citizen; that he should be politically interested, knowledgeable and rational. These investigators find that most voters are indeed politically apathetic, ignorant and far from rational in their political behavior.

25   Given the second theme one might have expected the authors to raise some pertinent questions concerning the sense, if any, in which we nevertheless do have a democracy, or possibly the sense in which we nevertheless *ought* to be able to have a democracy, if what we have now does not fit this concept. Or perhaps an attempt toward reformulating democratic norms in better accord with political realities, if the term "democracy" should be saved for new uses.

26   Nothing of the sort happens. Instead, the authors make the happy discovery that the *system of democracy* that we have "does meet certain requirements for a going political organization"; indeed, as it is said just before, "it often works with distinction" (p. 312). What is good and bad about the system is left in the dark, as is the question of criteria for "distinction." Instead, we are given a list of dimensions of citizen behavior, and are told that the fact that individuals differ on these various dimensions (*e.g.*, involvement—indifference) somehow is exactly what the modern democratic system requires. It all ends well, then; and in parting the authors leave us with this comforting if question-begging assurance: "Twentieth-century political theory—both analytic and *normative*—will arise *only* from hard and long observation of the actual world of politics, closely identified with the deeper problems of practical politics." (p. 323. Italics supplied.) *Only?*

27   Turn now to a widely and deservedly praised book with the promising title, *A Preface to Democratic Theory*. Robert Dahl explains his choice of title by asserting that "there is no democratic theory—only democratic theories. This fact sug-

gests that we had better proceed by considering some representative theories in order to discover what kinds of problems they raise..."[10] And in the landscape of behavioral literature this work does stand out as an impressive exercise in logical analysis. Excellent critical evaluations of the Madisonian and the populist-type democratic theories are offered; but subsequently Dahl changes his tack to what he calls (p. 63) the descriptive method: under "polyarchal democracy" he seeks to develop empirical criteria for a concept of democracy based on our knowledge of existing species. As we would expect of a competent behavioralist, the author develops some enlightening perspectives on how "the American hybrid" in fact appears to be functioning.

Penetrating as this account of the basic operating procedures 28 of the American democracy is, the author's criteria for evaluating the result are surprisingly inarticulate and *ad hoc*. He will *not* try to determine whether it is a desirable system of government, he assures us toward the end of the book; and then proceeds to do just that, but vaguely:

> It appears to be a relatively efficient system for reinforcing agreement, encouraging moderation, and maintaining social peace in a restless and immoderate people operating a gigantic, powerful, diversified, and incredibly complex society. This is no negligible contribution, then, that Americans have made to the arts of government—and to that branch, which of all the arts of politics is the most difficult, the art of democratic government.

These are Dahl's parting words.

Having subjected the assumptions, hypotheses, implied 29 definitions, and even the presumed value axioms of two theories of democracy to painstaking analysis, the author's ambition not to discuss the desirability of the American system of government would be difficult to understand for someone unacquainted with the currently prevailing fashions among behavioralists. To study the definitional characteristics of this hybrid species of government and of the genus, "polyarchal democracy," is a worthwhile endeavor, to be sure, but would in my opinion assume far greater significance if pursued within a framework of value assumptions, however tentatively presented, from which could be derived operational criteria for judging what aspects of a functioning democracy ought to be valued and strengthened, as against other aspects that should be deplored and, if possible, counteracted. Why does the author never say clearly whether in *his* views democracy is something to be valued in itself, and maximized (as he takes Madisonian theory to assert), or as valuable for some specified ends (for example, for maximizing political equality, after the fashion of populists)?

30   In a Preface to democratic theory, and one which demonstrates a high order of rigor in analyzing other theories of democracy, the author's reluctance even to begin to develop operating criteria toward making meaningful the present system, or to provide pointers toward its more meaningful further development, is as astounding as it is disappointing. Reluctantly one concludes that Dahl in this particular context behaves like most political behavioralists: he feels he can permit himself to write normatively about political purposes, it would seem, only if they are stated in terms of "democracy" and are reasonably indeterminate, lest the suspicion should arise that he is pleading for some politically partisan position. Thus, a demeanor of scientific objectivity is maintained, and so is a persistently implied commitment to a certain political bias, which favors democracy roughly as it now exists in the West, or in this country.

III

31   Leo Strauss charges the behavioralists with a bias toward liberal democracy, and rightly so, in comparison to his position. Yet in some respects the bias of much behavioralist political literature is profoundly conservative, although this is a species of conservatism rather different from Strauss's. Philosophically speaking, this behaviorally oriented conservatism frequently includes an *anti-political* dimension which is not found in Strauss's work.[11] What is anti-political is the assumption, explicit or implicit, that politics, or at any rate American politics, is and must always remain primarily a system of rules for peaceful battles between competing private interests, and not an arena for the struggle toward a more humane and more rationally organized society.

32   Consider S. M. Lipset's recent suggestion that the age-old search for the good society can be terminated, for we have got it now. Democracy as we know it "is the good society itself in operation." Not that our democracy cannot still be improved upon, but roughly speaking, it appears, "the give-and-take of a free society's internal struggles" is the best that men can hope for. Our society is so good that Lipset welcomes, at least for the West, what he sees as a trend toward replacing political ideology with sociological analysis.[12]

This is an extreme statement, although by a leading and 33 deservedly famous political sociologist. We cannot saddle behavioralists in general with responsibility for such phrasing. But in substance, as we shall see, the same tendency toward affirming the *status quo* and, what is worse, toward disclaiming the importance and even the legitimacy of political ideology, and ideals, is discernible in other leading behaviorally oriented works as well.

Let us note incidentally that all the behavioral works re- 34 ferred to so far wind up affirming that American democracy on the whole works well, while failing to articulate the criteria on which this judgment is based.[13] In fairness it should be added that probably all these writers would make an exception for the place of the Negro and certain other underprivileged groups or categories for whom our democracy admittedly does not work so well; there are flaws, then, but fundamentally all is well or else will become well without any basic changes.

What is more troublesome than this somewhat conser- 35 vative commitment to a somewhat liberal conception of democracy[14]—whether acknowledged or surreptitious—is the antipolitical orientation referred to a moment ago; the failure to see politics as potentially, at least, an instrument of reason, legitimately dedicated to the improvement of social conditions.

Within a brief space that allows no extensive documentation 36 perhaps the next best thing to do is to consider for a moment a recent example of a behavioralist approach in which, for a change, the underlying assumptions are spelled out with commendable clarity, and then let the reader judge to what extent other literature referred to above may not implicitly rest on similar starkly anti-political premises.

James M. Buchanan and Gordon Tullock have called their 37 book *The Calculus of Consent,* with subtitle *Logical Foundations of Constitutional Democracy.*[15] The task set for the book, we are told in the Preface, is "to analyze the calculus of the rational individual when he is faced with questions of constitutional choice"; the authors, both of whom have most of their training in economics, intend to develop what they take to be the rationale for group action in the public sector in a free society—*i.e.,* for political action.

The authors take pains to assert the value-free nature of their 38 approach to the science of politics. True, they choose to go along with "the Western philosophical tradition" in so far as they consider the human individual "the primary philosophical entity" (p. 11). From here on, supposedly, we are dealing with the political processes that flow from the desire of all individuals to try to maximize whatever they may value. "The grail-like search for some 'public interest' apart from, and independent of, the separate interests of the individual participants in social choice" (p. 12) is not the concern of *these* authors.

39   Only in one limited sense do the authors recognize a sort of collective interest in a free society: "it is rational to *have a constitution*" (p. 21), or a set of rules for deciding how decisions in the public sector are to be arrived at; *constitutional* issues are in principle to be settled by unanimity, while *operational* issues—all other political issues—must be settled according to constitutional provisions. The authors see no rationale for majoritarianism as a way of deciding, unless a constitution happens to require it in given contexts; consequently, constitutions can be changed only by unanimity, according to this "individualistic theory of political process," as one of the authors has lately named the theory.[16]

40   In his more recent statement, Buchanan recognizes as an "entirely reasonable interpretation" (p. 7) that this approach to political processes can be seen as a model for the defense of the *status quo*. His most important rejoinder is that "analysis must start from somewhere, and the existing set of rules and institutions is the only place from which it is possible to start" (p. 7).

41   The previously cited writings of leading behavioralists have been less explicit and also less bold in showing the way from assertedly value-free premises toward a conservative and in my sense anti-political orientation. Yet, in all the works given critical attention above, there are normative ambiguities wide enough to make room for a theory such as the one offered by Buchanan and Tullock. This is not to say that Eulau, Key, Berelson *et al.*, Dahl, or Lipset would concur with Buchanan and Tullock in their normative position. But their approach to politics is philosophically similar in its emphasis on prevailing behavior patterns here and now as the thing to study and in its rejection of the legitimacy of normative positions as frameworks for research (except in a normatively *ad hoc* policy science context). Buchanan and Tullock have been able to explicate in considerable detail *one* rationale for an implicit stance that appears to be widely shared by students of politics today.

42   If a similar orientation were to be adopted in medical literature, its scope would in the main be confined to studying how patients choose to cope or at any rate do cope with their pathologies, while omitting or neglecting fundamental study of conditions for possible treatment and prevention.

IV

Unlike other behavioral literature, modern works in compar- 43
ative politics almost always focus on real political problems;
when political institutions are compared cross-nationally or
cross-culturally, pseudopolitical behavior can more readily be
seen as dysfunctional in terms of some conception or other
of the public good; usually such conceptions are couched in
terms of "modernization" or "development," at least if comparisons are cross-cultural as well as cross-national. The point
is that developmental perspectives and therefore political purposes are ever-present in this literature, even if they are not
often well articulated. Yet, what is particularly impressive in
some of this literature is its conceptual and theoretical scope,
including the stress on psychological as well as social component explanations of political behavior, and on the need for
integrating microanalyses of personalities and small groups
with macro-analyses of large collectivities.[17]

Concerned as the modern students of comparative politics 44
have been with substantive problems, they have resisted temp-
tations to pursue their inquiries according to immediately
practical considerations such as the availability of operational
indices and techniques of measurement.[18] On the contrary,
insistent efforts have been made to innovate concepts that
would take account of variables which are not as yet accessible
to observation and quantification—concepts such as political
culture, political socialization, political identity, and political
style, for example. The long-term strategy appears to be to start
out with concepts broad enough to encompass all significant
aspects of political reality, and then work toward parcelling out
component concepts which come closer to corresponding to
variables that can be observed, perhaps indirectly and by tentative indices at first. Thus the theoretical working hypotheses
can gradually, it is hoped, be subjected to increasingly direct
and stringent tests. This is a far cry from the piecemeal approach to political (or pseudopolitical) reality in many other
works, which almost exclusively pays attention to disparate
empirical relationships while neglecting to consider the possible systematic-theoretical reasons we might have for taking
an interest in them.

There is also this to be said about the modern comparative 45
politics literature, however, that its conceptual and theoretical innovations have as yet failed to make a significant dent in
the same democratic myth that Almond himself—the leader in
this field—has warned us against years ago (above, p. 42). The

dilemma already discussed, of desiring to support democracy and adopt a stance of value neutrality, too, has not as yet been satisfactorily resolved in this literature, either. And this failure is paradoxical in this particular context, in part because the ostensible chief concern is with "development" or "modernization" as the dependent variable, so that the question of development toward *what* immediately suggests itself. The failure is paradoxical also because these scholars have coined bold new concepts on the independent side of the ledger, and some have written extensively about concepts as far removed from realms of observation as "political culture" and "political identity."[19] Yet a concept such as "human need" has not been touched, and discussions of key terms like "political development" or "modernization" have been hampered, it would seem, by an unwillingness to question whether democratic ways or what kinds of democratic ways are most conductive to satisfying human needs.[20]

46   In the most extensive recent discussion of these concepts La Palombara begins well with a warning that what many scholars appear to have in mind "when they speak of a modern or developed system is one that approximates the institutional and structural configuration that we associate with the Anglo-American (in any event, the Western) democratic systems" (p. 10). He calls this conceptualization culture-bound; yet in the same and the following chapter he goes to considerable lengths himself in arguing for the use of the same kinds of culture-bound criteria to evaluate development or modernity abroad. While he contributes a useful discussion of different dimensions along which political change can be measured, he never inquires whether in other countries there might be other criteria of development of equal or greater significance than his own essentially Anglo-Saxon criteria. "One of the great dilemmas of many of the developing countries," he writes, "is that they seem to want economic development more than freedom" (p. 41), and the last term he takes as a matter of course to refer to pluralist institutions. "Why should it not be possible to raise a belief in and desire for democracy to the same level?" (p. 58). And in conclusion La Palombara asserts that we Americans must expand our efforts to export not only technical know-how "but our political ideology and reasonable facsimiles of our political institutions and practices as well." Without such an effort, he adds, he is reasonably confident that "the probability of attaining democratic configuration in most of the newer states is very low indeed" (pp. 60–61).

47   The main difficulty with this reasoning is that men are motivated, also politically, by their immediate needs and

wants, and not by foreign orthodoxies. La Palombara speculates "whether it would not be possible to manipulate demands so that goals of political development enjoy a status equal to that of economic change" (p. 130), and suggests the encouragement of private as against collectively oriented enterprise for this end. The answer is surely a flat no: it is *not* possible, in most countries in which most people are economically underprivileged, to create a broad popular interest in pluralist democratic institutions. "Acceptance of the norms of democracy requires a high level of sophistication and ego security," writes Lipset, on the basis of a variety of loosely connected empirical data.[21] An active concern for the public welfare presupposes a liberation both from anxiety neuroses and from realistic fears concerning one's own and one's family's physical sustenance, welfare and security. To put it more succinctly, needs for food and safety take precedence over political interest; no amount of political manipulation could be expected to alter such priorities.

To be sure, individuals can be lured into "the game of politics" as advantageous careers under the right circumstances; but is this the kind of political development that the West should desire? If budding western-democracy-type pluralist institutions turn out to benefit only the middle and upper classes—as in many Latin American countries—then we should not be surprised if idealistic students and others with a passion for social justice, or for politics as distinct from pseudopolitics, may become disposed to reject the forms of pluralistic democracy altogether.[22]

Nevertheless, the trend among political behavioralists, including students of comparative politics, appears to be toward a clean break not only with Plato's concern with justice as something above democracy, for the true philosopher; also, it seems that the classical conception of democracy as a system of rational deliberation for settling issues of justice and welfare is on its way out, *even as a political ideal*. Reference has been made to the *ad hoc* attempts of Berelson *et al.* to bring the norms of democracy in better accord with the facts of what I have termed pseudopolitical behavior. In *The Civic Culture* Almond and Verba present and discuss a variety of usefully differentiated survey data collected in five countries (United States, Britain, West Germany, Italy and Mexico). "What we have done in this book," they conclude, "is to spell out methodically the mixture of attitudes that support a democratic system. If it can create a more sober and informed appreciation of the nature and complexity of the problems of democratization, it will have served its purpose."[23] But what kind of democracy?

The theoretical point of departure is neither in a conception of human needs nor in the classical theories of democracy, but in such literature as has been discussed above—notably Dahl's *Preface to Democratic Theory* and the last chapter in Berelson's *Voting*. In fact, Almond and Verba emphatically reject the classical "rationality-activist" ideal of democratic citizenship in favor of a more balanced "parochial-subject-participant" orientation; in a healthy, stable democracy as they conceive it (and American political culture comes close even though it does not quite embody this ideal), "the democratic citizen is called on to pursue contradictory goals; he must be active, yet passive; involved, yet not too involved; influential, yet deferential."[24]

50   Perhaps so, if the ultimate goal is democratic stability. And there is no denying, from my normative position, that democratic stability is valuable, and that many nations ought to have more of it. But is it the most important goal for political development; is it the goal that should serve as the basis for evaluating all other goals (whether wholly, in terms of instrumentality, or partially, in terms of compatibility)? Should we not instead hold, in Eulau's phrase, that "The Goal is Man?"

V

51   In the study of political behavior, "analysis must start from somewhere, and the existing set of rules and institutions is the only place from which it is possible to start," according to Buchanan. Students of comparative politics have nevertheless demonstrated the feasibility of analyzing political developments in some countries in terms of valuable outcomes achieved in others.[25] It remains to be shown that political behavior and institutions can be analysed also in terms of normative assumptions to the effect that the purpose of politics is to meet human needs and facilitate human development.

52   Contrary to an apparently prevailing assumption among political behavioralists, psychological phenomena are just as *real* as economic and voting behavior phenomena, even though admittedly less accessible to observation and measurement. Some more of the same conceptual boldness displayed in the recent literature on comparative politics is required if political inquiry is to become related to important human wants and needs. For one thing, we need to distinguish more clearly between pseudopolitical and more strictly political behavior, if we want to learn how to encourage the latter at the expense of the former.[26]

A major conceptual and theoretical task is to develop a sat- 53
isfactory theory of human needs and of the relationships between needs and *wants*—here referring to perceived or felt
needs. Wants (or, synonymously, desires) and demands can be
observed and measured by way of asking people or observing
their behavior. Needs, on the other hand, can only be inferred
from their hypothetical consequences for behavior or, more
manifestly, from the actual consequences of their frustration.
Whenever superficial wants are fulfilled but underlying needs
remain frustrated, pathological behavior is likely to ensue.

Prior to the development of a viable theory of political devel- 54
opment is at least a beginning toward a theory of individual
human development. Such a beginning exists in psychological literature, but it has so far been inadequately drawn on by
students of political behavior. Let me very briefly suggest the
direction of this theorizing, and some of its implications for
the study of political behavior.

Basic human needs are characteristics of the human organ- 55
ism, and they are presumably less subject to change than the
social or even the physical conditions under which men live.
Wants are sometimes manifestations of real needs, but, as Plato
and many other wise men since have insisted, we cannot always infer the existence of needs from wants. Wants are often
artificially induced by outside manipulation, or they may be
neurotically based desires whose satisfaction fails to satisfy
needs, or both. Emphasis on a civic-culture type of democracy as the goal for political development may well perpetuate a state of affairs in which human needs as seen by the
political-minded (in my strict sense of "political") will remain
in the shadow of much-advertised human wants as promoted
by pseudo-politicians and other enterprisers whose horizons
do not extend beyond their own occupational or career interests and status anxieties.[27]

I say *may*, for I am raising a question rather than adopt- 56
ing a position. In order to investigate the relationship between
needs and wants as they pertain to political functions we must
start out with a tentative conception of priorities among human needs. The best available point of departure, in my opinion, is in A. H. Maslow's theory of a hierarchy of human needs;
this theorizing ought to be drawn on until a more plausible and
useful theory becomes available.

Maslow lists five categories of needs in the order of their 57
assumed priority: (1) physical needs (air, water, food, etc.);
(2) safety needs (assurance of survival and of continuing satisfaction of basic needs); (3) needs to love and be loved;

(4) need for esteem (by self and others); and (5) need for self-actualization and growth. This list presents a hierarchy, according to Maslow, in the sense that the "less prepotent needs are minimized, even forgotten or denied. But when a need is fairly well satisfied, the next prepotent ('higher') need emerges, in turn to dominate the conscious life and to serve as the center of organization of behavior, since gratified needs are not active motivators."[28] Note, however, that whenever in the course of a human life the "higher" needs have become activated, they are not necessarily extinguished as a result of later deprivation of "lower" or more basic needs. For example, some individuals, provided they have once known physical safety, will unhesitatingly sacrifice all of it for love, or for standards of right conduct tied in with their self-esteem, etc.

58   In a recent volume, James C. Davies has suggested the utility of Maslow's theory as a generator of propositions regarding political behavior, and he illustrates the plausibility (without demonstrating the validity) of such propositions with a wealth of historical and contemporary political behavior data. For example, according to Davies's theorizing it is impractical to suggest, with La Palombara, that it might be "possible to manipulate demands" in economically underdeveloped countries so that widespread loyalties to democratic institutions could emerge: "Long before there can be responsible or irresponsible popular government, long before the question of dictatorship or democracy can be taken up, the problem of survival must be solved so that a political community itself can develop, so that people can direct some of their attention to politics."[29] In another context he says, "Propaganda cannot paint a picture which conflicts with reality as it is seen by individuals in the light of their basic needs" (p. 134); the picture can be painted all right, but it will be a wasted effort. And Davies quotes Kwame Nkrumah, whose implicit rejoinder to La Palombara's argument is hard to improve on: "We cannot tell our peoples that material benefits in growth and modern progress are not for them. If we do, they will throw us out and seek other leaders who promise more.... We have to modernize. Either we shall do so with the interest and support of the West or we shall be compelled to turn elsewhere. This is not a warning or a threat, but a straight statement of political reality" (p. 135).

59   One shortcoming in Davies's as well as Maslow's work, in my judgment, is that both authors seek to relate events and behavior directly to the elusive concept of "need," without the use of an intermediate and more manageable concept such as "want." Both concepts are badly needed, and their interrela-

tions and their application in hypotheses must be developed if we want to move toward a more adequate knowledge of political behavior. It must be granted that manifest wants are important aspects of our political reality, especially in democracies; what matters is that we also keep remembering, unlike many behavioralists, that there also are genuine needs to worry about, elusive though they may be to the researcher's conventional tools. The volume of competing loudspeakers, if I may use a metaphor, is in a pluralist democracy perhaps more likely to depend on the power of the purse than on the urgency of the need. Even the most democratic governments are likely to come to a bad end—to say nothing of the individuals living under them—unless they learn to become at least as responsive to the basic needs of all their citizens as they are to the most insistent wants of the various articulate influential interest groups and parties.

Most of Maslow's as well as Davies's discussion is highly 60 speculative; only a beginning has been made. But their theory does lend itself to the production of testable hypotheses. For example, Almond's theory of political "input functions" (political socialization and recruitment; interest articulation; interest aggregation; political communication) and "output functions" (rule making; rule application; rule adjudication),[30] would seem to provide a fertile field for exploring what the participation in or other ego-involvement with each type of function can mean, in satisfying individual personality needs as well as wants. Moving in this direction we can perhaps get away from the customary *clichés* about the value of democracy, toward research-based knowledge on what (aspects of) democratic institutions have what kinds of value for human development.

I have argued elsewhere that the human goals of poli- 61 tics should be conceived in terms of maximizing individual freedom—psychological, social and potential.[31] Democracy and indeed every law and constitutional clause should be judged as a means to this end. A comprehensive treatment of norms of liberty with interrelationships and empirical consequences is necessary for this purpose, and so is a theory of human needs such as Maslow's, which in effect predicts that with increasing satisfaction of sustenance and security needs men's tendency will be to become less anti-social, more capable of respecting and eventually perhaps insisting on respect for the basic needs and liberties of others.

The normative research[32] to be recommended can be done 62 with far more precision than was attempted or achieved in the work on freedom just referred to. Perhaps philosophers

working with political scientists can be expected to be active
on this research frontier in future years. One good example
of normative research of this kind, even though its reference
to empirical data is for purposes of normative interpretation
only, is Naess's study of Gandhi's ethics of conflict resolution.[33]
63   The burden of this paper, then, is to plead for an expansion and a more systematic articulation of the psychological
and the normative perspectives of political behavior research.
I propose as a normative basis the proposition that politics
exists for the purpose of progressively removing the most stultifying obstacles to a free human development, with priority for the worst obstacles, whether they hit many or few—in
other words, with priority for those individuals who are most
severely oppressed; as Harrington points out with respect to
the poverty-stricken in the United States, they are also the least
articulate, and the least likely to achieve redress by way of
the ordinary democratic processes.[34] It is argued in this paper
that the current preoccupation with pseudopolitical behavior
carries conservative and anti-political implications, and that
the best hope for a more politically useful reorientation of behavioral research—in addition to and beyond the comparative
politics perspective—is to study how the various functions of
government bear, and could bear, on the satisfaction of basic
needs as well as conscious wants.
64   Among the questions to ask are these: What kinds of enduring satisfactions tend to be associated, for example, with
particular participant and subject roles established by alternate forms of centralized or decentralized decision processes?
Under what socio-cultural and socio-economic circumstances
are majoritarian decision processes, of given types, likely to
produce substantive satisfaction of the basic needs of, in Harrington's phrase, society's "rejects"?
65   As so often in our human condition, the dimensions of our
ignorance appear to grow larger the closer we come to the most
enduringly important issues of our social life. Much conceptual
as well as basic psychological work remains to be done before
our technical proficiency in the study of the relation of political
forms to basic needs and to liberty can come to match the
current work on analysis of voting patterns. But in this work
political scientists should participate; our stakes in its progress
are as high as anyone else's.
66   One particular type of research that should be pushed, as
a much needed complement to the large supply of data on
pseudopolitical behavior, is work that would focus on just how
some citizens "graduate" from the role of pseudopolitical ac-

tor to that of political actor. Or, more accurately—for surely there are more pseudopolitical actors in the older age groups, "hardened in the school of life"—how it is that some categories of individuals (or individuals in some categories of situations) manage to remain concerned with ideals and with politics, *i.e.*, with the welfare of their fellow men, all their lives?

A theory of human development is implied in the re- 67 search approaches here recommended. It asserts that man is likely to become increasingly capable of being rational, or intellectual,[35] to the extent that he no longer needs the services of his beliefs and attitudes for the purpose of keeping his various anxieties in check. Deep-seated neurotic anxieties about one's worth as a human being predispose to right-wing or occasionally leftwing extremism, with glorification of ingroups or individuals, living or dead, along with hatreds against outgroups and deviants. Neurotic status anxieties predispose to eager adherence to whatever views appear expected in one's reference groups. Realistic fears about employment or future career prospects predispose against maintaining the luxury of political opinions at all, unless they are "safe." Only for individuals whose main anxiety problems have been faced and in some way resolved is it generally possible to think of and care about problems of politics in terms of standards of justice or the public interest, independently of personal worries.

The development of strictly political incentives in the indi- 68 vidual, then, depends on a gradual process of liberation from a preoccupation with personal anxieties and worries. Stages in this process can be identified by research, although our concepts and instruments need some improvement before we can with confidence relate specific categories of political irrationality to (repressed or acknowledged) anxieties associated with specific levels in a hierarchy of human needs. Human nature being complex, so is the task of fully comprehending the dynamics of political behavior. My essential argument here is that we must face up to but not complacently accept, as the pseudopolitical outlook does, the fact that most of our citizens live too harassed lives or lack the education or opportunities for reflection to permit them the real satisfactions and the full dignity of democratic citizenship. We must pose the empirical problem of how the more stultifying pressures on adults and pre-adults can be reduced. A premature ruling out of the classic democratic citizenship ideal, with its stress on reason as a crucial factor in politics, would seem particularly inappropriate in our age of rapid technological change; never was the need for politics in the strict sense greater.

69   It is conceivable that our prospects for developing much
larger proportions of political-minded citizens will improve
substantially if or when the "cybernetics revolution" does away
with our omnipresent worries about making a living.[36] On the
other hand, unless educational and cultural resources can be
expanded as rapidly, so that more people may be enabled to
base their sense of identity and self-esteem on their own attributes or ideals rather than on their occupational roles, status anxieties and despair about lack of purpose in life might
remain at present levels, and become aggravated for some. But
the over-all prospects surely would be brighter, to the extent
that more of the principal *real* worries on which our current
anxieties feed were removed.

70   In any event, let us not as political scientists rule out the possibility that a real *polity* may emerge eventually—a community
of people capable of giving some of their energies to political
as distinct from pseudopolitical reflection and activity. A less
utopian first step that may be hoped for is that many more
political scientists will adopt a more political (or a less pseudopolitical) perspective in their theorizing and research. As
the horizons of behavior research expand to encompass latent
need-behavior as well as manifest want-behavior, our political
science will not only produce a new order of intellectual challenge; it may also become a potent instrument for promoting
political development in the service of human development.

Notes

1. Alfred Cobban, "The Decline of Political Theory," *Political Science
   Quarterly*, Vol. 48 (1953), p. 335.
2. Heinz Eulau, *The Behavioral Persuasion in Politics* (New York,
   1963), p. 133 and pp. 133–37.
3. Robert Dahl, *Modern Political Analysis* (Englewood Cliffs, 1963),
   p. 6.
4. "Priorities" here refers to norms for guiding the choice among
   conflicting needs and demands. Political ideals and visions of the
   good life enter in here, and would do so even if our knowledge of
   needs and of human nature were as extensive as our knowledge
   of demands and of social determinants of "public opinion."
5. Karl Mannheim employs a similar dichotomy of terms, though
   with different concepts, in his *Man and Society in an Age of Reconstruction* (New York, 1954), pp. 51–60.
6. Gabriel A. Almond, *The American People and Foreign Policy* (New
   York, 1950), p. 4.
7. The term is from Leo Strauss. See his "Epilogue" in Herbert J.
   Storing, ed., *Essays on the Scientific Study of Politics* (New York,
   1962), p. 326.

8. New York, 1961.
9. Bernard R. Berelson, Paul F. Lazarsfeld and William N. McPhee, *Voting: A Study of Opinion Formation in a Presidential Campaign* (Chicago, University of Chicago Press, 1954).
10. Chicago, University of Chicago Press, 1956, p. 1.
11. This is not to deny that the Straussian position is more authoritarian and far less respectful of the right to radical dissent, as is to be expected when a corner on objective truth is being claimed. *Cf.* especially Leo Strauss, *What is Political Philosophy and Other Studies* (Glencoe, 1959); and his "Epilogue" in Herbert J. Storing, ed., *op. cit.* See also Walter Berns, "The Behavioral Sciences and the Study of Political Things: The Case of Christian Bay's *The Structure of Freedom*," *American Political Science Review*, Vol. 55 (1961), pp. 550–59.
12. Seymour Martin Lipset, *Political Man: The Social Bases of Politics* (Garden City, 1960), esp. pp. 403 and 415.
13. An interesting attempt to evaluate the 1952 Presidential election in terms of five criteria of democratic consent (as opposed to nonrational responses to manipulated processes) is reported in Morris Janowitz and Dwaine Marvick, *Competitive Pressure and Democratic Consent* (Ann Arbor, Bureau of Government, University of Michigan, 1956). The five criteria are chosen somewhat haphazardly, but they are carefully and ingeniously operationalized and brought to bear on available data. The study shows what could just as well be done, in years to come, within a more carefully and systematically stated framework of political objectives and norms.
14. Though perhaps paradoxical, the statement is not self-contradictory. A democracy that guarantees many liberties to people of most persuasions, and in theory to everybody, may well be considered a liberal democracy. Freedom of speech and related freedoms have a strong appeal to most intellectuals, many of whom may become staunch conservatives *because* they believe in preserving their liberal democracy. Some, indeed, will become fixated on the need for defense of the social order to the point of ignoring the plight of poverty-stricken fellow-citizens whose formal liberty may seem worthless to themselves.
15. Ann Arbor, University of Michigan Press, 1962.
16. James M. Buchanan, "An Individualistic Theory of Political Process." Paper prepared for delivery at the 1963 Annual meeting of the American Political Science Association in Commodore Hotel, New York City.
17. Some of the milestones in this literature are Gabriel A. Almond, "Comparative Political Systems," *Journal of Politics*, Vol. 18 (1956), pp. 391–409; Almond and James S. Coleman, eds., *The Politics of the Developing Areas* (Princeton, Princeton University Press, 1960); Almond and Sidney Verba, *The Civic Culture* (Princeton, Princeton University Press, 1963).
18. For contrast, consider this statement on the ways of other behavioralists: "The focus of the political behaviorist, however, does

not seem to be a result of the state of political theory. Elections have been intensively studied because they lend themselves to the methodology of empirical research into politics." Morris Janowitz, Deil Wright, and William Delany, *Public Administration and the Public—Perspectives Toward Government in a Metropolitan Community* (Ann Arbor, Bureau of Government, University of Michigan, 1958), p. 2.

19. *Cf.* Almond and Verba, *op. cit.*, and Lucian W. Pye, *Politics, Personality, and Nation Building: Burma's Search for Identity* (New Haven, Yale University Press, 1962).

20. Concepts of modernization or development are discussed by James S. Coleman in Almond and Coleman, eds., *op. cit.*, pp. 532–36; by Lucian W. Pye, ed., *Communication and Political Development* (Princeton, Princeton University Press, 1963), pp. 14–20; and by Joseph La Palombara in his (ed.) *Bureaucracy and Political Development* (Princeton University Press, 1963), chs. 1 and 2.

21. *Political Man, op. cit.*, p. 115 and ch. 4.

22. Fidel Castro's wide following in Latin American can be plausibly explained in these terms.

23. *Op. cit.*, p. 505 and ch. 15.

24. *Ibid.*, pp. 478–79 and 440–41.

25. See especially Robert E. Ward and Dankwart A. Rustow, *The Political Modernization of Japan and Turkey* (Princeton University Press, 1964).

26. However, we should not assume without inquiry that *all* pseudopolitical behavior is dysfunctional for all high-priority human wants and needs; not, of course, that all varieties of political behavior are to be preferred to pseudopolitical self-seeking or neurotic striving.

27. Joseph Tussman also stresses the danger of destroying the integrity of political communication when the modern bargaining approach to politics enters the "forum or tribunal" that a democratic electorate ought to constitute, according to classical theories of democracy. "We teach men to compete and bargain. Are we to be surprised, then, at the corruption of the tribunal into its marketplace parody?" *Obligation and the Body Politic* (New York, Oxford University Press, 1960), p. 100 and pp. 101–21.

28. Abraham H. Maslow, "A Theory of Human Motivation," *Psychological Review,* Vol. 50 (1943), p. 394 and pp. 370–96. See also his *Motivation and Personality* (New York, 1954).

29. *Human Nature in Politics* (New York, 1963), p. 28. Davies does not refer to La Palombara.

30. *Cf.* his introduction to Almond and Coleman, eds., *op. cit.*

31. *The Structure of Freedom* (Stanford, Stanford University Press, 1958, and New York, 1965).

32. The term "normative research" may be puzzling to some, who think of research exclusively as systematically re(peated) search for empirical data, in the real world or in contrived experimental worlds. And "research" has been one of the empirical social scientist's proud banners in his uphill fight against the sometime

supremacy of armchair speculators. In our time a less parochial use of "research" is called for, as a way of recognizing the close interplay between the empirical, normative and logical aspects of inquiry that, as the present paper argues, is necessary for the further development of our knowledge of political as of other human behavior.

33. Arne Naess, "A systematization of Gandhian ethics of conflict resolution," *Journal of Conflict Resolution,* Vol. 2 (1958), pp. 140–55; and also Johan Galtung and Arne Naess, *Gandhis poldiske etikk* (Oslo, Tanum, 1955).

34. Michael Harrington, *The Other America: Poverty in the United States* (Baltimore, Penguin Books, 1968; New York, 1969).

35. *Cf.* my "A Social Theory of Intellectual Development," in Nevitt Sanford, ed., *The American College* (New York, 1961), pp. 972–1005, esp. pp. 978 and 1000–1005.

36. W. H. Ferry and 25 associates have recently issued a statement that received front-page attention in the *New York Times* and other newspapers, under the title "The Triple Revolution: An Appraisal of the Major U.S. Crises and Proposals for Action" (Washington: Maurer, Fleischer, Zon and Associates, 1120 Connecticut Ave., 1964). Referring to the revolutions in cybernetics, in weaponry, and in human rights, but particularly to the first of the three, Ferry *et al.* argue that there "is an urgent need for a fundamental change in the mechanisms employed to insure consumer rights" (p. 9), now that the problem of production has been solved and the problem of full employment has become impossible to solve with our present system. "We urge, therefore, that society, through its appropriate legal and governmental institutions, undertake an unqualified commitment to provide every individual and every family with an adequate income as a matter of right. This undertaking we consider to be essential to the emerging economic, social, and political order in this country" (p. 16).

Bernard Susser

The Behavioural Ideology:
A Review and a Retrospect

1   From the end of the Second World War to the present, political science was rocked by two major upheavals. First of
these upheavals—the 'behavioural revolution'—was a spirited
but bloodless battle that set the tone of political research for
some two decades. In the middle-sixties a not always peaceful
protest movement from within the discipline once again began
to clamour for a reorientation of priorities, and by the end of
the sixties and the early seventies talk of a 'post-behavioural
revolution' was rife.[1]

2   These struggles divided the discipline into three more or less
identifiable groups: the pre-behaviouralists who retained traditional methods such as legal-institutional analysis and normative theory, the behaviouralists who emphasized the need
for scientific method, and the post-behaviouralists who felt
that exclusive reliance upon scientific method threatened the
'relevance' of the discipline. In recent years it has generally
been this last group that has posed the new questions and challenges for the discipline and that has attracted the generation
of aspiring political scientists.

3   If this schema is reasonably accurate, the owl of Minerva
is about ready to spread her wings over the gathering behavioural dusk. In a long retrospective look, the broad lines
of behavioural topography will become visible, signifying the
end of an era. While the author wishes to dissociate himself
from the wisdom of this prescient fowl, he would like to make
his own sortie over the behavioural terrain—from a lower altitude and with poorer visibility.

4   One of the most persistent criticisms of behaviouralism was
that it concealed ideological assumptions behind a veneer of
scientific objectivity. There was said to be a 'metaphysical
pathos,'[2] a series of intended and unintended consequences
that derived either directly from the application of scientific,
empirical and quantitative methods to human questions or,
more damning yet, an outright, if not always recognized, importation of values and preferences that found their way into
'scientific' conclusions.

5   While political conservatives generally focused their criticisms on the inability of scientific *method* to deal adequately

From *Political Studies*, 22 (1974), pp. 271–288. Reprinted by permission.

with human problems—only reason, wisdom, insight and cultivation (i.e., a return to the idealist tradition) could penetrate this most difficult of domains—radicals saw in the behavioural analysis of politics an attempt to vindicate ideological positions without recognizing them as such. They went on to decry the ulterior motives lurking behind many of the methodology-laden treaties, the jargoned 'scientism', the self-effacing 'neutrality'. 'Science', they claimed, 'is politics by other means'.

Perhaps the most telling indication that there was truth to 6 the radicals' claim is the way the discipline itself split over the issue. I think it may be said that the great majority of unreserved behaviouralists, as well as its most noted advocates, practitioners and defenders, were middle-of-the-road liberals who opposed major revisions to the basic structure of liberal democracy—whether offered from the right or the left. I think it true as well that many of the results of behavioural research on politics tended to buttress liberal democratic biases (e.g., pluralism, group theory, communications theory), while those which contradicted the accepted democratic values (most notably voting behavior, political participation, electoral responsibility) were assimilated into the liberal democratic persuasion through revisions, reinterpretations and reconciliation. Conservatives and radicals in contrast were, by and large, loathe to accept the behavioural methodology (mainly conservatives) or its conclusions (mainly radicals)—surely not a case of mere coincidence.[3]

If, as seems likely, behaviouralism reflected a political per- 7 spective as well as a research method, it becomes imperative to bring these underlying assumptions into the open, to appreciate them for what they are, and to determine the effect they had upon research. It is the object of this study to isolate, document and synthesize the various ideological strands that formed the matrix in which behaviouralism operated. My second aim will be to determine whether the enumerated preferences were a direct outcome of the method; i.e. does the scientific method itself as applied to politics yield certain ideological results, or are these values the product of conscious and unconscious borrowing? Simply stated, is the 'behavioural ideology' implicit in the method or supplied by its practitioners?

Two clarifications are necessary in order to avoid misunder- 8 standing. First, the behavioural movement is approached as an 'ideal type'. What is of interest is the main highway and not the many side roads, turn-offs and detours. While there are probably very few (if any) behaviouralists whose position is identical in all areas to the one presented below, there is nevertheless, I believe, a need to deal with eras and movements as if they had a collective, condensible character. Second, I mean by behaviouralism nothing more than the application of precise scientific methods to the study of politics. Its other more specific meanings are not considered.

Epistemology

9   Every *Weltanschauung* rests upon a sanctioned method of acquiring knowledge. It accepts the results of some cognitive procedures as valid, as constituting knowledge, while rejecting others because they fail to be either logical, dialectical, or existential; because they are not faith-centred and so on. The behavioural ideology as well, has both its methodological heroes and its *methoda non grata*. It accepts as admissible only knowledge that is inductive, quantifiable, objectively verifiable, specific, while rejecting as unsubstantiated, subjective or even worthless, propositions that rest on any other foundation. Most roundly condemned are those methods claiming justification through wisdom, insight and intuition.

10   If knowledge is founded upon a certain set scientific method, then clearly *training* in this method—and this training is likely to be of a technical nature—is of paramount importance. No amount of cultivation or common sense can replace the technical mastery of method for the social scientist. Thus the epistemological bias is not merely a philosophical commitment but implies a type of training and ultimately a type of professional personality.

11   Laswell states the matter flatly: '...the discovery of truth is an object of specialized research....'[4] Neither the people, nor the politicians, nor the philosophers are equipped for the pursuit of truths about society. Only the scientists, following certain prescribed methods, can penetrate the nature of social reality. Dahl, in a similar vein, rejects political theory 'in the grand manner' because it 'can rarely, if ever, meet rigorous criteria of truth'.[5] These criteria, Dahl goes on to elucidate, are the same severe standards of evidence required of scientific work. If these standards cannot be met, if political theory does not 'take the notion of testability seriously, it will have to take up permanent cohabitation with literary criticism'[6]— presumably, a less than enviable mate. Eugene Meehan, in his typically caustic style has the final word. 'Normative judgements obtained through the search of one's viscera are no more worthy of credence and serious consideration than "auspices"

obtained by scrutiny of the entrails of a dead chicken, though both may lead to interesting and suggestive results.'[7]

The training orientation that is the concomitant of this ap- 12 proach comes into stark outline when contrasted with the professional personality sought by, among others, C. Wright Mills, the great enemy of 'abstracted empiricism'.[8] Mills sees the role of the social scientist as one of committed participant, social critic, gadfly. The goal of his work is to vindicate freedom, human fulfilment and responsible, effective popular participation in the political process. As an educator 'it is his purpose to cultivate such habits of mind among men and women who are publicly exposed to him'.[9] Social knowledge must serve society; it must be turned from the university outward, it must seek—in the words of Mills' intellectual forbear—to change the world, not merely to understand it. The critical question is at all times: 'Knowledge for what?'[10]

By contrast, the behaviouralist's insistence on the desirabil- 13 ity of a 'value-free' science leads in an entirely different direction. Normative judgements and social relevance contradict the 'fact-value disjunction' that stands at the very base of modern positivism from which behaviouralism took its origin. Because the opinions of scientists are no better than those of the layman, the scientist *qua* scientist has nothing to add to debates over normative issues.[11] 'The ultimate goal of the student of political behaviour is the development of a science of the political process...',[12] not of public policy itself. He can attempt to spell out the probable consequences of a certain policy, he may even do cost-benefit analyses to determine which alternative course of action will 'pay off', but he may not step past the bounds of his expertise into prescribing what is desirable, moral or just. His legitimate role is the pursuit of truth, which must not be undermined by irresponsible adventures in the political thicket. Somit and Tanenhaus consider as one of 'the key behaviouralist articles of faith' the proposition that:

> Political science should abjure, in favor of 'pure' research, both applied research aimed at providing solutions to specific, immediate social problems, and meliatory programmatic ventures. These efforts, as the behaviourist sees it, produce little valid scientific knowledge and represent, instead, an essentially unproductive diversion of energy, resources and attention.[13]

Dahl converts this position into an abstract statement of professional policy: 'The empirical political scientist is concerned with what is...not with what ought to be.'[14] Eulau makes the

same distinction between the is and the ought correspond to
the roles of the good scientist and the good citizen: 'Let us not
confuse,' he warns, 'the role of the responsible citizen with the
role of the scientist.'[15] And finally Ranney:

> In sum, our professional skills and utility depend on the scien-
> tific quality of our special body of knowledge. Hence our pri-
> mary obligation as scholars and teachers is to improve upon
> that knowledge. If frequent trips to Washington or the state-
> house or city hall keep most of our best and creative minds
> from that nuclear task both political science and the students
> and policy makers who hope to profit from it will be much the
> poorer.[16]

14   Apart from prescribing methods for arriving at admissible
conclusions, and apart from fostering a certain professional
posture, the empirical bent of behaviourism has the effect of
encouraging certain avenues of research while discouraging
others. Gaining a 'broad overview' of the purpose, quality and
direction of social research, of the large tableau of contemporary political history as it unfolds, has far too much the smack
of undisciplined humanism to attract the specialized student.
Yehezkel Dror, a distinguished behaviouralist, complains that:

> Empirical research susceptible to statistical tests of validity and
> reliability is regarded as the only legitimate source of knowl-
> edge, while problems not susceptible to such methods are ex-
> cluded from the domain of investigation.

This, of course, causes 'general theories' to be 'regarded with
suspicion'. He concludes that:

> The net aggregative effect of these tendencies is a strong predis-
> position to concentrate on micro-issues. Macro issues of social
> structure and dynamics—including most problems of high pol-
> icy significance—are often regarded as subjects 'at present' not
> susceptible to 'scientific' examination, and therefore not to be
> dealt with by contemporary social sciences.[17]

The 'generalist', too, that member of a vanishing species who
stubbornly refuses to submit to the pressures toward specialization, may receive token endorsement—nostalgia perhaps—
but he has no real place in a world created in the behavioural
image.

Moreover, there is another very important sense in which *the* 15
method determines the matter. Kaplan irreverently dubs it 'the
law of instrument'. He formulates it as follows:

> Give a small boy a hammer, and he finds that everything he
> encounters needs pounding. It comes as no particular surprise
> to discover that a scientist formulates problems in a way which
> requires for their solution just those techniques in which he
> himself is especially skilled.[18]

Understandably, those areas—notably voting studies—that
adapt easily to the method will attract behavioural researchers, grants, and very likely produce important ground-
breaking work that reinforces the process. Fields impervious to
quantification, or posing difficulties for precision, will receive
only slipshod treatment.

Ironically, even after numerous behavioural studies have re- 16
peatedly and consistently shown that the electoral process is
not the centre of the political universe, but rather a dependent
variable falling far short of other critical factors, electoral research has kept on flowering, mainly it seems, because it suits
the soil of behaviouralism so well. As one critic has put it: 'the
choice of research subjects is typically made on essentially irrelevant (but not random) grounds'.[19]

Pluralism

If the empirical method affects the choice of research ar- 17
eas, does it also influence the substantive research conclusions
themselves? To some extent the answer would have to be 'yes'.

The pluralist bias provides a good case in point. Respond- 18
ing to the growing body of sociological literature that came
to *élitist* conclusions in the description of community power
structures, the pluralists, most significantly Dahl, presented
counter-arguments showing the basic inadequacies of the
'Hunter thesis'[20] and proposing alternate research strategies
and conclusions.[21] While the sociologists had emphasized a
structure of power, a system of complex intermeshing social
and political relations, a basic communal matrix in which various roles involving the exercise of power acquire meaning and
effectiveness, Dahl concentrates on single actors and specific
decisions. His celebrated conclusions need not detain us, but
we should not fail to be struck by the unmistakable *rapport* that
exists between his method and his substantive judgements.

19   His criticisms of the sociological approach can be briefly
summarized as 'not empirical, not verifiable, not scientific'. 'I
do not see', he insisted, 'how anyone can suppose that he has
established the dominance of a specific group in a community
...without basing his analysis on a careful examination of a
series of concrete decisions'.[22] All the talk of roles, structure
and interrelationships borders on mystification. These elusive
terms and the even more inaccessible reality they purport to
represent are not empirically derived; indeed, they probably
cannot, in the nature of things, undergo satisfactory empirical
treatment. The empirical scientist's hesitation with these sociological constructs is readily understandable. There are, to
this way of looking at things, not simply overt acts of power
that can be measured, but profoundly affecting socialized behaviour patterns and expectations that block certain alternatives and suggest others, that determine the limits of legitimate
action. An informal, often unconscious, highly conditioned network of nuanced assumptions regarding who may do what
with whom, under what circumstances and by what means,
is a behaviouralist's nightmare.

20   To extricate himself from this unnavigable swamp, the behaviouralist proposes a strikingly simple methodology—one
which demonstrates the power of 'the law of instrument'. Dahl
for example, concentrates on specific actors and specific decisions and arrives at pluralist conclusions. There was no single group, he claims, that determined public policy in all of
the three areas he examined. The source of this methodology
is obvious. As an empirical scientist, only overt, measurable
phenomena and concrete individuals in specific situations are
material for study. Hence the format of inquiry is virtually
predetermined.

21   The conclusions, too, show the marks of the method. For
if one is unwilling to grant the possible existence of a non-
empirically verifiable structure, the range of available conclusions is sharply delimited. The methodology has, in effect,
ruled out an entire genre of phenomena. Furthermore, and
this is the core of the matter, the necessity for emphasizing
specific individuals and groups in concrete situations leads to
atomistic conclusions. If reality can only be approached in its
empirically accessible aspect, i.e., in its particular, individual
manifestations, the result is likely to be a view that emphasizes
the multiplicity of factors at work, the independent and irreducible nature of these various factors—in short, pluralism,
polyarchy and group theory.

22   It is no coincidence that Dahl's major foray into 'power
theory',[23] if such it may be called, concentrates on determin-

ing the power of individual senators in specific decision areas and gives no attention whatever to the power structure of the Senate itself, the posts various senators held, the intricate background of personal interrelationships, in short, the senate as a *system*.[24] All systems, structures, relationships, communities, dissolve in the behaviouralists' cauldron into aggregations of individuals in specific conditions—rendering them measurable, distinct, plural.[25]

Neither is it coincidental that the rise of group theory was contemporaneous with the introduction of scientific methodology into the study of politics. Arthur Bentley, whose stated aim was to rid political inquiry of the 'spooks' that prevented precise measurement, is, of course, the father of modern group theory. Bentley saw the study of particular groups as the new axis of political research. If his suggestions were adopted, he assures his readers:

> We shall cease to be blocked by the intervention of unmeasurable elements, which claim to be themselves the real causes of all that is happening, and which by their spook-like arbitrariness make impossible any progress toward dependable knowledge.[26]

The inclination to break phenomena down into distinct factors that are empirically accessible, finds its way into virtually all behavioural research. In voting studies, for example—the behavioural staple—there is a clear tendency toward reduction to such empirically distinct factors as age, sex, income and education in establishing a voter's profile. Other elements not amenable to quantification, areas in which responses cannot be condensed into quantitatively manipulable statements of fact—such as values, moral considerations and conviction itself—tend to be relegated to the shadowy domain of quasi-phenomena, to Bentley's world of 'spooks'.

Social and Psychological Determinism

If conviction, moral outlook and values cannot penetrate the epistemological armour of the behavioural world, and if these convictions and the actions that stem from them can be analysed only in terms of being 'systematically related' to a series of empirically accessible factors, are we not very close to a full-blown doctrine (implicit though it may be) of social and psychological determinism? Conviction cannot justify itself but

must be stated in terms of some other supporting factor. It
follows that thought is a derivative conditioned process.

26   That this is not merely the logical implication of behavioural
research but the actual position of its practitioners is quite
clear. Easton writes that 'values can ultimately be reduced to
emotional responses conditioned by the individual's total life-
experience'.[27] Another behaviouralist claims that 'the total of
the strains within the individual resulting from his genetic input and variations in the input from his environment is often
referred to as his values'.[28] Bentley set the tone for these later
formulations when he wrote that 'there is no idea which is not
a reflection of social activity',[29] and that 'ideas can be stated
in terms of groups: the groups never in terms of the ideas'.[30] If
there is anywhere that the behavioural movement in political
science merges with its counterpart in psychology, it is here.[31]

27   Interestingly, this inclination to social and psychological reductionism or determination is, potentially at least, far more
impervious and thoroughgoing than the classic formulations
of Marx and Mannheim. Marx could speak of certain middle-
class intellectuals who, having grasped the direction of history,
overcame their social origins to become part of the proletarian
struggle. Mannheim, too, placed his hopes on the 'free-floating
intellectuals' who, thanks to their intellectual sophistication,
could rise above ideological particularism and gain a more or
less universal, objective view of social reality. Both these positions rest on the belief that convictions can be judged according to some standards of right and wrong. The intellectual, by
perceiving the truth, can lift himself above his immediate reality. For the consistent behaviouralist, however, all normative
judgements are irremediably subjective and arbitrary, trans-
latable only into factors accessible to empirical study, that is
to say, to conditioning. He has no way to relate to conviction besides correlating it to specific environmental factors.
Behavioural determinism is virtually watertight.[32]

28   In all fairness, it should be noted that the behaviouralist does
not technically ascribe causal dependence to the correlation he
finds between a conviction and a series of supporting factors.
He merely claims that the relationship exists. But this, I think,
is a deceptive Humeian formalism. Behaviouralists easily slip
from the descriptive to the causal mode and will almost invariably seek explanations of a causal nature to better understand
the 'raw' data they present. If there is no way to handle a belief
besides connecting it to a series of accompanying and recurring factors, the result will inexorably be—in effect—a causal
ascription.

Relativity and Democracy

Democracy is a delicate growth that requires a special, care- 29
fully controlled atmosphere to survive. The ideological climate
must not be too hot or stormy, it must be fed by a regular
stream of tolerance and mutual respect, and, to complete the
metaphor, it must be planted in the solid soil of consensus.
There is perhaps no doctrine more suitable for shoring up 30
this delicate balance than the behaviouralist's axiom that each
person's point of view is relatively conditioned and subjective.
'The recognition that a political adversary, no differently than
oneself, pieces together his position out of the material which
experience has provided, goes far in moderating the intensity,
the life and death character of political struggle. To recognize
that a person's conviction is a contingent and ultimately arbitrary affair and that there is no way of deciding between contending values, deflates ideological pretentions and leads to
the kind of tolerance that underlies a healthy democracy. Fanaticism and extremism—the political version of the struggle
of the children of light and the children of darkness—cannot
flourish when the very pillars upon which conviction stands
are critically undermined.[33] To recall once again Mannheim's
'free-floating intellectual', it is precisely his appreciation of the
relative nature of all ideology that provides him with the universalistic perspective which, Mannheim hoped, would moderate political conflict.
What remains after the absolute claims of ideology have col- 31
lapsed? Principally a structure of civilized and restrained political interaction. The 'rules of the game' take the place of the
absolutes that have failed.[34] No position can be so 'right' and
no opposing position so 'wrong' as to entitle a political actor
to break the rules. My adversary is not evil and the purpose
of politics is not to destroy him. The political process provides
an efficient framework in which opposing yet relative points
of view can negotiate, bargain and compromise. In short, the
relativist, reductionist position implicit in behaviourism mod-
erates ideological fervour, encourages toleration and supports
a consensual agreement on the 'rules of the game', all of which
may be compressed into a single term: Democracy.

Compromise, Accommodation, Equilibrium

Just as the behaviouralist studies only the process and 32
not the goals of politics, so he tends to emphasize as valu-

able the 'rules of the game' and not the game's outcome. Compromise—the give and take of a politics played with only limited liability—far from being only a salutory method of solving political conflicts and achieving, by and large, beneficial results, becomes in itself an independent good. It becomes axiomatic that negotiation and accommodation are *the* legitimate means of resolving conflict, regardless of the nature of the conflict or the nature of the compromise. While the following statement may be somewhat stark, it clearly expresses the point:

> Non-political decisions are reached by considering a problem in its own terms, and by evaluating proposals according to how well they solve the problem. The best available proposal should be accepted, regardless of who makes it or who opposes it, and a faulty proposal should be rejected or improved no matter who makes it. Compromise is always irrational; the rational procedure is to determine which proposal is best and accept it. In a political decision on the other hand, action is never based on the merits of a proposal but always on who makes it and who opposes it. Action should be designed to avoid complete identification with any proposal or any point of view no matter how good or how popular it may be. The best available proposal should never be accepted because it is best; it should be deferred, objected to, discussed, until major opposition disappears. Compromise is always a rational procedure, even when the compromise is between a good and bad proposal.[35]

33   The reasoning behind this type of position is manifest. Since the preservation of the 'decision structures' is the prime objective and prior condition of the political process, policy considerations must take second place to this goal.[36]

34   Compromise is, indeed, so critical a goal for the behaviouralist that central to his recommendations is a plan for 'social balance' whose dual object is the institutionalization of the necessity for compromise and the avoidance of unregulated conflict. Like Plato and Rousseau, who constructed societies that would of themselves tend to knowledge and the general will, the behaviouralist envisages a society that by virtue of its composition and structure will vindicate compromise and moderation. This latest entry in the tradition of social masterplans seeks to strike a balance between wealth and poverty, liberalism and conservatism, pragmatism and passion, consensus and cleavage, participation and passivity, activity and apathy, élitism and popular control.[37] Countervailing power is the behavioural utopia.

The only legitimate change in this kind of world is incremen- 35
tal. Continuity is the broad highway into the future. To ask for
too much too soon, to advocate more than the kind of change
that issues directly out of the existing reality itself, is to invite
catastrophe. Lucien Pye comments that:

> It has become the mark of non-scholarly innocence to believe
> that dramatic improvement could be expected in society, for
> change could at best be incremental. The mood was reinforced
> by such powerful concepts as equilibrium, the balance of power
> and countervailing forces. Wise men knew that the real need
> was to understand existing realities because they were going to
> be around for a long time, or, if change was to come it would
> have to be the modest consequence of the interplay of existing
> forces.[38]

Keeping tensions low is therefore the paramount aim of a 36
'healthy' society. Health and normalcy are defined politically
as 'homeostasis'.[39] Popular expectations, if they are aimed too
high, are likely to upset this fine balance; hence it may be necessary to deflate expectations to preserve equilibrium. Ithiel
de Sola Pool writes:

> The testimony of the developing world is that order depends
> on somehow compelling newly mobilized strata to return to a
> measure of passivity and defeatism from which they have re-
> cently been aroused by the process of modernization. At least
> temporarily the maintenance of order requires a lowering of
> newly acquired aspirations and levels of political activity.[40]

Laswell, in this respect, represents the anachronistic *avant* 37
garde of the movement for political homeostasis. Not only
does he consider government action necessary to solve conflicts, he applauds the educational goal of reducing 'the number of moral mavericks who do not share the democratic
preferences'.[41] For, as he writes elsewhere:

> The time has come to abandon the assumption that the prob-
> lem of politics is the problem of promoting discussion among
> all the interests concerned in a given problem. Discussion fre-
> quently complicates social difficulties, for the discussion by far-
> flung interests arouses a psychology of conflict which provides
> obstructive, fictitious and irrelevant values. The problem of pol-
> itics is less to solve conflicts than to prevent them; less to serve
> as a safety valve for social protest than to apply social energy
> to the abolition of recurrent sources of strain in society.[42]

The social psychiatrist with his stocked arsenal of 'socialized Freudianism' is to engineer human behaviour, root out the sources of conflict and set up 'the free man's commonwealth'.

38   The price of consensus is indeed high. It rests, among other things, on popular apathy, repressing unsettling popular demands and giving up on the good for the sake of compromise. Obviously, to be willing to pay so high a price for consensus it must be of the very highest priority.

39   Finally, moderation receives the enthusiastic approbation of communications theory. Extremism, according to Karl Deutsch, is 'an epistemological disaster'. Writing of extreme nationalism, he says:

> Like other forms of ideological extremism, it prefers ideologically encoded messages, even if they are in error to any messages in other codes or symbols, even if those messages should happen to be true. The extreme nationalist, like the adherent of any extreme ideology, thus becomes like a blind man with a very short white stick. He ignores reality until it hits him, and those few events or things that cannot be ignored, to him, as to all the blind, are sudden.

The 'world of fact' is outweighed, drowned out by the commitment to ideological positions Deutsch characterizes as extreme. Of an ideology:

> It is extreme to exactly that extent which urgent and relevant messages from reality are overridden by unrealistic or irrelevant messages which this ideology prefers. Conversely, nationalism or any other ideology is moderate within a given network of social communication to the extent that realistic messages are transmitted within it and still have a significant effect on the making of actual decisions.[43]

40   Moderation, apart from all its other virtues, is epistemologically sound, realistic, responsive, in direct touch with the facts. Extremism is out of touch with the world, blind, rigid, unintelligent, dangerous. In effect, the former knows the truth of the world, while the latter blunders in error.

Ideology

41   Although an anti-ideological bias has not been the exclusive possession of the behavioural movement,[44] it has, without doubt, found its most congenial home in just these quarters.

Neither is this difficult to understand. Ideology is a method of arranging and evaluating phenomena from a certain normative orientation. Like all other value judgements it is, for the behaviouralist, conditioned and arbitrary, having no interest save insofar as it becomes a causal factor in a specific behaviour pattern. Ideology is relevant solely for its effects, not for itself.

But this would render ideology not so much noxious as sim- 42
ply neutral. Behaviouralists, however, have gone far past this mild stance to describe ideological politics as backward, even dangerous. Almond and Powell write that 'an ideological style emerges when the individual develops a *specific* set of political orientations, but fails to develop the open, bargaining attitudes associated with full secularization'. Repeating much the same point as Deutsch, they characterize ideological politics as 'rigid and closed', as providing 'an inflexible image of political life to conflicting information and offering a specific explanation and code of political conduct for most situations.[45] A developed, mature politics, it clearly follows, is based on compromise, not ideology.

Warnings about the pernicious effects of ideology have also 43
been regularly issued. In its tendency to raise the level of political enthusiasm, ideology is a direct contributor to political conflict, instability, fanaticism and the rise of totalitarianism. An ideology of freedom is *ipso facto* a contradiction in terms. For example, Edward Shils' encyclopedia definition of ideology insists that:

> Complete subservience to the ideology is demanded of those who accept it, and it is regarded as essential and imperative that their conduct be completely permeated by it...all adherents of the ideology are urgently expected to be in complete agreement with each other.[46]

Raymond Aron, in his *The Opium of the Intellectuals*, peppers the argument against Marxist ideology with such phrases as 'irrational and foolish hope', 'political myths,' 'the idolatry of history', 'churchmen and the faithful' and 'secular clericalism',[47] and issues a call for a new age of 'doubt', of 'scepticism' that by undermining the various ideologies will give birth to tolerance and abolish fanaticism. These citations could be multiplied almost endlessly but the point is abundantly clear. Ideology is a false prism which distorts reality, a symptom of arrested political behaviour that will disappear with complete modernization and a dangerous catalyst of fanaticism and totalitarianism.[48]

44   The uneasiness of the behaviouralist with ideological politics is explicable on a number of grounds. As has already been
noted, ideology fails the test of verifiability and hence hovers
in the eternal twilight between fact and fiction. Secondly, the
professionally enforced posture of ideological neutrality, the
highly endorsed perspective of the detached observer, the necessity for translating ideology into a non-ideational vocabulary of conditioning, have a corrosive and undermining effect
on ideological commitment. For those who specialize in unmasking subjectivity, all the emperors—without exception—
have no clothes. Ideological commitments are often accompanied by an embarrassed sense of self-consciousness—often
resulting in a chronic inability to 'believe' spontaneously without attacks of self-doubt or the unsettling sense of cynicism and
déjà vu. Passion and enthusiasm seem the marks of adolescent
Sturm und Drang. The posture of neutrality, once adopted professionally, cannot be shed at will.

45   While these two attitudes are typically if not exclusively behaviouralist, a specifically behaviouralist response to ideology
is, in effect, to deny the need for it. De Sola Pool writes:

> The interesting issues in normative political theory [read ide-
> ology] are in the end generally empirical ones. Only rarely do
> arguments over policy turn on irreducible conflicts of values.
> More often they are arguments about the facts of situations to
> which the values are applied.[49]

Vernon Van Dyke makes the same point in methodological
terms:

> If he [the social scientist] wishes to spell out values in great
> detail, he will thereby be broadening the realm of ethical
> postulates—the realm of the normative. By the same token, he
> may be broadening the realm where emotion, faith, fervor and,
> perhaps, fanaticism operate, for these phenomena are associ-
> ated with values or ends. If the scholar chooses to regard all or
> virtually all events or states of affairs as means, he will thereby
> be broadening the realm of empirical and logical inquiry, en-
> larging the opportunities and potentialities for the use of reason.
> There is some basis for the view that the scholar should regard
> very little as self-justifying and that, conversely he should seek
> a situation in which he and others judge nearly all events and
> circumstances as means requiring justification. The positivist
> should especially desire this, for by making the realm of the nor-
> mative very small he minimizes his major failure—his inability
> to demonstrate the truth of ultimate value judgements.[50]

The 'end of ideology' school, behaviouralism's noisy step- 46
sister, reflects this new spirit precisely.[51] While predictions
about the 'decline' or 'end of ideology' came from many and
varied sources—from Herbert Marcuse to Lewis Feuer[52]—it
was the Lipset, Bell, Shils *et al.* group that welcomed it
as a salutory development. It promised to politics that long
sought after even keel of equilibrium, compromise and civility. Without the encitement of ideology, the 'low profile' political process could become reality. Moreover, there is only
a very minor substitution of terms necessary to convert de
Sola Pool's view that normative issues are in the end generally empirical ones, to a position like that of Lipset in which
ideological issues have been generally reduced to technical-
administrative ones.[53] How far is even Van Dyke's more moderate hope of methodologically reducing normative questions
to ones amenable to precision and verifiability, from a statement like that of an anti-ideological pragmatists like John
Kennedy who insisted that 'political labels and ideological approaches are irrelevant to the solutions' of social and economic
questions?[54]

Conservatism

Very few topics have been covered so often and so thoroughly 47
as the implicit conservative bias of behaviouralism. Times being what they were in the late sixties, very few who were so
inclined resisted the temptation to unmask, expose and otherwise embarrass the reigning king of political methodology.
I will spare the reader the ordeal of yet another repetition of
what has by now become the new 'conventional wisdom' and
merely point out what I see as the most basic and critical
tie between the behavioural methodology and political conservatism.

Science has no recourse to utopia. The physical laws the sci- 48
entist encounters are fixed. No talent or will can change them.
There is no sense in saying of a particular phenomenon, *qua*
scientist, that it is good or bad, or in calling for the reform
of one of Newton's laws. It is not given to the scientist to reconstruct the world, to rethink or second-guess God's work.
Consequently the first law the scientist learns is that reality
sets the absolute limit to his aspirations.

When social scientists took over the scientific method and 49
applied it to issues of social life, they adopted this outlook in
its totality. Reality, here too, set the limits to social scientists'
aspirations. To dream of another set of givens, to criticize real-

ity from the perspective of a vision of the potentially possible,[55] is to fall prey to what Eulau called 'the normative fallacy'. If representation, for example, fell short of what it was supposed to be, the social scientist had no more right to criticize representative institutions than did the natural scientist to find fault with gravity or photosynthesis. If the 'real' was not 'rational', the 'rational' was at fault.

> Because representative institutions did not work as preferred models of representation said they should work, the institutions were blamed rather than the models. It is an indication of the profound transformation in our approach to political phenomena that we have overcome the normative fallacy ... if there is a crisis, then, it is a crisis in the theory of representation and not in the institution of representation.[56]

50   Much the same approach is visible in Meehan's dictum that political theory is nothing but thought about politics—to be done by the same people and within the same framework as all other work on political phenomena.[57] This explicit rejection of critical standards that might derive from an independent source is the perfect translation of the natural scientific approach to the domain of the social scientist. Precisely here do we find that 'empirical conservatism' of which Marcuse so bitterly complained.[58]

51   Nowhere is the point more evident than in the truncation of language to fit the new and smaller perspective of the social scientist. A whole spate of terms that oscillated between the normative and descriptive poles have become locked into the smaller quarters now inhabited. 'Rational' intends only an action that is "'correctly" designed to maximize goal achievement'. 'Legitimate' means that which in practice has gained acceptance. There can be no court of higher appeal. Common to all these linguistic metamorphoses is the reduction of a multi-valent term to some variant of 'functional'.[59]

52   It is this same reality-centered spirit that animates much of the research done in the last decade on the relationship between democratic consensus, political participation and democratic stability.[60] Studies consistently indicate that while 'political operatives' and those of higher education and income are more or less agreed on a basic democratic value system, the population at large, particularly the lower socioeconomic classes, are far from understanding, to say nothing of accepting, the democratic consensus. What conclusions may be drawn from this disturbing data? Two different reactions are possible. The first, to see apathy as a blessing in disguise.

'Democratic viability is...saved by the fact that those who are most confused about democratic ideas are also likely to be politically apathetic and without significant influence.'[61] The second, to reason that since political participation and high educational and economic levels correlate with democratic consensus, true democratic 'viability' depends on including wider and wider circles in the political process while working to raise their socio-economic status.

In virtually all the behavioural research done, the first and 53 not the second conclusion was drawn. The inescapable 'why?' virtually poses itself. One might simply write the entire matter off as a patent case of 'scientized' ideology. This, I suspect, is unnecessarily harsh and indiscriminate. In the atmosphere of the late sixties, when an undeclared open season on the behavioural establishment existed, young scholars vied with one another in imputing the most sinister of motives to their adversaries. If we are to prepare an epitaph for a monument to a successful protest against a previous successful protest, we must, now that much of the dust of battle has settled, seek a more unbiased perspective with which to evaluate previous research.

While there can be no doubt that ideological factors were 54 relevant to the formulation of research programmes and conclusions, it seems forced, overly conspiratorial, 'vulgar' (in the sense of 'vulgar Marxism') to attribute—simply and directly— a causal relationship between them. There are, as we have shown, certain methodological commitments that are instrumental in fashioning both the *modus operandi* and conclusions of research. In our case, the scientific method confronted a state of affairs that contradicted a set of long-held ideals. Like the scientist, who, upon uncovering evidence which refutes an accepted theory, reformulates the theory to suit the newly discovered reality, the social scientist, operating within the confines of an identical world, does precisely the same. Democratic 'viability' must be reinterpreted in the light of reality rather than reality transformed to meet the demands of the ideal.

Behaviouralism's much-criticized 'obsession' with stability 55 and its insensitivity to change can be more fully appreciated if we recognize it as a concomitant of the scientific method and not merely another case of 'establishment politics'. Natural science is, of course, vitally concerned with change. But it is change of a certain type: change as development, as evolution, as unfolding. Nowhere does nature present us with discontinuity or revolt against its laws. The exertion of will from outside the ongoing process—will, not reducible to the mechanics of the process itself—is quite unacceptable in scientific terms, a form of discredited 'vitalism'. If nature is forever in flux, it is, for all that, functional and self-sustaining.

56   To apply this outlook to the social sciences is to incorporate a perspective on social change that is clearly confining. Change as development becomes *mutatis mutandis* incrementalism. Insofar as it does occur, change is viewed in terms of society's ongoing function; as a self-correcting and self-sustaining mechanism.[62] The notion of deep and basic structural transformation that results from conscious human agency, from criticism and will is foreign to an outlook taken over from the natural sciences.

Summary and Conclusion

57   To recapitulate: the epistemological bias of science has wide repercussions when applied to social phenomena. It creates a specific type of professional personality, together with a series of training priorities and educational objectives. It directly affects the responses and relationships of the political scientist to the political events affecting the community. Research is also affected, for it needs to be tailored to the dimensions of the method.

58   Because of the need for empirically accessible factors, the methodology is often instrumental in determining the range of possible research conclusions and even the nature of the conclusions themselves. The tendency to see the multiplicity and distinctness of phenomena seems built-in to the method.

59   Conviction and values, too, need to be broken down into a pattern of correlating empirical factors. The social determinism implied by the method is inescapable if conviction cannot be treated in its own terms.

60   Liberal democracy—i.e., ideological moderation, toleration and respect for the 'rules of the game'—results from the relativization of values. Scepticism of ideological finality makes for a 'low profile', compromise-oriented politics.

61   Bargaining, negotiation, accommodation, therefore, become the focal points of a healthy effective political system in which the process is clearly more important than the product. To maintain this low-conflict high-efficiency ratio, a certain social paradigm is suggested. It is a neatly balanced model which rests on the moderating, equilibrium-producing effect of countervailing power and incremental change.

62   The nemesis of homeostatic politics is ideology. It accompanies backwardness, subservience and fanaticism. But aside from its pernicious effects, ideology is simply unnecessary—

an anachronism that can be replaced by methods of empirical problem-solving. The 'end of ideology' is to be welcome, therefore, as politically salutory.

Coming full circle—the epistemological limits of the scientific method lead to a conservative political bias because of the denial of options implicit in non-critical, reality-bound research.   63

Having completed the survey, we now turn to our second question: In what measure is the behavioural outlook ideologically determined and to what degree is it the consequence of methodological priorities. We have, to some extent, anticipated our conclusions in the foregoing sections; it remains only to spell them out in greater detail.   64

The reader will have noticed that our presentation followed a deliberately logical outline. Step by step, from the most basic methodological commitments onward, the behavioural ideology took shape by implication, extrapolation and extension. It should be clear, nevertheless, that as a purely logical construct, standing only on the merit of internal coherence, it is seriously deficient. The democratic bias surely cannot be explained solely as a derivative of behaviouralist ethical relativism; any more than the antipathy to ideology, to conflict, to nonincremental change, are exclusively explicable by the limits of the scientific method. There is clearly a great deal of ideological mortar necessary for the structure to stand.[63] What may be said, however, is that insofar as the logical structure of methodological explanation is self-enclosed, and insofar as each step is not only necessary but also sufficient, the method bears the burden of the behavioural ideology.   65

More precise attribution to method or ideology is impossible—certainly not in the abstract. Even in specific cases no neat lines of demarcation can be drawn. There is, upon close examination, that inevitable blurring of motives that attends all sophisticated intellectual processes. Yet may we not be challenged on the grounds that the choice of method itself is an ideological decision? This hardly seems justified. The undisputed ascendency of scientific method in the past centuries is certainly reason enough for its adoption. The advantages of the scientific method are obvious, its accomplishments are legion and we require no tortured explanations to understand the desire to apply it to politics.   66

The ideological element—if it can be located in a particular segment of the intellectual process—flourishes not in the use of a particular method, nor even in the data the method produces. The onus of ideological design falls squarely upon the uncritical acceptance of *the parameters of the legitimate* that   67 are supplied by the scientific method. To accept the scientific method uncritically is to accept an 'uncritical' social science. And to accept an 'uncritical' social science is to accept the status quo.

68   If I understand the nature of the 'post-behavioural' era, it lies not in the rejection of the scientific method *per se*, but in the recognition of its limits. Precision and verifiability continue to be valued scholarly traits, but they have been wedded to a spirit of critical method.[64] If the pre-behavioural era was characterized by critical independence without precision and the behavioural era by precision without criticism, the 'cunning of Reason' has seen fit to effect an *Aufhebung* of these approaches in the post-behavioural era: i.e. precision with criticism.

Notes

1. Cf. G. J. Graham and G. W. Carey (eds.), *The Post-Behavioral Era: Perspectives on Political Science* (New York, 1972).
2. A. W. Gouldner, 'Metaphysical Pathos and the Theory of Bureaucracy,' *American Political Science Review*, 1955, 496–507.
3. In fairness it should be noted that most behaviouralists admit the impossibility of a 'value-free' political science. Nevertheless, they contend that values can be largely neutralized in the pursuit of scientific truth and that conclusions arrived at by the proper methods will be materially unaffected by either the researchers' own point of view or by the method itself. Probably the most authoritative and pervasive spokesman of the behavioural outlook is H. Eulau. See particularly his *The Behavioral Persuasion in Politics* (New York, 1963); 'Tradition and Innovation', in H. Eulau (ed.), *Behaviorism in Political Science* (New York, 1969), pp. 1–21; and 'Segments Susceptible to Behavioristic Treatment', in J. C. Charlesworth (ed.), op. cit., pp. 26–48.
4. *Psychopathology and Politics* (Chicago, 1930), p. 197.
5. 'Political Theory: Truth and Consequences', *World Politics*, 1960, p. 95.
6. Ibid., p. 98.
7. *Contemporary Political Thought: A Critical Study* (Homewood, Ill., 1967), pp. 46–7. For a thorough and balanced summary of the various positions see H. Eckstein, 'Political Theory and the Study of Politics: A Report of a Conference, *APSR*, 1956, pp. 475–87.
8. *The Sociological Imagination* (New York, 1959), pp. 50–75.
9. Ibid., pp. 187–8.
10. This position is not the monopoly of radicals like Mills. See, e.g., H. Morgenthau, 'The Commitments of Political Science,' in *Dilemmas of Politics* (Chicago, 1958), pp. 27–43. In recent years there have been defections from this position from the behavioral camp itself, most notably D. Easton's 'The New Revolution in Political Science', *APSR*, 1969, pp. 1051–61.

11. See A. Ranney, 'A Study of Policy Content: A Framework for Choice', in Ranney (ed.), *Political Science and Public Policy* (Chicago, 1968), pp. 3–21.
12. D. Truman, 'The Implications of Political Behavior Research', Social Science Research Council, *Items*, Dec. 1951, p. 39.
13. A. Somit and J. Tanenhaus, *The Development of American Political Science: From Burgess to Behavioralism* (Boston, 1967), p. 178.
14. R. A. Dahl, 'The Behavioral Approach in Political Science: Epitaph for a Monument to Successful Protest', *APSR*, 1967, pp. 770–1.
15. From Eulau's response to a paper by Morgenthau in J. C. Charlesworth (ed.), *A Design for Political Science: Scope, Objectives and Methods* (Philadelphia, 1966), pp. 115.
16. Ranney, loc. cit., pp. 20–21.
17. Y. Dror, 'The Barriers Facing Policy Science', in *American Behavioral Scientist*, 1965, p. 4.
18. A. Kaplan, *The Conduct of Inquiry* (San Francisco, 1964), p. 28.
19. M. Edelman, 'Research Orientations: Some Pitfalls and Some Strategic Suggestions', in H. S. Kariel (ed.), *The Frontiers of Democratic Theory* (New York, 1970), p. 361.
20. R. A. Dahl, 'A Critique of the Ruling Elite Model', *APSR*, 1958, pp. 463–9.
21. R. A. Dahl, *Who Governs?* (New Haven, 1961).
22. 'A Critique of the Ruling Elite Model', p. 466.
23. 'The Concept of Power', *Behavioral Science*, 1957, pp. 201–15.
24. See T. Anton, 'Power, Pluralism and Local Politics', *Administrative Science Quarterly*, 1962–1963, pp. 444–6.
25. A distinguished philosopher cites as the 'all important postulate' of modern science 'that valid explanations must always be in terms of small, elementary units in regularly changing relations'. E. A. Burtt, *The Metaphysical Foundations of Modern Science* (Garden City, 1954), p. 30.
26. A. Bentley, *The Process of Government* (Chicago, 1908), p. 202.
27. D. Easton, *The Political System* (New York, 1953), p. 221.
28. J. G. Miller, 'Introduction' to *Symposium: Profits and Problems of Homeostatic Models in the Behavioral Sciences* (Chicago, 1953), p. 7.
29. Bentley, op. cit., p. 177.
30. Ibid., p. 206.
31. Easton denies any connection whatever between the *behaviourist* in psychology and the *behaviouralists* in political science. Although he does note that Bentley was influenced by Watson, he contends that the extreme 'stimulus-response' position of Watson has been discarded by psychologists and is certainly not held by political scientists. Nevertheless, all standard definitions of behaviourism emphasize the 'objective' and 'accessible' nature of the facts the behaviourist studies, together with the rejection of subjectivity as irrelevant to science. It is this concentration on empirically accessible factors as the determinants of behaviour

that links the two schools. See Easton's, 'The Current Meaning of Behaviorism', in J. C. Charlesworth (ed.), *Contemporary Political Analysis* (New York, 1967), pp. 11–13.

32. Meehan takes 'all normative judgements as statements of fact about an individual's reaction to a situation ...'. By stating a normative judgement, one 'is only stating a fact about his own attitudes. To agree with him is to state another fact about another person's response to the same situation', op. cit., p. 45.

33. John Dewey repeatedly makes the pertinent observation that the respective 'spirits' of scientific inquiry and democracy go hand in hand. The experimental-pragmatic method in science—which is unwilling to accept any fixed, universal truths not vulnerable to revision, modification, even rejection—parallels the democratic notions of an open-ended future, resolution of problems through ongoing inquiry rather than *a priori* ideologies, etc. The behavioural sciences, from this perspective as well, are supportive of democracy'.

34. Lipset, for example, writes in a now celebrated passage, that 'democracy is not only or even primarily a means through which different groups can attain their ends or seek the good society; it is the good society itself in operation'. He goes on to elaborate that he means by democracy 'the give and take of a free society's internal struggles'. This give and take operates through institutions which support conflict and disagreement as well as those which sustain legitimacy and consensus—in short the 'rules of the game'. *Political Man* (Garden City, 1960), p. 439.

35. P. Diesing, *Reason in Society* (Urbana, 1962), pp. 231–2; for a general discussion see pp. 169–234.

36. Ibid., pp. 198, 203–4, 228.

37. G. A. Almond and S. Verba, *The Civic Culture* (Princeton, 1963), pp. 337–74; B. Berelson, P. Lazerfield and W. McPhee, *Voting* (Chicago, 1954), pp. 311 ff.; B. Berelson, 'Democratic Theory and Public Opinion', *Public Opinion Quarterly*, Fall, 1952, pp. 307–30.

38. 'Description, Analysis and Sensitivity to Change', in Ranney (ed.), op. cit., p. 248. See also R. A. Dahl and C. E. Lindblom, *Politics, Economics, and Welfare* (New York, 1954).

39. See W. Hield, 'The Study of Change in Social Science', *British Journal of Sociology*, 1954, pp. 1–11; and L. Coser, *The Functions of Social Conflict* (New York, 1956), pp. 15–31.

40. 'The Public and the Polity', in I. de Sola Pool (ed.), *Contemporary Political Science: Toward Empirical Theory* (New York, 1967), p. 26.

41. H. D. Laswell, *The World Revolution of our Times* (Stanford, 1951), p. 31.

42. *Psychopathology and Politics*, pp. 196–7.

43. 'Nation and World', in de Sola Pool (ed.), op. cit., pp. 208–9.

44. Cf. B. Crick, *In Defence of Politics* (London, 1966); I. Berlin, *Four Essays on Freedom* (Oxford, 1969); M. Oakshott, *Rationalism in Politics* (London, 1962). See also, J. Shklar's, *After Utopia* (Princeton, 1969).

45. *Comparative Politics* (Boston, 1966), p. 61.

46. *International Encyclopedia of the Social Sciences* (New York, 1968). See also Shil's 'Primordial, Personal, Sacred and Civil Ties', *British Journal of Sociology*, 1957, pp. 130–45; 'Ideology and Civility: On the Politics of the Intellectual', *The Sewanee Review*, 1958, pp. 450–80. Cf. P. H. Partridge, 'Politics, Philosophy, Ideology', *Political Studies*, 1961, pp. 217–35.

47. Cited by C. Geertz, 'Ideology as a Cultural System', in D. Apter (ed.), *Ideology and Discontent* (New York, 1964), p. 51. See Geertz, pp. 49–52 for a catalogue of anti-ideology statements and general comments on the subject.

48. Parsons writes that 'the problem of ideology arises where there is a *discrepancy* between what is believed and what can be established as scientifically correct'. 'An Approach to the Sociology of Knowledge', *Transactions of the 4th World Congress of Sociology* (Milan, 1959), pp. 25–49. In fact, Parsons credits the behavioural 'breakthrough' in the United States to the lack of ideological pressures that make for openness and receptivity. 'The Point of View of the Author', in M. Black (ed.), *The Social Theories of Talcott Parsons* (Englewood Cliffs, N.J., 1962), pp. 313–15, 360–2.

49. 'The Public and the Polity', p. 23.

50. *Political Science: A Philosophic Analysis* (Stanford, 1960), p. 12. The notion that social science can empirically dispose of value questions runs like a master thread through the essays in Ranney (ed.), op. cit.

51. See C. I. Waxman (ed.), *The End of Ideology Debate* (New York, 1968); M. Rejai (ed.), *Decline of Ideology* (Chicago, 1971).

52. See S. M. Lipset, 'Ideology and No End', *Encounter*, Dec. 1972, pp. 17–22.

53. Ideology is being replaced by sociology, by administration, Lipset tells us, because 'the fundamental problems of the Industrial Revolution have been solved'. *Political Man*, p. 406.

54. Cited by S. W. Rousseas and J. Farganis, 'American Politics and the End of Ideology', in Waxman (ed.), op. cit., p. 226.

55. See S. S. Wolin, 'Political Theory as a Vocation', op. cit., *APSR*, 1969, pp. 1062–82.

56. 'Changing Views of Representation', in de Sola Pool (ed.), op. cit., pp. 54–5. In less extreme form: 'Insofar as people do not live up to the ideal of the active citizen, democracy is a failure. If one believes that the realities of political life should be molded to fit one's theories of politics such an explanation is satisfactory. But if one holds to the view that theories of politics should be drawn from the realities of political life—a somewhat easier and probably more useful task—then this explanation of the gap between the rationality-activist model and democratic realities is less acceptable'. *The Civic Culture*, p. 340.

57. *Contemporary Political Thought*, p. 2 f.

58. *One Dimensional Man*. (London, 1970), pp. 105–60.

59. It is no coincidence that within the general 'behavioural mood' the most prevalent specific approaches are the functionalist and the analysis of systems. These, too, are taken over from the realm

of natural science where they are elementary. They are so basic
to the natural sciences because, in the absence of values or of independent criteria of judgement, a natural phenomenon must be
understood in terms of itself and its context. For this the concept
of function or system is perfectly appropriate. When these concepts are transferred to the social sciences, however, they impose
severe limits on the kinds of attitudes to social phenomena that
are possible.

60. J. W. Prothro and C. W. Grigg, 'Fundamental Principles of Democracy: Bases of Agreement and Disagreement', *Journal of Politics*,
1960, pp. 276–94; V. O. Key, 'Public Opinion and the Decay of
Democracy', *Virginia Quarterly Review*, 1961, pp. 481–94; H. A.
McClosky, 'Consensus and Ideology in American Politics', *APSR*,
1964, pp. 361–82; Berelson, Lazerfield and McPhee, op. cit., pp.
306 ff; J. Q. Wilson, *The Amateur Democrat: Club Politics in Three
Cities* (Chicago, 1962), pp. 340 ff; Lipset, *Political Man*, pp. 87–126;
L. W. Milbrath, *Political Participation* (Chicago, 1965), pp. 142–54.

61. McClosky, op. cit., p. 376.

62. A striking example of this kind of thinking is Coser's, *The Functions of Social Conflict*, op. cit. After castigating the negative attitude to conflict of the sociological establishment, he goes on to
show how conflict can be a beneficial element in social development. But once again it is conflict within an enduring framework,
conflict as functional, self-sustaining, self-correcting.

63. For a persuasive account of the ideological basis of political theorizing, see W. G. Runciman, *Social Science and Political Theory*
(Cambridge, 1963).

64. The new ideal image of the scholar 'unites the analytical precision
of a Dahl, the self-awareness of a Mannheim and the commitment
to social relevance of a C. Wright Mills'. W. Connolly, *Political
Science and Ideology*, p. 153.

CHAPTER TWO

SOCIAL SCIENCE AND THE PHILOSOPHY OF SCIENCE

Although our account of the behavioral controversy has covered the cardinal issues that divided defenders from detractors, it remains incomplete in one significant regard. The struggle between the various protagonists in the political science community was not exhausted by the relatively narrow and technical issue of how research should be carried out. Invariably, practical and operational questions were never far removed from issues of philosophic principle. In a critical sense, therefore, the behavioral controversy transcended professional loyalties in political science and focused on questions of epistemology and the reliability of knowledge. Indeed, in its most self-conscious and comprehensive moments, the controversy turned on the very nature, capacities, and limits of science.

Chronology is important here as well. The height of the behavioral dispute coincided with the high point of celebrity enjoyed by an epoch-making book published in 1962: Thomas Kuhn's *The Structure of Scientific Revolutions*. Kuhn's work challenged many widely held ideas regarding the nature of the scientific enterprise, and it was inevitable that his name, as well as those of many of his predecessors in the philosophy of science, should become profoundly embroiled in the struggle over behavioralism. We shall therefore need to make a rather lengthy detour from our discussion of behavioralism to explore the philosophical background issues that impinged heavily on the more practical methodological concerns.

To properly appreciate Kuhn's dramatic challenge to the reigning orthodoxies in the philosophy of science, we must make two preliminary stops. First we will need to describe the *positivist* position that dominated philosophic thinking in the early decades of the century and that, despite incessant batterings, stubbornly holds on to a sizable following to this day. (The term *positivist*, like the term *bourgeoisie*, has a large constituency even though few would admit to belonging.) Second, we will need to examine the challenge to positivism launched by one of the most remarkable of contemporary philosophers, Karl Popper. When these two preliminary tasks are behind us, we shall be well placed to assess the impact of Kuhn's challenge and to explore its consequences for the social sciences.

Although positivism has had many different meanings—some of which go back to the French nineteenth-century thinker Comte, and others that relate to twentieth-century legal theory—the term is used here in its most common modern meaning, that is, as a philosophical doctrine seeking to base itself solely on the positive data of observable and accessible sense experience. It rejects hypotheses that are not empirically verifiable and hence has little patience (and sometimes outright hostility) for metaphysical and value-oriented speculation. Without a mode of empirical verification, positivists argue, statements are only strings of words without a referent, mere "talk" lost in a verbal labyrinth that does not touch base with reality. Such statements provide no information about the world, and hence they can be classified neither as true nor as false. One well-known positivist thinker, A. J. Ayer, described such statements in the bluntest of terms: they are simply "nonsense."

Scientific statements, because they are verifiable, are model statements. They refer directly to observable phenomena. They can be confirmed by sense experience; in fact, that is the meaning of the term *experiment*: to submit an hypothesis to the confirmation of sense "experience." Although positivists did not strictly limit acceptable statements to those that could be immediately and directly confirmed in this way— for example, a statement hypothesizing the temperature on a distant planet is, despite its present unverifiability, in principle an observation statement—they made it abundantly clear that a good deal of what went under the rubric philosophy was a pompous churning of words and definitions to no avail.

Verifiability, in the positivist mind, normally meant induction. Science was a rigorous application of the inductive principle that proceeded by a number of steps that are well known to every high school student. First there is observation. The scientist observes a given reality, and if he is lucky, talented, and well informed, a pattern of regularities will begin to appear from among the great multitude of processes and events. This regularity is then formulated as an hypothesis. There is, the scientist hypothesizes, an enduring and significant relationship between A and B that will remain valid in all similar cases.

The next step is crucial. Data are gathered from many different cases, and the candidate hypothesis is checked against this cumulated experimental evidence. When the experimental verifications become sufficiently numerous and varied, scientists tend to speak of hypotheses as having been confirmed. Although it is impossible to specify in advance how many confirming cases add up to the verification of an hypothesis, it can nevertheless be said that at some reasonable point the weight of accumulated evidence justifies our saying that the regularity observed in the cases studied will hold in cases that we have not yet encountered. When, over time, many additional experimental confirmations are accumulated, hypotheses are "promoted" beyond their tentative hypothetical status to become full-blown and fully established laws. The object of scientific endeavor, according to this view, is to add to the reservoir of laws, to enrich the fund of confirmed knowledge.

In this version of the logic of science, hypotheses are both generated out of and confirmed by observation. In the initial stage, we hypothesize from the enduring patterns perceived among the many specific details we observe; in the final stage, we conclude on the basis of the many different cases in which we observe the hypothesis "in action." In a word, science begins and ends in careful observation. And because observation provides us with testable and secure knowledge of reality, our confidence in the findings of science is eminently justifiable.

This understanding of science retains a powerful hold over the public imagination—so powerful, indeed, that many readers will be asking themselves if there are any right-minded people who would wish to raise doubts about its accuracy. More important still, this understanding of the logic of science was close to the hearts of many leading behavioralists. Although the relationship between behavioralism and positivism was not a simple one and, consequently, is not always easy to formulate neatly, it may be said broadly that behavioralism tended to favor the positivist view of science.[1]

If the philosophy of science favored by behavioralists (and accepted in the popular mind) has been broadly positivist in character, philosophers of science, ironically, have increasingly distanced themselves from this view. Oddly, the view of science that behavioralists have defended has become more and more of a philosophical anachronism. In fact, behavioralists have been severely chastised for basing their view of what social scientists should be doing on outmoded cliches and long-rejected views of the scientific process. There is, so it is argued, a basic incongruity between the uncritical behavioralist vision of scientific endeavor and what has become a new consensus in the philosophy of science.[2]

A wide gamut of scholars and writers have attacked the positivist orthodoxy on a number of critical points: its naive empiricism, its misrepresentation of the process of scientific discovery, its uncritical faith in induction, its lack of sensitivity for the social context of science, and much more. Among these critics none stand out so prominently as Karl Popper; therefore, it is to his thought that we turn next.

Popper's rejection of positivism is of great interest, first, because of the power of the critique itself, and second because of the potential consequences it bears for a positivist-inspired social science. The initial and still most influential version of Popper's critique appeared in his *The Logic of Scientific Discovery*, first published in German in 1934. Popper's main aim was to show that induction and verification, in the positivist version, are misleading illusions. They are neither possible, nor can they ever be conclusive. In their place, Popper proposes a striking deductivist and refutation-based version of the scientific enterprise that turns much of the positivist view on its head.

Induction fails, Popper argues (following the eighteenth-century English philosopher David Hume), because its confidence that the future will be like the past is nothing but an undemonstrable faith with no solid foundation. When an hypothesis is examined experimentally, our basic aim is to project forward from the cases we have tested to those we have not. We wish to argue from the cases of which we have knowledge to a general rule, which is to say, to those cases we have not actually examined. This is critically important since it is impossible, in the nature of things, to study *all* the cases where a certain pattern is said to hold. Because a given regularity has held for the 100 or 1,000 cases that we have already studied, we feel justified in claiming that the pattern will hold for the 101st or the 1,001st case yet to be studied.

What is the source of this confidence, asks Popper. What obliges future cases to follow those of which we already have knowledge? The source of our confidence can only be that in the past we have not been disappointed in our anticipations. That is to say, the reason we feel justified in believing that the as-yet-undone experiments will follow those we have already done is that they have always followed in the past. But is this not a sleight of hand? We want to prove that the future cases will continue to follow the past cases, and how do we go about it? Only by saying that they have always done so in the past. But is this not precisely what we are trying to demonstrate, that future cases will *continue* to follow the past cases? Are we not assuming just what we have set out to prove? Induction is therefore a baseless conviction; it relies curiously only on itself to demonstrate its validity.

This may open a quite dizzying prospect to the nonphilosophical reader, but the very same idea can be expressed in quite practical and simple terms. Does the fact that a certain hypothesis has been verified by experience many times over make it more likely that it is in fact true? The aggressively commonsensical readers, hearing this question, are likely to reach for their revolvers. Even their more speculatively minded comrades will surely think this an odd and simple-minded query. But consider the following example. A person is lost in a labyrinth and, in searching for the way out, walks around a circular track convinced that because the path is always open, this must surely be the right road. At every turn the conviction grows stronger because it is constantly confirmed by the absence of obstacles. And yet these seeming verifications are nothing but a misleading waste of time.

Historically speaking, something quite similar actually took place. No series of hypotheses has ever been so widely tested and so universally confirmed as Newton's laws, but this did not prevent their profound adjustment by Einsteinian physics. All the thousands of verifications, like all the circular trekking of our hapless labyrinth wanderer, availed not at all. When the disconfirming cases came, all the verifications of the past seemed like so much self-deception. And if this is true of the most widely confirmed of all scientific laws, what conceivable confidence can we have in the multitude of garden-variety hypotheses that flood our intellectual market and appeal for our professional loyalty?

Induction's woes, Popper claims, begin long before the problems of demonstrating its conclusions. It commits its first fatal error at the very outset of its account of scientific discovery. It will be recalled that in the inductivist version, the scientist becomes aware of regularly recurring patterns through careful observations of reality. Popper enjoyed puncturing this account by turning to the students who filled his lecture halls and dramatically enjoining them to "observe." Their response, understandably, was confusion. They would look at each other sheepishly, not knowing what the august lecturer meant for them to look at. Popper would then triumphantly announce that they had learned the first lesson in the logic of scientific discovery, to wit, there can be no observation unless there is first a problem that directs us to what we should be looking at. Observation takes place in the context of a specific intellectual domain of discourse, never as a simple reporting of things seen. Imagine, he would conclude, the folly of the individual who went around for a full lifetime compulsively "observing" and compiling voluminous notes on all that he had seen. Would this, he asked mockingly, have any usefulness for science, or would it be, in fact, a compilation of random irrelevancies?

To say that observation is always contextual says more, perhaps, than meets the eye. If we require a specific context of scientific discourse to make sense of an observation, it must be true that our observations are mediated by what we know and expect, that the knowledge that we acquire depends on the knowledge we already have. There can be no seeing of reality *as it actually is*, that is, as something brute, uninterpreted, and given. The positivist notion of reality as simply "observed" is therefore placed into serious doubt. Moreover, it becomes clear that basing the claims of science on the "objectivity" of the scientist is a failing proposition. To be apprehended, reality must be filtered through categories that we as observers bring to the observation. These categories order what we see, highlight certain elements, and place others in the shadows. They "tame" reality and make it manageable and meaningful. Without these ordering categories and expectations, all would be a confused kaleidoscope of "motion and matter," a "buzzing, blooming confusion" (in the words of William James) lacking either sense or form. Perhaps newborn babies apprehend reality in this unenviable way.

But if the reality we observe is the reality that our particular problem context orients us toward, the source of our hypotheses becomes a serious dilemma. They cannot, on Popper's account, derive from observations pure and simple because reality is inevitably mediated through our prior conceptions of it. Popper responds with a revolutionary proposition: Our hypotheses are not formed out of observations at all; they are, he contends, nothing but bold guesses that have no empirical basis.

When faced with a problem situation in which our beliefs appear to contradict each other, or in which our results are incompatible, or in which the relationship among various events is bewildering, the scientific imagination is stimulated to seek a coherent resolution to the impasse. What we *do not* do under these conditions is to consult reality via experimentation. This would be a pointless exercise. It is precisely the experimental findings we have that are the source of our difficulty. The problem we confront would be only endlessly reproduced if we repeated the experiments that gave rise to it in the first instance. Without a novel idea that breaks the hold of these conventional findings on our imagination, or at least reconstructs their meaning in an innovative way, we are trapped within an intellectual cul-de-sac.

If not from observation, then where do such innovative ideas come from? From the depths of our creative imagination, answers Popper. We consider the problem as an intellectual conundrum and—again with luck, talent, and imagination—propose a solution that *satisfies our minds* without knowing if it *satisfies reality*. We propose solutions that seem reasonable and appealing to our speculative intelligence but that initially lack any verification in observable fact. Hypotheses are then conjectures that scientists throw out, as one would throw out a net, in an effort to "catch" some piece of reality. These conjectures precede the experimental process—as opposed to the positivist view, in which they derive from it— and set into motion the testing procedures whose objective it is to separate the true from the false.

In this creative effort, we are directed not only by our findings and our logic; certainly no less important in the pursuit of promising hypotheses is an inner quasi-aesthetic intuition that appeals to our sense of order, neatness, beauty, rightness in assessing candidate solutions. Popper speaks of scientists as leaping before they look, as stabbing into the dark; their only tools in this chancy endeavor are whatever knowledge they possess and an inscrutable conjectural sense. The scientific method, in this view, is more inspiration than observation. Scientists have no choice but to proceed blindly in this way, Popper insisted repeatedly, because there is nothing they can conceivably observe that would be of any help in proposing a solution to the problem they face.

Once an hypothesis is proposed, how are we to go about testing it? If Popper is right and induction/verification is a useless method, what can be done to test our conjectures? If by that question is meant, which method can provide us with the security that our conjecture is, in fact, *true*, Popper's answer is unequivocal: none. We can never be certain that our hypotheses are true because however many verifications have been accumulated, they are always liable to be disconfirmed by some future experiment. Oddly, all we can ever really know is that our hypotheses are in error. Of error at least we can be certain. In refuting an hypothesis, we establish at least one stable and indisputable point of reference.

Refutation succeeds where verification fails because there is a basic lack of symmetry between them. An hypothesis may have *many* verifying instances while being utterly false—as astrological predictions convincingly demonstrate. At the other pole, once a doctrine is disconfirmed, if only by a *single* refutation, the hypothesis is definitively disqualified. And knowing that an hypothesis is false is a very precious piece of knowledge indeed. It affords a fixed point by which we can orient our search, a mark of light on the map of our ignorance by which we can navigate our uncertain way.

No wonder, then, that for Popper, the refutation of an hypothesis is a cause for joy. As opposed to the conventional wisdom that mourns for failed hypotheses, Popper understands refutation as a breakthrough, the single form in which our knowledge can grow. All of science is directed to the moment when, through decisive refutation, reality gives us clear notice of errors committed.

If the prospect of refutation is so vital for the growth of knowledge, it will come as no surprise that refutability, that is, the vulnerability of a doctrine to disconfirmation, is the feature *sine qua non* of the scientific enterprise. Hypotheses that make claims that cannot be tested and refuted—as are quite common in religious doctrines—obviously do not fall into the category of science. More significant still, doctrines that make seemingly testable statements while refusing to specify in advance what evidence would constitute a refutation of their claims, fail the most basic test of science. Unless astrologers (and many other fellow travelers) are willing to make unambiguously clear what evidence is incompatible with their views, what evidence would force them to abandon their belief in the stars, their "knowledge" places itself outside the bounds of science.

Once an hypothesis is presented in refutable form, it becomes dissociated from its author. It no longer depends on his/her testimony, authority, objectivity, or reputation. Specifying in advance what would constitute a disconfirmation severs the proposal from its human source and renders it a possession of the scientific community as a whole. It becomes a self-standing proposition that can be dealt with entirely independently of the alleged "objectivity" of its author. Science does not depend on the good intentions or neutrality of the scientist—if it did we would be in some very deep trouble indeed. Rather, it rests on the ability of other scientists to subject a proposal to the most serious attempts at refutation. Science can do without objective scientists because the capacity to refute an hypothesis obviates the need for high-mindedness.

This quality of refutability is the basis of Popper's celebrated "line of demarcation." Science is demarcated from nonscience, from the ordinary stock of human speculations, fashions, faiths, and ideologies, by its testability—more specifically, by its refutability. What lies "above" the line of demarcation and enjoys the rubric *science* is not necessarily true, but, at least potentially, can be shown to be false. What lies on the nether side of the line of demarcation is not necessarily false. Yet because it will not allow itself to be falsified, because it is formulated in a way that frustrates attempts at refutation, it is condemned to hover in a cognitive limbo.

Popper singles out Marxism and psychoanalysis for dishonorable mention in this regard. They provide an object lesson in failed science. Both illustrate starkly the dangers of verification as well as the importance of refutability. Die-hard Marxists, Popper charges, cannot read through the daily newspaper without discovering verifications for their beliefs on every page, just as psychoanalysts will remarkably find that each case they treat only confirms more profoundly the views of human nature they already hold.

Certain particularly stubborn strains of Marxism and Freudianism, Popper charges, are so totally resistant to refutation that troubling findings are instinctively met with ready excuses; even the most grievous problems have a way of being converted into glowing endorsements. In the most extreme cases of all, the very attempt to refute the Marxist or psychoanalytic orthodoxy is understood by the faithful as a clear demonstration of the doctrine's truth—the misguided would-be challenger clearly being motivated by bourgeois interests or mechanisms of repression. In Popper's terms, these doctrines are compatible with any and all evidence. They forbid nothing. They are so protean in shape that they easily accommodate any eventuality. In a word, they are what happens to potentially interesting ideas that fail to discipline themselves through a refutation procedure.

For our purposes, the relevance of Popper's challenge to positivism (and, by extension, to behavioralism) lies in the doubt his critique casts on naive empiricism as a method of inquiry. If our access to social realities is necessarily mediated by the ideas and anticipations we bring to observation, if there is no theory-neutral way of describing reality, it becomes difficult to speak of a simple, passive, and direct apprehension of "out there facts." To a certain degree, at least, facts are not *given* but *taken*, that is, apprehended creatively through the categories and contexts that frame our observations. Neither does the mythology of the objective scientist so beloved of the behavioralists survive Popper's assault. Like all other mortals, scientists are prone to cook the evidence to suit their own needs. Moreover, if induction cannot predict future occurrences, and even the securest of our convictions is always only tentative and fragile, where does this leave the empirical generalizations toward which behavioralists aspire? If, in addition, all we can know is that we are mistaken, this does not bode well for the aggressively empirical and cognitively confident spirit that animates the positivist/behavioral consensus.

And yet Popper was anything but an intellectual defeatist. In fact, he spent the second half of his long career struggling against those who wished to derive skeptical or irrationalist conclusions from the ideas he proposed in the first. Although an acceptance of Popper's ideas would put something of a damper on behavioral brashness, there is little doubt that much of the behavioral project could be salvaged and reconstructed. To be sure, some of behavioralism's self-assurance might be shaken; the blow, however, would be far from fatal.

Admittedly, few behavioralists actively concerned themselves with the recondite issues raised by Popper. Their practical research orientation normally disdained the speculations of philosophers of science. And yet it is probably fair to say that the bulk of behavioralists would have responded to these challenges by saying that unfalsified hypotheses—whatever the ultimately tentative nature of scientific knowledge may be—are far superior to the murky theorizing of prebehavioral political science. In this response, ironically, they would have found an ally—probably unbeknownst to them—in Popper himself. Alarmed at the growing "intellectual defeatism" that his thought had spawned, the older Popper argued stubbornly that refutation provides us with real knowledge of an objective reality that is autonomous of our mode of inquiry or observation. The tentativeness of our knowledge has no bearing on the existence of "out there facts." That we are forced to make our way enveloped in the heavy fog of ignorance does not mean that the landscape through which we travel is illusory. Moreover, he insisted (incongruously, his critics maintained) that hypotheses that consistently withstand attempts at refutation can be spoken of as possessing a quasi-truth content or "verisimilitude," as he liked to call it. The behavioralist project, in other words, was still a going concern.

But let us now consider the unsettling thought of Thomas Kuhn. Kuhn radicalizes Popper's position in one cardinal respect: he denies that refutation is a viable scientific strategy. This is a dramatic claim, and its elucidation will require some prefatory explanation. It will be best to proceed via a concrete (although necessarily simplified) historical illustration. This is advisable first because it is the method that Kuhn himself utilizes, and second because the stages of scientific change emerge most clearly when placed within a specific historical schema.

Ptolemaic astronomy dominated Western thought for a great many centuries. Its central feature for our purposes was, of course, its geocentric view of the universe, that is, the belief that the earth is at the very center of things, with all other heavenly bodies revolving around it. By the late Middle Ages, Ptolemaic astronomy had accumulated a vast infrastructure of tabulations, predictions, calendars, timetables, maps, stellar charts, and other guides. For the most part, these served well enough for the purposes of those who utilized them. Where discrepancies nevertheless appeared, all manner of correcting devices and ad hoc interpolations were utilized to adjust what was known to what was expected.

The difficulties with the Ptolemaic system were there for all to see, but the ordinary reaction to these incongruities was to work on improving the adjustments and corrections rather than to conceive of alternative ways of picturing the heavens. Enter the Polish astronomer Copernicus

(1473–1543). When he began to speculate on the problems associated with orthodox astronomy, he was faced with a rich and not unsuccessful tradition that appeared unable to account for all the phenomena it observed. Kuhn makes it clear that considerations of prudence should have led Copernicus to devote his considerable talents to amending and sharpening the existing system rather than striking out into heavenly *terra incognita*, where all he had on his side was his speculative imagination.

What is critical to understand, Kuhn (in full agreement with Popper) argues, is that simple observation of the heavens would provide Copernicus with no clues in his search for an answer. Copernicus' astronomical revolution took place in his head; it did not derive from any findings. In fact, if the criterion for accepting a particular scientific hypothesis is how many findings it can account for, Ptolemaic astronomy offered an incomparably better record than the untested and unsupported musings of a lone reasoner. What is it, then, that moved Copernicus to abandon the known and secure geocentric account of the heavens and venture what was no more than a half-baked and unsubstantiated hypothesis lacking any evidence to speak of?

Kuhn believes that Copernicus was seduced by a flash of imaginative intuition whose emotional appeal, aesthetic satisfaction, and intellectual promise were irresistible. No gradual transformation took place. Copernicus did not make piecemeal improvements in the geocentric view by reacting to the specific problems and incongruous findings it confronted. Heliocentric astronomy did not simply pass beyond Ptolemaic discourse by cleansing it of its errors. It was a clean break and a fresh start, a dramatic and total reordering of all that was previously known according to a new key; to use Kuhn's well-known term, it can be understood as a "conversion process." In a single inspired speculative flash, the terms of astronomical discourse were invented anew.

What, however, can account for the lure that the Copernican image of the heavens had for other practitioners? After all, it lacked any basis in observation or evidence. More important still, its acceptance entailed jettisoning the solid framework of accumulated knowledge—much of it still quite serviceable—that Ptolemaic astronomy offered. As a simple question of cognitive "economy," that is, in terms of the costs and benefits for knowledge, it was a bad deal. To ask the question in more broadly abstract terms, if the radical change in scientific perspectives does not result from observation and evidence, what can account for it? If scientific revolutions begin with only unsubstantiated conjectures, how do they make any headway in the scientific community?

Mainly, Kuhn argues, by kindling the imagination of a younger generation of scholars who warm to the promise of a new idea. They become sufficiently roused by its future potential to trade the familiar and prosaic for the adventure of discovery. This wave of exhilarated expectations spreads quickly through the ranks of the newly initiated members of the discipline. Their especial vulnerability to the lure of intellectual adventure is not difficult to grasp. As opposed to their senior colleagues, who have devoted significant parts of their lives to working with certain concepts and assumptions, they are as yet relatively uncommitted. Besides, they have careers to make, and for that purpose fallow soil is more beckoning and malleable than the crowded and well-trodden terrain of the familiar. In a word, the underlying causes of scientific revolutions and the reasons for their success are, to no small degree, extra-scientific in character. Kuhn contends that they are more readily explicable in terms of the sociology and psychology of the scientific community than by the logic of scientific discovery.

As the revolutionary conception sweeps through the community of scientists, it understandably confronts dogged resistance from those committed to the status quo ante. Interestingly, Kuhn asserts, the debate between the old and the new world views is a futile one. It cannot be resolved by appeal to "facts" because how to determine what will count as a fact and what the relative importance of these facts may be, is in itself a matter of dispute. In Kuhn's celebrated term, the views are "incommensurate," that is, built of such different materials as to be beyond comparison in the light of a single standard of rationality. (Try, for example, to visualize a discussion between a medieval theologian/scientist and a modern physicist.) If the new view wins, it is not because of its superior cogency but because of its supporters' greater life expectancy. The old view dies with the older generation of scholars, and the new perspective begins the process of settling into scientific routine.

For what was revolutionary must, inexorably, become routine. As exhilarating and unfettered as the moments of creation may be, the ideas that inspired them must congeal into a reigning orthodoxy in order for scientific activity to become ordered and stable. In Kuhn's view, there is the sharpest of distinctions between revolutionary science and science that has become routine. The first is limited only by the outer reaches of the scientist's imagination, whereas the second is severely constrained by a virtual Hobbesian *Leviathan* of authoritative doctrines and mandatory procedures. Ironically, it is the second and not the first characteristic that is truly favorable for scientific progress.

Without broad consensus on how scientific activity should be conducted, without fundamental agreement on what it is that our knowledge is for, without a shared conception of intellectual virtues and vices, without—perhaps above all—an accepted vision of what the world is like and in what way it is accessible to our inquiry, no scientific *discipline* is possible. Science is organized activity, and like all organized activity it requires authoritative structures and binding norms to order its operation. When no such structures or norms exist, science may enjoy the free-for-all of a give-and-take without rules, axioms, or constraining standards—it may even experience a time of irrepressible creativity—but it will never flourish or progress. These are periods of what Kuhn calls "extraordinary science." Although they are often tumultuous in their intellectual fervor, they are, for the most part, barren in terms of scientific accomplishment.

As opposed to "extraordinary science," Kuhn emphasizes the importance of those periods marked by what he calls "normal science." These are the times in which "textbook" wisdom rules. Education takes place according to universally accepted principles of what a fledgling astronomer or biologist or psychologist must know to become a professional. What constitutes good science and what entails mere quackery is easily resolvable according to widely shared principles. Similarly, the "gatekeepers" of science—those who decide which research projects will be funded, which articles published, which applicant offered the job—operate according to a prevalent consensus of what constitutes meritorious scientific achievement. To this overarching and authoritative consensus regarding the nature of science, the world it describes, its objectives, methods, and proper subject, Kuhn gives the term *paradigm.** A shared paradigm is the condition for normal science, and normal science is the condition for scientific progress.

Because paradigms strictly limit what is scientifically acceptable, they create a common language and common standards. They also encourage a common focusing on certain problems that are consensually regarded as requiring solution. For example, after Copernicus proposed his revolutionary heliocentric paradigm, it was clear what needed to be done to convert these abstract speculations into a functioning scientific enterprise. A great deal of hard empirical work was needed to fill in the as-yet missing details (which were so richly present in the well-researched Ptolemaic system). Copernican "normal scientists" directed their concerted energies to the challenges posed by the great knowledge gaps in the new paradigm. (Notably, Kuhn refers to this kind of normal scientific activity that spells out the detailed consequences of a paradigm as "puzzle solving.") Armed with the paradigm's assumptions, they set off to explore its explanatory potential. In brief, the paradigm provided the direction, the tools, the method, the issues, the discipline, and the shared understanding that made the new form of scientific activity a going concern.

Like a jealous sovereign who demands full obeisance to his will as the condition for keeping the forces of anarchy at bay, the paradigm demands strict compliance with its norms as the condition for order and progress in science. Hence, all truly fruitful scientific activity must take place within the paradigm's boundaries. Hypotheses that violate its assumptions are ipso facto disqualified. Indeed, they cannot even be casually entertained

*Although the term has been severely criticized for its ambiguity, and although Kuhn himself has recently turned to more hesitant and restrictive formulations, the term *paradigm* has achieved such currency in academic discussion that it is wise to retain it, whatever its flaws. It should be mentioned, however, that the term's popularity has not added to its clarity. There are probably few contemporary terms that are used so frequently and to such different ends as *paradigm*.

without the guilty party suffering a severely tarnished reputation, without his "soundness" as a scientist coming into question.

Why this should be so is well illustrated by the case of Uri Geller and his bent spoons. Let us assume that, despite careful scrutiny, scientists are unable to identify any "trick" Geller uses to do what he appears to be doing. Can they accept what they seem to be seeing—that a man using telepathic powers is able to bend cutlery—as a fact? Consider the choice that our flabbergasted scientist confronts. He appears to be witnessing a phenomenon that undermines all he knows and believes about the natural world. To accept it as fact would entail nothing less than a total reconstruction of science and a drastic revision of the world with which he is familiar. Geller cannot be dismissed as a curious single exception to physical laws; if what the scientist sees is what is really happening, the entire paradigm of modern science is in jeopardy. To accommodate what he appears to be seeing, the scientist would need to pay the price of doubting everything else that he knows. Either Geller is a fraud or modern science is about to be overturned. Hardly a difficult choice to make!

Clearly, the choice our scientist confronts is not made on the basis of the "evidence" he appears to have. The evidence seems to constitute a striking "refutation" of the modern scientific paradigm, and yet he dismisses it, without good substantive reasons, as charlatanism or hocus pocus. What may be called "cognitive economy" leaves him little choice. He must either abandon what he knows of nature or refuse to believe the authenticity of what he sees. It is either the paradigm or this peculiar anomaly. And it goes without saying that paradigms are incomparably more valuable and irreplaceable than any particular ostensible refutation.

All this leads to one very non-Popperian conclusion: Our most basic scientific convictions cannot be refuted by "mere" evidence. In a basic sense, paradigms are above refutation. For Kuhn, a paradigm can be overturned only when another paradigm takes its place. Because evidence must be evaluated in terms of the reigning paradigm's assumptions and procedures, any challenge to the paradigm itself must be formulated in paradigmatic terms or be ignored. And, clearly, if the paradigm defines from the very start what is acceptable, challenges do not stand much of a chance. As in the case of Uri Geller, our scientist's paradigmatic assumptions disallowed the evidence of his senses for no better reason than that what he was seeing was simply impossible. To be sure, second-order findings, those that flesh out the paradigmatic framework, are refutable because the paradigm does not hinge on their validity. But no argument that challenges the authoritative context of argument itself has any chance of being given a second thought.

If paradigms cannot be refuted, they may nevertheless be replaced. Replacement, however, does not derive from a critical, progressive, evidence-based process of trial and error; rather, it represents (as was explained earlier) a rupture with the past, a rapid and overwhelming reorientation of axioms and objectives. Replaced paradigms are not refuted as much as they are overtaken and forced into obsolescence. It is not difficult to sense the paradox involved in these bold assertions. Where refutation is possible (in second-order propositions), it is of less-than-critical importance; where the proposition is of critical importance (i.e., of a paradigmatic character), refutation is impossible.

In Kuhn's view, therefore, Popper's falsification criterion needs to be rethought. Far from being the *sine qua non* of science, it is a prescription for chaos and sterility. Where falsification of paradigmatic propositions is possible, scientific progress is not. Science demands conformity, at least in regard to its basic assumptions. As an organized discipline, science is, in fact, recognizable by the *non*falsifiability of its paradigmatic beliefs. It thrives only when these fundamental beliefs become unassailable, when normal scientists direct their energies exclusively toward second-order "puzzles" that the paradigm creates. Only when reality is perceived through unquestioned and unquestionable categories, when scientific first principles become axiomatic, when orthodoxy is binding and universal, does the "republic of science" thrive. (This is, indeed, a far cry from the positivist view that "out there facts" as they are observed by objective scientists direct and validate the scientific enterprise.)

Intriguingly, Kuhn recounts that it was his experience with the social sciences that alerted him to the fool's paradise of "extraordinary science." The freedom from paradigmatic constraints meant that the social sciences were hardly a *discipline* at all. The most elementary issues remained unresolved. As opposed to the virtual unanimity in regard to substance and method that he found in the natural sciences, social science confronted him with a Tower of Babel, a motley mix of unruly and competing approaches that luxuriated in their sheer multiplicity. And this proliferation of credos was no peaceful affair; many of the contending schools of thought were prepared to accuse their adversaries, often in the most caustic terms, of anything from venality to heartlessness to stupidity.[3] Marxists can hardly carry on a useful (much less a civil) dialogue within neoconservatives, it is difficult to see Straussians and sociobiologists doing anything but shouting past each other, and even behavioralists and antibehavioralists have been known to lose their patience with each other.

Unable to agree about basics, social scientists conduct endless and fruitless wrangles about definitions and first principles. They have been compared (unkindly and probably unjustly) to carpenters who perpetually sharpen their tools and do no work. The work they manage to do nevertheless is fitful and discouraging because, with no common basis for evaluation, what is received glowingly in some academic quarters is cold-shouldered in others. And without strict agreement about what is to be done, the ebb and flow of intellectual vogues and ephemeral fads is particularly powerful. Textbooks teach different materials and different skills, important terms are given radically different meanings, what con-

stitutes proof or evidence varies radically from school to school, method-
ologies are so different that one school is often unable to understand what
the other is talking about, and, perhaps most fundamentally, the ideal
object of scientific knowledge, what it means to be knowledgeable or
wise or intellectually preeminent, is anything but self-evident. Indeed,
putting down one social science journal and picking up another often entails changing professional gears so sharply that one can understandably
wonder if they belong to the same discipline.

Viewed through Kuhn's eyes, the behavioral revolution can be seen in
two quite different ways. Behavioralism was, first of all, a spirited attempt
by a young and ambitious cadre of scholars to close ranks around a particular paradigm and to make of it a binding orthodoxy for political science.
To be sure, from a Kuhnian perspective, behavioralism did not constitute
an advance over earlier paradigms so much as an effective rallying point
for the reorganization of the discipline. And yet, in its organizational
enthusiasm, it created the conditions for stability and progress. The behavioralists' success in replacing the older legal-institutional approach,
their buoyant hopes that the new empirical methods would pay rich
dividends in understanding, their gradual capturing of the discipline's
institutions and publications (some of which is outlined in Dahl's "The
Behavioral Approach in Political Science: Epitaph for a Monument to
a Successful Revolution")—all of this follows Kuhn's model of scientific
revolution quite closely. Insofar as the newly emerging paradigm replaced
the lackadaisical regime of prebehavioralism with a stern, coercive, and
universal regimen of assumptions, methods, and objectives, it held out
the promise of introducing the order and discipline that are the necessary
conditions for a thriving scientific enterprise.

But from another Kuhn-based perspective, the behavioral position
could not bear careful analysis. The contention that empiricism provided an "inside track" on reality, for example, was indefensible. Reality
was accessible only through specific frameworks of analysis; to see at all
required choosing a delimited perspective from which to make one's observations. And, of course, what one saw depended on where one stood.
The idea (championed by the more insistent behaviorists) that political
scientists could transcend the intellectual context of which they were
inexorably a part, observe the "brute data" they confronted disinterest-
edly, and derive scientific conclusions unaffected by the anticipations,
assumptions, and interests mandated by the reigning paradigm, was given
a sound thrashing in Kuhn's account of scientific activity.

Even a falsification-based methodology that avoids resting on the personal objectivity of the researcher and bases its findings on the impersonal nature and privileged status of refutation cannot save the day. As
we noted previously, falsification for Kuhn is an available strategy only in
regard to hypotheses that arise *within* the paradigmatic context; it is un-
availing in regard to the paradigm itself. Here only a total revolutionary
transformation is possible.

Ironically, this was the exact fate that overtook behavioralism. The behavioral paradigm was, of course, never definitively falsified. In fact, it continues at present to command a sizable constituency of enthusiastic followers—perhaps even a majority of current practitioners. But the combined effect of the Vietnam War, the black revolt, student activism, and a host of other sociohistorical factors that converged during the late 1960s, rendered its socially detached and ideologically uncommitted nature unpalatable to a new generation of scholars. Political science, in their minds, required a more humane and engaged character than what was offered in the behavioral persuasion. It was challenged, therefore, not for specific failures of which it was guilty but rather because another, more gratifying and timely vision of what political inquiry should look like contested its hegemony.

And yet the challenge did not remain as amorphous and undifferentiated as the preceding discussion might lead the reader to believe. There followed specific attacks of great power that exposed weaknesses in the behavioral approach—weaknesses that even behavioralists were forced to acknowledge. The insufficiency of focusing exclusively on overt political behavior was, for example, hammered home by Bachrach and Baratz in their seminal article "Two Faces of Power."[4] Still, loyal Kuhnians would tend to see these arguments, astute and cogent though they were, not as the direct cause of the retreat from behavioralism, but as the explicit and reasoned arguments given by the disenchanted to justify abandoning an approach that no longer held moral or intellectual appeal for them.

Whatever position one takes on the Kuhnian challenge, it has had one indisputable effect on contemporary academic thinking: a heightened sensitivity to the social psychology of scientific practice. It is no longer possible to speak *tout court* of the inherent "logic" of scientific discovery as the exclusive factor accounting for its character. Kuhn has forced us to give serious attention to science as a social and communitarian form of behavior, a conformity-enforcing discipline, a paradigm-dominated activity. Science, in other words, is an enterprise moved by many important organizational, psychological, and authority-related considerations—considerations that lie beyond the likes of logic, methodology, and analysis.

The older, idealized picture of the scientific community as a "fellowship of discovery" set on an unconditional course of free inquiry appears quaint and gullible by comparison. The community of science, Kuhn would have us believe, is a "political" community, one that regulates, enforces, socializes, arbitrates, allocates, and punishes—and all of this by the authority of an ascendant and sovereign paradigm. It is no wonder, therefore, that in the post-Kuhnian era there were many who, faced with the behavioral revolution, were more disposed to anticipate a politicization of science than a "scientization" of politics.

What becomes incontrovertibly clear from this discussion is the lack of synchronization between developments in neighboring fields. The behavioral revolution based itself on a conception of science that the bulk of contemporary philosophers of science would find outmoded and unsophisticated. Similarly, the skeptical speculations of the philosophers of science would appear alien, tortured, and fanciful to those involved in hands-on research. Each, apparently, marches to the rhythm of a different drummer.

NOTES

1. See, for example, Heinz Eulau's *The Behavioral Persuasion in Politics* (New York, Random House, 1963).

2. For a good discussion, see John C. Gunnel, *Philosophy, Science and Political Inquiry* (Morristown, N. J., General Learning Press, 1975). See also Michael Shapiro, *Language and Political Understanding: The Politics of Discursive Practice* (New Haven, Conn., Yale University Press, 1981), esp. Ch. 1.

3. Suffice it to say that a course in "Approaches to the Study of Modern Physics" would not have much to offer. Insofar as there are differences among physicists, Kuhn would contend that they are of a nonparadigmatic, second-order nature.

4. *American Political Science Review*, 56 (1962) pp. 947–52.

SUGGESTIONS FOR FURTHER READING

Gunnel, J., *Philosophy, Science and Political Inquiry* (Morristown, N. J., General Learning Press, 1975).

Hempel, C. G., "General Laws in History," in *Aspects of Scientific Explanation and Other Essays in the Philosophy of Science* (New York, The Free Press, 1965), pp. 231–243.

Kuhn, T., *The Structure of Scientific Revolutions* (Chicago, University of Chicago Press, 1962).

Popper, K., *The Logic of Scientific Discovery* (London, Hutchinson, 1959).

Stephens, J., "The Kuhnian Paradigm and Political Inquiry," *American Journal of Political Science*, 17 (1973), pp. 467–488.

Richard von Mises

Positivism

I

1   The word "positivism" is used, as are all terms of this kind, with many different and partly contradictory meanings. Therefore it seems appropriate to say something about the sense in which it will be used in this book. But a complete discussion of the term "positivism" is clearly impossible here, since that would mean anticipating the content of the book. What we can attempt is only this: to start within a frame of reference familiar to the reader and to introduce him gradually, step by step, into the lines of thought which we call positivism.

2   Presumably the reader knows what he would regard as a reasonable or judicious attitude in most situations of life. No doubt a major component of such an attitude is, in the first place, to judge on the grounds of experience, that is, the remembrance of the contingencies of one's own life and the knowledge of those of others. Furthermore, such an attitude requires a continual readiness to give up a judgment once made or to change it if new experiences require. It also implies a lack of prejudice, superstition, obstinacy, blind trust in authority, mystical thinking, fanaticism. Evidently, nobody can be a perfect embodiment of all these qualities all of the time; but one should certainly be ready to repudiate actions and judgments as soon as one becomes aware that they were not consonant with those requirements.

3   As a first tentative and quite rough approach to the definition of positivism, we may say that whoever, when confronted with any practical or theoretical problem, acts as we have just described it is a positivist.

4   For several hundred years there has been, in all civilized countries, an area of life in which positivistic conduct has become almost an unconditional rule. This is the realm of scientific research; and by this we by no means refer only to research in the natural sciences. Those who study the laws of phonetic development of the Romance languages, or try to clear up the circumstances under which Julius Caesar was murdered, are engaged in positive scientific investigation. The situation is more difficult in those sciences whose subject matter is closer to the life of the scientist himself or of those persons for whom

From *Positivism: A Study in Human Understanding* (New York, Dover Publications), pp. 1–15 used by permission of Harvard University Press.

he cares. The stars of the astronomer are detached enough, but the social sciences, which, if the term is used in the widest sense, include even theology, deal with questions that make it difficult for the researcher to maintain the disinterested attitude of the scholar. Nevertheless one can say that, apart from the most extreme cases, everybody who claims for himself the name of a scientist must accept, at least *in principle,* the rules that we have outlined above as the marks of "reasonable conduct." With this in mind, we may say, a little more precisely, but still in a very preliminary way, that he is a positivist who, when confronted by a problem, acts in the manner in which a typical contemporary scientist deals with his problems of research.

At this point it might be appropriate to say a word about 5 what positivism in our conception is *not.* In the history of art the problem arises of determining the period of origin of a work handed down to us from a remote past. One scholar derives his assertions from a study of similarities and differences in artistic style, another draws his conclusions from a chemical analysis of the material. It is *not* positivism to accept the second method only and to reject, as a matter of principle, the first one. No procedure based on systematic observations from which conclusions may be drawn is declined by positivism. Those who demand that a physician, when he treats a patient, must use physical and chemical methods *only,* cannot claim a positivistic tenet as support. Even less than the method are the subject matter and the aim of research subject to limitations from the standpoint of positivism. The observations about telepathy so far seem not very promising; but positivism does not recommend that they be discontinued. Nor does a positivist think that man "lives by bread alone" or, for that matter, has only intellectual needs; but more about that later.

What are the things which in our mind definitely have to be 6 regarded as antipositivistic? First of all is the idea that there exists an area of problems in which the intellect is not "competent," in which one *cannot* think or *must* not think. Next is the conception that there exists a realm of "truth" which cannot be shaken by any experience, previous or future. It is typical "negativism" to use the intellect in order to prove that the intellect is worthless and must not be used, either anywhere or in certain fields.

This book, however, will deal with much more subtle ques- 7 tions. It will turn out that deviations from "reasonable conduct" creep in almost everywhere, even in the work of the scientist in the so-called exact sciences, unless he continually uses the greatest care. The manner in which the means of language are applied in description and communication requires, at every period in the development of science, a new act of purification, a "purge," which usually lasts only for a short time. In every branch of science that really progresses, there arise continually new auxiliary concepts and the people who learn them are only too prone to misunderstand the tentativeness of their role. It is astounding to see to what degree men tend to misuse the intellectual (and, for that matter, the material) means that they have created themselves. A consequence is that those who go beyond narrowly limited technical fields, or areas of life in which they are at home, find themselves confronted by irresolvable contradictions, unless they are willing to change their conceptions every time. But neither contradictions nor continual changes of viewpoint are reconcilable with reasonable judgments and actions.

8   We now add to the previous conceptual delineations of positivism the more specific but just as tentative one: It is the aim of positivistic theory to review and to sum up the stock of experience acquired by men in a uniform picture so that mutually consistent judgments are possible in all situations of life.

II

9   The first and greatest difficulty in striving for reasonable judgments and in constructing a consistent world picture lies in *language*. It is true and is often stated that our language contains deep wisdom, but it is the wisdom of the primitive, the childhood of mankind. All linguistic elements—words, locutions, grammatical rules—originate in the need to find one's way about in the maze of everyday life. They can be adjusted only with great difficulty to the complicated requirements set by our present stock of knowledge and experience. Anyone who knows a language takes words such as "cause" and "effect," or rules about contingent and causal sentences, as something given, and he can get along with these means in almost all practical situations. But as soon as one tries to go a little deeper into situations that are farther removed from everyday life, it turns out that the world is much less simple than men thought several thousand years ago (when our language was created). All school philosophers from Plato through Kant and Hegel to Husserl and Heidegger have tried to solve the unsolvable problem of deriving a consistent world image by using (and slightly modifying) the stock of ready-made expres-

sions in their language. Present-day logical positivism (which has had rather early predecessors, too) starts from the fact that the "logic" stored in our language represents a primitive stage of science. The positivist, like everybody else, has to use colloquial language in order to make himself understood; but he uses it critically. He knows that all terms in use are conventions which refer to a limited area of experience and beyond that mean nothing. Over and over again he returns to the question: What are the actual experiences and observations that find their expression in a specific word, a sentence, or a theory?

For the positivist, every word, every phrase, of colloquial lan- 10 guage means a dissection of the world into three classes. The first class consists of things or situations to which the word, according to the existing linguistic conventions, applies without any doubt. The second class comprises those things for which the word in question is definitely not meant; and the third is formed by all those phenomena for which the linguistic conventions are not sufficient to enable one to decide whether or not the given expression applies. This holds for the simplest words such as "table" and "bed," "above" and "below," "walking" and "running," as well as for more complicated terms such as "cause" and "effect," "body" and "soul," "good" and "evil." In most situations of everyday life and in wide areas of science, we can make use of these familiar linguistic means without having to fear misunderstandings. But these expedients are not sufficient if we go too far beyond the primitive experiences for which they were originally created.

The analysis and critique of language by positivism do not 11 aim to restrict or to prohibit the legitimate use of the standard linguistic means in everyday life, in science, or in poetry. A simple analogy will make this immediately clear. For the greater part of our lives, we regard the earth not as a curved surface but as a plane. We measure distances, distinguish directions, we speak of mountains and valleys, of above and below, as though the surface of the earth were a flat disk. It is only when we undertake a trip around the world, or deal with the time of day on a different hemisphere, that we have to take notice of the spherical shape of the earth. All this is familiar today to everyone who has gone through grammar school. In the not-too-distant future, we hope, men will also understand that concepts such as cause and effect, body and soul, and other expedients of this kind, are not adequate concepts for the conquest of more difficult intellectual problems.

The metaphysician's attitude toward language is entirely dif- 12 ferent. He thinks that a word, e.g., the word "justice," corresponds, independently of all conventions, to some specific entity, and he seeks to *discover* this entity, i.e., to find the "true" and correct definition of justice. To the positivist the question "What is justice?" can mean only one of two things. Either one wants to find out what in the course of time was denoted by this word within different cultural areas (historical semantics), or one seeks, with a specific aim in mind, to fix a new concept of justice, that is to say, to suggest a new linguistic convention for use within some limited field of action or of science. In the exact sciences the second procedure is the common one. What in mechanics is called "force" or "work" can in no wise be derived from the meanings that these words carry in everyday language.

III

13   Everyone who makes efforts to gain knowledge in any field has the natural desire to see this knowledge secured forever. Since scientific assertions are nothing but predictions about future experiences (in what sense this holds also for historical sciences and the other humanities will be explained later), this is nothing but another expression of the general longing for security in life. Hence it is no wonder that at a very early time, the ideal of an unchangeable *"eternal" truth* made itself felt.

14   For a long time we have known a class of assertions that seemed to satisfy this ideal—the mathematical theorems. That two times six equals twelve, or that thirteen is not divisible by any positive integer but itself and 1, seem entirely without doubt and certain for all future time. Most of Kant's and his successors' epistemology is devoted to the problem how one could arrive at results of the same absolute certainty in other areas, such as, e.g., astronomy. But in Kant's time and even before, there were wiser scholars (above all the English positivists such as Locke and Hume) who knew that these attempts were illusory. However, a satisfactory analysis of the whole situation was initiated only recently, by Ludwig Wittgenstein.

15   In his *Tractatus Logico-Philosophicus* of 1922, Wittgenstein shows that the theorems of pure mathematics or of logic say absolutely nothing about reality (about the experienceable, observable world), but are, in a specific sense of the word, *tautologies*. This of course does not mean that they are superfluous or self-evident. Sometimes they are very intricate transformations of certain symbol complexes according to fixed rules. Theorems of logic or pure mathematics are

said to be "correct" if they are in agreement with the system of accepted definitions and rules, just as in chess only those moves are accepted which are in accordance with the rules of the game. One who knows these rules can decide *once and for all* whether a tautological assertion is true or false (unless there turns out to be an inconsistency in the system), but he has thereby said nothing about any matter of observable fact. That twelve is divisible by three, while thirteen is not, is absolutely correct, but a shepherd can no more divide twelve sheep than thirteen into three absolutely "equal" parts.

The last example also shows in what manner mathematical theorems are applicable to reality. The symbols and transformation rules of logic correspond as an *approximation* to certain facts and relations of everyday life. The wool of each group of four sheep in a flock is approximately equal and, if we are satisfied with this degree of approximation, it is possible to say that a herd of twelve is divisible into three parts and one of thirteen is not. But in this proposition there is nothing left of the absoluteness and exactness of the mathematical theorem. The situation is no way different in the more complicated problems of geometry or physics in general. The theorems of Euclidean, as well as of non-Euclidean, geometry derived from different systems of axioms are both absolutely correct. The spatial relations, however, that are open to observation correspond only approximately to one or the other system of geometry. Which one we have to use in a given case is a question of better approximation, that is to say, of greater utility, and is thus to a certain degree arbitrary. 16

Our answer to the Kantian problem of epistemology is therefore this: One can construct in many ways tautological systems in which there exist—according to fixed rules—absolutely correct statements; but if one wants to state anything about relations between observable phenomena, e.g., in astronomy, then one is subject to control by future experiences. The application of mathematical methods can never guarantee the correctness of a nonmathematical proposition. 17

The opponents of positivism usually claim that we, the positivists, too, believe in certain dogmas and therefore contradict ourselves. Such a dogma of the positivist is allegedly, for instance, the statement: "There are no eternal truths." If we accept this, we are supposed to believe in at least one eternal truth (namely, the foregoing statement), and therefore we refute ourselves. The quoted assertion, however, does not appear in the vocabulary of positivism. As epistemologists we do nothing but what every scientist does: we describe what we observe. We see that there are tautological systems in which 18 one operates with fixed symbols according to accepted rules. We see that the majority of all statements which play any role in practical life and in science originate in observations and are continually tested by experience. Aristotle's mechanics, according to which the circle is the natural orbit of a body, has been replaced by Newton's mechanics, in which the straight line is the path of a body left to itself. In order to take later observations into account, Newton's theory has been replaced by Einstein's, which one can interpret by saying that the inertial orbits are straight lines in a space with a non-Euclidean geometry. Whether or not, sooner or later, even this conception will have to be modified, is something we certainly do not know, or care to make assertions about.

19   But we also observe that metaphysicians make propositions which are framed in such a way that they neither form parts of an established tautological system nor are testable in experience. Such propositions, if stated by one author, are as a rule opposed by all, or almost all, others. Sometimes they find a group of disciples that is geographically and temporally limited. If one wants to give to these theories, or to one of them, the name "eternal truth," then this is a manner of speaking whose usefulness everybody may judge for himself.

IV

20   We do not claim that a scientific theory, either in physics, or in economics, or in any other field, is uniquely determined by the observable facts. Theories are inventions, constructions. A theory is useful if it predicts the phenomena correctly. Different theories may make the same predictions with respect to large areas of facts. Under otherwise equal circumstances one will prefer that theory which covers a larger field of phenomena or which from some point of view appears to be the "simpler." This preference is subjective, and accordingly the acceptance or rejection of a specific theory is to a certain extent arbitrary. The attempts, sometimes made, to decide the usefulness of a theory "scientifically," as for instance by means of the so-called calculus of probability, must be rejected. The calculus of probability itself is a scientific theory of the same kind as any other branch of the exact natural sciences. Its area of application is that of long sequences of repeating occurrences or of mass phenomena. But scientific problems and competing theories in any field do not occur en masse; therefore, it is not possible to ascribe to them a numerical probability. Experience teaches that all theories are constantly subject to larger or smaller modifi-

cations and that, as Ernst Mach expressed it, science consists of a continually progressing *adaptation of ideas to facts.*

The positivistic philosophy of science seeks, in the first place, 21 to determine the features that all branches of science have in common. In this sense it speaks of a *unity of science* without overlooking the sometimes wide differences of methodology in the separate disciplines. We prefer not to propose a classification of the sciences in the sense of a hierarchy or a pyramid, because too many points of view cross each other and because the boundaries are unstable. This shows itself in every small sector; the experiment, i.e., observation under artificially produced conditions, plays the main role in physics and chemistry, but almost no role today in astronomy or geology. As far as the extent of the application of mathematical means is concerned, astronomy and geology stand perhaps at opposite ends. There is a continuous formation of theories in physics as well as in geology. The boundary between physics and chemistry is gradually disappearing, astronomy changes into astrophysics, and geology comes to use more and more the methods of physics. As time passes the situation changes quickly, areas split off, others grow into one, and, in the course of one generation, the map of the sciences may assume an entirely different appearance.

The main problem arises when we study the mutual relation 22 of those two groups of sciences which, as a rule, are regarded as complete opposites and even as incompatible: the natural sciences and the humanities. According to a conception that predominates primarily in Germany, not only are these two groups distinct in their methods of research and in the principal meaning of their results, but even the kind of "understanding" of matters of fact that each employs is allegedly totally different. The point of view of this study is essentially that this dichotomy is untenable. Physics, biology, psychology, the social sciences, history, form a complicated, interconnected web which cannot be bisected by a simple cut. The more we learn about psychosomatic phenomena, the less it is possible to split off a part of psychology as belonging to the "humanities." The social sciences, whose relation to psychology is becoming closer and closer, are accepting in many branches more and more the methods of the natural sciences. The idea that the use of mathematical formalism is a measure of the "scientificness" of a discipline is not shared by us.

Since the time of Ernst Mach, natural scientists have known 23 that the explanation or the theory of a group of phenomena is only a description of the facts on a higher level. In history, the advocates of dualism claim that there are no theories at all but only pure and objective descriptions of occurrences. But such an "objective" report does not exist; otherwise, new historians could not always give new expositions of the same happenings. Even if we leave aside such explicit theories of history as that of Marxism or that of Spenglerism, the theory of a historian consists inherently in the selection and correlation of the facts he mentions. He implies that from certain premises which he reports the adduced occurrences follow and thereby he predicts or implies that under approximately the same circumstances in the future approximately the same thing will happen again. The meteorologist proceeds in the same manner when he describes the course of the weather, which, as a whole, is just as unique an event as the history of men and peoples or the history of the earth, the development of animal species and human races. It is always the search for, and the exposition of, typical and recurring elements *within the unique course of the world* that is the subject of science.

V

24   The positivism represented here tries to avoid some exaggerations of which other authors in earlier or even recent times have been guilty. For us, metaphysics is not nonsense, poetry is not superfluous, the fine arts and music are legitimate forms of communication among men.

25   So-called "logical positivism," which was created in the first quarter of this century, has carried through for the first time the idea that epistemology is nothing but a logical study of the language in which scientific results are expressed. Among the founders of the "Vienna Circle" it was particularly Carnap and Neurath who developed in detail the theory that the scientific language can be built up in a consistent manner from uniform simple elements. The element sentences are short, immediately understandable statements about simple sensations (receptions). Later we shall see that this theory is only another form of Mach's doctrine of elements. It is also closely related to Bridgman's so-called "operationalism."

26   The Vienna scientists have drawn from the logical analysis of the language of science the conclusion that the propositions of metaphysics which cannot be constituted in the above-mentioned manner are meaningless and do not say anything. This is the point in which the present study does not follow the logical positivists. In our conception the decisive concept is that of *connectibility*. The statements of science and the carefully formulated sentences of everyday language are con-

nectible among each other and with a certain stock of linguistic rules. The assertions of metaphysics do not belong to this area. With them the single words or groups of words do not have the meaning that can be derived from or traced back to element sentences. Nevertheless, metaphysical statements can in most cases be given a more or less vague meaning; this is due to the fact that here, too, within limited areas a certain connectibility exists, namely, between the works of a limited metaphysical school and certain rules of language which for them (and only for them) are accepted as valid. In other words, if two physicists talk about the phenomenon of heat conduction they always mean the same thing by the same expressions; but if two metaphysicians develop theories about cause and effect, they usually speak about different things.

The aim of intellectual endeavor of man may in the last 27 analysis consist in the attempt to arrive, for all phenomena that are of some interest, at a description that is connectible across the boundaries of all fields. We are very far, at present, from achieving this final aim. In the meantime the gaps are filled by nonscientific theories, i.e., theories that are not connectible with the language of science. They appear in the form of metaphysics or of religious systems or of poetry. But we do not mean to say that these types of intellectual activity will disappear within the foreseeable future. Anyone who knows a little physics is aware that men continually use up the store of energy of the earth and that the entropy of the planet on which we live continually increases. But the prophecy that sometime all available energy will be exhausted and that we will have to suffer an entropy death does not frighten us. We do not make such extrapolations since *all* conditions change in time; the word "eternity" does not appear in scientific language.

Expressions such as *"eternity"* and *"the beyond," "beauty"* and 28 *"love,"* are familiar words in another language which is called the language of poetry. We do not think of lyrical poetry only or of verses in general, but of all those communications to which the concepts truth and validity are applied in a different sense than to the assertions of everyday life. The story of a novel is not true in the historical sense, but one ascribes to it validity if it agrees with certain experiences of life and if the author has given us insights that stand the test of later experiences. Even lyrical poetry, so far as it is to be taken seriously, expresses experiences of a specific sort. Connectibility is even more limited here than in metaphysics, if one thinks of different single works of poets. But certain basic elements of the poetic language are familiar to such a wide circle of educated men that what is expressed in it seems understandable to more people than scientific theories.

29   Science and art are much more closely related to each other than the popular (and also the logical) positivism will have us believe. Every work of art can be considered as a *theory* of a specific small section of real life—at any rate, much better as a theory than as an imitation or reproduction. A drama describes the development of a human character by showing us a few single actions or a few moments of his life. A sculpture with the title "The Thinker" even shows only a single face and a single position and claims to tell us something about the nature of an individual engaged in intellectual work. A work of art is neither true nor false, but it can, to a greater or lesser degree, agree with our experiences, previous or future.

30   Evaluations of works of art are customarily framed with expressions that are related to the word "beauty." Today there will hardly be anyone who still believes that there exists a standard of beauty valid for all times and all peoples. It is the task of a sufficiently general sociology to study in what manner esthetic judgments depend upon the race, the environment, the education, and the personal experiences of the individual. The same holds for all "valuations" in metaphysical systems. At any rate, the positivist does not deny the existence of esthetic needs and he is not opposed to undertakings directed toward their satisfaction.

VI

31   Most of the expositions of positivism avoid dealing with the complex of questions pertaining to the modes of conduct of men, usually called *ethics.* We shall not limit ourselves in this way here, particularly since we do not see a sharp dividing line between the intellectual endeavors of men directed toward regulation of general conduct and the other subjects of our investigation.

32   If an engineer computes the relation between the dimensions of the girders of a bridge and the load that the bridge can stand, he can phrase the result in the form: The bridge *must* have these dimensions. If the physician determines by scientific tests that a certain drug kills certain bacteria, he can make the prescription: The patient *ought* to take this drug. If sociological studies lead us to believe that a specific way of rearing children badly influences their development at a later age, one may fix by law: This kind of upbringing is *prohibited.* In all of these cases the connection between statements of fact and

the ought-sentences derived from them is evident. We can formulate it thus: Ought-sentences are elliptic statements; they suppress one part of the implication.

Common opinion has it that there exist also imperatives of 33 another kind. It is felt that the commandments Thou shalt not steal or Thou shalt not kill are more than expressions of the general experience that the community life of men would be decisively disturbed if stealing and murder were to be practiced to the full extent. Just what this "more" consists of that these ought-sentences allegedly imply is not commonly agreed upon. Some think that certain ethical rules are inherent in men, much as the ability to breathe is. Others believe that certain groups of rules of conduct were communicated to men at a specific historical period by revelation, i.e., without interference of their own intellect.

The first of these assumptions is contradicted by the fact that 34 there are primitive peoples who simply do not know some of the rules of life that seem self-evident to us. The second, religious, conception of the moral laws is invalidated by the fact that the allegedly revealed commandments are so vague and incomplete that their application requires continually new interpretation which, after all, is a work of the intellect. Nobody can say with certainty whether the seventh commandment allows the lending of money at an arbitrarily high rate of interest, whether the fifth commandment includes the case of suicide, of self-defense, of killing in war, and whether it prohibits the sacrifice of an unborn infant in order to save the life of the mother. There can be no doubt that the rules according to which we live and act are an elaborate result of tradition, of continued control by experience, and of conventional decisions.

One usually regards as the main task of ethics the setting 35 up and justification of systems of norms. A justification of a prescription can, as we have seen, only consist of statements that express the relation between the prescribed conduct and certain consequences. Among these consequences the acquisition of feelings of security, of an inner satisfaction, of peace of mind or peace of soul, of general recognition, and so on, take a particular place. Since the reaching of such an aim depends essentially upon the extent to which the same or similar norms of conduct are accepted by others and followed by them, the dispersion of uniform systems of ethics among large communities is a prerequisite for their existence. As a matter of fact, only a few religious doctrines—and these are not so very different from each other in their ethics—have historically survived. Nobody will deny the tremendous influence which the

Hellenistic, the Jewish-Christian, the Islamic, the Buddhistic religions, and Confucianism have exerted upon the civilization of mankind. But we see no reason in this fact why every single assertion of such a doctrine should not be subject to the same kind of logical critique and continual control by experience as any claim of a scientific theory.

36   Questions of ethics are frequently raised in connection with the concepts of *value* and *evaluation*. People think that it is possible not only to ascribe to single actions and to the total conduct of a man expressions such as good and evil, but even to bring all actions into an ordered sequence of increasing moral values. Now, it is very easy to order a group of a hundred individuals according to their height or weight, but very difficult or hardly possible in a consistent manner to determine their order with respect to their strength. Further, if one asks for the degree of bodily or mental health of the hundred individuals, the uncertainty and the variety of incompatible points of view become so large that agreement without the explicit introduction of arbitrary standards is entirely unthinkable. In our conception, it is only *one more step* in the same direction if a classification of moral conduct is sought. The question whether there "exists" an objective standard which we just do not know may be neglected by us. It is certain that agreement on moral values, except in quite rough cases, can be accomplished only within limited communities that have a great part of their life experiences in common.

37   The introduction and the discussion of such standards of value which fulfill some useful purpose (to which, of course, the satisfaction of feelings of happiness belongs) is without doubt a worthy task; but no useful purpose is served if one tries to mislead oneself or others about the fact that *all* moral systems, including their justification, are creations of the human intellect of a similar kind to scientific theories.

VII

38   The most serious objections raised against accepting the positivistic point of view are that it leaves unsatisfied essential needs of men, and that it often proves preferable in one's life not to act strictly according to logic and the scientific method. To a certain extent both of these points are well taken.

39   As to the first we may make our answer very brief. The aim of a scientific exposition can never be other than an intellectual one, that is to say, to offer information, enlightenment, eluci-

dation of relationships, no matter what feelings of pleasure or displeasure result from these for an individual. Other types of communication, such as poetry, have, in addition, the purpose of creating pleasure, by stimulating certain vague associations with one's previous experience. We are quite aware that a strict delineation of these various forms of mental endeavor is impossible, and we maintain that, as we have stressed above, positivism does not stand for the elimination of any of them. Those who seek satisfaction of their esthetic wants (in the most general sense of the word) from sources other than scientific discourse do not thereby stand in opposition to positivism as we understand it.

To discuss the matter of the pragmatic value, or lack of it, 40 of positivism is much more difficult. The criticism here comes from so many directions and can take on so many different meanings that it is hardly possible even to enumerate them all. We can mention only the most important of these antipositivistic approaches.

"Too clear an insight into the limitations and uncertainties 41 of a theory hinders the creative scientist in his work, which is mainly guided by instinct." Many valuable scientific discoveries, it is true, are due to men who, consciously or unconsciously, kept free of philosophical scruples, who had absolute faith in the validity of the currently accepted auxiliary concepts, and who did not care for questions of epistemology at all. Textbooks of any branch of science are an intertwined mixture of definitions (tautological elements), statements of observation, inductive generalizations, and conclusions of various degrees of exactitude. Not every specialist in a field can analyze or have a full understanding of this entire complex. But it cannot be denied that the great turning points in the development of science were decisively influenced by advances in philosophical enlightenment of a positivistic nature. Newton's creation of the structure of deterministic physics was, in its origin, not independent of the principles of clearness and distinctness of ideas proclaimed about fifty years earlier by Descartes. And in our time, everyone knows that the theory of relativity and the ensuing reorientation of all of physics had their roots in Mach's critique of the foundations of Newtonian mechanics. Presumably it will take another step in the positivistic direction to clear up certain difficulties and inconsistencies in quantum physics, and thus to bring to perfection the present phase of the development of the physical sciences. In the small, in the individual steps or in routine work one may question the usefulness of positivism; in the large it is indispensable.

42   As far as ordinary happenings in everyday life are concerned, the situation is not much different. Undoubtedly in many cases an instinctive, unpremediated act is successful, while careful examination of all pros and cons leads to failure. However, what we today, in civilized society, call instinct is to a large extent the product of early training, upbringing, and education, which become effective in not too unusual situations. If one is confronted by difficult tasks, by circumstances that deviate more noticeably from the normal, one seldom relies on intuition or inspiration and is very rarely successful with them.

43   Occasionally one hears the assertion that the practical consequences of positivism have been invalidated by certain newer results of natural science. Psychoanalysis has uncovered the role of the unconscious in human conduct, and the so-called uncertainty relation of quantum physics, it is alleged, has proved that even in the realm of physics not everything can be subject to measurement. The answer to this is that the "unconscious" of psychoanalysis and the "uncertainty" of quantum mechanics are entirely rational concepts; they may be interpreted in terms of metaphysics only in the same sense in which previously people saw a metaphysical element in the "action-at-a-distance" of gravitation or in all electrical phenomena. In the same category belongs the quaint belief that certain psychosomatic phenomena, once they are thoroughly studied, will be something else than just a new chapter of the rational explanation of nature.

44   The most decided opposition to the positivistic point of view comes from those circles which claim the existence of an absolute (religious) authority for the solution of all vital problems. As pointed out above, a system that anticipates all situations that might ever occur is impossible, and a new interpretation of the laws of religion by intellectual means continually proves necessary. History shows how much, in spite of all its apparent conservatism, the practical position of the Church with respect to factual questions (e.g., in the treatment of heretics) changes. Those who close their eyes to such changes and, in their daily lives, follow the prescriptions of their Church as they stand at the given movement can gain peace of soul and happiness to which positivism has nothing comparable to offer. However, whether a Christian Scientist who later becomes aware that, by neglecting rational actions, he has caused permanent damage to his own or other people's lives can keep his peace of soul is, to say the least, questionable.

45   Positivism does not claim that all questions can be answered rationally, just as medicine is not based on the premise that

all diseases are curable, or physics does not start out with the postulate that all phenomena are explicable. But the mere possibility that there *may* be no answers to some questions is no sufficient reason for not looking for answers or for not using those that are attainable.

This is particularly true for that complex of questions so 46 vital to all of us that arise from the community life of large and ever larger groups of people. The problem has been the same for thousands of years: to find a just balance between, on one hand, the social requirements of planning and organization made necessary by the steady increase and the growing density of population, and, on the other hand, the desire for individual freedom. The two strongest political powers of the present, take pains to emphasize exclusively either one or the other of these two extremes, and each regards those who pay heed to the other side as moral enemies. On both sides scholars try to prove, by what are apparently the available scientific means, that this one-sidedness is justified. In the last analysis, they base their attempts (not with full justification) upon ideological systems of an extremely metaphysical character—the one side upon the doctrines of the Church, and the other upon Hegel's absolutistic world of ideas. If this goes on, the predictions of those who believe that the next step toward the solution of the basic sociological problems must come from the physical annihilation of one of the two groups of people will be borne out.

In our opinion the only way out is less loose talk and more 47 criticism of language, less emotional acting and more scientifically disciplined thinking, less metaphysics and more positivism.

Karl R. Popper

Science: Conjectures and Refutations

Mr. Turnbull had predicted evil consequences... and was now doing the best in his power to bring about the verification of his own prophecies.

ANTHONY TROLLOPE

I

1   When I received the list of participants in this course and realized that I had been asked to speak to philosophical colleagues I thought, after some hesitation and consultation, that you would probably prefer me to speak about those problems which interest me most, and about those developments with which I am most intimately acquainted. I therefore decided to do what I have never done before: to give you a report on my own work in the philosophy of science, since the autumn of 1919 when I first began to grapple with the problem, *'When should a theory be ranked as scientific?'* or *'Is there a criterion for the scientific character or status of a theory?'*

2   The problem which troubled me at the time was neither, 'When is a theory true?' nor, 'When is a theory acceptable?' My problem was different. I *wished to distinguish between science and pseudo-science;* knowing very well that science often errs, and that pseudo-science may happen to stumble on the truth.

3   I knew, of course, the most widely accepted answer to my problem: that science is distinguished from pseudo-science— or from 'metaphysics'—by its *empirical method,* which is essentially *inductive,* proceeding from observation or experiment. But this did not satisfy me. On the contrary, I often formulated my problem as one of distinguishing between a genuinely empirical method and a non-empirical or even a pseudo-empirical method—that is to say, a method which, although it appeals to observation and experiment, nevertheless does not come up to scientific standards. The latter method may be exemplified by astrology, with its stupendous mass of empirical evidence based on observation—on horoscopes and on biographies.

4   But as it was not the example of astrology which led me to my problem I should perhaps briefly describe the atmosphere

From *Conjectures and Refutations: The Growth of Scientific Knowledge* (New York: Basic Books, 1962), pp. 33–59.

in which my problem arose and the examples by which it was stimulated. After the collapse of the Austrian Empire there had been a revolution in Austria: the air was full of revolutionary slogans and ideas, and new and often wild theories. Among the theories which interested me Einstein's theory of relativity was no doubt by far the most important. Three others were Marx's theory of history, Freud's psycho-analysis, and Alfred Adler's so-called 'individual psychology.'

There was a lot of popular nonsense talked about these theories, and especially about relativity (as still happens even today), but I was fortunate in those who introduced me to the study of this theory. We all—the small circle of students to which I belonged—were thrilled with the result of Eddington's eclipse observations which in 1919 brought the first important confirmation of Einstein's theory of gravitation. It was a great experience for us, and one which had a lasting influence on my intellectual development. 5

The three other theories I have mentioned were also widely discussed among students at that time. I myself happened to come into personal contact with Alfred Adler, and even to cooperate with him in his social work among the children and young people in the working-class districts of Vienna where he had established social guidance clinics. 6

It was during the summer of 1919 that I began to feel more and more dissatisfied with these three theories—the Marxist theory of history, psychoanalysis, and individual psychology; and I began to feel dubious about their claims to scientific status. My problem perhaps first took the simple form, 'What is wrong with Marxism, psycho-analysis, and individual psychology? Why are they so different from physical theories, from Newton's theory, and especially from the theory of relativity?' 7

To make this contrast clear I should explain that few of us at the time would have said that we believed in the *truth* of Einstein's theory of gravitation. This shows that it was not my doubting the *truth* of those other three theories which bothered me, but something else. Yet neither was it that I merely felt mathematical physics to be more *exact* than the sociological or psychological type of theory. Thus what worried me was neither the problem of truth, at that stage at least, nor the problem of exactness or measurability. It was rather that I felt that these other three theories, though posing as sciences, had in fact more in common with primitive myths than with science; that they resembled astrology rather than astronomy. 8

I found that those of my friends who were admirers of Marx, Freud, and Adler, were impressed by a number of points com- 9 mon to these theories, and especially by their apparent *ex-planatory power*. These theories appeared to be able to explain practically everything that happened within the fields to which they referred. The study of any of them seemed to have the effect of an intellectual conversion or revelation, opening your eyes to a new truth hidden from those not yet initiated. Once your eyes were thus opened you saw confirming instances everywhere: the world was full of *verifications* of the theory. Whatever happened always confirmed it. Thus its truth appeared manifest; and unbelievers were clearly people who did not want to see the manifest truth; who refused to see it, either because it was against their class interest, or because of their repressions, which were still 'un-analysed' and crying aloud for treatment.

10   The most characteristic element in this situation seemed to me the incessant stream of confirmations, of observations which 'verified' the theories in question; and this point was constantly emphasized by their adherents. A Marxist could not open a newspaper without finding on every page confirming evidence for his interpretation of history; not only in the news, but also in its presentation—which revealed the class bias of the paper—and especially of course in what the paper did *not* say. The Freudian analysts emphasized that their theories were constantly verified by their 'clinical observations'. As for Adler, I was much impressed by a personal experience. Once, in 1919, I reported to him a case which to me did not seem particularly Adlerian, but which he found no difficulty in analysing in terms of his theory of inferiority feelings, although he had not even seen the child. Slightly shocked, I asked him how he could be so sure. 'Because of my thousandfold experience,' he replied; whereupon I could not help saying: 'And with this new case, I suppose, your experience has become thousand-and-one-fold.'

11   What I had in mind was that his previous observations may not have been much sounder than this new one; that each in its turn had been interpreted in the light of 'previous experience,' and at the same time counted as additional confirmation. What, I asked myself, did it confirm? No more than that a case could be interpreted in the light of the theory. But this meant very little, I reflected, since every conceivable case could be interpreted in the light of Adler's theory, or equally of Freud's. I may illustrate this by two very different examples of human behaviour: that of a man who pushes a child into the water with the intention of drowning it; and that of a man who sacrifices his life in an attempt to save the child.

Each of these two cases can be explained with equal ease in Freudian and in Adlerian terms. According to Freud the first man suffered from repression (say, of some component of his Oedipus complex), while the second man had achieved sublimation. According to Adler the first man suffered from feelings of inferiority (producing perhaps the need to prove to himself that he dared to commit some crime), and so did the second man (whose need was to prove to himself that he dared to rescue the child). I could not think of any human behaviour which could not be interpreted in terms of either theory. It was precisely this fact—that they always fitted, that they were always confirmed—which in the eyes of their admirers constituted the strongest argument in favour of these theories. It began to dawn on me that this apparent strength was in fact their weakness.

With Einstein's theory the situation was strikingly differ- 12 ent. Take one typical instance—Einstein's prediction, just then confirmed by the findings of Eddington's expedition. Einstein's gravitational theory had led to the result that light must be attracted by heavy bodies (such as the sun), precisely as material bodies were attracted. As a consequence it could be calculated that light from a distant fixed star whose apparent position was close to the sun would reach the earth from such a direction that the star would seem to be slightly shifted away from the sun; or, in other words, that stars close to the sun would look as if they had moved a little away from the sun, and from one another. This is a thing which cannot normally be observed since such stars are rendered invisible in daytime by the sun's overwhelming brightness; but during an eclipse it is possible to take photographs of them. If the same constellation is photographed at night one can measure the distances on the two photographs, and check the predicted effect.

Now the impressive thing about this case is the *risk* involved 13 in a prediction of this kind. If observation shows that the predicted effect is definitely absent, then the theory is simply refuted. The theory is *incompatible with certain possible results of observation*—in fact with results which everybody before Einstein would have expected.[1] This is quite different from the situation I have previously described, when it turned out that the theories in question were compatible with the most divergent human behaviour, so that it was practically impossible to describe any human behaviour that might not be claimed to be a verification of these theories.

These considerations led me in the winter of 1919–20 to con- 14 clusions which I may now reformulate as follows.

(1) It is easy to obtain confirmations, or verifications, for nearly every theory—if we look for confirmations.

(2) Confirmations should count only if they are the result of *risky predictions;* that is to say, if, unenlightened by the theory in question, we should have expected an event which was incompatible with the theory—an event which would have refuted the theory.

(3) Every 'good' scientific theory is a prohibition: it forbids certain things to happen. The more a theory forbids, the better it is.

(4) A theory which is not refutable by any conceivable event is nonscientific. Irrefutability is not a virtue of a theory (as people often think) but a vice.

(5) Every genuine *test* of a theory is an attempt to falsify it, or to refute it. Testability is falsifiability; but there are degrees of testability: some theories are more testable, more exposed to refutation, than others; they take, as it were, greater risks.

(6) Confirming evidence should not count *except when it is the result of a genuine test of the theory;* and this means that it can be presented as a serious but unsuccessful attempt to falsify the theory. (I now speak in such cases of 'corroborating evidence'.)

(7) Some genuinely testable theories, when found to be false, are still upheld by their admirers—for example by introducing *ad hoc* some auxiliary assumption, or by re-interpreting the theory *ad hoc* in such a way that it escapes refutation. Such a procedure is always possible, but it rescues the theory from refutation only at the price of destroying, or at least lowering, its scientific status. (I later described such a rescuing operation as a *'conventionalist twist'* or a *'conventionalist stratagem'*.)

15   One can sum up all this by saying that *the criterion of the scientific status of a theory is its falsifiability, or refutability, or testability.*

II

16   I may perhaps exemplify this with the help of the various theories so far mentioned. Einstein's theory of gravitation clearly satisfied the criterion of falsifiability. Even if our measuring instruments at the time did not allow us to pronounce on the results of the tests with complete assurance, there was clearly a possibility of refuting the theory.

17   Astrology did not pass the test. Astrologers were greatly impressed, and misled, by what they believed to be confirming

evidence—so much so that they were quite unimpressed by any unfavourable evidence. Moreover, by making their interpretations and prophecies sufficiently vague they were able to explain away anything that might have been a refutation of the theory had the theory and the prophecies been more precise. In order to escape falsification they destroyed the testability of their theory. It is a typical soothsayer's trick to predict things so vaguely that the predictions can hardly fail—that they become irrefutable.

The Marxist theory of history, in spite of the serious efforts 18 of some of its founders and followers, ultimately adopted this soothsaying practice. In some of its earlier formulations (for example, in Marx's analysis of the character of the 'coming social revolution'), their predictions were testable, and in fact falsified.[2] Yet instead of accepting the refutations the followers of Marx re-interpreted both the theory and the evidence in order to make them agree. In this way they rescued the theory from refutation; but they did so at the price of adopting a device which made it irrefutable. They thus gave a 'conventionalist twist' to the theory; and by this stratagem they destroyed its much advertised claim to scientific status.

The two psycho-analytic theories were in a different class. 19 They were simply non-testable, irrefutable. There was no conceivable human behaviour which could contradict them. This does not mean that Freud and Adler were not seeing certain things correctly: I personally do not doubt that much of what they say is of considerable importance, and may well play its part one day in a psychological science which is testable. But it does mean that those 'clinical observations' which analysts naively believe confirm their theory cannot do this any more than the daily confirmations which astrologers find in their practice.[3] And as for Freud's epic of the Ego, the Super-ego, and the Id, no substantially stronger claim to scientific status can be made for it than for Homer's collected stories from Olympus. These theories describe some facts, but in the manner of myths. They contain most interesting psychological suggestions, but not in a testable form.

At the same time I realized that such myths may be de- 20 veloped, and become testable; that historically speaking all— or very nearly all—scientific theories originate from myths, and that a myth may contain important anticipations of scientific theories. Examples are Empedocles' theory of evolution by trial and error, or Parmenides' myth of the unchanging block universe in which nothing ever happens and which, if we add another dimension, becomes Einstein's block universe (in which, too, nothing ever happens, since everything is, four-dimensionally speaking, determined and laid down from the beginning). I thus felt that if a theory is found to be non-scientific, or 'metaphysical' (as we might say), it is not thereby found to be unimportant, or insignificant, or 'meaningless,' or 'nonsensical.'[4] But it cannot claim to be backed by empirical evidence in the scientific sense—although it may easily be, in some genetic sense, the 'result of observation'.

21   (There were a great many other theories of this pre-scientific or pseudo-scientific character, some of them, unfortunately, as influential as the Marxist interpretation of history; for example, the racialist interpretation of history—another of those impressive and all-explanatory theories which act upon weak minds like revelations.)

22   Thus the problem which I tried to solve by proposing the criterion of falsifiability was neither a problem of meaningfulness or significance, nor a problem of truth or acceptability. It was the problem of drawing a line (as well as this can be done) between the statements, or systems of statements, of the empirical sciences, and all other statements—whether they are of a religious or of a metaphysical character, or simply pseudo-scientific. Years later—it must have been in 1928 or 1929—I called this first problem of mine the *'problem of demarcation'*. The criterion of falsifiability is a solution to this problem of demarcation, for it says that statements or systems of statements, in order to be ranked as scientific, must be capable of conflicting with possible, or conceivable, observations.

III

23   Today I know, of course, that this *criterion of demarcation*— the criterion of testability, or falsifiability, or refutability—is far from obvious; for even now its significance is seldom realized. At that time, in 1920, it seemed to me almost trivial, although it solved for me an intellectual problem which had worried me deeply, and one which also had obvious practical consequences (for example, political ones). But I did not yet realize its full implications, or its philosophical significance. When I explained it to a fellow student of the Mathematics Department (now a distinguished mathematician in Great Britain), he suggested that I should publish it. At the time I thought this absurd; for I was convinced that my problem, since it was so important for me, must have agitated many scientists and philosophers who would surely have reached

my rather obvious solution. That this was not the case I learnt from Wittgenstein's work, and from its reception, and so I published my results thirteen years later in the form of a criticism of Wittgenstein's *criterion of meaningfulness.*

Wittgenstein, as you all know, tried to show in the *Tracta-* 24 *tus* (see for example his propositions 6.53; 6.54; and 5) that all so-called philosophical or metaphysical propositions were actually non-propositions or pseudo-propositions: that they were senseless or meaningless. All genuine (or meaningful) propositions were truth functions of the elementary or atomic propositions which described 'atomic facts', i.e.—facts which can in principle be ascertained by observation. In other words, meaningful propositions were fully reducible to elementary or atomic propositions which were simple statements describing possible states of affairs, and which could in principle be established or rejected by observations. If we call a statement an 'observation statement' not only if it states an actual observation but also if it states anything that *may* be observed, we shall have to say (according to the *Tractatus,* 5 and 4.52) that every genuine proposition must be a truth-function of, and therefore deducible from, observation statements. All other apparent propositions will be meaningless pseudo-propositions; in fact they will be nothing but nonsensical gibberish.

This idea was used by Wittgenstein for a characterization of 25 science, as opposed to philosophy. We read (for example in 4.11, where natural science is taken to stand in opposition to philosophy): 'The totality of true propositions is the total natural science (or the totality of the natural sciences).' This means that the propositions which belong to science are those deducible from *true* observation statements; they are those propositions which can be *verified* by true observation statements. Could we know all true observation statements, we should also know all that may be asserted by natural science.

This amounts to a crude verifiability criterion of demarca- 26 tion. To make it slightly less crude, it could be amended thus: 'The statements which may possibly fall within the province of science are those which may possibly be verified by observation statements; and these statements, again, coincide with the class of *all* genuine or meaningful statements.' For this approach, then, *verifiability, meaningfulness, and scientific character all coincide.*

I personally was never interested in the so-called problem of 27 meaning; on the contrary, it appeared to me a verbal problem, a typical pseudo-problem. I was interested only in the problem of demarcation, i.e. in finding a criterion of the scientific character of theories. It was just this interest which made me see at once that Wittgenstein's verifiability criterion of meaning was intended to play the part of a criterion of demarcation as well; and which made me see that, as such, it was totally inadequate, even if all misgivings about the dubious concept of meaning were set aside. For Wittgenstein's criterion of demarcation— to use my own terminology in this context—is verifiability, or deducibility from observation statements. But this criterion is too narrow (*and* too wide): it excludes from science practically everything that is, in fact, characteristic of it (while failing in effect to exclude astrology). No scientific theory can ever be deduced from observation statements, or be described as a truth-function of observation statements.

28   All this I pointed out on various occasions to Wittgensteinians and members of the Vienna Circle. In 1931–2 I summarized my ideas in a largish book (read by several members of the Circle but never published; although part of it was incorporated in my *Logic of Scientific Discovery*); and in 1933 I published a letter to the Editor of *Erkenntnis* in which I tried to compress into two pages my ideas on the problems of demarcation and induction.[5] In this letter and elsewhere I described the problem of meaning as a pseudo-problem, in contrast to the problem of demarcation. But my contribution was classified by members of the Circle as a proposal to replace the verifiability criterion of *meaning* by a falsifiability criterion of *meaning*—which effectively made nonsense of my views.[6] My protests that I was trying to solve, not their pseudo-problem of meaning, but the problem of demarcation, were of no avail.

29   My attacks upon verification had some effect, however. They soon led to complete confusion in the camp of the verificationist philosophers of sense and nonsense. The original proposal of verifiability as the criterion of meaning was at least clear, simple, and forceful. The modifications and shifts which were now introduced were the very opposite.[7] This, I should say, is now seen even by the participants. But since I am usually quoted as one of them I wish to repeat that although I created this confusion I never participated in it. Neither falsifiability nor testability were proposed by me as criteria of meaning; and although I may plead guilty to having introduced both terms into the discussion, it was not I who introduced them into the theory of meaning.

30   Criticism of my alleged views was widespread and highly successful. I have yet to meet a criticism of my views.[8] Meanwhile, testability is being widely accepted as a criterion of demarcation.

IV

I have discussed the problem of demarcation in some detail 31 because I believe that its solution is the key to most of the fundamental problems of the philosophy of science. I am going to give you later a list of some of these other problems, but only one of them—the *problem of induction*—can be discussed here at any length.

I had become interested in the problem of induction in 1923. 32 Although this problem is very closely connected with the problem of demarcation, I did not fully appreciate the connection for about five years.

I approached the problem of induction through Hume. 33 Hume, I felt, was perfectly right in pointing out that induction cannot be logically justified. He held that there can be no valid logical[9] arguments allowing us to establish *'that those instances, of which we have had no experience, resemble those, of which we have had experience'*. Consequently *'even after the observation of the frequent or constant conjunction of objects, we have no reason to draw any inference concerning any object beyond those of which we have had experience'*. For 'shou'd it be said that we have experience'[10]—experience teaching us that objects constantly conjoined with certain other objects continue to be so conjoined—then, Hume says, 'I wou'd renew my question, *why from this experience we form any conclusion beyond those past instances, of which we have had experience'*. In other words, an attempt to justify the practice of induction by an appeal to experience must lead to an *infinite regress*. As a result we can say that theories can never be inferred from observation statements, or rationally justified by them.

I found Hume's refutation of inductive inference clear and 34 conclusive. But I felt completely dissatisfied with his psychological explanation of induction in terms of custom or habit.

It has often been noticed that this explanation of Hume's is 35 philosophically not very satisfactory. It is, however, without doubt intended as a *psychological* rather than a philosophical theory; for it tries to give a causal explanation of a psychological fact—*the fact that we believe in laws,* in statements asserting regularities or constantly conjoined kinds of events—by asserting that this fact is due to (i.e. constantly conjoined with) custom or habit. But even this reformulation of Hume's theory is still unsatisfactory; for what I have just called a 'psychological fact' may itself be described as a custom or habit—the custom or habit of believing in laws or regularities; and it is neither very surprising nor very enlightening to hear that such a custom or habit must be explained as due to, or conjoined with, a custom or habit (even though a different one). Only when we remember that the words 'custom' and 'habit' are used by Hume, as they are in ordinary language, not merely to *describe* regular behaviour, but rather to *theorize about its origin* (ascribed to frequent repetition), can we reformulate his psychological theory in a more satisfactory way. We can then say that, like other habits, *our habit of believing in laws is the product of frequent repetition*—of the repeated observation that things of a certain kind are constantly conjoined with things of another kind.

36   This genetico-psychological theory is, as indicated, incorporated in ordinary language, and it is therefore hardly as revolutionary as Hume thought. It is no doubt an extremely popular psychological theory—part of 'common sense', one might say. But in spite of my love of both common sense and Hume, I felt convinced that this psychological theory was mistaken; and that it was in fact refutable on purely logical grounds.

37   Hume's psychology, which is the popular psychology, was mistaken, I felt, about at least three different things: (a) the typical result of repetition; (b) the genesis of habits; and especially (c) the character of those experiences or modes of behaviour which may be described as 'believing in a law' or 'expecting a law-like succession of events.'

38   (*a*) The typical result of repetition—say, of repeating a difficult passage on the piano—is that movements which at first needed attention are in the end executed without attention. We might say that the process becomes radically abbreviated, and ceases to be conscious: it becomes 'physiological.' Such a process, far from creating a conscious expectation of law-like succession, or a belief in a law, may on the contrary begin with a conscious belief and destroy it by making it superfluous. In learning to ride a bicycle we may start with the belief that we can avoid falling if we steer in the direction in which we threaten to fall, and this belief may be useful for guiding our movements. After sufficient practice we may forget the rule; in any case, we do not need it any longer. On the other hand, even if it is true that repetition may create unconscious expectations, these become conscious only if something goes wrong (we may not have heard the clock tick, but we may hear that it has stopped).

39   (*b*) Habits or customs do not, as a rule, *originate* in repetition. Even the habit of walking, or of speaking, or of feeding at certain hours, *begins* before repetition can play any part whatever. We may say, if we like, that they deserve to be called 'habits' or 'customs' only after repetition has played its typical part;

but we must not say that the practices in question originated as the result of many repetitions.

(c) Belief in a law is not quite the same thing as behaviour 40 which betrays an expectation of a law-like succession of events; but these two are sufficiently closely connected to be treated together. They may, perhaps, in exceptional cases, result from a mere repetition of sense impressions (as in the case of the stopping clock). I was prepared to concede this, but I contended that normally, and in most cases of any interest, they cannot be so explained. As Hume admits, even a single striking observation may be sufficient to create a belief or an expectation—a fact which he tries to explain as due to an inductive habit, formed as the result of a vast number of long repetitive sequences which had been experienced at an earlier period of life.[11] But this, I contended, was merely his attempt to explain away unfavourable facts which threatened his theory; an unsuccessful attempt, since these unfavourable facts could be observed in very young animals and babies—as early, indeed, as we like. 'A lighted cigarette was held near the noses of the young puppies,' reports F. Bäge. 'They sniffed at it once, turned tail, and nothing would induce them to come back to the source of the smell and to sniff again. A few days later, they reacted to the mere sight of a cigarette or even of a rolled piece of white paper, by bounding away, and sneezing.'[12] If we try to explain cases like this by postulating a vast number of long repetitive sequences at a still earlier age we are not only romancing, but forgetting that in the clever puppies' short lives there must be room not only for repetition but also for a great deal of novelty, and consequently of non-repetition.

But it is not only that certain empirical facts do not support 41 Hume; there are decisive arguments of a *purely logical* nature against his psychological theory.

The central idea of Hume's theory is that of *repetition, based* 42 *upon similarity* (or 'resemblance'). This idea is used in a very uncritical way. We are led to think of the water-drop that hollows the stone: of sequences of unquestionably like events slowly forcing themselves upon us, as does the tick of the clock. But we ought to realize that in a psychological theory such as Hume's, only repetition-for-us, based upon similarity-for-us, can be allowed to have any effect upon us. We must respond to situations as if they were equivalent; *take* them as similar; *interpret* them as repetitions. The clever puppies, we may assume, showed by their response, their way of acting or of reacting, that they recognized or interpreted the second situation as a repetition of the first: that they expected its main element, the objectionable smell, to be present. The situation was a repetition-for-them because they responded to it by *anticipating* its similarity to the previous one.

43   This apparently psychological criticism has a purely logical basis which may be summed up in the following simple argument. (It happens to be the one from which I originally started my criticism.) The kind of repetition envisaged by Hume can never be perfect; the cases he has in mind cannot be cases of perfect sameness; they can only be cases of similarity. Thus *they are repetitions only from a certain point of view*. (What has the effect upon me of a repetition may not have this effect upon a spider.) But this means that, for logical reasons, there must always be a point of view—such as a system of expectations, anticipations, assumptions, or interests—*before* there can be any repetition; which point of view, consequently, cannot be merely the result of repetition. (See now also appendix *X, (1), to my *L.Sc.D.*)

44   We must thus replace, for the purposes of a psychological theory of the origin of our beliefs, the naive idea of events which *are* similar by the idea of events to which we react by *interpreting* them as being similar. But if this is so (and I can see no escape from it), then Hume's psychological theory of induction leads to an infinite regress, precisely analogous to that other infinite regress which was discovered by Hume himself, and used by him to explode the logical theory of induction. For what do we wish to explain? In the example of the puppies we wish to explain behaviour which may be described as *recognizing or interpreting* a situation as a repetition of another. Clearly, we cannot hope to explain this by an appeal to earlier repetitions, once we realize that the earlier repetitions must also have been repetitions-for-them, so that precisely the same problem arises again: that of *recognizing or interpreting* a situation as a repetition of another.

45   To put it more concisely, similarity-for-us is the product of a response involving interpretations (which may be inadequate) and anticipations or expectations (which may never be fulfilled). It is therefore impossible to explain anticipations, or expectations, as resulting from many repetitions, as suggested by Hume. For even the first repetition-for-us must be based upon similarity-for-us, and therefore upon expectations—precisely the kind of thing we wished to explain.

46   This shows that there is an infinite regress involved in Hume's psychological theory.

47   Hume, I felt, had never accepted the full force of his own logical analysis. Having refuted the logical idea of induction he was faced with the following problem: how do we actually obtain our knowledge, as a matter of psychological fact,

if induction is a procedure which is logically invalid and rationally unjustifiable? There are two possible answers: (1) We obtain our knowledge by a noninductive procedure. This answer would have allowed Hume to retain a form of rationalism. (2) We obtain our knowledge by repetition and induction, and therefore by a logically invalid and rationally unjustifiable procedure, so that all apparent knowledge is merely a kind of belief—belief based on habit. This answer would imply that even scientific knowledge is irrational, so that rationalism is absurd, and must be given up. (I shall not discuss here the age-old attempts, now again fashionable, to get out of the difficulty by asserting that though induction is of course logically invalid if we mean by 'logic' the same as 'deductive logic', it is not irrational by its own standards, as may be seen from the fact that every reasonable man applies it *as a matter of fact:* it was Hume's great achievement to break this uncritical identification of the question of fact—*quid facti?*—and the question of justification or validity—*quid juris?*

It seems that Hume never seriously considered the first alternative. Having cast out the logical theory of induction by repetition he struck a bargain with common sense, meekly allowing the re-entry of induction by repetition, in the guise of a psychological theory. I proposed to turn the tables upon this theory of Hume's. Instead of explaining our propensity to expect regularities as the result of repetition, I proposed to explain repetition-for-us as the result of our propensity to expect regularities and to search for them.

Thus I was led by purely logical considerations to replace the psychological theory of induction by the following view. Without waiting, passively, for repetitions to impress or impose regularities upon us, we actively try to impose regularities upon the world. We try to discover similarities in it, and to interpret it in terms of laws invented by us. Without waiting for premises we jump to conclusions. These may have to be discarded later, should observation show that they are wrong.

This was a theory of trial and error—of *conjectures and refutations*. It made it possible to understand why our attempts to force interpretations upon the world were logically prior to the observation of similarities. Since there were logical reasons behind this procedure, I thought that it would apply in the field of science also; that scientific theories were not the digest of observations, but that they were inventions—conjectures boldly put forward for trial, to be eliminated if they clashed with observations; with observations which were rarely accidental but as a rule undertaken with the definite intention of testing a theory by obtaining, if possible, a decisive refutation.

V

51   The belief that science proceeds from observation to theory is still so widely and so firmly held that my denial of it is often met with incredulity. I have even been suspected of being insincere—of denying what nobody in his senses can doubt.

52   But in fact the belief that we can start with pure observations alone, without anything in the nature of a theory, is absurd; as may be illustrated by the story of the man who dedicated his life to natural science, wrote down everything he could observe, and bequeathed his priceless collection of observations to the Royal Society to be used as inductive evidence. This story should show us that though beetles may profitably be collected, observations may not.

53   Twenty-five years ago I tried to bring home the same point to a group of physics students in Vienna by beginning a lecture with the following instructions: 'Take pencil and paper; carefully observe, and write down what you have observed!' They asked, of course, *what* I wanted them to observe. Clearly the instruction, 'Observe!' is absurd.[13] (It is not even idiomatic, unless the object of the transitive verb can be taken as understood.) Observation is always selective. It needs a chosen object, a definite task, an interest, a point of view, a problem. And its description presupposes a descriptive language, with property words; it presupposes similarity and classification, which in its turn presupposes interests, points of view, and problems. 'A hungry animal', writes Katz,[14] 'divides the environment into edible and inedible things. An animal in flight sees roads to escape and hiding places.... Generally speaking, objects change ... according to the needs of the animal.' We may add that objects can be classified, and can become similar or dissimilar, *only* in this way—by being related to needs and interests. This rule applies not only to animals but also to scientists. For the animal a point of view is provided by its needs, the task of the moment, and its expectations; for the scientist by his theoretical interests, the special problem under investigation, his conjectures and anticipations, and the theories which he accepts as a kind of background: his frame of reference, his 'horizon of expectations'.

54   The problem 'Which comes first, the hypothesis (H) or the observation (O),' is soluble; as is the problem, 'Which comes first, the hen (H) or the egg (O)'. The reply to the latter is, 'An earlier kind of egg'; to the former, 'An earlier kind of hypothesis'. It is quite true that any particular hypothesis we choose will have been preceded by observations—the observations, for

example, which it is designed to explain. But these observations, in their turn, presupposed the adoption of a frame of reference: a frame of expectations: a frame of theories. If they were significant, if they created a need for explanation and thus gave rise to the invention of a hypothesis, it was because they could not be explained within the old theoretical framework, the old horizon of expectations. There is no danger here of an infinite regress. Going back to more and more primitive theories and myths we shall in the end find unconscious, *inborn* expectations.

The theory of inborn *ideas* is absurd, I think; but every organism has inborn *reactions* or *responses;* and among them, responses adapted to impending events. These responses we may describe as 'expectations' without implying that these 'expectations' are conscious. The new-born baby 'expects', in this sense, to be fed (and, one could even argue, to be protected and loved). In view of the close relation between expectation and knowledge we may even speak in quite a reasonable sense of 'inborn knowledge'. This 'knowledge' is not, however, *valid a priori;* an inborn expectation, no matter how strong and specific, may be mistaken. (The newborn child may be abandoned, and starve.)   55

Thus we are born with expectations; with 'knowledge' which, although not *valid a priori,* is *psychologically or genetically a priori,* i.e. prior to all observational experience. One of the most important of these expectations is the expectation of finding a regularity. It is connected with an inborn propensity to look out for regularities, or with a *need* to *find* regularities, as we may see from the pleasure of the child who satisfies this need.   56

This 'instinctive' expectation of finding regularities, which is psychologically *a priori,* corresponds very closely to the 'law of causality' which Kant believed to be part of our mental outfit and to be *a priori* valid. One might thus be inclined to say that Kant failed to distinguish between psychologically *a priori* ways of thinking or responding and *a priori* valid beliefs. But I do not think that his mistake was quite as crude as that. For the expectation of finding regularities is not only psychologically *a priori,* but also logically *a priori:* it is logically prior to all observational experience, for it is prior to any recognition of similarities, as we have seen; and all observation involves the recognition of similarities (or dissimilarities). But in spite of being logically *a priori* in this sense the expectation is not valid *a priori.* For it may fail: we can easily construct an environment (it would be a lethal one) which, compared with our   57

ordinary environment, is so chaotic that we completely fail to
find regularities. (All natural laws could remain valid: environments of this kind have been used in the animal experiments
mentioned in the next section.)

58   Thus Kant's reply to Hume came near to being right; for
the distinction between an *a priori* valid expectation and one
which is both genetically *and* logically prior to observation,
but not *a priori* valid, is really somewhat subtle. But Kant
proved too much. In trying to show how knowledge is possible,
he proposed a theory which had the unavoidable consequence
that our quest for knowledge must necessarily succeed, which
is clearly mistaken. When Kant said, 'Our intellect does not
draw its laws from nature but imposes its laws upon nature',
he was right. But in thinking that these laws are necessarily
true, or that we necessarily succeed in imposing them upon
nature, he was wrong.[15] Nature very often resists quite successfully, forcing us to discard our laws as refuted; but if we
live we may try again.

59   To sum up this logical criticism of Hume's psychology of
induction we may consider the idea of building an induction
machine. Placed in a simplified 'world' (for example, one of
sequences of coloured counters) such a machine may through
repetition 'learn', or even 'formulate', laws of succession which
hold in its 'world'. If such a machine can be constructed (and
I have no doubt that it can) then, it might be argued, my theory must be wrong; for if a machine is capable of performing
inductions on the basis of repetition, there can be no logical
reasons preventing us from doing the same.

60   The argument sounds convincing, but it is mistaken. In constructing an induction machine we, the architects of the machine, must decide *a priori* what constitutes its 'world'; what
things are to be taken as similar or equal; and what *kind*
of 'laws' we wish the machine to be able to 'discover' in its
'world'. In other words we must build into the machine a
framework determining what is relevant or interesting in its
world: the machine will have its 'inborn' selection principles.
The problems of similarity will have been solved for it by its
makers who thus have interpreted the 'world' for the machine.

VI

61   Our propensity to look out for regularities, and to impose
laws upon nature, leads to the psychological phenomenon of
dogmatic thinking or, more generally, dogmatic behaviour: we
expect regularities everywhere and attempt to find them even

where there are none; events which do not yield to these attempts we are inclined to treat as a kind of 'background noise'; and we stick to our expectations even when they are inadequate and we ought to accept defeat. This dogmatism is to some extent necessary. It is demanded by a situation which can only be dealt with by forcing our conjectures upon the world. Moreover, this dogmatism allows us to approach a good theory in stages, by way of approximations: if we accept defeat too easily, we may prevent ourselves from finding that we were very nearly right.

It is clear that this *dogmatic attitude*, which makes us stick 62 to our first impressions, is indicative of a strong belief; while a *critical attitude*, which is ready to modify its tenets, which admits doubt and demands tests, is indicative of a weaker belief. Now according to Hume's theory, and to the popular theory, the strength of a belief should be a product of repetition; thus it should always grow with experience, and always be greater in less primitive persons. But dogmatic thinking, an uncontrolled wish to impose regularities, a manifest pleasure in rites and in repetition as such, are characteristic of primitives and children; and increasing experience and maturity sometimes create an attitude of caution and criticism rather than of dogmatism.

I may perhaps mention here a point of agreement with 63 psycho-analysis. Psycho-analysts assert that neurotics and others interpret the world in accordance with a personal set pattern which is not easily given up, and which can often be traced back to early childhood. A pattern or scheme which was adopted very early in life is maintained throughout, and every new experience is interpreted in terms of it; verifying it, as it were, and contributing to its rigidity. This is a description of what I have called the dogmatic attitude, as distinct from the critical attitude, which shares with the dogmatic attitude the quick adoption of a schema of expectations—a myth, perhaps, or a conjecture or hypothesis—but which is ready to modify it, to correct it, and even to give it up. I am inclined to suggest that most neuroses may be due to a partially arrested development of the critical attitude; to an arrested rather than a natural dogmatism; to resistance to demands for the modification and adjustment of certain schematic interpretations and responses. This resistance in its turn may perhaps be explained, in some cases, as due to an injury or shock, resulting in fear and in an increased need for assurance or certainty, analogous to the way in which an injury to a limb makes us afraid to move it, so that it becomes stiff. (It might even be argued that the case of the limb is not merely analogous to the dogmatic response, but an instance of it.) The explanation of any concrete case will have to take into account the weight of the difficulties involved in making the necessary adjustments—difficulties which may be considerable, especially in a complex and changing world: we know from experiments on animals that varying degrees of neurotic behaviour may be produced at will by correspondingly varying difficulties.

64   I found many other links between the psychology of knowledge and psychological fields which are often considered remote from it—for example the psychology of art and music; in fact, my ideas about induction originated in a conjecture about the evolution of Western polyphony. But you will be spared this story.

VII

65   My logical criticism of Hume's psychological theory, and the considerations connected with it (most of which I elaborated in 1926-7, in a thesis entitled 'On Habit and Belief in Laws'[16]) may seem a little removed from the field of the philosophy of science. But the distinction between dogmatic and critical thinking, or the dogmatic and the critical attitude, brings us right back to our central problem. For the dogmatic attitude is clearly related to the tendency to *verify* our laws and schemata by seeking to apply them and to confirm them, even to the point of neglecting refutations, whereas the critical attitude is one of readiness to change them—to test them; to refute them; to *falsify* them, if possible. This suggests that we may identify the critical attitude with the scientific attitude, and the dogmatic attitude with the one which we have described as pseudo-scientific.

66   It further suggests that genetically speaking the pseudo-scientific attitude is more primitive than, and prior to, the scientific attitude: that it is a pre-scientific attitude. And this primitivity or priority also has its logical aspect. For the critical attitude is not so much opposed to the dogmatic attitude as super-imposed upon it: criticism must be directed against existing and influential beliefs in need of critical revision—in other words, dogmatic beliefs. A critical attitude needs for its raw material, as it were, theories or beliefs which are held more or less dogmatically.

67   Thus science must begin with myths, and with the criticism of myths; neither with the collection of observations, nor with the invention of experiments, but with the critical discussion of myths, and of magical techniques and practices. The scientific

tradition is distinguished from the pre-scientific tradition in having two layers. Like the latter, it passes on its theories; but it also passes on a critical attitude towards them. The theories are passed on, not as dogmas, but rather with the challenge to discuss them and improve upon them. This tradition is Hellenic: it may be traced back to Thales, founder of the first *school* (I do not mean 'of the first *philosophical* school', but simply 'of the first school') which was not mainly concerned with the preservation of a dogma.

The critical attitude, the tradition of free discussion of theo- 68 ries with the aim of discovering their weak spots so that they may be improved upon, is the attitude of reasonableness, of rationality. It makes far-reaching use of both verbal argument and observation—of observation in the interest of argument, however. The Greeks' discovery of the critical method gave rise at first to the mistaken hope that it would lead to the solution of all the great old problems; that it would establish certainty; that it would help to *prove* our theories, to *justify* them. But this hope was a residue of the dogmatic way of thinking; in fact nothing can be justified or proved (outside of mathematics and logic). The demand for rational proofs in science indicates a failure to keep distinct the broad realm of rationality and the narrow realm of rational certainty: it is an untenable, an unreasonable demand.

Nevertheless, the role of logical argument, of deductive logi- 69 cal reasoning, remains all-important for the critical approach; not because it allows us to prove our theories, or to infer them from observation statements, but because only by purely deductive reasoning is it possible for us to discover what our theories imply, and thus to criticize them effectively. Criticism, I said, is an attempt to find the weak spots in a theory, and these, as a rule, can be found only in the more remote logical consequences which can be derived from it. It is here that purely logical reasoning plays an important part in science.

Hume was right in stressing that our theories cannot be 70 validly inferred from what we can know to be true—neither from observations nor from anything else. He concluded from this that our belief in them was irrational. If 'belief' means here our inability to doubt our natural laws, and the constancy of natural regularities, then Hume is again right: this kind of dogmatic belief has, one might say, a physiological rather than a rational basis. If, however, the term 'belief' is taken to cover our critical acceptance of scientific theories—a *tentative* acceptance combined with an eagerness to revise the theory if we succeed in designing a test which it cannot pass—then Hume was wrong. In such an acceptance of theories there is nothing irrational. There is not even anything irrational in relying for practical purposes upon well-tested theories, for no more rational course of action is open to us.

71   Assume that we have deliberately made it our task to live in this unknown world of ours; to adjust ourselves to it as well as we can; to take advantage of the opportunities we can find in it; and to explain it, *if* possible (we need not assume that it is), and as far as possible, with the help of laws and explanatory theories. *If we have made this our task, then there is no more rational procedure than the method of trial and error—of conjecture and refutation:* of boldly proposing theories; of trying our best to show that these are erroneous; and of accepting them tentatively if our critical efforts are unsuccessful.

72   From the point of view here developed all laws, all theories, remain essentially tentative, or conjectural, or hypothetical, even when we feel unable to doubt them any longer. Before a theory has been refuted we can never know in what way it may have to be modified. That the sun will always rise and set within twenty-four hours is still proverbial as a law 'established by induction beyond reasonable doubt'. It is odd that this example is still in use, though it may have served well enough in the days of Aristotle and Pytheas of Massalia—the great traveller who for centuries was called a liar because of his tales of Thule, the land of the frozen sea and the *midnight sun.*

73   The method of trial and error is not, of course, simply identical with the scientific or critical approach—with the method of conjecture and refutation. The method of trial and error is applied not only by Einstein but, in a more dogmatic fashion, by the amoeba also. The difference lies not so much in the trials as in a critical and constructive attitude towards errors; errors which the scientist consciously and cautiously tries to uncover in order to refute his theories with searching arguments, including appeals to the most severe experimental tests which his theories and his ingenuity permit him to design.

74   The critical attitude may be described as the conscious attempt to make our theories, our conjectures, suffer in our stead in the struggle for the survival of the fittest. It gives us a chance to survive the elimination of an inadequate hypothesis—when a more dogmatic attitude would eliminate it by eliminating us. (There is a touching story of an Indian community which disappeared because of its belief in the holiness of life, including that of tigers.) We thus obtain the fittest theory within our reach by the elimination of those which are less fit. (By 'fitness' I do not mean merely 'usefulness' but truth.) I do not think that this procedure is irrational or in need of any further rational justification.

VIII

Let us now turn from our logical criticism of the *psychology* 75 *of experience* to our real problem—the problem of *the logic of science.* Although some of the things I have said may help us here, in so far as they may have eliminated certain psychological prejudices in favour of induction, my treatment of the *logical problem of induction* is completely independent of this criticism, and of all psychological considerations. Provided you do not dogmatically believe in the alleged psychological fact that we make inductions, you may now forget my whole story with the exception of two logical points: my logical remarks on testability or falsifiability as the criterion of demarcation; and Hume's logical criticism of induction.

From what I have said it is obvious that there was a close link 76 between the two problems which interested me at that time: demarcation, and induction or scientific method. It was easy to see that the method of science is criticism, i.e. attempted falsifications. Yet it took me a few years to notice that the two problems—of demarcation and of induction—were in a sense one.

Why, I asked, do so many scientists believe in induction? I 77 found they did so because they believed natural science to be characterized by the inductive method—by a method starting from, and relying upon, long sequences of observations and experiments. They believed that the difference between genuine science and metaphysical or pseudo-scientific speculation depended solely upon whether or not the inductive method was employed. They believed (to put it in my own terminology) that only the inductive method could provide a satisfactory *criterion of demarcation.*

I recently came across an interesting formulation of this be- 78 lief in a remarkable philosophical book by a great physicist— Max Born's *Natural Philosophy of Cause and Chance.*[17] He writes: 'Induction allows us to generalize a number of observations into a general rule: that night follows day and day follows night....But while everyday life has no definite criterion for the validity of an induction,...science has worked out a code, or rule of craft, for its application.' Born nowhere reveals the contents of this inductive code (which, as his wording shows, contains a 'definite criterion for the validity of an induction'); but he stresses that 'there is no logical argument' for its acceptance: 'it is a question of faith'; and he is therefore 'willing to call induction a metaphysical principle'. But why does he believe that such a code of valid inductive rules must exist?

This becomes clear when he speaks of the 'vast communities of people ignorant of, or rejecting, the rule of science, among them the members of anti-vaccination societies and believers in astrology. It is useless to argue with them; I cannot compel them to accept the same criteria of valid induction in which I believe: the code of scientific rules.' This makes it quite clear that *'valid induction' was here meant to serve as a criterion of demarcation between science and pseudo-science.*

79   But it is obvious that this rule or craft of 'valid induction' is not even metaphysical: it simply does not exist. No rule can ever guarantee that a generalization inferred from true observations, however often repeated, is true. (Born himself does not believe in the truth of Newtonian physics, in spite of its success, although he believes that it is based on induction.) And the success of science is not based upon rules of induction, but depends upon luck, ingenuity, and the purely deductive rules of critical argument.

80   I may summarize some of my conclusions as follows:

(1) Induction, i.e. inference based on many observations, is a myth. It is neither a psychological fact, nor a fact of ordinary life, nor one of scientific procedure.

(2) The actual procedure of science is to operate with conjectures: to jump to conclusions—often after one single observation (as noticed for example by Hume and Born).

(3) Repeated observations and experiments function in science as *tests* of our conjectures or hypotheses, i.e. as attempted refutations.

(4) The mistaken belief in induction is fortified by the need for a criterion of demarcation which, it is traditionally but wrongly believed, only the inductive method can provide.

(5) The conception of such an inductive method, like the criterion of verifiability, implies a faulty demarcation.

(6) None of this is altered in the least if we say that induction makes theories only probable rather than certain.

IX

81   If, as I have suggested, the problem of induction is only an instance or facet of the problem of demarcation, then the solution to the problem of demarcation must provide us with a solution to the problem of induction. This is indeed the case, I believe, although it is perhaps not immediately obvious.

82   For a brief formulation of the problem of induction we can turn again to Born, who writes: '...no observation or experiment, however extended, can give more than a finite number of

repetitions'; therefore, 'the statement of a law—B depends on A—always transcends experience. Yet this kind of statement is made everywhere and all the time, and sometimes from scanty material.'[18]

In other words, the logical problem of induction arises from (*a*) Hume's discovery (so well expressed by Born) that it is impossible to justify a law by observation or experiment, since it 'transcends experience'; (*b*) the fact that science proposes and uses laws 'everywhere and all the time'. (Like Hume, Born is struck by the 'scanty material', i.e. the few observed instances upon which the law may be based.) To this we have to add (*c*) *the principal of empiricism* which asserts that in science, only observation and experiment may decide upon the *acceptance or rejection* of scientific statements, including laws and theories. 83

These three principles, (*a*), (*b*), and (*c*), appear at first sight to clash; and this apparent clash constitutes the *logical problem of induction*. 84

Faced with this clash, Born gives up (*c*), the principle of empiricism (as Kant and many others, including Bertrand Russell, have done before him), in favour of what he calls a 'metaphysical principle'; a metaphysical principle which he does not even attempt to formulate; which he vaguely describes as a 'code or rule of craft'; and of which I have never seen any formulation which even looked promising and was not clearly untenable. 85

But in fact the principles (*a*) to (*c*) do not clash. We can see this the moment we realize that the acceptance by science of a law or of a theory is *tentative only;* which is to say that all laws and theories are conjectures, or tentative *hypotheses* (a position which I have sometimes called 'hypotheticism'); and that we may reject a law or theory on the basis of new evidence, without necessarily discarding the old evidence which originally led us to accept it.[19] 86

The principle of empiricism (*c*) can be fully preserved, since the fate of a theory, its acceptance or rejection, is decided by observation and experiment—by the result of tests. So long as a theory stands up to the severest tests we can design, it is accepted; if it does not, it is rejected. But it is never inferred, in any sense, from the empirical evidence. There is neither a psychological nor a logical induction. *Only the falsity of the theory can be inferred from empirical evidence, and this inference is a purely deductive one.* 87

Hume showed that it is not possible to infer a theory from observation statements; but this does not affect the possibility of refuting a theory by observation statements. The full appre- 88

ciation of this possibility makes the relation between theories
and observations perfectly clear.

89   This solves the problem of the alleged clash between the
principles (*a*), (*b*), and (*c*), and with it Hume's problem of induction.

X

90   Thus the problem of induction is solved. But nothing seems
less wanted than a simple solution to an age-old philosophical problem. Wittgenstein and his school hold that genuine
philosophical problems do not exist;[20] from which it clearly
follows that they cannot be solved. Others among my contemporaries do believe that there are philosophical problems, and
respect them; but they seem to respect them too much; they
seem to believe that they are insoluble, if not taboo; and they
are shocked and horrified by the claim that there is a simple,
neat, and lucid, solution to any of them. If there is a solution,
it must be deep, they feel, or at least complicated.

91   However this may be, I am still waiting for a simple, neat,
and lucid criticism of the solution which I published first in
1933 in my letter to the Editor of *Erkenntnis*,[21] and later in
The Logic of Scientific Discovery.

92   Of course, one can invent new problems of induction, different from the one I have formulated and solved. (Its formulation
was half its solution.) But I have yet to see any reformulation
of the problem whose solution cannot be easily obtained from
my old solution. I am now going to discuss some of these re-
formulations.

93   One question which may be asked is this: how do we really
jump from an observation statement to a theory?

94   Although this question appears to be psychological rather
than philosophical, one can say something positive about it
without invoking psychology. One can say first that the jump
is not from an observation statement, but from a problem-
situation, and that the theory must allow us *to explain* the observations which created the problem (that is, *to deduce* them
from the theory strengthened by other accepted theories and
by other observation statements, the so-called initial conditions). This leaves, of course, an immense number of possible
theories, good and bad; and it thus appears that our question
has not been answered.

95   But this makes it fairly clear that when we asked our question we had more in mind than, 'How do we jump from an ob-

servation statement to a theory?' The question we had in mind was, it now appears, 'How do we jump from an observation statement to a *good* theory?' But to this the answer is: by jump- ing first to *any* theory and then testing it, to find whether it is good or not; i.e. by repeatedly applying the critical method, eliminating many bad theories, and inventing many new ones. Not everybody is able to do this; but there is no other way.

Other questions have sometimes been asked. The original 96 problem of induction, it was said, is the problem of *justifying* induction, i.e. of justifying inductive inference. If you answer this problem by saying that what is called an 'inductive in- ference' is always invalid and therefore clearly not justifiable, the following new problem must arise: how do you justify your method of trial and error? Reply: the method of trial and error is a *method of eliminating false theories* by observation state- ments; and the justification for this is the purely logical rela- tionship of deducibility which allows us to assert the falsity of universal statements if we accept the truth of singular ones.

Another question sometimes asked is this: why is it reason- 97 able to prefer non-falsified statements to falsified ones? To this question some involved answers have been produced, for ex- ample pragmatic answers. But from a pragmatic point of view the question does not arise, since false theories often serve well enough: most formulae used in engineering or navigation are known to be false, although they may be excellent approxima- tions and easy to handle; and they are used with confidence by people who know them to be false.

The only correct answer is the straightforward one: because 98 we search for truth (even though we can never be sure we have found it), and because the falsified theories are known or be- lieved to be false, while the non-falsified theories may still be true. Besides, we do not prefer *every* non-falsified theory—only one which, in the light of criticism, appears to be better than its competitors: which solves our problems, which is well tested, and of which we think, or rather conjecture or hope (consid- ering other provisionally accepted theories), that it will stand up to further tests.

It has also been said that the problem of induction is, 'Why 99 is it *reasonable* to believe that the future will be like the past?', and that a satisfactory answer to this question should make it plain that such a belief is, in fact, reasonable. My reply is that it is reasonable to believe that the future will be very different from the past in many vitally important respects. Admittedly it is perfectly reasonable to *act* on the assumption that it will, in many respects, be like the past, and that well-tested laws will continue to hold (since we can have no better assumption to act upon); but it is also reasonable to believe that such a course of action will lead us at times into severe trouble, since some of the laws upon which we now heavily rely may easily prove unreliable. (Remember the midnight sun!) One might even say that to judge from past experience, and from our general scientific knowledge, the future will *not* be like the past, in perhaps most of the ways which those have in mind who say that it will. Water will sometimes not quench thirst, and air will choke those who breathe it. An apparent way out is to say that the future will be like the past *in the sense that the laws of nature will not change*, but this is begging the question. We speak of a 'law of nature' only if we think that we have before us a regularity which does not change; and if we find that it changes, then we shall not continue to call it a 'law of nature'. Of course our search for natural laws indicates that we hope to find them, and that we believe that there are natural laws; but our belief in any particular natural law cannot have a safer basis than our unsuccessful critical attempts to refute it.

100   I think that those who put the problem of induction in terms of the *reasonableness* of our beliefs are perfectly right if they are dissatisfied with a Humean, or post-Humean, sceptical despair of reason. We must indeed reject the view that a belief in science is as irrational as a belief in primitive magical practices— that both are a matter of accepting a 'total ideology', a convention or a tradition based on faith. But we must be cautious if we formulate our problem, with Hume, as one of the reasonableness of our *beliefs*. We should split this problem into three—our old problem of demarcation, or of how to *distinguish* between science and primitive magic; the problem of the rationality of the scientific or critical *procedure*, and of the role of observation within it; and lastly the problem of the rationality of our *acceptance* of theories for scientific and for practical purposes. To all these three problems solutions have been offered here.

101   One should also be careful not to confuse the problem of the reasonableness of the scientific procedure and the (tentative) acceptance of the results of this procedure—i.e. the scientific theories—with the problem of the rationality or otherwise *of the belief that this procedure will succeed*. In practice, in practical scientific research, this belief is no doubt unavoidable and reasonable, there being no better alternative. But the belief is certainly unjustifiable in a theoretical sense, as I have argued (in section v). Moreover, if we could show, on general logical grounds, that the scientific quest is likely to succeed, one could

not understand why anything like success has been so rare in the long history of human endeavours to know more about our world.

Yet another way of putting the problem of induction is in terms of probability. Let t be the theory and e the evidence: we can ask for $P(t, e)$, that is to say, the probability of t, given e. The problem of induction, it is often believed, can then be put thus: construct a *calculus of probability* which allows us to work out for any theory t what its probability is, relative to any given empirical evidence e; and show that $P(t, e)$ increases with the accumulation of supporting evidence, and reaches high values—at any rate values greater than $\frac{1}{2}$. [102]

In *The Logic of Scientific Discovery* I explained why I think that this approach to the problem is fundamentally mistaken.[22] To make this clear, I introduced there the distinction between *probability* and *degree of corroboration or confirmation*. (The term 'confirmation' has lately been so much used and misused that I have decided to surrender it to the verificationists and to use for my own purposes 'corroboration' only. The term 'probability' is best used in some of the many senses which satisfy the well-known calculus of probability, axiomatized, for example, by Keynes, Jeffreys, and myself; but nothing of course depends on the choice of words, as long as we do not *assume*, uncritically, that degree of corroboration must also be a probability—that is to say, that it must satisfy the calculus of probability.) [103]

I explained in my book why we are interested in theories with a *high degree of corroboration*. And I explained why it is a mistake to conclude from this that we are interested in *highly probable* theories. I pointed out that the probability of a statement (or set of statements) is always the greater the less the statement says: it is inverse to the content or the deductive power of the statement, and thus to its explanatory power. Accordingly every interesting and powerful statement must have a low probability; and *vice versa*: a statement with a high probability will be scientifically uninteresting, because it says little and has no explanatory power. Although we seek theories with a high degree of corroboration, *as scientists we do not seek highly probable theories but explanations; that is to say, powerful and improbable theories.*[23] The opposite view—that science aims at high probability—is a characteristic development of verificationism: if you find that you cannot verify a theory, or make it certain by induction, you may turn to probability as a kind of '*Ersatz*' for certainty, in the hope that induction may yield at least that much. [104]

Notes

1. This is a slight oversimplification, for about half of the Einstein effect may be derived from the classical theory, provided we assume a ballistic theory of light.

2. See, for example, my *Open Society and Its Enemies*, ch. 15, section iii, and notes 13–14.

3. 'Clinical observations', like all other observations, are *interpretations in the light of theories* (see below, sections iv ff.); and for this reason alone they are apt to seem to support those theories in the light of which they were interpreted. But real support can be obtained only from observations undertaken as tests (by 'attempted refutations'); and for this purpose *criteria of refutation* have to be laid down beforehand: it must be agreed which observable situations, if actually observed, mean that the theory is refuted. But what kind of clinical responses would refute to the satisfaction of the analyst not merely a particular analytic diagnosis but psycho-analysis itself? And have such criteria ever been discussed or agreed upon by analysts? Is there not, on the contrary, a whole family of analytic concepts, such as 'ambivalence' (I do not suggest that there is no such thing as ambivalence), which would make it difficult, if not impossible, to agree upon such criteria? Moreover, how much headway has been made in investigating the question of the extent to which the (conscious or unconscious) expectations and theories held by the analyst influence the 'clinical responses' of the patient? (To say nothing about the conscious attempts to influence the patient by proposing interpretations to him, etc.) Years ago I introduced the term *'Oedipus effect'* to describe the influence of a theory or expectation or prediction *upon the event which it predicts* or describes: it will be remembered that the causal chain leading to Oedipus' parricide was started by the oracle's prediction of this event. This is a characteristic and recurrent theme of such myths, but one which seems to have failed to attract the interest of the analysts, perhaps not accidentally. (The problem of confirmatory dreams suggested by the analyst is discussed by Freud, for example in *Gesammelte Schriften*, III, 1925, where he says on p. 314: 'If anybody asserts that most of the dreams which can be utilized in an analysis ... owe their origin to [the analyst's] suggestion, then no objection can be made from the point of view of analytic theory. Yet there is nothing in this fact', he surprisingly adds, 'which would detract from the reliability of our results.')

4. The case of astrology, nowadays a typical pseudo-science, may illustrate this point. It was attacked, by Aristotelians and other rationalists, down to Newton's day, for the wrong reason—for its now accepted assertion that the planets had an 'influence' upon terrestrial ('sublunar') events. In fact Newton's theory of gravity, and especially the lunar theory of the tides, was historically speaking an offspring of astrological lore. Newton, it seems, was most reluctant to adopt a theory which came from the same stable as for example the theory that 'influenza' epidemics are due to

an astral 'influence'. And Galileo, no doubt for the same reason, actually rejected the lunar theory of the tides; and his misgivings about Kepler may easily be explained by his misgivings about astrology.

5. My *Logic of Scientific Discovery* (1959, 1960, 1961), here usually referred to as *L.Sc.D.*, is the translation of *Logik der Forschung* (1934), with a number of additional notes and appendices, including (on pp. 312–14) the letter to the Editor of *Erkenntnis* mentioned here in the text which was first published in *Erkenntnis*, **3**, 1933, pp. 426 f.

Concerning my never published book mentioned here in the text, see R. Carnap's paper '*Ueber Protokollstäze*' (On Protocol-Sentences), *Erkenntnis*, **3**, 1932, pp. 215–28 where he gives an outline of my theory on pp. 223–8, and accepts it. He calls my theory 'procedure B', and says (p. 224, top): 'Starting from a point of view different from Neurath's' (who developed what Carnap calls on p. 223 'procedure A'), 'Popper developed procedure B as part of his system.' And after describing in detail my theory of tests, Carnap sums up his views as follows (p. 228): 'After weighing the various arguments here discussed, it appears to me that the second language form with procedure B—that is in the form here described—is the most adequate among the forms of scientific language at present advocated...in the...theory of knowledge.' This paper of Carnap's contained the first published report of my theory of critical testing. (See also my critical remarks in *L.Sc.D.*, note 1 to section 29, p. 104, where the date '1933' should read '1932'.)

6. Wittgenstein's example of a nonsensical pseudo-proposition is: 'Socrates is identical'. Obviously, 'Socrates is not identical' must also be nonsense. Thus the negation of any nonsense will be nonsense, and that of a meaningful statement will be meaningful. *But the negation of a testable (or falsifiable) statement need not be testable,* as was pointed out, first in my *L.Sc.D.*, (e.g. pp. 38 f.) and later by my critics. The confusion caused by taking testability as a criterion of *meaning* rather than of *demarcation* can easily be imagined.

7. The most recent example of the way in which the history of this problem is misunderstood is A. R. White's 'Note on Meaning and Verification', *Mind*, **63**, 1954, pp. 66 ff. J. L. Evans's article, *Mind*, **62**, 1953, pp. 1 ff., which Mr. White criticizes, is excellent in my opinion, and unusually perceptive. Understandably enough, neither of the authors can quite reconstruct the story. (Some hints may be found in my *Open Society*, notes 46, 51 and 52 to ch. 11).

8. In *L.Sc.D.* I discussed, and replied to, some likely objections which afterwards were indeed raised, without reference to my replies. One of them is the contention that the falsification of a natural law is just as impossible as its verification. The answer is that this objection mixes two entirely different levels of analysis (like the objection that mathematical demonstrations are impossible since checking, no matter how often repeated, can never make it quite

certain that we have not overlooked a mistake). On the first level, there is a logical asymmetry: one singular statement—say about the perihelion of Mercury—can formally falsify Kepler's laws; but these cannot be formally verified by any number of singular statements. The attempt to minimize this asymmetry can only lead to confusion. On another level, we may hesitate to accept any statement, even the simplest observation statement; and we may point out that every statement involves *interpretation in the light of theories,* and that it is therefore uncertain. This does not affect the fundamental asymmetry, but it is important: most dissectors of the heart before Harvey observed the wrong things—those, which they expected to see. There can never be anything like a completely safe observation, free from the dangers of misinterpretation. (This is one of the reasons why the theory of induction does not work.) The 'empirical basis' consists largely of a mixture of *theories* of lower degree of universality (of 'reproducible effects'). But the fact remains that, relative to whatever basis the investigator may accept (at his peril), he can test his theory only by trying to refute it.

9. Hume does not say 'logical' but 'demonstrative', a terminology which, I think, is a little misleading. The following two quotations are from the *Treatise of Human Nature,* Book I, Part III, sections vi and xii. (The italics are all Hume's.)

10. This and the next quotation are from *loc. cit.,* section vi. See also Hume's *Enquiry Concerning Human Understanding,* section IV, Part II, and his *Abstract,* edited 1938 by J. M. Keynes and P. Sraffa, p. 15, and quoted in *L.Sc.D.,* new appendix *VII, text to note 6.

11. *Treatise,* section xiii; section xv, rule 4.

12. F. Bäge, 'Zur Entwicklung, etc.', *Zeitschrift f. Hundeforschung,* 1933; cp. D. Katz, *Animals and Men,* ch. vi, footnote.

13. See section 30 of *L.Sc.D.*

14. Katz, *loc. cit.*

15. Kant believed that Newton's dynamics was *a priori* valid. (See his *Metaphysical Foundations of Natural Science,* published between the first and the second editions of the *Critique of Pure Reason.)* But if, as he thought, we can explain the validity of Newton's theory by the fact that our intellect imposes its laws upon nature, it follows, I think, that our intellect *must succeed* in this; which makes it hard to understand why *a priori* knowledge such as Newton's should be so hard to come by.

16. A thesis submitted under the title *'Gewohnheit und Gesetzerlebnis'* to the Institute of Education of the City of Vienna in 1927. (Unpublished.)

17. Max Born, *Natural Philosophy of Cause and Chance,* Oxford, 1949, p. 7.

18. *Natural Philosophy of Cause and Chance,* p. 6.

19. I do not doubt that Born and many others would agree that theories are accepted only tentatively. But the widespread belief in

induction shows that the far-reaching implications of this view are rarely seen.
20. Wittgenstein still held this belief in 1946.
21. See note 5 above.
22. *L.Sc.D.* (see note 5 above), ch. x, expecially sections 80 to 83, also section 34 ff. See also my note 'A Set of Independent Axioms for Probability', *Mind*, N.S. **47**, 1938, p. 275. (This note has since been reprinted, with corrections, in the new appendix *ii of *L.Sc.D.*
23. A definition, in terms of probabilities (see the next note), of $C(t, e)$, i.e. of the degree of corroboration (of a theory t relative to the evidence e) satisfying the demands indicated in my *L.Sc.D.*, sections 82 to 83, is the following:

$$C(t, e) = E(t, e)(1 + P(t)P(t, e)),$$

where $E(t, e) = (P(e, t) - P(e))/(P(e, t) + P(e))$ is a (non-additive) measure of the explanatory power of t with respect to e. Note that $C(t, e)$ is not a probability: it may have values between -1 (refutation of t by e) and $C(t, e) < +1$. Statements t which are lawlike and thus non-verifiable cannot even reach $C(t, e) = C(t, t)$ upon empirical evidence e. $C(t, t)$ is the *degree of corroborability* of t, and is equal to the *degree of testability* of t, or to the *content* of t. Because of the demands implied in point (6) at the end of section I above, I do not think, however, that it is possible to give a complete formalization of the idea of corroboration (or, as I previously used to say, of confirmation).

(Added 1955 to the first proofs of this paper:)

See also my note 'Degree of Confirmation', *British Journal for the Philosophy of Science*, **5**, 1954, pp. 143 ff. (See also **5**, pp. 334.) I have since simplified this definition as follows (*B.J.P.S.*, 1955, **5**, p. 359:)

$$C(t, e) = (P(e, t) - P(e))/(P(e, t) - P(et) + P(e))$$

For a further improvement, see *B.J.P.S.* **6**, 1955, p. 56.

Thomas S. Kuhn

The Essential Tension:
Tradition and Innovation
in Scientific Research

1   I am grateful for the invitation to participate in this important conference, and I interpret it as evidence that students of creativity themselves possess the sensitivity to divergent approaches that they seek to identify in others. But I am not altogether sanguine about the outcome of your experiment with me. As most of you already know, I am no psychologist, but rather an ex-physicist now working in the history of science. Probably my concern is no less with creativity than your own, but my goals, my techniques, and my sources of evidence are so very different from yours that I am far from sure how much we do, or even *should*, have to say to each other. These reservations imply no apology: rather they hint at my central thesis. In the sciences, as I shall suggest below, it is often better to do one's best with the tools at hand than to pause for contemplation of divergent approaches.

2   If a person of my background and interests has anything relevant to suggest to this conference, it will not be about your central concerns, the creative personality and its early identification. But implicit in the numerous working papers distributed to participants in this conference is an image of the scientific process and of the scientist; that image almost certainly conditions many of the experiments you try as well as the conclusions you draw; and about it the physicist-historian may well have something to say. I shall restrict my attention to one aspect of this image—an aspect epitomized as follows in one of the working papers: The basic scientist "must lack prejudice to a degree where he can look at the most 'self-evident' facts or concepts without necessarily accepting them, and, conversely, allow his imagination to play with the most unlikely possibilities" (Selye, 1959). In the more technical language supplied by other working papers (Getzels and Jackson), this aspect of the image recurs as an emphasis upon "divergent thinking, . . . the freedom to go off in different directions, . . . rejecting the old solution and striking out in some new direction."

From *The Essential Tension* (Chicago: University of Chicago Press, 1977). Reprinted by permission from *The Third (1959) University of Utah Research Conference on the Identification of Scientific Talent*, ed. C. W. Taylor (Salt Lake City: University of Utah Press, 1959), pp. 162–74. ©1959 by the University of Utah.

I do not at all doubt that this description of "divergent think- 3
ing" and the concomitant search for those able to do it are
entirely proper. Some divergence characterizes all scientific
work, and gigantic divergences lie at the core of the most significant episodes in scientific development. But both my own
experience in scientific research and my reading of the history
of sciences lead me to wonder whether flexibility and open-
mindedness have not been too exclusively emphasized as the
characteristics requisite for basic research. I shall therefore
suggest below that something like "convergent thinking" is just
as essential to scientific advance as is divergent. Since these
two modes of thought are inevitably in conflict, it will follow
that the ability to support a tension that can occasionally become almost unbearable is one of the prime requisites for the
very best sort of scientific research.

I am elsewhere studying these points more historically, 4
with emphasis on the importance to scientific development of
"revolutions."[1] These are episodes—exemplified in their most
extreme and readily recognized form by the advent of Coperni-
canism, Darwinsim, or Einsteinianism—in which a scientific
community abandons one time-honored way of regarding the
world and of pursuing science in favor of some other, usually
incompatible, approach to its discipline. I have argued in the
draft that the historian constantly encounters many far smaller
but structurally similar revolutionary episodes and that they
are central to scientific advance. Contrary to a prevalent impression, most new discoveries and theories in the sciences
are not merely additions to the existing stockpile of scientific
knowledge. To assimilate them the scientist must usually rearrange the intellectual and manipulative equipment he has
previously relied upon, discarding some elments of his prior
belief and practice while finding new significances in and new
relationships between many others. Because the old must be
revalued and reordered when assimilating the new, discovery
and invention in the sciences are usually intrinsically revolutionary. Therefore, they do demand just that flexibility and
open-mindedness that characterize, or indeed define, the divergent thinker. Let us henceforth take for granted the need for
these characteristics. Unless many scientists possessed them to
a marked degree, there would be no scientific revolutions and
very little scientific advance.

Yet flexibility is not enough, and what remains is not ob- 5
viously compatible with it. Drawing from various fragments
of a project still in progress, I must now emphasize that revolutions are but one of two complementary aspects of scientific

advance. Almost none of the research undertaken by even the greatest scientists is designed to be revolutionary, and very little of it has any such effect. On the contrary, normal research, even the best of it, is a highly convergent activity based firmly upon a settled consensus acquired from scientific education and reinforced by subsequent life in the profession. Typically, to be sure, this convergent or consensus-bound research ultimately results in revolution. Then, traditional techniques and beliefs are abandoned and replaced by new ones. But revolutionary shifts of a scientific tradition are relatively rare, and extended periods of convergent research are the necessary preliminary to them. As I shall indicate below, only investigations firmly rooted in the contemporary scientific tradition are likely to break that tradition and give rise to a new one. That is why I speak of an "essential tension" implicit in scientific research. To do his job the scientist must undertake a complex set of intellectual and manipulative commitments. Yet his claim to fame, if he has the talent and good luck to gain one, may finally rest upon his ability to abandon this net of commitments in favor of another of his own invention. Very often the successful scientist must simultaneously display the characteristics of the traditionalist and of the iconoclast.[2]

6   The multiple historical examples upon which any full documentation of these points must depend are prohibited by the time limitations of the conference. But another approach will introduce you to at least part of what I have in mind—an examination of the nature of education in the natural sciences. One of the working papers for this conference (Getzels and Jackson) quotes Guilford's very apt description of scientific education as follows: "[It] has emphasized abilities in the areas of convergent thinking and evaluation, often at the expense of development in the area of divergent thinking. We have attempted to teach students how to arrive at 'correct' answers that our civilization has taught us are correct.... Outside the arts [and I should include most of the social sciences] we have generally discouraged the development of divergent-thinking abilities, unintentionally." That characterization seems to me eminently just, but I wonder whether it is equally just to deplore the product that results. Without defending plain bad teaching, and granting that in this country the trend to convergent thinking in all education may have proceeded entirely too far, we may nevertheless recognize that a rigorous training in convergent thought has been intrinsic to the sciences almost from their origin. I suggest that they could not have achieved their present state or status without it.

Let me try briefly to epitomize the nature of education in 7 the natural sciences, ignoring the many significant yet minor differences between the various sciences and between the approaches of different educational institutions. The single most striking feature of this education is that, to an extent totally unknown in other creative fields, it is conducted entirely through textbooks. Typically, undergraduate *and* graduate students of chemistry, physics, astronomy, geology, or biology acquire the substance of their fields from books written especially for students. Until they are ready, or very nearly ready, to commence work on their own dissertations, they are neither asked to attempt trial research projects nor exposed to the immediate products of research done by others, that is, to the professional communications that scientists write for each other. There are no collections of "readings" in the natural sciences. Nor are science students encouraged to read the historical classics of their fields—works in which they might discover other ways of regarding the problems discussed in their textbooks, but in which they would also meet problems, concepts, and standards of solution that their future professions have long since discarded and replaced.

In contrast, the various textbooks that the student does en- 8 counter display different subject matters, rather than, as in many of the social sciences, exemplifying different approaches to a single problem field. Even books that compete for adoption in a single course differ mainly in level and in pedagogic detail, not in substance or conceptual structure. Last, but most important of all, is the characteristic technique of textbook presentation. Except in their occasional introductions, science textbooks do not describe the sorts of problems that the professional may be asked to solve and the variety of techniques available for their solution. Rather, these books exhibit concrete problem solutions that the profession has come to accept as paradigms, and they then ask the student, either with a pencil and paper or in the laboratory, to solve for himself problems very closely related in both method and substance to those through which the textbook or the accompanying lecture has led him. Nothing could be better calculated to produce "mental sets" or *Einstellungen*. Only in their most elementary courses do other academic fields offer as much as a partial parallel.

Even the most faintly liberal educational theory must view 9 this pedagogic technique as anathema. Students, we would all agree, must begin by learning a good deal of what is already known, but we also insist that education give them vastly more.

They must, we say, learn to recognize and evaluate problems to which no unequivocal solution has yet been given; they must be supplied with an arsenal of techniques for approaching these future problems; and they must learn to judge the relevance of these techniques and to evaluate the possibly partial solutions which they can provide. In many respects these attitudes toward education seem to me entirely right, and yet we must recognize two things about them. First, education in the natural sciences seems to have been totally unaffected by their existence. It remains a dogmatic initiation in a pre-established tradition that the student is not equipped to evaluate. Second, at least in the period when it was followed by a term in an apprenticeship relation, this technique of exclusive exposure to a rigid tradition has been immensely productive of the most consequential sorts of innovations.

10   I shall shortly inquire about the pattern of scientific practice that grows out of this educational initiation and will then attempt to say why that pattern proves quite so successful. But first, an historical excursion will reinforce what has just been said and prepare the way for what is to follow. I should like to suggest that the various fields of natural science have not always been characterized by rigid education in exclusive paradigms, but that each of them acquired something like that technique at precisely the point when the field began to make rapid and systematic progress. If one asks about the origin of our contemporary knowledge of chemical composition, of earthquakes, of biological reproduction, of motion through space, or of any other subject matter known to the natural sciences, one immediately encounters a characteristic pattern that I shall here illustrate with a single example.

11   Today, physics textbooks tell us that light exhibits some properties of a wave and some of a particle: both textbook problems and research problems are designed accordingly. But both this view and these textbooks are products of an early twentieth-century revolution. (One characteristic of scientific revolutions is that they call for the rewriting of science textbooks.) For more than half a century before 1900, the books employed in scientific education had been equally unequivocal in stating that light was wave motion. Under those circumstances scientists worked on somewhat different problems and often embraced rather different sorts of solutions to them. The nineteenth-century textbook tradition does not, however, mark the beginning of our subject matter. Throughout the eighteenth century and into the early nineteenth, Newton's *Opticks* and the other books from which men learned science taught almost all students that light was particles, and research guided by

this tradition was again different from that which succeeded it. Ignoring a variety of subsidiary changes within these three successive traditions, we may therefore say that our views derive historically from Newton's views by way of two revolutions in optical thought, each of which replaced one tradition of convergent research with another. If we make appropriate allowances for changes in the locus and materials of scientific education, we may say that each of these three traditions was embodied in the sort of education by exposure to unequivocal paradigms that I briefly epitomized above. Since Newton, education and research in physical optics have normally been highly convergent.

The history of theories of light does not, however, begin with Newton. If we ask about knowledge in the field before his time, we encounter a significantly different pattern—a pattern still familiar in the arts and in some social sciences, but one which has largely disappeared in the natural sciences. From remote antiquity until the end of the seventeenth century there was no single set of paradigms for the study of physical optics. Instead, many men advanced a large number of different views about the nature of light. Some of these views found few adherents, but a number of them gave rise to continuing schools of optical thought. Although the historian can note the emergence of new points of view as well as changes in the relative popularity of older ones, there was never anything resembling consensus. As a result, a new man entering the field was inevitably exposed to a variety of conflicting viewpoints; he was forced to examine the evidence for each, and there always was good evidence. The fact that he made a choice and conducted himself accordingly could not entirely prevent his awareness of other possibilities. This earlier mode of education was obviously more suited to produce a scientist without prejudice, alert to novel phenomena, and flexible in his approach to his field. On the other hand, one can scarcely escape the impression that, during the period characterized by this more liberal educational practice, physical optics made very little progress.[3]

The preconsensus (we might here call it the divergent) phase in the development of physical optics is, I believe, duplicated in the history of all other scientific specialties, excepting only those that were born by the subdivision and recombination of pre-existing disciplines. In some fields, like mathematics and astronomy, the first firm consensus is prehistoric. In others, like dynamics, geometric optics, and parts of physiology, the paradigms that produced a first consensus date from classical antiquity. Most other natural sciences, though their problems were often discussed in antiquity, did not achieve a first con-

sensus until after the Renaissance. In physical optics, as we
have seen, the first firm consensus dates only from the end
of the seventeenth century; in electricity, chemistry, and the
study of heat, it dates from the eighteenth; while in geology
and the nontaxonomic parts of biology no very real consensus
developed until after the first third of the nineteenth century.
This century appears to be characterized by the emergence of
the first consensus in parts of a few of the social sciences.

14   In all the fields named above, important work was done before the achievement of the maturity produced by consensus.
Neither the nature nor the timing of the first consensus in these
fields can be understood without a careful examination of both
the intellectual and the manipulative techniques developed before the existence of unique paradigms. But the transition to
maturity is not less significant because individuals practiced
science before it occurred. On the contrary, history strongly
suggests that, though one can practice science—as one does
philosophy or art or political science—without a firm consensus, this more flexible practice will not produce the pattern
of rapid consequential scientific advance to which recent centuries have accustomed us. In that pattern, development occurs
from one consensus to another, and alternate approaches are
not ordinarily in competition. Except under quite special conditions, the practitioner of a mature science does not pause to
examine divergent modes of explanation or experimentation.

15   I shall shortly ask how this can be so—how a firm orientation toward an apparently unique tradition can be compatible
with the practice of the disciplines most noted for the persistent production of novel ideas and techniques. But it will help
first to ask what the education that so successfully transmits
such a tradition leaves to be done. What can a scientist working within a deeply rooted tradition and little trained in the
perception of significant alternatives hope to do in his professional career? Once again limits of time force me to drastic
simplification, but the following remarks will at least suggest
a position that I am sure can be documented in detail.

16   In pure or basic science—that somewhat ephemeral category
of research undertaken by men whose most immediate goal is
to increase understanding rather than control of nature—the
characteristic problems are almost always repetitions, with
minor modifications, of problems that have been undertaken
and partially resolved before. For example, much of the research undertaken within a scientific tradition is an attempt to
adjust existing theory or existing observation in order to bring
the two into closer and closer agreement. The constant examination of atomic and molecular spectra during the years since

the birth of wave mechanics, together with the design of theoretical approximations for the prediction of complex spectra, provides one important instance of this typical sort of work. Another was provided by the remarks about the eighteenth-century development of Newtonian dynamics in the paper on measurement supplied to you in advance of the conference.[4] The attempt to make existing theory and observation conform more closely is not, of course, the only standard sort of research problem in the basic sciences. The development of chemical thermodynamics or the continuing attempts to unravel organic structure illustrate another type—the extension of existing theory to areas that it is expected to cover but in which it has never before been tried. In addition, to mention a third common sort of research problem, many scientists constantly collect the concrete data (e.g., atomic weights, nuclear moments) required for the application and extension of existing theory.

These are normal research projects in the basic sciences, 17 and they illustrate the sorts of work on which all scientists, even the greatest, spend most of their professional lives and on which many spend all. Clearly their pursuit is neither intended nor likely to produce fundamental discoveries or revolutionary changes in scientific theory. Only if the validity of the contemporary scientific tradition is assumed do these problems make much theoretical or any practical sense. The man who suspected the existence of a totally new type of phenomenon or who had basic doubts about the validity of existing theory would not think problems so closely modeled on textbook paradigms worth undertaking. It follows that the man who does undertake a problem of this sort—and that means all scientists at most times—aims to elucidate the scientific tradition in which he was raised rather than to change it. Furthermore, the fascination of his work lies in the difficulties of elucidation rather than in any surprises that the work is likely to produce. Under normal conditions the research scientist is not an innovator but a solver of puzzles, and the puzzles upon which he concentrates are just those which he believes can be both stated and solved within the existing scientific tradition.

Yet—and this is the point—the ultimate effect of this 18 tradition-bound work has invariably been to change the tradition. Again and again the continuing attempt to elucidate a currently received tradition has at last produced one of those shifts in fundamental theory, in problem field, and in scientific standards to which I previously referred as scientific revolutions. At least for the scientific community as a whole, work within a well-defined and deeply ingrained tradition seems more productive of tradition-shattering novelties than work in which no similarly convergent standards are involved. How can this be so? I think it is because no other sort of work is nearly so well suited to isolate for continuing and concentrated attention those loci of trouble or causes of crisis upon whose recognition the most fundamental advances in basic science depend.

19   As I have indicated in the first of my working papers, new theories and, to an increasing extent, novel discoveries in the mature sciences are not born *de novo*. On the contrary, they emerge from old theories and within a matrix of old beliefs about the phenomena that the world does *and does not* contain. Ordinarily such novelties are far too esoteric and recondite to be noted by the man without a great deal of scientific training. And even the man with considerable training can seldom afford simply to go out and look for them, let us say by exploring those areas in which existing data and theory have failed to produce understanding. Even in a mature science there are always far too many such areas, areas in which no existing paradigms seem obviously to apply and for whose exploration few tools and standards are available. More likely than not the scientist who ventured into them, relying merely upon his receptivity to new phenomena and his flexibility to new patterns of organization, would get nowhere at all. He would rather return his science to its preconsensus or natural history phase.

20   Instead, the practitioner of a mature science, from the beginning of his doctoral research, continues to work in the regions for which the paradigms derived from his education and from the research of his contemporaries seem adequate. He tries, that is, to elucidate topographical detail on a map whose main outlines are available in advance, and he hopes—if he is wise enough to recognize the nature of his field—that he will some day undertake a problem in which the anticipated does *not* occur, a problem that goes wrong in ways suggestive of a fundamental weakness in the paradigm itself. In the mature sciences the prelude to much discovery and to all novel theory is not ignorance, but the recognition that something has gone wrong with existing knowledge and beliefs.

21   What I have said so far may indicate that it is sufficient for the productive scientist to adopt existing theory as a lightly held tentative hypothesis, employ it *faute de mieux* in order to get a start in his research, and then abandon it as soon as it leads him to a trouble spot, a point at which something has gone wrong. But though the ability to recognize trouble when confronted by it is surely a requisite for scientific advance, trouble must not be too easily recognized. The scientist requires a thoroughgoing commitment to the tradition

with which, if he is fully successful, he will break. In part this commitment is demanded by the nature of the problems the scientist normally undertakes. These, as we have seen, are usually esoteric puzzles whose challenge lies less in the information disclosed by their solutions (all but its details are often known in advance) than in the difficulties of technique to be surmounted in providing any solution at all. Problems of this sort are undertaken only by men assured that there is a solution which ingenuity can disclose, and only current theory could possibly provide assurance of that sort. That theory alone gives meaning to most of the problems of normal research. To doubt it is often to doubt that the complex technical puzzles which constitute normal research have any solutions at all. Who, for example, would have developed the elaborate mathematical techniques required for the study of the effects of interplanetary attractions upon basic Keplerian orbits if he had not assumed that Newtonian dynamics, applied to the planets then known, would explain the last details of astronomical observation? But without that assurance, how would Neptune have been discovered and the list of planets changed?

In addition, there are pressing practical reasons for com- 22 mitment. Every research problem confronts the scientist with anomalies whose sources he cannot quite identify. His theories and observations never quite agree; successive observations never yield quite the same results; his experiments have both theoretical and phenomenological by-products which it would take another research project to unravel. Each of these anomalies or incompletely understood phenomena could conceivably be the clue to a fundamental innovation and scientific theory or technique, but the man who pauses to examine them one by one never completes his first project. Reports of effective research repeatedly imply that all but the most striking and central discrepancies could be taken care of by current theory if only there were time to take them on. The men who make these reports find most discrepancies trivial or uninteresting, an evaluation that they can ordinarily base only upon their faith in current theory. Without that faith their work would be wasteful of time and talent.

Besides, lack of commitment too often results in the scien- 23 tist's undertaking problems that he has little chance of solving. Pursuit of an anomaly is fruitful only if the anomaly is more than nontrivial. Having discovered it, the scientist's first efforts and those of his profession are to do what nuclear physicists are now doing. They strive to generalize the anomaly, to discover other and more revealing manifestations of the same effect, to give it structure by examining its complex interrelationships with phenomena they still feel they understand. Very few anomalies are susceptible to this sort of treatment. To be so they must be in explicit and unequivocal conflict with some structurally central tenet of current scientific belief. Therefore, their recognition and evaluation once again depend upon a firm commitment to the contemporary scientific tradition.

24   This central role of an elaborate and often esoteric tradition is what I have principally had in mind when speaking of the essential tension in scientific research. I do not doubt that the scientist must be, at least potentially, an innovator, that he must possess mental flexibility, and that he must be prepared to recognize troubles where they exist. That much of the popular stereotype is surely correct, and it is important accordingly to search for indices of the corresponding personality characteristics. But what is no part of our stereotype and what appears to need careful integration with it is the other face of this same coin. We are, I think, more likely fully to exploit our potential scientific talent if we recognize the extent to which the basic scientist must also be a firm traditionalist, or, if I am using your vocabulary at all correctly, a convergent thinker. Most important of all, we must seek to understand how these two superficially discordant modes of problem solving can be reconciled both within the individual and within the group.

25   Everything said above needs both elaboration and documentation. Very likely some of it will change in the process. This paper is a report on work in progress. But, though I insist that much of it is tentative and all of it incomplete, I still hope that the paper has indicated why an educational system best described as an initiation into an unequivocal tradition should be thoroughly compatible with successful scientific work. And I hope, in addition, to have made plausible the historical thesis that no part of science has progressed very far or very rapidly before this convergent education and correspondingly convergent normal practice became possible. Finally, though it is beyond my competence to derive personality correlates from this view of scientific development, I hope to have made meaningful the view that the productive scientist must be a traditionalist who enjoys playing intricate games by pre-established rules in order to be a successful innovator who discovers new rules and new pieces with which to play them.

26   As first planned, my paper was to have ended at this point. But work on it, against the background supplied by the working papers distributed to conference participants, has sug-

gested the need for a postscript. Let me therefore briefly try to eliminate a likely ground of misunderstanding and simultaneously suggest a problem that urgently needs a great deal of investigation.

Everything said above was intended to apply strictly only to 27 basic science, an enterprise whose practitioners have ordinarily been relatively free to choose their own problems. Characteristically, as I have indicated, these problems have been selected in areas where paradigms were clearly applicable but where exciting puzzles remained about how to apply them and how to make nature conform to the results of the application. Clearly the inventor and applied scientist are not generally free to choose puzzles of this sort. The problems among which they may choose are likely to be largely determined by social, economic, or military circumstances external to the sciences. Often the decision to seek a cure for a virulent disease, a new source of household illumination, or an alloy able to withstand the intense heat of rocket engines must be made with list reference to the state of the relevant science. It is, I think, by no means clear that the personality characteristics requisite for pre-eminence in this more immediately practical sort of work are altogether the same as those required for a great achievement in basic science. History indicates that only a few individuals, most of whom worked in readily demarcated areas, have achieved eminence in both.

I am by no means clear where this suggestion leads us. The 28 troublesome distinctions between basic research, applied research, and invention need far more investigation. Nevertheless, it seems likely, for example, that the applied scientist, to whose problems no scientific paradigm need be fully relevant, may profit by a far broader and less rigid education than that to which the pure scientist has characteristically been exposed. Certainly there are many episodes in the history of technology in which lack of more than the most rudimentary scientific education has proved to be an immense help. This group scarcely needs to be reminded that Edison's electric light was produced in the face of unanimous scientific opinion that the arc light could not be "subdivided," and there are many other episodes of this sort.

This must not suggest, however, that mere differences in edu- 29 cation will transform the applied scientist into a basic scientist or vice versa. One could at least argue that Edison's personality, ideal for the inventor and perhaps also for the "oddball" in applied science, barred him from fundamental achievements in the basic sciences. He himself expressed great scorn for scientists and thought of them as wooly-headed people to be hired when needed. But this did not prevent his occasionally arriving at the most sweeping and irresponsible scientific theories of his own. (The pattern recurs in the early history of electrical technology: both Tesla and Gramme advanced absurd cosmic schemes that they thought deserved to replace the current scientific knowledge of their day.) Episodes like this reinforce an impression that the personality requisites of the pure scientist and of the inventor may be quite different, perhaps with those of the applied scientist lying somewhere between.[5]

30   Is there a further conclusion to be drawn from all this? One speculative thought forces itself upon me. If I read the working papers correctly, they suggest that most of you are really in search of the *inventive* personality, a sort of person who does emphasize divergent thinking but whom the United States has already produced in abundance. In the process you may be ignoring certain of the essential requisites of the basic scientist, a rather different sort of person, to whose ranks America's contributions have as yet been notoriously sparse. Since most of you are, in fact, Americans, this correlation may not be entirely coincidental.

Notes

1. *The Structure of Scientific Revolutions* (Chicago, 1962).
2. Strictly speaking, it is the professional group rather than the individual scientist that must display both these characteristics simultaneously. In a fuller account of the ground covered in this paper that distinction between individual and group characteristics would be basic. Here I can only note that, though recognition of the distinction weakens the conflict or tension referred to above, it does not eliminate it. Within the group some individuals may be more traditionalistic, others more iconoclastic, and their contributions may differ accordingly. Yet education, institutional norms, and the nature of the job to be done will inevitably combine to insure that all group members will, to a greater or lesser extent, be pulled in both directions.
3. The history of physical optics before Newton has recently been well described by Vasco Ronchi in *Histoire de la lumière*, trans. J. Taton (Paris, 1956). His account does justice to the element I elaborate too little above. Many fundamental contributions to physical optics were made in the two millennia before Newton's work. Consensus is not prerequisite to a sort of progress in the natural sciences, any more than it is to progress in the social sciences or the arts. It is, however, prerequisite to the sort of progress that we now generally refer to when distinguishing the natural sciences from the arts and from most social sciences.

4. A revised version appeared in *Isis* 52 (1961): 161–93.
5. For the attitude of scientists toward the technical possibility of the incandescent light see Francis A. Jones, *Thomas Alva Edison* (New York, 1908), pp. 99–100, and Harold C. Passer, *The Electrical Manufacturers, 1875–1900* (Cambridge, Mass., 1953), pp. 82–83. For Edison's attitude toward scientists see Passer, ibid., pp. 180–81. For a sample of Edison's theorizing in realms otherwise subject to scientific treatments see Dagobert D. Runes, ed., *The Diary and Sundry Observations of Thomas Alva Edison* (New York, 1948), pp. 205–44, passim.

CHAPTER THREE

SYSTEMS ANALYSIS

The behavioralist's commitment to "methodological individualism" involved them in a problematic relation with such holistic notion as "the state," "society" and the "nation." These deceptively familiar terms, behavioralists claimed, could easily become sloppy and unthinking short-hands; that is, they could lead us to forget that they really stood for specific individuals involved in discrete events. It was among the most pressing of behavioral priorities to puncture "holistic mystifications" such as these and reveal the concrete and particular realities for which they stood. Unless "the state" and "society" were understood as meaning no more than the sum of their parts, they were dubious, if not downright misleading, terms. Empirical research was, in fact, the most effective antidote to these broad abstractions since it limited the investigator to observable phenomena, and these were invariably individual and concrete.

This quest for "hard data" was the behavioralist's consuming passion. And yet it created a novel theoretical challenge unknown to political theorists of the past. If specific occurrences and concrete individuals were all that science could legitimately investigate, how could the mass of accumulated data be organized into an intelligible whole? How could a theoretical framework be constructed that would be sufficiently substantial and credible to integrate the mass of data that poured in, while remaining loyal to behavioralism's strictures against regarding "wholes" as real? How could a movement that rigorously restricted itself to the empirical and concrete generate overall meaning and significance? Could data become coherent and compelling without the introduction of unifying frameworks—frameworks that came perilously near the tabooed idea of "totality"? And, finally, where could these organizing frameworks possibly come from if all genuine scientific knowledge was of an empirical kind?

At first glance, answering these questions seems akin to squaring the circle. On the one hand, a theoretical construct that could translate the scattered bricks of data into a livable, unified edifice would have to stray from the strict empiricism that behavoralism enjoined. On the other hand, a consistent commitment to the concrete and specific courted the danger of atomistic confusion.

This, of course, is not to say that behavoralists refused to indulge in generalization and abstraction. No intelligible discourse on social behavior can remain at the level of factsheets, brute data, or simple reportage. Without generalization there is no meaning, no illumination, no understanding. At stake in the behavioral position was, therefore, not the inevitability of abstactions per se but rather the cognitive status to be accorded them. Were these abstractions merely linguistic shortcuts, manners of speaking, kinds of unavoidable fictions that treated individuals as if they were more than individuals? To be sure, behavioralists sometimes spoke as if this was the case. But there was more than a hint of hesitation in their words. After all, the intelligibility and significance they sought in their research seemed to adhere to the generalizations they made rather than to the individual facts they gathered. There seemed to be no exit.

The theoretical challenge was more daunting still because, as opposed to the "grand theories" of classical political philosophy that unashamedly interpreted and appraised public life, this new breed of theories was strictly forbidden, by the first and most uncompromising of behavioral commandments, to indulge in such explicit evaluative activity. Value statements lacked an observable, empirical base and were hence to be rigorously avoided by political scientists who cared for their scientific credentials. What was needed was sometimes called an "empirical theory," but was this not a contradiction in terms? If it was theoretical, in what sense could it be empirical—and vice versa? Without an interpreting perspective, how was one to make sense of what one saw? Could the hard data by itself, without any forbidden nonempirical additions, ever add up to a meaningful and coherent picture? What would a theory look like that was simultaneously value-free, ideologically neutral, intellectually credible, effective for research, and coherence-contributing?

The most interesting attempts to deal with this conundrum have concentrated on the concept of a *system*. David Easton's work in this regard has been particularly influential. In a series of books that culminated in *A Systems Analysis of Political Life*, he explored the possibilities of viewing political life in systemic terms. Because his work represents probably the clearest and least complex of all "input-output" (as systems analysis is sometimes called) frameworks, it is the best place to start.

What special attributes does the concept "system" have that recommend it to the behaviorally oriented theorist? First of all, system is a "totality" simulating concept. If the term "system" is understood to mean a persistent co-variance, a substantial degree of coherence, endurance, and interdependence between a complex of units, we appear to be having our cake and eating it too. Without violating the prohibitions against "wholes" that "methodological individualism" imposes, systems nevertheless act very much like integrated realities. They cohere without their constituent parts losing their individuality. We can speak of a political system "as if" it was an integral unity while being fully cognizant that it is, in truth, only a series of individual units interrelating. Systems are not "real" or "essential," Easton cautions his readers, they are no more than artificial constructions with heuristic value. Indeed, the concept of a system is the farthest behavioralists can go in the direction of "wholes" without trespassing into forbidden unscientific terrain.

Systems are, moreover, value-neutral and ideologically indeterminate. They have no appraising content, nor do they appear to add an interpretive dimension to the processed data. Viewing political life in systemic terms organizes our findings around a single focus: the co-variance and interdependence of the units that make up the system. Systems theory postulates axiomatically that changes in one element will not be limited to that unit alone; there is a presumption that they will influence other proximate elements in the system. Systems involve regular patterns holding between constituent elements; a weakening of police surveillance, for example, can be expected to have certain specifiable consequences for crime levels. When a political system fails, therefore, what is involved has nothing to do with some vital essence being slain; it means nothing more than that the individual units involved cease to be interdependent.

We seem then to have the answer to our conundrum: the concept of a system lends coherence to a complex reality without violating empirical individuality; it organizes data without interpreting or appraising it; its axiomatic assumption of interdependence appears to be eminently reasonable, and it holds out the promise of effectively ordering research and categorizing findings. Understandably, therefore, the idea of political life as a cohering system of interdependent units has been a favorite image of behavioral political science. As we shall see below, it has been given a number of different treatments, each with its own unique variation on the general theme. Moreover, the terminology associated with systems analysis has become so pervasive that it is off-handedly used by many who no longer recognize its source.

But how are we to identify specifically political systems from the many other systems into which human behavior is organized? To distinguish political activity from all the rest, Easton proposes a definition of the "political" that has become standard to the point of cliché: politics, he tells us, involves "the authoritative allocation of social values." Because social values or resources are invariably in short supply (it is impossible, barring messianic categories, to envisage a reality in which everyone could have everything they wanted whenever they wanted it), a mechanism for their distribution is mandatory.

Social values range from the familiar material kind to those possessing the most spiritual qualities. They run the gamut from budgetary allocations to the apportionment of prestige and honor to definitions of what is to be counted good. Politics is the struggle between individuals and groups for dominion over these social values. Because in even the most egalitarian design for a theater someone will be privileged to sit fifth row center while someone else will need to sit in the balcony, a criterion for seat allotment cannot be avoided. Should the better seat be given to the one who is willing to pay more money for it, should it perhaps be alloted by a system of rotation or lottery or first-come-first-serve, maybe according to aristocratic lineage, according to religious status, by gender, by rank within the party, government or army, etc.? (Each of these criteria have, in fact, been utilized by different political systems at one time or another.)

Politics organizes collective decisions such as these and announces the victors and the vanquished. And because human interests are often as incompatible as they are highly charged, these distributions cannot be voluntary. Politics is a world in which there must be a last word and it must be binding. To speak of a political system, therefore, is to distinguish activity that is directed to the "authoritative allocation of social values" from other systems of human activity (for example, the economic system) that revolve around a different axis.

A distinction between the political and the economic systems does not mean to imply that any kind of real border exists between them in actual public life. Easton's distinction is purely conventional; it aims only at demarcating systems for the purpose of study. In practice, no such system is autonomous or closed. They interpenetrate so thoroughly as to be inextricable. In fact, each system receives most of its inputs from other neighboring systems while passing most of its outputs on to them as well. Taxation policy, for example, clearly appertains to the economic system. The various interests that compete to determine the nature of the tax structure (although they originate within the economic system) converge on the political system in search of a favorable resolution to the issue. When an authoritative political determination has been made, taxation policy—the political system's output—now reenters the economic system as an economic input. All of which is only to say that the commerce across system lines is both rich in itself and, moreover, imperative in order for each system to survive.

There is little point in fleshing out in detail the many elements that go into constituting a political system; Easton's essay is clear, enlightening, and self-explanatory. It will be sufficient for us to briefly develop some of the more significant themes that are involved. It is recommended at this point that the reader turn to Easton's essay. The discussion below is best read afterwards because it assumes some familiarity with the ideas that Easton presents.

Inputs, Easton asserts, are comprised of demands and supports. Demands on a political system come in a virtually infinite variety of forms: from demands for financial support, to demands for services, to demands for the enforcement of certain moral principles, to demands for symbolic recognition. Demands drive the motor of politics, and politics operates to convert demands into authoritative policy outputs.

Unregulated demands spell the doom of a political system. Were these protean demands to come pouring into a political system unselectively, it would very rapidly suffer from flooding, overload, and breakdown. (By contrast, when demands, for whatever reason, do not reach the political process, system "starvation" is said to occur. Although it is less prevalent than overload, it is no less fatal). "Systems maintenance" requires that demand processing be kept to a manageable level. To accomplish this end, all political systems establish filtering devices that select and limit the demands that actually enter the determining stages of the political process. Institutional, cultural, and structural "gatekeepers" of various kinds guard the entrance to the "conversion process." They disqualify those demands that do not conform to very severe specifications of importance, consensuality, feasibility, etc.

Where political systems are simple, the demands they generate as well as the institutions that deal with these demands tend to be commensurately simple. With the introduction of complexity into a political community—and complexity is an invariable concomitant of modernization—the need for a more structurally differentiated processing mechanism becomes vital. For the vast quantities of demands that characterize modern states to be expeditiously processed requires a degree of specialization and institutional differentiation provided only by a diversified bureaucratic structure.

Were demands the only input, political systems could not long survive. Alongside demands, political systems require what Easton calls "supports." For the system's arbitration between competing demands to be acceptable and definitive, supports must underwrite the mechanism of choice. Supports may be based on cultural, ideological, or national loyalties. They may also rest on coercion, fear, and the lack of available alternatives. Whatever their source, supports provide effective criteria— one might speak of them as natural gatekeepers—for the selection process between demands. Those that are deemed "inappropriate" to the system are disqualified before they get very far. In addition, supports validate and fortify the rules of the decision process. And finally, they authorize the binding nature of the system's outputs.

Political systems, therefore, are the totality of the process in which inputs are converted into outputs. The actual conversion of input to output is effected by the various governmental institutions expressly designed for these ends. These are the cauldrons of politics into which the prepared input material is poured and out of which issues the finished output product. (Parenthetically, it is typical of the behavioral distaste for institutional analysis that Easton speaks almost not at all of actual organizations that effect the conversion. They are for him a "black box" into which inputs stream and out of which outputs emerge.)

This, however, is hardly the end of the process. Outputs need to travel full-circle and return, via the feedback loop, to the input side of the conversion process. Outputs that are deemed satisfactory by major elements within the system generate renewed supports and put to rest the original demands that set the conversion process into motion. Outputs that are judged inadequate may well erode supports and dangerously intensify the level of demands. The interdependence and co-variance of the various units that make up a system are nowhere more clearly visible than here.

In a sense, the political system has a kind of reflexive self-consciousness that is sensitive to its own activity. It regularly monitors its own pulse and responds to its own malfunctioning by attempting to restore a dynamic balance. When the system goes somewhat askew—as, for example, when certain significant demands are consistently unfulfilled—the pressure mounts for a corrective operation to restore system equilibrium. The feedback loop, the system's responding to itself, endows it with a form of intelligence. Indeed, many commentators have seen in Easton's systems what can almost be called a will to restore its own stability. It is here, when the system acts as an almost sentient unit, that the behavioralist comes closest to violating his own prohibition against ascribing to many concrete individuals the character of a whole.

Critiques of systems analysis have come from many quarters, two of which stand out as broadly typical. The first argues that Easton's notion of a political system is too transparently axiomatic to be of real use. The second contends that despite its protestations of value-neutrality, Easton's system betrays clear signs of the politically liberal intellectual context in which it had its origins. Let us take up these critiques by turns.

For all its appealing simplicity and clarity, many have observed that Easton's brand of "input-output" analysis figures very little in actual research; it is more contemplated than worked with. Although it represents a striking example of what political theorizing in the modernist key would entail—clean cold lines of glass and steel rather than the warmly idiosyncratic and baroque shape of classical thought—the theory fails to accomplish its declared purpose of providing a serviceable template for research. Where it has been used, its contribution turns out to be more terminological than real. Easton's system is, its detractors claim, a heuristic model possessing a purely deductive and axiomatic quality rather than a tool which aids the investigator in the field. Easton's model of the political system, they claim, is far too generic and tautological to be useful. In other words, it is a restatement of the essential elements in the political process stripped bare of any and all specific characteristics, a minimalistic conceptualization that gains clarity at the price of abstraction.

To put Easton's concepts into operation would require specifying which concrete demands and supports are typical of a particular system. The bare categories "demands" and "supports," of course, tell us nothing, so a firm grasp of the sociological, economic, cultural, ideological, and religious attributes of the system being studied is required. And because demands and supports (even if they are fleshed out with the aforementioned attributes) cannot be adequately studied in a dimensionless present, using Easton's concepts would also require exploring the system's past, its development, and its distinctive historical sensitivities and strengths. Moreover, since a system's inputs and outputs derive from and issue into neighboring systems, the study of a political system would require careful attention to the many other systems that form its natural environment.

Without all this, it would be impossible to distinguish between the significant and the trivial concerns of a system, between its episodic and enduring issues. Lacking knowledge of a system's historical and cultural peculiarities would make it impracticable to compare the system either to itself (in other periods) or to others. It would be difficult to discriminate between crisis situations and normal ones, between weakening supports and mere verbal bravado, between marginal and mainstream demands, and so on. But if it is imperative that the wealth of sociological and historical information be processed to comprehend the system's distinctive nature, what, Easton's critics ask, do the rather feeble categories of demands, supports, conversion process, and policy outputs contribute to our understanding? Are we not merely translating familiar and known phenomena into generic terms and empty jargon? To what extent do these terms truly aid us in better understanding political life or in directing our research efforts?

In the charged partisan atmosphere of the 1960s, it was perhaps inevitable that Easton's ostensibly value-neutral analysis would be scrutinized for tell-tale ideological loyalties. Many anti-behavioralists expended great energy and creativity in revealing the liberal assumptions they discerned at the heart of Easton's work. Systems analysis, they charged, was a politically loaded conceptualization that masqueraded as dispassionate science. Above all, they pointed out that conceiving of the political system as an equilibrium-seeking, self-balancing entity betrayed clear ideological inclinations. Like the liberal consensualist position, Easton's system's "normal" state was one of adaptive dynamic stability; it remained in balance until disturbed. What required explanation was why systems failed to adapt, why their balance-restoring mechanisms were defeated by the forces of imbalance and disintegration. System stress, overload, starvation, output paralysis, feedback loop blockage, and the like, were the pathologies of politics, a system gone wrong.

That this view differs from radical Marxist conceptions of politics goes without saying. For Marxists, stress, contradiction, conflict, and imbalance characterize the "normal" condition of the modern state. They require no special explanation. Eastonian equilibrium, Marxists contend, is necessarily contrived and, in the end, illusory. What does need to be accounted for from the Marxist perspective is the ability of the political system to survive in the face of the incessant batterings it suffers. It should, by all objective measures, succumb to revolutionary violence. Politics, for the Marxist, is only the ultimately futile attempt of the ruling interests to artificially and temporarily right the balance, which is, in fact, radically askew. Consequently, Easton's claim that his equilibrium-seeking system is ideologically neutral cannot be accepted at face value. A comparison of Marxist ideas with the presumptions built into Easton's work, his critics charge, dramatizes how profoundly his own liberal axioms are woven into the fabric of his thought.

This genre of criticism goes further still. It challenges Easton's account of demands and their relation to the conversion process. Easton understands demands as being initiated by an undefined social reservoir and, subsequently, undergoing a selection process mediated by a network of "gatekeepers." The system's policy outputs are generated by the demands that actually reach the conversion process. Easton's systemic analysis has no room for those demands that fail to pass the gatekeepers. Outputs, similarly, are judged only in relation to the demands that actually make their way into the governmental process. A system that succeeds in adequately processing its demand inputs—converting them into policy outputs and passing successfully through the judgment of the feedback loop—is, presumably, in fine form.

But is it? What kinds of demands actually succeed in reaching the critical moment when inputs are converted into outputs? Are certain types of demands systematically thwarted in their drive to get a fair hearing? Are there particular categories of demands that, despairing of success, will not even attempt to become system outputs? Easton's critics charge that his consensualist liberal analysis overlooks the following: (1) demands do not derive from an undifferentiated social base; (2) they do not receive equal treatment at the hands of the gatekeepers; and (3) the feedback assessment of outputs is not uniformly sensitive to the judgments of all groups. Certain kinds of demands—let us call them "establishment" demands—will have an inside track on success while others, representing ineffective or repressed groups, can hope for little attention.

Politically ineffective groups, however, are not necessarily politically unimportant groups. The demands of a vast voiceless underclass, of national or racial minorities, of impoverished rural farmers, of a revolutionary underground, of "dissident" elements in authoritarian regimes, and of many other potentially destabilizing groups will often fail to make much headway in having their demands heard. Such groups are either incapable of translating their interests into articulate demands or, when such demands are successfully articulated, to carry them to a favorable conclusion. Nor are their grievances effectively felt in the feedback process. Typically, groups such as these are unable to generate sufficient political velocity to breech the political fortress—either because they are unable to mount an effective offensive or because their offensive is forcibly repelled.

The frustration of groups whose demands are consistently defeated cannot be calibrated with the machinery of Easton's system. Similarly, the erosion of their support will not register because the support of the politically "relevant" groups is all the system is geared to monitor. Although their frustrations may be potentially critical for the system's stability and survival—even in the short run—they nevertheless go unrecorded. But demands that are rejected or ignored over time do not, of course, go away. They may both intensify and seek other avenues of expression. Groups having poor access to the political forum may take their needs elsewhere, outside the system, perhaps in a revolutionary manner. A revolutionary situation may, in fact, be in the offing without showing up in the demands the system processes. Although such systems may be deeply divided and tenuous, they will give an illusory impression of stability.

Critics draw two conclusions from these arguments. First, Easton's liberal predispositions have insinuated themselves into the seemingly transparent analytical scheme he proposes. These predispositions are evidenced in the affinity of systems analysis to equilibrium-seeking images of politics as well as in its proclivity to focus on politically dominant supports and demands. Second, the categories of systems analysis are not very useful in the conduct of political research. In the actual analysis of political realities, one is bound to dispense with Easton's categories and rely on those sources of information that knowledgeable observers have used immemorially. For example, to correct the bias of systems analysis toward politically dominant forces would require going outside Easton's notion of inputs as those demands and supports that actually impinge on the conversion process. It would involve including all those forces that a general sociological, economic, cultural, and historical knowledge of the system would make apparent. But, the critics ask, if we are to base our understanding of political life on these familiar and accessible sources, what does systems analysis have to offer?

SUGGESTIONS FOR FURTHER READING

Easton, D. *A Systems Analysis of Political Life* (New York, Wiley, 1965).

Easton, D. *A Framework for Political Analysis* (Englewood Cliffs, N.J., Prentice Hall, 1965).

Kaplan, M. *System and Process in International Politics* (New York, Wiley, 1957).

Sutherland, J. W. *A General Systems Philosophy for the Social and Behavioral Sciences* (New York, George Braziller, 1973).

David Easton

Categories for the
Systems Analysis of Politics*

The question that gives coherence and purpose to a rigor- 1
ous analysis of political life as a system of behavior is: How
do political systems manage to persist in a world of both stability and change? Ultimately, the search for an answer will
reveal what we may call *the life processes of political systems*—
those fundamental functions without which no system could
endure—together with the typical modes of response through
which systems manage to sustain them. The analysis of these
processes, and of the nature and conditions of the responses, I
posit as a central problem of political theory.

Political Life as an Open and Adaptive System

Although I shall end by arguing that it is useful to interpret 2
political life as a complex set of processes through which certain kinds of inputs are converted into the type of outputs we
may call authoritative policies, decisions, and implementing
actions, it is useful at the outset to take a somewhat simpler
approach. We may begin by viewing political life as a system
of behavior imbedded in an environment to the influences of
which the political system itself is exposed and in turn reacts.
Several vital considerations are implicit in this interpretation,
and it is essential that we become aware of them.

First, such a point of departure for theoretical analysis as- 3
sumes, without further inquiry, that political interactions in
a society constitute a *system* of behavior. This proposition is
deceptive in its simplicity. The truth is that if the idea *system* is used with the rigor it permits and with all its currently

*This essay is a slightly revised version of Chapter Two of my book, A *Systems Analysis
of Political Life* (New York: John Wiley & Sons, Inc., 1965). It is reprinted here with
permission of the publishers. In effect this essay summarizes my book, A *Framework for
Political Analysis* (Englewood Cliffs, N.J.: Prentice-Hall, Inc., 1965) and points forward
to the more detailed elaboration of my views now to be found in A *Systems Analysis of
Political Life*. The value of its presence here is not only that it offers an overview of the
analytic structure developed in both of these values, but also that it represents strategy
toward a general theory substantially different from the strategies presented in the other
essays in this book.

From David Easton, ed., *Varieties of Political Theory* (Englewood Cliffs, N.J., Prentice-
Hall, 1966), pp. 143-154. Reprinted by permissionof the author and University of Chicago
Press.

inherent implications, it provides a starting point that is already heavily weighted with consequences for a whole pattern of analysis.

4   Second, to the degree that we are successful in analytically isolating political life as a system, it is clear that that system cannot usefully be interpreted as existing in a void. It must be seen as surrounded by physical, sociological, social, and psychological *environments*. Here again, the empirical transparency of the statement ought not to distract us from its crucial theoretical significance. If we were to neglect what seems so obvious once it is asserted, it would be impossible to lay the groundwork for an analysis of how political systems manage to persist in a world of stability or change.

5   This brings us to a third point. What makes the identification of the environments useful and necessary is the further presupposition that political life forms an *open* system. By its very nature as a social system that has been analytically separated from other social systems, such a system must be interpreted as lying exposed to influences deriving from the other systems in which it is embedded. From them flows a constant stream of events and influences that shape the conditions under which the members of the system must act.

6   Finally, the fact that some systems do survive, whatever the buffets received from their environments, awakens us to the fact that they must have the capacity to *respond* to disturbances and thereby to adapt to the conditions under which they find themselves. Once we are willing to assume that political systems may be adaptive, and need not just react passively to their environmental influences, we shall be able to cut a new path through the complexities of theoretical analysis.

7   In a political system's internal organization, a critical property that it shares with all other social systems is an extraordinarily variable capacity to respond to the conditions under which it functions. Indeed, political systems accumulate large repertoires of mechanisms by which they may try to cope with their environments. Through these mechanisms, they may regulate their own behavior, transform their internal structure, and even go so far as to remodel their fundamental goals. Few types of systems, other than social systems, have this potentiality. In practice, students of political life cannot help but take this into account; no analysis could even begin to appeal to common sense if it did not do so. Nevertheless, this potentiality is seldom built into a theoretical structure as a central component; certainly its implications for the internal behavior of political systems have never been set forth and explored.[1]

Equilibrium Analysis and Its Shortcomings

It is a major shortcoming of the one form of inquiry latent 8 but prevalent in political research—equilibrium analysis—that it neglects such variable capacities of systems to cope with environmental influences. Although the equilibrium approach is seldom explicitly elaborated, it has permeated a good part of political research, especially group politics[2] and international relations. Of necessity, an analysis that conceives of a political system as seeking to maintain a state of equilibrium must assume the presence of environmental influences. It is these that displace the power relationships in a political system from their presumed stable state. It is then customary to analyze the system, if only implicitly, in terms of a tendency to return to a presumed preexisting point of stability. If the system should fail to do so, it would be interpreted as moving on to a new state of equilibrium; and then this would need to be identified and described. A careful scrutiny of the language used reveals that *equilibrium* and *stability* are usually assumed to mean the same thing.[3]

Numerous conceptual and empirical difficulties stand in the 9 way of an effective use of the equilibrium idea for the analysis of political life.[4] Among these difficulties, there are two that are particularly relevant for present purposes.

In the first place, the equilibrium approach leaves the im- 10 pression that the members of a system have only one basic goal as they seek to cope with change or disturbances: namely, to re-establish the old point of equilibrium or to move on to some new one. This is usually phrased, at least implicitly, as the search for stability, as though stability were sought above all else. In the second place, little if any attention is explicitly given to formulating the problems relating to the path that the system takes in seeking to return to its presumed old point of equilibrium or to attain a new one. It is as though the pathways taken to manage the displacements were an incidental, rather than a central, theoretical consideration.

But it is impossible to understand the processes underlying 11 the capacity of some kind of political life to sustain itself in a society if either the objectives or the form of the responses are taken for granted. A system may well have other goals than that of reaching one or another point of equilibrium. Even though the idea of a state of equilibrium were to be used only as a theoretical norm that is never achieved,[5] such a conception would offer a less useful theoretical approximation of reality than one that takes into account other possibilities. We would find it more helpful to devise a conceptual approach that recognized that members in a system may at times wish to take positive actions to destroy a previous equilibrium or even to achieve some new point of continuing disequilibrium. This is typically the case when the authorities seek to keep themselves in power by fostering internal turmoil or external dangers.

12   Furthermore, with respect to these variable goals, it is a primary characteristic of all systems that they are able to adopt a wide range of actions of a positive, constructive, and innovative sort for warding off or absorbing any forces of displacement. A system need not react to a disturbance just by oscillating in the neighborhood of a prior point of equilibrium or by shifting to a new one. It may cope with the disturbance by seeking to change its environment so that the exchanges between its environment and itself are no longer stressful; it may seek to insulate itself against any further influences from the environment; or the members of the system may even fundamentally transform their own relationships and modify their own goals and practices so as to improve their changes of handling the inputs from the environment. In these and other ways, a system has the capacity for creative and constructive regulation of disturbances.

13   It is clear that the adoption of equilibrium analysis, however latent it may be, obscures the presence of system goals that cannot be described as a state of equilibrium. It also virtually conceals the existence of varying pathways for attaining these alternative ends. For any social system, including a political one, adaptation represents more than simple adjustment to the events in its life. It is made up of efforts—limited only by the variety of human skills, resources, and ingenuity—to control, modify, or fundamentally change either the environment or the system itself, or both together. In the outcome, the system may succeed in fending off or incorporating successfully any influences stressful for it.

Minimal Concepts for a Systems Analysis

14   A systems analysis promises a more expansive, inclusive, and flexible theoretical structure than is available even in a thoroughly self-conscious and well-developed equilibrium approach. To do so successfully, however, a systems analysis must establish its own theoretical imperatives. At the outset, we may define a *system* as any set of variables regardless of the degree of interrelationship among them. The reason for preferring this definition is that it frees us from the need to argue

about whether or not a political system is really a system. The only question of importance about a set selected as a system to be analyzed is whether this set constitutes an interesting system. Does it help us to understand and explain some aspect of human behavior of concern to us?

As I have argued in *The Political System,* a *political* system 15 can be designated as those interactions through which values are authoritatively allocated for a society; this is what distinguishes a political system from other systems is its environment. This environment itself may be divided into two parts: the intrasocietal and the extrasocietal. The first consists of those systems in the same society as the political system which are not political systems due to our definition of the nature of political interactions. Intrasocietal systems include such sets of behavior, attitudes, and ideas as the economy, culture, social structure, and personalities; they are functional segments of the society of which the political system is itself a component. In a given society, the systems other than the political system are the source of many influences that create and shape the conditions under which the political system itself must operate. In a world of newly emerging political systems, we do not need to pause to illustrate the impact that a changing economy, culture, or social structure may have upon political life.

The second part of the environment, the extrasocietal, in- 16 cludes all those systems that lie outside the given society itself. They are functional components of an international society, a suprasystem of which any single society is part. The international cultural system is an example of an extrasocietal system.

Taken together, these two classes of systems—the intra- and 17 extra-societal—which we conceive to lie outside a political system, comprise the *total environment* of a political system.[6] From these sources arise influences that are of consequence for possible stress on the political system. *Disturbances* is a concept that we may use to refer to those influences from the total environment of a system that act upon the system, and thereby change it. Not all disturbances need strain the system: Some may be favorable to the persistence of the system; others may be entirely neutral with regard to stress. But many can be expected to contribute to stress.

When may we say that *stress* occurs? This question involves 18 us in a rather complex idea, one that embodies several subsidiary notions. All political systems as such are distinguished by the fact that if we are to be able to describe them as persisting, we must attribute to them the successful fulfillment of two functions. They must be able to allocate values for a society, and they must manage to induce most members to accept these allocations as binding, at least for most of the time. These two properties distinguish political systems from other kinds of social systems.

19   Hence, these two distinctive properties—the allocations of values for a society and the relative frequency of compliance with them—are the *essential variables* of political life. But for their presence, we would not be able to say that a society has any political life. And we may here take it for granted that no society could exist without some kind of political system; elsewhere I have sought to demonstrate this in detail.[7]

20   One of the important reasons for identifying these essential variables is that they give us a way of establishing when and how the disturbances acting upon a system threaten to cause it stress. We can say that stress occurs when there is a danger that the essential variables will be pushed beyond what we may designate as their *critical range*. What this means is that something may be happening in the environment—the system suffers total defeat at the hands of an enemy, or a severe economic crisis arouses widespread disorganization in and disaffection from the system. Let us assume that, as a result, either the authorities are consistently unable to make decisions, or the decisions they do make are no longer regularly accepted as binding. Under these conditions, authoritative allocations of values are no longer possible, and the society collapses for want of a system of behavior to fulfill one of its vital functions.

21   Here we cannot help but accept the interpretation that the political system had come under stress, so severe that any and every possibility for the persistence of a system for that society had disappeared. But frequently the disruption of a political system is not that complete; even though stress is present, the system continues to persist in some form. Severe as a crisis may be, it still may be possible for the authorities to be able to make some kinds of decisions and to get them accepted with at least minimal frequency, so that some of the problems typically subjected to political settlements can be handled.

22   In other words, it is not always a matter of whether or not the essential variables are operating. It is possible that they may only be somewhat displaced, as when the authorities are partially unable to make decisions or to get them accepted with complete regularity. Under these circumstances, the essential variables remain within some normal range of operation; they may be under stress, but not to a sufficient degree to displace them beyond a determinable critical point. As long as the sys-

tem keeps its essential variables operating within their critical range, some kind of system can be said to persist.

As we have seen, every system has the capacity to cope with 23 stress on its essential variables. Not that systems always do so; a system may collapse precisely because it has failed to take measures appropriate for handling the impending stress. But it is the existence of the capacity to respond to stress that is of paramount importance. The kind of response (if any) actually undertaken will help us to evaluate the probability that the system will be able to ward off the stress. Raising the question of the nature of the response to stress points up the special objectives and merit of a systems analysis of political life. It is especially suited for interpreting the behavior of the members in a system in the light of the consequences this behavior has for alleviating or aggravating stress upon the essential variables.

The Linkage Variables Between Systems

But a fundamental problem remains: How do the potentially 24 stressful conditions from the environment communicate themselves to a political system? After all, common sense tells us that there is an enormous variety of environmental influences at work on a system. Do we have to treat each change in the environment as a separate and unique disturbance, the specific effects of which have to be independently worked out?

If this were indeed the case, the problems of systematic anal- 25 ysis would be virtually insurmountable. But if we can devise a way for generalizing our method for handling the impact of the environment on the system, there would be some hope of reducing the enormous variety of influences into a manageable number of indicators. This is precisely what I seek to do through the use of the concepts of *inputs* and *outputs*.

How are we to describe these inputs and outputs? Because 26 of the analytic distinction that I have been making between a political system and its parametric or environmental systems, it is useful to interpret the influences associated with the behavior of persons in the environment as *exchanges* or *transactions* that can cross the boundaries of the political system. *Exchanges* will be used when we wish to refer to the mutuality of the relationships between the political system and the other systems in the environment. *Transactions* will be used when we wish to emphasize the movement of an effect in one direction, from an environmental system to the political system,

or the reverse, without being concerned at the time about the
reactive behavior of the other system.

27   Up to this point, there is little to dispute. If systems were
not in some way coupled together, all analytically identifiable
aspects of behavior in society would be independent of each
other, a patently unlikely condition. What makes the fact of
this coupling more than a mere truism, however, is the proposal of a way to trace out the complex exchanges so that we
can readily reduce their immense variety to theoretically and
empirically manageable proportions.

28   To accomplish this, I have proposed that we condense the
major and significant environmental influences into a few indicators. Through the examination of these we should be able
to appraise and follow through the potential impact of environmental events on the system. With this objective in mind,
I have designated the effects that are transmitted across the
boundary of a system toward some other system as the outputs
of the first system and hence, symmetrically, as the inputs of
the second system. A transaction or an exchange between systems will therefore be viewed as a linkage between them in the
form of an input-output relationship.

Demands and Supports as Input Indicators

29   The value of inputs as a concept is that through their use we
shall find it possible to capture the effect of the vast variety of
events and conditions in the environment as they pertain to the
persistence of a political system. Without using the concept of
inputs, it would be difficult to delineate the precise operational
way in which the behavior in the various sectors of society
affects what happens in the political sphere. Inputs will serve
as *summary variables* that concentrate and mirror everything
in the environment that is relevant to political stress. Thereby
the concept of inputs serves as a powerful analytic tool.

30   The extent to which inputs can be used as summary variables will depend, however, upon how we define them. We
might conceive of them in their broadest sense. In that case,
we would interpret them as including any event external to
the system that alters, modifies, or affects the system in any
way.[8] But if we used the concept in so broad a fashion, we
would never be able to exhaust the list of inputs acting upon a
system. Virtually every parametric event and condition would
have some significance for the operations of a political system
at the focus of attention; a concept so inclusive that it does not

help us to organize and simplify reality would defeat its own purposes.

But as I have already intimated, we can greatly simplify the 31 task of analyzing the impact of the environment if we restrict our attention to certain kinds of inputs that can be used as indicators to sum up the most important effects, in terms of their contributions to stress, that cross the boundary from the parametric to the political systems. In this way, we would free ourselves from the need to deal with and trace out separately the consequences of each type of environmental event.

As the theoretical tool for this purpose, it is helpful to view 32 the major environmental influences as focusing in two major inputs: *demands* and *support*. Through them, a wide range of activities in the environment can be channeled, mirrored, summarized, and brought to bear upon political life. Hence, they are key indicators of the way in which environmental influences and conditions modify and shape the operations of the political system. If we wish, we may say that it is through fluctuations in the inputs of demands and support that we shall find the effects of the environmental systems transmitted to the political system.

Outputs and Feedback

In a comparable way, the idea of *outputs* helps us to organize 33 the consequences flowing from the behavior of the members of the system rather than from actions in the environment. Our primary concern is, to be sure, with the functioning of the political system. For understanding political phenomena, we would have no need to be concerned with the consequences in and of themselves that political actions have for the environmental systems. This is a problem that can be better handled by theories dealing with the operations of the economy, culture, or any of the other parametric systems.

But the activities of the members of the system may well 34 have some importance for their own subsequent actions or conditions. To the extent that this is so, we cannot entirely neglect those actions that do flow out of a system into its environment. As in the case of inputs, however, there is an immense amount of activity that takes place within a political system. How are we to isolate the portion relevant to an understanding of the way in which systems manage to persist?

A useful way of simplifying and organizing our perceptions 35 of the behavior of the members of the system (as reflected in their demands and support) is to do so in terms of the effects these inputs have on what we may call the *political outputs*. These are the decisions and actions of the authorities. Not that the complex political processes internal to a system that have been the subject of inquiry for so many decades in political science will be considered in any way irrelevant. Who controls whom in the various decision-making processes will continue to be a vital concern, since the pattern of power relationships helps to determine the nature of the outputs. But the formulation of a conceptual structure for this aspect of a political system would draw us onto a different level of analysis. Here, I am only seeking economical ways of summarizing—not of investigating—the outcomes of these internal political processes, which can, I suggest, be usefully conceptualized as the outputs of the authorities. Through them, we are able to trace out the consequences of behavior within a political system for its environment.

36   Outputs not only help to influence events in the broader society of which the system is a part, but also, in doing so, they help to determine each succeeding round of inputs that finds its way into the political system. There is a *feedback loop*, the identification of which helps us to explain the processes through which the system may cope with stress. Through it, the system may take advantage of what has been happening by trying to adjust its future behavior.

37   When we speak of the systems as acting, however, we must be careful not to reify the system itself. We must bear in mind that all systems, to make collective action possible, have those who usually speak in the name or on behalf of the system. We may designate these as the *authorities*. If actions are to be taken to satisfy demands or create conditions that will do so, information must be fed back, at least to these authorities, about the effects of each round of outputs. Without information-feedback about what is happening in the system, the authorities would have to operate in the dark.

38   If we take as our analytic point of departure the capacity of a system to persist, and if we view as one of the possible and important sources of stress a possible drop in support below some specifiable minimum, we can appreciate the importance of information-feedback to the authorities. The authorities need not necessarily seek to bolster the input of support for themselves or for the system as a whole. But if they should wish to do so—and their own survival may well force them to do so—information about the effects of each round of outputs and about the changing conditions under which the

members finds themselves is essential. It enables them to take whatever action they feel is necessary to keep support at some minimal level.

For this reason, a model of this kind suggests that explo- 39 ration of the operations of the feedback processes is of vital significance. Anything that serves to delay, distort, or sever the flow of information to the authorities interferes with their capacity to take action, if so desired, to keep support at a level high enough to ensure the persistence of the system.

The feedback loop itself has a number of parts worthy of 40 detailed investigation. It consists of the production of outputs by the authorities, a response by the members of the society to these outputs, the communication of information about this response to the authorities, and finally, possible succeeding actions by the authorities. Thereby, a new round of outputs, response, information-feedback, and reaction by the authorities is set in motion, forming a seamless web of activities. What happens in this feedback thus has a profound influence on the capacity of a system to cope with stress and persist.

A Flow Model of the Political System

It is clear from what has been said that this mode of analysis 41 enables and indeed compels us to analyze a political system in dynamic terms. Not only do we see that a political system gets something done through its outputs, but we are also sensitized to the fact that what the system does may influence each successive stage of behavior. We appreciate the urgent need to interpret political processes as a continuous and interlinked flow of behavior.

If we were to be content with what is basically a static pic- 42 ture of a political system, we might be inclined to stop at this point. Indeed, most political research today does just this. It is concerned with exploring all those intricate subsidiary processes through which decisions are made and put into effect. Therefore, insofar as we were concerned with how influence is used in formulating and putting into effect various kinds of policies or decisions, the model to this point would be an adequate if minimal first approximation.

But the critical problem confronting political theory is not 43 just to develop a conceptual apparatus for understanding the factors that contribute to the kinds of decisions a system makes—that is, to formulate a theory of political allocations. As I have indicated, theory needs to find out how any kind of system manages to persist long enough to continue to make such decisions, and how it deals with the stress to which it may be subjected at any time. For this reason we cannot accept outputs as the terminus of either the political processes or our interest in them. Thus it is important to note, as part of this model, that the outputs of the conversion process characteristically feed back upon the system and thereby shape its subsequent behavior. It is this feature, together with the capacity of a system to take constructive actions, that enables a system to try to adapt or to cope with possible stress.

44   Thus, a systems analysis of political life rests on the idea of a system imbedded in an environment and subject to possible environmental influences that threaten to drive the essential variables of the system beyond their critical range. Such an analysis suggests that, to persist, the system must be capable of responding with measures that alleviate that stress. The actions of the authorities are particularly critical in this respect. But if they are to be able to respond, they must be in a position to obtain information about what is happening so that they may react insofar as they desire, or are compelled, to do so. With information, they may be able to maintain a minimal level of support for the system.

45   A systems analysis poses certain major questions, answers to which would help to flesh out the skeletal outline presented here: What precisely is the nature of the influences acting upon a political system? How are they communicated to a system? In what ways, if any, have systems typically sought to cope with such stress? What kinds of feedback processes must exist in any system if it is to acquire and exploit the potential for acting so as to ameliorate these conditions of stress? How do different types of systems—modern or developing, democratic or authoritarian—differ with regard to their types of inputs, outputs, and internal conversion and feedback processes? What effects do these differences have upon the capacity of the system to persist in the face of stress?

46   The task of theory construction is not of course to give substantive answers to these questions initially. Rather, it is both to formulate the appropriate questions and to devise appropriate ways for seeking answers.[9]

Notes

1. K. W. Deutsch, in *The Nerves of Government* (New York: Free Press of Glencoe, Inc., 1963), has considered the consequences of the response capacity of political systems in international affairs, although in very general terms. Some work has also been done for formal organizations. See J. W. Forrester, *Industrial Dynamics* (New

York: MIT Press and John Wiley & Sons, Inc., 1961); and W. R. Dill, "The Impact of Environment on Organizational Development," in S. Mailick and E. H. Van Ness, *Concepts and Issues in Administrative Behavior* (Englewood Cliffs, N.J.: Prentice-Hall, Inc., 1962), pp. 94–109.

2. See David Easton, *The Political System* (New York: Alfred A. Knopf, Inc., 1953), Chapter Eleven.
3. In "Limits of the Equilibrium Model in Social Research," *Behavioral Science*, I (1956): 96–104, I discuss difficulties created by the fact that social scientists typically fail to distinguish between stability and equilibrium. We often assume that a state of equilibrium must always refer to a stable condition, but in fact there are at least two other kinds of equilibria: neutral and unstable.
4. Easton, "Limits of the Equilibrium Model."
5. J. A. Schumpeter, *Business Cycles* (New York: McGraw-Hill Book Company, 1939), especially in Chapter Two, discusses the idea of equilibrium as a theoretical norm.
6. The total environment is presented in Table 1, Chapter Five, of *A Framework for Political Analysis*. That volume also includes a full discussion of the various components of the environment.
7. In David Easton, *A Theoretical Approach to Authority*, Office of Naval Research, Technical Report No. 17 (Stanford, California: Department of Economics, 1955).
8. I am confining my remarks here to external sources of inputs. For the possibility of inputs deriving from internal sources and therefore constituting "withinputs," see *A Framework for Political Analysis*, Chapter Seven.
9. I have addressed myself to these objectives in *A Framework for Political Analysis* and *A Systems Analysis of Political Life*.

CHAPTER FOUR

STRUCTURE-FUNCTIONALISM

The terminological and conceptual apparatus of functionalism is probably more widely utilized in Western political science than that of any other broad-gauged approach to the subject. Professional literature is full to bursting with references to the "functions" of political systems, to the relation between "structure and function," and so on. Very often, perhaps even most often, this usage is casual and unpremeditated, a mere linguistic fashion without any necessary connection to the deeper ramifications of the functionalist position, which is only to say that functionalism is more popular terminologically than it is espoused philosophically. It is the deeper theoretical allegiances, entailed by functionalism, that will occupy us below.

In practice, structure-functionalism often presupposes a "systems" view of the political world. There are, indeed, a host of similarities that link functionalism to systems analysis. Both focus on "input-output" analysis; both have an affinity to view political systems as striving to homeostasis or equilibrium; and both incorporate important "feedback" elements into their analysis. Yet functionalism is historically, conceptually, and operationally different in a number of significant ways. Unlike systems analysis, which made its appearance on the social scientific scene fairly recently, functionalism has had a long and venerable history that goes back at least to Aristotle's teleological conceptions of nature and society. In the modern age, Montesquieu's celebrated doctrine of the separation of powers rests on a notion of essential governmental functions that are best dissevered from each other to ensure maximal stability and security. Furthermore, each type of state, Montesquieu tells us, has a certain spirit (a "spirit of the laws," he called it) that is functional to its existence.

Functionalism became a major perspective in thinking about human behavior with the advent of Darwin's evolutionary theories. Darwin had conceived of the struggle for survival in functional terms. Biological units were functioning, adaptive systems in a life and death competition with each other. Each part of the system played its role in the functioning and the survival of the whole. Systems that could not adapt their functioning to the fresh challenges that nature was constantly posing went the way of the brontosaurus and the saber-tooth tiger. Moreover, the good of nature as a functioning whole was served by this competition among the many rival species. In a changing and perilous reality with scarce resources and fierce conflict, the efficient functioning of all system elements for the sake of survival of the whole was the key to evolutionary success.

It was not long before these ideas were borrowed by certain observers of human behavior and applied to social affairs. Whatever its worth as political philosophy, "Social Darwinism" imported these same "functionalist" categories into social analysis. Social Darwinists argued that science itself underwrote the policy of laissez-faire, that the general social benefit was served by unrestrained competition between units, that functional adaptability was the highest of virtues, and, least savory of all, that attempts to protect the weak or the set-upon hampered the optimal functioning of the social whole.

These ideas enjoyed something of a vogue toward the end of the nineteenth century, and, as is not uncommon in intellectual history, they transcended their narrowly polemical and ideological origins and entered into academic discourse. Most notably, functionalist ideas influenced the fledgling discipline of anthropology. From anthropology they were transmitted to a neighboring but also infant discipline, sociology. Implicitly at first in the thought of Emile Durkheim and later explicitly in the work of Talcott Parsons and Robert Merton, these ideas made their way to center stage of the social sciences. Gabriel Almond's "Introduction" to *The Politics of Developing Areas*, originally published in 1960, represents the fullest and most often cited attempt to apply functionalist ideas to political life.

For a first approximation to what functionalism entails for social scientific analysis, we can do no better than to quote one of its early anthropological protagonists, A. Radcliffe-Brown:

> The concept of function applied to human society is based on an analogy between social life and organic life. It is through and by the continuity of the functioning that the continuity of the structure is preserved. "Function" is the contribution that a partial activity makes to the total activity of which it is a part. The function of a particular social usage is the contribution it makes to the total social system. Such a view implies that a social system has a certain kind of unity. We may define it as a condition in which all parts of the system work together with a sufficient degree of harmony or internal consistency, i.e., without producing persistent conflicts which can neither be resolved nor regulated.[1]

A number of overlapping elements stand out in Radcliffe-Brown's account. First, the elements of a social system have roles to perform in supporting the whole; second, the functional whole takes on an autonomy and self-standing nature that is difficult to reduce to the simple sum of its constituent parts; and third, the base analogy to be invoked in picturing human social life is an organic one.

Let us stop to consider this last point. Analogies for the political system that are based on mechanical rather than organic images imply a certain looseness of association between the parts. The parts of a motor do indeed function as a unit, but the independence of the constituent parts and their removability and replaceability make the union less than essential. The parts can easily be conceived of as existing autonomously. Not so the organic image. "Spare parts" of an organic kind belong to the domain of science fiction. Here the interrelating units form a union that cannot be disassembled without the direst of consequences. Individual elements depend on the whole for their maintenance. The quality of "unity" that binds the various parts is therefore significantly greater than in the mechanical analogy. Mechanical images are basically structural and anatomical in quality; organic ones, Almond insists, perceive the deeper physiological dimension as well. There is, in short, more involved in the organic metaphor than the simple covariance we found in Easton's notion of a system.

The jealous defender of "methodological individualism" will hardly find Radcliffe-Brown's ideas to his taste. A serious commitment to organically inspired conceptions of society can easily stray into nonempirical mystifications. Consequently, many contemporary functionalists have tended to attenuate this organic bond into something less objectionable methodologically. Nevertheless, it remains true that functionalists have tended to view social and political units in more holistic-organic terms than strict behavioral orthodoxy can easily accommodate. (Almond, for example, makes express reference to organic analogies in his "Introduction").

If the organic image with which the functionalist operates is responsible for its share of methodological predicaments, it is nonetheless thought to invest the functional approach with a significant interpretive advantage. Viewing a political unit in functional terms ascribes a certain meaning and purpose to action. Beyond simple covariance, social practices are said to have a functional role in sustaining the system as a whole. As such, analyzing a system involves an appreciation of the purposefulness of its constituent parts and of its integral coherence. Functionalism is therefore more than a transparent or generic model of the political system. It views political behavior as taking place within an intelligible, goal-oriented whole.

To be sure, there is no need here to understand behavior in terms of explicit values, norms, or ideologies that are external to the political system. Such values are, of course, rejected outright by behavioralists as inappropriate to social scientific analysis. The functionalist renders political behavior meaningful without such overt violations of scientific propriety by understanding purposes as inherent in the system itself. It is this recognition of purposefulness without express values that provides functionalism with its peculiar appeal as an approach.

Almond's "Introduction" appears in the context of a book on politics in "developing areas." This is significant because developing non-Western political systems are inaccessible via the institutional analysis

that prevailed before the behavioral revolution. Armed with only structural categories, the comparative analysis of political systems breaks down
as the difference between the compared structures increases. Comparing
the institutions or the structural characteristics of a highly differentiated,
specialized Western democracy with the "government" of an African
tribe, for example, would be an exercise in futility. The two are so lacking in comparability that it is difficult to conceive how such an exercise
could be conducted.

Functions, by contrast, are eminently comparable. To speak of political systems in functional terms is to render all such systems—from
the undeveloped to the modernizing to the modern—on an analytic par.
(Indeed, it is often observed that functionalism entered the social sciences via the anthropological study of "primitive" peoples because the
other more formal tools of analysis were inapplicable.) If a prime minister and a tribal chief are difficult to compare institutionally, they may
nevertheless embody comparable political functions. As such they may
be analytically commensurate despite their vastly disparate institutional
structures.

The functionalists' underlying axiom might read as follows: If the
structures of political rule are infinitely various, the functions that political systems must perform are essentially universal. Structures are variable, functions are constant. Whether these functions are **manifest**, that
is, performed intentionally, or **latent**, that is, unrecognized and unintended by participants—they must be discharged. If political systems are
to maintain themselves, certain basic functions are imperative regardless
of the system's level of development, ideological character, or cultural
peculiarities. To return to the organic analogy: all living things—from
the amoeba to homo sapiens—must seek nutrition, excrete waste, and
reproduce. These functions are basically comparable among all living
creatures despite the vast difference in levels of sophistication and differentiation that each employs to dispense its functions.

It is not only the actual functions political systems perform that may
be compared in this way; no less significant is our ability to compare the
relationship between the sociopolitical structures a system designs and
the functions it must discharge. (It is this focus on the connection between structures and functions that made the name "structure-function"
analysis so popular.) Some systems have undifferentiated multipurpose
structures that perform a host of very different functions. Others create
specialized structures that are responsible for defined and specific tasks.

While it is impossible, Almond contends, to achieve a one-to-one
relationship in which each structure is narrowly responsible for one and
only one function, the growing specialization of structures is perhaps the
clearest sign that a process of modernization is under way. Undeveloped
political systems assign many very different functions to a single personality or institution. A tribal chief, for example, may simultaneously
fulfill the roles of leading political officer, chief of staff, high priest, main

judge, foremost educator, and leading procreator. Modern political systems will, of course, replicate these functions, but they will be discharged by a small (perhaps not so small) army of officials and institutions. It is this interplay between the fluid and dynamic functions a system must discharge and the more fixed and static structures that it designs for itself that is perhaps the most characteristic attribute of functionalist political literature.

What, then, are the functions that are common to all political systems? Almond enumerates seven: political socialization, interest articulation, interest aggregation, political communication, rule making, rule application and rule adjudication. The first four belong to the input side of the system's functioning, the last three to its policy outputs. Political communication, last of the input functions, also serves to link inputs to outputs in a manner that is functionally equivalent to the "feedback loop."

Almond's essay explores these categories thoroughly, so there is little point in repeating his analysis. What should be remarked, nevertheless, is the significantly richer and more substantial nature of Almond's categorization when compared with the rather meager and unenlightening "demands and supports" that Easton's systems analysis offers. Indeed, many of Almond's categories have become fields of research in themselves. (Political socialization is a good example.) Furthermore, Almond does not gloss over the transformation of inputs into outputs by merely referring to a nondescript "conversion process." Here, too, the flesh and blood of politics—its physiology as well as its anatomy, as Almond notes—are more clearly represented. Indeed, scores of studies on many different aspects of politics have been inspired by and designed according to Almond's categories. This is the sincerest form of compliment that academe can pay.

Functionalism is subject to many of the same criticisms that are leveled at systems analysis. First, despite what has just been said, there are many who remain unhappy with what they see as the axiomatic, generic, and tautological character of the approach. In the end, it is not substantially more than a translation of familiar and known phenomena into blandly broad categories, a terminological rather than an essential transformation in the discipline. Although there is surely greater specificity and serviceability to Almond's functional taxonomy than is the case with systems analysis, it is often charged, nevertheless, that functional categories are too undifferentiated to be of real help in actual research. To be sure, structure-function analysis creates a useful research vocabulary and perhaps even an ambitious research program, but only to a far lesser extent does it create genuinely useful tools to deal with the recalcitrant complexities that political realities invariably present.

Second, it is often alleged that enumerating the functional requisites of political systems creates a trap into which functionalists regularly fall.

A deductive list of necessary functions is created, and then, predictably, the appropriate structures fulfilling these requirements are found. That empirical contortions are performed in order to satisfy the preexisting conceptual scheme is perhaps not a surprising eventuality. Yet, in all fairness, it should be cautioned that this type of critique is common to many academic exercises and is not specific to functionalism. In the end, the responsibility for abusing functionalist categories lies, at least in this regard, with the individual researcher rather than with the approach itself.

Third, and certainly the most oft-repeated attack on functionalism, is that it harbors an ideological slant. This charge comes in two overlapping forms. First, it is argued that functionalism (like systems analysis, only more so) has an ideological proclivity for adaptive, moderate, liberal politics. Second, it is said, at least as often, that functionalism tends to underwrite a politics of conservatism, stability, and the **status quo**. Since it is axiomatically assumed that political systems discharge their requisite functions in order to lessen system stress and to maintain system equilibrium, their adaptive, compromising, integrative, incrementalist character appears to be manifest. How far is functionalism, its critics ask censuringly, from identifying the dysfunctional with the undesirable? How far from saying that—like health for an organism—the functional is the good? How easy it is to slide imperceptibly from the statement that an existing structure performs a system-sustaining function, to the conclusion that it is functional, that is, beneficial? In other words, is there not here a subtle and implicit assimilation of what exists to what ought to be?

Critics saw in many of the functionalist postulates a translation of Anglo-American political norms in methodological terminology, an illicit smuggling of the liberal pluralist ideal into a research program. There was, no doubt, much to this allegation in regard to certain functionalists who wrote as if every (or virtually every) pattern of action served the functioning of the whole system. Similarly, it certainly held for those who used seemingly neutral language to advocate very definite political norms of thought and action.

For the sake of balance, however, it must be added that there were those in the functionalist camp (Robert Merton is probably best known among them) who rejected both these tendencies quite strenuously. Nor can we forget that despite the hefty sack of complaints that has accumulated against structure-functionalism, much of what was best in the political research of an entire generation was often couched in its terms. Even those who would abandon it for other and fresher pastures often find themselves inadvertently speaking in its characteristic terminology. Although it appears, at present, to be in a process of steady decline, it is fair to speak of structure-functionalism as the "war horse" of a generation of political scientists.

NOTE

1. See A. R. Radcliffe-Brown, "On the Concept of Function in Social Science," *American Anthropologist*, 37 (1935), p. 394.

SUGGESTIONS FOR FURTHER READING

Coser, L. A., *The Functions of Social Conflict* (New York, Free Press, 1956).

Coser, L. A., and Rosenberg, B., eds., *Sociological Theory*, 4th ed. (New York, Macmillan, 1976), pp. 490–533.

Jones, R. E., *The Functional Analysis of Politics: An Introductory Discussion* (London, Routledge and Kegan Paul, 1967).

Merton, R. K., *Social Theory and Social Structure*, enlarged ed. (New York, Free Press, 1968).

Turner, J. H., and Maryanski, A., *Functionalism* (Menlo Park, Calif., Benjamin Cummings, 1979).

Gabriel A. Almond

A Functional Approach
to Comparative Politics

This book is the first book to compare the political systems 1
of the "developing" areas, and to compare them systematically
according to a common set of categories. To accomplish this it
has been necessary to experiment with the conceptual vocabulary of political science. The old rubrics served us fairly well
during the long era of political dominance of the Western European culture area. As long as scholars carried in the backs
of their minds the history and anthropology of the area, the
gross changes in the functional characteristics of governmental institutions which occurred in the nineteenth and twentieth
centuries placed no great strain on the existing vocabulary.
They corrected as they went along, adding empirical functions and questioning normative ones, making comparisons
from one country to the next and offering causal explanations
based upon inferences from historical experience and social
structural and cultural differences.

But despite this apparent good health of the discipline of 2
comparative government in its special area of competence, the
conceptual scheme of political science steadily lost its capacity to grapple even with the phenomena of Western European
politics in the course of the last fifty years. The concepts of
separation of powers and of representation had arisen at a
time of a relatively narrow suffrage, when public office was
the monopoly of aristocratic or middle-class notables, when
party and interest groups were informal and relatively limited phenomena, and when the "public" was limited to men
of substance and culture. Since that time suffrage has become
universal, political recruitment has lost its class character, political parties have developed formal and mass organization,
associational interest groups have emerged, universal education and the media of mass communication have developed.
These enormous changes in the political cultures and political
structures of the West have not been accompanied by thoughtful conceptual adaptations. Until recent experiments began,
we were endeavoring to handle the complexity of the political
phenomena of the modern world with a legal and institutional
vocabulary.

Introduction from Gabriel A. Almond and James S. Coleman, eds. *The Politics of the Developing Areas*, (Princeton, N.J.: Princeton University Press, 1960), pp. 3–64. Reprinted by permission.

3   To find concepts and categories appropriate for the comparison of political systems differing radically in scale, structure, and culture—to say nothing of dealing adequately with the familiar phenomena of Western Europe—we have had to turn to sociological and anthropological theory. Some of the concepts we use in this book, such as *political system, political role, political culture, political structure,* and *political socialization,* have acquired a certain currency among scholars in the field. Perhaps their utility may be said to have been tested. The additional categories which we introduce here have had only a preliminary trial in the area analyses of this present group of collaborators.

4   It ought also to be pointed out that the search for new concepts reflected in these terms is not an *ad hoc* matter. It reflects an underlying drift toward a new and coherent way of thinking about and studying politics that is implied in such slogans as the "behavioral approach." This urge toward a new conceptual unity is suggested when we compare the new terms with the old. Thus, instead of the concept of the "state," limited as it is by legal and institutional meanings, we prefer "political system"; instead of "powers," which again is a legal concept in connotation, we are beginning to prefer "functions"; instead of "offices" (legal again), we prefer "roles"; instead of "institutions," which again directs us toward formal norms, "structures"; instead of "public opinion" and "citizenship training," formal and rational in meaning, we prefer "political culture" and "political socialization." We are not setting aside public law and philosophy as disciplines, but simply telling them to move over to make room for a growth in political theory that has been long overdue.

5   If we pause for a moment and consider the interconnection among these terms, how they all rest on an "action" or a "behavioral" base, how one suggests another, and how open they are to the other components of the social process, it becomes evident that we are not simply adding terms to an old vocabulary, but rather are in the process of developing or adapting a new one. And, to put all of our cards on the table, this is not only a matter of a conceptual vocabulary; it is an intimation of a major step forward in the nature of political science as science. The joyous barks of the few formal logicians who have emerged in political science may still be worse than their bites, but there can be no doubt that we are moving slowly forward toward a probabilistic theory of politics. The concepts used here contribute to this ultimate goal, as we shall attempt to show at the conclusion of this chapter.

I. The Political System

If the concept of political system is to serve the purpose to 6
which we wish to put it—that is, separate out analytically the
structures which perform political functions in all societies
regardless of scale, degree of differentiation, and culture—we
shall have to specify what we mean by politics and the political system. Without such a sharp definition we will be unable to compare the differentiated modern political systems
with the relatively undifferentiated primitive ones, the secular
modern systems with the traditional and theocratic ones. The
definitions of politics which identify it with such general societal functions as "integration" and "adaptation" fail us from
this point of view. It is of course true that political systems
typically perform the functions of maintaining the integration
of a society, adapting and changing elements of the kinship,
religious, and economic systems, protecting the integrity of
political systems from outside threats, or expanding into and
attacking other societies. But to identify politics with social
integration and adaptation is a regressive step, scientifically
speaking. It represents a return to a dull tool, rather than an
advance to a sharper one, for if in pursuit of the political system we follow the phantoms of integration and adaptation, we
will find ourselves including in the political system churches,
economies, schools, kinship and lineage groups, age-sets, and
the like.

If we consult the current literature for adequate definitions 7
of politics and the political, we find considerable variety and
some help. Weber's celebrated definition is of the "state," rather
than of the political system in our sense of the term: "Today,
however, we have to say that a state is a human community
that (successfully) claims the monopoly of the legitimate use
of physical force within a given territory. Note that 'territory'
is one of the characteristics of the state. Specifically, at the
present time, the right to use physical force is ascribed to other
institutions or to individuals only to the extent to which the
state permits it."[1] Schapera's point that the Weber definition
would rule out as political systems small, undifferentiated societies in which there is no *monopoly* of the legitimate use
of physical force is well taken. On the other hand, Schapera
himself simply sets aside Weber's definition of the state, and
does not offer an alternative definition, even though he insists
that the Bergdama and Bushmen, for example, have political organization.[2] He throws away one tool but does not offer
another. Levy's definition is not confined to the state: "Political

allocation for the purposes of this study has been defined above
as the distribution of power over and responsibility for the actions of the various members of the concrete structure concerned, involving on the one hand coercive sanctions, of which
force is the extreme form in one direction, and, on the other,
accountability to the members and in terms of the structure
concerned, or to the members of other concrete structures."[3]
But what these coercive and other sanctions are is left in doubt,
as are the structures which perform these sanctions. Hence, the
definition points indecisively in all directions in the society and
does not enable us to pick out a specific system which we can
relate to other systems and properties of a given society, or
compare with the political systems of other societies.

8   Definitions of the sociologically inclined political scientists
are suggestive, but still leave something to be desired for comparative purposes. Lasswell and Kaplan define political power
in these terms: "Power is a special case of the exercise of influence: It is the process of affecting policies of others with
the help of (actual or threatened) severe deprivations for nonconformity with the policies intended."[4] Here again, "severe
deprivations" does not distinguish the political system from
other social systems. David Easton[5] offers a definition with
three components: (1) The political system allocates values (by
means of policies); (2) its allocations are authoritative; and (3)
its authoritative allocations are binding on the society as a
whole. Elaborating on the meaning of "authoritative," Easton
points out: "...a policy is clearly authoritative when the feeling prevails that it must or ought to be obeyed...that policies,
whether formal or effective, are accepted as binding."[6] The
difficulty with this definition, as with others, is that "author-
itativeness" as defined by Easton does not differentiate political systems from churches, business firms, and the like. But
his combination of comprehensiveness of application plus "au-
thoritativeness" comes close to the kind of tool we need in the
work of comparing political systems of differing scales and degrees of differentiation. We may sharpen Easton's definition by
turning his conception of authority into "legitimate physical
compulsion"—in other words, building back into the definition the explicitness of Max Weber's formulation—at the same
time that we broaden the Weber definition in order to be able
to include types of political organization other than the state.
Certainly the comparative politics of modern times must be in
a position to handle primitive and traditional systems which
are political but are not states in the sense of Weber's definition, as well as transitional and revolutionary systems in

which there may be no "monopoly of the legitimate use of physical force within a given territory." What we propose is that the political system is that system of interactions to be found in all independent societies which performs the functions of integration and adaptation (both internally and vis-à-vis other societies) by means of the employment, or threat of employment, of more or less legitimate physical compulsion. The political system is the legitimate, order-maintaining or transforming system in the society. We use the term "more or less" to modify legitimacy because we do not want to exclude from our definition political systems, like the totalitarian ones, where the degree of legitimacy may be very much in doubt; revolutionary systems, where the basis of legitimacy may be in process of change; or non-Western systems, in which there may be more than one legitimate system in operation. We use the term "physical compulsion" since we believe that we can distinguish political systems from other social systems only by such a specific definition, but this is by no means the same thing as reducing politics to force. Legitimate force is the thread that runs through the inputs and outputs of the political system, giving it its special quality and salience and its coherence as a system. The inputs into the political system are all in some way related to claims for the employment of legitimate compulsion, whether these are demands for war or for recreational facilities. The outputs of the political system are also all in some way related to legitimate physical compulsion, however remote the relationship may be. Thus, public recreational facilities are usually supported by taxation, and any violation of the regulations governing their use is a legal offense.

With the conceptions of input and output we have moved 9 from the definition of "political" to that of "system," for if by the "political" we mean to separate out a certain set of interactions in a society in order to relate it to other sets, by "system" we mean to attribute a particular set of properties to these interactions. Among these properties are (1) comprehensiveness, (2) interdependence, and (3) existence of boundaries. The criterion of comprehensiveness means that when we speak of the political system we include all the interactions—inputs as well as outputs—which affect the use or the threat of use of physical coercion. We mean to include not just the structures based on law, like parliaments, executives, bureaucracies, and courts, or just the associational or formally organized units, like parties, interest groups, and media of communication, but *all of the structures in their political aspects,* including undifferentiated structures like kinship and lineage, status and caste groups, as well as anomic phenomena like riots, street demonstrations, and the like.

10   By "interdependence" we mean that a change in one subset of interactions (e.g., the electoral reforms of 1832 in England) produces changes in all the other subsets (e.g., the characteristics of the party system, the functions of parliament and cabinet, and so forth). Or, to borrow from an earlier comment on the interdependence of the political system: " ... the emergence of pressure groups in the present century produced certain changes in the party system and in the administrative and legislative processes. The rapid expansion of executive bureaucracy was one of the factors that triggered off the development of legislative bureaucracy and pressure group bureaucracy. Changes in the technology of communication have transformed the electoral process, the characteristics of political parties, the legislature, the executive. The concepts of system and of interdependence lead us to look for these changes when any specific role changes significantly. It suggests the usefulness of thinking at the level of the system and its interdependence rather than in terms of discrete phenomena, or limited bilateral relationships occurring only within the formal-legal role structure."[7]

11   By the existence of a boundary in the political system, we mean that there are points where other systems end and the political system begins. We may illustrate this point in the following way. The murmurs and complaints in the bazaar in Baghdad are not in the political system until they break out, for example, in an act of violence—an anomic act of interest articulation—or when Haroun-el-Rashid, disguised as a water bearer, overhears the murmurs and translates them into political claims. As the diffuse and inarticulate murmur is translated into a claim on the use of "public authority," it passes the boundary and enters the political system as an act of "interest articulation."

12   In a more modern setting the police agent or informant in the Soviet Union observes a decline in labor productivity in a particular plant. He may overhear conversations and read cues in faces that lead him to infer that the decline is due to a special shortage of consumer goods. The conversations themselves and the cues from which motive was inferred are not in the political system. They pass the boundary into the political system when the agent translates them in his report to higher authorities into claims for public policy or bureaucratic action.

While we can say that the religious organization and the so- 13
cial stratification of a society influence the political system, we
would not say that they are part of it. Only when a religious
group makes claims upon the political system through religious authorities, or through specialized structures such as religious interest groups, religious political parties, or a religious
press, do the intermittent political actions of the clergy, or the
regular action of the specialized religio-political structures, become part of the political system. What kinds of structures man
the boundaries of the political system is of the utmost importance in the functioning of the political system. These structures process the inputs, establish and maintain the contact
between the polity and the society.

The boundaries between the society and polity differ from 14
political system to political system. In a primitive society the
shift from economy to church to polity may in one case be
hardly perceptible. It may involve only a change of insignia
or location of the action. But even in the "omnifunctional"
primitive band some signaling occurs. On the other hand, the
boundaries between the political and other social systems of
primitive societies may be most sharply marked, as in war
dances, sacrificial rites, and dramatic changes of costume.
When we talk about good and bad boundary maintenance,
we must use criteria appropriate to the system. In one case
diffuseness and intermittency may be appropriate boundary
maintenance; in another specialized secular structures are appropriate. We shall return to this concept of boundary maintenance when we deal with the functions of the political system
in detail.

II. The Common Properties of Political Systems

The Universe of Political Systems. We suggested above that 15
the discipline of political science until recent years has been
working in a limited sector of man's experience with politics—
the modern, complex, primarily Western states. Thus out of the
many thousands of experiments with politics which have occurred in history and exist today, political science derives its
generalizations from the study of a relatively small number.
Furthermore, the political scientist is not aware—nor can he
be—of how special and peculiar are the political forms and
processes which he does study, since he is not aware of the
composition of the total universe, of the range of complexity,
and the kinds and frequencies of patterns to be found in it.

The capacity to identify the peculiar properties of a particular species of politics, and the conditions with which it is associated, is dependent upon the variety of contrasting species with which one can compare it.

16   Even in the absence of this compelling scientific justification for broadening the scope of comparative politics, practical policy motives have forced the modern political scientist to concern himself with the whole range of political systems which exist in the modern world—from African kingdoms and tribal organizations to traditional oligarchies such as Saudi Arabia, and transitional, modernizing systems such as Burma and India.

17   An extraordinary enrichment of the discipline of political science is bound to result from the inclusion of these non-Western systems. For while the interdependences of the different components of the political system and of the political system with other social systems may elude us when we focus on the modern, specialized political systems of the West, they are inescapable when we examine them in the context of the less fully differentiated non-Western systems.

18   An illustration or two may make this point clear. Political scientists know in a general way that political control in a society is just one of a number of social control systems, such as religion, the family, the economic organization, and the like. What he is less likely to be aware of is the fact that the form and content of the political system in a society will vary with the form and content of the religious, family, and other systems in a society. Thus a society in which threats to social order are handled largely through a witchcraft system may have a less differentiated political system than one which does not. The essential point here is that crucial interrelations which we may miss when we examine the fully differentiated, more or less autonomous political systems in the West stand out more clearly in primitive and non-Western contexts.

19   If we are to extend the boundaries of the universe of comparative politics and include in it the "uncouth" and exotic systems of the areas outside Western Europe, it will be useful to specify the properties which all the individuals in this universe have in common. We shall have to break through the barriers of culture and language and show that what may seem strange at first sight is strange by virtue of its costume or its name, but not by virtue of its function. What are the common properties of all political systems? What makes the Bergdama band and the United Kingdom members of the same universe? We would suggest that there are four characteristics which all

political systems have in common, and in terms of which they may be compared.

1. First, all political systems, including the simplest ones, have political structure. In a sense it is correct to say that even the simplest societies have all of the types of political structure which are to be found in the most complex ones. They may be compared with one another according to the degree and form of structural specialization.

2. Second, the same functions are performed in all political systems, even though these functions may be performed with different frequencies, and by different kinds of structures. Comparisons may be made according to the frequency of the performance of the functions, the kinds of structures performing them, and the style of their performance.

3. Third, all political structure, no matter how specialized, whether it is found in primitive or in modern societies, is multifunctional. Political systems may be compared according to the degree of specificity of function in the structure; but the limiting case, while specialized, still involves substantial multifunctionality.

4. Fourth, all political systems are "mixed" systems in the cultural sense. There are no "all-modern" cultures and structures, in the sense of rationality, and no all-primitive ones, in the sense of traditionality. They differ in the relative dominance of the one as against the other, and in the pattern of mixture of the two components.

The Universality of Political Structure.   There is no such thing 20 as a society which maintains internal and external order, which has no "political structure"—i.e., legitimate patterns of interaction by means of which this order is maintained. Furthermore, all the types of political structures which are to be found in the modern systems are to be found in the non-Western and primitive ones. The interactions, or the structures, may be occasional or intermittent. They may not be clearly visible, but to say that there are no structures would be to argue that the performance of the political function is random. What may be involved are intermittent actions of the oldest male of a band in response to situations, or an informally formulated consensus by the group dealing with some serious threat to internal order, or some problem of external relations. The articulative, aggregative, communicative, rule-making, and rule-application functions may spill over into one another without formal partitions between them, as a part of a single continuous action. But this is not a case of no political structures, but of a special kind of political structure. In other words, we are arguing that the classic distinction between primitive societies which are states and those which are not should be reformulated as a distinction between those in which the political structure is quite differentiated and clearly visible and those in which it is less visible and intermittent. We are dealing with a continuum and not a dichotomous distinction.

21   This rejection of the "state and non-state" classification, which is found throughout the anthropological, sociological, and political science literature is not simply a verbal quibble. It is a matter of theoretical and operational importance. Such a dichotomous classification could come only from an approach to politics which identifies the political with the existence of a specialized, visible structure, and which tends to restrict the political process to those functions performed by the specialized structure. With this approach an analysis of the politics of a non-Western or primitive society may begin and end with a description of the properties and functions of a specific chieftainship or kingship which in the visible sense may perform only the functions of legislation and administration. The articulative, aggregative, and communicative functions may be performed diffusely within the society, or intermittently through the kinship or lineage structure. An adequate analysis of a political system must locate and characterize all of these functions, and not simply those performed by the specialized political structure. Indeed, it is this emphasis on the specialized structures of politics which has led to the stereotyped conception of traditional and primitive systems as static systems, since the political structures most likely to be differentiated are executive-legislative and adjudicative structures. The mechanics of political choice are there as well, but in the form of *intermittent* political structures. The rule to follow which we suggest here is: If the functions are there, then the structures must be, even though we may find them tucked away, so to speak, in nooks and crannies of other social systems.

22   *The Universality of the Political Functions.* But if all the structures which are to be found in specialized Western systems are also to be found in the non-Western, we are able to locate them only if we ask the correct functional questions. It is true that political systems may be compared with one another structurally, all the way from the intermittent political system of a primitive band like the Bergdama of Schapera and the Eskimo of Hoebel to the modern Western state system. But structural comparison is of only limited utility. It is

like a comparative anatomy without a comparative physiology. It is like comparing an amoeba and a mammal strictly in structural terms—saying that this one is multicellular and that one is unicellular; this one has specialized organs and that one does not have them. We have not compared them as functioning, living organisms. To do this, we have to ask functional questions—e.g., how is the motility function performed? how is the sensory-nervous function performed? how is the digestive function performed? how is the reproductive function performed?

In other words, in comparing political systems with one an- 23 other, we have made only a beginning when we describe the specialized structures. Furthermore, we may be misled if we follow structural lines in our comparative efforts. Suppose we take interest groups as an example, and attempt a comparison of American interest groups with those of Indonesia. We might say that the United States has many formally organized, large-membership interest associations. Indonesia has relatively few; they are poorly organized, inadequately financed, have highly fluctuating memberships, and so forth.

Suppose we put the problem the other way around, and 24 ask a functional rather than a structural question. Suppose we ask in regard to both countries: how are interests articulated? what structures are involved? how do they articulate interests? These questions open our minds to the whole range of interest phenomena in a society. We are not structure-bound. Thus we find in Indonesia that the few and relatively poorly organized trade unions or business associations are not the important interest-articulating structures, that we have to look at the bureaucracy, status groups, kinship and lineage groups, and anomic phenomena to discover how interests are articulated. Only when we ask this functional question are we led to an accurate representation of a dynamic process.

If we then look to the theory of political science for help in 25 formulating these functional questions, we find ourselves gazing into a stagnant pool. Nothing much has happened to the functional theory of politics since the doctrine of separation of powers and the lively discussion of it in the great era of constitution-making in the United States. Between the Federalist Papers and Frank J. Goodnow's *Politics and Administration,* published in 1900, no formal theoretical attack on the functional theory of politics was undertaken. In the Federalist Papers only the authoritative governmental, or output, functions are treated. The political, or input, functions are treated generally as a representation or election function with little indication of the problems which have to be solved in the po-

litical process. The Federalist theory of authoritative governmental functions emphasized the inherent inequality of governmental functions and stressed the necessity for mingling
powers among the structures if they were to be kept separate
and autonomous.

26   Goodnow's critique of the separation-of-powers theory[8] rejects the possibility of locating any single function in a single structure. It is a positivist critique of the legal conception
of division of powers among the authoritative governmental
structures. Goodnow argues that there are two functions of
government, politics and administration. The function of politics, which is concerned with constitution-making, legislation,
the selection of governmental officers, and the control over administration, is performed by a variety of structures, including
parties, parliaments, bureaucracies, and courts. "It is impossible to assign each of these functions to a separate authority,
not merely because the exercise of governmental power cannot
be clearly apportioned, but also because as political systems
develop, these two primary functions of government tend to be
differentiated into minor and secondary functions."[9]

27   These systematic and creative leads of Goodnow were not
followed up in later work. Functional theory in political science followed an unsystematic course. Students of political
parties developed theories of the party which rejected normative notions and stressed empirical, implicitly probabilistic
ones. Students of the courts and of constitutional law stressed
the legislative as well as the adjudicative powers of the courts.
Students of bureaucracy stressed the legislative and judicial
functions of administration. Students of parliaments and legislatures stressed the decline of the legislative function of these
bodies.

28   But no one in political science, prior to very recent and very
provisional efforts, confronted the problem of political function and structure in a direct and systematic way. Two interesting recent efforts are David Easton's "An Approach to the
Analysis of Political Systems"[10] and Harold D. Lasswell's *The
Decision Process.*[11] Easton elaborates his conception of the political system by distinguishing "inputs," which he divides into
"demands" and "supports," and "outputs," which are authoritative decisions or policies. The conceptual simplicity of Easton's model, with its three functions—demands, supports, and
policies—will not carry us very far in our efforts at political
comparison. It is still too close to the generic model of a system, with its interdependence, its boundaries, and its inputs
and outputs, to be particularly discriminating in the politi-

cal field. But certainly Easton's work is moving in the general direction of systematic functional theory.

While Easton's functional approach is derived from general systems theory, Lasswell's approach arose out of empirical efforts at comparing judicial processes, and out of dissatisfaction with separation-of-powers "functional" theory for these purposes. The specific categories of functional analysis which Lasswell developed were tested in "...studies of comparative political science and jurisprudence."[12] Lasswell makes no claims for the definitiveness of his seven categories: "Classifications are serviceable when they are tentative and undogmatic, and when they guide scholarly activity in directions that are presently accepted as valuable."[13] He also makes the point made by Goodnow as to the multifunctionality of all political structure, a point which we will develop in some systematic detail below. 29

Lasswell's seven categories of functional analysis are as follows: 30

1. Intelligence—Information, prediction, planning
2. Recommendation—Promoting policy alternatives
3. Prescription—The enactment of general rules
4. Invocation—Provisional characterizations of conduct according to prescriptions
5. Application—The final characterization of conduct according to prescriptions
6. Appraisal—The assessment of the success or failure of the policy
7. Termination—The ending of prescriptions, and of arrangements entered into within their framework.[14]

It is quite clear from an examination of these categories that they were designed primarily for governmental and particularly judicial comparison. Thus the political or, in Easton's terms, the input functions are handled in two rather formal categories, "intelligence" and "recommendation"—gentle concepts which hardly do justice to the vigor of politics. Nevertheless, this is to be expected. If functional categories are to be instrumental to research, they must be adapted to the particular kind of comparison which is contemplated. Research on the foreign–policy-making process in the United States also illustrates the difficulties which arise in trying to develop a set of categories of functional analysis which may be used for all kinds of comparisons. In a series of studies[15] which were intended to describe the functions performed by the Execu- 31 tive, the Congress, pressure groups, and the press in the making of foreign policy, some eight more or less distinctive activities or functions developed from the coding of interview responses. These were initiation, authorization, modification, vetoing, representation, communication, advocacy, and interpretation. Initiation, communication, and advocacy were the main foreign-policy-making functions attributed to the Executive. Initiation, authorization, modification, vetoing, and representation were the main functions attributed to the Congress. Representation, communication, advocacy, and interpretation were attributed to pressure groups; and communication, advocacy, and interpretation to the press.

32   These examples make clear that the functional categories which one employs have to be adapted to the particular aspect of the political system with which one is concerned. This is not to reject the possibility that in time some consensus may develop as to appropriate categories for functional comparison. But we are certainly far from such a mature theoretical position today. The particular functional categories which we employ in this book were developed for the purpose of comparing political systems as whole systems; and particularly for comparing the modern Western ones with the transitional and traditional.

33   They were derived in a very simple way. The problem essentially was to ask a series of questions based on the distinctive political activities existing in Western complex systems. In other words, we derived our functional categories from the political systems in which structural specialization and functional differentiation have taken place to the greatest extent. Thus the functions performed by associational interest groups in Western systems led us to the question, "How are interests articulated in different political systems?" or the *interest articulation* function. The functions performed by political parties in Western political systems led us to the question, "How are articulated demands or interests aggregated or combined in different political systems?" or the *aggregative function*. The functions performed by specialized media of communication of Western political systems led us to the question, "How is political information communicated in different political systems?" or the *political communication function*. The existence in all political systems of methods of political recruitment and training led us to the question, "How are people recruited to and socialized into political roles and orientations in different political systems?" or the *recruitment* and *socialization function*. Finally, the three authoritative governmental functions, *rule-making, rule application,* and *rule adjudication,* are the old

functions of "separation of powers," except that an effort has been made to free them of their structural overtones—rule-making rather than "legislation," rule application rather than "administration." Indeed, this taking over intact of the three functions of "separation of powers" reflects the political bias of this undertaking. It was the conviction of the collaborators in this study that the political functions rather than the governmental ones, the input functions rather than the output, would be most important in characterizing non-Western political systems, and in discriminating types and stages of political development among them.

Our functional categories therefore are as follows: 34

A. Input functions
  1. Political socialization and recruitment
  2. Interest articulation
  3. Interest aggregation
  4. Political communication
B. Output functions
  5. Rule-making
  6. Rule application
  7. Rule adjudication

The Multifunctionality of Political Structure.   The differences 35 between Western and non-Western political systems have generally been exaggerated. This is in part due to the fact that the "limiting case" models of the Western system, on the one hand, and of the traditional and primitive systems, on the other, have been greatly overdrawn. The model of the Western system has overstressed the functional specificity of political structure, while that of the traditional system has overstressed the undifferentiated and diffuse character of political and social structure. If we examine the literature of political science in the past forty or fifty years, we find that one of its great accomplishments has been the demonstration of the multifunctionalism of modern political institutions. Thus it has shown that the courts not only adjudicate but also legislate; that the bureaucracy is one of the most important sources of legislation; that legislative bodies affect both administration and adjudication; that pressure groups initiate legislation and participate in administration; and that the media of communication represent interests and sometimes initiate legislation. In the American system this multifunctionalism is partly intended (legally based), as in the "checks and balances" doctrine of the framers of the American Constitution, and partly an inescapable consequence of the nature of the political system. It is impossible to have political structures in relation to one another in a common process without multifunctionalism. What we mean when we speak of modern systems as being specialized is that certain structures emerge which have a functional distinctiveness, and which tend to perform what we may call a regulatory role in relation to that function within the political system as a whole. Thus the development of a modern party system means that the performances of the political recruitment function by other structures, such as interest groups and the media of communication, tend to pass through and be processed by the party system before they emerge as acts of political recruitment. The development of specialized associational interest groups means that there is a tendency for the articulations of interest which are performed by such structures as legislatures, bureaucracies, informal status and lineage groupings, and institutions such as churches and corporations to pass through and be processed by the associational interest groups before they emerge as acts of interest articulation. Although acts of interest aggregation on the part of political parties, interest groups, media of communication, and the bureaucracy may take the form of legislative projects which are enacted unchanged by legislatures or parliaments, they must pass through the legislative body before they become acts of "rule-making."

36   The development of these specialized regulating structures creates the modern democratic political system and the peculiar pattern of boundary maintenance which characterizes the internal relations between the subsystems of the polity and the relations between the polity and the society. But this is by no means the same thing as saying that the relation between structure and function in the modern system is of a one-to-one order. What is peculiar to modern political system is a relatively high degree of structural differentiation (i.e., the emergence of legislatures, political executives, bureaucracies, courts, electoral systems, parties, interest groups, media of communication), with each structure tending to perform a regulatory role for that function within the political system as a whole.

37   At the other extreme, our impression of primitive and traditional systems have exaggerated their compactness and lack of differentiation. Even the simplest ones contain political systems. It is no more correct to think of the primitive band as a kinship group, a religious system, or an economy than it is to think of it as a polity. Indeed, it is all of these things and no more one than any of the others. At the extreme limit of sim-

plicity, societies tend to be "omnifunctional structures" which are intermittently family, economy, church, and political system. While it is true that primitive, traditional, and transitional systems have more intermittent political structures, the modern ones have them, too. A few examples illustrating the relation between intermittency and level of differentiation and specialization of political structure may be in point.

In the Eskimo community it would appear that, with the pos- 38 sible exception of the headman, all the political structures are intermittent.[16] At a higher level of differentiation, executive, legislative, and adjudicative structures may have developed in specialized form, but the political functions of communication, interest articulation, and aggregation may be intermittently performed by lineage, status, religious, and similar groupings. At an even higher level of differentiation and specialization, as for example in "modernizing" or transitional systems, we may find differentiated governmental and political structures operating along with traditional and intermittent ones. The traditional and intermittent structures are not regulated by the modern ones, but continue to operate inside and outside the bureaucracy, parliament, parties, interest groups, and media of communication. The traditional and intermittent structures are not penetrated by or fused to the modern ones. They continue to function autonomously and legitimately. Unlike the modern system, their performance of political functions is not regulated by the differentiated and specialized structures. The modern political system does not eliminate intermittency and traditionality; it tends to regulate and control it. Diffuse and primary structures perform governmental and political functions within the modern structures. Other social systems and structures in the society—such as the family, the church, the educational system, the economy—are parts of the political system as intermittent political socializers, recruiters, interest articulators, and communicators. No political system, however modern, ever fully eliminates intermittency and traditionality. It can penetrate it, regulate it, translate its particularistic and diffuse impacts into the modern political language of interest articulation, public policy, and regulation.

The Culturally Mixed Character of Political Systems. The final 39 point in our argument as to the homogeneity of the universe of political systems is that certain kinds of political structure which we have usually considered to be peculiar to the primitive are also to be found in modern political systems, and not as marginal institutions, but having a high functional im-

portance. Perhaps the best way to develop this argument is
to refer to a recent body of research which is illustrative—the
discovery in *The People's Choice* and subsequent studies[17] of
the great importance of informal opinion leadership and face-
to-face communication in the processes of individual decision-
making. What is most interesting is the point made by Elihu
Katz about the research design of the first of these studies,
The People's Choice: "...the design of the study did not anticipate the importance which interpersonal relations would
assume in the analysis of the data. Given the image of the
atomized audience which characterized so much of mass media research, the surprising thing is that interpersonal influence attracted the attention of the researchers at all."[18] In
other words, the emergence of the specifically modern media
of mass communication had so captured the imagination of
scholars that they had developed a model of the communications process which counterposed a society or an electorate
consisting of atomized individuals to a system of mass media
which were assumed to monopolize the communication process. It is a tribute to the faithful empiricism of this research
undertaking that their findings did not confirm this model, but
uncovered a face-to-face communication and interest articulation system below the mass media of communication and the
interest group system—a "particularistic," "diffuse," and "ascriptive" system very much like that described in studies of the
politics of primitive societies. The typical opinion leader was
found to be a trusted individual whose political influence was
often a diffuse consequence of other roles.

40   Subsequent studies have suggested hypotheses as to how
these two systems of communication and influence are interrelated, and how they affect one another. The "two-step flow of
communication" hypothesis is one of these. In Katz's words:
"...it is the opinion leader's function to bring the group into
touch with this relevant part of the environment through whatever media are appropriate. In every case, influentials have
been found to be more exposed to these points of contact with
the outside world. Nevertheless, it is also true that, despite
their greater exposure to the media, most opinion leaders are
primarily affected not by the communication media but by
still other people."[19] Given our present state of knowledge, we
can conclude tentatively that, in modern political systems, the
specialized structures of interest articulation (interest groups),
aggregation (political parties), and communication (the mass
media) exist in relation to persisting non-specialized structures
which are certainly modified by the existence of the special-

ized ones, but are by no means assimilated to them. In other words, the modern, mass, bureaucratically organized, political party has not supplanted the informal coteries of notables which preceded it, but combines with this "more primitive" type of structure in what amounts to a mixed system. Similarly, the distinctively modern associational interest groups have not supplanted informal groupings of a status or interest kind, but are combined with them in a mixed system, just as the mass media of communication combine with the primary communication system.

Studies of the importance of the primary group and informal organization in governmental and industrial bureaucracies are too well known for detailed comment here.[20] Though research on the informal organization of Western parliaments and legislative bodies is only in its beginnings, certainly here, too, one would expect to find an informal primary-group system combined with the legal normative structure. This combination of formal-legal structure and diffuse and particularistic primary structure is not too different from the situation which obtains in many non-Western parliaments where, within the formal framework of parliamentary norms, there exists a normative structure and decision system based on kinship and status groups. There are significant differences, without question, between Western and non-Western parliaments, but both of them contain informal, primary groups.

If this general proposition regarding the "cultural" dualism of political systems is correct—and the evidence suggests that it is—then it brings into question certain applications of Parsonian social theory to the study of political systems. Some of Talcott Parsons' theoretical work[21] has as its point of departure the central concepts of Max Weber—in particular, his types of social action.[22] The "pattern variables" of Parsons build in large part on Weber's four types of social action—the affectual, the traditional, the instrumentally rational, and the absolute-value rational. Indeed Parsons' "diffuseness-specificity," "ascription-achievement," and "universalism-particularism" variables are specifications of some of the elements of Weber's general concepts of "rationality" and "traditionality." In the sense that an accurate specification of the elements of general concepts is a step in the direction of precision, the elaboration of the "pattern variables" from Weber's "traditionality" and "rationality" represents an interesting and promising theoretical development. However, certain uses of these pattern variables in the construction of models of political systems create serious problems if the position advanced in this chapter as to the persistence of "primitive" or "pre-modern" political structure in modern systems is a correct one.

43   There have been two recent efforts at constructing conceptual models of political systems from Parsons' pattern variables, one by Francis X. Sutton,[23] and a later one by Fred W. Riggs,[24] which is specially concerned with comparative administration. Both Sutton and Riggs develop models of industrial and agricultural political systems in which three of Parsons' pattern variables are the more important discriminating concepts. The industrial type of political system is characterized by universalistic, achievement, and functionally specific norms and structures and the agricultural type of political system is characterized by particularistic, ascriptive, and functionally diffuse norms and structures. Put in other terms the industrial model is characterized by law, social mobility, and the differentiation of specialized structures, while the agricultural systems are characterized by custom, status, and the relative absence of specialization. Sutton suggests the usefulness of these two models of political systems in the following terms: "The major societies of the modern world show varying combinations of the patterns represented in the ideal types I have sketched out. Some stand close to the model of industrial society; others are in various transitional states which hopefully may be understood better by conceptions of where they have been and where they may be going."[25]

44   There can be little question of the usefulness of these theoretical efforts, but if the dualism hypothesis which we have advanced is correct, it would appear that the "pattern variable" concept has led to an unfortunate theoretical polarization. A model appropriate for the analysis of modern political systems would have to take into account the interrelations between the differentiated, specialized structures of parliaments, bureaucracies, courts, political parties, interest groups, and media of communication, and the "pre-modern" structures which persist as political structures of great importance. One would have to argue that the modern "industrian" system, to use Riggs' term, never exists by itself, but always has an "agrarian" system inside it.

45   This dualism of political structure is not only characteristic of modern Western political systems but of non-Western and primitive ones; i.e., there are both primary and secondary structures in primitive and traditional political systems and the secondary structures have modern (specific, universalistic, and achievement) features.

If both Western and traditional systems are dualistic in this 46
sense, in what respects do they differ? Verba suggests that there
are two main differences. First, in modern Western systems the
secondary structures and relationships are far more differentiated and significant; and, second, the primary structures in
modern systems tend to be affected by (modernized by) the
secondary ones.[26]

To illustrate we may refer again to our comparison of a Western 47
and a non-Western legislative body. Both have formal and informal structures. But in the Western parliament, the loyalty of the
parliamentarian to the formal parliamentary norms would be
greater in comparison to his loyalty to the norms of his primary
groups than would be the case in the non-Western parliament.
The secondary structure, in other words, would be more effective.
Second, and perhaps more important, the informal structure
of a non-Western parliament would be of a different kind than
that found in a Western one. In the non-Western parliament,
the informal structure may be based on extended aristocratic
family ties, on caste, on religious sect. In a very real sense these
groupings, rather than legislative committees or party factions,
may constitute the decision-making structure of the parliament.
In a Western parliament, the informal structure would tend to
be adapted to the formal structure, i.e., it would tend to be more
modern in its culture (more specific, universalistic, achievement-
oriented). The informal groups might take the form of interest
or regional blocs, informal leaders of party groups and their
followings, friendships based on common interest or residence,
and the like. Thus the dualism of the non-Western parliament
may really amount to a subversion of the formal by the informal;
the dualism of the Western, to a penetration and domestication
of the informal by the formal.

But while such a sweeping differentiation between Western 48
and non-Western dualism may be true in general, a simple pair
of models such as this may be quite misleading and tend to
exaggerate the differences between Western and non-Western
systems. It is quite clear that no political system is ever quite
modern or Western in the sense in which we have been using the
term, just as in the same sense no individual is ever fully "mature"
and emancipated from primary ties and diffuse dependences.
All political systems—the developed Western ones as well as the
less-developed non-Western ones—are transitional systems, or
systems in which cultural change is taking place.

We may distinguish among them according to the kind of 49
relationship which exists between the "modern" and the "tra-

ditional" components. Let us take as an example the British
political system. The relation between the diffuse, affective,
particularistic, and ascriptive elements of the British political
culture and the more universalistic, specific, instrumental elements tends to be one of *fusion.* In other words, all the way
from right to left among the British public, the modern and the
pre-modern attitudes are combined in such a way as to produce a homogeneous political culture, secular and traditional
in content. In addition, British political structures—interest
groups, political parties, parliament, cabinet, and monarchy
manifest the same fusional dualism. What is so interesting in
Robert McKenzie's recent book[27] on British political parties
is his demonstration of the fact that the British Labor Party,
antitraditional and rationalistic in ideology and formal organization though it may be, has actually tended to take on the same
pattern of traditional-rational fusion which is characteristic of
the Conservative Party.

50   In contrast, in a country such as France there is a polarization
of political culture, with some elements and regions manifesting
traditionality and others manifesting rationality. According to
our analysis, both subcultures of France are dualistic; but the
traditional "areas" would manifest the kind of dualism which
we attributed to non-Western societies above, while the other
components would manifest the modern form of dualism.

51   Thus the French political culture is not fusional in its acculturative characteristics. Traditionality and modernity are not
uniformly distributed, but are concentrated in different parts
of French society. The relationship between these components
has tended to be isolative. In some non-Western countries where
a modern culture has been introduced in the cities and large-
scale modernizing efforts have been introduced in the villages,
we may speak of an *incorporative* pattern—i.e., the modern and
pre-modern elements have not combined, or fused, and at the
same time they are not sharply antagonistic. The two systems
exist side by side; the acculturative process continues, and the
outcome may turn out to be fusional or isolative, depending on
events.[28]

52   What is useful in these concepts of multifunctionalism, cultural dualism, and political acculturation is that they set aside
once and for all the geographic, cultural, and analytical polarizations which have plagued our efforts at social and political
comparison. We have been talking of "modern" and "pre-
modern," "developed" and "underdeveloped," "industrial" and
"agrarian," "Western and non-Western"; or the Parsonian syndromes of universalism-specificity-achievement-affective neu-

trality, versus particularism-diffuseness-ascription-affectivity. The universe of political systems is less tractable to simple contrasts than we have supposed. We need dualistic models *rather than* monistic ones, and developmental *as well as* equilibrium models, if we are to understand differences precisely and grapple effectively with the processes of political change.

III. The Functions of the Political System

Political Socialization and Recruitment. In his recent book [53] on political socialization, Hyman comments on the relative imbalance of research in the field of political behavior, the emphasis on motivational and emotional factors, and the relative neglect of cognitive elements. He states: "men are urged to certain ends but the political scene in which they act is perceived and given meaning. Some cognitive map accompanies their movement towards their ends."[29] Hyman's own treatment of political socialization views it as a continuous learning process involving both emotional learning and manifest political indoctrination, and as being mediated by all of the participations and experiences of the individual and not simply by early family experiences.[30]

Actually Hyman is criticizing only one of the prevailing the-[54]ories of political socialization—the one which has stemmed from the psychoanalytic theory of personality and psychoanalytically oriented anthropology. This theory in turn was a reaction against the rational voluntarist theory of man and citizenship of the Enlightenment and liberalism, a theory which stressed political and social history and formal educational and propaganda practices in the development of the political attitudes and "civic spirit" of nations and peoples. Furthermore it is hardly accidental that psychiatrists, psychologists, and anthropologists should have developed a theory of political socialization which stressed unconscious or latent attitudes and the family as the primary mediators of the basic political "learning process." The libido theory and the unconscious were, after all, the great discoveries of psychoanalytic psychology. And the kinship group was clearly the central institution of primitive societies. A theory of political socialization stemming from specialists in unconscious psychological processes and primitive societies could hardly avoid being a "latent, primary group" theory, just as a theory of political socialization stemming from the study of intellectual and social history and political ideology could not avoid overstressing the manifest, rational, indoctrinative aspects of political socialization.

55   With Hyman, our own conception of political socialization
endeavors to combine these two intellectual tendencies. It is
a conception that recognizes both the latent and the manifest
components of the process of induction into citizenship roles
and orientations, and which examines the later as well as the
earlier and more primary "socializing" institutions and influences.

56   What do we mean by the function of political socialization?
We mean that all political systems tend to perpetuate their
cultures and structures through time, and that they do this
mainly by means of the socializing influences of the primary
and secondary structures through which the young of the society pass in the process of maturation. We use the qualifier
"mainly" deliberately, since political socialization, like learning in general, does not terminate at the point of maturation,
however this is defined in different societies. It is continuous
throughout life. A great war or a depression, an experience like
Italian Fascism or German Nazism, is an enormous learning
experience which is not mediated through any particular social institution. Nevertheless the early participations tend to
define the limits of later adult learning experiences. Thus it is
striking that, with all the learning that attended the collapse
of Nazism, so much of the earlier political culture of Germany
survives into the present.

57   In a sense the socialization experiences of childhood and
early adulthood—family, church, school, work group, voluntary associations—are pre-political citizenship experiences.
The individual is inducted into a sequence of decision-making
systems with particular authority and participation patterns,
and with particular kinds of claim or demand inputs and policy outputs. It need not follow that all of these pre-political
citizenship patterns are consistent with one another and with
the adult citizenship pattern which emerges. That they influence one another there can be no doubt.

58   A second qualification to our definition of political socialization is necessary. When we say that all political systems
tend to perpetuate their cultures and structures through time,
we do not intend to convey a static impression. Insofar as the
culture and structure are adapting and changing, the socialization patterns are likely also to be changing. But again this
is a matter of degree and involves differences in the rates of
change in the various subsystems of the society. One of the
most important factors making for resistance to social and political change is the conservatism of primary groups and the
early family socialization process.

Political socialization is the process of induction into the po- 59
litical culture. Its end product is a set of attitudes—cognitions,
value standards, and feelings—toward the political system, its
various roles, and role incumbents. It also includes knowledge
of, values affecting, and feelings toward the inputs of demands
and claims into the system, and its authoritative outputs.

In comparing the political socialization function in different 60
political systems, it becomes necessary to examine the structures which are involved in the function and the style of the
socialization. Thus, in a modern Western political system such
as the United States, family, church, peer group, community,
school, work group, voluntary associations, media of communication, political parties, and governmental institutions all
share in the function of political socialization, and the associations, relationships, and participations of adult life continue
the process.

The socialization may be manifest or latent. It is manifest 61
political socialization when it takes the form of an explicit
transmission of information, values or feelings vis-à-vis the
roles, inputs, and outputs of the political system. It is latent
political socialization when it takes the form of a transmission
of information, values, or feelings vis-à-vis the roles, inputs,
and outputs of other social systems such as the family which
affect attitudes toward analogous roles, inputs, and outputs of
the political system.

The psycho-cultural school of political socialization is quite 62
correct when it argues that latent or "analogous" political socialization is the first and undoubtedly the most basic stage
of the political socialization process. The first years of life in
the family, the experience of authority and discipline and of
the family "political process" and "public policy" constitute
the most rapid and binding stage of socialization. More of an
impact occurs here than at any other point in the process. But
the way in which the family citizenship analogy affects adult
citizenship is quite complex and rarely, if ever, takes the form
of a direct repetition of early childhood patterns.

As the child matures, the rate of latent political socialization 63
drops off as the rate of manifest political socialization accel-
erates. Thus, in the early family, latent or analogous socialization is most important, and manifest or explicit political
socialization is relatively unimportant. In the school, latent
and manifest political socialization takes place, with the latter
becoming of increasing importance in the higher educational
levels. In later experience via work relationships, participation
in voluntary associations and political parties, exposure to the

media of communication, and to government, manifest socialization is of much greater importance, although latent socialization continues. In other words, even in later life there is a
carryover into political citizenship patterns of the analogous
citizenship patterns of the adult family, work group, church,
and voluntary association memberships.

64   The style of the political socialization may be specific or
diffuse, depending on the extent of differentiation and specificity of the political structure. Thus, in the Bergdama band,
socialization into family authority and participation patterns
is hardly separated from socialization into the political system, the religious community, or the work group, just as the
boundaries of the various social systems of the society are not
sharply drawn. It is easy to see how anthropologists, concerned
as they have been with societies of only a slightly higher order
of complexity than the simple band, should have produced a
theory of homogeneity of authority and "public policy" patterns in cultures. Where the boundaries of the social systems
of a society are diffuse, their capacity to generate significant
differences in culture and structure are greatly limited. Where
the boundaries are sharply drawn, autonomous development
becomes possible. Thus a modern society may have one form
of authority and participation in the family, another in the
economy, and still a third in the political system. Each one of
these involves a separate socialization process and, while they
affect one another, they do not determine one another. At the
primitive level, socialization into authority and participation
is diffuse and hence more alike from one system to the next.

65   The political socialization function in different societies
may be compared according to the way in which particularistic and universalistic elements are combined. In a modern
Western society, political socialization is both universalistic and particularist. It produces kinsman, friend, religious
communicant, member of a status group, as well as interest group member, party member, and citizen with a set
of explicit rights and duties. Each one of these roles makes
its separate claims, and the most general role of all—that
of citizen—under certain circumstances may take precedence
over all of them. In many primitive societies, even though
there may be membership in a political system constituted
on the basis of territorial jurisdiction—in other words, a
kind of "subject" or citizenship status with general obligations to the political system—kinship, lineage, or village tends
to constitute the dominant group membership, and membership in the larger political system tends to be constituent—
i.e., membership in the kinship, lineage, or village group—

rather than individual and direct. Kinship or narrow local affiliations tend to define the most enduring political relationships, the basic units of jurisdiction with claims on loyalty more powerful than general membership in the larger political system. In other words, political socialization tends to be to the particular kinship, lineage, or village group as a subsystem of the larger territorial jurisdictional system, rather than directly to the larger system. In larger, more complex societies, caste and religious community, along with village and other local affiliations, may constitute particularistic subsystems; and membership in the larger territorial system and political socialization into it may be via these subsystems. What is unique in the modern political system is a political socialization function which creates a distinct loyalty and membership on the part of the individual in the general political system, and a tendency to penetrate and affect the socialization processes of other social systems, such as the family and church, so that they introduce general citizenship content into their socialization processes.

Finally, the political socialization function in different societies may be compared according to the way in which affective and instrumental elements are combined. All political socialization involves an affective component—the inculcation of loyalty to, love of, respect for, and pride in the political system—and often, perhaps usually, negative affect of differing kinds and intensities for other political systems. The systems differ in the way in which these affective elements are combined with instrumental components. Thus, in a primitive political system, love of the polity tends to be a simple and direct affective attachment with relatively little cognitive discrimination and instrumentalism—i.e., policy preferences, strategies of influence, and the like. But it would be a great mistake to minimize the extent to which instrumental attitudes and strategies of influence enter into even the most primitive political system. The love felt by the citizen for the modern political system is more of a civic love. The affect may be strong even unto death, when the chips are down, so to speak. But it combines with affective ties for other groups, with an instrumental attitude toward the behavior or policy of the loved object, and with rationally calculated strategies of influence. 66

We may conclude this treatment of the political socialization function by pointing out that in a certain sense in political development, as in biological development, political ontogeny recapitulates phylogeny. That is to say, the early stages of the political socialization process are the same in all political systems, regardless of their degree of complexity. It is essentially 67 a latent, primary process—diffuse, particularistic, ascriptive, and affective. Political socialization in primitive societies tends to stop at this stage or, rather, involves only to a relatively limited extent secondary and manifest socialization into special- ized political roles. In the modern system, political socialization continues beyond latent, analogous political so- cialization into a whole sequence of manifest political social- ization experiences via the primary and secondary structures of the society. But no citizen of whatever modern political sys- tem ever fully escapes from the effects of his latent primary so- cialization experiences, or can ever fully suppress his needs for the intimacy and the stability of primary group relationships which bring into human proportion the secondary structures of the secular mass society. Hence the cultural and structural dualism of the modern political system.

68   The analysis of the political socialization function in a par- ticular society is basic to the whole field of political analysis, since it not only gives us insight into the pattern of politi- cal culture and subcultures in that society, but also locates for us in the socialization processes of the society the points where particular qualities and elements of the political cul- ture are introduced, and the points in the society where these components are being sustained or modified. Furthermore, the study of political socialization and political culture are essen- tial to the understanding of the other political functions. For, if political socialization produces the basic attitudes in a so- ciety toward the political system, its various roles, and public policy, then by studying political culture and political social- ization we can gain understanding of one of the essential condi- tions which affect the way in which these roles are performed, and the kinds of political inputs and outputs which these roles produce.

69   The relationship between the political socialization function and the *political recruitment function* is comparable to the re- lationship between Linton's "basic personality" and "status" or "role" personality.[31] All members of societies go through common socialization experiences. Differences in the political cultures of societies are introduced by differences in the polit- ical socialization processes in the subcultures of that society, and by differences in socialization into different status groups and roles.

70   The political recruitment function takes up where the gen- eral political socialization function leaves off. It recruits mem- bers of the society out of particular subcultures—religious communities, statuses, classes, ethnic communities, and the like—and inducts them into the specialized roles of the po-

litical system, trains them in the appropriate skills, provides them with political cognitive maps, values, expectations, and affects.

In comparing the political recruitment function in different 71 political systems, we have again to consider—as we did in the analysis of the political socialization function—the social and political structures which perform the function and the style of the performance. We have to examine in each political system the role of family, kinship, and lineage in recruitment to specialized political roles, status and caste, religious community, ethnic and linguistic origins, social class, schooling and training institutions. We have to examine the structures affecting specific induction patterns—political parties, election systems, bureaucratic examining systems, "in-role political socialization," and channels of recruitment and advancement within the political and authoritative governmental structures. The recruitment function, in other words, consists of the special political role socializations which occur in a society "on top of" the general political socialization. They include orientation to the special role and the political system of which it is a part, and to political inputs and outputs.

Styles of political recruitment may be compared according 72 to the way in which ascriptive and particularistic criteria combine with performance and universalistic criteria. Thus, in a modern Western political system, recruitment is affected both by ascriptive and by performance criteria. Kinship, friendship, "school ties," religious affiliation, and status qualities affect recruitment in various important ways, but the more thoroughgoing the political modernization, the more these ascriptive criteria are contained within or limited by achievement criteria—educational levels, performance levels on examinations, formal records of achievement in political roles, and the like. But the recruitment pattern is both structurally and culturally dualistic. Similarly, in the primitive or traditional political system the recruitment function is dualistic, but the achievement or performance criterion is less explicitly and generally applied. A chief or headman is selected because of his place in a lineage. He may be removed for poor performance according to either sacred or secular norms. He is replaced again by ascriptive criteria.

Similarly, particularistic and universalistic criteria are com- 73 bined differently in the performance of the recruitment function in modern and traditional systems. While, in a formal sense, in modern systems political recruitment is open to all members of the society fulfilling certain general requirements, particularistic structures such as family, friendship, religion, status, and informal groupings in the specifically political and governmental structures enter into the recruitment function throughout the political system. In traditional systems, while particularistic criteria are relatively more important in the performance of the recruitment function, general criteria enter in as well, as in the allocation of members of the society to social and political roles according to age and sex.

74   *Interest Articulation.* Every political system has some way of articulating interests, claims, demands for political action. The function of interest articulation, as we have already pointed out, is closely related to the political socialization function and the patterns of political culture produced by it. Among the input functions, interest articulation is of crucial importance since it occurs at the boundary of the political system. The particular structures which perform the articulation function and the style of their performance determine the character of the boundary between polity and society.

75   In characterizing the interest articulation function in a political system and in comparing it with that of other political systems, we have to discover first what kinds of structures perform the function and, second, the style of their performance. Four main types of structures may be involved in interest articulation: (1) institutional interest groups, (2) non-associational interest groups, (3) anomic interest groups, and (4) associational interest groups.

76   By institutional interest groups we have in mind phenomena occurring within such organizations as legislatures, political executives, armies, bureaucracies, churches, and the like. These are organizations which perform other social or political functions but which, as corporate bodies or through groups within them (such as legislative blocs, officer cliques, higher or lower clergy or religious orders, departments, skill groups, and ideological cliques in bureaucracies), may articulate their own interests or represent the interests of groups in the society.

77   By non-associational interests we have in mind kinship and lineage groups, ethnic, regional, religious, status and class groups which articulate interests informally, and intermittently, through individuals, cliques, family and religious heads, and the like. Examples might be the complaint of a tribal chief to a paramount chief about tributes or law enforcement affecting his lineage group; a request made by a landowner to a bureaucrat in a social club regarding the tariff on grains; or the complaint of an informal delegation from a linguistic group regarding language instruction in the schools.

The distinguishing characteristic of the institutional interest 78 group is the fact that a formally organized body made up of professionally employed officials or employees, with another function, performs an interest articulation function, or constitutes a base of operations for a clique or subgroup which does. The distinguishing characteristic of the non-associational interest is that the structure of interest articulation is intermittent and often informal.

By anomic interest groups we mean more or less sponta- 79 neous breakthroughs into the political system from the society, such as riots and demonstrations. Their distinguishing characteristic is their relative structural and functional liability. We use the term "relative" advisedly, since riots and demonstrations may be deliberately organized and controlled. But even when organized and controlled they have the potentiality of exceeding limits and norms and disturbing or even changing the political system. Though they may begin as interest articulation structures, they may end up performing a recruitment function (i.e., transferring power from one group to another), a rule-making function (i.e., changing the constitution, enacting, revising, or rescinding statutes), a rule application function (i.e., freeing prisoners, rescinding a bureaucratic decision), a rule adjudication function (i.e., "trying" and lynching), an aggregative or a communication function (drawing other interest groups to it, or publicizing a protest).

Associational interest groups are the specialized structures 80 of interest articulation—trade unions, organizations of businessmen or industrialists, ethnic associations, associations organized by religious denominations, civic groups, and the like. Their particular characteristics are explicit representation of the interests of a particular group, orderly procedures for the formulation of interests and demands, and transmission of these demands to other political structures such as political parties, legislatures, bureaucracies.

The performance of the interest articulation function may 81 be manifest or latent, specific or diffuse, general or particular, instrumental or affective in style. A manifest interest articulation is an explicit formulation of a claim or a demand. It is latent when it takes the form of behavioral or mood cues which may be read and transmitted into the political system. The demand or claim may be specific or diffuse. It is specific when it takes the form of a request for a particular piece of legislation or a subsidy; it is diffuse when it takes the form of a general statement of dissatisfaction or preference (i.e., "We need a change," "The political system is rotten," "We need socialism," and the like). Demands and claims may be general or particular. They are general when they are couched in class or professional group terms (i.e., "The rich ought to be taxed more," "The big estates should be divided"), particular, when they are couched in individual or family terms (i.e., "I'll give you my vote or something of value if you lower my taxes"). Finally, the articulation of interest may be instrumental or affectively neutral or affective. It is instrumental when it takes the form of a bargain with consequences realistically spelled out (i.e., "If you don't vote for this law, we'll campaign against you in the next election"); it is affective when it takes the form of a simple expression of gratitude, anger, disappointment, and the like.

82 The structure and style of interest articulation define the pattern of boundary maintenance between the polity and the society, and within the political system affect the boundaries between the various parts of the political system— parties, legislatures, bureaucracies, and courts. For example, a high incidence of anomic interest articulation will mean poor boundary maintenance between the society and the polity, frequent eruptions of unprocessed claims without controlled direction into the political system. It will affect boundary maintenance within the political system by performing aggregative, rule-making, rule application, and rule adjudication functions outside of appropriate channels and without benefit of appropriate process.

83 A high incidence of institutional interest articulation is also an indication of poor boundary maintenance between the polity and the society and within the political system. Thus the direct impingement of a church (or parts of a church) or of business corporations on the political system introduces raw or diffuse claims and demands difficult to process or aggregate with other inputs into the political system. Within the political system a high incidence of interest articulation by bureaucratic or military groups creates boundary difficulties among rule application, rule-making, articulative, and aggregative structures, and may indeed result in their atrophy. A high incidence of non-associational interest articulation—in other words, the performance of the interest articulation function intermittently by individuals, informal groups, or representatives of kinship or status groups, and so forth—similarly may represent poor boundary maintenance between the polity and the society. We have in mind here modern or transitional political systems, and not simple, primitive ones where this form of interest articulation is appropriate. Finally, a high incidence of associational interest articulation may indicate good boundary main-

tenance between society and polity and may contribute to such maintenance within the subsystems of the political system. Good boundary maintenance is attained by virtue of the regulatory role of associational interest groups in processing raw claims or interest articulations occurring elsewhere in the society and the political system, and directing them in an orderly way and in aggregable form through the party system, legislature, and bureaucracy.

With regard to the style of interest articulation, the more la- 84 tent, diffuse, particularistic, and affective the pattern of interest articulation, the more difficult it is to aggregate interests and translate them into public policy. Hence a political system characterized by these patterns of interest articulation will have poor circulation between the rest of the society and the political system, unless the society is quite small and has good cue-reading authorities. On the other hand, the more manifest, specific, general, and instrumental the style of interest articulation, the easier it is to maintain the boundary between the polity and society, and the better the circulation of needs, claims, and demands from the society in aggregable form into the political system. A political system with an interest articulation structure and style of this kind can be large and complex and still efficiently process raw demand inputs from the society into outputs responsive to the claims and demands of that society.

It may be useful for illustrative purposes to describe the in- 85 terest articulation function in a number of types of political systems. In the British political system we begin with a homogeneous, fusional (i.e., mixed secular and traditional) political culture. As a consequence, the members of the society and the political elites are homogeneously oriented toward the polity, and the orientation combines "civility" (from the secular component) and deference (from the traditional component). Though institutional, non-associational, and even (on rare occasion) anomic interest groups are present,[32] there is a thoroughly elaborated system of associational interest groups which regulates the impact of the other interest structures, and mitigates their particularistic, diffuse, ascriptive, and affective impacts, translates these into explicit, general, and bargaining demands for public policies, and works out strategies of influence and access.

In the British political system, "...the functions of inter- 86 est groups and political parties are sharply differentiated. Interest groups articulate political demands in the society, seek support for these demands among other groups by advocacy and bargaining, and attempt to transform these demands into authoritative public policy by influencing the choice of political personnel, and the various processes of public policy-making and enforcement. Political parties tend to be free of ideological rigidity, and are aggregative, i.e., seek to form the largest possible interest group coalitions by offering acceptable choices of political personnel and public policy. Both the interest group systems and the party systems are differentiated, bureaucratized, and autonomous. Each unit in the party and interest group systems comes into the 'market,' so to speak, with an adjustive bargaining ethos. Furthermore, the party system stands between the interest group system and the authoritative policy-making agencies and screens them from the particularistic and disintegrative impact of special interests. The party system aggregates interests and transforms them into a relatively small number of alternative general policies. Thus this set of relationships between the party system and the interest group system enables choice among general policies to take place in the cabinet and parliament, and assures that the bureaucracy will tend to function as a neutral instrument of the political agencies."[33] Thus in the British political system a differentiated, secular system of associational interest groups contributes to effective boundary maintenance between the society and the polity, and among the subsystems of the polity.

87   We may take a second illustration of the performance of the interest articulation function from the French political systems of the Third and Fourth Republics. First, the French political culture is not a homogeneous, fusional culture. Traditional and rational components are distributed in different proportions in the society. The rational part of the culture takes the form of an absolute-value rationality rather than a bargaining, instrumental rationality. Its rationality tends to be apocalyptic rather than civic or pragmatic; and this has been as true of French Catholic intellectuals as it has been true of French Radicals, Socialists, and Communists.

88   While associational interest groups exist in large numbers and with large memberships in France, institutional and anomic interest groups are of far greater importance than in England. In fact, the significance of institutional and anomic interest groups is directly related to the uneven effectiveness of associational interest groups, the absence of an effectively aggregative party system, and its fragmented or isolative political culture. Parties and interest groups in France do not constitute differentiated, autonomous political subsystems. They interpenetrate one another. There are some parties which more or less control interest groups (e.g., the Communist Party and the Communist-dominated trade unions, and to a lesser

extent the Socialist Party and the Socialist trade unions). The most powerful institutional interest group, the Catholic Church, controls other interest groups (e.g., the CFTC) and strongly influences political parties (e.g., the MRP).

"When parties control interest groups they may, and in France do, inhibit the capacity of interest groups to formulate pragmatic specific demands; they impart a political-ideological content to interest group activity. When interest groups control parties they inhibit the capacity of the party to combine specific interests into programs with wider appeal. What reaches the legislative process from the interest groups and through the political parties thus are the 'raw,' unaggregated demands of specific interests, or the diffuse, uncompromising, or revolutionary and reactionary tendencies of the Church and the movements of the right or left. Since no interest group is large enough to have a majority, and the party system cannot aggregate different interests into a stable majority and a coherent opposition, the electoral and legislative processes fail to provide alternative, effective choices. The result is a legislature penetrated by relatively narrow interests and uncompromising ideological tendencies, a legislature which can be used as an arena for propaganda, or for the protection of special interests, by veto or otherwise, but not for the effective and timely formulation and support of large policy decisions. And without a strong legislature, special interests and ideological tendencies penetrate the bureaucracy, and undermine its neutral, instrumental character."[34]

Thus the absence in France of an autonomous, secular interest group system is one of the factors contributing to poor boundary maintenance between the society and the political system, and among the various parts of the political system. The high incidence of anomic interest articulation (*"Poujadism"*) reflects the incapacity of the associational interest groups to receive demands from the society, assimilate them and transform them into aggregable claims, and transmit them to the party system, legislature, cabinet, and bureaucracy from which they may emerge as impacts upon public policy and regulation.

The Function of Aggregation. Every political system has some way of aggregating the interests, claims, and demands which have been articulated by the interest groups of the polity. Aggregation may be accomplished by means of the formulation of general policies in which interests are combined, accommodated, or otherwise taken account of, or by means of the recruitment of political personnel, more or less committed to a particular pattern of policy. The functions of articulation and aggregation overlap, just as do those of aggregation, recruitment, and rule-making. In certain political systems, such as the authoritarian and the primitive ones, the three functions of articulation, aggregation, and rule-making may be hardly differentiated from one another. In what appears to be a single act, a headman of a primitive society may read cues in his people, aggregate different cues and complaints, and issue an authoritative rule. We might say that he is intermittently interest articulator, aggregator, and rule-maker in the course of this process. In other systems, such as the modern Western ones, there are partitions in the process and separate structures or subsystems with boundaries take a distinctive part. Certainly, in the Anglo-American mass democracies this threefold division in function maintains the flow from society to polity and from polity to society (from input to output to input again) in an especially efficient manner. Thus, to attain a maximum flow of inputs of raw claims from the society, a low level of processing into a common language of claims is required which is performed by associational interest groups. To assimilate and transform these interests into a relatively small number of alternatives of policy and personnel, a middle range of processing is necessary. If these two functions are performed in substantial part before the authoritative governmental structures are reached, then the output functions of rule-making and rule application are facilitated, and the political and governmental processes become calculable and responsible. The outputs may be related to and controlled by the inputs, and thus circulation becomes relatively free by virtue of good boundary maintenance or division of labor.

92 The distinction between interest articulation and aggregation is a fluid one. The narrowest event of interest articulation initiated by a lineage head in a primitive political system, or the smallest constituent unit of a trade association, involves the aggregation of the claims of even smaller groups or of individuals or firms. Modern interest groups—particularly the "peak" associations—carry aggregation quite far, sometimes to the point of "speaking for" whole classes of the society— "labor," "agriculture," "business."

93 In our definition we reserve the term "aggregation" for the more inclusive levels of the combinatory processes, reserving the term "articulation" for the narrower expressions of interest. This is not the same thing as identifying interest articulation with "pressure groups" and aggregation with "political parties," though again in the developed modern systems these

agencies have a distinctive and regulatory relation to these functions.

Actually the aggregative function may be performed within 94 all of the subsystems of the political system—legislative bodies, political executives (cabinets, presidencies, kingships, chieftainships), bureaucracies, media of communication, party systems, interest groups of the various types. Parties, factions, blocs in legislatures; cliques or factions in political executives and bureaucracies; individual parties or party coalitions outside the legislature; and individual interest groups (in particular the civic or "general interest" groups) or *ad hoc* coalitions of interest groups—all perform an aggregative function, either by formulating alternative public policies or by supporting or advocating changes in political personnel.

But again it is the party system which is the distinctively 95 modern structure of political aggregation and which in the modern, developed, democratic political system "regulates" or gives order to the performance of the aggregative function by the other structures. Without a party system the aggregative function may be performed covertly, diffusely, and particular- istically, as in a political system such as Spain. Spain has asso- ciational, institutional, and non-associational interest groups, but aggregation occurs under the surface by cliques in the Falangist Party, the bureaucracy, army, or in the staff of the Caudillo. The relationship between interest articulation and aggregation is obscure and partly latent, the result of "deals," the reading of cues from unarticulated interests, and the like.

In the five area analyses which make up this book, party 96 systems are classified under four headings (1) authoritarian, (2) dominant non-authoritarian, (3) competitive two-party sys- tems, and (4) competitive multiparty systems. Authoritarian party systems may in turn be classified into the totalitarian and authoritarian varieties. Totalitarian parties aggregate in- terests by means of the penetration of the social structure of the society and by the transmission and aggregation of de- mands and claims through the party structure. Overt interest articulation is permissible only at the lowest level of individ- ual complaints against the lower-echelon authorities. Above this level, interest articulation and aggregation are latent or covert. The democratic critique of totalitarianism as a political system lacking in any interest articulation and aggregation is not correct. We know of the existence of interest groups ("fami- lies," bureaucratic cliques advocating policies and allocations) and of factions in the party which aggregate interests into alternative policies or advocate political personnel changes.

What is true of totalitarian systems is that they are characterized by a high rate of coercive social mobilization. The output
of authoritative policy is not paralleled by, but only somewhat
mitigated by, the input of demands and alternative policies.
Nevertheless there is an upward flow of significance and, while
difficult to characterize, it is essential that we be aware of it if
we are to avoid misleading polarizations.

97   Authoritarian parties such as the Republican People's Party
after the Turkish revolution have some of the properties of totalitarian parties, except that the penetration of the party into
the social structure is less complete and some interest groups
are permitted to articulate demands overtly. Hence there is
more of an upward flow of claims and demands, more of an
overt performance of the input functions. The absence of a free
party system and an open electoral process usually reduces the
aggregative function to the formulation of policy alternatives
within the authoritarian party and authoritative governmental
structures such as the bureaucracy and army. Where a religious
group is powerful, as in Catholic Spain, the Church may perform an aggregative function as well as an interest articulation
function.

98   Dominant non-authoritarian party systems are usually to be
found in political systems where nationalist movements have
been instrumental in attaining emancipation. Most of the significant interest groups, associational and non-associational,
have joined in the nationalist movement around a common
program of national independence. In the period following
emancipation the nationalist party continues as the greatly
dominant party, opposed in elections by relatively small left-
wing or traditionalist and particularist movements. This type
of party system is a formally free one, but the possibility of
a coherent loyal opposition is lacking. Hence the dominant
party is confronted by a complex problem of interest aggregation. Since highly dissimilar groups (traditionalist, secularist,
socialist, conservative, and so forth) are included in the nationalist movement, it is difficult to adopt a policy which aggregates their interests effectively. The cohesion of the party is
difficult to maintain. In order to avoid divisive issues, decisions
are postponed, and policy proposals take the form of diffuse
programs selected more for their unifying symbolism than for
their effective coping with demands emanating from the society or the various political elites. Thus circulation and boundary maintenance are poor in these party systems. Much will
depend on the purposes of the political elites of these parties.
They may have the goal of political modernization and seek
to introduce functionally specific associational interest groups

and a loyal, coherent opposition party, and to perform the political socialization function in such a way as to modernize the political culture. Where they do this, we call these systems "tutelary democracies." Where they fail to do so, a dominant non-authoritarian party may turn into an authoritarian party and transform the system into an oligarchy either of a modernizing type (e.g., Turkey between the wars) or of a conservative type (e.g., Poland between the wars).

The third type of party system is the competitive two-party 99 system exemplified by the United Kingdom, the members of the old Commonwealth, and the United States. Here a homogeneous, secular, bargaining political culture and an effective and autonomous system of associational interest groups introduce claims into the party system, legislature, political executive, and bureaucracy which are combinable into responsive, alternative public policies. Boundary maintenance between society and polity and among the articulative, aggregative, and rule-making structures is good. The whole process tends to be overt and calculable and results in an open circulatory flow of inputs and outputs.

Multiparty systems may be divided into two classes—the so- 100 called "working" multiparty systems of the Scandinavian area and the Low Countries, and the "immobilist" multiparty systems of France and Italy. In the Scandinavian version of the multiparty system, some of the parties are broadly aggregative (e.g., the Scandinavian Socialist parties, the Belgian Socialist and Catholic parties). Secondly, the political culture is more homogeneous and fusional of secular and traditional elements. Hence the relations between parties and interests are more consensual, which makes stable majority and opposition coalitions possible. "Thus though the party systems fail to aggregate interests as thoroughly as in the British case, the public policy-making function of the legislature is not undermined to the same extent as in the French and Italian cases. What appears to happen in the Scandinavian and the Low Countries is that the function of interest aggregation and general policy formulation occurs at both the party and parliamentary levels. The parties are partly aggregative of interests, but 'majority-minority' aggregation takes place finally in the coalition-making process in the legislature. This coalition-making process may be organized by parties in the formation of cabinets and the enactment of legislation or it may take the form of interest coalitions organized around issues of public policy. The capacity for stable majority-minority party coalitions and for relatively flexible issue-oriented interest coalitions is dependent upon the existence of a basic political consensus which affects both parties and interest groups. These appear to be the properties of the so-called 'working multi-party systems.' "[35]

101   The characteristics of the "immobilist" type of multiparty system have been referred to in the discussion of the articulation function above. In comparison to the working multiparty system, with its relatively homogeneous political culture, the political socialization processes in countries such as France and Italy tend to produce a fragmented, isolative political culture, and as a consequence the relations between interest groups and parties are not of an instrumental bargaining kind. The boundaries between the articulative and aggregative functions are poorly maintained. The aggregation performed by the parties is relatively narrow, and coalitions are fragile because of the cultural differences between political movements. The poor circulation of inputs from the society into the polity, and the difficulty of combining different inputs into outputs of rules and rule applications produces an alienation between the society and the polity which is general throughout the society, but is usually marked among particular groups (e.g., workers, obsolescent economic groups, and so forth).

102   We may also compare the performance of the aggregative function in different political systems in terms of its style. We may distinguish three different kinds of parties from this point of view: (1) secular, "pragmatic," bargaining parties; (2) absolute value-oriented, *Weltanschauung* or ideological parties; and (3) particularistic or traditional parties. The secular, pragmatic, bargaining type of party is instrumental and multivalue-oriented and its aggregative potential is relatively high. It is capable of generalized and adaptive programs intended to attract the maximum of interest support. Parties such as this may be broad- or narrow-based. Thus, in some Latin American countries, parties may emerge only at election time as the small following of a single politician or group of politicians. Without penetrating the countryside, they may bargain for the support of interest groups and then go out of business between elections. Or, a pragmatic party may develop its own structure in the countryside and be in a position to mobilize voters directly through its own organization. Naturally such a party can aggregate more effectively, since it is not as thoroughly dependent on interest groups as a narrow-based *ad hoc* party.

103   The *Weltanschauung* or ideological party is absolute value-oriented and is usually revolutionary, reactionary, or oriented toward national independence or power. The Fascist and Nazi versions of this type of party combined all three ideological elements. In their earlier manifestations ideological parties have

an appeal among alienates or cultural deviants in the society, usually consisting of small coteries of intellectuals and agitators. In other words, they are narrow-based. In their full-blown version they become the "parties of total integration" of Sigmund Neumann.[36] In this form they penetrate deeply into the society, almost replace all other social structures and, once securely rooted, are most difficult to dislodge by means short of violence.

The "particularistic" party is limited in its aggregate po-   104
tential by being identified completely with the interests of a particular ethnic or religious group. Just as the totalitarian version of the ideological party is an integrator and general social mobilizer rather than an aggregator, the particularistic party is more of an interest articulator than an aggregator. In this sense, functionally it is like the interest group of the West, differing primarily in the fact that it presents candidates in elections as well as advocating policies. Development toward a modern political system will reduce the particularistic party to an associational interest group, properly speaking.

The mode of performance of the aggregative function is cru-   105
cial to the performance of the political system as a whole. Thus the aggregative function in the British political system is distinctively performed by the party system. Interest aggregations occurring in the bureaucracy are controlled and to some extent assimilated into the aggregative processes of the party system. The parties are broad-based and hence can maintain their boundaries distinct from interest groups. Because of this autonomy and their secular bargaining culture, they can effectively aggregate these interests into general policy alternatives. The consequences of these structural and cultural patterns for the performance of the aggregative function in the British political system are the following. A high degree of interest aggregation occurs in the British system. This aggregation occurs in large part prior to the performance of the authoritative governmental functions and hence renders responsibility for outputs unambiguously clear. The pragmatic-instrumental quality of the aggregative process regulates the impact of latent, diffuse, particularistic, and affective components in the political system. It contributes to a relatively high mobility in the aggregative process, i.e., a relatively free movement of interest groups among political parties.

In a transitional country such as India there is a relatively   106
low degree of interest aggregation through the party system as such. The boundaries between party, legislature, and bureaucracy are poorly maintained by virtue of the fact that much of the aggregative function is performed within the bureau-

cracy in a process which does not separate aggregation, rule-making, and rule application. In the party system the aggregative function is performed in some measure particularistically, diffusely, symbolically, and ideologically, rather than pragmatically. Hence circulation from social needs and demands to articulation, to aggregation, to rule-making, to rule application, and back to society is not a fully open, responsive, and responsible process. The particularisms and ideological tendencies in the party and interest group systems ("communal" movements, linguistic-ethnic interests, traditional groups, sectarian socialist movements) produce relatively low mobility of interest groups in the party system, and a relatively low potential for stable coalitions among political parties.

107   *The Political Communication Function.*   All of the functions performed in the political system—political socialization and recruitment, interest articulation, interest aggregation, rule-making, rule application, and rule adjudication—are performed *by means of* communication. Parents, teachers, and priests, for example, impart political socialization through communication. Interest group leaders and representatives and party leaders perform their articulation and aggregation functions by communicating demands and policy recommendations. Legislators enact laws on the basis of information communicated to them and by communicating with one another and with other elements of the political system. In performing their functions, bureaucrats receive and analyze information from the society and from various parts of the polity. Similarly, the judicial process is carried on by means of communication.

108   At first thought, it might appear that there is no political communication function as such, that communication is an aspect of all of the other political functions. But a view such as this comes into conflict with the fact that in the modern political system differentiated media of communication have arisen which have developed a vocational ethics of "neutral" or objective communication. This ethics requires that the dissemination of information ought to be separated from the other political functions such as interest articulation, aggregation, and recruitment.

109   The separating-out of the communication function is not unique to modern political systems. The Greek Pantheon had a specialized communicator in Mercury; the Old Testament had its dusty messengers, usually carriers of tragic news, who frequently failed to survive the act of communication. Primitive political systems have their drummers and runners, medieval

towns had their criers, noblemen and kings their heralds. Even when there is no specialized political communicator, we can distinguish in the combined performance of, for example, the interest articulation and communication function the articulaive event from the event of communicating the act of articulation. Thus a labor news medium may both advocate a trade union policy and communicate the content of that policy.

Failure to separate out the political communication function from the other political functions would deprive us of an essential tool necessary for distinguishing among political systems and characterizing their performance. It is not accidental that those political systems which have homogeneous political cultures and autonomous and differentiated structures of interest articulation and aggregation—the United Kingdom, the old Commonwealth, and the United States—also have to the greatest extent autonomous and differentiated media of communication. Nor is it accidental that the political systems with fragmented political cultures and relatively undifferentiated structures of interest articulation and aggregation—France and Italy, for example—also have a "press" which tends to be dominated by interest groups and political parties. The whole pattern of function in these political systems is affected by and tends to sustain a fragmented political culture. The control over the media of communication by parties and interest groups means that the audience for political communications is fragmented.

Thus it is essential in characterizing a political system to analyze the performance of the communication function. Just because of the fact that all the political functions are performed by means of communications, political communication is the crucial boundary-maintenance function. When there is an autonomous system of communication, covert communications in the bureaucracy, the interest groups, and political parties may to some extent be regulated and controlled by publicity. Similarly latent interests in the society may be made explicit through neutral media of communication. Autonomy in the media of communication makes possible a free flow of information from the society to the polity and, in the polity, from political structure to political structure. It also makes possible an open feedback from output to input again. One may liken the communication function to the circulation of the blood. It is not the blood but what it contains that nourishes the system. The blood is the neutral medium carrying claims, protests, and demands through the veins to the heart; and from the heart through the arteries flow the outputs of rules, regulations, and adjudications in response to the claims and demands.

112   The general specialization of political structure in modern
political systems, the autonomy and regulatory role of the individual structures with respect to individual functions, rests on
a neutral system of communications. While associational interest groups in the modern democratic political system perform a regulatory role both in the polity and in the society
with reference to the articulation function, the communication
function in turn regulates the interest articulation function.
Thus it facilitates the articulation of latent interest independently of the associational interest groups, and communicates
the articulations of interest emanating from political parties,
legislatures, and bureaucracies, which can thereby correct actions of the associational interest groups. Similarly it limits
the regulatory power of the political parties in the performance
of the aggregative function; that of the legislature and political executive with respect to the rule-making function; that of
the bureaucracy with respect to the rule application function.
An autonomous communication system "regulates the regulators" and thereby preserves the autonomies and freedoms of
the democratic polity.

113   One might even argue that the crucial control in the totalitarian political system is not coercion—although it is
essential—but the monopoly of the media of communication.
By means of it coercion may be limited to occasional events of
anomic interest articulation or incidental to acts of mobilization. Totalitarian communication directs the inflow of information to a single political structure, and limits the outflow of
communication to the purposes of the Communist elite. Thus
only that elite has the necessary information on the basis of
which it can calculate, devise strategies, control and eliminate
anomic potentialities. The dependence, the instrumental character of other political structures are maintained by controlling the information available to them. Only the bureaucratic
apparatus of the Communist Party at the very top level has a
complete switchboard. All other structures plug in only to the
central, where their communications can be received, moni-
tored, and relayed at the discretion of the central. Effective
political action must be based on rational calculation, which
in turn requires information. A democratic system provides
for a relatively free, multidirectional flow of information, thus
making it possible for all the structures to calculate and to act
effectively.

114   In particular, an autonomous, neutral, and thoroughly penetrative system of communication is essential to the development and maintenance of an active and effective electorate
and citizenship. The effective performance of the recruitment

function by an electorate (i.e., choosing candidates in relation to needs and demands) is dependent on an open and multidirectional flow of communications reporting on the performance of the other functions by the incumbents of the authoritative offices to the mass of citizens. There is still another aspect of the communication function in a democratic polity which calls for comment. The availability of neutral information about the functioning of the political system tends to create an informed stratum of citizens—public policy-oriented, rather than interest-oriented in the narrow sense—a stratum which sustains the regulatory role of the media of communication in the polity. For the existence of an "attentive" informed audience is not only sustained by an adequate system of communication; it in turn provides an audience or market for high-quality political information. In other words, it creates and sustains a sector in the communication elite which carries on an analytical, open, and informed discussion of public policy issues within the polity as a whole, more or less independently of interest groups, parties, legislators, executives, and bureaucrats. In addition, this attentive stratum constitutes a special political subculture in which special kinds of interest groups thrive—interest groups concerned with general policy problems rather than with special interests.

The performance of the communication function in different political systems may be compared according to the structures performing it and the style of its performance. We have already pointed out that all of the political structures—governmental agencies, parties, interest groups, media of communication—and all of the social structures—families, kinship and lineage groups, face-to-face groups, neighborhoods, communities, villages, caste, status and class groups, ethnic and linguistic groups—may be involved in the performance of the communication function. What distinguishes a modern political system from a traditional or primitive one is the fact that in the modern system the specialized communication structure is more elaborate, and that it penetrates the unspecialized or intermittent structures of political communication. Thus Katz's point referred to above as the "two-step flow of communication" is a demonstration of the penetration of the informal and intermittent structures of political communication by the specialized mass media. Traditional or primitive political communication is performed intermittently by kinship, lineage, status, and village groups. Specialized media of communication are present only to a limited degree, if they are present at all. 115

Political systems may also be compared according to the ways in which they combine communication styles. Styles of 116 political communication may be distinguished according to whether they are manifest or latent, specific or diffuse, particularistic or "generalistic," affectively neutral or affective. A manifest political communication is an explicit message; a latent one is a mood readable only from behavioral or expressive cues. A specific message is a statement of a political event or potential event which separates the political from the non-political and involves explicit cognitive discrimination. A specific political event is reported as having occurred, as occurring, or as likely to occur, with the estimate of probability, and sometimes with the consequences, spelled out. A particularistic message is one which by virtue of its language, or of its esoteric properties, cannot be easily transmitted throughout the polity as a whole. It requires political interpreters if it is to be transmitted at all beyond the limits of the esoteric audience. A general or universal message is one that is so couched as to be more or less transmissible throughout the entire communication network of the polity. An affectively neutral communication is an objective report of an event or events which may be combined with other reports and other data and be the ready object of analysis and inference. An affective communication creates difficulties in analysis and inference. It cannot be as readily appraised or weighed, and fed into the stream of political inputs and outputs.

117   But here, as in the treatment of other functions, we have to avoid polarizations. The political communication networks of modern political systems are full of latent, diffuse, particularistic, and affective messages. But with the existence of autonomous and specialized media of communication, associational interest groups, and aggregative parties these traditional messages tend to get translated into modern ones. Furthermore, in this process of translation the messages tend to get placed in envelopes with the correct political addresses.

118   In order to illustrate this mode of analysis of the political communication function, it may be useful to compare its performance in a modern Western system such as the United States with its performance in a transitional political system such as India. The comparison may be made in four respects: (1) the homogeneity of political information; (2) the mobility of information; (3) the volume of information; (4) the direction of the flow of information.

119   With respect to the homogeneity of political information, the point has already been made that the existence of autonomous and specialized media of communication and their penetration of the polity as a whole in modern Western political systems do not eliminate latent, diffuse, particularistic, and affective

messages but only tend to afford opportunities throughout the political system for such messages to be couched in a manifest, specific, general, and instrumental language of politics. There is, in other words, a system whereby these messages are made manifest and homogeneous. If what has been written about the opinion leader in the United States is correct, a modern political system does not eliminate esoteric communication; it works through a system of widely distributed interpreters which tend to penetrate these primary communication cells and connect them with the secondary media of communication. In contrast, in a transitional political system the messages in the communication network are heterogeneous. In the urban, relatively modern areas, specialized media of communication are to be found, but they tend to be organs of interest groups or political parties. Even in the cities, among the illiterate and uneducated elements of the urban population, the impact of the specialized media of communication is relatively limited. The illiterate and certainly the newly urbanized elements of the population tend to persist in a traditional, rural-type network of communication, with kinship, lineage, caste, and language groupings performing the political communication function intermittently, diffusely, and particularistically.

Although here too there are interpreters standing between 120 the modernized and the non-modernized sectors of the urban populations, the problem of interpretation is much more difficult than in the modern Western system. The opinion leader in the United States receives information from the mass media and interprets it for his "opinion followers." These opinion followers tend to speak the same language, share the same values, and have cognitive maps similar to the ones conveyed in the mass media. The politician or interest group leader in an Indian urban area faces a far greater gap between the communication content of the literate modern sector of the Indian city and the illiterate and traditional sector. The gap is one of culture; it may include language in the specific sense, values, and cognitive maps differing radically in amount and specificity of information and in the range of political objects which they include. What has been said of the communication gap in the urban areas of a country like India is true to an even greater extent of connections between the urban and rural and village areas. Here, the problem of interpretation is a massive one. The interpreter, whether he be a bureaucrat, interest group leader, or party leader, cannot readily find equivalents in language, values, and cognitive material to make an accurate translation. There is a genuine block in communication between the urban central and the rural and village periphery.

No real penetration by communication is possible, and the audience of the polity consists of a loosely articulated congeries of subaudiences.

121   This takes us to the second major point of contrast between a modern Western and a transitional system of political communication—the mobility of information. In a modern Western system, neutral information flows freely throughout the polity, from the initiators of information into the neutral secondary media of communication, and into the capillaries of primary communication. In a transitional system, information circulates relatively freely in the urban areas, but never penetrates fully the diffuse and undifferentiated networks of the traditional and rural areas. Obstacles to mobility exist in both the input and the output process.

122   Third, in the modern Western system, the volume of political information passing through the communication network is far greater than in a transitional system. A differentiated and autonomous system of communication creates information, by bringing covert communication into "the open," by making latent information manifest. Its very mobility creates animated discussion and controversy among the various political role incumbents. Thus a large volume of information is pumped rapidly throughout the polity. The assimilation of information is rapid, and calculations may be made relatively quickly and accurately. The volume of flow in a transitional system is uneven. Much information remains covert and latent, and it is consequently difficult to make political estimates accurately and quickly.

123   Finally, there are important differences in the direction of the flow of information. The output of messages from the authoritative governmental structures in a transitional system tends to be far larger than the input of messages from the society. The government employs the mass media and operates through its own media as well. To be sure, governmental messages cannot be accurately transmitted to "tribesmen," "kinsmen," and "villagers." They may hear the messages over the radio, but they cannot register their meaning precisely. Nevertheless the messages get there physically. On the input side, much important information regarding the needs of the base and periphery of the society never gets explicated, and cannot therefore be fully taken account of by other elements in the political system.

124   This brief comparison of the communication function in a modern and a transitional political system is sufficient to suggest how important the communication function is in the operations and cohesion of political systems. An examination of other systems, such as the varieties of traditional ones, and

the various forms of authoritarianism and totalitarianism in terms of the communication function, would be useful not only in gaining a more precise understanding of their functioning but in developing a more adequate theory of political communication.

The Governmental Functions: Rule-Making, Rule Application, 125 *Rule Adjudication.* In the individual area analyses which follow, far greater stress has been placed on the political functions than on the governmental. The primary reasons for this are the indeterminacy of the formal governmental structures in most of the non-Western areas, and the gross deviations in the performance of the governmental functions from the constitutional and legal norms. Most of these political systems either have had, have now, or aspire to constitutions which provide for legislatures, executives, and judiciaries. In the distribution of legal powers they follow either the British, the American, or the French model. But it is the exceptional case in which these institutions perform in any way corresponding to these norms. A careful examination of governmental structures and their formal powers would have yielded little of predictive value.

On the other hand, a careful examination of the polit- 126 ical culture of these political systems, the factors making for change, the political socialization processes, patterns of recruitment into politics, and the characteristics of the infrastructure—interest groups, political parties, and media of communication—yield some insight into the directions and tempo of political change. Hence our emphasis on political structure and function both in the theoretical discussion and in the area analyses.

In a recent paper Shils[37] classifies the "new states" of the 127 non-Western world into five groups: (1) political democracies, (2) "tutelary" democracies, (3) modernizing oligarchies, (4) totalitarian oligarchies, and (5) traditional oligarchies. Although these are classes of *political systems,* they each imply a particular state of governmental structure.

The political democracies are those systems with function- 128 ing and relatively autonomous legislatures, executives, courts, and with differentiated and autonomous interest groups, political parties, and media of communication. In the non-Western areas, Japan, Turkey, Israel, and Chile are examples which approximate this type.

Tutelary democracies are political systems which have 129 adopted both the formal norms of the democratic polity— universal suffrage, freedom of association, and of speech and publication—and the structural forms of democracy. In addition, the elites of these systems have the goal of democratizing their polities even though they may be unclear as to the requirements—in particular, the requirements in political infrastructure and function. In reality, as Shils points out, these systems are characterized by a concentration of power in the executive and the bureaucracy. The legislature tends to be relatively powerless, and the independence of the judiciary has not been fully attained. A country such as Ghana comes close to this model.

130   Modernizing oligarchies are political systems controlled by bureaucratic and/or army officer cliques in which democratic constitutions have been suspended or in which they do not exist. The goals of the elites may or may not include democratization. The modernizing impulse usually takes the form of a concern for efficiency and rationality, and an effort to eliminate corruption and traditionality. Modernizing oligarchies are usually strongly motivated toward economic development. The governmental structure of modernizing oligarchies concentrates powers in the hands of a clique of military officers or bureaucrats who are usually placed in control of the chief ministries. Turkey under Atatürk and contemporary Pakistan and the Sudan are examples of modernizing oligarchies.

131   Totalitarian oligarchy such as exists in North Korea and Viet Minh differs from modernizing oligarchy by the degree of penetration of the society by the polity, the degree of concentration of power in the ruling elite, and the tempo of social mobilization. There have been two types of totalitarianism—the Bolshevist and the traditionalist, such as Nazi Germany and Fascist Italy. Two criteria distinguish the Bolshevist version from the traditional version. National Socialism and Fascism left some autonomy to other institutions, such as the Church, economic interest groups, and kinship and status groups. In addition, its goals took the form of an extremely militant and charismatic nationalism. The Bolshevist version is more thoroughly penetrative of the society, and its goals are revolutionary and global.

132   Traditional oligarchy is usually monarchic and dynastic in form, based on custom rather than constitution or statute. The ruling elite and the bureaucracy are recruited on the basis of kinship or status. The central governmental institutions control local kinship, lineage, or territorial units only to a limited extent. The goals of the elite are primarily maintenance goals; the capacity and mechanisms for adaptation and change are present only to a limited extent. Nepal, Saudi Arabia, and Yemen are examples of traditional oligarchy.

Shils distinguishes the traditional regime from the "tradition- 133 alistic"[38] or traditional "revival" regime. These are conservative reactions against modernizing tendencies or threats. But because they are reactions against modernizing tendencies or threats which require mobilization and modernization, these traditionalistic systems tend to rationalize the governmental structure and mitigate the autonomies of kinship, status, and local units. In other words, the traditionalistic regime cannot avoid some modernization and consequently tends to overlap with the modernizing oligarchy. It is distinguished from it primarily by its "defensive" and limited modernization.

The most frequent types of political systems to be found in 134 the non-Western areas are tutelary democracies and modernizing and traditionalistic oligarchies. From a functional point of view, the tutelary democracy tends to concentrate—to a far greater extent than is true of developed democracies—the rule-making function and the rule application function in the executive and the bureaucracy. Because of the rudimentary character of the party system, the interest group system, and the modern media of communication, the executive and the bureaucracy are far more dominant in the performance of the political functions than they are in developed democracies. Furthermore, the cultural dualism of the tutelary democracy is either "isolative" or "incorporative," rather than "fusional," in character. Nevertheless the elites of the tutelary democracies have in their goal system, more or less clearly spelled out, the functional properties of the modern differentiated, fusional political system, with its autonomies and its boundary maintenance pattern.

The modernizing oligarchies are characterized to an even 135 greater extent by the concentration of functions in a ruling clique and in the bureaucracy, and by the absence of a competitive party system. The activities of associational interest groups, to the extent that they exist, are greatly limited, and the media of communication are controlled. But though the activities of interest groups are limited, there is an overt, pluralistic system of interest articulation in which local communities, informal status and lineage groups, and institutional groups take part. Like the tutelary democracy, the modernizing oligarchy is characterized by an incorporative or isolative dualism. Particularistic, diffuse, and ascriptive groups perform the political functions, along with groups that are characterized by "modern" styles although not necessarily penetrated by them.

The development of modern structure in traditionalistic oli- 136 garchies is defensive. Thus only the army, the police, and parts of the civil bureaucracy are rationalized in order to control or prevent modernizing tendencies in the society. Thus, while a modernizing oligarchy may use an authoritarian party as an instrument of mobilization and aggregation, this is less likely in a traditionalistic oligarchy where the aggregative, articulative, and communication functions are usually performed by the bureaucracy and/or the army, as well as by kinship or tribal units, status groups, and local units such as villages.

137   While there is justification for having underplayed the governmental structures in this study, their neglect in the development of the theory of the functions of the polity represents a serious shortcoming in the present analysis. The threefold classification of governmental or output functions into rule-making, rule application, and rule adjudication will not carry us very far in our efforts at precise comparison of the performance of political systems. The experiments referred to above in the development of more adequate functional categories make this clear. Cohen and Almond in their studies of the American foreign policy-making process[39] found it necessary to break down the rule-making function into three sub-functions—initiation, modification, vetoing. This threefold breakdown resulted empirically from efforts at coding the contents of responses of individuals who regularly participated in the foreign policy-making process. Lasswell in his work cited above[40] uses five functions to break down the governmental functions. Two of these—prescription and termination—are divisions of the rule-making function; two—invocation and application—are subdivisions of the rule application function; and two—rule application and appraisal—are subdivisions of the rule adjudication function. Neither of these experiments in functional categorization satisfies our need for a set of conceptual tools which can bring out the differences in the performance of governmental functions in different kinds of political systems. Perhaps we shall have to work empirically in a sequence of bilateral comparisons until a more generally useful classification emerges.

138   In characterizing the governmental functions in a political system, we have to specify the structures performing the functions, the style of their performance, and the way in which the problem of cultural dualism is solved. We have already illustrated this mode of analysis briefly in our functional comparison of tutelary democracies and oligarchies. In the performance of the rule-making function we may have a division among executive, legislature, and courts, as in the United States; or it may take the parliamentary form, with cabinet and parliament being dominant in the performance of the function, and the courts having far less general rule-making

importance. Similarly, the division of the rule-making function may be confederal, federal, or unitary. In each case some rule-making is performed by local governmental structures, but the degree of autonomy varies.

A federal system, in the constitutional sense, is different from 139 a traditional system, in which kinship, lineage, ethnic, and local groups may enjoy great autonomy. The traditional system tends to be particularistic, diffuse, and ascriptive. Thus to the extent that the local unit coincides with lineage, or a group of lineages, there is no general citizenship. Similarly, the penetration of the rule-making of the central authorities may be limited to taxation, tribute, the obligation to military service, or an external contact through the local authorities. In all other respects, rule-making in both process and content may be limited to the specific local unit, and may differ substantially from one local unit to the next, particularly if there are significant differences among them in culture and social structure.

A constitutional or legally based federal system is charac- 140 terized by a penetration of the local political systems by the central one, and by the existence of general rules governing the distribution of powers among the central and the local units. A legal federal system is more particularistic than a legal unitary one. However, it is a "particularism" within a "universalism" — that is, the powers of the local units are exercised within a framework of general rules distributing powers. Furthermore, the central system works directly in the local units within its competence, and not outside it and through the authorities of the local system.

The particularism of pluralistic traditional systems may in- 141 volve a particularism to the point of closure. The central authorities may differ in culture and structure from the local ones and they may operate only through the local authorities, with no direct contact with the individuals of the local units. There is an obvious parallelism with confederal systems, but again there are differences which it is not necessary to go into here.

Perhaps the best way to illustrate the functional approach to 14: the comparison of governmental structure is to contrast modern Western democratic systems with transitional non-Western ones from this point of view. On the whole, it would be correct to say that boundary maintenance tends to be good in modern Western democratic systems such as the United States and England and relatively poor in transitional ones. In the United States the Congress and the Presidency in its legislative role tend to regulate the rule-making activities which are delegated to and performed by the bureaucracy. Thus, even though quantitatively many more general rules may be made by the bureaucracy, they are usually made within grants of power from the Congress and the President. The grants of power may be rescinded or modified. In the British cabinet-parliamentary system, the boundaries are drawn differently, but nevertheless there is a similar regulatory control by the cabinet and parliament over the rule-making function performed by the bureaucracy. In both the British and American systems the boundaries between the courts and the other governmental structures are maintained effectively. The courts in both countries have a regulatory role with reference to the performance of the adjudicative function by other governmental structures. Again the pattern differs as between the United States and the United Kingdom. Through the power of judicial review in the United States, the courts may exercise a generally regulatory role with reference to the performance of the rule-making, rule application, and rule adjudicative functions by the other federal structures, and also regulate the division of powers between the central government and the states. In the British system, the regulatory role of the courts tends to be confined to the performance of the adjudicative function.

143   In both the British and the American political systems there are informal primary structures within the formal ones. The informal structures take the form of diffuse, ascriptive, and particularistic relationships which may be quite important in the performance of the governmental functions. But these informal structures tend to be penetrated by and acculturated to the primary and secondary formal structures.

144   In contrast, in transitional political systems, boundary maintenance between governmental structures is less effective. The legislative bodies are far less effective in regulating the performance of the rule-making function by the bureaucracy. The rule-making function tends to be performed by the executive and the bureaucracy. Furthermore, within the governmental structures and particularly at the provincial or local levels, informal, primary groups are of the "communal" kind—i.e, based on lineage, caste, and language. It would not be correct to say that the formal secondary structure has penetrated this informal structure. Rather they tend to operate with equal legitimacy, with the result that the universalistic, specific, and affectively neutral political culture of the modern structures is stalemated by the particularistic, diffuse, and affective political culture of the traditional ones.

145   Finally, there is a serious problem of continuity between the central governmental structures and the local ones. Village government tends to be assimilated to the traditional lineage, caste, and status structure. Thus, though a mayor may wear

the trappings of his formal office, it may really be a caste leader or a headman who is speaking. A modern system of local courts may be subverted by a traditional system of adjudication, as for example by the Koranic interpreters. Thus a transitional system has not as yet eliminated the planes of cleavage which exist both within the central governmental structures and between the central governmental structure and the local units.

IV. Toward a Probabilistic Theory of the Polity

In recent years there has been growing interest among polit- 146 ical scientists in the possibilities of applying formal logic and mathematics to the study of politics. This impulse toward rigor and precision is a sound and constructive one, even though some of the first efforts have not produced impressive results. Perhaps the most serious problem confronting efforts of this kind is the absence of a theory of the political system specifying its properties in such form as to lend itself to statistical and mathematical formulation.

The functional theory of the polity which we have elabo- 147 rated above does specify the elements of the polity in such form as may ultimately make possible statistical and perhaps mathematical formulation. What we have done is to separate political function from political structure. In other words, we have specified the elements of two sets, one of functions and one of structures, and suggested that political systems may be compared in terms of the probabilities of performance of the specified functions by the specified structures. In addition, we have specified styles of performance of function by structure which makes it possible for us at least to think of a state of knowledge of political systems in which we could make precise comparisons relating the elements of the three sets—functions, structures, and styles—in the form of a series of probability statements.

If this appears to be too rash a projection into the future, 148 the point should be made that the statements about politics now to be found in the political science literature are codable into such functional-structural statements of probability. Dahl has already shown that it is possible to take propositions in political theory, translate them into statements of probability, develop operational indices, and test them against empirical data.[41] It is similarly possible to take the monographic literature on political and governmental institutions and code much of their content into statements of probability of performance of function by structure. Much of what David Truman

has to say about interest groups in the political process takes
the form of statements about the functions performed by interest groups, the conditions facilitating the performance of
these functions, and the effect of the performance of these
functions on other functions and the political system as a
whole.[42] Similarly V. O. Key's comments on parties and pressure groups may be coded into statements of probability of
performance of functions by structures.[43] But these statements
tend to be implicit probabilistic statements. The estimates take
the form of qualifiers such as "by and large," "in general,"
"with great frequency," "with increasing (or decreasing) frequency." Similarly, the propositions about the performance of
function by structure in the body of the present theoretical
chapter are estimates of "more or less," or of "increases" and
"decreases."

149   What we are suggesting is that great advantage would be
gained if we were to make explicit the essentially statistical
nature of our propositions about the structures, functions, and
styles of the polity. This is by no means pedantry, as an example or two may make abundantly evident.

150   When we say that pressure groups in the United States perform certain functions in certain ways, we are saying in effect
that there is a universe of pressure group actions—i.e., performances of functions by pressure groups—and that in this
universe there is a given probability that these functions will
be performed by pressure groups with certain frequencies and
in certain ways. A significant step is taken in the direction of
precision by the simple recognition of the statistical nature
of the proposition, for it immediately and explicitly brings to
bear on the problem the theories of sampling and of probability. It is now no longer possible to leave diffuse the evidential
nature of the proposition. If such a proposition implies a universe of events, then we must specify the limits and content
of the universe. We can examine our evidence and ask of it, to
what extent does it sample this universe?

151   We know that each member of this universe—each performance of function by pressure groups—is a unique individual;
but like human populations it has a stratification (e.g., age,
sex, occupation, education, and so forth). The stratification of
the universe of pressure group events is affected by the nature
of the policy issue, its place or salience in the context of public
policy issues, the urgency of the issue, its novelty and contro-
versiality, as well as a number of other conditions. If we simply
look at our evidence from the point of view of these evidential
requirements, we can at least become aware of how imprecise
we are and must be in view of the enormity of the research

implied. But to explicate our imprecision is in itself a step in the direction of precision.

We will also have discovered that there are ways of sam- 152 pling this universe. Once we set up the problem in a statistical matrix, our knowledge and intelligence can help us select the probable well-populated cells, and eliminate the empty and poorly populated ones. Thus our sampling of the universe can proceed in an orderly way, step by step, and gradually develop a rigorous theory of interest groups or any other political structure with which we might be concerned.

We do not minimize the problem of finding quanities to place 153 in the cells of our matrices, but, once having thought of the problem in these terms, we have at least liberated our capacities to look for appropriate indices and establish the problems, costs, and values of quantification. Indeed we may conclude that, at least at the present state of our knowledge and resources, we cannot establish quantitative values. Nevertheless statistical thinking is still of great value and may produce greater precision, if not quantitative precision.

We may take as an illustration of this the strategy of case 154 studies of public policy decisions. Quite a library of such case studies, both political and administrative, have accumulated in the last decade or so. But we still do not know how to use them for the purpose of developing political theory. What is a case study, anyway? It is an effort at reconstructing, by documentary research and interviewing of informants, a public policy individual. In this public policy individual will be found the specific performances of political and governmental functions by the structures of the polity. Once we think of case studies in these terms, our capacity to draw from the case study hypotheses or theories of the functioning of the polity, and our capacity to devise a strategy of case studies, have been liberated. The first question we would ask is, what stratum of our universe of public policy decisions does our case study purport to represent? How well does it represent it? What other strata must we sample before we can formulate a theory of the polity which is actually representative of its population? The earlier work of Cohen and Almond referred to above illustrates the method. Thus in order to characterize the foreign-policy-making process in the United States in the post-World War II period eight case studies were made, each one being selected because it tapped a different cell in the foreign policy matrix. This kind of case study approach enables us to develop a typology of foreign-policy-making and a set of "if-then" propositions respecting the conditions which affect foreign-policy-making profiles.

155   Thus, regardless of the possibilities and costs of quantification, making explicit the statistical basis of our science provides us with far better canons than have guided us in the
past. It is this aspiration, rather than rashness or fanaticism,
which leads us to conclude our discussion of the functions of
the polity with a statement of some of the problems which
would have to be solved in the development of a probabilistic
theory of the polity.

156   Throughout this chapter we have been suggesting that political systems may be compared with one another in terms
of the frequency and style of the performance of political
functions by *political* structures. The set of political functions
which we have proposed is most preliminary. We cannot really say that we have developed a set of functional categories
which will prove satisfactory for purposes of analyzing and
comparing political systems. We must be even more tentative about the structural categories. Here we have simply used
the nomenclature of political and social institutions without
pretending to have arrived at clearly defined, universally applicable categories of structure. Finally, in comparing styles
of performance of function by structure we have relied in
the main upon the pattern variable concepts of Parsons and
Shils.[44]

157   Assuming that we had solved the problem of categorization
of function, structure, and style, our next problem would be
to form the product of these three sets, which would give us a
matrix with several hundred cells. If we were then to attempt
to sample the actions of a number of polities over a given period of time in order to arrive at precise comparisons of these
polities in terms of frequencies of performance of function, by
structure, by style, we would have set ourselves a research task
of ridiculous proportions.

158   The point should be clear, however, that the intellectual exercise of thinking of the polity as being representable by a set
of frequencies recorded on a series of matrices is not a research
design. It simply states the problem in its fully explicated form.
It makes explicit the operational assumptions of what many
of us have been pretending to be able to say about the political systems of the United Kingdom, the United States, France,
Germany, and the many other polities with which political scientists are concerned. With this explication of assumptions in
mind, we are in a better position to judge the adequacy of the
evidence that we have to support these propositions.

159   Thus, in having specified the elements of these sets of functions, structures, and styles, we have taken a step in the direction of a probabilistic theory of the polity, but perhaps it is only

a small step. Theoretical imagination may enable us to select a limited number of indicators of the performance of function by structure, and research ingenuity may enable us to get quantitative evidence of these performances. The election studies carried on in the United States have yielded quantitative evidence of the relative importance of primary, diffuse, and particularistic communication structures as compared with secondary, specific, and universalistic mass communication structures, in the performance of the function of political recruitment. It should be possible to make similar studies of the recruitment function in other polities.

It is conceivable that a well-executed series of case studies 160 in a number of countries of the performance of the interest articulation function by different kinds of structures, and with different kinds of styles, would enable us to spell out what we mean by the forms of cultural dualism to which we have referred above, and might also enable us to specify what we mean when we say that in the United Kingdom and the United States associational interest groups regulate the performance of the interest articulation function, while in other countries such as France and Italy they fail to do so. It is only through such approximative research undertakings, carried on, however, within the framework of a statistical model of the polity, that we will be able to settle the question of which aspects of the polity are susceptible of quantitative representation, and which are not, and what the costs and problems of such operations are likely to be.

There is an even more challenging prospect which this ap- 161 proach to the study of the polity holds out. In our presentation of the functional theory, we have continually stressed the point that all political structure is multifunctional, and all political culture is dualistic. The peculiar properties of "modernity" of structure and culture are a particular mode of solution of the problems of multifunctionality and cultural dualism. In the modern Western system, each of the functions has a specialized structure which regulates the performance of the particular function by other structures. We have characterized this "modern" solution of the problem of multifunctionality as a regulation of the performance of the function within the polity by a specialized autonomous structure with a boundary of its own and a capacity to "enforce" this boundary in the system as a whole. We have characterized the "modern" solution of the problems of cultural dualism as a penetration of the "traditional" styles of diffuseness, particularism, ascriptiveness, and affectivity, by the "rational" styles of specificity, universalism, achievement, and affective neutrality.

162   If somehow the problem of finding reliable indicators for
these concepts of functional regulation and cultural penetration can be solved, we may be able to take a step along the way
toward the development of a formal theory of political modernization, a step which would improve our capacity to predict
the trend of political development in modernizing states from
carefully selected indicators.

163   To be able to do this implies a state of knowledge of the
performance of modern Western polities far beyond what we
have attained today. It also implies the obsolescence of the
present-day divisions of the study of politics into American,
European, Asiatic, Middle Eastern, African, and Latin American "area studies." The political scientist who wishes to study
political modernization in the non-Western areas will have to
master the model of the modern, which in turn can only be
derived from the most careful empirical and formal analysis
of the functions of the modern Western polities. In his efforts
at predicting what might happen, or in explaining what did
happen, he will not only have to know the properties of the
systems we call modern, but should be able to call upon, with
relative freedom, the experience of the polities of the other non-
Western areas as a means of gaining insight into the processes
of change in those areas in which he specializes.

164   The magnitude of the formal and empirical knowledge required of the political scientist of the future staggers the imagination and lames the will. We have been accustomed to working in a dim and fitful light. As we learn that a stronger and
steadier illumination is possible, our first reaction is to blink
and withdraw in pain. And yet as those who carry on the traditions of one of the most ancient of sciences, which is intended
to maximize man's capacity to tame violence and employ it
only for the humane goals of freedom, justice, and welfare, we
cannot hesitate in the search for a greater illumination. Suppose many of the problems of developing a formal theory of
the polity prove intractable and their solution eludes us for
generations to come. Casting our problems in terms of formal
theory will direct us to the kind and degree of precision which
are possible in the discipline, and will enable us to take our
place in the order of the sciences with the dignity which is reserved only for those who follow a calling without limit and
condition.

Notes
   1. Max Weber, "Politics as a Vocation," in Gerth and Mills, *From Max
   Weber,* New York, 1946, p. 78.

2. I. Schapera, *Government and Politics in Tribal Societies*, London, 1956, p. 119.
3. Marion Levy, Jr., *The Structure of Society*, Princeton, N.J., 1952, p. 469.
4. H. D. Lasswell and Abraham Kaplan, *Power and Society*, New Haven, Conn., 1950, p. 76.
5. David Easton, *The Political System: An Inquiry into the State of Political Science*, New York, 1953, pp. 130ff.
6. *Ibid.*, p. 133.
7. Gabriel A. Almond, "Comparative Political Systems," *Journal of Politics*, Vol. XVIII, No. 3, August 1956, pp. 395–396.
8. Frank J. Goodnow, *Politics and Administration*, New York, 1900.
9. *Ibid.*, p. 17.
10. *World Politics*, Vol. IX, No. 3, April 1957, pp. 383ff.
11. Bureau of Governmental Research, University of Maryland, 1956.
12. *Ibid.*, p. 1.
13. *Ibid.*, p. 2.
14. *Ibid.*, p. 2.
15. Conducted by graduate students of the Woodrow Wilson School of Princeton University under the supervision of Bernard C. Cohen and myself.
16. E. Adamson Hoebel, *Law of Primitive Man*, Cambridge, Mass., 1954, pp. 67ff.
17. Paul F. Lazarsfeld, Bernard Berelson, and Hazel Gaudet, *The People's Choice*, New York, 1948; Robert K. Merton, "Patterns of Influence: A Study of Interpersonal Influence and Communications Behavior in a Local Community," in Paul Lazarsfeld and Frank N. Stanton, eds., *Communications Research, 1948–1949*, New York, 1949; Paul F. Lazarsfeld, Bernard Berelson, and William N. McPhee, *Voting: A Study of Opinion Formation in a Presidential Campaign*, Chicago, 1954; Elihu Katz and Paul F. Lazarsfeld, *Personal Influence: The Part Played by People in the Flow of Mass Communications*, Glencoe, Ill., 1955.
18. Elihu Katz, "The Two-Step Flow of Communication: An Up-to-Date Report on an Hypothesis," *Public Opinion Quarterly*, Vol. XXI, No. 1, Spring 1957, pp. 61ff.
19. *Ibid.*, p. 77.
20. For a summary of the literature on the primary group, see E. A. Shils, "The Study of the Primary Group," in Daniel Lerner and Harold Lasswell, eds., *The Policy Sciences*, Stanford, Calif., 1951, pp. 44ff. See also Sidney Verba, "The Experimental Study of Politics" (Ph.D dissertation, Department of Politics, Princeton University, 1959), pp. 17ff.
21. See in particular Talcott Parsons' introduction to Max Weber, *The Theory of Social and Economic Organization*, trans. by A. M. Henderson and Talcott Parsons, New York, 1947, pp. 8ff., and Talcott Parsons and Edward A. Shills, *Toward a General Theory of Action*, Cambridge, Mass., 1951, pp. 53ff.; Talcott Parsons, *The Social System*, Glencoe, Ill., 1951, pp. 58ff.

22. See Weber, *The Theory of Social and Economic Organization, op. cit.*, pp. 115ff.
23. "Social Theory and Comparative Politics," a paper prepared for a conference of the Committee on Comparative Politics, Social Science Research Council, held at Princeton in June 1954.
24. "Agraria and Industria—Toward a Typology of Comparative Administration," in W. J. Siffin, ed., *Toward a Comparative Study of Public Administration,* Bloomington, Ind., 1957, pp. 23–116.
25. "Social Theory and Comparative Politics," *op.cit.*
26. Verba, *op.cit.*, pp. 21ff.
27. Robert T. McKenzie, *British Political Parties,* London, 1955, pp. 581ff.
28. I have taken these three models of culture contact and change from Evon Z. Vogt's "The Navaho," in Edward H. Spicer, ed., *New Perspectives in American Indian Culture Change.*
29. Herbert Hyman, *Political Socialization,* Glencoe, Ill., 1959, p. 18.
30. *Ibid.*, p. 25.
31. Ralph Linton, *The Cultural Background of Personality,* New York, 1945, pp. 125ff.
32. Even anomic interest articulation tends to be domesticated in the British political system. Hence "Hyde Park" and the exaggerated concern that the most extreme and unpopular of claims and ideas have a protected opportunity and place for expression.
33. Gabriel A. Almond, Rapporteur, "A Comparative Study of Interest Groups and the Political Process," *American Political Science Review,* Vol. LII, No. 1, March 1958, p. 275.
34. *Ibid.*, p. 276.
35. Almond, "Comparative Interest Groups," op.cit., pp. 276–277. See Dankwart Rustow, "Scandinavia: Working Multiparty Systems," in Sigmund Neumann, ed., *Modern Political Parties,* Chicago, 1956, pp. 169ff.
36. Neumann, op.cit., p. 405.
37. Edward Shils, *"Political Development in the New States"* (mimeographed paper prepared for the Committee on Comparative Politics, Social Science Research Council, 1959).
38. *Ibid.*, p. 53.
39. *Supra*, p. 16.
40. *The Decision Process* (see note 11).
41. Robert A. Dahl, *A Preface to Democratic Theory,* Chicago, 1956.
42. See *The Governmental Process,* New York, 1951, in particular Ch. 16.
43. V. O. Key, Jr., *Politics, Parties, and Pressure Groups,* New York, 1958, pp. 142ff.
44. Talcott Parsons and Edward Shils, *Toward a General Theory of Action,* op.cit., pp. 53ff.

CHAPTER FIVE

COMMUNICATIONS THEORY

Inevitably, political scientists are influenced by the intellectual developments that take place around them. The organic images of which we spoke in the functionalist context were derived from ideas that prevailed outside political science. In much the same way, current cognitive fashions have made their impact on how the world of politics is perceived. This is particularly true in regard to the technological-intellectual 'revolutions' (here, this much overused word is entirely appropriate) that have taken place in information processing, cybernetics, communications, computer technology, and artificial intelligence.

Although both systems analysis and functionalism already incorporate information-processing elements and foreshadow the cybernetic understanding of politics—the notion of 'feedback' is, after all, a significant part of them both—in neither case was this the primary focus for construing the political system. Karl Deutsch's book *The Nerves of Government*, which appeared in 1963, takes up the challenge raised by these novel ideas about learning, control, and self-monitoring. The question he poses can be loosely formulated as follows: What are the implications for our understanding of the political system if we conceive of it as a vast information storing, receiving, processing, transmitting network? If we compare the political process to what we know of learning, responding to new stimuli, self-correction, and self-regulation, are our traditional assumptions about politics still adequate and serviceable?

Perhaps the single most important insight provided by this exercise is the novel conception of the political system as a "self-conscious" network that responds to itself. Government, as the title of Deutsch's book indicates, is a series of "nerves" extending throughout the body politic; these nervous connections bring messages from a command center to the periphery, and vice versa. So, if the regnant image of the functionalists is that of an organism, here the operative analogy is that of a nervous system.

When the political system is so conceived, our attention is drawn to those sources of information and those channels of transmission that effectively initiate and restrain action. What would a study concentrating on the relative speed and effectiveness with which different kinds of messages were transmitted tell us about a political system? Clearly, it would tell us very different things than a formal legal analysis of institutions and constitutional documents. These traditional approaches tell us little about (1) the patterns of information dissemination, (2) the susceptibility of certain messages to be recognized and acted upon while others are consistently rejected, or (3) the ability of a system to ingest new information and adapt itself accordingly. On the other hand, avenues of inquiry like political socialization and political culture, whose underlying subject is the creation of selective receptiveness to certain kinds of information, would appear to be of cardinal importance.

A communications perspective also has the effect of reorienting political science away from its perennial concern with "power" to more information-based criteria of political capacities. Just as the nervous system initiates the movement of the body's powerful muscle masses, so, in a cybernetic approach to the body politic, information transmissions activate the organs of power. In the final analysis, it is, no doubt, the real organs of power that actually make contact with the hard realities of the here and now; it is, nevertheless, the political mind, the command center together with its many message-carrying offshoots and tributaries, that orchestrates their activities and accounts for their effectiveness. As such, the cybernetic approach to political inquiry argues that political analysis, particularly in regard to modern political communities, would do well to replace the traditional concentration on power ("how many divisions does he have," Stalin reputedly asked about the pope), with a fresh look at political systems as information-processing networks.

"Power" as the focus of political analysis fails, in Deutsch's estimation, because it is usually not power, i.e., the wielding of force against resistance, that is the hub of modern politics. Power is a currency of last resort rather than the coin in which most political transactions are carried out. Primarily, politics is conducted through the medium of steering and decision making, with the power-wielding "divisions" usually waiting far in the background.

Deutsch provides a striking analogy to illustrate his point. Only the wildly naive believe that the money I have deposited in my local bank branch is actually set aside for me in the safe. Not only is my money not kept ready at hand by the bank, but the ratio between the money that the bank in all its branches has available at any one moment and the actual deposits it has received from all its customers is anything but 1:1. (Deutsch also speaks at another level of the gold in Fort Knox as totally insufficient to cover all the American paper money that is based upon it.) The greater part of a bank's assets are, at any given moment, not liquid; its debts to its depositors far outrun its cash on hand. Were a bank's depositors to come en masse and withdraw their savings, bankruptcy would quickly result.

Are banks then merely fraudulent institutions that take the public's money without the ability to return it? Hardly! Banks are based on the **trust** that the public has in them, trust that when Jane Doe does appear at the teller's window, the cash she asks to withdraw will be given to her without hesitation. It is, in fact, for this very reason—the trust we have in the institution of banking—that we do not, at this very moment, dash over to our bank (which does not, after all, have funds sufficient to cover all its deposits) and withdraw our savings. In a word, were banks forced to pay what they owe, they would all fail. They flourish only because we trust them and therefore, ironically, do not ask them to make good on their commitments.

Power, Deutsch wishes us to understand, is very much like cash in the safe. We could never have enough of it if everyone continually challenged a government's legitimacy and refused to obey any law. Were there to be a "run" on a government's power (like a run on the bank's assets), one armed soldier or policeman would have to be assigned to each citizen twenty-four hours a day. And like the bank pressured by its depositors, such a government would not have long to live. Probably no government could continue to rule for any length of time if it needed to rely only on wielding force against omnipresent resistance. The cost would be so prodigious that even the mightiest regime would be reduced to destitution in no time at all.

Like liquid cash, power is effective when it is not called upon, when the very belief that it is there prevents it from actually being used. More exactly formulated, power is effective when its legitimacy is unquestioned and hence its implementation is superfluous. It is therefore the vast grid of information in which we are placed and to which we respond—and not the actual wielding the power—that accounts for better parts of our political lives.

Viewed in this information-related manner, a "nation," for example, is neither a union of volk souls nor yet an aggregation of individuals simply residing within the national borders; it needs to be approached as a relatively coherent and enduring information network. The nation ends, so to speak, where there is a sharp drop-off in shared information. In a very simplistic form then, a nation would be a human grouping that, because of common and specific linguistic, cultural, historical, etc., sensibilities, processes information in a similar way. There is therefore a special receptivity, speed, accessibility, and sensitivity that marks communication traveling within the national network.

Modernization, usually thought of in the quantitative terms of industrial production, road building, urbanization, etc., can also be viewed as the process of transforming systems of information dissemination and reception. Developing nations go through a far-reaching and profound transformation in the kinds of information available, the sources that initiate its dissemination, the channels through which it flows, the receptors that ingest and decode it, and so on. Modernization (and the very often associated process of "nation building") is in large measure the process of restructuring communication networks. When a rural, tribal, traditional people urbanize and take on a "modern" character, old information networks are discarded, and, in a transitional period of communicative fallowness, new national links are fashioned.

From Deutsch's perspective, the primary image of the political process needs to be that of "navigation" and "steering," a coordination of efforts, rather than a system of force and compulsion. The **process** of decision making rather than the brute **implementation** of decisions is his central concern. To put this idea in the familiar terms of a "ship of state": rather than concentrating on the boiler room, which supplies energy to drive the turbines and propel the ship forward, the proper focus for Deutsch is the captain at the helm, the decisions that he and his officers make, and the speed and efficiency with which they are implemented. Although these decisions, in themselves, involve little energy, they engage the gears of action and account for the thrust of power that follows.

This lack of symmetry between the small amounts of energy involved in information flow and decision making, on the one hand, and the immense quantities of energy they activate, on the other, is perhaps the typical feature of cybernetic analysis. Deutsch notes that a small key or combination (which both are, after all, nothing but coded messages) can move the tons of steel and the complex locks and tumblers of a massive bank vault door. Modern politics is about these keys and these messages. Understanding the political process entails an appreciation of how information controls, initiates, regulates, harnesses, channels, and monitors the energies of a political community. It is about the kinds of messages that, if directed to the right receptors at a timely moment, can launch major campaigns and set masses of individuals into motion.

One immediate advantage of this approach is that the "message units" responsible for political navigation become substantially easier to measure—even though such things are never really easy. As opposed to power with its notorious elusiveness and lack of standards of comparability, information can be calibrated, traced, and compared. We can follow a message, its content, style of delivery, speed of access, etc., from the moment of its sending until it reaches its destination and effects its change (if any) in the receptor. Information grids can be mapped, dissemination patterns can be charted, the efficacy of similar messages in different contexts can be compared, and the learning capacity of a system can be appraised.

Arguably, therefore, the information-processing approach provides more concrete tools for analysis than the approaches we have studied to this point. It is especially close to real events and consequently is less generic and heuristic than some of the other input-output schemes. This appears all the more convincing when it is considered that Deutsch does not limit the concept "information" to the narrow and conventional sense of the term, that is, to "units of knowledge, facts or data." In his formulation, information includes virtually any transfer of people and commodities, alongside the more familiar transmitting of messages.

Drawing a map of mail flow, bus routes, airline traffic, telephone conversations, commerce ties, road networks and so on, brings us very close
indeed to the nerves of government that Deutsch seeks to expose.

A political system's viability depends heavily on its ability to (1) absorb
information from both within and without its borders, (2) to process it
expeditiously, (3) to respond appropriately, and (4) to evaluate its own
response. Absorbing information, the first stage of this process, is not
an automatic matter. To receive information requires receptors that are
adjusted to the right frequency and sensitive to the kinds of information
being sent. Some kinds of messages are difficult for a system to absorb.
For example, information that challenges widely held beliefs may be
dismissed outright because it does not match our anticipations. That
President Sadat of Egypt would cross the Suez Canal and attack Israel
in the 1973 Yom Kippur War was not seriously considered by Israel's
intelligence community—despite the overwhelming evidence that it was
about to happen—because it violated their most basic assumptions.
   Political systems that fail to absorb changing patterns of information
from their environments suffer from a kind of selective deafness. They
filter out those messages that do not suit their anticipations and hence act
in the absence of what is important for them to know in order to respond
intelligently. Deutsch identifies the major source for such communication failures as excessively rigid ideologies. When ideologies—usually of
an extreme and doctrinaire kind—act as impervious filtering devices that
severely limit what the receptors are capable of absorbing, when they jam
what is threatening or novel, the system's learning capacity is seriously
impaired. Ideologies of this kind, Deutsch believes, are "epistemological catastrophes" because they fail to recognize the response-demanding
changes, the novel imperatives, that their political environment constantly poses.
   Does this mean that political realities are best navigated without the
aid of any ideology at all? It is seductive to believe that, unencumbered by
any ideological anticipations, learning capacity and response flexibility
would be virtually limitless. It would be seductive, perhaps, but quite
misleading. Lacking any framework for the processing of information
would be no less catastrophic than being limited by a doctrinaire orthodoxy. Without a frame of values or anticipations, incoming information
would be utterly unprocessable; we would lack elementary categories and
hierarchies through which to organize and relate to what we experience.
   What is needed, Deutsch believes, is a flexible ideological frame that
organizes, catalogs, and interprets incoming data broadly and prelim-
inarily without suffering the gridlock of dogma. Ideologies that have
substantial learning capacity built into them, that remain at least partly
agnostic, pragmatic, and uncommitted, that are open to accommodate
fresh patterns of response, are in information-processing terms optimal
for growth and survival.

The processing of incoming information depends, of course, on the quality and quantity of what has been absorbed both from within and without. Lacking adequate receptors or being ideologically deaf to uncomfortable information means that what becomes available for processing is either meager or distorted. But for exposition's sake, let us assume there is an adequate and reasonably undistorted information flow. This information now must be processed; that is, it must be interpreted, evaluated, and responded to. Policy must be fashioned, decisions made, and directives given. Deutsch's approach focuses great energies on studying the ease, speed, discrimination, accuracy, balance, method, etc., in which incoming information is converted into decisions and policy. Does the information flow unimpeded between the various decision-making bodies? Do rival and mutually undermining information flows take place simultaneously? Are certain institutions characteristically sluggish or unbalanced or slipshod in the way they transform the stimulating information into responses? Are certain kinds of information more easily and expeditiously dealt with than others?

Another critical element in Deutsch's research program is the link between the decision-making process and the actual response on the ground. Brilliant decisions are, of course, useless if they fail to translate into action. Here, too, those following Deutsch's lead are particularly concerned with how the flow of information from the decision-making bodies affects those who are charged with implementation. Does information regarding the decision reach the implementors fully, faithfully, and rapidly? Do decisions translate quickly and accurately into execution? Are certain areas of the polity (say, peripheries) less responsive to decisions taken at its center? Are certain kinds of decisions regularly expedited and others regularly "sabotaged" by different bodies and institutions, etc.?

But it is in the analysis of politics as a self-monitoring and self-correcting system that the cybernetic approach is perhaps most sophisticated and innovative. For Deutsch, the ability of political systems to evaluate their own performance against their objectives, their capacity to learn from mistakes and change direction appropriately, allows us to understand them as sentient and intentional systems—in a certain sense, even as "conscious." Consequently, Deutsch would have us focus on the learning capacity of political systems and on their ability to acknowledge error and to correct their decisions accordingly.

When such errors are diagnosed, how long does it take to redirect efforts to where they properly belong? Does the recognition of error mean that the system will overreact in the opposite direction? Will the political system—like an inexperienced driver who turns too sharply to avoid danger and then is unable to overcome the subsequent skiddings first to the right and then to the left—miss the first obstacle only to head into a permanent condition of oscillation and disequilibrium? How, in short, are political responses intentionally moderated, adjusted, and improved in the light of objectives the system chooses to pursue?

The criticisms leveled at the cybernetic approach should be familiar at this point because they are quite similar to those we have already discussed in regard to systems analysis and functionalism. Predictably, the ideological critique stands front and center here as well. There is no getting away from the charge that very determinate political convictions lurk not very far from the surface of Deutsch's formulations. As in all input-output analysis, we cannot avoid the allegation that the liberal values of equilibrium, self-maintenance, and stress reduction are the implicit objectives of the political system.

In Deutsch's case, however, the charge that he had inveigled liberal pluralist norms into his approach took a more specific direction as well. Deutsch's ideological enemies were quick to accuse him of utilizing academic terminology and a sophisticated conceptual apparatus in order to both bludgeon ideologies of the left and the right for which he had no sympathy and to place his preferred pragmatic liberalism on a scientific pedestal. After all, Deutsch had explicitly spoken of nonpragmatic ideologies as selectively deaf to reality, as misleading, wrong-headed, incapable of learning, and as likely as not to lead the believer into unmitigated catastrophe. Liberal pluralism, by contrast, possesses great "learning capacity," large reserves of "uncommitted resources," and far greater innovative capabilities. Whatever we may think of these contentions as committed political individuals, can we fail to distinguish here between the character of partisan ideological convictions and that of disinterested academic methodology?

SUGGESTIONS FOR FURTHER READING

Deutsch, K. W., *Nationalism and Social Communication: An Inquiry into the Foundation of Nationality* (Cambridge, MIT Press, 1966).

Deutsch, K. W., "Social Mobilization and Political Development," *American Political Science Review*, 55, (1961), pp. 493–514.

Dobuzinskis, Laurent, *The Self-Organizing Polity: An Epistemological Analysis of Political Life* (Boulder, CO, Westview Press, 1987).

Merritt, R. L., and Russett, B. M., *From National Development to Global Community: Essays in Honor of Karl W. Deutsch* (London, Allen and Unwin, 1981).

Taylor, C. L., and Jodice, D. A., *World Handbook of Social and Political Indicators*, 2 vols. (New Haven, Yale University Press, 1983).

Karl W. Deutsch
A Simple Cybernetic Model

1   Mechanic, organismic, and historical models were based, substantially, on experiences and operations known before 1850, even though many of their implications were worked out more fully only later. A major change in this situation began in the 1940's. Its basis was in the new development in communications engineering, with its extensive use of self-monitoring, self-controlling, and self-steering automatic processes. By making equipment that fulfills the functions of communication, organization, and control, significant opportunities were gained for a clearer understanding of the functions themselves.

2   These new developments in science and engineering were the beneficiaries of long-standing developments in social organization. Communication was social before it became elaborately technological. There were established routes for messages before the first telegraph lines. In the nineteenth century, factories and railroads required accurate coordination of complex sequences of human actions—a requirement that became central in the assembly-line methods and flow charts of modern mass production. The same age saw the rise of general staffs, and of intelligence organizations for diplomatic as well as for military purposes. These staffs and organizations, just as the modern large-scale industrial research laboratory itself, represent in a very real sense assembly lines of information, assembly lines of thoughts. Just as the division of manual labor between human hands preceded the division of labor between human hands and power-drive mechanisms, so the increasing division of intellectual labor between different human minds preceded today's divisions of labor between human minds and an ever-growing array of electronic or other communications, calculating, and control equipment.

3   What have the new machines of communication and control to offer for a further understanding of historical and social processes? For thousands of years, the operations of communication and control were largely carried on inside the nerve systems of human bodies. They were inaccessible to direct observation or analysis. They could be neither taken apart nor reassembled. In the new electronic machines of communication and control, messages or control operations can be taken

From *The Nerves of Government: Models of Political Communication and Control* (New York, Free Press, 1966), pp. 75-97. Reprinted by permission.

apart, studied step by step, and recombined into more efficient patterns.

The Viewpoint of Cybernetics

The science of communication and control, which has been derived from this technology and which Norbert Wiener has called "cybernetics," is therefore a new science about an old subject. In investigating the old subject of communication and control, it uses the facilities of modern technology to map out step by step the sequence of actual events involved.[1]

Cybernetics, the systematic study of communication and control in organizations of all kinds, is a conceptual scheme on the "grand scale," in J. B. Conant's sense of the term.[2] Essentially, it represents a shift in the center of interest from drives to steering, and from instincts to systems of decisions, regulation, and control, including the noncyclical aspects of such systems. In its scope, it is comparable to Lavoisier's stress on quantitative chemistry, or to Darwin's concept of evolution. As to its performance and success, the future will have to tell, but it is perhaps safe to say that social science is already being influenced by the interests implicit in cybernetics at this time.

The fundamental viewpoint of cybernetics and its relevance to social science have been well expressed by Norbert Wiener:

> The existence of Social Science is based on the ability to treat a social group as an organization and not as an agglomeration. Communication is the cement that makes *organisations*. Communication alone enables a group to think together, to see together, and to act together. All sociology requires the understanding of communication.
>
> What is true for the unity of a group of people, is equally true for the individual integrity of each person. The various elements which make up each personality are in continual communication with each other and affect each other through control mechanisms which themselves have the nature of communication.
>
> Certain aspects of the theory of communication have been considered by the engineer. While human and social communication are extremely complicated in comparison to the existing patterns of machine communication, they are subject to the same grammar; and this grammar has received its highest technical development when applied to the simpler content of the machine.[3]

7   In other words, the viewpoint of cybernetics suggests that all organizations are alike in certain fundamental characteristics and that every organization is held together by communication. Communication is a process different from transportation on the one hand and from power engineering on the other. Transportation transmits physical objects such as liquids in pipelines, or boxes or passengers in trains or on escalators. Power engineering transmits quantities of electric energy. Communication engineering, by contrast, transmits neither tons of freight nor kilowatts of power. It transmits messages that contain quantities of information, and I shall say more about this concept of information later in this chapter. It is communication, that is, the ability to transmit messages and to react to them, that makes organizations; and it seems that this is true of organizations of living cells in the human body as well as of organizations of pieces of machinery in an electronic calculator, as well as of organizations of thinking human beings in social groups.[4] Finally, cybernetics suggests that steering or governing is one of the most interesting and significant processes in the world, and that a study of steering in self-steering machines, in biological organisms, in human minds, and in societies will increase our understanding of problems in all these fields.

Analogies and Convergent Developments

8   Why should anyone think that this viewpoint represents a conceptual scheme and not a mere analogy? Actually, the meaning of the term *analogy* is often poorly understood. Analogy means limited structural correspondence. All mathematics is based on analogies, and so is a large part of every science. Darwin himself tells us that it was his perception of the analogy between Malthus' theory of human population and certain processes in the animal kingdom that led him to his theory of evolution. When scientists speak disparagingly of "mere analogies," they mean, more accurately, "false analogies" or "poor analogies." The test by which we discriminate between a false analogy and a good analogy consists in the extent of actual structural correspondence between the two systems from which the analogy is drawn.[5] How many and how significant are the instances in which the analogy holds good, and how numerous and how important are the instances in which it fails to work? These are the questions by which we test analogies and which serve to unmask the many false analogies

which look plausible at first glance but fail completely after the early stages of the application. The test of a good analogy, conversely, is that it continues to be confirmed after we have penetrated more deeply into the subjects it purports to connect and that it becomes more fruitful of new ideas and of new investigations as we continue to apply it. Darwin's analogy with the work of Malthus was a good analogy in this sense, and so was Torricelli's analogy between the atmosphere and a "sea of air." It is suggested that cybernetics is currently proving itself a good analogy or conceptual scheme in a similar manner.

The rise of the viewpoint of communications in the present 9 period has not been fortuitous. Rather, it has been the result of convergent developments in a whole series of different sciences. Among these trends is the development of mathematical and statistical methods for the study of randomness and order, and thus of probability, leading to the mathematical theory of communication as developed by Norbert Wiener, Claude Shannon, and others. During the same decades the concept of homeostasis was developed by Claude Bernard, and later by Walter B. Cannon and Arturo Rosenblueth in physiology. This medical work found its parallel in the mathematical and empirical studies of control mechanisms, from Clark Maxwell's early paper on the governor in steam engines to the highly developed automatic control engineering of today. Problems of flow in various organizations were studied in production engineering, traffic engineering, city planning, and the design of telephone systems. Advances in the design of automatic switchboards eventually merged with the long-standing efforts to design effective calculating machines, from the early days of Leibniz and later of Charles Babbage to the analogue computer constructed by Vannevar Bush and the big digital computers of today. These advances in mathematics and the study of physical systems were paralleled by Ivan Pavlov's emphasis on the material nature of psychological processes, and on the discrete structure of the conditioned reflexes on which many of them were based. This emphasis was balanced by the rise of the school of *Gestalt* psychology led by Kurt Koffka and Wolfgang Köhler, emphasizing the importance of pattern and order, and the rise of the depth psychology of Sigmund Freud and his followers.

It is the experience of this new group of sciences that finds 10 its reflection in some of the major ideas of cybernetics, such as the notion of the physical reality of patterns and of information and of the statistical nature of the latter, as well as the related notions of the physical nature of control processes, memory, and learning.

11   Taken together, the new experiences and notions promise to
      replace the classic analogues or models of mechanism, organ-
      ism, and process, which so long have dominated so much of
      scientific thinking. All three of these models have long been
      felt to be inadequate. Mechanism and the equilibrium concept
      cannot represent growth and evolution. Organisms are inca-
      pable of both accurate analysis and internal rearrangement;
      and models of historical processes lacked inner structure and
      quantitative predictability.

12   In the place of these obsolescent models, we now have an
      array of self-controlling machines that react to their environ-
      ment, as well as to the results of their own behavior; that store,
      process, and apply information; and that have, in some cases,
      a limited capacity to learn.

13   None of this is *thought* in the human sense of the word, as
      we find it in the behavior of individuals or groups, but it has
      significant parallels to it. Above all, the storage and treatment
      of information in machines, and its application to the control
      of the machines themselves, are taking place under conditions
      where every step can be traced distinctly and where every sys-
      tem can be taken apart for study and reassembled again. This
      is a research advantage that it would be neither easy nor en-
      tirely desirable to parallel in the case of human beings.

14   The test of the usefulness of this new science, as that of
      any science, must be its results. In the field of scientific the-
      ory it must offer new concepts rather than mere explanations.
      The analogies cybernetics may suggest between communica-
      tion channels or control processes in machines, nerve systems,
      and human societies must in turn suggest new observations,
      experiments, or predictions that can be confirmed or refuted
      by the facts. They must be meaningful, that is, capable of being
      tested by practicable operations, and they should be fruitful,
      that is, lead to new operations and new concepts.

The General Concept of a Self-Controlling System

15   To the extent that we can demonstrate that such analogies
      exist, and that they are fruitful in research, we may derive
      from them a generalized concept of a *self-modifying communi-
      cations network* or *"learning net."* Such a "learning net" would
      be any system characterized by a relevant degree of organiza-
      tion, communication, and control, regardless of the particular
      processes by which its messages are transmitted and its func-
      tions carried out—whether by words between individuals in a

social organization, or by nerve cells and hormones in a living body, or by electric signals in an electronic device.[6]

How does a modern communications mechanism look and what concepts can be derived from it? 16

Let me refer here to a brief sketch I gave elsewhere: 17

A modern radar tracking and computing device can "sense" an object in the air, interacting with its beam; it can "interpret" it as an airplane (and may be subject to error in this "perception"); it can apply records of past experience, which are stored within its network, and with the aid of these data from "memory" it can predict the probable location of the plane several seconds ahead in the future (being again potentially subject to error in its "recollections" as well as in its "guess," and to "disappointment," if its calculation of probability was correct, but if the airplane should take a less probable course); it can turn a battery of antiaircraft guns on the calculated spot and shoot down the airplane; and it can then "perceive," predict, and shoot down the next. If it should spot more than one airplane at the same time, it must become "infirm of purpose," or else decide ("make up its mind") which one to shoot down first....

Man-made machines actually operating or designable today have devices which function as "sense organs," furnish "interpretations" of stimuli, perform acts of recognition, have "memory," "learn" from experience, carry out motor actions, are subject to conflicts and jamming, make decisions between conflicting alternatives, and follow operating rules of preference or "value" in distributing their "attention," giving preferred treatment to some messages over others, and making other decisions, or even conceivably overriding previous operating rules in the light of newly "learned" and "remembered" information.

None of these devices approach the overall complexity of the human mind. While some of them excel it in specific fields (such as the mechanical or electronic calculators), they are not likely to approach its general range for a long time to come. But, as simplified models, they can aid our understanding of more complex mental and social processes, much as sixteenth-century pumps were still far simpler than the human heart, but had become elaborate enough to aid Harvey in his understanding of the circulation of the blood.[7]

What are some of the notions and concepts that can be de- 18
rived from this technology? Perhaps the most important is the notion of information.

The Concepts of Information,
Message, and Complementarity

19   Power engineering transfers amounts of electric energy: *communications engineering transfers information*. It does not transfer events; it transfers *a patterned relationship between events*. When a spoken message is transferred through a sequence of mechanical vibrations of the air and of a membrane; thence through electric impulses in a wire; thence through electric processes in a broadcasting station and through radio waves; thence through electric and mechanical processes in a receiver and recorder to a set of grooves on the surface of a disk; and finally played and made audible to a listener—what has been transferred through this chain of processes, or channel of communication, is not matter, nor any one of the particular processes, nor any significant amount of energy, since relays and electronic tubes make the qualities of the signal independent from a considerable range of energy inputs. Rather it is *something* that has remained unchanged, invariant, over this whole sequence of processes.

20   The same principle applies to the sequence of processes from the distribution of light reflected from a rock to the distribution of black or white dots on a printing surface, or the distribution of electric "yes" or "no" impulses in picture telegraphy or television. What is transmitted here are neither light rays nor shadows, but information, the pattern of relationships between them.

21   In the second group of examples, we could describe the state of the rock in terms of the distribution of light and dark points on its surface. This would be a *state description* of the rock at a particular time. If we then take a picture of the rock, we could describe the state of the film after exposure in terms of the distribution of the dark grains of silver deposited on it and of the remaining clear spaces; that is, we should get another state description. Each of the two state descriptions would have been taken from a quite different object—a rock and a film—but a large part of these two state descriptions would be identical whether we compared them point by point or in mathematical terms. There would again be a great deal of identity between these two descriptions and several others; such as the description of the distribution of black and white dots on the printing surface, or of the electric "yes" or "no" impulses in the television circuits, or the light and dark points on the television screen. The extent of the physical possibility to transfer and

reproduce these patterns corresponds to the extent that there is "*something*" unchanging in all the relevant state descriptions of the physical processes by which this transmission is carried on. That "something" is *information—those aspects of the state descriptions of each physical process that all these processes had in common.*[8]

To the extent that the last state description in such a se- 22 quence differs from the first, information has been lost or distorted during its passage through the channel. From the amount of information transmitted as against the information lost, we may derive a measure of the *efficiency* of a channel, as well as of the relative efficiency or *complementarity* of any parts or states of the channel in relation to the others.

These patterns of information can be measured in quantita- 23 tive terms, described in mathematical language, analyzed by science, and transmitted or processed on a practical industrial scale.

This development is significant for wide fields of natural and 24 social sciences. Information is indeed "such stuff as dreams are made on." Yet it can be transmitted, recorded, analyzed, and measured. Whatever we may call it, information, pattern, form, *Gestalt*, state description, distribution function, or negative entropy, it has become accessible to the treatment of science. It differs from the "matter" and "energy" of nineteenth-century mechanical materialism in that it cannot be described adequately by their conservation laws.

But it also differs, if not more so, from the "idea" of "idealis- 25 tic" or metaphysical philosophies, in that it is based on physical processes during every single moment of its existence, and in that it can and must be dealt with by physical methods. It has material reality. It exists and interacts with other processes in the world, regardless of the whims of any particular human observer; so much so that its reception, transmission, reproduction, and in certain cases its recognition, can be and sometimes has been mechanized.

These, then, were the main developments that came to a 26 head after 1940. Cybernetics as the science of communication and control arose in response to a technological and social opportunity. It was made possible by advanced and parallel developments in neurophysiology and psychology, in mathematics, and in electrical engineering, and by the growing need for cooperation among these and other sciences.[9] The result of these developments was a new body of experience, going beyond classic organism in its rationality, that is, in its ability to be retraced step by step in its workings.

27   The concept of information grew out of this new body of
experience, and particularly out of the separation of communications engineering from power engineering. Information is
what is transferred in telephony or television: it is not events
as such, but a patterned relationship between events. Information has physical, "material" reality; without exception, it
is carried by matter-energy processes. Yet it is not subject to
their conservation laws. Information can be created and wiped
out—although it cannot be created from nothing or destroyed
completely into nothingness.[10] Finally, it differs from the classic notion of "form" in that it can be analyzed into discrete
units that can be measured and counted.

28   Information consists of a transmitted pattern that is received
and evaluated against the background of a statistical ensemble
of related patterns. The classic example for this is the standardized birthday telegram transmitted by telegraphing a single
two-digit number indicating the message to be selected from
the limited set of prefabricated messages held ready by the
company. All information at bottom involves the indication of
some pattern out of a larger statistical ensemble, that is, an
ensemble that is already stored at the point of reception.

29   From this it follows that recognition can be treated as a
physical process and can, in fact, be mechanized in many instances. Current mechanical devices embodying operations of
matching and recognition range all the way from the lowly
fruit-grading and candling machines to the Moving Target Indicator and the Friend and Foe Identification device of the
Armed Forces.[11] Similar standardized recognition processes
are embodied in processes that have been only partly mechanized thus far and that still embody standardized human operations at some stages. Examples of such semimechanized
recognition processes include qualitative analysis in chemistry
and the Crocker-Henderson odor classification scheme and its
successor, the flavor profile, according to which each of five
hundred well-known smells can be identified by a four-digit
number.[12] These recognition devices have grown up empirically, but the application of the theory of information forms
part of the current development work on more complex devices
of recognition—devices that are to be used to permit the deaf
to understand spoken messages and the blind to read printed
books, as well as for work on machines that will transcribe
dictation or translate printed matter from one language into
another.[13] Work on all these problems has been under way
since the 1950's at several institutions of research.

Memory and Recognition

Since information has physical reality, its storage, that is 30
to say, *memory*, is also a physical process. Most processes of
thought can be represented in terms of a seven-stage process:

First, abstraction or coding of incoming information into ap- 31
propriate symbols;

Second, storage of these symbols by means of quasi- 32
permanent changes in the state of some appropriate physical
facilities, such as the patterns of electric charges in certain
electronic devices, the activity patterns of cells in nervous tis-
sue, or the distribution of written marks on paper;

Third, dissociation of some of this information from the rest; 33

Fourth, recall of some of the dissociated items, as well as of 34
some of the larger assemblies;

Fifth, recombinations of some of the recalled items into new 35
patterns that had not been present among the input into the
system;

Sixth, new abstraction from the recombined items preserv- 36
ing their new pattern, but obliterating its combinatorial origin.
Steps five and six together make up the operation of creating
novelty; and

Seventh, transmission of the new item to storage or to ap- 37
plications to action. This application of novelty to behavior we
may call *initiative.*

A similar multistep sequence could consist of matching an 38
incoming pattern of information against another pattern recalled from storage or memory. Both patterns are exposed to a
critical process, that is to say, a physical process the outcome of
which depends critically on the degree of correspondence between the two patterns to which it is applied. If the difference
between the two patterns is smaller than a certain threshold
given by the process, the critical process will have one result;
if the difference is larger, the process will have another outcome. The process of recognition is completed by applying the
outcome of the critical process to the behavior of the system.

An Operational Approach to Quantity and Quality

In a much more general aspect the notions of information 39
and complementarity might be used to clarify the notion of
quality that has sometimes baffled social scientists. From Plato
and Aristotle to Oswald Spengler, Otto Strasser, and Ernst

Jünger, authoritarian philosophers and political theorists have invoked qualitative judgments, the "all or nothing" reactions of taste or esthetic appreciation, as weapons against rationality or democracy. Only the coarse and simple things of social life can be counted and measured, so the argument has run, while all truly subtle and important things defy quantification and step-by-step analysis. Their imponderable and incommensurable peculiarities make them a law unto themselves and a proper analogue to the superiority of mankind's privileged individuals, classes, or races. By contrast, if those social scientists who favored privilege have invoked quality in its defense, some of those who attacked privilege have tried to ignore problems of quality altogether.

40   Perhaps definitions of quantity and quality might be developed in terms of the operations from which they are derived, that is, from the operations involved in the processes of recognition and of measurement. At Massachusetts Institute of Technology a preliminary survey has been made of six processes involving *recognition*. These six systems are in actual use. Two of them are mechanical: the Yale lock and the automatic sorting of punched cards. Two are electronic: the equipment for the Identification of Friend or Foe (I.F.F.) and the Moving Target Indicator (M.T.I.). The last two involve biological or chemical processes within a systematized sequence of steps of human labor: the Crocker-Henderson odor classification scheme, and the scheme of qualitative analysis in chemistry.

41   In all cases it was found that the critical step in the recognition of quality was the establishment of a structural correspondence between a part of the recognizing system and the system that was recognized, and the testing of that correspondence by a *critical process,* that is, a physical process the outcome of which depends critically on the extent of that correspondence.[14] Quality is recognized, therefore, by the matching of two structures. The decisive step is to establish whether or not such matching has occurred.

42   *Quantity* in this view would appear to be really a more complicated notion that quality. It can be measured only *after* some qualitative matching has occurred or has been established; and it consists, then, in the matching of these matchings, that is, in comparing these operations of matching with each other, so as to derive a result of "more" or "less" from this comparison, or in comparing them with some counting structure, so as to record the number of complete matchings.

43   Quality in this view is derived from simple matching; quantity is derived from second-order matching. Despite this fact,

quality has appeared to some writers as the more complex of the two notions, since quantitative measurement occurred only in those relatively well-understood situations where qualitative recognition had already taken place and where the latter could, therefore, already be taken for granted. The situations where qualitative problems were conspicuous were precisely those more difficult cases where structural matching had not yet been accomplished well enough to permit quantitative comparisons. There is reason to suspect that many of the qualitative problems in social and political science may turn out to be problems of matching and complementarity in social communication.[15]

Feedback and Equilibrium

Another significant concept elaborated since the 1940's is that of the "feedback." The feedback pattern is common to self-modifying communications networks, whether they are electronic control devices, nerve systems, or social organizations. "In a broad sense [feedback] may denote that some of the output energy of an apparatus or machine is returned as input. ... [If] the behavior of an object is controlled by the margin of error at which the object stands at a given time with reference to a relatively specific goal ... [the] feedback is ... negative, that is, the signals from the goal are used to restrict outputs which would otherwise go beyond the goal. It is this ... meaning of the term feedback that is used here."[16] "By output is meant any change produced in the surroundings by the object. By input, conversely, is meant any event external to the object that modifies this object in any manner."[17]

In other words, by feedback—or, as it is often called, a servomechanism—is meant a communications network that produces action in response to an input of information, and *includes the results of its own action in the new information by which it modifies its subsequent behavior.* A simple feedback network contains arrangements to react to an outside event (for example, a target) in a specified manner (such as by directing guns at it) until a specified state of affairs has been brought about (the guns cover the target perfectly, or the automatic push-button tuning adjustment on a radio has been accurately set on the wavelength approached). If the action of the network has fallen short of reaching fully the sought adjustment, it is continued; if it has overshot the mark, it is reversed. Both continuation and reversal may take place in proportion to the extent to which the goal has not yet been reached. If the feedback is well designed, the result will be a series of diminishing mistakes—a dwindling series of under- and over-corrections converging on the goal. If the functioning of the feedback or servomechanism is not adequate to its task (if it is inadequately "dampened"), the mistakes may become greater. The network may be "hunting" over a cyclical or widening range of tentative and "incorrect" responses, ending in a breakdown of the mechanism. These failures of feedback networks have specific parallels in the pathology of the human nervous system ("purpose tremor") and perhaps even, in a looser sense, in the behavior of animals, men, and whole communities.[18]

46   This notion of feedback—and its application in practice— is at the heart of much of modern control engineering. It is a more sophisticated concept than the simple mechanical notion of equilibrium, and it promises to become a more powerful tool in the social sciences than the traditional equilibrium analysis.

47   If we say that a system is in *equilibrium,* we make a number of rather specific suggestions. We suggest that it will return to a particular state when "disturbed"; that we imagine the disturbance is coming from outside the system; that the system will return with greater force to its original state the greater has been the disturbance; that the high or low speed with which the system reacts or with which its parts act on each other is somehow irrelevant (and we term this quality "friction" to denote that it is a sort of imperfection or blemish that has no proper place in the "ideal" equilibrium); and finally we suggest that no catastrophes can happen within the limits of the system, but that, once an equilibrium breaks down, next to nothing can be said about the future of the system from then on.

48   Such equilibrium theories are based on a very restricted field of science, called "steady state dynamics." They are not well suited to deal with so-called *transients;* that is, they cannot predict the consequences of *sudden* changes within the system or in its environment, such as the sudden starting or stopping of a process. Altogether, in the world of equilibrium theory there is no growth, no evolution; there are no sudden changes; and there is no efficient prediction of the consequences of "friction" over time.

49   On all these points the feedback concept promises improvements. Instead of pushing the effect of "friction" into the background, feedback theory is based on the measurement of *lag* and *gain.* *Lag* is the time that elapses between the moment a negative feedback system reaches a certain distance from its goal and the moment it completes corrective action corre-

sponding to that distance. *Gain* means the extent of the corrective action taken. An inexperienced automobile driver tends to have slow reflexes: he responds tardily to the information of his eyes that his car is heading for the right-hand ditch. His lag, in feedback terms, is high. Yet when he acts, he may turn his steering wheel sharply—with a high gain—and head for the left-hand ditch until he notices the overcorrection and corrects his course again. If we know three quantities—the speed of his car and extent of his lags and of his gains—we can try to predict the wobbliness of his resulting course.

Lag and *gain*, in the feedback approach, are the most important variables to work on. Of the two, *lag* is the more important. It can be reduced by improving the system, as when our novice driver learns to react faster; or lag can be compensated for by a lead—a prediction of a future distance from the goal—as when an experienced driver compensates for an anticipated skid at the first sign of its onset. What *lag* still remains will permit control engineers to calculate just how much gain—how drastic a self-correction at each step—the system can afford under known conditions without endangering its stability.

To sum up, equilibrium analysis is based on a restricted part of dynamics; it is restricted to the description of steady states. Cybernetics is based on full dynamics including changes of state; and it combines these full dynamics with statistics. Cybernetics is the study of the full dynamics of a system under a statistically varying input. The potential usefulness of this approach to such economic problems as, for example, the so-called "cobweb theorem" has been stressed by some economists.[19]

From a historical point of view, the rise of equilibrium analysis meant the neglect of problems of purpose. Cybernetics offers not only a gain in technical competence but also a possibility of restoring to problems of purpose their full share of our attention.

Learning and Purpose

Even the simple feedback network shows the basic characteristics of the "learning process" described by John Dollard in animals and men. According to Dollard, "there must be (1) drive, (2) cue, (3) response, and (4) reward." In a man-made feedback network, "drive" might be represented by "internal tension," or better, by mechanical, chemical, or electric "disequilibrium"; input and output would function as "cue" and "response"; and the "reward" could be defined analogously for both organisms and man-made nets as a "reduction in intensity" (or extent) of the initial "drive" or internal disequilibrium.[20]

54   A simple feedback mechanism implies a measure of "purpose" or "goal." In this view a goal not only exists within the mind of a human observer; it also has relative objective reality within the context of a particular feedback net, once that net has physically come into existence. Thus a *goal* may be defined as "a final condition in which the behaving object reaches a definite correlation in time or in space with respect to another object or event."[21]

55   This definition of a goal, or purpose, may need further development. There is usually at least one such external goal (that is, one relation of the net as a whole to some external object) that is associated with one state encompassing the relatively lowest amount of internal disequilibrium within the net. Very often, however, an almost equivalent reduction of internal disequilibrium can be reached through an internal rearrangement of the relations between some of the constituent parts of the net, which would then provide a more or less effective substitute for the actual attainment of the goal relation in the world external to the net. There are many cases of such surrogate goals or *ersatz* satisfactions, as a short circuit in an electronic calculator, intoxication in certain insects, drug addiction or suicide in a man, or outbursts against scapegoat members of a "tense" community. They suggest the need for a distinction between merely internal readjustments and those that are sought through pathways that include as an essential part the reaching of a goal relationship with some part of the outside world.

56   This brings us to a more complex kind of learning. Simple learning is a goal-seeking feedback, as in a homing torpedo. It consists in adjusting responses, so as to reach a goal situation of a type that is given once for all by certain internal arrangements of the net; these arrangements remain fixed throughout its life. A more complex type of learning is the self-modifying or *goal-changing* feedback. It allows for feedback readjustments of those internal arrangements that implied its original goal, so that the net will change its goal, or set for itself new goals that it will now have to reach if its internal disequilibrium is to be lessened. Goal-changing feedback contrasts, therefore, with Aristotelian teleology, in which each thing was supposed to be characterized by its unchanging *telos*, but it has parallels in Darwinian evolution.[22]

57   We can now restate our earlier distinction as one between two kinds of goal-changing by internal rearrangement. Internal rearrangements that are still relevant to goal-seeking in

the outside world we may call "learning." Internal rearrangements that reduce the net's goal-seeking effectiveness belong to the pathology of learning. Their eventual results are self-frustration and self-destruction. Pathological learning resembles what some moralists call "sin."

Perhaps the distinction could be carried further by thinking 58 of several orders of purposes.

A first-order purpose in a feedback net would be the seeking 59 of *immediate satisfaction*, that is, of an internal state in which internal disequilibrium would be less than in any alternative state, within the range of operations of the net. This first-order purpose would correspond to the concepts of "adjustment" and "reward" in studies of the learning process. Self-destructive purposes or rewards would be included in this class.

By a second-order purpose would be meant that internal and 60 external state of the net that would seem to offer to the net the largest probability (or predictive value derived from past experience) for the net's continued ability to seek first-order purposes. This would imply *self-preservation* as a second-order purpose of the net, overriding the first-order purposes. It would require a far more complex net.[23]

A third-order purpose might then mean a state of high proba- 61 bility for the continuation of the process of search for first- and second-order purposes by a group of nets beyond the "lifetime" of an individual net. This would include such purposes as the *preservation of the group* or "preservation of the species." Third-order purposes require several complex nets in interaction. Such interaction between several nets, sufficiently similar to make their experiences relevant test cases for one another, sufficiently different to permit division of labor, and sufficiently complex and readjustable to permit reliable communication between them—in short, such a *society*—is in turn essential for the higher levels of the learning process that could lead beyond third-order purposes.

Among fourth-order purposes we might include states of- 62 fering high probabilities of the *preservation of a process* of purpose-seeking, even beyond the preservation of any particular group or species of nets. Such purposes as the preservation or growth of "life," "mind," "order in the universe," and all the other purposes envisaged in science, philosophy, or religion, could be included here.

The four orders overlap; their boundaries blur; and there 63 seems to be no limit to the number of orders or purposes we may set up as aids to our thinking. Yet it may be worthwhile to order purposes in some such fashion, and to retain, as far as possible, the model of the feedback net that permits us to

compare these purposes to some degree with physical arrangements and operations. The purpose of this procedure would not
be to reduce intellectual and spiritual purposes to the level of
neurophysiology or mechanics. Rather it would be to show
that consistent elaboration of the simpler processes can elevate their results to higher levels.

Values and the Capacity to Learn

64   The movements of messages through complex feedback networks may involve the problem of "value" or the "switchboard
problem," that is, the problem of choice between different possibilities of routing different incoming messages through different channels or "associative trails"[24] within the network. If
many alternative channels are available for few messages, the
functioning of the network may be hampered by indecision; if
many messages have to compete for few channels, it may be
hampered by "jamming."

65   The efficient functioning of any complex switchboard requires, therefore, some relatively stable operating rules, explicit or implied in the arrangements of the channels. These
rules must decide the relative preferences and priorities in the
reception, screening, and routing of all signals entering the
network from outside or originating within it.

66   There are many examples of such rules in practice: the priority given fire alarms in many telephone systems; or the rules
determining the channels through which transcontinental telephone calls are routed at different loads of traffic; these last
include even the "hunting" of an automatic switchboard for a
free circuit when the routing channels are fully loaded. They
illustrate the general need of any complex network to decide
in some way on how to distribute its "attention" and its priorities in expediting competing messages, and how to choose
between its large number of different possibilities for combination, association, and recombination for each message.

67   What operating rules accomplish in switchboards and calculating machines is accomplished to some extent by "emotional
preference" in the nervous systems of animals and men, and
by cultural or institutional preferences, obstacles, and "values"
in groups or societies. Nowhere have investigators found any
mind of that type that John Locke supposed "to be, as we say,
white paper." Everywhere they have found structure and relative function.

68   In much of the communications machinery currently used,
the operating rules are rigid in relation to the content of the in-

formation dealt with by the network. However, *these operating rules themselves may be made subject to some feedback process.* Just as human directors of a telephone company may react to a traffic count by changing some of their network's operating rules, we might imagine an automatic telephone exchange carrying out its own traffic counts and analyses, and modifying its operating rules accordingly. It might even modify the physical structure of some of its channels, perhaps adding or dropping additional microwave beams (which fulfill the function of telephone cables) in the light of the traffic or financial data "experienced" by the network.[25]

What seems a possibility in the case of man-made machinery 69 seems to be a fact in living nerve systems, minds, and societies. The establishment and abolition of "conditional reflexes" have long been studied in animals and men, and so have the results of individual and group learning. Such processes often include changes in the "operating rules" that determine how the organism treats subsequent items of information reaching it.

Any network whose operating rules can be modified by feed- 70 back processes is subject to *internal conflict* between its established working preferences and the impact of new information. The simpler the network, the more readily internal conflicts can be resolved by automatically assigning a clear preponderance to one or another of two competing "channels" or "reflexes" at any particular moment, swinging from one trend of behavior to another with least delay. The more complex, relatively, the switchboards and networks involved, the richer the possibilities of choice, the more prolonged may be the periods of indecision or internal conflict. Since the net acquires its preferences through a process of history, its "values" need not all be consistent with each other. They may form circular configurations of preference, which later may trap some of the impulses of the net in circular pathways of frustration. Since the human nervous network is complex, it remains subject to the possibilities of conflicts, indecision, jamming, and circular frustration. Whatever pattern or preferences or operating rules govern its behavior at any particular time can only reduce this affliction, but cannot abolish it.[26]

Since the network of the human mind behaves with some 71 degree of plasticity, it can change many of its operating rules under the impact of experience. It can learn, not only superficially but fundamentally: with the aid of experience the human mind can change its own structure of preference, rejections, and associations. And what seems true of the general plasticity of the individual human mind applies even more to the plasticity of the channels that make up human cultures and social institutions and those particular individual habit patterns that go with them. Indeed, this cultural learning capacity seems to occur in some proportion to the ability of those cultures to survive and to spread.

72   Since all learning including changes in goals or values consists in physical internal rearrangements, it depends significantly on material resources. The *learning capacity* of any system or organization, that is, the range of its effective internal rearrangements, can thus be measured to some extent by the number and kinds of its *uncommitted resources*. Such resources need not be idle; but they must be reassignable from their current functions. There is a qualitative element in learning capacity, since it depends not only on the amount of uncommitted resources but also on their configurations. Yet, since learning capacity consists in an over-all performance, a particular configuration of internal elements can be replaced, in many cases, by some functionally equivalent configuration of others. This is the more probable, the richer the range of available rearrangements, and thus, again, the greater the amount of uncommitted resources, and of facilities for their quick and varied recommitment.

73   Learning capacity can be tested by two independent sets of operations: first, by outside tests of a system's over-all performance in a given situation, much as the learning capacity of rats is tested in a maze and that of armies is tested in battle; and second, by analysis of its inner structure. Thus the greater learning capacity of rats compared to frogs can be predicted from the greater size and complexity of the rat's central nervous system, and the greater learning capacity or adaptability of one army relative to another can be predicted if, other things being equal, it has greater facilities of communication and transport and a greater "operational reserve" of uncommitted man power and equipment. Since over-all performance tests are cheap in rats, but expensive in armies, or in the defense of cities against atom bombs, the prediction of probable learning capacity from structural analysis and the suggestions for probable improvements by the same method may have considerable practical importance.

74   So far we have described two kinds of feedback: "goal-seeking," the feedback of new external data into a net whose operating channels remain unchanged, and "learning," the feedback of external data for the changing of these operating channels themselves. A third important type of possible feedback is the feedback and simultaneous scanning of highly selected internal data, analogous to the problem of what usually is called "consciousness."

Notes

1. N. Wiener, *Cybernetics*, 2nd ed., New York, Wiley, 1961, and *The Human Use of Human Beings*, Boston, Houghton Mifflin, 1950; cf. also W. Ross Ashby, *An Introduction to Cybernetics*, New York, Wiley, 1956; and, for a brief account, G. T. Guilbaud, *What Is Cybernetics?* tr. Valerie MacKay, New York, Grove, 1960.
2. *Science and Common Sense*, New Haven, Yale University Press, 1961, pp. 47–49. Cf. also Conant, *On Understanding Science*, New Haven, Yale University Press, 1947, pp. 16–20, 23–28.
3. Wiener, Communication, M.I.T., 1955.
4. Cf. Wiener, *Cybernetics* and *The Human Use of Human Beings*, both passim; Colin Cherry, *On Human Communication*, Cambridge-New York, M.I.T. Press-Wiley, 1957; and J. Ruesch and G. Bateson, *Communication: The Social Matrix of Psychiatry*, New York, Norton, 1951.
5. Cf. G. Polya, "Analogy," in *How to Solve It*, Princeton, Princeton University Press, 1946, pp. 37–46.
6. On this whole subject, see also A. Rosenblueth, N. Wiener, and J. Bigelow, "Behavior, Purpose and Teleology," *Philosophy of Science*, X, January, 1943, 18–24; W. S. McCulloch and W. Pitts, "A Logical Calculus of the Ideas Immanent in Nervous Activity," *Bulletin of Mathematical Biophysics*, V, 1943, pp. 115–133; F. S. C. Northrop, "The Neurological and Behavioristic Psychological Basis of the Ordering of Society by Means of Ideas," *Science*, 107, No. 2782, April 23, 1948, pp. 411–416; J. Ruesch and G. Bateson, "Structure and Process in Social Relations," *Psychiatry*, XII, 2, May, 1949, pp. 105–124. On the learning aspects, cf. also Wiener, *Cybernetics*, 2nd ed., pp. 169–180; W. Ross Ashby, *Design for a Brain*, 2nd ed., New York, Wiley, 1960, pp. 11, 113, 234. Cf. also the essays in Peter Laslett, ed., *The Physical Basis of Mind*, Oxford, Blackwell, 1957, and W. Russell Brain, *Mind, Perception and Science*, Oxford, Blackwell, 1951.
7. K. W. Deutsch, "Higher Education and the Unity of Knowledge," in L. Bryson et al., eds., *Goals for American Education*, New York, Harper, 1950, pp. 110–111.
8. Somewhat differently phrased, a communications *network* is "a system of physical objects interacting with each other in such a manner that a change in the state of some elements is followed by a determinate pattern of changes in other related elements, in such a manner that the changes remain more or less localized, and independent of changes in the system from other sources" (W. Pitts); a communication *channel* is a "physical system within which a pattern (or *message*) is more or less isolated from other changes in the system" (Norbert Wiener); "A *state description* of a network or part of it" (Pitts); or again, somewhat differently stated, "a message is a reproducible pattern regularly followed by determinate processes depending on that pattern" (Wiener). Oral Communication, M.I.T. (Spring, 1949). Cf. also Claude E. Shannon and Warren Weaver, *The Mathematical Theory of Com-*

munication, Urbana, Ill., University of Illinois Press, 1949, pp. 99–106 ("Information").

9. For a discussion of this entire subject, see N. Wiener, *Cybernetics*, Shannon and Weaver, op. cit.; for a much simplified account, cf. E. C. Berkeley, *Giant Brains*, New York, Wiley, 1949.

10. On "Information" and "Matter," see also John E. Burchard, ed., *Mid-Century: The Social Implications of Scientific Progress*, Cambridge-New York, M.I.T. Press-Wiley, 1950, p. 228, n. 52.

11. Peter B. Nieman, "The Operational Significance of Recognition," B.S. thesis, M.I.T., 1949 (unpublished). Cf. also Cherry, *On Human Communication*, pp. 256–273.

12. Cf. S. E. Cairncross and L. B. Sjöström, "Flavor Profiles—A New Approach to Flavor Problems," *Food Technology*, 4:8, 1950, pp. 308–311; Sjöström, Cairncross, and Jean F. Caul, "Methodology of the Flavor Profile," ibid., 11:9, 1957, pp. 20–25; Caul, Cairncross, and Sjöström, "The Flavor Profile in Review," *Perfumery and Essential Oil Record*, 49, pp. 130–133, London, March, 1958; "Physicochemical Research on Flavor," *Analytical Chemistry*, 30, Feb., 1958, pp. 17A–21A; Caul, "Geruchs- und Geschmacksanalysen mit der Profilmethode, II. Welche Rolle spielt der Geschmack bei Verbrauchsgütern," *Die Ernährungswirtschaft*, 7:9, 1960, pp. 398–402.

13. For this last topic, cf. W. N. Locke and A. D. Booth, eds., *Machine Translation of Languages*, Cambridge-New York, M.I.T. Press-Wiley, 1955.

14. Neiman, op. cit.; Cherry, loc. cit.

15. Cf. the essays in Daniel Lerner, ed., *Quantity and Quality*, New York, The Free Press of Glencoe, 1961.

16. Rosenblueth-Wiener-Bigelow, op. cit., p. 19. A more refined definition would put "output information" in place of "output energy," in accordance with the distinction between "communications engineering" and "power engineering." Cf. Wiener, *Cybernetics*, 2nd ed., pp. 39, 42.

17. Rosenblueth-Wiener-Bigelow, op. cit., p. 18. There is also another kind of feedback, different from the negative feedback discussed in the text: "The feedback is...positive [if] the fraction of the output which reenters the object has the same sign as the original input signal. Positive feedback adds to the input signals, it does not correct them...." Ibid., p. 19; see also Wiener, *Cybernetics*, 2nd ed., pp. 95–115. Only self-correcting, i.e., negative, feedback is discussed here.

18. Wiener, loc. cit.

19. Harry G. Johnson, Review of Norbert Wiener's *Cybernetics*, in the *Economic Journal*, Vol. LIX, N. 236, London, December, 1949, pp. 573–575. For an early attempt to apply feedback analysis to economics, see. A. Tustin, *The Mechanism of Economic Systems*, Cambridge, Harvard University Press, 1953. Cf. also the special issue on "automatic control" of *Scientific American*, 187:3, September, 1952.

20. Cf. John Dollard, "The Acquisition of New Social Habits," in Ralph Linton, *The Science of Man in the World Crisis*, New York, Columbia University Press, 1945, p. 442; with further references. "Drives... are 'rewarded,' that is... they are reduced in intensity... " A. Irving Hallowell, "Sociopsychological Aspects of Acculturation," in Linton, op. cit., p. 183; cf., in the same volume, Clyde Kluckhohn and William H. Kelly, "The Concept of Culture," pp. 84–86; and E. R. Hilgard, *Theories of Learning*, New York, Appleton-Century-Crofts, 1948. Cf. also the references to Wiener and Ashby in Note 6, above.
21. Rosenblueth-Wiener-Bigelow, op. cit., p. 18. "By behavior is meant any change of an entity with respect to its surroundings.... Accordingly any modification of an object, detectable externally, may be denoted as behavior."—Ibid.
22. The performance of a human goal seeker who strives for new goals on reaching each old one has been immortalized in Goethe's *Faust:*

> "Im Weiterschreiten find't er Qual und Glück
> Er, unbefriedigt jeden Augenblick."

Analytical undersanding of this process need not diminish its sublimity, and its emotional impact on us in our experience of recognition. *Faust* becomes no more trivial by our knowledge of goal-changing feedbacks than a sunrise becomes trivial by our knowledge of the laws of refraction.
23. The nature of "self" to be preserved by this order of purposes will be discussed in a later chapter.
24. Vannevar Bush, "As We May Think," *Atlantic Monthly*, 176, July, 1945, pp. 101–108.
25. An automatic telephone exchange capable of opening new channels in response to its own traffic counts was reported under construction by the Phillips Company of Eyndthove, Holland (*Science News Letter*, Washington, D.C., April 10, 1948, p. 233). A telephone exchange that would install such a channel control itself would represent one more extension of the same principle.
26. "Man is the only organism normally and inevitably subject to psychological conflict" (J. S. Huxley, *Man Stands Alone*, New York, Harper, 1941, pp. 22–26, with examples).

CHAPTER SIX

GAMES, STRATEGIES, AND RATIONAL ACTOR THEORY

Rationality is not the transparent term it appears to be. Those who deal regularly with this slippery concept testify that it eludes simple definitions, frustrates many common-sensical intutions, and not rarely leads to acute exasperation. And yet without some minimal notion of rational action, without a sense that humans are (at least intermittently) rational creatures, the entire project of the social sciences is in serious danger of collapsing.

Among the problems involved in profitably using the concept of rationality, none induces more headaches than the difficulty of distinguishing a rationality of ends from a rationality of means. The rationality of means is fairly easy to specify: a means is rational if it pursues a given objective efficiently, that is, with the greatest chance of achieving it at the lowest possible price. This is all quite straightforward—which is probably the reason that most political scientists who deal with rational political action focus exclusively on the rationality of means.

The rationality of ends, on the other hand, is an intellectual bog usually avoided by empirical researchers. After all, it threatens to suck us into a morass of ethical speculations about what our human objectives ought to be in the light of reason: not a very promising subject for research. It would force us to make undemonstrable normative statements and contend pointlessly about value-inspired and idiosyncratic worldviews and ideologies. Presumably, this is best left to intrepid philosphers, who are not bound by the same methodological constraints as political scientists.

This would then appear to be a convenient division of labor; the political scientist focuses on the rationality of actions in terms of their capacity to achieve given ends while philosphers take up the rationality of the ends themselves. But can this distinction hold? Are means and ends indeed water-tight categories with no commerce between them? Can one give a meaningful account of rational means without a glance at the ends to which they are aimed? It will not take much thought to realize that this is simply another way of formulating the question we grappled with in our first chapter on behavioralism and its critics: can politics be meaningfully studied oblivious of the human ends it pursues?

Initial difficulties are confronted when we recognize how easily the term *rational* can be trivialized when used exclusively in its instrumental sense. Consider the following case. A woman is profoundly moved by and committed to the feminist cause. Her boyfriend, a neanderthal type with no appreciation for the finer points of consciousness raising, loses his cool whenever she goes to feminist-sponsored activities. She loves her boyfriend (despite his flaws) and wants to maintain the relationship. Consequently, she decides to forgo her feminist involvement. Can we describe her decision as rational? Would we not, at some point of the analysis, be forced to confront the substantive rather than the merely instrumental issues raised by the case in order to deal with it adequately? Would an analysis that merely took her decision as the means to a given end have anything enlightening to tell us?

It is not difficult to devise even more radical scenarios. A drunkard, for whom every moment of noninebriated life is painful, regularly drinks himself to oblivion. Could we soberly speak of his action as rational? Or what of the self-destructive, suicidal person who yearns for the peace of the grave and drives her car off a cliff? The point is clear: discussions of rationality that remain solely at the instrumental level consistently beg the larger, more demanding question. The rationality of means in isolation leads a flat, one-sided, and, in the end, unsatisfying existence.

Games such as chess or bridge have the great advantage of having their objective—winning—written into the very nature of the activity. To play chess is to play to win. Here, the means and the ends are perfectly suited to one another. Moreover, there are never conflicting ends between which the player must choose. The only choice that confronts competitors is which of the many means at their disposal is best suited to the pursuit of victory. It is precisely the pristine clarity that the game possesses, the calculability and logic of its moves, and the simplicity of its objectives that inspired political scientists to envisage political contests in game-theoretical terms. What, they asked, could be gained by viewing political competition for power and position as a kind of game or contest in which the politician-players seek to use the most rational means to further their ends?

Although there is the occasional playfulness, politics is hardly a game. And yet it is surely a **contest** replete with rules, constraints, attacks, defenses, victors, and vanquished. We each act to maximize our own benefit in a world of limited resources, a world in which only very rarely can we all be winners. Our actions, insofar as they are balanced and rational, take into account the actions and possible reactions of others. We attempt to receive the greatest possible benefit at the smallest possible cost. We defend ourselves when attacked and assume that others will do so as well. Our political strategy is planned with the clear understanding that our rivals, in deliberating their moves and countermoves, are seriously considering our tactics as well as our potential reaction to their maneuvers.

Politics is in large measure the craft of assessing correctly what others will do. It is hardly surprising then that the idea of politics as a game should have struck root and that a large body of theory has developed, exploring the different kinds of contests, strategies, defenses, plans, ploys, expectations, gambits, maneuvers, resolutions, etc. Over time this body of theory has become increasingly rigorous, formalized, and mathematical. As Schelling puts it; "*Game Theory* is the formal study of the rational, consistent expectations that participants can have about each other's choices."

At the simplest levels of decision making involving a single or very few actors, in which the information necessary for deciding on a course of action is complete, the parties to the decision are completely rational, the environment is fixed and predictable, etc., the outcome of rational calculations is not difficult to determine. If the shortest, fastest, cheapest, most pleasant, and least crowded route from point A to point B is known, it can be predicted without fail which route will be chosen by motorists who wish to traverse the distance. These cases are so clear that no special method is necessary to predict outcomes.

The game becomes more interesting—and sophisticated theory becomes increasingly relevant—when the deciding individual has only partial control over the decision context, when his decisions depend on his expectations of what others will do, when the variables are greater in number, more complex in character, when information is not complete, when the decision must be made in a dynamic and changing reality, and when the various interests and objectives pull in a number of different directions at once. If our motorists were forced to choose between the speed and the pleasantness of the drive, what would they say then? If the fastest route were also the most expensive one, what would their decision be? Most complex of all, if motorists needed to make their decision on the basis of how other drivers would decide—in order to avoid crowded highways—how would they assess the response of others to one of the above problems and how would they factor this information into their own choice?

It should be made clear that, as opposed to those approaches deriving directly from the empirical-behavioral credo, game theory stands somewhat apart. It does have its rigorous and quantitative mathematical side, to be sure, but it is nevertheless deductive rather than empirical in character. It deals in abstract reasoning, not with what decision makers do in practice. For the most part, it models choice situations rather than doing "field work." It concerns itself with the rationality of decisions rather than with the actual motives that generate them.

In a certain sense, game theory does have a predictive quality. But it is not prediction in the behavioralist mode. Game theorists do not normally forecast what will actually happen; rather they are concerned with identifying the rational course of action given certain objectives, constraints, and contingencies. In this narrow sense it is "normative" as well, that is, directed to ideal or optimal solutions. (It is, of course, not normative in the conventional sense of advocating specific substantive values over others—unless one accepts the commitment to rationality as such a value.) Game theorists seek to specify what should be done in order to rationally maximize one's interests; they do not presume to tell us what those interests ought to be.

Because of its theoretical and formalized nature, game theory is potentially applicable to the most various of conflict situations. Martin Shubik composed the following register of potential areas for its use:

> In the context of political science the game may involve generals engaged in battle; diplomats involved in bargaining and negotiations; politicians attempting to influence their voters; legislators trying to put together the appropriate coalitions; medieval princes concerned with power or modern mayors fighting their way through the morass of municipal affairs. In economics or political economy the conflict situation may be labor unions striking against the firm; firms in oligopolistic competition; members of a cartel negotiating market shares or legislatures devising "fair" taxation schemes.[1]

Before imaginations run riot, however, it should be remarked that game theory historically came to politics via economics where enlightened rational behavior in conditions of market competition has been intensively studied. In political analysis, game theory has been used most extensively in the field of international relations. It has been found to be particularly suitable to the study of deterrents and to the theory of threats. (Probably the single most cited work of this kind is Thomas Schelling's *Strategy of Conflict*.)

Game theorists are especially concerned with classifying the kinds of decision-contexts that political actors are likely to confront and to specify the strategies relevant to each. Perhaps the most important and well known distinction they draw is between those contests in which there exists a resolution that can, at least minimally, satisfy all the participants and those contests in which there can only be winners and losers. A football game is a good example of the latter. In principle, there is no strategy that both sides can jointly adopt for their mutual benefit. Football rivals do not have the option of observing an attack on their goal with equanimity. Every advantage that one team gains necessarily means a disadvantage to the other; each victory entails, indeed is predicated upon, a concomitant defeat. These kinds of conflicts are conventionally called "zero-sum" games.

These are all-out contests, and for all their fierceness, they introduce a certain order, clarity, and predictability into game theoretical discussions. There is little doubt here that each attack in our football game will be met with a resolute defense; both sides and all observers understand the all-or-nothing nature of the contest. (This is probably what makes a football game so agitating and inflaming.) The rules of most sporting events are, in fact, rigorously constructed to prevent the possibility of the game becoming bogged down in negotiated or mutually satisfactory resolutions.

Politics, by contrast, as the old adage tells us, is the "art of the possible." In politics, zero-sum games tend to be the exception rather than the rule. More often than not, there exists the possibility of negotiating a settlement that satisfies at least some of each side's basic needs. Politics has a creative and open quality to it that engages our mediating, bargaining, and reconciling imagination. Only in all-out war and in some other uncompromisingly radical choice-contexts does a zero-sum situation unquestionably exist. In most cases, at least some maneuvering room mitigates the extreme starkness of the zero sum situation.

Even realities that produce bellicose rhetoric with express zero-sum formulations are not necessarily what they appear to be. Such rhetoric, in fact, may be nothing but an effort to frighten an opponent into compromising. Indeed, even the actual outbreak of hostilities does not necessarily mean that the conflict is essentially of a zero-sum nature.

A good example is the Arab-Israeli dispute. It can be debated—long and hard—whether this fierce and protracted conflict belongs to one or the other category. What this debate will likely turn up is that one's position depends on one's assessment of the various protagonists' intentions. Those who come to the conclusion, for example, that something like a "two state" solution—the one Jewish, the other Palestinian—can meet the basic needs of both sides, and that it can promote long-term stability in the region, will argue that the conflict is, at bottom, of a non-zero-sum character. Each side can have its basic needs met without mortally wounding the other. Those who are convinced, by contrast, that the Arab world (whatever its official pronouncements may be) will never truly accept Israel's existence, or that Israel will never accept the claims of Palestinians to self-determination, or that each side's basic needs include territorial claims incompatible with the other's existence, or that whatever the formal possibility of resolution, the passions involved in the conflict make it nonnegotiable, will understandably opt for the zero-sum designation.

We are led ineluctably to the disconcerting conclusion that the categories "zero-sum" and "non-zero-sum" do not really refer to the objective character of the conflict as such, but rather to an appreciation of the motives, interpretations, anticipations, fears, and intent of those who are involved in it. Conflicts are not between interests per se—in which case game theory would be directly relevant and eminently suitable—but between interests as they happen to be perceived at any given moment by the parties involved. That is only another way of stating what is a standard critique of game theory: it avails us little without a full understanding of the cultural, historical, psychological, religious, etc., peculiarities that happen to obtain in a specific reality.

Dealing with choice situations in a game theoretical vacuum that has rationality as its dominant standard produces academic resolutions that often have little to do with the rough-and-tumble world of real political conflict. Applying game theoretical constructs to a conflict, the animating passions of which are so explosive that rational bargaining solutions cannot be considered, will not prove to be particularly enlightening. It is just when hatreds and suspicions are deep-seated and long-standing, that is, when resolutions are most urgently needed, that game theory has least to offer. In politics it often turns out that the rational line between two points is not always the shortest one. In this regard, it has been charged that game theory does, in fact, come close to the analysis of parlor games, i.e., it considers conflicts as if they were conundrums that, like those of bridge or chess, are pristine, self-enclosed, and rationally soluble. Critics therefore charge that game theory tends to possess a scholastic and nonpolitical character that often achieves its results at the price of radically simplifying and abstracting political realities.

And yet, against these strictures three compensatory remarks need to be made. First, the percentage of conflicts involving rationally calculating protagonists is, arguably, very large. Second, in clarifying the areas of rational compromise that are potentially available to protagonists, game theorists are capable of shedding a very positive light on what might presently appear to be a tangled and unnavigable situation. They can point to where the solution might be profitably pursued, even if, at present, the protagonists are unwilling to give it a serious hearing. Third, it is not fully accurate to claim that game theory deals only with situations lacking personal idiosyncrasy and containing perfect information. True, these are the realities that game theorists prefer because they render calculations easiest to handle. But, in fact, variables often are introduced that simulate less than perfectly rational conditions. Still, it must be admitted that their introduction involves growing complexity and, what is more problematic, growing uncertainty in regard to conclusions.

There appears then to be an unavoidable tradeoff that game theorists confront. When variables are few and streamlined, there is the gnawing suspicion that what is being offered is naive and unrealistically designed or that the reality has been denuded to suit methodological imperatives. When, at the other pole, the variables introduced are adequately complex and multifarious, the fear is that they will be neither manageable for analysis nor sufficiently intelligible and distinct to support reliable conclusions. In either case, the elemental worry persists that political variables are not the precise quantities that game theorists would have us believe; there is at least a prime facie argument for understanding them as vague, subtle, and controversial qualities.

Although the most frequent utilization of game theory has been in regard to threats, deterrents, first strikes, and counter strikes, there have been a number of very notable attempts to apply the logic of gaming situations to the dynamics of government. Three such uses deserve at least brief mention: first, the understanding of democratic competition in marketing-bargaining terms, second, the appreciation of coalition formation as an attempt to maximize payoffs while minimizing costs, and third, the application of "minimax" strategies to political reasoning. Let us begin with the last.

What is the most rational strategy to be adopted in conditions of great uncertainty and lack of knowledge? Should we, under such circumstances, take a chance on radical solutions to our problems or would it be wiser to hedge our bets and, at the very least, prevent major setbacks? Dahl and Lindblom, in their 1953 study, *Politics, Economics and Welfare* (see also, David Braybrooke and Charles Lindblom's *A Strategy of Decision*), argue that such conditions of uncertainty prevail in regard to large-scale political decisions. In even the best of political circumstances, our knowledge of a decision's consequences is likely to be limited and partial. So many different and unpredictable developments, repercussions, and effects are possible, including many which undermine the objectives we seek to achieve, that boldness is hardly to be seen as a virtue. They conclude that the rational strategy to be adopted politically is one of incrementalism or of a cautious, gradualist, step-by-step policy. In conditions of ignorance, we need to minimize the risk of suffering the maximal harm—minimax, in game theoretical jargon—rather than strike out daringly in what will often turn out to be foolhardy ventures.

Interestingly, John Rawls, the contemporary ethical philosopher whose (1971) book, *A Theory of Justice*, has had an enormous influence on recent political thought, finds the minimax strategy of great use as well. He asks us to consider the following case: A group of people need to establish the rules and standards by which their society will operate. They need to decide on the principles that will regulate the distribution of income, privilege, rights, punishments, etc. For the sake of this exercise, however, they are understood to find themselves behind a "veil of ignorance." This ignorance, to be sure, does not refer to their general knowledge of the world, to their understanding of the broad sociological and psychological characteristics of human association. This kind of knowledge they do, in fact, possess. What they do not know are the particulars regarding their own nature, attributes, and circumstances as individuals. They do not know, for example, whether they are intelligent or dull, good-looking or homely, wealthy or destitute, talented or inept, of privileged or common stock, skilled or simple laborers, etc. They do not know whether they are optimists or pessimists, daring or cautious, or even what their philosophy of life is. From behind this veil, they need to create the charter of the sociopolitical community that they will henceforth inhabit.

Would they, under these circumstances, choose a regime that distributed goods according to a capitalist market mechanism? In other words, would they agree upon a competitive, skill-based, initiative-centered system with strong property rights that would inexorably lead to a hierarchical class system? Rawls thinks not. From behind the veil, each of the deliberators would be haunted by the fear that they would find themselves among the disadvantaged and unendowed, that is, at the bottom of the heap. To prevent this worst of all possible scenarios, our veiled deliberators would gravitate rationally to a minimax strategy. They would seek to avoid the worst, even if it meant forgoing a chance at the best. And this, Rawls believes, would entail agreeing upon social arrangements with a substantial egalitarian component.

Returning to more practical and conventional subject matter, the formation of political coalitions has been a prime target for the utilization of gaming theories. William Riker's path-breaking *Theory of Political Coalitions* (1961) set off an intense stir of activity (which has not yet subsided) centered on the strategies that control coalition formation. The considerations that govern coalitions, Riker contends, are those of rational, benefit-seeking groups and individuals—the desire to maximize payoffs and minimize costs. What kind of coalition meets these conditions? What kind of coalition ensures the coalition-making party or individual that it will receive the greatest possible benefit while paying the smallest possible price? Riker's well-known answer is a "minimum winning coalition."

Such a coalition is drawn between two objects: it needs to create an effective ruling block while keeping its size down to a minimum. For each additional coalition partner that is added for the sake of winning and security, there will inevitably be an additional price to pay. Riker's contention is that rational coalition creators will gravitate to that spot in the tradeoff between these two objectives that provides a winning coalition at the lowest price, or a minimum winning coalition.

All this, however, requires that the parties to the coalition possess complete information about each other. Only then would a coalition of, say, fifty-one in a parliament of one hundred be the rational strategy. If, by contrast, the coalition-forming group were uncertain of how one or more of the partners to this minimal coalition would act in a time of crisis (would this partner bolt the coalition and leave it to face defeat?), it would not be wise to form a coalition without at least some extra margin of security. The reason that minimum winning coalitions do not prevail universally, Riker tells us, is that the real political world is hardly one of full and perfect information. Consequently, Riker appends a critical corollary to his initial rule:

> The greater the degree of imperfection or incompleteness of information, the larger will be the coalitions that coalition-makers seek to form and the more frequently will winning coalitions actually formed be greater than minimum size. Conversely, the nearer information approaches perfection and completeness, the smaller will winning coalitions actually formed be close to minimum size.[2]

This corollary, together with the minimum winning principle, has been debated, tested, emended, extended, applied, and criticized in the years since their initial presentation. It cannot be said that Riker's contribution has turned into a reigning orthodoxy. It has nevertheless (and this may be the more substantial contribution) formed the basis for enlightening debate and for fruitful disagreement.

Another very ambitious attempt at utilizing game theory to explicate the nature of political processes is Anthony Downs' *An Economic Theory of Democracy* (1957). Downs' book, although severely criticized in some quarters, has had the virtue of initiating serious debate over the years. Despite its age, it serves to dramatically illustrate some of the main strengths and weaknesses of the approach. Downs' object is to construct a model of rational political behavior that takes into account the costs of alternative decisions, within the context of democratic government. An economist by training, Downs seeks to understand the political process in terms of the classic economic problem of the efficient utilization of scarce resources.

The master axiom of his model, from which all other propositions are drawn, is that the object of politics is power. Power is politics' desirable but scarce resource. Rational political choices are therefore those that maximize the power accruing to a particular individual or group. Decisions that do not aim at power as their end are, in these terms, "irrational," even "neurotic." Consequently, Downs must exclude from the category of rational all those political objectives that do not necessarily enhance power: these would include social welfare, ideological conviction, and social fraternity. This rather draconic axiom does not apply solely to those in government; individual voters are thought to behave irrationally as well if they do not support the party that offers them more benefits than any other.

One critical corollary of Downs' power-centered gaming perspective is that parties design policies in order to maximize votes. Because votes are the main power resource in a democracy, party leaders who act in a politically rational manner do not adopt positions out of ideological conviction or because of their perception of the national good. Political positions are vote-getting devices, and rational political behavior treats them as such. Political leaders act much as a commercial producer would. If there is a market for a certain product and the profits are good, it will be produced and marketed with little concern for its genuine usefulness or necessity. Ideology, like packaging or advertising slogans, can be instrumental in augmenting sales, but advertising claims do not motivate the producer to sell his product.

Viewed as a marketing strategy, ideology serves power, and not vice versa. The position a party adopts depends on what positions have been taken by other political entrepreneurs and what remaining segments of the electoral market are most promising. For example, a political vacuum caused by the disappearance of a party in a multiparty system will cause the two parties adjacent to it on the left and the right to adapt their ideology and move toward the vacated position to maximize their electoral appeal. Similarly, in two-party systems, the parties will tend to converge on the ideological center because the center offers the optimal position from which to woo voters from all parts of the political spectrum. Political choices are, in short, marketing choices; the democratic process is best understood as a single-minded attempt on the part of the various political contenders to capture that scarce commodity, power, by the rational utilization of all the means allowed by democratic government.

Not surprisingly, many have complained that Downs' conception of rationality is excessively narrow and idiosyncratic. Moreover, it is not always clear whether he is developing a purely deductive and theoretical model of political rationality on the basis of certain posited axioms or whether he is trying to tell us something about the real world of politics. Is it a standard of rational performance in some normative sense that he is advocating, or is it a description of the underlying tendencies of political life? Would, for example, the finding that ideological conviction possesses substantial independent standing—not reducible to the pursuit of power—cause him to revise his model?

If the foregoing has conveyed the impression that rational actor analysis is exhausted by game theory, it is an impression that should be quickly corrected. Game theory is, in fact, only one of the many uses to which the rationality assumption has been applied. It has been used, for example, to distinguish those cases in which individuals will choose to abandon failing institutions from those in which they tend to stay on and fight for reform from within.[3] It has been extensively utilized to evaluate the properties and relevant strategies of various voting systems; it has had a rich career in analyzing the agendas and committee activities of Congress; it has been applied to assessing the viability of various proposed constitutional reforms. Most especially, it has been used broadly to examine the rationality of public policy choices. Although this large body of research possesses some very disparate characteristics and divergent assumptions,[4] it is all informed by the underlying belief that, as Steven Brams puts it, "the postulation of rational behavior is a powerful engine for systematically generating hypotheses from a small set of explicit assumptions."[5]

The name *public choice* is associated with much of this research. Although its roots are deeply planted in economic theory, public choice has made something of an academic migration over the past few decades and, at present, is well represented in political science research. As opposed to game theorists, who generally focus on individual actors (or groups acting as units) and the strategies best suited to maximize their interests as against those of rival actors, public choice analysis is interested in how public choices can accommodate indivdual preferences. Public choice aims at understanding the considerations that go into public decisions seeking to maximize the interests of individuals: How can actors who decide collectively choose in such a way that the selected policy will suit each of them as individuals? What, public choice theorists typically ask, are the optimally rational strategies that a public should pursue in order to satisfy the interests of those individuals affected by a decision?

At first sight, this may not appear a particularly difficult question to answer—policies that meet more needs of more people would seem to rank highest on the rationality scale—but first sight here is badly misleading. Analyses of the logic of social choices have turned up some quite perverse and paradoxical effects that complicate matters very significantly.[6] Clarifying these complexities, devising standards of rational optimality—all these have made public choice a growth industry in political research.

For those unhappy with such formalized, hypothetical, axiomatic descriptions of rationality, an analysis of the actual psychological motives and drives that underlie political behavior will seem like a welcome corrective. This will be our subject in the next chapter.

NOTES

1. Shubik, "The Uses of Game Theory," in James C. Charlesworth, ed., *Contemporary Political Analysis* (New York, Free Press, 1967) p. 240.

2. Piker, *The Theory of Political Coalitions* (New Haven, Yale University Press, 1962), pp. 88–89.

3. Albert D. Hirschman, *Exit, Voice and Loyalty: Responses to Decline in Firms, Organizations and States* (Cambridge, Cambridge University Press, 1970).

4. For an elaboration on the various types of rational actor theories and research see Russell Hardin "Rational Choice Theories," in *Idioms of Inquiry: Critique and Renewal in Political Science* ed. by Terence Ball (Albany, N.Y., State University of New York Press, 1987) pp. 67–94 and William C. Mitchell "Virginia, Rochester, and Bloomington: Twenty-Five Years of Public Choice and Political Science," in *Public Choice* (1988) 56: 101–119. The latter article has a good bibliography for further reading.

5. Brams, *Rational Politics: Decisions, Games and Strategies* (Washington, DC, CQ Press, 1985), p. 4.

6. The founding father of the field is Kenneth Arrow, and his *Social Choice and Individual Values* (New Haven, Yale University Press, 1952) remains the classical text.

SUGGESTIONS FOR FURTHER READING

Brams, S. J., *Game Theory and Politics* (New York, Free Press, 1975).

Brams, S. J., *Superpower Games: Applying Game Theory to Superpower Conflict* (New Haven, Yale University Press, 1985).

Davis, M. D., *Game Theory: A Nontechnical Introduction* (New York, Basic Books, 1983).

Hirschman, A. O., *Exit, Voice and Loyalty* (Cambridge, Harvard University Press, 1970).

Ordeshook, P. C., *Game Theory and Political Theory* (Cambridge, Cambridge University Press, 1987).

Shubik, M., *Game Theory in the Social Sciences: Concepts and Solutions* (Cambridge, MIT Press, 1982).

Schelling, T. C., *The Strategy of Conflict* (Cambridge, Harvard University Press, 1960).

Steven J. Brams

The Study of Rational Politics

1   Politics is a subject difficult to pin down, though discussions of politics have a long and venerable history. No less a figure than Aristotle propounded his views in a book called *Politics* more than two thousand years ago. Of course, politics certainly predated Aristotle, manifesting itself, for example, in events reported in the Bible. To further complicate the subject, the politics of the twentieth century is vastly different in scope and substance, if not in form, from the politics of the ancients. Thus, it is not unreasonable to be perplexed about the meaning of politics.

2   There is, however, a core to politics that usefully distinguishes it from other human activities. Political relationships are characterized by *conflict*, which may be about any variety of matters, from civil rights to education, from agriculture to the environment, from the international economy to nuclear deterrence. What makes conflicts political is that they are not purely private matters but have a public dimension: they impinge on and involve other people besides the protagonists. The origin of the word *politics* reflects its public aspect—the Greek word *polis* means city or state, which is also the root of *polites* (citizen) and *politeia* (government or constitution). In other words, politics by its very nature embraces a larger community—the public, or the citizens of a state—and how it is governed.

3   If politics is about *public* conflicts, then conflicts in the family, the office, and other more or less private arenas are outside the domain of politics, at least as the term will be used here. But this does not mean that politics is solely concerned with matters of government or state in which public participation is officially sanctioned. To limit politics to controversies connected with governing by official bodies or representatives is to take too restrictive a view. It shuts out conflicts that are indisputably political in the sense of affecting the lives and fortunes of many individuals, even the well-being of nation-states. Some multinational corporations, for example, are more powerful than some countries, if one's criterion is the impact they have on political leaders as well as ordinary citizens.

4   To exclude the quarrels of home, office, and other small-scale arenas but to include certain battles set in motion outside gov-

From Steven J. Brams, *Rational Politics: Decisions, Games and Strategies* (Washington D.C., CQ Press, 1985).

ernment requires a definition that avoids indelible boundaries yet establishes a general area of inquiry centered around conflict that affects the public. Different kinds of conflict will be distinguished later with the aid of game theory, including conflicts that never break into the open because they are deterred by threats.

The study of politics, even limited to the discussion of certain 5 kinds of conflict, still requires a focus if it is to be understood as a coherent whole rather than a set of myriad details. The focus here will be on the analysis of *rational politics,* which can be defined as politics involving the *calculation of advantage and disadvantage by rational actors in situations of conflict, resulting in choices whose consequences affect significant numbers of people and the actions of governments.*

To act rationally means, in general terms, to choose better 6 alternatives over worse ones. Since the ranking of alternatives depends on an actor's goals, rationality cannot be divorced from the goals that give it direction.

Political actors have all manner of goals. Some hunger for 7 fame, whereas others prefer quiet, behind-the-scenes manipulation; still others seek mastery of a public policy issue or try to exploit such an issue because they have an ideological ax to grind. To the extent that actors achieve their goals as efficiently and effectively as possible, they are being rational. This is true even if they are not fully conscious of their goals but act *as if* they have them—that is, in a manner consistent with attaining certain goals.

Thus, to be rational is to strive for what one desires—or at 8 least to act as if one were pursuing some end. But it is not simple to determine exactly what a rational course of action is that satisfies these desires or ends in a particular situation. Also, it is no mean task to check that a certain course of action was actually selected in order to test empirical hypotheses that are derived from a rational-choice model.

The rationality assumption explains political behavior well, 9 including that which seems on occasion paradoxical. Indeed, insofar as rational-choice models illuminate nonobvious aspects of politics, the use of these models seems justified.

To be sure, the models developed [in the rational study of 10 politics] differ substantially in the assumptions they make. Nevertheless, all share the same structure: consequences are deduced from assumptions, which makes the models deductive. To the degree that these consequences can be interpreted in terms of real-world politics, the models offer a palpable understanding of such politics, particularly of why conflicts break out and how they may be resolved or controlled.

11   In contrast to deduction, induction involves searching for patterns or regularities directly in the empirical data at hand rather than using data to test consequences derived from a model. Induction does not presume starting from an explicit logical structure that is rooted in relatively few assumptions. Instead, the inductive study of politics begins with the empirical description of the actual choices of political actors, the behavior of political institutions, and the like. Such description and the generalizations drawn from it, however, explain little if it is not clear why some alternatives were selected over others. For this reason it is usually insufficient to explain political behavior by observing it: it does not often speak for itself, no matter how carefully it is scrutinized or measured. Some prior assumptions are generally helpful and sometimes necessary for sorting out and making sense of the confusions and contradictions of political life, especially in trying to account for the choices political actors make that appear to violate common sense.

12   A deductive structure facilitates logically relating political choices to each other through a set of hypotheses, which are simply the consequences of a model interpreted or operationalized so as to be testable. The hypothetico-deductive method thus provides an economical means for going from an abstract deductive structure to a testable theory; it has become the hallmark of the natural sciences, which until the eighteenth century were largely descriptive and typological.

13   The hypothetico-deductive method is still not common in the social sciences. But there is no reason why, in principle, the study of politics should be impregnable to this method. In fact, it is our rationality that makes our activities intelligible. The assumption of rationality is now generally accepted in the field of economics, at least for explaining the behavior of individuals and households in microeconomic theory.

14   Political science has still not generally accepted this assumption, but not because political actors are less rational than economic ones. Rather, there is a paucity of rational-choice models—wedding the rationality assumption to the hypothetico-deductive method—to explain their behavior. This situation is changing, however, as it becomes more and more evident that political actors also think carefully about the options they have available and choose those that best enable them to achieve their goals. In short, the rationality assumption is by and large a realistic one.

It would be strange indeed if this were not the case, par- 15
ticularly when the decisions of actors have momentous consequences, for themselves as well as for the public. The only
behavior that might be construed as irrational is random behavior, but even randomness can be shown to be optimal in
certain situations and so may not be devoid of purpose. On
the contrary, being utterly predictable may be utterly foolish
in politics.

Politics, of course, connotes more than theoretical calcula- 16
tion, whether of the sinister variety associated with machina-
tion and subterfuge or the ennobling variety associated with
courage and heroism. It is also about the actual decisions of
citizens and elites, whose rationality may be severely circumscribed by many factors. Lack of information, for example,
may significantly impede the ability of actors to make strategic calculations, as in the "fog of war."

Not only may information be imperfect, but political actors 17
also may be constrained by limited resources, poor communication, their inability to make complex calculations, and a host
of other real-life mitigating factors. These constraints, however,
do not negate the actors' rationality. In fact, when one makes
strategic choices in a murky or recalcitrant political environment, one is likely to be *more* prudent than if the obstacles are
known and therefore can be anticipated.

The postulation of rational behavior is a powerful engine 18
for systematically generating hypotheses from a small set
of explicit assumptions. In addition, since optimal strategies
are sometimes far from obvious, the deductive structure of
rational-choice models enables one not only to sort out better from worse strategies but also to analyze their sensitivity
to different modeling assumptions. Behavior inexplicable by
one set of assumptions may be eminently rational according
to another set.

Rational-choice models...differ substantially not only in 19
their assumptions—except for rationality, in one form or
another—but also in the topics to which they are applied.
[They may be applied to] individualistic calculations of players in games with radically different settings; [to the delineation of] what coalitions of players are likely to form and
remain stable in electoral politics and international relations;
[to the analysis of] the properties of voting systems used in
small committees, legislatures, large conventions, and international organizations; and [to the characterization of] different
situations vulnerable to the exercise of power. Starting from
the assumption that actors are rational with respect to some

goals in each case, consequences of their rationality [can be] deduced and compared with their actual behavior—insofar as this is possible—to test the empirical validity of the different models.

20   Such tests help one to determine whether there is a rhyme and reason to political choices beyond the peculiar circumstances of the moment. In the tens of thousands of public elections held every year in the United States, for example, it is reasonable to suppose that candidates face common and recurrent strategic decisions for which rational-choice models may provide both general insights and verifiable hypotheses.

21   Of course, such models need to be generalized further, and logical connections among them must be tightened or made more parsimonious. They also have to be applied to new empirical situations, which will suggest revisions that make them less arbitrary and hence more germane to other situations. My larger aim here, however, is not to parade before the reader a series of models and their applications but rather to show the merits of an overall conception of politics that takes as a starting point that political choices are made by thoughtful (and usually intelligent) decision makers who want to realize certain ends. They may be impeded in making rational choices by various environmental constraints, but this does not impugn their rationality as such, only their ability to exercise it.

22   In fact, certain problems of social choice are ineradicable, ... and hence pose difficulties that no rational calculations can surmount. From the normative perspective of the reformer, the study of rational politics pinpoints where these difficulties lie and, consequently, what possible trade-offs can be made to ameliorate them.

23   Although there certainly may be differences about the best means to achieve goals, the most wrenching conflicts in politics usually arise because of disagreements in the goals themselves. Yet even if the goals of actors are antithetical, understanding this fact may not only facilitate understanding their behavior but also clarify differences and identify where (if anywhere) reconciliation may be possible. Thereby rational-choice models may be used for normative purposes—if not to eliminate conflict, then at least to explain why it persists and how, possibly, it may be abated.

24   Rational-choice models offer not only a calculus for understanding political behavior but also a basis for changing it. Whereas developing and testing models may help explain political phenomena and processes, political reformers seek more than scientific explanation. They wish to change the system by eliminating aspects they consider inimical or unethical.

Reformers will be aided in their task if they better under- 25
stand the source of the problems they perceive and can model
the probable effects of the reforms they propose. In fact, the
scientific and the normative study of politics often complement
each other. Reformers become more persuasive if their assessments are grounded in rigorous analysis and hard evidence;
scientists, when stimulated by reformers, are encouraged to
go beyond the here and now and to consider the possible as
well as the actual.

Ideally, the study of rational politics will encourage a useful 26
dialogue, even if the goals of scientists and reformers—not to
mention the practitioners of politics—differ. In fact, one can
be both a scientist and a reformer: after having completed a
scientific analysis, a scientist who concludes that reforms are
in order and feasible can switch hats and become an advocate.
In short, the study of rational politics fosters both good science
and good reform, which, after all, are two sides of the same
analytic coin.

T. C. Schelling

What Is Game Theory?

1   You are on the station platform, ready to board the train, and meet an old friend who has reserved a seat in a different car from yours. You agree to meet in the diner. After you board the train a steward comes through making reservations, and you discover that there is a first-class diner and a second-class buffet car. You'd somewhat rather eat in first class, you suspect that your friend would prefer the buffet car, but mainly you want to make a reservation that coincides with his. Do you elect the diner or the buffet car?

2   Again you are on the platform and meet a friend you are trying to avoid; he is going to coax you onto some committee. Your reservations are in different cars, but he suggests meeting in the diner. When the steward comes through you discover to your relief that there are two diners, first-class and buffet, and if you choose correctly you may "innocently" miss your friend. You have to be careful; he can guess that you'll evade him if you can. Normally you'd dine first class and he knows it. For which car do you make your lunch reservation?

3   Once again, you are on the train without a reserved seat. You find a seat but a few passengers are left standing. When the steward announces lunch, the standing passengers watch eagerly to see who will vacate a seat in favor of lunch. If you go to the diner you will have no claim to your seat when you return. If you do not vacate your seat you cannot eat; if you do not eat nobody gets your seat, not even for the time you would like to be in the diner. What arrangement can you work out?

4   Finally, you are in your air-conditioned parlor car when the steward gives you your ballot. Passengers are asked whether they wish smoking to be permitted in these cars. You suspect it will be a close vote. A second item on the ballot asks whether, if smoking is permitted in response to the passengers' wishes, it should be confined to cigarettes. You'd love a cigar, which is all you ever smoke, would evidently answer no to the second question, but suspect that all nonsmokers and some cigarette smokers would vote to exclude cigars. How do you vote? Can you make a deal with someone?

5   As you leave your parlor car at the station, the steward stands expecting his tip. Fifty cents would be a reasonable tip, but the steward disposes of enough favors to make it worth

From James C. Charlesworth, ed., *Contemporary Political Analysis* (New York, Free Press, 1967), pp. 212–238. Reprinted by permission.

some small expense to be among his favorites. You suspect that some of the other regular commuters try to tip a little above average. You'd like to tip a little above average. How much do you give the steward?

Interdependent Decisions

Game Theory is the formal study of rational decision in sit- 6 uations like these. Two or more individuals have choices to make, preferences regarding the outcomes, and some knowledge of the choices available to each other and of each other's preferences. The outcome depends on the choices that both of them make, or all of them if there are more than two. There is no independently "best" choice that one can make—it depends on what the others do.

For some problems, like choosing the route that minimizes 7 distance from home to office, you can reach a solution without solving anybody else's problem at the same time. To drive through an intersection, though, you want to know what the other driver is going to do—to stop, slow down, speed up, or just keep going—and you know that a main element in his decision is what he thinks you are going to do. Any "solution" of a problem like this is necessarily a solution for *both* participants. Each must try to see the problem from the other's point of view, but when he does he sees himself trying to reach a decision.

What game theory did was to identify this class of situations 8 as one of practical importance and intellectual challenge, and to propose that any satisfactory solution for rational participants ought to be a solution for them jointly. Each must base a decision on his expectations. Unless we are willing to suppose one or more among them merely to expect wrong—and then we have to decide *ad hominem* who is going to be wrong—there must be some consistency, not only of their choices with their expectations but among their expectations of each other. Game theory is the formal study of the rational, consistent expectations that participants can have about each other's choices.

It is, though, abstract and deductive, not the empirical study 9 of how people make decisions but a deductive theory about the conditions that their decisions would have to meet in order to be considered "rational," "consistent," or "noncontradictory." Of course, defining "rational," "consistent," or "noncontradictory" for interdependent decisions is itself part of the business of game theory. Take the case of the man whom we do not want to meet in the diner: could there be a theory that tells us unequivocally which diner to choose in order not to meet him? Only if we deny our opponent access to the theory. If logic could tell us which diner to choose, the same logic could tell him which diner we would choose, and as von Neumann and Morgenstern said in the monumental work that launched game theory two decades ago, we can hardly be satisfied with the generality of any theory whose success depends on its not becoming known!

10   Strictly speaking, this kind of theory is not predictive. It is what is sometimes called "normative" theory in contrast to predictive or explanatory theory. Still, it is doubtful whether theorists would put forth so much energy and receive so much attention if their deductions were not felt to provide some bench mark for the analysis of actual behavior. This method, which might be called "vicarious problem-solving," has been traditional in economics; for the study of how business firms maximize profits, even for the study of whether they try to, it is helpful to know how they would behave if they actually tried and succeeded.[1]

Solving the Problem

11   Let us look, now, at how the problems that began this essay are approached through game theory. First, with an exception to be noted later, from the point of view of game theory none of these problems involves dining cars. The dining cars are merely an interpretation; the man I did not want to meet in the diner could as well be a disarmament inspector along whose route I do not want to leave evidence of violation, or a submarine commander about to fire a torpedo in the direction he thinks my ship will go. Second, the problem does not involve particular individuals; game theory eschews solutions based on personal idiosyncrasy or the ability of one individual to outguess another. Third, in game theory one does not care why the one individual wants to meet the other and the second wants to avoid the first; they are treated as "rational" in the way they try to achieve their goals, but their goals are *their* business, and game theory takes them as data.

12   In the case of *opposed interests*, if either of us has to make his choice first, in a way that the other can see, the solution is easy: the first loses, however he chooses, and the second wins. This result is trivial but its implications are not. It points to the value of postponing decision, of gaining intelligence about

the choice another has already made and denying intelligence in case one has to move first.

This dining-car case is simplified by the occurrence of only 13 two possible outcomes, *meet* and *don't meet*, and using S and F for success and failure, the problem an be depicted in a 2 × 2 matrix:

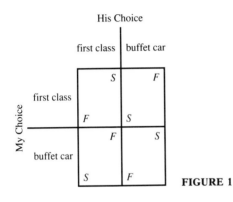

FIGURE 1

In the lower left corner of each cell is the outcome from my point of view, I being the one whose decision corresponds to choosing the upper or lower row; and in the upper right corner of each cell is the outcome from his point of view, his decision corresponding to the choice of the left or right column. We can make the problem look somewhat quantitative by using numerical scores in place of S and F—a 1 for success and a 0 for failure, or perhaps a −1 for failure, choosing numbers for sheer mnemonic and typographic convenience, just remembering that the larger of the two numbers means success. We may as well use the same pair of numbers for both players, although this again is just for convenience. We can now say that each player tries "to maximize his score," but this merely means that he tries to achieve success or to maximize his chances of success.

This is one of the situations that in game theory is known as 14 "zero-sum." It is often described as a situation in which he loses what I gain and vice versa, but actually in game theory the scoring systems of the two individuals are invariably treated as incommensurate. If two feudal noblemen play a game of cards, one to lose his thumb if he loses and the other to lose his eyesight, the game is "zero-sum" (as long as neither cares about the other's loss) though nobody's loss is the other's gain and there may be no way of comparing what they risk losing. It is precisely *because* their value systems are incommensurable that, if their interests are strictly opposed, we can arbitrarily represent them by scales of value that make the scores or pay-offs add up in every cell to zero. Visually it is often more convenient to use positive numbers and zeros; the sum then will be some positive number.

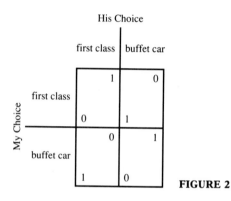

FIGURE 2

What, now, does game theory say about this dining-car or disarmament-inspection or torpedo-target problem that is abstractly represented in our matrix? The reader can probably guess: it says that each participant should have a fifty-fifty chance of succeeding. Why? Because the positions are symmetrical and in game theory we agree not to pick favorites. Is it quite true that their positions are symmetrical, when one wants to meet and the other wants not to meet? Yes, the same situation arises in matching pennies; one wants both coins heads or tails and the other wants a head and a tail, but if we match a nickel against a penny it is arbitrary whether we call the Indian or the buffalo "head." So we not only eliminate the dining car, we eliminate the concept of "meeting." We can interchange columns in the matrix and get another that is superficially changed but essentially the same; "meet" and "not meet" are only labels, and in game theory we ignore the labels unless there are special reasons for using labels as part of the communication process.

15   We might say that it is a "tossup" who wins this game and indeed one may as well flip a coin. But I can flip the coin for either of two reasons, because I just don't care and, like a person who doesn't know which shoe to put on first, want some

arbitrary way to decide, or alternatively because if I deliberately flip a coin you cannot guess what I will do, any better than you can guess the toss of a coin. In game theory it is discovered that some games of wits (usually, "zero-sum" games of pure conflict) can be converted into games of chance by appropriate randomization of one's decision.

There is a consistency here: if I flip a coin you can have no 16 better than a fifty-fifty chance at meeting me, and if you flip a coin I can have no better than a fifty-fifty chance of avoiding you. In game theory, this fifty-fifty chance of success or failure for each participant is considered the "value of the game," and the "solution." This does not quite say that a person should flip a coin. What it says is that two rational participants, in this situation with alternative outcomes, cannot rationally expect more than a fifty-fifty chance of success unless there are special reasons for supposing that one of the opponents just does not understand the game. If you can think of any line of reasoning by which to choose one car or the other with a better than fifty-fifty chance of meeting me, I can spoil your strategy by flipping a coin. No mediator could talk the two of us into any scheme that gave odds of less than, or more than, a fifty-fifty chance of meeting, because one of us could always do better by flipping a coin.

Where is all the mathematics? The mathematics is of two 17 sorts. One relates to logical generalization: it is interesting to know whether every problem of this kind has this kind of solution, and what kinds may not. Second, if we complicate the problem it may take some practical mathematics to figure out what kind of coin to flip. Suppose for example that there is one dining car in which your acquaintance is bound to find you but another in which he has only a fifty-fifty chance even if you both go to that car. The latter is like two dining cars coupled together, and to decide where to go you must choose among the equivalent of three dining cars, rolling dice to determine which of the three to go to. He then has one chance in three of finding you, and could himself guarantee one chance in three by choosing one or the other dining car with odds of two to one. Complicate the problem all you please, the principle remains the same; complicate it all you please, and the services of a mathematician or a computer become necessary. The intellectual achievement is in recognizing which complicated problems of disarmament inspection, torpedo fire control, and dining-car selection can be reduced to the general principle of flipping a coin or using random numbers. For generations people presumably chose safe combinations at random in order not to be outguessed by burglars, but it was game theory that saw the same principle (with the odds suitably chosen) in the allocation of a quota of on-site disarmament inspections among the months of a year or the sections of a territory.

18   Notice that communication is of no significance in this strictly adversary relation. The submarine commander and the captain of the target ship can have no rational interest in sending each other messages; any message worth sending is not worth reading, unless somebody thinks that he is a little smarter than his adversary and can think one step further in a game of mutual deceit.

Alternative Solutions

19   Now turn to the two friends who want to meet in the same dining car. They succeed or fail together. (If we want symmetrical terminology we can call the situation a "zero-difference game" in exactly the same sense as the pure-conflict situation is called a "zero-sum game.") Their choices are represented in the following matrix:

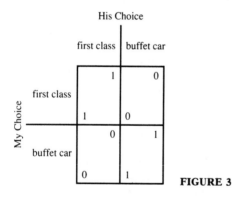

FIGURE 3

Their problem is an "embarrassment of solutions." There are two, and they do not know which to choose. If either can move first, letting the other follow, the situation is trivially easy. This is a "team" situation (to use Jacob Marschak's term) and it takes only one-way communication, or a leader-follower relation, or a "rule" known to both participants, to solve their problem.[2] If they flip coins they guarantee the same fifty-fifty chance that the adversaries did. What they might do is search for clues; a clue is a kind of signal that each can recognize as an arbitrary instruction worth following in the interest of getting together. Here is the place where "labels" can make a difference, but only as a kind of surrogate for an instruction or a communication. If one dining car is named "The Rendezvous" and the other "Solitaire," they may agree tacitly that they have the signal they need. Members of a squad separated in combat, two people with a lunch date who failed to mention where to meet, or two cars keeping to opposite sides of the road need such clues and signals. Communication makes the problem trivial, but communication is not always available. What is interesting conceptually about this problem is that there are too many "solutions," posing a problem.

Consider now the man who will lose his seat if he goes to 20 the diner. His interest, and that of the man who wants his seat, are neither strictly opposed nor wholly coincident. Both will be better off if the man can reclaim his seat when he returns, because if he can he will eat, and the other will get to sit down for a while. The "solution," if the man would rather sit than eat and has no way of reclaiming his seat, is an *inefficient* one: he goes without lunch, the other stands up all the way. What is needed is a one-way promise that the man who sits down will get up, or an enforceable contract, or a scheme to rearrange the incentives of the man who takes the seat (such as his going to the dining car second, not first, and being hungry enough to vacate his seat when the first returns). Game theory helps to discover some of these "inefficient" situations; it can also try to discover some rules or procedures, legal arrangements, or enlargement of the range of strategies available, to achieve better outcomes for both participants. Game theory also provides a framework for studying the bargaining that then occurs if there are two or more such outcomes and they discriminate differently among the participants.

A Framework for Analysis

So far I have mentioned only some rudiments of game the- 21 ory, and none of the subtle or elaborate analysis that has attracted the attention of mathematics. But what may be of most interest to a social scientist is these rudiments. The rudiments can help him to make his own theory, and make it in relation to the particular problems that interest him. One of the first things that strike a social scientist when he begins to experiment with illustrative matrices is how rich in variety the relationships can be even between two individuals, and how many different meanings there are for such simple notions as "threat," "agreement," and "conflict." He is struck by how many configurations of information and misinformation there are, how many different communication systems, and what a variety of alternative "legal" constraints on bargaining and tactics. Even the simplest of situations, involving two individuals with two alternatives apiece to choose from, cannot be exhaustively analyzed and catalogued. Their possibilities are almost limitless. For this reason, game theory is more than a "theory," more than a set of theorems and solutions; it is a framework for analysis. And for a social scientist the framework can be useful in the development of his own theory. Whether the theory that he builds with it is then called game theory, sociology, economics, conflict theory, strategy, or anything else, is a jurisdictional question of minor importance.

22   Consider two individuals with two choices each, four possible outcomes. For each participant, rank the four outcomes from first choice to fourth, without yet using numbers to represent the intensity of preferences; eliminate ties, that is, assume that no two outcomes are equally attractive or unattractive for either of the participants. How many different 2 × 2 situations can we get? The answer is 78. Furthermore, in 66 of these situations the positions of the two participants are different; and there are a total of 144 different positions a man can be in vis-à-vis his partner.

23   This number is large enough to surprise most people; but if it seems manageably small, we need only to make allowance for some tied preferences and the number of distinguishable 2 × 2 matrices exceeds a thousand. Just give each participant three alternatives to choose among, rather than two, with nine outcomes that can result from the joint decision, and the number of distinguishable positions a man could be in a vis-à-vis his partner is more than a billion. That is to say, if we prepare a table with three rows and three columns and put, in each of the nine cells, one of the numbers from one to nine for the player who chooses column, and similarly for the one who chooses row, there are more than a billion different ways of inserting those numbers, even after we eliminate all the duplications that result from arbitrarily rearranging rows and columns. (To be more exact: the number is $[9|]^2 \div [3|]^2 = 3,659,830,400$.)

24   No wonder there is no exhaustive catalogue of even the simplest kinds of interdependence that can exist between the decisions of two people. Add a third person, or add for each person his estimate of the other person's preferences, or add an opportunity for one person to make his choice conditional on the other's choice, and the number of different possibilities quickly becomes astronomical. Let the population explosion go to any

imaginable extreme and form all the possible pairs of human beings on this planet; there will not be enough pairs to illustrate the full variety of the situations that can occur when two people contemplate between them a dozen possible outcomes they jointly determine by choosing, in a brief sequence of moves, among three or four alternatives each.

These numbers are not meant to daunt the theorist but to encourage him. Since a definitive catalogue of even the simplest situations and their analyses could not be physically provided nor humanly read if it could be, and since evidently not all differences are important differences, one needs a system, or some criteria, for handling whole classes of situations that, though different, need not be distinguished. One needs to identify the models that have the greatest generality or some unique interest. And one needs a few theorems that permit him to make general statements based on a few salient characteristics of a model, without having to examine all the possibilities.[3]

Some Illustrative "Moves"

The use of matrices and explicit preferences can be helpful both in discovering and in communicating distinctions that need to be made (and in recognizing false distinctions or inessential ones). How does one distinguish a threat from a warning? How does one distinguish the potency of a threat from its credibility? How does one distinguish a bluff from an insufficiently credible threat? When does a threat need to be coupled with a reassurance to be effective? In what situations can both parties be interested in threats, in what situations can only one party have an interest? When is misinformation of value to both parties, when is it of value to one party, and when harmful to both? What is the minimum communication system required for the effectiveness of a threat, of a promise, of a threat coupled with a promise; and what kinds of insurance against failure will enhance the credibility of a threat, what kinds will degrade it? What definitions break down, or have to be replaced by more complicated notions, if the number of relevant alternatives increases from two to three, or from three to some larger number?

It turns out that many of these concepts and distinctions can be operationally defined by reference to an explicit "payoff matrix" that shows the preferences of two parties among the several outcomes. It also turns out that some cannot, and it is useful to see explicitly why they cannot. Some concepts can be operationally defined, and quite simply represented, as

a change in a single number or preference ranking in a single
cell of a matrix; some can be defined as simultaneous changes
in two or more of the pay-offs—two pay-offs of the same person
in different cells, or one pay-off for each of the players.

28   This is hardly high-powered theory, and surely does not yet
involve mathematics, but it can lead to discoveries and it can
reduce ambiguity in communication.

29   We can make threats that are bluffs or bets that are bluffs:
does "bluff" have the same meaning in both cases? My dictio-
nary says that to bluff is to frighten someone by threats that
cannot be made good. What about "will not" be made good?
Is there a difference? What is it if I make a threat that I want
you not to believe will be made good? Am I bluffing if I try
to make you underrate either my capability or my willingness
to do what I said? As von Neumann and Morgenstern pointed
out, in situations like poker one may not only bluff to win an
occasional hand on poor cards but also, quite rationally, bluff
to be occasionally caught bluffing, so that a partner may think
one is bluffing when one is not and put more money in the pot.
It is extraordinary how rich in alternative meanings some of
these apparently simple concepts are; the surest way I know
to identify the necessary distinctions, to get away from verbal
ambiguities, even to discover significant motives and actions
that one had not thought of, is to use some of the rudimentary
paraphernalia of game theory in making a model that one can
manipulate.

30   Another superficially simple concept is *immunity*. An important problem in a rebellious area is to get people to give information that they want to give but are afraid to. The same
problem arises in getting Negroes to testify when their rights
have been violated, or hotels integrated whose owners are
afraid of reprisal. Medical authorities have the same problem
in getting dope addicts to seek medical advice, since disclo-
sure of the addiction makes the patient subject to prosecution.
Grand juries often have to grant a witness immunity from self-
incrimination. (A committee can even give an immunity that a
witness does not want, to deny him the excuse that otherwise
resides in the danger of self-incrimination.) In elections the secret ballot is mandatory, not an optional privilege, so that no
one can give evidence of how he voted and thus cannot be made
to comply with a bribe or a threat. This concept of immunity
is susceptible to formal analysis, and the analysis could lean
on some of the concepts and techniques of game theory. The
situation is a "game" of *n* persons, where *n* is typically three
or more but can be as small as two; there are pay-offs to be
identified, channels of communication and a structure of infor-

mation, a distinction between verbal communication and evidence, and a set of choices that go in a certain sequence. There are alternative ways of providing immunity, such as privacy, protection, and coercion. Privacy can be personal or statistical; the protection can be based on defense against third parties or deterrence of them; the coercion can be secret, or it can be made visible to third parties to discourage countercoercion. These situations do not especially belong to economics, law, political science, criminology, strategic intelligence, or any of the traditional disciplines; it cuts across them.

Still another example is the interesting subject of locks, 31 alarms, warnings, and safety catches. We usually do not need much theory to help us buy a lock for the garage door, but a lock on nuclear weapons is rich in its theoretical possibilities. There are many kinds of locks and many motives, and even a classification of them requires something that looks a little like game theory. A lock on radium in a doctor's office has, among its purposes, the anomalous one of protecting the thief himself. A lock on the bathroom door is intended to keep people out who prefer to stay out and is equivalent to a sign saying "occupied"; and in bathrooms in some new buildings, to keep children from locking themselves in, there is an anomalous lock that can be unlocked from either side of the door. A lock on an ammunition chest may be designed to keep the contents from being used by somebody, and a mechanism that destroys the contents when the box is violated is almost as good as one that keeps the thief out; if the lock is to keep someone from destroying our ammunition, though, a destruct mechanism merely eases his task. A lock that makes the ammunition explode when the mechanism is joggled will not protect the ammunition if it works secretly, but if the burglar knows that it will explode in his face it can deter him. Some locks are designed only to measure the urgency of entry and are designed to give way under stress; fire alarms and emergency brakes are protected by a piece of glass to which a small metal hammer is conveniently attached. Some locks are meant to catch the intruder by blocking escape, some to catch his identity by photograph, some merely to report his intrusion by giving an "alarm," and they are hidden or made conspicuous according to whether one wants to trap the burglar or to deter him. And some, like the time lock on a bank vault, are designed to keep the owners themselves from being able to open them, so that they are immune to coercion during times of day that the place is unprotected.

And so on. Similar problems arise in handling confidential 32 information, the reaction to a radar alarm and the authority to launch warfare, systems to guard the legal rights of apprehended suspects, and disciplinary systems. What we are discussing is devices or institutions that can be construed as a "move" in an n-person game, where interesting values of n may be anywhere from one up to half a dozen and the game can profitably be described by reference to the pay-offs, the information structure, and the strategies available to the participants. The garage door, as I said, may be an easy one, but designing an appropriate device for a nuclear weapon, a fallout shelter, or an ammunition convoy in Vietnam requires explicit attention to the rich array of alternatives, the trade-offs and compromises, the probabilities of contingent events, the relative magnitudes of pay-offs, and what needs to be communicated, what guarded against revelation. The richness of the problem, and the value of explicit analysis, is occasionally brought home to us on those occasions when we lose a credit card, lock ourselves out of a house, or can't find something we hid to keep it away from the children.

33   I am not trying to advertise something called "game theory" that will provide instant insight into these interesting problems, but rather to make vivid the kind of problem that stimulated the development of game theory and to show how ubiquitous these problems are.

Voting Strategy as an Example

34   Voting schemes provide nice illustrations of the domain of game theory. Voting is notorious for inviting strategy—the calculation of how one ought to cast his ballot in view of how others may cast their ballots. Someone who dislikes public housing may vote in favor of a civil rights amendment he despises, knowing that only with the amendment can the bill itself be killed on a subsequent ballot. Voting also invites coalitions; and implicit coalitions can be exploited by designing "package" proposals to be voted all at once as a means of enforcing the coalition. "Packages" eliminate alternatives; a rule obliging the President to enact or to veto an appropriations bill in its entirety permits the Congress to exploit the President's preferences.

35   I am going to work through an example, and to keep it simple I shall restrict the number of voters to two. I can do that if I use a rule of unanimity. You and I are members of a two-man committee to determine the career of an employee who would normally be considered for promotion but has been charged with a blunder that he might be fired for. Our committee has

to decide two things. First, is the man's over-all record so excellent that, leaving the blunder aside, we ought to promote him? Second, is he guilty of this blunder? If his record is excellent and he is innocent he will be promoted, if his record is only ordinary and he is guilty he will be fired. If we find him guilty, but find his record excellent, he will be demoted but not fired; if we find him innocent but of ordinary record he will be kept but neither promoted nor demoted.

I have been through the evidence and reached the conclu- 36 sion that, all things considered, the man ought to be demoted, but I'd rather keep him than fire him, even promote him than fire him. You are convinced the man ought to be fired; if you can't fire him you'd like him demoted, least of all promoted. Under the rules we must vote on both issues, his record and his innocence. Under the rules, it takes two to find him guilty of the blunder, and two to award him an excellent. Under the rules, we do not vote whether to promote, keep, demote or fire the man; we vote these two issues.

a) The normal procedure is to vote first on guilt or innocence 37 and, having that out of the way, to proceed with whether his record is excellent or ordinary. If both of us prefer, however, to take his record up first, we may. So together we first vote on which question to take up first, unanimity being required to take up his record first.

b) Both of us are interested in the *outcome*, not in the abstract 38 notions of innocence and excellence. And both of us have made no secret of our preferences.

We can sketch this problem in the form of a branching tree 39 (Figure 4). There are eight ways that the balloting can go in arriving at one of these four results. The first branching point at the top determines which issue is taken up first; the second determines the answer on that first issue and the third the issue voted last. The numbers in the sketch refer to how many votes it takes to determine the choice; at the top of the diagram the 2 means that it takes two favorable votes to elect the right-hand procedure (under which his record is voted before his innocence or guilt), the 1 means that it takes only one vote to have his guilt taken up first. It would take three unanimous ballots to reach the right-hand outcome where the man is promoted; either of us can bring about the outcome on the left because it takes only one vote for guilt to be considered first, one vote to find him innocent, and one vote to deny him an excellent rating. Under one procedure, if I vote him guilty you can alone decide to have him fired; under the alternative procedure, if you vote him a good record I can get him promoted by finding him innocent. How should we expect each other to vote?

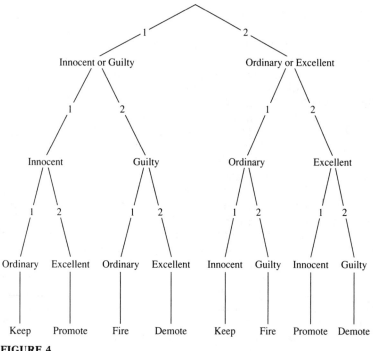

FIGURE 4

One way to work this problem is to start from the final votes and work up. At the far left (at the point reached if either of us votes for the normal procedure and if either of us votes him innocent) the final ballot (nominally on his excellence) is a choice between *promote* and *keep*, and it takes two to promote him. Evidently we'll both vote to keep him. At the final vote second from the left the choice is between firing and demoting, and it takes two to find his record excellent and thus to demote him; you prefer to fire him, and your vote would do it. Foreseeing this, at the preceding stage when we vote innocent or guilty, we know that the choice is between keeping him and firing him, so I shall vote him innocent, after which we shall both find his record ordinary. This means that if either of us supports the normal procedure on the first ballot, the result will be that the man is kept.

40   Similarly, on the far right if we have found him excellent, we shall both vote to demote him; if instead we have found him ordinary I shall vote to keep him. So when we vote on his rating we know we are voting to demote or to keep him, and

we both vote "excellent" in order to demote him at the next stage.

So, if we both vote to reverse the normal procedure and 41 take up his record first, we can expect the man to be demoted. Since we both prefer his demotion to his merely being kept, we should both vote to reverse the normal procedure, then to find his record good, then to find him guilty.

There are several points to note. First, *the procedure makes* 42 *a difference;* the man is demoted or merely kept according to which of the two questions we vote first. Second, one of the two procedures is *less satisfactory for both of us* than the other procedure, even though our interests do not coincide. Third, the reason why voting first on guilt or innocence leads to this less satisfactory outcome is that I must expect you to find his record poor after we both find him guilty. Because I do, I have to find him innocent. It is your power of decision on the final ballot that diverts me down another branch, to an outcome that we both like less than demotion. If you could promise in advance to vote his record good, I could go ahead and vote him guilty and we'd both be better off. The alternative procedure, down the right-hand branch, can be thought of as a way for you to give me that promise; by voting a good record in advance, you deny yourself the possibility to get the man fired after I vote him guilty, leaving me free to vote him guilty.

Each of us would have to re-examine his strategy if the 43 other's preferences were switched. If you knew that I really wanted him promoted, for example, you would not dare to vote as you just did; nor would I if I knew that you wanted him promoted.

A Matrix of Strategies

One technique of game theory is to identify all of these 44 "strategies"—all of the different contingent plans that the voter may have for deciding along the way how to vote next. If I had to be absent, and sent a deputy to represent me, I could not simply tell him how to vote on each ballot. Each vote should depend on how the preceding ballot went. I can, however, if I'm willing to be sufficiently explicit, anticipate all possibilities and tell my deputy what to do in each case that could arise. I could say, for example, "Vote yes on the first ballot; if that loses, vote no on the next two ballots, but if it wins, vote yes on the next ballot and yes again if it wins or no if it fails."

45   This is a *sufficient* instruction; it tells him how to do everything I would have done as the situation unfolds. In the
language of game theory, this is a "strategy." Every such contingent instruction, if it covers all possible contingencies, is
a "strategy." In this voting problem, the number of different
strategies is limited, and any advance plan or instruction that
covers every contingency can be thought of as a selection of
one strategy from among all the possible strategies. If we identify all of the alternative strategies, we can construct a matrix
consisting of all possible plans that the two of us might have,
and thus convert our dynamic sequential problem to a static
simultaneous-choice equivalent, in which I merely choose a
strategy in advance, considering all the strategies open to you,
and you do the same, and the outcome is the joint result of
these two strategies.

46   To see how this is done, without cluttering the page with too
large a matrix, suppose that we have already voted to reverse
the usual procedure and to take up excellence first, and are
about to decide on our remaining strategies. Since a no vote
is decisive while a yes vote can carry or lose, I have one completely definite strategy: voting no on both ballots with the
result that the man is kept, independently of how you vote. I
also can vote no on the first ballot and yes on the second; if I
want him fired, this may be a way of achieving my aim. If I
vote yes on the first ballot there are four possible plans I could
have for continuing: (1) to vote him guilty whether or not the
first ballot finds his record excellent, (2) to vote innocent however the first ballot comes out, (3) to vote guilty if his record is
found excellent, otherwise innocent, and (4) to find him innocent if his record is found excellent, otherwise guilty. I have,
then, a total of six possible ways of playing the game when
two ballots remain. You have the same alternatives, so there
are thirty-six different ways our contingent plans can combine
in reaching one of four possible outcomes. These are shown in
Figure 5.

47   The numbers have to be explained. To represent my preferences I have arbitrarily given a score of 3 to *demote*, 2 to *keep*,
1 to *promote*, 0 to *fire*. Since your preference order is *fire*, *demote*, *keep*, *promote*, I've scored you with 3 if he is fired, 0 if
he is promoted, etc. These numbers just remind us of our preference order; the magnitudes do not matter. (A little later we
shall see where numerical values would make a difference.)

48   Neither of us has a "dominant" strategy, that is, a strategy
that he would be satisfied to have chosen no matter what the
other chose. Row 6 looks good to me unless you choose Col-

My Strategies	No No	No Yes	Yes No	Yes No/Yes *	Yes Yes	Yes Yes/No **
No, No	1 / 2	1 / 2	1 / 2	1 / 2	1 / 2	1 / 2
No, Yes	1 / 2	3 / 0	1 / 2	3 / 0	3 / 0	1 / 2
Yes, No	1 / 2	1 / 2	0 / 1	0 / 1	0 / 1	0 / 1
*Yes, No/Yes	1 / 2	3 / 0	0 / 1	0 / 1	0 / 1	0 / 1
Yes, Yes	1 / 2	3 / 0	0 / 1	0 / 1	2 / 3	2 / 3
**Yes, Yes/No	1 / 2	1 / 2	0 / 1	0 / 1	2 / 3	2 / 3

*Vote *yes*, followed by *no* if it carries, *yes* if it fails.

**Vote *yes*, followed by *yes* if it carries, *no* if it fails.

Outcomes:

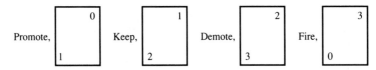

Promote, [0 / 1]   Keep, [1 / 2]   Demote, [2 / 3]   Fire, [3 / 0]

FIGURE 5

umn 3 or 4, in which case I'd rather have chosen Row 1. Column 5 looks good to you if I choose Row 2, bad if I choose Row 3 or 4, pretty good if I choose Row 5. There are some columns you might choose that leave me indifferent—Column 1, for example. There are some columns in which my score can be anything from 0 up to 3 according to what row I pick.

49   Though no row or column is an obvious "best" choice, we can still ask whether there is a pair of expectations we can have about each other that will lead us to choices that confirm those expectations. Is there a column such that if I expect you to choose it I will choose precisely the row that, if you expected it, would lead you to choose that column? Yes, Row 6 and Column 5 have that "equilibrium" property. If I expect you to choose Column 5 I am content with Row 6, and if you expect me to choose Row 6 you are content with Column 5. We cannot quite say that I "prefer" Row 6 when you choose Column 5, because I would do just as well in Row 5, but if you expected me to choose 5 you would choose Column 2. The intersection of Row 6 and Column 5 is an "equilibrium point," or an "equilibrium pair" of strategies. It has the property that if we both make the corresponding choices, each expecting the other to do so, each has behaved correctly in accordance with his expectations and each has confirmed the other's expectations.

50   Furthermore, the intersection of Row 6 and Column 5 is an "efficient" outcome, as economists use the term. There is no other cell in the matrix that can improve the outcome for one player without worsening it for the other. The same cannot be said for the cell in the upper left corner, which is also an equilibrium point but a weak one. (It is a "weak" one, a kind of "neutral equilibrium," because neither of us has an actual preference for that cell above any others in the corresponding row or column.)

51   If we draw up the corresponding matrix for the two-stage ballot under the normal procedure, with guilt or innocence being decided first, we get the matrix in Figure 6.

52   This matrix differs from Figure 5 in several ways. One is that you now have a dominant strategy: Column 3 in every row is as good as any other column and sometimes better. You can eliminate the other 5 from consideration. Since you can, I can assume you will, and I choose Row 1 or 2.

53   But though 3 dominates, your outcome is not especially favorable. Knowing your choice, I pick a row that gives me a score of 2 and you but 1. You cannot wish that you had chosen differently, all you can wish is that I could have expected you to. Then I might have chosen differently.

54   If Columns 3 and 4 could be suppressed I would have a dominant strategy, Row 6, and you could choose Column 5 or 6 and both of us would be ahead. But in the matrix as it stands, the two of us cannot hold a consistent pair of expectations that would lead us to Row 6, Column 5. This pair of strategies has not the equilibrium quality; there is no line of reasoning by which we can reasonably expect each other to expect it.

My Strategies:

	No No	No Yes	Yes No	Yes No/Yes *	Yes Yes	Yes Yes/No **
No, No	1 / 2	1 / 2	1 / 2	1 / 2	1 / 2	1 / 2
No, Yes	1 / 2	0 / 1	1 / 2	0 / 1	0 / 1	1 / 2
Yes, No	1 / 2	0 / 1	3 / 0	3 / 0	3 / 0	3 / 0
*Yes, No/Yes	1 / 2	0 / 1	3 / 0	3 / 0	3 / 0	3 / 0
Yes, Yes	1 / 2	0 / 1	3 / 0	3 / 0	2 / 3	2 / 3
**Yes, Yes/No	1 / 2	1 / 2	3 / 0	3 / 0	2 / 3	2 / 3

*Vote *yes*, followed by *yes* if it carries, *no* if it fails.
**Vote *yes*, followed by *yes* if it carries, *no* if it fails.

Outcomes:

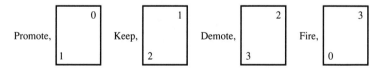

Promote, 0 / 1   Keep, 1 / 2   Demote, 2 / 3   Fire, 3 / 0

FIGURE 6

The Complete Matrix

The very first ballot, then, deciding the order in which to take up the two questions, can be construed as a ballot for deciding which of these two matrices to confront. We could of course construct a matrix corresponding to the whole three-ballot game. It would be hard to get on a single page, but we can at least ask what it should look like.

55 How many rows and columns would it have? A complete strategy has to indicate how to vote on the first ballot and how to vote thereafter in either of two cases. Since it takes two of us to reverse the normal procedure, one to keep it, a vote of no on the first ballot need only be coupled with a choice of a row (or column) in the matrix (Figure 6) corresponding to the left-hand branch. So there are six complete strategies corresponding to a vote of no on the first ballot. If I vote yes on the first ballot, my strategy must specify a row in each matrix, since I shall have to choose a row in whichever matrix the first ballot selects. There are, thus, 36 possible strategies containing a yes vote on the first ballot. Altogether, then, there are 42 strategies for me and the same number for you. This 42 × 42 matrix has 1764 cells, each containing one of the four outcomes. What else do you know about it without taking the trouble to draw the matrix?

56 We know, without any more theory, that the outcome is bound to be asymmetrical; no outcome has the same rank in our two preference scales. We might guess, and with a little more theory we would know, that this large matrix shows an equilibrium pair of strategies corresponding to a yes on the first ballot for both of us and Row 6, Column 5, of the matrix in Figure 5. That is, the solution we arrived at by working backwards from final outcomes corresponds to an equilibrium pair in our larger matrix.

57 Actually, there is a further characteristic that game theory tells us to expect. There is at least one "dominated" row or column in the matrix—a row or column that is inferior to some other row or column in at least one cell and nowhere superior. If we strike out dominated rows and columns, compressing the matrix, we shall still find dominated rows and columns (because some that were originally not dominated are dominated after the eliminations). We can go on doing this until the residual matrix contains only cells with the *demote* outcome. Game theory is interested in which kinds of problems generate matrices that have various properties, like this one.

58 A few more things can be observed in this example. One is that a "dominant" strategy is not necessarily a good strategy *to have*. It is necessarily a good strategy *to play*, because no matter what the partner does, the dominant strategy proves never to have been inferior to any other choice. But its mere availability can induce the other player to make a choice that condemns one to a poor outcome.

Another point, not illustrated in our matrix, is that in gen- 59
eral a matrix need not show an equilibrium pair of strategies;
it may show more than one; if it shows more than one they
may differ, and they may differ by both pay-offs' being lower
in one cell than another or by one pay-off's being lower, the
other higher. (Game theory also tells us that if a matrix shows
no equilibrium pair of strategies one can be generated by a
randomized choice, with suitable odds, among some or all of
the strategies in the matrix; this procedure, though, requires
that there be a suitable interpretation of the numerical values
of the pay-offs.)

Collection Decisions

This voting example illustrates that a "gamelike" situation 60
can be viewed as a *collective-decision* process—a process by
which two or more individuals jointly decide on an outcome.
The analysis also has ethical implications: we assumed the
voters to be concerned with outcomes, not with strategies for
their own sake; with consequences, not actions; with ends, not
means; with justice, not truth. A voting scheme also illustrates
how the organization of authority, leadership, and bargaining
arrangements can affect the outcomes—can affect whether an
outcome is efficient, can affect in whose favor the outcome
discriminates. And evidently if we had been willing to enlarge
our committee and have a majority-vote procedure, coalitions
would have been important; communication might have been
important to coalitions, and so might discipline. And it is evidently important what people know, or think they know, about
each other's preferences.

The "legal" arrangements are important. If binding promises 61
can be enforced, the alternative voting procedure is unnecessary; you merely promise to vote the man excellent if I will join
in finding him guilty. In fact, the first ballot can be thought of
as a "bargain" that you have an incentive to keep because I
have a credible incentive to vote for promotion if you back out
of the bargain.

Probabilistic Uncertainty and Numerical Preferences

The numbers in our matrices had only ordinal significance. 62
To illustrate how the numerical values could assume importance and how numerical values are assigned in game theory,

suppose that any award of excellence or verdict of guilty is subject to a review procedure that we believe to have only a fifty-fifty chance of confirming our unanimous vote. If a man is found innocent and excellent, there is a fifty-fifty chance that he will be kept or promoted; if a man is found guilty and excellent, there are equal probabilities of .25 that he will be promoted, kept, demoted or fired.

63   To handle the problem we now need a more complicated set of preferences. It is not enough to know that I prefer demoting to keeping the man, keeping to promoting, and promoting to firing. We now have to know whether I'd rather keep the man or take a fifty-fifty chance between demoting and firing. And we may have to know whether I'd prefer a fifty-fifty chance between demoting and firing or a four-way split over the four outcomes. We can assume a few things, such as that if I prefer demoting the man to keeping him I prefer a fifty-fifty chance between demoting and keeping to the certainty of keeping him, and prefer any odds between demoting and keeping to any odds between promoting and firing.

64   Two points are worth mentioning. First, not only can these "critical odds" or "critical risks" be subjected to certain consistency postulates in a way that may permit us to go ahead and solve our problem, but it even turns out to be possible and convenient (though not necessary) to derive numerical values for the different outcomes from a limited number of expressed critical-risk preferences. These numbers can be operated on *as though* one were trying to maximize the mathematical expectation, i.e., the expected value in a probabilistic sense. One can alternatively just postulate that a decision maker associates numerical values with all the outcomes and tries to maximize expected value; but the postulate need not be that heroic. It needs only to be that he can answer a few simple questions like those we asked above about the critical odds between a pair of outcomes that would make him just willing to settle for the certainty of a third that lies between the other two. If our man then obeys a few other "consistency" rules to avoid some kind of contradiction, we can often handle the problem. For convenience we can attach numerical values to outcomes, based on these critical odds, even calling these numbers "utilities" or something of the sort, but this is only a convenience for combining and compounding a limited set of expressed preferences in the form of critical odds.

65   The second point is that the need for numerical values arises only in the presence of uncertainties of this sort (and only when

the number of alternative outcomes is at least three), when one has to place his bets in a probabilistic environment. (The uncertainty may be about another's choice or, in case of deliberate randomization or faulty control, about one's own.) If there is no such uncertainty, numerical values prove unnecessary (as they were in our original voting situation). And in the face of uncertainty one *has* to make choices of this kind, so it is not an outlandish assumption that one actually can. "Numerical utilities," though often thought unique to game theory, are by no means peculiar to game theory; they arise in the same fashion in any theory of decision under uncertainty.[4]

These numerical values are arrived at separately for all the participants, and there is no intended interpersonal comparability among value scales. In some calculations it may appear that arithmetic is done on the numerical values of two or more players together, but it invariably turns out in game theory that an expression involving the "utilities" of two participants contains only *ratios of increments*, from which any units of measure would cancel out.

It is of some philosophical interest whether the value scales of two individuals are *assumed* inherently incommensurable, or instead we just mean that we don't yet *know how* to compare them. Game theory typically assumes the first position. Some writers treat this as a limitation of the theory and look forward to some way to compare the scales of value between people. I know of none, though, that has indicated how he would use such knowledge if it were available. Just as absolute-cost comparisons in international trade are unnecessary and usually meaningless—the notion of "comparative advantage" or "comparative cost" being sufficient to solve every problem of interest in international-trade economics—the notion of *comparative* ratios of *utility increments* (in which any absolute scales would cancel out) is sufficient in game theory. In fact, so far as game theory is concerned, there really are no "utility scales" to compare. There are merely preference rankings among outcomes that have to incorporate numerical probabilities when some of the outcomes themselves are probabilistic. To say that a rational individual "maximizes utility" is a little like saying that nature "conserves" momentum or that water "seeks" its own level. These figures of speech save a lot of circumlocution; but when we forget that they are figures of speech and try to compare actual measures of utility, or to measure the "frustration" of water when a valve opposes it, it is time to abandon the metaphor and get back to operational statements.

An Apotheosis of "Rationality"?

68   The question is often raised whether game theory restricts
its empirical applicability by postulating mental giants with
nerves of steel—perfectly rational amoral deciders who have
access ex officio to the theoretical results of game theory.

69   The answer is: not quite. In principle there is no difficulty
in imputing misinformation rather than true information, in
supposing that calculation is costly or that people make mistakes or suffer from bad memories or display idiosyncracies
in their choices. In our voting scheme, for example, we can
easily suppose that when a man votes on excellence he cannot remember whether or not a vote has already been taken
on guilt or innocence; and in fact our review-board procedure
can easily be interpreted as the likelihood that a vote will be
recorded wrong or that one of the voters will shy away from
the word "guilty" for unconscious reasons.[5]

70   But to handle these departures from perfection one has to
specify them explicitly. And it greatly complicates the problem to depart from perfection, whether it be perfect memory
or perfect absence of memory, perfect knowledge or perfect
absence of knowledge, perfect calculation or perfectly random
choice. The man with the perfect memory and the man without a memory are the easiest to handle in abstract analysis.
To allow for an imperfect memory requires that we specify
precisely how his memory misbehaves (and whether he knows
how it misbehaves, whether his partner knows how it misbehaves, and whether he knows whether his partner knows how
it misbehaves, and so forth). Pretty soon we are tempted to give
him either a perfect memory or no memory at all, or perhaps
to provide him a simplified and idealized "imperfect" memory
such that exactly half the time he forgets everything, knows
that he does, and his partner knows it, too.

71   But this is not a limitation of game theory; it is a limitation of any theory that tries to deal with the full multidimen-
sional complexity of imperfect decision-makers. Game theory
indeed usually assumes perfect knowledge or perfect absence
of knowledge, because these are simple and unambiguous assumptions to make. Anything between the two extremes requires detailed specification, and game theorists can at least
be forgiven for solving the simpler problems first and saving
the more complicated ones for later.

72   Game theory usually supposes a few other things, such as
that a man's ethics are what have recently been called "situation ethics"; he is concerned with *outcomes*, not intermediate

processes. (In our voting example he is not seeking "truth" as to guilt or excellence, but defines justice in terms of what is done with the man.)[6] The decision-maker is assumed not trying to be bold or novel for the sake of boldness or novelty, not trying to surprise us for the sake of surprise itself; he is not concerned with *why* his partner may choose a particular strategy, but what strategy his partner will choose. Nothing but the *outcomes* enter his value system. If a man has good will or malice towards his partner, a conscience or a bent for mischief, it is all assumed to be reflected in his valuation of the final outcomes. It is assumed that all the elements of his value system are displayed—everything that matters to him is allowed for—in the ranking or valuation of cells in the matrix.

How much a limitation this is depends, as in any theory, 73 on whether an abstract, somewhat perfectionist bench mark can be helpful, and whether we can keep in mind that the result is only an abstract perfectionist bench mark. Newton's laws don't work if atmospheric resistance is present; purely inertial motion is hard to observe in the earth's gravitational field; some voters are shrewd parliamentarians, some are naive or inept. Game theory runs the same danger as any theory in being too abstract, even in the propensity of theorists to forget, when they try to predict or to prescribe, that all their theory was based on some abstract premises whose relevance needs to be confirmed. Still, game theory does often have the advantage of being naked so that, unlike those of some less explicit theories, its limitations are likely to be noticeable.

Games, Theories, and Social Science

A word needs to be said about the name of this discipline, 74 "game theory." The name has frivolous connotations. It is also easily confused with "gaming," as in war gaming, business, gaming, crisis gaming—confused, that is, with simulations of decision or conflict.

The name arises from the observation that many parlor 75 games have the key quality of interdependence among players' decisions. The best move in a chess game, the best way to bid or the best card to lay down in a bridge game, depends on what one's opponents are likely to do, even on what one's partners are likely to do. Furthermore, these games are usually well defined; there is an explicit and efficient set of rules; the information available to the players is specified at every point (even if in a probabilistic sense); and the scoring system is complete. If we had a more general name for the subject now known as "game theory" it would be found that a great many parlor games fit the definition. It was this that led the authors of the first great work in the field to call their book *Theory of Games and Economic Behavior,* and "game theory" stuck like a nickname.

76   Two decades of usage have got professionals so used to the name that they occasionally forget that "game" is not only a technical term but a word in the English language. If they say that war is a *game,* elections are a *game,* industrial disputes or divorce negotiations are *games,* they usually have nothing playful in mind but are merely using a term that grew out of the recognition that some games, too, are *games.*

77   There is another problem of nomenclature: *game theory* already has the word "theory" in its name. We find it useful to draw distinctions between economics and economic theory, statistics and statistical theory, decisions and decision theory; but there is no accepted name for whatever the field is of which "game theory" refers to the theoretical frontier. Most game theory in fact has been substantially mathematical; some people prefer even to define it as the application of mathematics to this subject, and any bibliography of the discipline is almost dominated by accomplished mathematicians. Often the mathematicians have been more interested, for natural professional reasons, in mathematics than in law, social structure, diplomacy, economics, or sociology. Game theorists, and social scientists who deal with the subject of which game theory is the mathematical frontier, are out of touch with each other in a way that, say, economists and economic theorists are not, for a number of reasons including, often, the absence of a sufficient common interest to keep them in touch. The mathematical barrier is not the only one. There is an unusual dichotomy between the subtle, elegant, mathematical accomplishments of game theorists and the interests of social scientists.

78   Nothing in this essay begins to describe what mathematical game theorists actually do or even to give the flavor of it. For the social scientist, what is rudimentary and conceptual about game theory will be, for a long time, the most valuable. And it will be valuable not as "instant theory" just waiting to be applied but as a framework—one with a great deal of thought now behind it—on which to build his own theory in his own field.

79   Take the pay-off matrix itself. This is hardly "theory," although a good deal of theory underlies the definition of strategies and the interpretation of pay-offs. Yet by itself, as a way of identifying alternatives and ordering choices, of laying out the

structure of a situation to facilitate analysis, comparison and communication, the pay-off matrix may be, for the analysis of interdependent decision, what double-entry bookkeeping was for accounting, national-income accounts for economics, the truth table for logic, or even the equation for mathematics.[7]

Notes

1. Impressive support for this approach is in Jerome S. Bruner, Jacqueline S. Goodnow, and George A. Austin, *A Study of Thinking* (New York: Wiley, 1957). In studying experimentally the process of "concept attainment" the authors use the term, "strategy," to refer to a "pattern of decisions in the acquisition, retention and utilization of information that serves to meet certain objectives, i.e., to insure certain forms of outcome and to insure against certain others [p. 54]." Furthermore—and this is an interesting step beyond the restrictions of game theory—the authors do not demand that the subject be conscious of his strategy. "Psychology has been celebrating the role of 'emotional factors' and 'unconscious drives' in behavior for so long now that man's capacity for rational coping with his world has come to seem like some residual capacity that shows its head only when the irrational lets up.... Man is not a logic machine, but he is certainly capable of making decisions and gathering information in a manner that reflects better on his learning capacity than we have been as yet ready to grant." (p. 79.)

2. Jacob Marschak, "Theory of an Efficient Several-Person Firm," *American Economic Review: Papers and Proceedings*, 50 (May, 1960), pp. 541–548. The cost of information in the presence of coinciding preferences is a central part of Marschak's theory of organization.

3. Interesting attempts to characterize and classify two-person situations, by reference to some kind of pay-off matrix, are in Kellogg V. Wilson and V. Edwin Bixenstine, "Forms of Social Control in Two-Person Two-Choice Games," *Behavioral Science*, Vol. 7 (1962), pp. 92–102, reproduced in Shubik (see bibliographical note); and in John W. Thibaut and Harold H. Kelley, *The Social Psychology of Groups* (New York: Wiley, Inc., 1959). There are many twofold classifications that can be combined; the original distinction between zero-sum and nonzero-sum is one, the distinction between "cooperative" and "noncooperative" games another. See Luce and Raiffa (bibliographical note), esp. Chaps. 4, 5, and 6. Two-by-two and larger games can also be classified according to the type of "solution" they admit, to their symmetry or asymmetry, to the order of moves, to the dominance of strategies, and so forth. The "best" method of classification will usually depend on what the analyst wants to bring out.

4. See, for example, Robert Schlaifer, *Probability and Statistics for Business Decisions*, New York, McGraw-Hill, 1959, esp. Chap. 2. Luce and Raiffa (see footnote 7) give an excellent account of "numerical utilities" in their Chap. 2; and a highly persuasive presentation is in Armen A. Alchian, "The Meaning of Utility Mea-

surement," *American Economic Review,* Vol. 43 (March, 1953), pp. 26–50.

5. A perfect example is in the work of Bruner et al., referred to in footnote 1 in which the limitations on memory show up in the difference between "in the head" and "on the board" records. They even allow for the "comforting" quality of certain strategies. Their work is impressive evidence that one of the best ways to study "irrational" (or, better, "imperfectly rational") decisions is to look at specific departures from perfection rather than to start from no base line at all.

6. Lying, murder, abortion, suicide, violence and nonviolence, adultery, and presumably voting are to be judged by their consequences, not by reference to absolute laws (which, if plural, are bound to conflict occasionally), in "the new morality," which Joseph Fletcher characterizes as "a method of 'situational' or 'contextual' decision-making." Joseph Fletcher, *Situation Ethics* (Philadelphia, Westminster Press, 1966), esp. pp. 11–39, 64–68, 71–75. The question whether "deterrence" is evil if it threatens something awful (massive retaliation, capital punishment) and it works, so that what is threatened need not be done (and indeed is not expected to be done), is a question to which "situation ethics" will give a different answer from the more traditional ethics. In some of these questions the central issue is how the consequences of an action depend on the way it influences someone else's choice; thus not only does game theory typically assume a "situation ethics," but "situation ethics" needs game theory. (Fletcher, p. 188, even supports a game-theoretical attempt "to assign numerical values to the factors at stake in problems of conscience.")

7. *Bibliographical note:* The definitive survey of game theory is still R. Duncan Luce and Howard Raiffa, *Games and Decisions* (New York: Wiley, 1957); though ten years old it has not been surpassed and is not likely to be. A good sampling of game theory pertinent to social science is in Martin Shubik (ed.), *Game Theory and Related Approaches to Social Behavior* (New York: Wiley, 1964); the 75-page introduction by Shubik should be read by anyone who found this essay worthwhile. A professional treatment of zero-sum games, with illustrative applications to military tactics, is Melvin Dresher, *Games of Strategy: Theory and Applications* (Englewood Cliffs, N.J.: Prentice-Hall, 1961). For some of this author's work see T. C. Schelling, *The Strategy of Conflict* (Cambridge: Harvard University Press, 1960). *The Journal of Conflict Resolution* and, somewhat less, *Behavioral Science,* are the journals to watch for suggestive uses of the concepts and apparatus of game theory in the social sciences. The original classic is John von Neumann and Oscar Morgenstern, *Theory of Games and Economic Behavior* (Princeton: Princeton University Press, 1944); it is a stunning architectural achievement even if not, now, the best route of access for most social scientists.

PSYCHOLOGY AND POLITICS

Historical ages are often associated with the dominant image of human character that prevails. For some eras, the attributes of **Homo economicus** were central, others focused on the rational qualities of humans as thinking beings, still others emphasized the faith-centered and spiritual character of human strivings. That ours is (alongside whatever else it might be) an era of psychological self-consciousness, the age of **Homo psychologicus,** can hardly be doubted. It is not merely that psychology as a professional discipline has come into its own in our age, but that the psychological mode of appreciating human thought and action has penetrated all aspects of our contemporary culture: from the pop culture of the mass media to our most sophisticated works of literature and philosophy.

It was well-nigh inevitable that this new-found tool should be applied to the study of politics. Apart from the natural migration of concepts and methods from field to field and beyond the obvious proximity of political behavior to other aspects of human behavior that psychology explored, there is something in the nonrational quality politics often exhibits that seems to call out for psychological analysis. Politics appears to go beyond the rational calculations of cost and benefit on which game theorists, among others, set such great store. Politics is a world visibly dominated by compulsive drives, by self-destructive courses of action, by relations of dominance and submission, by catharsis, megalomania, aggression, loyalty, hatred, adulation, messianism, and anxiety.

Notably, these less-than-rational qualities are not limited to individuals uncontrollably possessed by political ambitions. Nor do they refer merely to the macabre sideshow of politics where lunatic fringes act out crackpot ideas before tiny groups of eccentrics. Political madness has seized whole communities, enlightened communities, for long periods of time. Indeed, a momentously important part of twentieth-century politics remains utterly impenetrable without a proper regard for the dark labyrinths of human motivation.

Political psychology is not, however, merely in the business of studying pathology. Although the politically extraordinary has, not surprisingly, tended to grab the biggest research headlines, much of the most significant work in political psychology relates to subjects far closer to the familiar and the ordinary. These include studies of the nature of political learning (how individuals apprehend and internalize political values), the relation between psychological needs and political participation, the psychological aspects of decision making, the effect of images that candidates project on the electorate, and, of course, the attempt to psychologically interpret the perceptions and behavior of prominent political figures.

The first and most general of the psychological analyses of politics belongs to the realm of political theory. While these psychopolitical theories are not "approaches" to the study of politics in the strict sense in which we have used the term, a word on their character and direction is nevertheless quite in place. Perhaps the most basic issue here, one that has a long and controversial history in political philosophy, is whether the basic drives that motivate us as individuals and as collectives are internally determined and fixed—this being the view of Freud—or derive more broadly from a mix of internal and social influences—the position defended by Adler, Erikson, Fromm, Sullivan, and Horney. If the former view is accepted, the prospects for a truly meaningful change in our public lives are remote if not impossible. External changes, however radical they may be, cannot affect the permanent and deep-seated motives that eventuate in discontent, animosity, conflict, and war. If, however, it is accepted that the underlying sources of our thoughts and actions are determined, at least to some degree, by social and historical factors, the prospects for creative political activity, for reform and reconstruction, become viable political strategies.

In the broadest sense, these philosophical or metapsychological analyses agree that the surface level of political activity—the coalitions, ideologies, parties, struggles for power, and so on—is reflective of needs and drives that are not simply what they appear to be. The political drama is fueled by motives with sources deep in the structure of our psyches and our interrelations, sources that will consistently escape mundane empirical analysis. As it is in our personal lives, so it is in our public existence: there is more to our actions as groups and communities than meets the unaided eye. Whether this public drama is best understood in terms of the collective unconscious, libidinal drives and their management, life and death drives (Eros and Thanatos, as Freud calls them), or the need for father figures, it is clear that the deep "truth" of a political reality requires elucidation beyond what mass survey research or rational gaming theories can turn up. Indeed, the attempt to see human public life in terms of its exoteric and declared objects is just what the classical psychological approaches to politics reject.

Although many of the psychological approaches to politics that will occupy us below are empirical in method and lack the speculative ambition of these classical theories, they tend to perpetuate this underlying characteristic: to peer beyond the given and obvious to those sources of political life which are often eclipsed or camouflaged in everyday political discourse and action. For example, political scientists conventionally see political systems in terms of institutions, power, governmental processes, rules, and culture; the political psychologist, by contrast, asks about the relation between the prevalence of certain personality types and the prevalent political ethos. Are different personality types more likely to predominate in different political regimes? Is there a definable democratic personality type that underlies the democratic political process? And conversely, what relation does the authoritarian personality have to the character of Fascist or Communist totalitarianism? Do certain collective childhood experiences create an identifiable political style when these children grow into adulthood? Are authoritarian (or democratic) personality traits relatively isolated and self-enclosed characteristics that are randomly compatible with a wide range of different attitudes and tastes? Or do they perhaps form an intelligible and unified syndrome? In other words, are authoritarian personality attributes prone to appear as a systematic clustering of attitudes possessing a certain internal psychological coherence?

Incomparably the most influential study of this kind is Theodor Adorno et al.'s *The Authoritarian Personality* (1950). In spite of the decades that have passed since its publication and in spite of the many substantive and methodological reservations that have been raised, this monumental study remains the starting point for any discussion. A simple list of the secondary literature addressing the issues raised by Adorno and his research group would take dozens of pages to encompass—and the list grows each year.

Adorno's team initially set out to study anti-semitism in postwar America. They quickly understood, however, that they were dealing with a social syndrome considerably more complex than anti-semitism itself. Anti-semitism, they found, was only a single manifestation of a considerably broader pattern. This pattern they initially formulated in the following terms:

> [the tendency to] stereotypes, adherence to middle class values, the tendency to regard one's own group as morally pure in contrast to the immoral outgroup; opposition to and exaggeration of prying and sensuality; extreme concern with dominance and power; . . . fear of moral contamination; fear of being overwhelmed and victimized; the desire to erect social barriers in order to separate one group from another and to maintain the dominance of one's own group. [1]

If this clustering of attitudes was found to hold for anti-semitism, the Adorno team speculated that it should also hold for other less specific attitudes as well. Would this clustering of attributes be maintained in regard to general ethnocentrism (the tendency to be hostile to foreigners or to outgroups) as well? What of the relationship between these traits and the tendency to accept ideologies of political and economic conservatism? And, finally, what of their relevance to those who manifested an antidemocratic potential and were prone to respond favorably to authoritarian political ideologies and regimes? [2]

These speculations turned out to be well founded. The cluster of attitudes held for ethnocentrism, conservatism, and authoritarianism as well. Moreover, the attitudes in regard to the four areas studied (the three mentioned above in addition to anti-semitism) were shown to cluster together. Knowing what an individual felt in one area was the basis for a reasonably safe forecast about what he or she felt in regard to another. This general clustering was understood to be more than a random aggregation of attitudes and opinions; it possessed, the authors argued, a basic coherence and organization as well as a tendency to maintain stability over time. Anti-semitism, ethnocentrism, political and economic conservatism, and authoritarianism together constituted an integrated personality system. Anti-semitism, the initial focus of the study, was therefore properly understood not as a specific and isolated prejudice but rather as a "general frame of mind."

Most famous of the measures developed by the Adorno group was the F (for Fascist) Scale. It was intended to measure the antidemocratic potential of a people, its vulnerability to authoritarian appeals. Here, they found a notable correlation between attitudes. When one element was present (anti-semitism, ethnocentrism, political and social conservatism), it could be fairly safely predicted that authoritarian antidemocratic potential could be found as well. Antidemocratic potential, they concluded, constitutes an internally consistent attitudinal syndrome.

Adorno's project would be of distinctly limited value if this attitudinal clustering and the authoritarian syndrome it describes lacked any real political consequences, that is, if these attitudes were merely individual attitudes without implications for community behavior. Underlying the Adorno research project, however, are the following critical premises: first, that the attitudes of individuals somehow become transmuted into real behavior and, second, that this behavior of individuals then determines the character of a political community's activity.

Admittedly, these premises seem to have a certain common-sense plausibility. And yet they certainly cannot be taken for granted. Suffice it to say that they have come in for their share of heated criticism.[3] Is it in fact true that the character of regimes is a reasonably accurate expression of the popular attitudes prevailing among the people? More starkly and simply put: do attitudes necessarily translate into congruent behavior? Are attitudes and dispositions perhaps too complex, latent, unsystematic, unexamined, undifferentiated, volatile, or nonobligatory to provide us with anything near adequate information in regard to what actor X will actually do in situation Y? Reversing the question does not make it any easier. Does the fact that individual X acts in manner Y meaningfully entail the existence of underlying attitude Z? What *can* be said confidently is that these correlations are imperfect at best. No less confident is the rather discouraging remark that too often this questionable shortcut—the facile deduction of an attitude from behavior and vice versa—takes the place of hard evidence.

Whereas the Adorno project focused on the attitudes of very large publics, other scholars chose to illuminate much smaller and more sharply circumscribed subjects. James D. Barber, for example, in a well-known, controversial study[4] set about constructing a typology of psychological characteristics with which to analyze presidential performance. His basic premise is quite simple: if we can discover the basic psychological and behavioral patterns that have emerged in the life of a political personality, we have powerful tools with which to assess and predict the patterns of behavior that will prevail under the typical strains and prerogatives of the presidency. Barber's analysis becomes more daring when he specifies what he takes to be the critical determinants that shape the presidential character. In his own words:

> The core of the argument... is that presidential character—the basic stance a man takes toward his Presidential experience—comes in four varieties. The most important thing to know about a president or candidate is where he fits among these types, according to (a) how active he is and (b) whether he gives the impression he enjoys his political life.[5]

The "four varieties" of presidential character that Barber analyses exhaust the possible combinations of (a) and (b).

1. Some presidents are both dynamically active in the pursuit of their duties and positive in their attitudes toward what they do.
2. Others are active when judged by the quantity of their efforts, but tend to find little emotional reward in their exertions.
3. Still others are passive, receptive, and compliant in discharging their duties while apparently enjoying the office they fill.
4. Last are the passive-negative types. They lack assertiveness in their approach to presidential duties and find the powers they must exercise a burden they are duty-bound to shoulder.

But Barber is not merely a taxonomist displaying a collection of species. His main interest lies in using his categories to make predictions about the actual performance of presidents, to organize presidential styles into recognizable packages, to operationalize the typologies he presents into usable guides for analysis, and to forecast the success and failure of presidential performances. It is a bold and challenging thesis that Barber presents. Even if the often-heard charge of "reductionism"—the argument that too many factors are being coerced into too neat a scheme—is valid, Barber's work must be counted as one of the more interesting attempts to apply psychosocial categories to the analysis of politics.

Robert Jervis' equally influential study, *Perception and Misperception in International Politics*,[6] turns the tools of psychological analysis onto the foreign policy decision-making process. Rather than concentrating on the deep, intimately personal, character structures of political leaders, Jervis chooses to remain closer to the surface of the messages, the information processing, the expectations, the perceptions, and the misperceptions that go into policy outcomes. Above all, he is interested in seeking out the sources of cognitive distortion—why decision makers often fail to respond appropriately to information they receive—and to recommend methods by which the tendency toward these kinds of often fatal misunderstandings can be remedied.

Based on the evidence available from both psychological and historical research, Jervis contends that overwhelmingly the most serious danger to judicious policy formation is the proclivity of decision makers to fit the information they absorb into the theories they already hold. What they know and recognize determines what they will notice and emphasize. Their expectations select, structure, and interpret the incoming messages so as to avoid cognitive dissonance. They perceive what they expect to perceive. Actors who are dead sure of the theories they hold will fail to perceive (or mistakenly interpret) the disconfirming evidence that comes across their desks.

Jervis' analysis is far too detailed and elaborate to permit adequate summary, but here is one typical example of a self-serving cognitive mechanism that Jervis dissects. He cautions decision makers to be on the alert for attitudes that contain suspiciously "consistent or supporting beliefs that are not logically linked." So as to keep our mental world tidy, we tend to build consistent and integrated views in which the various elements harmonize with and uphold each other systematically. Although there is no empirical necessity that belief in A demands belief in B, we tend to slide imperceptibly from A to B in order to sustain our ordered world views. In so doing, B becomes an unexamined and potentially dangerous assumption. Although this kind of consistency may be a logical (or even a psychological) virtue, it can easily turn into a decision maker's vice.

As an illustration, most of those who felt it was imperative to emerge victorious from the war in Vietnam believed that a meaningful victory was, indeed, possible. Conversely, those who were convinced that defeat was an acceptable outcome tended to believe simultaneously that the United States could not win the war. Similarly, Israeli doves, who tend to be solicitous of Palestinian rights, are also confident that Palestinian self-determination does not pose unacceptable security risks to their country. Israeli hawks, by contrast, tend to fuse the arguments questioning Palestinian rights with others that claim the implementation of these rights would be suicidal for Israel. In neither case do the two arguments strictly entail each other. In both instances there is a tendency to substitute emotional and psychological coherence for objective analysis.

Another intriguing attempt to interpret political behavior in terms of psychological attitudes has been undertaken by Ronald Ingelhart.[7] His interest is in generational change in contemporary Western politics. He sets out to understand the style and content of postwar politics on the basis of the various formative childhood experiences of different generations and groups. The ideological transformations characteristic of Western politics in recent decades, he argues, have resulted from a profound reorientation of the attitudes and anticipations acquired in childhood.

Until fairly recently, most political parties in Western democracies tended to be rather clearly aligned along a class-based axis. Economic factors tended to play a decisive role in political conflict. There are many indications, however, that this is changing. As affluence replaces scarcity as the dominant economic condition of the Western world, classic economic issues become distinctly less important. At high levels of economic development, the old left right continuum becomes increasingly inadequate; there is a "diminishing utility" to economic explanations. The old scarcity-based political issues tend to be replaced by another set of values and concerns that Ingelhart calls postmaterialist.

Notably, the poorer European states such as Greece and Ireland (where issues of poverty and class remain critical) maintain their old-style political polarizations. To illustrate: support for standard left-wing policies such as nationalization of industry, government management of the economy, and reducing economic inequality ranks high in the priorities of Greek and Irish citizens. At the other end of the economic spectrum, wealthy countries such as Denmark and Germany show relatively scant support for such policies. As economic development increases, the agenda of the classical Left seems to be running out of steam.

It would be easy to conclude from the above that the politics of the Left have failed and that unmitigated laissez-faire capitalism is the wave of the future. It would also be wrong. Ingelhart contends that it is precisely the success of conventional left-wing policies such as social security, reduction of inequality, and so on that has diminished their urgency and reduced their appeal. Their very success in reducing inequality and securing the lives of the disadvantaged has curtailed their salience for these affluent states. A return to nineteenth-century laissez-faire would, however, reawaken the class antagonisms that the egalitarian policies of the last century have succeeded in moderating. Postmaterialist politics therefore do not entail a rejection of the older program of social equality so much as a going beyond it to new issues and concerns that its very success has made possible.

This broad social transformation, Ingelhart believes, is inextricable from a dramatic change in the kinds of attitudes that Europeans acquire in childhood. The decrease of economic scarcity, want, and anxiety is systematically related to postmaterialist value systems. These are instilled in youth and tend to persist throughout an individual's life. The value priorities of those who grew up with scarcity and economic insecurity are increasingly giving way to a generation whose formative experiences were affluence and security. This younger generation no longer views politics in terms of simple pocketbook interests, although these, of course, persist. This generation tends to be drawn to more principled issues such as environmentalism, feminism, and nuclear disarmament. It responds positively to issues of conscience related to "the sense of community" and "the nonmaterial quality of life."

Postmaterialism is understandably more prevalent among those belonging to the postwar generation, especially to the more prosperous among them. Rather than supporting parties of the Right, as privileged groups traditionally have, they tend to shift to the parties of the Left and, in so doing, to transform the agendas of these parties toward nonmaterial concerns. By contrast, working-class individuals, or at least a sizable portion of them, tend to be drawn to the parties of the Right. There are two complementary explanations for this political about-face. They abandon the Left, first, because of a backlash against the postmaterialist values they identify with the privileged and, second, because of their own insecure economic conditions they encourage a reaffirmation of materialist values such as economic growth, military security, law and order—values that are close to the programs of right-wing parties. The conventional polarization of Western politics according to class interests therefore has undergone a process of obsolescence as the realignment along the materialist/postmaterialist axis takes place. Social class voting, that is, the support of the Left by working-class voters and of the Right by middle-class voters, becomes steadily weaker as the new generation with its postmaterial concerns replaces the older generation with its traditional class-based interests and security needs.

For our purposes, what is of particular interest in Ingelhart's very complex and sophisticated argument is his analysis of formative childhood experiences and their effect on political culture. Influenced by the work of psychologist Abraham Maslow, Ingelhart distinguishes six degrees of "need priority," that is, an ascending ladder of human needs and requirements. Our primary physiological needs are for food, water, and shelter and our basic security need is for safety and freedom from fear. Only when these elemental needs are met are we open to pursue the needs "higher" on the human hierarchy. In ascending order these needs are belongingness, love, self-esteem, and the drive to self-actualization.[8]

Broadly speaking, Ingelhart (supported by much empirical evidence) contends that those whose formative childhood experiences were the depression and the Second World War tend to be fixed in the syndrome characteristic of the early stages of the need hierarchy. Their central concerns were, and remain, the materialist values of economic and military security, of order and stability. By contrast, those who grew up in the relatively prosperous and secure postwar years tend to concentrate less on these materialist issues and to be more concerned with subjects that derive from the higher stages of the need hierarchy. The "New Politics," as Ingelhart calls it, is based on the divide between two outlooks and temperaments rather than on the simple difference between class-based interests. It distinguishes between a psychological disposition created in times of scarcity and insecurity and a very different one that arose amidst the wealth and peace of the postwar years. These basic psychological dispositions are in the process of transforming the meaning of Left and Right, reconstructing the ideological paradigms of the past, and creating a new political agenda for the future.

Social psychologists have relatively little difficulty in determining the attitudes of great numbers of individuals because (1) survey research has, in recent decades, succeeded in perfecting its methods of mass polling and (2) what interests them are surface-level opinions and viewpoints rather than the deeper and less accessible levels of personality. By contrast, those psychologists of politics who focus their research on prominent political individuals enjoy neither of these advantages. Assembling the relevant information is the first obstacle. How are they to gather their data about figures whom they may never have met, figures who may have died long before the research began, figures who, in any case, they will never have the opportunity of analyzing on the psychiatrist's couch? Because the kind of information necessary for depth analysis is incomparably more complex, profound, and elusive than what can be learned from questionnaires, culled from the formal texts their subjects may have authored, or inferred from the policies they advocated, is there not an inevitable frailty and precariousness to these psychological studies?

These are daunting obstacles, but they have not frightened a goodly number of intrepid scholars. Dozens of such psychoportraits have been written with mixed results. They have covered a remarkably wide gamut of political figures: Karl Marx, Woodrow Wilson, Mahatma Gandhi, Adolf Hitler, Richard Nixon, and Moshe Dayan. Despite the frequently intriguing nature of the psychological speculations that are entertained, these studies for the most part suffer from an irremediable impressionism. There is often no rigorous or binding method to speak of, frequently only meager and unreliable information to go on, little in the way of definitive demonstration of conclusions, and a tendency to fanciful flights of the imagination whose suitability and relevance is anyone's guess.

To be sure, some studies, like Alexander and Juliette George's study of Woodrow Wilson,[9] appear to escape many of these formidable difficulties. Because of a singularly successful convergence of relevant information, tight reasoning, and an unusually strict validation procedure, the Georges present a portrait of Wilson that many believe withstands careful examination. It is in any event considerably less impressionistic than is the norm for this genre of analysis.

One enterprising way of dodging this set of difficulties is to avoid studying the prominent political figure—who is unlikely to submit to extensive psychoanalytic examination—and to focus instead on the inner political world of a "face in the crowd." These "average" citizens can be sounded out quite extensively in regard to their views and feelings. Closely drawn portraits of such personalities and their inner world of political ideas could conceivably elucidate the politics of the "common man"—a politics that so often eludes and frustrates the political scientist's designs.

This strategy was employed by Robert Lane in a series of studies[10] with interesting if inconclusive results. Were the fifteen individuals he studied representative of the American populace? What could be inferred from their sometimes fascinating political ideas about the American political system? In Lane's case, the "micro-macro bridge" seemed virtually impassible.

Whatever the methodological difficulties it poses, the psychological approach to politics is inevitable, and irreplaceable. There would be virtually universal agreement, for example, that Lyndon Johnson's character is critical for understanding the United States' role in the Vietnam War. Who would wish to disavow the intimate link between Hitler's psychopathology and the phenomenon of National Socialism? Could we consider severing Stalin's personal idiosyncracies from the great purges of the 1930s or Saddam Hussein's from the Gulf Crisis of 1990–1991? Would anyone seriously contend that the dramatic power needs exhibited by many political leaders are explicable without psychological categories? In short, the psychological aspect of political behavior is manifest and critical even though our ability to get at it with precision and reliability leaves much to be desired. It is a case where our methods—at least as they stand at present—cannot keep up with our intuitions.

NOTES

1. T. W. Adorno, E. Frenkle-Brunswick, D. J. Levinson, and R. N. Sanford, *The Authoritarian Personality* (New York, Harper, 1950), p. 100.

2. Adorno and his team identified authoritarianism with Fascism. One of the central critiques of the study was that authoritarianism is a left-wing as well as a right-wing phenomenon. Critics charged that Communist authoritarianism, for all its uniqueness, was no less authoritarian than that of the Fascists. Whether the various "scales" devised by the Adorno group apply equally to left-wing authoritarianism and whether a unidimensional right-left continuum is relevant to the study of authoritarianism are questions about which there is massive secondary literature.

3. A well-known skeptical position is presented by David Marsh in "Political Socialization: Implicit Assumptions Questioned," *British Journal of Political Science*, I, 1971, pp. 453–465.

4. *The Presidential Character: Predicting Performance in the White House* (Englewood Cliffs, N.J., Prentice Hall, 1972). Updates of the book made in 1977 and 1985 carry the analysis into the Reagan presidency.

5. Ibid., p. 4.

6. (Princeton, Princeton University Press, 1976). An early and condensed formulation of Jervis's ideas can be found in "Hypotheses on Misperception," *World Politics*, 20, (1968), pp. 454–479.

7. Ingelhart's research is presented in a number of books and articles. See his *Silent Revolution* (Princeton, Princeton University Press, 1977) and his summary article, "Value Change in Industrial Societies," *American Political Science Review* 81, no. 4, (1987), pp. 1289–1303.

8. See Abraham Maslow, *Motivation and Personality* (New York, Harper and Row, 1954).

9. Alexander and Juliette George, *Woodrow Wilson and Colonel House: A Personality Study* (New York, Dover, 1964).

10. Probably Robert Lane's best-known work is *Political Ideology* (New York, Free Press, 1962).

SUGGESTIONS FOR FURTHER READING

Barber, J. D., *The Presidential Character* (Englewood Cliffs, N.J., Prentice Hall, 1972).

George, A. L., "The Operational Code: A Neglected Approach to the Study of Political Leaders and Decision Making," *International Studies Quarterly*, 13 (1969), pp. 190–222.

Greenstein, F., *Personality and Politics* (Princeton, Princeton University Press, 1987).

Hermann, M. G., ed., *Political Psychology: Contemporary Problems and Issues* (San Francisco, Jossey-Bass, 1986).

Janis, I. L., *Groupthink: Psychological Studies of Policy Decisions and Fiascos*, 2nd ed. (Boston, Houghton Mifflin, 1982).

Jervis, R., Stein, J., and Lebow, R. W., *Psychology and Deterrence* (Baltimore, Johns Hopkins University Press, 1984).

Verzberger, Y. I., *The World in Their Minds* (Stanford, Stanford University Press, 1990).

Robert Jervis

Additional Thoughts on Political Psychology and Rational Choice

1   Let me [turn now to] the contrast between political psychology and rational choice. In doing so, I will place [especial] emphasis on the strengths of the former.... Of course, neither approach is—or seeks to be—a united entity. Nevertheless, a few broad contrasts between them can be drawn. I should stress that this is done not in the spirit of claiming that political psychology is in all ways and for all problems more appropriate than rational choice. In fact, I think that both approaches can be useful....Furthermore, the two are not entirely incompatible. Political psychology may be necessary to provide the beliefs and perceptions that are used in rational choice models.

2   Most kinds of political psychology see people as quite heterogeneous. Although I [have previously] noted...that this strand of thought has been weakened in some formulations, many perspectives from political psychology sensitize us to the fact that different individuals will behave differently in different situations. Linked to this are cultural differences—we should not expect people in other societies to react the same way we do or to form the same institutions and patterns that characterize American society. Although a rational choice perspective can accommodate individual and cultural differences—at the cost of some parsimony—the current tendency is not to do so. It is analytically convenient to regard all people and all cultures as very similar to one another. Indeed, this is consistent with the once-popular view that implicitly or explicitly America is the model for the rest of the world. But it is a convenience that comes at a descriptive and prescriptive price many of us are not willing to pay.

3   A belief in diversity is linked to political psychology's argument that simple stimulus-response models will rarely be sufficient. Rational choice, by contrast, often implies that people respond to changes in incentive structures in fairly straightforward ways. But this will not be the case if what appears to an observer—or to one of the actors—as a reward is taken by the other person as a punishment. I certainly do not want to deny the importance of incentives in explaining human be-

From *Political Psychology*, Vol. 10, No. 3, 1989.

havior. But the very fact that some of us have chosen academic pursuits instead of investment banking reminds us of the obvious fact that people differ in the extent to which they value various kinds of rewards. Indeed, we need to do a better job of understanding the different incentive systems that operate (see, e.g., Payne, 1972; Payne *et al.*, 1984). Furthermore, variance in experienced incentives is compounded by the affective and cognitive mediations between stimulus and response. Political psychology explores the diverse ways in which people think they can reach their goals. Too often, rational choice approaches assume simple and direct linkages; this is unwarranted and is likely to produce misleading results.

Third, several kinds of political psychology stress the impor- 4 tance of development, change, and history. Some—but not all (see, e.g., North and Thomas, 1973; Cox, 1987)—rational choice approaches often are timeless—actors simply are in a given situation and we need not pay much attention to how they got there. But political psychology sensitizes us to the fact that in any situation individuals and states are not just in a situation; they have arrived there through some historical path which influences the beliefs, hopes, fears, and expectations which they bring to the situation. One reason for Britain's appeasement policy of the 1930s was the preceding experience of World War I; one reason for the Western policy of deterrence and containment after World War II was the preceding experience of the 1930s. Often, we cannot understand what actors will do without knowing where they have been and what they have done.

I want to discuss at greater lengths the final point, which is 5 linked to the two previous ones. Political psychology is committed to heavy doses of empiricism. Abstract theorizing is crucial, but we must also examine a great many cases if our understanding is to advance. Not only are data needed to test and modify our theories, but carefully looking at lots of behavior can lead us to develop important ideas. Of course "facts" never speak for themselves, but there is no substitute for the careful and detailed study of how actors have behaved in specific situations. Rational choice theory often adopts the economists' charming notion of "stylized facts," which are simple, convenient accounts that are at best oversimplified and at worst highly distorted. This approach has its utility, and we all use it on some occasions. But one of the strengths of political psychology is a commitment to the detailed empirical work which is necessary for both scholarly understanding and adequate public policy.

6   A fine and socially important example is provided by Philip
Treiseman's (1985) work on why many black students do badly
in college mathematics classes and, even more importantly,
what can be done about it. He started with five propositions
that seemed almost certainly correct—e.g., the high failure rate
among blacks could be explained by lack of high school prepa-
ration, motivation, or parental support. But he found that none
of the propositions were correct. More significantly, he did not
abandon his investigation, but instead spent 18 months following the students around in something like anthropological field
work. Only after this prolonged, intensive, and detailed study
did he find that the operating incentive structure differed from
what he had assumed from the outside. Instead, much related
to the students' beliefs and self-images. Thus because these
young men and women viewed themselves as strong students,
the extra classes could not be touted as remedial and in fact the
assignments had to include extremely difficult problems. Because most of them had succeeded in high school by resisting
peer pressure, they had to be brought to the idea that working
with their fellow students could be a way to gain mutual benefit. I do not mean to suggest that all of us would have done
what Treiseman did, although I wish that were the case. But I
think that political psychology predisposes us not to take apparent facts for granted but rather to explore the diverse yet
patterned ways that people develop and pursue their goals,
perceive and act in their environments, and make sense of their
lives.

7   To take a second example from a very different area, recently
game theorists have rediscovered the concepts of reputation
and credibility whose importance Schelling made clear almost
30 years ago (Schelling, 1960; Wilson, 1985, 1989). They develop ingenious models of the causes and effects of increases or
decreases in actors' reputations for behaving in various ways.
But, unlike Schelling, they display little curiosity about the
crucial empirical questions of how actors in fact gain and lose
various reputations. In international politics, for example, we
need to know whether reputation actually is as important as
the models would lead us to believe. Some investigations indicate that it is not (Snyder and Diesing, 1977, pp. 498–500).
If it is important, do perceivers pay most attention to whether
a state has lived up to its commitments—what I have elsewhere called its signaling reputation (Jervis, 1970, reprinted
ed., 1989a)—or to its general record of behavior, irrespective
of the pledges it has made? A related question is whether re-

solve transfers from one area to another. That is, if a state is willing to run high costs to prevail on one issue, will others infer that it will do so in a very different substantive area? For example, when Ronald Reagan fired the air controllers, did our adversaries and allies believe that he was more likely to be tough on foreign policy issues? This leads to another question: does reputation attach to the individual statesman or to his or her country? If Reagan established a reputation for standing firm, will this transfer to an America led by Bush? We also need to know whether reputations are established by making a great effort or by succeeding. For example, did its willingness to fight in Vietnam earn the United States the reputation for being willing to try to protect its allies even though it did not succeed in that case? Another question is whether a reputation for carrying out threats is gained, preserved, and damaged in the same manner as is a reputation for giving rewards.

This list of questions could easily be lengthened. The central point is that reputation and credibility are in the eye of the beholder. It is unlikely that rational choice or game theory can give us these answers, in part because not all perceivers are alike. What is needed is psychologically informed empirical research. Of course these investigations must be guided by and interpreted in light of relevant theories. Indeed, preliminary work indicates that attribution theory will prove particularly helpful. Thus Hopf (1989) has found that the inferences that Soviet observers have drawn from American defeats in the Third World were mediated by their judgments about American public opinion; Blum (1989) has found that the Soviet analyses of the causes of American behavior after Afghanistan were strongly driven by their prior beliefs; Mercer (unpublished ms) discovered that cases from 19th-century European diplomatic history provided some confirmation for the expectations derived from attribution theory that it is particularly difficult for states to acquire reputations for living up to promises and for failing to carry out threats.

Here as elsewhere what is required, then, is the application of psychological theories and detailed empirical research. I doubt that even our best theories will account for all the inference processes that are at work and so we must take care lest we, like those whom we study, be excessively theory-driven. But the main point in this context is that in trying to determine how states infer how others will behave in the future from how they have behaved in the past we cannot ignore either psychological theory or empirical evidence.

10   In summary, although no one approach can capture all of reality, political psychology's commitment to diversity, complexity, and historically grounded empirical research provides firm foundations for a rich and powerful social science.

References

Blum, D. (1989). Soviet perceptions of American foreign policy after Afghanistan. In Snyder, J., and Jervis, R. (eds.), *Dominoes and Bandwagons: Strategic Beliefs and Superpower Competition in the Eurasian Rimland,* Oxford University Press, New York.

Cox, G. (1987). *The Efficient Secret: The Cabinet and the Development of Political Parties in Victorian England,* Cambridge University Press, Cambridge.

Hopf, T. (1989). Soviet inferences from their victories in the periphery: visions of resistance or cumulating gains? In Snyder, J., and Jervis, R. (eds.), *Dominoes and Bandwagons: Strategic Beliefs and Superpower Competition in the Eurasian Rimland,* Oxford University Press, New York.

Jervis, R. (1970), reprinted ed., 1989a). *The Logic of Images in International Relations,* Princeton University Press, Princeton and Columbia University Press, New York.

Mercer, J. (1988). Attribution error and threat and promise credibility (unpublished ms), Department of Political Science, Columbia University, New York.

North, D., and Thomas, R. (1973). *The Rise of the Western World,* Cambridge University Press, Cambridge.

Payne, J. (1972). *Incentive Theory and Political Processes,* Lexington Books, Lexington, Mass.

Payne, J., Woshinsky, O., Veblen, E., Loogan, W., and Bigler, G. (1984). *The Motivations of Politicians,* Nelson-Hall, Chicago.

Snyder, G., and Diesing, P. (1977). *Conflict among Nations,* Princeton University Press, Princeton, N.J.

Schelling, T. (1960). *The Strategy of Conflict,* Harvard University Press, Cambridge, Mass.

Treiseman, P. (1985). *A Study of the Mathematics Performance of Black Students at the University of California, Berkeley,* Unpublished dissertation in Mathematics and Mathematical Education, University of California, Berkeley, Calif.

Wilson, R. (1985). Reputations in games and markets. In Roth, A. (ed.), *Game-theoretic Models of Bargaining,* Cambridge University Press, Cambridge.

Wilson, R. (1989). Deterrence in oligopolistic competition. In Stern, P., Axelrod, R., Jervis, R., and Radnor, R. (eds.), *Perspectives on Deterrence,* Oxford University Press, New York.

Fred I. Greenstein

Can Personality and Politics be Studied Systematically?

The personalities of political actors impinge on political af- 1
fairs in countless ways, often with great consequences. Political life regularly generates such contrary-to-fact conditionals
as "If Kennedy had lived, such-and-such would or would not
have happened." Counterfactual propositions are not directly
testable, but many of them are so compelling that even the
most cautious historian would find them persuasive. Most historians would agree, for example, that if the assassin's bullet
aimed at President-Elect Franklin D. Roosevelt in February
1933 had found its mark, there would have been no New Deal,
or if the Politburo had chosen another Leonid Brezhnev, Kon-
stantin Chernenko or Yuri Andropov rather than Mikhail Gorbachev as General Secretary of the Communist Party of the
Soviet Union in 1985, the epochal changes of the late 1980s
would not have occurred, at least not at the same time and in
the same way.

The seemingly self-evident effects of many changes in lead- 2
ership, including changes of a much lesser order in lesser entities than the national governments of the United States and the
Soviet Union, along with the innumerable other events in the
political world that are difficult to account for without taking cognizance of the actors' personal peculiarities, lead the
bulk of nonacademic observers of politics, including journalists, to take it for granted that personality is an important determinant of political behavior. It may seem truistic to those
members of the scholarly community whose interests direct
them to read a journal entitled *Political Psychology* that such
lay political observers are correct and that there is need for
systematic study of personality and politics. Yet it is rare in
the larger scholarly community for specialists in the study of
politics to make personality and politics a principal focus of
investigation. Instead, they tend to concentrate on impersonal
determinants of political events and outcomes, even those in
which the participants themselves believe personality to have
been significant. Or, if they do treat individual action as important, they posit rationality, defining away personal characteristics and presuming that the behavior of actors can be
deduced from the logic of their situations (cf. Simon, 1985).

From *Journal of Political Psychology*, vol. 12, no. 4 (1991). Reprinted with permission of
Plenum Publishing Corporation.

3   My argument in this paper is that the study of personality and politics is possible and desirable, but that systematic
intellectual progress is possible only if there is self-conscious
attention to evidence, inference, and conceptualization. In setting that argument forth, I build on, augment, and modify
my previous writings on problems of explanation in political psychology (Greenstein, 1969; 1975), selectively incorporating later scholarship, particularly the extensive work in recent years on political cognition. My formulation builds on the
very controversies that often impede the study of personality
and politics.

4   The study of personality and politics sometimes appears to
have more critics than practitioners. Some of the controversy
is no more than the usual methodological and empirical disagreements within the ranks of those who seek to unravel a
complex and varied real-world phenomenon, but the most important disagreements for the purposes of this essay are over
whether in principle there *is* a need for the study of personality and politics, and, if so, what the scope of such study might
be.

5   Reservations have been expressed about the utility of studying the personalities of political actors on the grounds that (1)
political actors are randomly distributed in roles and therefore their personalities "cancel out"; (2) political action is determined more by the actors' political environments than by
their own characteristics; (3) the particular stratum of the psyche many political scientists equate with *personality*, psycho-
dynamics and the ego defenses, does not have much of a political impact; (4) the social characteristics of political actors
are more important than their psychological characteristics;
and (5) individuals are typically unable to have much effect
on political outcomes. On analysis, each of these reservations
or disagreements proves to have important conceptual implications for the study of personality and politics. The debate
about scope has roots in the definitional ambiguity of the basic terms *personality* and *politics* and is best dealt with before
the objections and their positive implications for systematic
inquiry.

Definitional Questions

6   Narrowly construed, the term *politics* in *personality and
politics* refers to the politics most often studied by political scientists—that of civil government and of the extra-

governmental processes that more or less directly impinge upon government, such as political parties and interest groups. Broadly construed, it refers to politics in all of its manifestations, whether in government or any other institution, including many that are rarely studied by political scientists—for example, the family, school, and workplace. By this broader construction, the common denominator is the various referents of *politics*, including the exercise of influence and authority and the diverse arts of interpersonal maneuver, such as bargaining and persuasion, connoted by the word *politicking*, none of which are monopolized by government.

Personality also admits of narrow and broad definitions. In 7 the narrow usage typical of political science, it excludes political attitudes and opinions and often other kinds of subjective states that are of a political nature (for example, the ideational content associated with political skill) and applies only to nonpolitical personal differences, or even to the subset of psychopathological differences that are the preoccupation of clinical psychology. In psychology, on the other hand, the term has a much broader referent—in the phrase of the personality theorist Henry Murray (1968), it "is the most comprehensive term we have in psychology." Thus, in their influential study of *Opinions and Personality*, the psychologists M. Brewster Smith, Jerome Bruner, and Robert White (1956, p. 1) use a locution one would not expect from political scientists, describing opinions as "an integral part of personality."

Although usage is a matter of convention and both the nar- 8 row and the broad definitions encompass phenomena worthy of study, this seemingly semantic controversy has a significant bearing on what scholars study. As Lasswell (1930, pp. 42–45) argued long ago, there are distinct advantages to adopting the broader definition. A perspective that transcends governmental politics encourages study of comparable phenomena, some of which may happen to be part of the formal institutions of governance and some of which may not. Browning and Jacobs (1964), for example, compared the needs for power, achievement, and affiliation of businessmen and public officials in highly diverse positions that imposed sharply divergent demands. They found that the public officials were by no means all cut from the same psychological cloth, but that there were important similarities between certain of the public officials and businessmen. The underlying principle appears to be that personality tends to be consistent with the specific demands of roles, whether because of preselection of the role incumbents or because of in-role socialization.

The Distribution of Individuals in Roles

9   Even if the first of the reservations sometimes expressed about the value of studying personality and politics—the claim that individuals are randomly distributed in political roles and therefore their impact is somehow neutralized—is empirically sound, it is by no means a reason not to study personality and politics. If one visualizes political processes as analogous to intricately wired computers, political actors can be viewed as key junctures in the wiring, for example circuit breakers. If anything, it would be *more*, not less, urgent to know the performance characteristics of the circuit breakers if their operating properties were random, with some capable of tripping at inappropriate times, losing valuable information, and others failing to trip, exposing the system to the danger of meltdown.

10   In the real political world, events sometimes do more or less randomly assign individuals with unanticipated personal styles and proclivities to political roles, often with significant consequences. This was the case of two of the national leaders referred to in the opening of the article: neither Franklin Roosevelt's nor Mikhail Gorbachev's contemporaries anticipated the innovative leadership they displayed in office. As the Browning and Jacobs study suggests, however, people do not appear to be randomly distributed in political roles, though the patterns of their distribution appear to be complex and elusive. Ascertaining them, examining their political consequences and determining the "fit" between role and personality are important parts of the intellectual agenda for the study of personality and politics (George, 1974).

Personality and Environment

11   The second reservation about the study of personality and politics—that environment has more impact than personality on behavior—and the other three reservations need to be considered in the context of a general clarification of the types of variables that in principle can affect personality and politics and their possible interconnections. An important example of such a clarification is M. Brewster Smith's (1968) well-known "map for the study of personality and politics." (See also Stone and Schaffner's [1988, p. 33] depiction of "political life space.") The representation that I will employ (Greenstein, 1975) is introduced in segments in Figures 1 and 2 and set forth in its entirety in Figure 3.

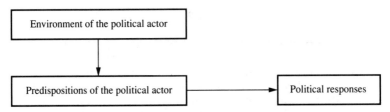

FIGURE 1 Basic antecedents of political behavior:E→P→R

The most fundamental distinction in the map is the rudi- 12
mentary one that, as Kurt Lewin (1936, pp. 11–12) put it, "behavior or any kind of mental event...depends on the state of
the person and at the same time on the environment." Figure 1
depicts the links between the two broad classes of behavioral
antecedent Lewin refers to and behavior itself, using the terminology of Lasswell and Kaplan (1950, pp. 4–6), who ground
an entire conceptual framework for the analysis of politics on
the equation that human response (R) is a function of the re-
spondent's environment (E) and predispositions (P):E→P→ R.
Here again, terminology is a matter of convenience. Instead
of *predispositions*, it would have been possible to use many
other of the 80 terms Donald Campbell (1963) enumerates in
his account of the logic of studying "acquired behavioral dispositions." Such terms as *situation, context,* and *stimulus* are
common alternative labels for all or part of the environment
of human action.

The E→P→R formula provides a convenient way of visual- 13
izing the fallacy in the claim that behavior is so much a function of environments that individuals' predispositions need not
be studied (reservation two). In fact, environments are always
mediated by the individuals on whom they act; environments
cannot shape behavior directly, and much politically important action is not reactive to immediate stimuli. Indeed, the
capacity to be *proactive* (Murray, 1968) and transcend existing perceptions of what the environment dictates is at the core
of effective leadership. But the debate about whether environments determine political behavior is a reminder of the endless interplay of individuals and the political contexts in which
they find or place themselves.

Some contexts are indeed associated with the kind of be- 14
havior that leads social determinists to be skeptical about the
need to study personality. Informed of the impending collapse
of a building, everyone—irrespective of temperament and personality type—will seek to leave it. Other contexts illustrate

Gordon Allport's (1937, p. 325) aphorism that "that same heat that hardens the egg, melts the butter." Still others are virtual ink blots, leading individuals with varying characteristics to project their inner dispositions onto them. The connection between personality and context is so integral that this relationship has become the basis of an important approach to personality theory known as interactionism (Magnusson and Endler, 1977; Pervin and Lewis, 1978; Endler, 1981). By systematically analyzing personality and politics in interactional terms, the analyst is sensitized to the kinds of contingent relationships that make the links between personality and politics elusive.

15   A good example of a contingent relationship in which the impact of personality is mediated by the environment is to be found in the work of Katz and Benjamin (1960) on the effects of authoritarianism in biracial work groups in the North and the South. Katz and Benjamin compared white undergraduates in the two regions who scored low and high on one of the various authoritarian personality measures to see how they comported themselves in interracial problem-solving groups. They found that in the South authoritarianism (which previous studies showed to be associated with race prejudice) was associated with attempts of white students to dominate their black counterparts, but that in the North the authoritarians were more likely than the nonauthoritarians to be *deferential* to blacks. The investigators' conclusion was that the sociopolitical environment of the Southern authoritarians enabled them to give direct vent to their impulses, but that the liberal environment of the Northern university led students with similar proclivities to go out of their way to avoid coming in conflict with the prevailing norms.

16   The relative effect of environment and personality on political behavior varies. Ambiguous environments—for example, new situations and political roles that are only sketchily defined by formal rules (Budner, 1962; Greenstein, 1969, pp. 50–57)—provide great latitude for actors' personalities to shape their behavior. Structured environments—for example, bureaucratized settings and contexts in which there are well-developed and widely known and accepted norms—tend to constrain behavior. The environment also is likely to account for much of the variance in political behavior when strong sanctions are attached to certain possible courses of action.

17   The dramatic reduction of political repression in the Soviet Union And Eastern Europe in the late 1980s led to an outpouring of political action. Just as the absence of authoritarian rule leads individuals in the aggregate to express their personal po-

litical proclivities, its presence magnifies the effects of leaders, assuming that the authoritarian system is one in which the individual or individuals at the top have more or less absolute power (Tucker, 1965). The striking capacity of leaders' personalities to shape events in an authoritarian system was evident in the leeway Gorbachev appears to have had at the time of the initiation of glasnost and perestroika, if not later when the forces of pluralism began to bedevil him.

Just as environments vary in the extent to which they foster 18 the expression of individual variability, so also do predispositions themselves vary. There is an extensive literature on the tendency of people to subordinate themselves to groups and consciously or unconsciously suppress their own views when they are in the company of others. But some individuals are remarkably resistant to such inhibitions and others have compliant tendencies (Asch, 1956; Allen, 1975; Janis, 1982). The intensity of psychological predispositions promotes expression of them. Most people suppress their impulses to challenge the regimes of authoritarian systems, but those with passionate convictions and strong character-based needs for self-expression or rebellion are more likely to oppose such regimes. (In doing so, they alter the environment, providing social support for their more compliant fellows to join them.)

Psychopathological and Other Political Motivation

One of the ways in which humans vary is in the extent to 19 which they manifest emotional disturbance and ego defensiveness. Equating all of personality with the psychological stratum that traditionally concerns clinical psychologists, some students of politics voice the third of the reservations about the study of personality and politics, arguing that the links between psychopathology and politics are rare and unimportant. A specific exploration of the general question of whether ego-defense motivation is common in politics can be found in the extensive empirical literature on the student political protest movements of the 1960s. Some research findings appeared to indicate that protest was rooted in "healthy" character traits, such as inner strength to stand by one's convictions and the cognitive capacity to cut through propaganda, whereas other reports suggested the possible influence of the kinds of neurotic needs that might, for example, arise from repressed resentment of parents or other everyday-life authority figures.

In order to consider the general issue of the role of psy- 20 chopathology in politics and the specific issue of the roots of protest, it is necessary to elaborate the E→P→R formula. Figure 2 expands the personality panel in Figure 1. The panel is constructed so as to suggest, in a metaphor common in personality theory (Hall and Lindzey, 1970), "levels" of psychic functioning. The level closest to the surface and most directly "in touch" with the environment is the perceptual. Perceptions can be thought of as a cognitive screen that shapes and structures environmental stimuli, sometimes distorting them, sometimes reflecting them with considerable verisimilitude. In the 1970s and 1980s there was burgeoning inquiry into political perception and cognitive psychology more generally (Jervis, 1976; Jervis, Lebow and Stein, 1985; Lau and Sears, 1986; Vertzberger, 1990). Also at the surface, in the sense that they are conscious or accessible to consciousness, are political orientations such as attitudes, beliefs and convictions. Psychologists commonly conceive of dispositions at this level as composites of the more basic processes of cognition (thought), affect (emotion), and conation (proclivities toward action).

21   The subpanel of Figure 2 labeled "functional bases of conscious orientations" and, more or less synonymously, "basic

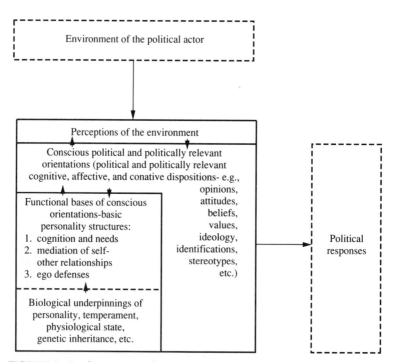

FIGURE 2 Predispositions of the political actor

personality structures," represents the level of psychic activity that political scientists often have in mind when they speak of personality. Different personality theorists emphasize the importance of different underlying personality structures, but most of them distinguish (in varied terminology) three broad classes of inner processes—those bearing on thought and perception, on emotions and their management (including feelings of which the individual may have little conscious understanding) and on the relation of the self to significant others. The terms used for these processes in Figure 2 are *cognition, ego defense* and *mediation of self-other relations.* Figure 2 also includes a subpanel identifying the genetic and acquired physical states that contribute to personality and diffuse into political behavior (Masters, 1989; Park, 1986).

Both the broad question of whether psychopathology man- 22 ifests itself in political behavior and the narrow question of what motivates political rebels can be illuminated by reference to Figure 2. One way of thinking about political attitudes and behavior is in terms of the functions they serve for the personality (Smith, Bruner, and White, 1956; Pratkanis, Breckler, and Greenwald, 1989)—hence the use of the phrase "functional bases of conscious orientations." What might on the surface seem to be the same belief or class of action, may serve different functions in the motivational economies of different people. For one individual a certain view—for example, a positive or negative racial stereotype—may result from the available information in the environment, mainly serving needs for cognitive closure. For another, the view might be rooted in a need to take cues from (or be different from) significant others. For a third, it might serve the ego-defensive function of venting unacknowledged aggressive impulses. (More often than not, a political behavior is likely to be fueled by more than one motivation but with varying mixes from individual to individual.)

The incidence of psychopathological and other motivational 23 bases of political orientations needs to be established by empirical inquiry. Just as some environmental contexts leave room for the play of personality in general, some are especially conducive to the expression of ego defenses. These include stimuli that appeal to the powerful emotional impulses that people are socialized to deny but that remain potent beneath the surface. There is an especially steamy quality to political contention over issues that bear on sexuality like abortion and pornography. Nationalistic issues such as flag burning and matters of religious doctrine also channel political passions (Davies, 1980), for reasons that have not been adequately explained.

Extreme forms of behavior are also likely (though not certain) to have a pathological basis, as in the behavior of American presidential assassins such as Ronald Reagan's would-be killer, John Hinckley, Jr. (Clarke, 1990).

24   The circumstances under which psychopathology and its lesser variants find their way into politics are of great interest, as are those under which the other motivational bases of political behavior come into play. Depending upon the basic personality systems to which a given aspect of political performance is linked, differences can be expected in the conditions under which it will be aroused and changed, as well as in the detailed way it will manifest itself. Opinions and actions based in cognitive needs will be responsive to new information. Those based on social needs will respond to changes in the behavior and signals provided by significant others. Those based on ego defenses may be intractable, or only subject to change by extensive efforts to bring about self-insight, or by certain manipulative strategies such as suggestion by authority figures (Katz, 1960).

25   The functional approach to the study of political orientations provides a useful framework for determining whether and under what circumstances political protest has motivational sources in ego-defensive needs. There is much evidence bearing on this issue, at least as it applies to student protest. A remarkable number of empirical studies were done of student protest activity of the late 1960s and early 1970s in the United States and elsewhere, no doubt because that activity occurred in contexts where numerous social scientists were available to conduct research. A huge literature ensued, abounding in seemingly contradictory findings, many of which, however, appear to fit into a quite plausible larger pattern, once one takes account of the diversity of the institutions in which protest was studied and of the particular periods in the cycle of late-1960s and early 1970s student protest in which the various studies were conducted.

26   The earliest student protests of the 1960s occurred in colleges and universities with meritocratic admissions policies and upper-middle-class student bodies. The first studies of this period, those by Flacks (1967) of University of Chicago students, suggested that student protest was largely a cognitive manifestation—the response of able students to the perceived iniquities of their political environment. Later analyses of data collected in the same period on similar populations (students at the University of California, Berkeley) suggested a more complex pattern in which some of the ac-

tivists did seem to have the cognitive strengths and preoccupations that Flacks had argued were the mark of *all* of them, but others appeared to be channeling ego-defensive needs (based in troubled parent-child relations) into their protest behavior. The students who the later analysts concluded had ego-defensive motivations and those who they concluded were acting out of cognitive needs showed different patterns of protest behavior, the first directing their activity only on the issues of national and international politics, the second taking part in local reform activities (Block, Haan, and Smith, 1969).

The psychological correlates of student activism changed 27 over time in the United States, as activism became transformed from the activity of a few students in the "elite" universities to a widespread form of behavior, which at the time of the Nixon administration's incursion into Cambodia and the killing of student protesters at Kent State University manifested itself on virtually every American college and university campus. Studies conducted at that time found little evidence that protesters had distinctive distinguishing characteristics (Dunlap, 1970; Peterson and Bilorusky, 1971).

Personality, Historical Context, and Social Background

Variation according to historical context and change over 28 time are so important in determining how personality becomes linked with politics that the map around which this article is organized needs to be expanded, as it is in Figure 3, which encompasses the time dimension and differentiates the immediate and remote features of the political environment. Figure 3 suggests that the fourth reservation about the utility of studying personality and politics—the claim that social backgrounds are more important than psychological characteristics—is grounded in a confusion which can be readily dissolved. The social backgrounds of political actors (panel 2 of Figure 3) influence their actions but only as mediated by the individual's developing predispositions (panel 3) and the different levels of personality they shape (panels 4, 5 and 6). Thus, to take a final example from the literature on student protest in the 1960s, it was (as Block et al., 1969, pointed out at the time) fallacious for Lipset (1968) to argue that because so many student activists were young middle-class Jews, personality was not an important determinant of activism. To the extent that Jewish background was connected with activism,

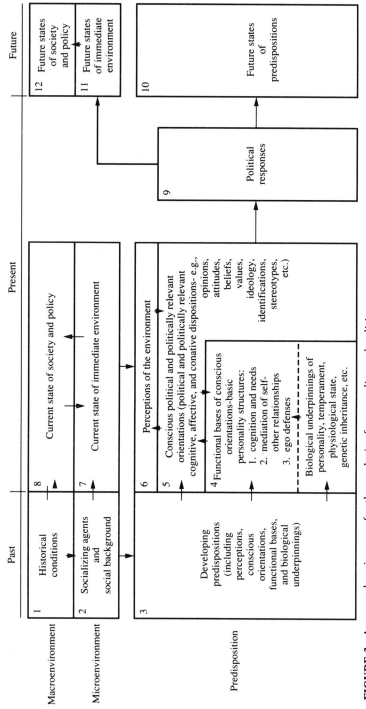

FIGURE 3 A comprehensive map for the analysis of personality and politics

it had to be part of a causal sequence in which developmental experiences specific to Jews contributed to their psychological orientations. The latter, not Jewish background per se, would have been the mediator of behavior.

The study of how ethnicity, class, and other of the so-called 29 background characteristics affect political behavior is important and highly relevant to (but no substitute for) the study of personality and politics. To the extent that a characteristic becomes part of an actor's personal make-up, it is no longer "background"—it is an element of the psyche. But evidence about whether background experience distinguishes members of one social group from those of others is grist for political psychologists. Lipset may have been correct in sensing that Jewish political activists of the 1960s had some distinctive qualities that were important for their behavior. The observation that many student protesters were Jewish not only fails to prove this, but also forecloses systematic inquiry.

An appropriate program of inquiry into Lipset's claim 30 would entail specifying the precise psychological dynamics that ostensibly make Jewish protesters distinctive and comparing Jewish and non-Jewish protesters with comparable non-protesters in order to determine whether the imputed patterns existed. If they did, one would want to know whether they resulted from particular developmental histories, whether they had predictable consequences for political behavior, and why some Jews protested and some did not. Whether a distinctly Jewish psychology of political protest exists is an empirical question and is part of a broader set of questions that can be asked about how group membership affects personality and political behavior.

The Impact of Personality on Events

The last of the reservations about the study of personality 31 and politics derives from the view that individuals are not likely to have much impact on events. Such a premise underlies many theories of history. In the 19th century the question of whether historical actors have an impact on events was the basis of a fruitless grand controversy, with such social determinists as Herbert Spencer denying the efficacy of historical actors and such Great Man theorists as Thomas Carlyle proclaiming their overriding importance (Kellerman, 1986, pp. 13–57). Contemporary leadership theorists typically describe themselves as interactionists, emphasizing the interdependence of leaders and their environments and the contingent nature of the leader's impact on larger events (Burns, 1978; Tucker, 1981).

32   The debate about whether actors can shape events concerns the causal chain from personality (panels 4–6 of Figure 3), through political response (panel 9), to future states of the immediate and more remote political and social environment (panels 11 and 12). Claims that a particular actor's personality did or did not affect a particular historical outcome usually prove to be claims about *action dispensability* and *actor dispensability* (Greenstein, 1969, pp. 40–46) — that is, about whether the outcome in question would have taken place in the absence of that individual's actions and whether the actions in question were ones that any similarly placed actor would have taken. The second issue is one I have already explored under the heading of personality and environment. The first requires clarification.

33   The capacity of actors to shape events is a variable, not a constant. The sources of variation are parallel to the determinants of success in the game of pool. The number of balls a player will be able to sink is in part a function of the location of the balls in the table. The parallel in politics is the malleability of the political environment (Burke and Greenstein, 1989, p. 24). The second determinant of success in the pool room is the position of the cue ball. This is analogous to the actor's position in the relevant political context. Roosevelt and Gorbachev could not have had an impact from lower-level administrative positions. The third class of variable has the same labels in the games of pool and politics—skill, self-confidence, and the other personal requisites of effective performance.

Personality Theory, Role, Culture

34   The distinctions summarized in Figure 3 represent many of the basic categories in the multitude of personality theories that offer partial visions of psychic structure and function. The seeming Babel of competing personality theories and alternative nomenclatures conceals basic commonalities: all theories necessarily take cognizance that humans are thinking, feeling creatures who exist in social environments and have inner qualities that shape their response to those environments.

35   Beyond that, personality theories differ from one another in what they emphasize. The various personality theorists— Freud, Jung, Allport, Murray and the many others—differ in the extent to which they emphasize one class of motivation over another, in their sensitivity to the individual's environ-

ment, in the weight they put on biology, in the extent to which they view personality to be structured, and in many other respects. For the present purposes it is not appropriate to recommend a particular personality theory. The advice Hall and Lindzey (1970, p. 602) offer all students of personality is equally sound for students of personality and politics. After becoming broadly acquainted with the field of personality, become immersed in a particular personality theory and "wallow in it, revel in it, absorb it, learn it thoroughly, and think that it is the best possible way to conceive of behavior," but "reserve in one small corner of [the] mind the reservation that the final crucible for any theory is the world of reality studied under controlled conditions." Then "set about the cold hard business of investigation."

Figure 3 does not make explicit provision for two important 36 concepts for the student of political psychology—role and culture. What is their conceptual standing? The first of these terms has already appeared with some regularity in this paper. It is difficult to envisage an extended discussion of political psychology that does not take account of the way political actors perform their roles, and of the fit between role and personality and related matters. Yet, as Levinson (1959) shows, the referents of *role* are systematically ambiguous. Sometimes the term is used to refer to political behavior itself (Figure 3, panel 9), as in "His role in the Cuban Missile Crisis was critical." Sometimes it refers to the expectations in an individual's environment about what behavior is appropriate for someone filling that individual's position, in which case the referent would be mapped in panels 7 and 8 of Figure 3. And sometimes the term refers to the role-incumbent's own assumptions about what the role entails (panel 5). As long as the referent is specified, an investigator may use the term in any of these senses, depending on his or her theoretical assumptions and concerns. Indeed, the mere act of recognizing the diversity of meaning may suggest fruitful hypotheses—for example, about whether and to what extent incumbents in particular roles and the individuals with whom they interact have shared conceptions of what the roles entail.

If the term role is ambiguous, culture is ambiguity run riot 37 (Kroeber and Kluckhohn, 1952; Merelman, 1984). A simple solution would be to conceive of the term as the counterpart at the collective level to personality at the individual level. If personality is used as an omnibus term to encompass the various elements of an individual's subjectivity, culture then would be used to encompass those elements at the collective level for societies, polities, and lesser entities. In Figure 3, the referent would be the environmental panels (7 and 8). Such a usage, however, would leave no referent for terms like "acculturate," which refer to the individual's incorporation of cultural norms and assumptions. And it would bypass the issues that make culture such a protean term to begin with—for example, the debates about whether cultures are marked by structure and about what kinds of orientations are and are not parts of a culture. (If the term is simply synonymous with public opinion, it is redundant.) As with role, there seems to be no single usage that will command agreement. Because the various usages refer to different (and, in many cases, potentially interesting) phenomena, it is essential for investigators to specify the sense in which they are using the term.

Kinds of Personality and Politics Analysis

38   Every human being is in certain ways like all other human beings, in certain ways more like some human beings than others, and in certain ways unique (Kluckhohn and Murray, 1953). Each of these resemblances is reflected in an analytically distinct kind of personality-and-politics analysis. The universality of human qualities is explored in writings that seek in some broad way to make the connection stated in the title of Graham Wallas' *Human Nature and Politics* (1908). Sigmund Freud's *Civilization and its Discontents* (1930), Fromm's *Escape from Freedom* (1941), Norman O. Brown's *Life Against Death* (1959) and Herbert Marcuse's *Eros and Civilization* (1966) are notable contributions to this tradition. At their best such works provide fascinating and provocative perspectives on the human condition. Many of them are rich in insights that suggest testable hypotheses.

39   Because they seek to explain the variable phenomena of political behavior with a constant, such efforts are not themselves subject to confirmation or disconfirmation. In contrast, it *is* possible to conduct systematic, replicable inquiries into political actors' unique qualities (*single-case analysis*) and the qualities that make them more like some individuals than others (*typological analysis*). The ways in which individual and typical political psychology affects the performance of political processes and institutions (*aggregation*) can also be studied systematically.[1]

40   Single-case personality analysis is more important in the field of personality and politics than it has come to be in personality psychology generally, because students of politics are concerned with the performance of specific leaders and their

impact on events. There have been noteworthy personality-and-politics studies of leaders as diverse in time, culture and the circumstances of their leadership as Martin Luther (Erikson, 1958), Louis XII (Marvick, 1986), Woodrow Wilson (George and George, 1964), Kemal Ataturk (Volkan and Itzkowitz, 1984), and Josef Stalin (Tucker, 1973), as well as many others. There also have been valuable single-case psychological analyses of figures whose political importance derives from their impact on leaders—for example, George and George's analysis (1964) of the influence of Colonel Edward House on Woodrow Wilson and Kull's (1988) of defense policy advisers. In addition, there is a tradition in the field of personality and politics of single-case analyses of "faces in the crowd"—people who are without policy influence but who illustrate in depth the psychological process that can only be examined more superficially in surveys (Riesman and Glazer, 1952; Smith, Bruner, and White, 1956; Lane, 1962).

Typological study of political and other actors is of potentially great importance: if political actors fall into types with known characteristics and propensities, the laborious task of analyzing them *de novo* can be obviated, and uncertainty is reduced about how they will perform in particular circumstances. The notion of a psychological *type* can be stretched to include all efforts to categorize and compare the psychology of political actors, even straightforward classifications of the members of a population in terms of whether they are high or low on some trait such as ego strength, self-esteem, or tolerance of ambiguity. The more full-blown political psychology typologies parallel diagnostic categories in medicine and psychiatry. They identify syndromes—patterns of observable characteristics that reflect identifiable underlying conditions, result from distinctive developmental histories, and have predictable consequences.

Of the many studies that employ the first, simpler kind of psychological categorization, the studies by Herbert McClosky and his students are particularly valuable because of their theoretical and methodological sophistication and the importance of the issues they address (e.g., McClosky, 1967; Di Palma and McClosky, 1970; Sniderman, 1974; McClosky and Zaller, 1984). Political personality typologies of the second, more comprehensive variety go back at least to Plato's account in the eighth and ninth books of *The Republic* of the aristocrat, the democrat, the timocrat and the tyrant—political types that Plato believed were shaped in an intergenerational dialectic of rebellion of sons against their fathers' perceived shortcomings. (For a gloss on Plato's account, see Lasswell, 1960). Latter-day typologies that have generated important bodies of literature are the authoritarian, dogmatic, and Machiavellian personality classifications (Adorno, Frenkel-Brunswick, Levinson and Sanford, 1950; Rokeach, 1960; Christie and Geis, 1970).

43   Within political science, the best-known personality typology has been James David Barber's (1985) classification of the character structures of American presidents. Within psychology, the best-known has been that of the authoritarian personality. Both typologies have engendered methodological controversies that for a time, at least, threatened to submerge the insights in the works in which they were originally set forth (George, 1974; Kirscht and Dillehay, 1967), but both contain important insights and may eventually stimulate cumulative bodies of scholarship.

44   This can occur even after a long dormant period, as can be seen by the tangled history of studies of authoritarianism. By the late 1960s, the massive literature exploring the implications of that construct appeared to be at a dead end. But in the 1980s an ingenious and rigorous program of inquiry by Altemeyer (1981, 1988) furnished persuasive empirical evidence that the original authoritarian construct was an approximation of an important political-psychological regularity—the existence in some individuals of an inner makeup that disposes them to defer to authority figures.

45   Single-case and typological studies alike make inferences about the inner quality of human beings (panels 4, 5, and 6) from outer manifestations—their past and present environments (panels 1, 2, 7, and 8) and the pattern over time of their political responses (panel 9). They then use those inferred constructs to account for the same kind of phenomena from which they were inferred—responses in situational contexts. The danger of circularity is obvious, but tautology can be avoided by reconstructing personality form some response patterns and using the reconstruction to explain others.

46   The failure of some investigators to take such pains contributes to the controversial status of the personality-and-politics literature, as does the prevalence of certain other practices. Some biographers, for example, impose diagnostic labels on their subject, rather than presenting a systematic account of the subject's behavior in disparate circumstances (George, 1987). Some typological analysts categorize their subjects without providing the detailed criteria and justifications for doing so. Some analysts of individuals as well as of types have engaged in the fallacy of observing a pattern of behavior and simply attributing it to a particular developmental pattern, without documenting causality, and perhaps

even without providing evidence that the pattern existed. Finally, some analysts commit what might be called the psychologizing and clinical fallacies: they explain behavior in terms of personality without considering possible situational determinants, or conclude that it is driven by psychopathology without considering other psychological determinants, such as cognition. Both fallacies were evident in a body of literature attributing the high scores of poor blacks and other minorities on the paranoia scale of the Minnesota Multiphasic Personality Inventory (MMPI) to emotional disturbance. The scores appear actually to have reflected cognitively based responses to the vicissitudes of the ghetto environment (Gynther, 1972; Newhill, 1990).

It is not surprising that some personality-and-politics studies are marked by methodological shortcomings. Certain of the inferences mapped in Figure 3 pose intrinsic difficulties. Claims about the determinants of personality characteristics (that is, of the connections between panels 1 and 2 and panels 3–6) are unlikely to be conclusive. Characterizations of personality structures themselves are never wholly persuasive, if only because of the absence of uniformly accepted personality theories with agreed-upon terminologies. Fortunately, the variables depicted in Figure 3 that *can* be characterized with great confidence are those closest to and therefore most predictive of behavior: the environments in which political action occurs (panels 7 and 8) and the patterns that action manifests over time (panels 9, 10, etc.). Those patterns are themselves variables, and they can be treated as indicators of an important further dimension of personality and politics—*political style*. 47

Two examples of political biographies that provide impressively comprehensive accounts of the precise patterns of their subjects' behavior are Walter's study of Australian Prime Minister Gough Whitlam (1980) and Landis's (1987) of Senator Joseph McCarthy. Richard Christie's (Christie and Geis, 1970) studies of the types of people who manifest the Machiavellian syndrome—the characterological proclivity to manipulate others—provide a model of careful measurement and theoretically sophisticated analysis in which contingent relationships are carefully explored. People who score high on tests of Machiavellianism do not differ in their behavior from non-Machiavellians in all contexts, only in contexts in which their manipulative impulses can be effective—for example, in situations that permit improvisation and in situations requiring face-to-face interaction. 48

Personality is likely to interest most political scientists only if it has aggregate consequences for political institutions, pro- 49 cesses, and outcomes. The literature on the aggregate effects of personality on politics is varied because the processes of aggregation are varied. Broadly speaking, political psychology affects the performance of political systems and processes through the activities of members of the public and the deliberations and decision-making of leaders. The impact of mass publics on politics, except through elections and severe perturbations of public opinion, is partial and often elusive. On the other hand, the political impact of leaders and others in the active political stratum, more generally, is direct, readily evident, and potentially momentous in its repercussions.

50   The first efforts to understand the psychology of mass populations go back to the accounts by writers in the ancient world, such as Tacitus, of the character of the inhabitants of remote tribes and nations. Such disquisitions are an antecedent of the vexed post-World War II national character literature in which often ill-documented ethnographic reports and cultural artifacts such as child-rearing manuals, films, and popular fiction were used to draw sweeping conclusions about model national character traits. That literature came therefore to be known to students of politics mainly for its methodological shortcomings, but it anticipated later, more systematic studies of political culture (Inkeles and Levinson, 1967; Inkeles, 1983).

51   By the 1950s, there was broad scholarly consensus that it is inappropriate simply to attribute psychological characteristics to mass populations on the basis of anecdotal or indirect evidence. Direct assessment of publics through survey research became the dominant mode of studying mass populations. Studies like those of McClosky and his associates provide survey data on basic personality processes such as ego-defenses and cognitive styles and how they affect political opinion. But basic personality processes have not been persuasively linked to the aspect of mass behavior that most clearly and observably has an impact on political institutions and processes—electoral choice. Most members of the general public appear to be too weakly involved in electoral politics for their voting choices to tap deeper psychological roots, and many of those who are involved appear to take their cues from party identifications formed in their early years and short-run situational stimuli.

52   If what is commonly thought of as personality is not linked to electoral choice, attitudinal political psychology most definitely is. The literature on electoral choice (Niemi and Weisberg, 1984) is too vast to begin to review here, but the research of Kelley (1983) is of particular interest in that it is explicitly aggregative; it reveals the precise distributions of attitudes and beliefs about issues and candidates that were as-

sociated with post-World War II American election outcomes. So is the research of Converse and Pierce (1986), who have convincingly linked certain attributes of the French political system to the distinctive ways members of that nation's electorate orient themselves to political parties.

In contrast to the ambiguous links between mass publics 53 and political outcomes other than elections, the connections between political decision-makers and political outcomes are direct and palpable. Nevertheless, many historical reconstructions of political decision-making are insufficiently specific about which actors in what precise contexts took which actions with what consequences. Sometimes the historical record does not contain the appropriate data. Often, however, the difficulty is not with the record but with the way it has been analyzed.

The questions the analyst needs to ask of an historical record 54 are suggested by two of the analytic distinctions introduced above—*action dispensability* and *actor dispensability*. Establishing whether an individual's actions were necessary for a particular outcome to have taken place calls for reconstructing the determinants of the outcome, asking whether it would have occurred if the actions of the individual in question had not occurred. Establishing whether that individual's personality shaped the outcome calls for a different and more complex reconstruction that asks whether the situation of the actor in question would have imposed the same course of action on anyone who might plausibly have occupied that individual's position. This calls for examining not only the psychology of the individual in question, but also the historical context, including the other significant actors and their claims, demands, perceptions, and personal qualities.

A good example of an historical reconstruction that ad- 55 dresses both issues is the analysis by George and George of Woodrow Wilson's role in the crisis over ratification of the Versailles Treaty. The intense, uncompromising qualities of Wilson the man, at least in certain kinds of conflicts, are an essential part of any account of the ratification fight. There is abundant evidence that the political context did not impose a course of action on Wilson that would have kept him from achieving his goal of ratification. All that was required was that he accept certain nominal compromises that his supporters urged upon him, pointing out that they had no practical significance. Moreover, Wilson's actions are necessary to explain the outcome. Wilson's supporters were lined up for a favorable ratification vote, but were unprepared to act unless he authorized them to accept mild qualifying language. This he refused to do.

56   The explanatory logic of propositions about whether an individual's actions and characteristics were consequential in
some episode is that of counter-factual reasoning. This is the
only available alternative in analyses of single events to the
quantitative analysis that would be called for if data existed
on large numbers of comparable episodes. Counter-factual reasoning is not falsifiable, but it can be systematic. To be so it
must be explicit and addressed to bounded questions—not conundrums about remote contingencies. "Was Lyndon Johnson's
action necessary for the 1965 American escalation in Vietnam
to have occurred?" is an example of a question that is susceptible to investigation (Burke and Greenstein, 1989). "If Cleopa-
tra's nose had been an inch longer, how would world history
have been changed?" is an example of one that is not.

57   Personality and political psychology more generally affect political processes not only through the actions taken by leaders
more or less on their own, but also through group processes
such as the collective suspension of reality testing manifested
in what Irving Janis (1983) has characterized as groupthink.
Groupthink occurs in highly cohesive decision-making groups.
The members of such groups sometimes become so committed to their colleagues they more or less unconsciously suspend their own critical facilities in order to preserve group
harmony. Janis, who is scrupulous about setting forth the criteria for establishing whether a group has engaged in groupthink, analyzes a number of historical episodes (the most striking
example being the Bay of Pigs) in which a defective decision-
making process appears to have led able policy-makers to make
decisions on the basis of flawed assumptions and defective information. To the extent that groupthink is a purely collective
phenomenon, emerging from group interaction, it is a manifestation of social psychology rather than personality psychology. But, as Janis suggests, personality probably contributes
to groupthink in that some personalities are more likely than
others to suspend their critical capacities in group settings.

Concluding Remarks

60   Political institutions and processes operate through human
agency. It would be remarkable if they were *not* influenced by
the properties that distinguish one individual from another.
In examining that influence, I have emphasized the logic of
inquiry. In doing so I have not attempted a comprehensive review of the literature. For a variety of useful reviews and com-
pendia, readers should consult Greenstein and Lerner (1971),

Knutson (1973), Stone (1981), Herman (1986) and Simonton (1990).

To the extent that this article brings out possible pitfalls [61] in studies of personality and politics, its message to cautious scholars may *seem* to be the following: Find pastures that can be more easily cultivated. Even daring scholars might conclude that the prospects for the systematic study of personality and politics are too remote to justify the investment of scholarly time and effort. Nothing in this article is meant to support such conclusions. In a parable on the shortcomings of scientific opportunism, Kaplan (1964, pp. 11, 16-17) relates the story of a drunkard who lost his keys in a dark alley and is found searching for them under a street lamp, declaring, "It's lighter here." The drunkard's search is a poor model. If the connections between the personalities of political actors and their political behavior are obscure, all the more reason to illuminate them.[2]

Notes

1. It should be stressed that although types of personality-and-politics inquiry can be distinguished analytically, a comprehensive analysis of some real-world political phenomenon—for example, presidential leadership—is likely to draw on more than one kind of analysis.

2. This article expands upon Greenstein (forthcoming). I am indebted to Alexander L. George, Richard Merelman and M. Brewster Smith for comments on an earlier draft.

References

Adorno, T. W., Frenkel-Brunswick, E., Levinson, D. J. and Sanford, R.N. (1950). *The Authoritarian Personality*, Harper, New York.

Allen, V. L. (1975). Social Support for Nonconformity. *Advances in Social Psychology* 8:1–43.

Allport, G. W. (1937). *Personality: A Psychological Interpretation*, Holt, New York.

Altemeyer, B. (1981). *Right-Wing Authoritarianism*, University of Manitoba Press, Winnipeg.

Altemeyer, B. (1988). *Enemies of Freedom: Understanding Right-Wing Authoritarianism*, Jossey-Bass, San Francisco.

Asch, S. E. (1956). Studies of Independence and Conformity: A Minority of One Versus a Unanimous Majority. *Psychological Monographs* 70:9, Whole No. 406.

Barber, J. D. (1985). *The Presidential Character: Predicting Performance in the White House*, 3d ed., Prentice-Hall, Englewood Cliffs, N.J.

Block, J. H., Haan, N. and Smith, M. B. (1969). Socialization Correlates of Student Activism. *Journal of Social Issues* 25: 143–77.

Brown, N. O. (1959). *Life Against Death*, Wesleyan University Press, Middletown, Conn.

Browning, R. P. and Jacobs, H. (1964). Power Motivation and the Political Personality. *Public Opinion Quarterly* 24: 75–90.

Budner, S. (1962) Intolerance of Ambiguity as a Personality Variable. *Journal of Personality* 30: 22–50.

Burke, J. P. and Greenstein, F. I. (1989). *How Presidents Test Reality: Decisions on Vietnam, 1954 and 1965*, Russell Sage Foundation, New York.

Burns, J. M. (1978). *Leadership*, Harper and Row, New York.

Campbell, D. T. (1963). Social Attitudes and Other Acquired Behavioral Dispositions. In S. Koch (ed.). *Psychology: A Study of A Science* 6, McGraw Hill, New York; pp. 94–172.

Christie, R. and Geis, F. L., (1970). *Studies in Machiavellianism*, Academic Press, New York.

Clarke, J. W. (1990). *On Being Mad or Merely Angry: John W. Hinckley Jr. and Other Dangerous People*, Princeton University Press, Princeton, N.J.

Converse, P. E. and Pierce, R, (1986). *Political Representation in France*, Harvard University Press, Cambridge, Mass.

Davies, A. F. (1980). *Skills, Outlooks and Passions: A Psychoanalytic Contribution to the Study of Politics*, Cambridge University Press, Cambridge, Mass.

Di Palma, G. and McClosky, H. (1970). Personality and Conformity: The Learning of Political Attitudes. *American Political Science Review* 64: 1054–73.

Dunlap, R. (1970). Radical and Conservative Student Activists: A Comparison of Family Backgrounds. *Pacific Sociological Review* 13: 171–81.

Endler, N. S. (1981). Persons, Situations, and their Interactions. In A. I. Rabin, J. Aronoff, A. M. Barclay and R. A. Zucker, eds., *Further Explorations in Personality*, Wiley, New York, pp. 114–51.

Erikson, E. H. (1958). *Young Man Luther: A Study in Psychoanalysis and History*, Norton, New York.

Flacks, R. (1967). The Liberated Generation: An Exploration of the Roots of Student Protest. *Journal of Social Issues* 25: 52–75.

Freud, S. (1930). *Civilization and its Discontents*. In Stratchey, J., *The Standard Edition of the Complete Psychological Works of Sigmund Freud*, vol. 17, Hogarth, London.

Fromm, E. (1941). *Escape from Freedom*, Rinehart, New York.

George, A. L. (1969). *Personality and Politics: Problems of Evidence, Inference and Conceptualization*, Markham, Chicago. (Current edition Princeton University Press, 1987).

George, A. L. (1971). Some Uses of Dynamic Psychology in Political Biography: Case Materials on Woodrow Wilson. In Fred I. Greenstein and Michael Lerner, eds., *A Source Book for the Study of Personality and Politics*, Markham, Chicago. [Reprinted in G. Cocks and T. L. Crosby (eds.)., *Psycho/History: Readings in the Method of Psychology, Psychoanalysis and History*, Yale University Press, New Haven, Conn., 1987, pp. 132–156.]

George, A. L. (1974). Assessing Presidential Character. *World Politics* 26: 234–82.

George, A. L. (1980). *Presidential Decisionmaking in Foreign Policy: The Effective Use of Advice and Information,* Westview Press, Boulder, Colorado.

George, A. L. and J. L. George (1956). *Woodrow Wilson and Colonel House: A Personality Study,* John Day, New York. (Reprinted by Dover, 1964).

Greenstein, F. I. (1975). Personality and Politics. In F. I. Greenstein and N. W. Polsby (eds.), *The Handbook of Political Science: Micropolitical Theory* 2, Addison-Wesley, Reading, Mass., pp. 1–92.

Greenstein, F. I. (forthcoming). Personality and Politics. In M. Hawkesworth and M. K. Kogan, eds., *Routledge Encyclopedia of Government and Politics.*

Greenstein, F. I. and Lerner, M. (1971). *A Source Book for the Study of Personality and Politics,* Markham, Chicago.

Gynther, M. (1972). White Norms and Black MMPIs: A Prescription for Discrimination. *Psychological Bulletin* 78:386–402.

Hall, C. S. and Lindzey, G. eds. (1970). *Theories of Personality,* 2d ed., Wiley, New York.

Herman, M. G., ed. (1986). *Political Psychology,* Jossey-Bass, San Francisco.

Inkeles, I. (1983). *Exploring Individual Modernity,* Columbia University Press, New York.

Inkeles, I. and Levinson, D. J. (1967). National Character: The Study of Modal Personality. In Lindzey, G. and Aronson, E., eds., *The Handbook of Social Psychology* 4, 2nd. ed., Addison-Wesley, Reading, Mass.

Janis, I. L. (1982). *Groupthink: Psychological Studies of Policy Decisions and Fiascos,* 2d. ed., Houghton Mifflin, Boston, Mass.

Jervis, R. (1976). *Perception and Misperception in International Politics.* Princeton University Press, Princeton, N.J.

Jervis, R, Lebow, R. N. and Stein, J. (1985). *Psychology and Deterrence,* Johns Hopkins University Press, Baltimore.

Kaplan, A. (1964). *The Conduct of Inquiry: Methodology for Behavioral Sciences,* Chandler, San Francisco.

Katz, D. (1960). The Functional Approach to the Study of Attitudes. *Public Opinion Quarterly* 24: 163–204.

Katz, I. and Benjamin, L. (1960). The Effects of Authoritarianism on Biracial Work Groups. *Journal of Abnormal and Social Psychology* 61: 448–56.

Kellerman, B., ed. (1986). *Political Leadership: A Source Book,* University of Pittsburgh Press, Pittsburgh, Penna.

Kelley, S. K., Jr. (1983). *Interpreting Elections,* Princeton University Press, Princeton, N.J.

Kirscht, J. P. and Dillehay, J. P. (1967). *Dimensions of Authoritarianism,* University of Kentucky Press, Lexington.

Kluckhohn, C. and Murray, H. A. (1953). Personality Formation: The Determinants. In Kluckhohn, C. and Murray, H. A., eds., *Personality in Nature, Society and Culture,* 2nd edition, Knopf, New York, pp. 53–67.

Knutson, J. N. (1973). *Handbook of Political Psychology*, Jossey-Bass, San Francisco, Calif.

Kroeber, A. L. and Kluckhohn, C. (1952). Culture: A Critical Review of Concepts and Definitions. In *Papers of the Peabody Museum of American Archaeology and Ethnology* 47:1, Harvard University, Cambridge, Mass.

Kull, S. (1988). *Minds at War: Nuclear Reality and the Inner Conflict of Defense Policymakers*, Basic Books, New York.

Landis, M. (1987). *Joseph McCarthy: The Politics of Chaos*, Associated Universities Presses, Cranbury, N.J.

Lane, R. E. (1962). *Political Ideology: Why the Common Man Believes What He Does*, The Free Press of Glenco, New York.

Lasswell, H. D. (1930). *Psychopathology and Politics*, University of Chicago Press, Chicago. (University of Chicago Press Midway Reprint, 1986).

Lasswell, H. D. (1960). Political Character and Constitution. *Psychoanalysis and Psychoanalytic Review* 46:1–18.

Lasswell, H. D. and Kaplan, A. (1950). *Power and Society: A Framework for Political Inquiry*, Yale University Press, New Haven, Conn.

Lau, R. R. and Sears, D. O., eds. (1986). *Political Cognition*, Lawrence Erlbaum Associates, Hillsdale, N.J.

Levinson, D. J. (1959). Role, Personality, and Social Structure in the Organizational Setting. *Journal of Abnormal and Social Psychology* 58:170–80.

Lewin, K. (1935).*Principles of Topological Psychology*, McGraw Hill, New York.

Lipset, S. M. (1968). The Activists: A Profile. In Daniel Bell and Irving Kristol, eds., *Confrontation: The Student Rebellion and the Universities*, Basic Books, New York, pp. 44–57.

Magnusson, D. and Endler, N. S., eds. (1977). *Personality at the Crossroads: Current Issues in Interactional Psychology*, Lawrence Erlbaum Associates, Hillsdale, N.J.

Marcuse, H. (1966). *Eros and Civilization*, revised edition, Beacon, Boston, Mass.

Marvick, E. W. (1986). *Louis XIII: The Making of a King*, Yale University Press, New Haven, Conn.

Masters, R. D. (1989). *The Nature of Politics*. Yale University Press, New Haven, Conn.

McClosky, H. (1967). Personality and Attitude Correlates of Foreign Policy Orientations. In Rosenau, J.N., ed., *Domestic Sources of Foreign Policy*, The Free Press of Glencoe, New York, pp. 51–109.

McClosky, H. and Zaller, J. (1984). *The American Ethos: Public Attitudes Toward Capitalism and Democracy*, Harvard University Press, Cambridge, Mass.

Merelman, R. M. (1984). *Making Something of Ourselves: On Culture and Politics in the United States*, University of California Press, Berkeley, Calif.

Murray, H. A. (1968). Personality: Contemporary Viewpoints: Components of an Evolving Personological System. *International Encyclopedia of the Social Sciences* 12, Macmillan, New York.

Newhill, C. E. (1990). The Role of Culture in the Development of Paranoid Symptomatology. *American Journal of Orthopsychiatry* 60: 176–85.

Niemi, R. and Weisberg, H. E. (1984). *Controversies in Voting Behavior,* 2d. ed., Congressional Quarterly Press, Washington, D.C.

Park, B. E. (1986). *The Impact of Illness on World Leaders,* University of Pennsylvania Press, Philadelphia, Penna.

Pervin, L. A. and Lewis, M., eds. (1978). *Perspectives on Interactional Psychology,* Plenum, New York.

Peterson, R. E. and Bilorusky, J. A. (1971). *May 1970: The Campus Aftermath of Cambodia and Kent State,* The Carnegie Foundation for the Advancement of Teaching, New York.

Pratkanis, A. R., Breckler, S. J., Greenwald, A. G., eds. (1989). *Attitude Structure and Function,* Lawrence Erlbaum Associates, Hillsdale, N.J.

Riesman, D. and Glazer, N. (1952). *Faces in the Crowd: Individual Studies of Character and Politics,* Yale University Press, New Haven, Conn.

Rokeach, M. (1960). *The Open and the Closed Mind: Investigations into the Nature of Belief Systems and Personality Systems,* Basic Books, New York.

Simon, H. A. (1985). Human Nature in Politics: The Dialogue of Psychology with Political Science. *American Political Science Review* 79: 293–304.

Simonton, D. K. (1990). Personality and Politics. In Pervin, L. A., ed., *Handbook of Personality: Theory and Research,* Guilford, New York, pp. 670–692.

Smith, M. B. (1968). A Map for the Study of Personality and Politics. *Journal of Social Issues* 24: 15–28.

Smith, M. B., Bruner, J. S. and White, R. W. (1956). *Opinions and Personality.* Wiley, New York.

Sniderman, P. M. (1974). *Personality and Democratic Politics,* University of California Press, Berkeley, Calif.

Stone, W. F. (1981). Political Psychology: A Whig History. In Long, S.L., ed., *The Handbook of Political Behavior* 1, Plenum, New York.

Stone, W. F. and Schaffner, P. E. (1988). *The Psychology of Politics,* 2d ed., Springer Verlag, New York.

Tucker, R. C. (1965). The Dictator and Totalitarianism. *World Politics* 17: 555–83.

Tucker, R. C. (1973). *Stalin as Revolutionary, 1879–1929: A Short Study in History and Personality,* Norton, New York.

Tucker, R. C. (1981). *Politics as Leadership,* University of Missouri Press, Columbia, Missouri.

Vertzberger, Y. Y. I. (1990). *The World in their Minds: Information Processing, Cognition, and Perception in Foreign Policy Decisionmaking,* Stanford University Press, Stanford, Calif.

Volkan, V. D. and Itzkowitz, N. (1984). *The Immortal Ataturk: A Psychobiography,* University of Chicago Press, Chicago.

Wallas, G. (1908). *Human Nature and Politics,* 3d ed., Crofts, New York.

Walter, J. (1980). *The Leader: A Political Biography of Gough Whitlam,* University of Queensland Press, St. Lucia, Queensland.

CHAPTER EIGHT

THE TRADITIONALIST PROTEST
OF LEO STRAUSS

While mainstream political scientists debated the merits of the various approaches created in the 1950s and 1960s, there were those who looked upon the entire tumult with disdain and aversion. These were the traditionalists who remained stubbornly loyal to the status quo ante. They refused to give up the conviction that political science is a philosophic and normative enterprise whose paramount objective is to uncover the *true* ends of political life. Among these traditionalists, incomparably the most influential was Leo Strauss.

As an intellectual phenomenon, Leo Strauss is unique. Although he was by all accounts a bookish, erudite man who disdained the limelight and had little use for power, he succeeded in creating the closest thing to an intellectual dynasty that exists in North American academe. Many scholars, no doubt, have had their devoted students and their professional following, but Strauss excited intellectual passions that went well beyond ordinary scholarly loyalties. Over the years, both his person and his views became enveloped in such veneration and homage that, in the eyes of the faithful, criticism had about it the odor of sacrilege. Indeed, it would be difficult to challenge the proposition that Leo Strauss kindled emotions more charged and controversial than any other figure in contemporary North American political science.

On their face, the bare facts of Strauss's curriculum vitae make such a development seem most improbable. He was an expatriate German trained in philosophy with a substantial Jewish education. (He was, one reviewer wrote, "an exotic flower transplanted from Central Europe to the plains of the American Midwest."[1]) He displayed an unusual obsession with meticulous textual exegesis. He harbored a profound hostility for the prevalent relativist assumptions of modern intellectual life, a taste for the speculations of classical Greek philosophy, a belief in the radical superiority of the wise over ordinary men, and an unshakable conviction that the authentic philosopher (and only the authentic philosopher) was able to know the Truth.

When Leo Strauss passed away in October 1973, he left behind a tight-knit fraternity of followers and emulators with representatives in many of the finest departments of political science in the United States and Canada. While no one scholar has taken his place as beacon and mentor to the next generation of epigones, the Straussian fellowship continues to flourish. Indeed, its missionizing zeal persists unabated. Whatever one's final judgment in regard to the Straussian approach to the study of politics, it cannot be denied that they are a force to be reckoned with.

To his followers, Strauss was simply the "master." He was "the best, the wisest and the most just," a man of "a different order."[2] He was regularly compared to Socrates. His style of argumentation, which often caused frustration and anger in opponents, was said to be reminiscent of the great Athenian philosopher. The singularity of his commitment to truth was deemed to be Socratic as well. So was the role he adopted of philosophical gadfly, that is, the desire to awaken our jaded intellectual sensibilities by means of stinging provocations. Perhaps most of all, the likeness to Socrates was based on the ridicule and derision he suffered at the hands of those who were, so his followers insist, both unworthy and incapable of his lofty purposes.

Although Strauss was a prodigious scholar of the history of political ideas, it was not for his scholarship that he was revered. Learning in itself was not his object; in his eyes it was a mere anteroom to learning's purpose: wisdom. And wisdom, true philosophical wisdom, is not a chimera. It is available to the endowed and sincere seeker. Strauss's central teaching, tirelessly repeated, is that modernism with its skepticism and cognitive defeatism has poisoned our minds. It has caused us to believe that philosophy can teach us nothing about Truth, that there are no fixed criteria by which to judge actions and ideas, that ideas invariably reflect the transient social interests of their authors, that reality is created in the observer's perceptions and that morality is situational, individual and subjective. On the contrary, Strauss exhorted, there is a single transhistorical, transcultural, incontrovertible Truth and it is knowable exclusively to philosophy. From a position of magnificent isolation, Strauss argued this very unpopular position with such persistence and verve—and in a manner so unusual for the detached reticence of ordinary academic life—that he succeeded in creating a generation of enthusiastic followers.

Understandably, many who have little patience with the Straussian fellowship dismiss it as an academic cult with all the typical trappings of such sectarian groups. It is charged that Straussians speak in a language of the initiated that is often impenetrable to the outsider, that they affect certain predictable intellectual postures and conceits, that they are convinced that they alone preserve the truth while ignorance and darkness prevail all around them. The fact that they adopt something of a crusading approach toward the unconverted and that they have achieved no small political influence—normally right-wing conservative in character—only aggravates the antagonism they provoke in those who do not share their convictions.

These antagonisms belong to the realm of academic warfare. They are not arguments. To join the argument, it is imperative that the essential elements of Strauss's position be understood. Because much of the exposition of Strauss's ideas is taken up in the article included in the readings, these prefatory remarks will attempt to give a flavor of the Straussian style of argumentation—for the most part in his own words. A few very central tenets of his position will be presented in citations from his work, interspersed with only the minimal connecting passages necessary for the sake of coherence.

The modern age, Strauss contends, has shattered our links to philosophical transcendence. In innumerable and insidious ways we have been taught that the good, the just, the virtuous—what ought to be— are subjective matters fit for the personal deliberations of each individual. It is said that these are not questions given to definitive philosophical or scientific resolution. We are taught incessantly that there is no single incontrovertible answer to these most weighty of questions.

> The crisis of modernity reveals itself in the fact, or consists in the fact, that modern Western man no longer knows what he wants—that he no longer believes that he can know what is good and bad, what is right and wrong. Until a few generations ago, it was generally taken for granted that man can know what is right and wrong, what is the just or the good or the best order of society—in a word, that political philosophy is possible and necessary. In our time this faith is impossible: it was a dream, a noble dream, but at any rate a dream.[3]

Social scientists incorporate these modernist axioms as well. They prohibit the intrusion of "value judgments" and of "ought" into scientific discourse. Scientists, they teach, are exclusively concerned with discovering what is; they have no business offering their idiosyncratic opinions on questions of morality or politics. Having abandoned the belief that authentic knowledge of the "ought" is available to us, science must make do with the "is." The merely empirical is all that remains after the truly important questions of philosophy are declared to be illegitimate.

These views, Strauss exhorts, are both dehumanizing and untenable.

> If there is no standard higher than the ideal of our society, we are utterly unable to take a critical distance from that ideal. But the mere fact that we can raise the question of the worth of the ideal of our society shows that there is something in man that is not altogether in slavery to his society, and therefore that we are able, and hence obliged, to look for a standard with reference to which we judge of the ideas of our own as well as of any other society. That standard cannot be found in the needs of the various societies, for the societies and their parts have many needs that conflict with one another: the problem of priorities arises. This problem cannot be solved in a rational manner if we do not have a standard with reference to which we can distinguish between genuine

needs and fancied needs and discern the hierarchy of the various types of genuine needs. The problem posed by the conflicting needs of society cannot be solved if we do not possess knowledge of natural right.[4]

If we lack knowledge of this kind, if it is, in principle, impossible to distinguish between good and bad, better and worse, our entire intellectual edifice crumbles to dust. "The contemporary rejection of natural right leads to nihilism—nay, it is identical with nihilism."[5] And nihilism, Strauss continues, creates the most serious psychological and practical consequences.

Once we realize that the principles of our actions have no other support than our blind choice, we really do not believe in them any more. We cannot wholeheartedly act upon them any more. We cannot live any more as responsible beings. In order to live, we have to silence the easily silenced voice of reason, which tells us that our principles are in themselves as good or as bad as any other principles. The more we cultivate reason, the more we cultivate nihilism: the less we are able to be loyal members of society. The inescapable practical consequence of nihilism is fanatical obscurantism.[6]

Nowhere is this moral nihilism more dramatic and objectionable than in the social sciences.

According to our social science, we can be or become wise in all matters of secondary importance, but we have to be resigned to utter ignorance in the most important respect: we cannot have any knowledge regarding the ultimate principles of our choices, i.e., regarding their soundness or unsoundness; our ultimate principles have no other support than our arbitrary and hence blind preferences. We are then in the position of beings who are sane and sober when engaged in trivial business and who gamble like madmen when confronted with serious issues—retail sanity and wholesale madness.[7]

This moral agnosticism is especially problematic in regard to politics. For to forbid the issue of value in the study of politics is tantamount to misconstruing its nature utterly.

Political things are by their nature subject to approval or disapproval, to choice and rejection, to praise and blame. It is of their essence not to be neutral but to raise a claim to man's obedience, allegiance, decision, or judgment. One does not understand them as what they are, as political things, if one does not take seriously their explicit or implicit claims to be judged in terms of goodness or badness, or of justice or injustice, i.e., if one does not measure them by some standard of goodness or justice. To judge soundly one must know the true standards. If political philosophy wishes to do justice to its subject matter, it must strive for genuine knowledge of these standards.[8]

Having abandoned the central question of human affairs—What is to be done?—social science becomes quite pathetic and ridiculous.

Many social scientists of our time seem to regard nihilism as a minor inconvenience which wise men would bear with equanimity, since it is the price to pay for obtaining that highest good, a truly scientific social science.[9]

A social science from which values are excised is a travesty of human social life.

Do we not know petrification or spiritual emptiness when we see it? And if someone is incapable of seeing phenomena of this kind, is he not disqualified by this very fact from being a social scientist, just as much as a blind man is disqualified from being an analyst of painting.[10]

It comes as no surprise then that Strauss judges modern empirical, value-free social science as worthless.

Generally speaking, one may wonder whether the new political science has brought to light anything of political importance which intelligent political practitioners with a deep knowledge of history, nay intelligent and educated journalists, to say nothing of the old political science at its best, did not know at least as well beforehand.[11]

An authentic social science, Strauss proclaims, would be one that sought answers to important rather than secondary questions. It would not waste its time polling unintelligent people about subjects they were ignorant of and then act as if these findings represented important contributions to scientific truth. It would not fiddle inconclusively and sophistically with data that remained meaningless without moral criteria by which to judge it. It would desist from its ubiquitous "methodolotry," that is, the risible belief that the mere proper use of some prescribed method equalizes unequal minds.

The shabby modern tendency to pander to mass tastes by saying that one person's preferences and opinions are as good as those of another would be the first implicit social scientific assumption to be thrown aside. The existence of a great range of predilections in human history and society—from cannibalism to satan worship—should not lead us to become dutiful recorders of the variety of human foolishness. It should lead us instead to look for the true opinion, that is, for the opinion that is not merely an opinion.

As little as man's varying notions of the universe prove that there is no universe or that there cannot be *the* true account of the universe or that man can never arrive at true and final knowledge of the universe, so little seem man's varying notions of justice to prove that there is no natural right or that natural right is unknowable. The variety of notions of justice can be understood as the variety of errors, which variety does not contradict, but presupposes the existence of the one truth regarding justice.[12]

The quest for this one truth is the political philosopher's animating drive. Political philosophy seeks to disentangle opinion from knowledge, the part from the whole, the conventional from the necessary, the transient from the permanent. This pursuit of truth, as opposed to the mere spinning out of ideology or the accumulation of facts, is the distinguishing mark of political philosophy.

A political thinker who is not a philosopher is primarily interested in, or attached to, a specific order or policy; the political philosopher is primarily interested in, or attached to, the truth.[13]

The genuine political philosophers were all engaged in this quest.

The whole galaxy of political philosophers from Plato to Hegel... assumed that the fundamental political problem is susceptible of a final solution. This assumption ultimately rests on the... answer to the question of how men ought to live.[14]

By contrast to these philosophers, especially to the classical Greek philosophers, so much of modern political thought is sterile and defeatist. It is based on the express denial of philosophy's aspirations. It operates according to the assumption that "the fundamental distinction between philosophic and historical questions cannot, in the last analysis, be maintained."[15] For the likes of these, political philosophy is nothing more than the "history of political philosophy." Strauss argues that

to replace political philosophy by the history of political philosophy means to replace a doctrine which claims to be true by a survey of more or less brilliant errors. The discipline which takes the place of political philosophy is the one which shows the impossibility of political philosophy.[16]

Strauss asserts that modern political philosophy gives up its unconditional pursuit of truth and concerns itself instead with mundane, all-too-common questions of welfare and utility.

Modern political philosophy comes into being when the end of philosophy is identified with the end which is capable of being pursued by all men. More precisely, philosophy is now asserted to be essentially subservient to the end which is capable of being actually pursued by all men.... In this respect, the modern conception of philosophy is fundamentally democratic. The end of philosophy is now no longer what one may call the disinterested contemplation of the eternal, but relief of man's estate [i.e., contribution to human welfare].[17]

To recapture the nature of the true philosophical quest it is necessary to go back to the time before it was corrupted, to the ancients, to the classics.

If the history of human thought is studied in the spirit of modern science, one reaches the conclusion that all human thought is "historically conditioned" or that the attempt to liberate one's thought from one's historical situation is quixotic. . . . Once this state has been reached, the original meaning of philosophy is accessible only through recollection of what philosophy meant in the past, i.e., for all practical purposes, only through the reading of old books.[18]

Returning to the classics, to Plato and Aristotle, puts us into direct contact with genuine political understanding. For the few that can ascend the ladder of philosophy and emerge from the "cave" of opinion into the open air of truth, the horizon that reveals itself is of transcending sublimity. To pursue political philosophy in its uncorrupted form is then the highest of human pursuits: it is "the rightful queen of the social sciences, the sciences of man and of human affairs."[19]

NOTES

1. Stephen Holmes, "Truths for Philosophers Alone?" *Times Literary Supplement* (1–7 December 1989), p. 1324.

2. See W. Berns, "The Achievement of Leo Strauss," *National Review* (7 December 1973) p. 1347, and A. Bloom, "Leo Strauss: September 20th 1899–October 1973" *Political Theory*, 2 (1974) pp. 372–92.

3. Strauss, "The Three Waves of Modernity," in Hilail Goldin, ed., *Political Philosophy: Six Essays* (Indianapolis, Pegasus, 1975), pp. 81–82.

4. Strauss, *Natural Right and History* (Chicago, University of Chicago Press, 1953), p. 3.

5. Ibid., p. 5.

6. Ibid., p. 6.

7. Ibid., p. 4.

8. Strauss, "Epilogue," *Essays on the Scientific Study of Politics*, ed. Herbert Storing (New York, Rinehart and Winston, 1962).

9. Strauss, *Natural Right and History*, p. 49.

10. Ibid., p. 50.

11. Strauss, *Liberalism Ancient and Modern* (New York, Basic Books, 1968), p. 212

12. Strauss, *Natural Right and History*, pp. 97–98.

13. Strauss, *What is Political Philosophy?* (New York, Free Press, 1959), p. 12.

14. Strauss, *Natural Right and History* (Chicago, Chicago University Press, 1953), pp. 35–36.

15. Strauss, *What is Political Philosophy?* p. 57.

16. Ibid., p. 12.

17. Strauss, *Liberalism Ancient and Modern*, pp. 19–20.

18. Strauss, *Persecution and the Art of Writing* (Westport, Conn, Greenwood Press, 1973), p. 157.

19. Strauss, *The City and Man* (Chicago, Rand McNally, 1964), p. 1.

SUGGESTIONS FOR FURTHER READING

Berns, W., Storing, H. J., Jaffa, H. V., and Kannhauser, "The Achievement of Leo Strauss," *National Review*, 25 (7 December 1973).

Drury, S. B., *The Political Ideas of Leo Strauss* (London, Macmillan, 1988).

Gunnel, J., "The Myth of Tradition," *American Political Science Review*, 72 (1978), pp. 123–134.

Schaefer, D. L., "The Legacy of Leo Strauss: A Bibliographic Introduction," *Intercollegiate Review*, 9, no. 3 (1974), pp. 139–148.

Schaar, J., and Wolin, S., Review *Essays on the Scientific Study of Politics*, *American Political Science Review*, 57, no. 1, (1963), pp. 125–150.

Storing, H. J., *Essays on the Scientific Study of Politics* (New York, Holt, Rinehart and Winston, 1962).

Bernard Susser

Leo Strauss: the Ancient as Modern

1   Probably no figure in the recent history of American political science has generated as much light *and* heat as Leo Strauss.[1] While there were none to impugn his prodigious learning, there were many who found his root and branch dismissal of modern social science outrageous, his idiosyncratic reading of texts exasperating and, above all, his uncompromising belief in absolute truths regarding man, morality and politics breathtakingly anachronistic and not a little pretentious. Many, however, saw him as a modern guide for the perplexed leading the way out of dead-end relativism, value-free (and as he put it 'valueless') quantitative social science, a master of the forgotten art of seriously reading the texts of great thinkers, especially the Classics, and, above all, an extraordinary teacher who rose above conflicting opinions with a purity that intimated the absolute.

2   Part of the reason for the acrimonious controversy surrounding Strauss is, no doubt, that he wished to supplant political science as it is widely practised with a radically different kind of discipline. He advocated nothing less than a 'new' paradigm, for the study of politics. It is no wonder then that accounts of his thought are divided between the abusive and the hagiographical. Moreover, the divide between his defenders and defamers is reproduced in the organization of the American political science discipline itself. The Straussian fraternity forms an intellectual community apart, a community that because of assumptions and methods 'incommensurate' with those widely held outside their circle, generally keeps its intellectual distance. Although Straussians constitute what is arguably the most distinct and cohesive subgrouping in the American discipline, there is little intellectual commerce across the border that divides them from their adversaries, and when such trafficking in ideas does occur, it often issues in angry, fruitless and irresolvable wrangles over basics.

3   The object of the following study is threefold. First, it aims to make accessible in a systematic way what Strauss stood for and what continues to be the core persuasion of his followers. My intentions are not ecumenical. Understanding will not increase affection. I am concerned to right a long-standing imbalance. For while Straussians cut their teeth on the orthodoxies of modern political science (so as to stake out their own rea-

From *Political Studies*, 34 (1988), pp. 497–514. Reprinted by permission.

soned alternative) political scientists outside their circle have only vague and clichéd notions of the challenge that Strauss posed and the alternative he championed. Both the challenge and the alternative are important: first of all, because they constitute what is perhaps the most radical and sustained critique of the empirical—quantitative turn taken by political science in the past four decades and secondly, because there is probably no finer way for those who are part of these contemporary developments to sharpen their professional credos than by confronting them with the acutely critical intelligence of Leo Strauss. Secondly, while the Straussian challenge is an unavoidable presence in American political science, across the Atlantic his thought is not at all well known. Here too, it is, I believe, beneficial to redress the imbalance. Thirdly, Strauss's thought is prone to strike readers as basically incongruous; that is, constituted out of incompatible elements. In the quarrel between the ancients and the moderns, his sympathies are clearly with the ancients, yet there were few who manipulated the modernist battery of forensic weapons to more devastating effect. The corpus of his writings is, on the one hand, a panegyric to the sublimity of the philosophical life, yet on the other hand, readers are likely to come away with the impression of an intensely combative personality who is implacably rancorous in argument. Accounting for this incongruity brings us near the heart of Strauss's thought.

It should be made clear at the outset that exploring Strauss's 4 thought involves far more than a report on narrow professional loyalties. His quarrel with modern political science is not comparable to, say, the dispute between the Adlerians and orthodox Freudians in psychology or the verificationists and falsificationists in the philosophy of science. In both these cases the controversy takes place against the background of many shared assumptions, with a largely common vocabulary and in more or less the same tradition of intellectual discourse. The charges that Strauss levelled against contemporary political science are, by contrast, so generic that discourse between the opposing positions is largely precluded. Those expecting point by point critique and alternative will, therefore, surely be disappointed. Both Strauss's argument and his alternative are pitched at an entirely different level of discourse.

Strauss's critique is, indeed, only obliquely directed to mod- 5 ern social science. His main target is nothing less than the modern intellectual temper taken as a whole. Strauss's alternative, therefore, includes academic recommendations but is not exhausted by them. His critique of political science is a single instance of a comprehensive critique of contemporaneity, one that challenges virtually all the prevailing beliefs about morality, philosophy and political practice.

6   What these prevailing beliefs actually are is perhaps the single point of agreement between Strauss and his adversaries. In the broadest terms, modernism involves a turning away from the traditional understanding of truth as an independently existing, accessible and knowable quality. In one form or another, the modernist perspective has contextualized thought. The acceptance of its conventional, derivative and circumstantial nature has filtered into virtually every domain of intellectual activity. Cognition is understood to be socially constructed, culturally generated, psychologically derived, historically bounded. What results is a relativism of cognitive perspectives, a tendency to intellectual 'unmasking' in argumentation, subjectivism in ethics, tolerance and equalitarianism in politics, a basic uneasiness with normative questions that are not amenable to definitive resolution.[2] What remains is only the pursuit of narrowly empirical questions, or as Strauss might have put it: empiricism is what is left when the truly important questions are declared illegitimate.

7   Relativism was his enemy. It could not, he insisted, be distinguished from nihilism without undermining itself; that is, without recourse to some question-begging non-relative standard that was either groundless or self-contradictory.[3] There were for him only two choices: nihilism or the belief in an accessible, transhistorical, universal absolute. All those cagey and unthinking attempts to square the relativist circle by granting its assumptions, while simultaneously speaking of decency, reason, justice, authenticity and so on were at best pathetically deluded and at worst unaware of how close to the brink they trod. Relativism, Strauss warned, 'is not a cab which one can stop at his convenience'.[4] It has an inexorable logic and tolerates no *via media*.

8   Strauss was regularly at hand to upbraid those thinkers who abandoned the absolute anchor and to demonstrate that there was no resting place available to them save in nihilism, if nihilism can qualify as a place of rest. 'I contend', Strauss wrote very typically,

> that Weber's thesis [the fact—value disjunction] necessarily leads to nihilism or to the view that every preference, however evil, base or insane, has to be judged before the tribunal of reason as legitimate as any other preference.[5]

Isaiah Berlin's observation that 'no skeptical conclusions seem to me to follow' from the recognition that human principles are historically accountable and transitory earned a similar rebuke: Berlin seeks refuge in the very house he has destroyed. Being unable to 'live without an absolute basis' and yet unable to justify 'an absolute basis', he is precipitated into fraudulence, trying to inhabit 'an absolute middle ground between relativism and absolutism'.[6]

In itself, of course, the terror of nihilism does not disqualify it. Strauss does not believe that philosophers should be afraid of the dark or that they are in the business of providing pleasant truths for a popular constituency. 'Even by proving that a certain point of view is indispensable for living well, one proves only that the view in question is a salutary myth: one does not prove it to be true. Utility and truth are two entirely different things'.[7] For Strauss the ultimate warrant for truth lies not in its consequences but rather in the very nature of the philosophic experience, an experience that Strauss understands to be so compelling and unmistakable that it distinguishes itself forthwith from the other lesser products of thought. It 'is so high, so pure, so noble an experience that Aristotle could ascribe it to his God'.[8]

The juxtaposition of Aristotle and the genuine philosophic experience is anything but chance. Strauss's rejection of modernism and its 'anti-philosophical' bias is of a piece with his efforts at restoring the 'Ancients'—particularly Plato and Aristotle—to their proper place as the most reliable sources available to the sincere seeker after truth. His labours at rendering their thought alive and relevant were undertaken to revive our jaded ontological sensibilities and to permit a generation corrupted by relativist cynicism to speak of truth without feeling compelled to add a pair of mocking inverted commas.

What stands out most conspicuously about Strauss's 'restorative ontology' is precisely its being an attempt at restoration, an attempt to resurrect a generally moribund intellectual tradition. Terms like natural law, objective cosmic order, moral absolutes, right reason, etc. are for our age gravestones in the intellectual cemetery of the past. Strauss's ontological declarations are, therefore, a polemic in the midst of a modernist monopoly, the missionary voice of a prophet in the wilderness, discourse and disputation at once.

Ironically, however fiercely Strauss rejected relativism, it was the mainspring of his thought, *the* problem to be mastered. His absolutism is conceived in opposition to it rather than emerging naturally out of a supportive intellectual environment. Strauss is not above wielding the weapons of the modernist cognitive style against his adversaries, at times with exquisite vindictiveness. All of which is only another way of saying that Strauss's thought, first impressions notwithstanding, is thoroughly modern and that the exigencies of the modernist intellectual temper govern its structure and generate its typical utterances.

13   What emerges then is a unique conflation of idioms. *Substantively*, Strauss is a voice out of a scholarly tradition whose golden age was centuries, even millennia ago. He recreates with peculiar force, the intellectual universe in which the thought of Plato, Aristotle, Aquinas and Maimonides took shape. But the *form* of disputation that he utilizes against his modern enemies comes largely from the modernist idiom itself. If he challenges the implicit relativism of the sociology of knowledge and the is/ought disjunction or the loss of moral autonomy entailed by Freudian psychology, he does so by turning their own weapons against them. Many of his readers remark on the apparent delight he took in toying with the relativist tangled in his own relativism, the proponent of value-freedom unable to vindicate his position without recourse to values, the Freudian desperately calling for moral courage. There is a curious familiarity to Strauss's argumentation, curious, that is, for a position so remote from contemporary intellectual concerns.

14   However intensely Strauss condemns relativism, he never attempts to belittle the dimensions of the problem. On the contrary, it is for him 'the spirit of our time',[9] *the* axiomatic premise of modern thought, and as such worthy of all the cautionary respect accorded to a powerful enemy. No modern thinker can proceed on his way without first making peace with or declaring war upon this most central of modern prejudices. It is, he declares without unqualification, 'the most urgent question for political philosophy'.

15   Although relativist resignation is apparently urged upon us by the recognition that 'all human thought belongs to specific historical situations', and consequently 'is bound to perish with the situation to which it belongs',[10] Strauss rejects this conclusion. Indeed, it is through the ever-changing multiplicity of beliefs that we are made aware of the absolute. Because the relative in its question-begging variety is patently insufficient, it intimates the existence of a more permanent conceptual sphere beyond itself. 'The variety of opinions about right and justice not only is compatible with the existence of natural right or the idea of justice but it is required by it.' We are urged on towards the truth because of the untenable irresolu-

tion in the world of opinion and the patent insufficiency of the contradictions it expresses.

> Recognizing the contradiction one is forced to go beyond opinions toward the consistent view of the nature of the thing concerned. The consistent view makes visible the relative truth of the contradictory opinions.[11]

True philosophy and the world of opinion are, in fact, inseparable. 'Opinion is the element of society' which the philosopher 'after long and concentrated study' is able to see in its proper relative setting. In a word, knowledge and opinion are not synonyms for truth and falsehood. Philosophy perfects opinion, it does not cancel it.[12]

But the variety of opinions regarding justice (for example) 16 leads to the absolutely just in yet a more basic way. To find a never-ending and universal struggle over the meaning of the just—spanning millennia, continents and cultures—betokens for Strauss the existence of a quintessential justice that excites our reason and humanity to its discovery. The definitive answer may elude us but the fact that the philosophic itch to determine its character does not cease to arouse the passions of the mind, this alone witnesses the presence of an independent stimulating force.[13]

What is more, Strauss conditions the very ability to pursue 17 the absolute on the prevalence of a critical, anti-traditional intellectual disposition. Traditional truths must become problematic, chastened by the relativist dilemma, before they can emerge philosophically mature and self-conscious. Without the presence of doubt that dissolves certainties and creates a gallery of contending possibilities to be explored, the contestable nature of the good can neither be initially perceived nor finally transcended in an absolute resolution.[14] And authority is doubted only when different social codes, opposing conventions, antagonistic cultural assumptions, force 'the question to arise as to which code is the right code and which account of the first things is the true account'.[15]

But if philosophy must begin with a plurality of opinions 18 in order to rise to its full cognitive stature, it is the trademark of Strauss's intellectual position to insist, nevertheless, on the most uncompromising divide between knowledge and opinion. Opinion may well be the starting point of all genuine knowledge but knowledge is not merely refurbished opinion. Against the background of a motley parade of opinion there rises the single, eternal and universal vision of philosophy.

So radically different are these two worlds that, in Strauss's view, 'the philosopher and the non-philosopher cannot have genuinely common deliberations. There is a fundamental disproportion between philosophy and the city.'[16] Philosophical knowledge is the hard-won exception to the fortuitous world of available ideas; in Strauss's words, the ascent 'from public dogma to essentially private knowledge'.[17]

19   The philosopher's unique intimacy with the truth consists in seeing beyond the perpetual reenactments of the human comedy to the heart of the matter: to those 'unchangeable standards founded in the nature of man and the nature of things'.[18] Transcending the lure of immediacy, the true philosophic intelligence perceives the 'unchanging framework which persists in all changes of human knowledge'. But this perception of unvarying 'frameworks' is merely an antechamber to substantive, specific knowledge of unqualified validity, or as Strauss dubs it, natural right.

> There cannot be natural right if human thought ... is not capable of solving the problem of the principles of justice in a genuine and hence universally valid manner. More generally expressed, there cannot be natural right if human thought is not capable of acquiring genuine, universally valid, final knowledge ... [19]

To exclude any doubt on this score, Strauss's most oft-repeated conviction is that such knowledge is not only possible, it is the alpha and omega of philosophy. 'Political philosophy' he typically declares, 'as a quest for the final truth regarding the political fundamentals is possible and necessary'.[20]

20   What is it that lifts knowledge so incommensurably above opinion? Strauss's answer cannot be mistaken: opinion is partisan, fragmented and partial; philosophy by contrast, is total, integrative and comprehensive. Indeed, by philosophy Strauss intends precisely the quest for 'the comprehensive truth or for the truth about the whole or for the science of the whole'.[21] In contrast to relative and mutually undermining opinions, the philosophic view, 'the consistent view, proves to be the comprehensive or total view. The opinions are thus seen to be fragments of the truth, soiled fragments of the pure truth'. Each 'taken by itself is merely an opinion about the whole or an inadequate articulation of the fundamental awareness of the whole and this points beyond itself toward an adequate articulation'.[22] To rise from opinion to knowledge is therefore identical with rising from the part to the whole.

21   Assuming, however, that opinion reaches out for the whole as well, why does it fail where philosophy succeeds? What

accounts for the apparently serendipitous way in which true knowledge chooses among its many suitors? Surely it cannot be merely a matter of favouring the intellectually gifted or the spiritually inspired. For if this were the case, we would legitimately expect people such as these to be scattered randomly among the centuries and cultures and not, as Strauss believes, virtually extinct in the modern philosophical wilderness, yet cramped densely into a single century in Classical Athens. Are we not compelled to account for this efflorescence of knowledge by relating it to the peculiar intellectual fertility of a specific historical juncture or, more formally expressed, to a sociology of knowledge? If the necessity for such an explanation is granted, have we not returned with painful circuitry to the very dilemma from which Strauss seeks to extricate himself?

Queries of this sort would have had only the remotest significance for the Athenian thinkers that Strauss commends as philosophic models. But Strauss, whatever his personal sympathies, is fully a man of his own time and hence, inexorably, a participant in the contemporary rhetoric of disputation. As such, the uneven appearance of real knowledge is a formidable claim requiring justification. This justification comes, ironically, in an ingenious twist of the historicist argument, a turning of the intellectual tables of which Strauss is most fond. He propounds an idiosyncratic sociology of knowledge that, like so many other modernist *ruses de guerre*, accepts the ubiquity of relativism but endeavours to vindicate a specific kind of knowledge as privileged in the pursuit of truth.

With a studied casualness that belies the boldness of the argument, Strauss observes that the sociology of knowledge examines

> impartially everything that pretends to be knowledge as well as genuine knowledge. Accordingly, one should expect that it would devote some attention also to the pursuit of genuine knowledge of the whole or to philosophy. Sociology of philosophy would thus appear to be a legitimate subdivision of sociology of knowledge.[23]

In effect, Strauss is suggesting a 'sociology of truth', a setting down of the conditions that permit a transient historical moment to catch sight of knowledge of the whole. Even the radical historicists, Strauss lectures his adversaries, cannot rule out 'the obvious possibility' that 'the situation to which one particular doctrine is related, is particularly favourable to the discovery of truth, whereas all other situations may be more or less unfavourable'.[24]

24   As opposed to the moderns, whose relation to the *res publica*
is already refracted through a tradition of theorizing that keeps
political reality at a bookish distance, Strauss believes that the
Classics were unburdened by any such legacy and able to confront politics with a peerless clarity and immediacy. The political 'thing-in-itself' became available to them because they
sought it free of inherited categories.[25] Post-classical political
thinking suffers from being a mediated and derivative enterprise that is heavy with the intellectual accretions of the past.
It cannot reach the absolute philosophic moment because its
learning is an obstacle to its knowing. The Classics, however,
were not subordinated to a tradition; theirs was a morning of
discovery, a pure beginning, an Archimedean point.

25   Although the transparency of the classical era has never returned, the tradition that emerged out of this philosophic moment of grace preserved the relationship with totality 'to a
certain extent'.[26] Periodically, when the tradition is shaken and
reality exposed to direct view, political thinking once again re-
covers some of its old lustre. The extraordinary perspicacity
of a Hobbes, for example, is attributed by Strauss to his having 'philosophised in the fertile moment when the classical
and theological tradition was already shaken and a tradition
of modern science had not yet formed and established'.[27] If we
were to ask irreverently what it is that enables Strauss himself
to contend so successfully with the truth, the answer would be
much the same. Contemporary cracks in the tradition allow
the light to shine through. As Strauss formulates it, 'genuine
understanding' has been

> rendered possible by the shaking of all traditions; the crisis of
> our time may have the accidental advantage of enabling us to
> understand in an untraditional or fresh manner. This may ap-
> ply especially to classical political philosophy which has been
> seen for a considerable time only through the lenses of modern
> political philosophy and its various successors.[28]

26   The absolute knowledge made accessible by these cracks in
the tradition is, of course, immutable. As it appeared to the
Classics, so it appears to its fortunate contemporary custodi-
ans. But if truth is one and eternal, so must the nature of the
good society be enduring and invariable; an unchanging philosophical imperative mandates a social order that is similarly
constant. Strauss presents in his thought what he would have
in the world of practice: an essentially unalterable world of
sovereign norms accessible only to a philosophical elite and
hence authoritatively interpretable only by them.

Strauss finds nothing amiss in this unity of philosophy and 27
practice. But, as is so typically the case with the modernist 'unmasking' style, he unfailingly sniffs it out in the thought of others. For example, the all-too-cosy relation between liberalism
and science (and particularly social science), is one of Strauss's
perennial themes.[29] Like equalitarian liberal democracy, scientific method is 'the greatest equalizer of unequal minds'.[30]
Just as liberalism sets prosperity and progress as its goal, so
science—abandoning truth as an 'end in itself'—is 'in the service of human power, of a power to be used for making human
life longer, healthier, more abundant'.[31] As science is value free,
so liberalism is committed to tolerance. Both are materialis-
tic, anti-philosophical, secular, instrumental, anti-ideological,
progressive, and Strauss cares for the one no more than for the
other. So that when liberalism appeals to the scientific ideal
to validate its claims, it is, in effect, hearing the inner echo of
its own closed system.

This genre of 'relativizing argument' seeks to debunk the 28
pretence of certainty by relating it to partisan perspectives. By
establishing the incriminating alliances between the liberal
social order and its scientific patron, the claims to definitive
validation are demoted to the status of a sophisticated battle
cry or a pretentious value judgement. It is at this modernist
art of burrowing beneath an adversary's position to reveal its
merely relative foundations—surely the most common rhetor-
ical weapon in current ideological disputation—that Strauss
ranks as an international grand master.

Understandably, the first and essential step of all relativizing 29
arguments is to impugn relativism itself, to reveal its merely
relative standing. Strauss disposes of relativism predictably: it
is a peculiarly modern affliction with roots in our idiosyncratic
cognitive malaise. Relativism, he charges, reflects the small-
minded and smug character of the modern mind.[32] Besides, it
is untenable as a doctrine because, logically, it entails its own
self-destruction. Moreover, when the doctrine of relativism is
translated into practice, it issues in the same impossible *cul
de sac*. Tolerance, relativism's operational analogue, is either
intolerant of intolerance, in which case it has smuggled an
absolute standard into the domain of principled agnosticism,
or it tolerates intolerance in which case it has breached its
own rule and accepted its contradiction.[33] Either tolerance 'is
in accordance with reason' and based on the assumption 'that
men know what is good', leading to intolerance of the bad; or
tolerance is baseless and no better than intolerance.[34]

If relativism is untenable as universal doctrine, it is never- 30
theless a marvellous weapon and Strauss uses it unsparingly.

A very few examples of this familiar strategy must suffice. Conservativism of the traditional Burkeian variety, Strauss laments, has forsaken the idea of a transcendent good and hence seeks its ends in the merely ancestral. But the ancestral is, by definition, the accidental. Burke can offer no more than the contextually prudential and prescriptive and how are we to distinguish true prudence from the *faux amis* masquerading as prudence if not on the basis of a non-traditional standard?[35]

31   Empiricism's insistence on its own especially direct relation to reality is similarly shown to be an absolute claim with only relative justification. Relying on its own empirical standards, empiricism cannot prove its axioms: 'Empiricism cannot be established empiricistically. It is not known through sense data that the only possible objects of perception are sense data.'[36] Which leads us back to the familiar charge: if empiricism is not established by empirical means but is nevertheless held to be *the* true doctrine, there must be a non-empirical standard that has been smuggled into the argument. Is it any wonder then that empiricist *hubris* is so irresistible a target for historicist unmasking; indeed, that historicism follows positivism not accidentally but necessarily?

32   Of all Strauss's relativizing polemics, the most incisive and well known is his debate with the ghost of Max Weber.[37] Seemingly neutral categories such as 'the routinisation of charisma', the tripartite division of traditional, legal-rational and charismatic authority and the identification of politics with 'power politics' are shown to have only relative historical validity. For example, Weber's 'ethic of responsibility', that enjoins striking a noble posture in the midst of an inscrutable reality, is pilloried by Strauss as an example of relativism hiding from its own consequences. What place have 'nobility', 'responsibility' and 'honesty' if cannibalism is quite as justified as philanthrophy? Weber's island of immovable human virtue is a preposterous shelter once the deluge of relativism has been loosed. Why, Strauss taunts, 'should one not prefer pleasing delusions or edifying myths to truth?' How can we 'take seriously this belated insistence on responsibility, this inconsistent concern with consistency, this irrational praise of rationality'.[38]

33   The relativizing critique also underlies Strauss's distinction between ideology and philosophy: ideology is relative, philosophy is true. Positions antagonistic to his own—in which category are included virtually all Western political doctrines since Machiavelli—are tainted with the relativism of ideology. Only those that preserve the authentic contemplative posture, that recognize elitism as necessary and moderation as paramount, that eschew revolution, subversion and irresponsible politi-

cal adventures,[39] are said to belong to the sovereign kingdom of philosophy. Whereas classical political philosophy authentically pursued truth, modern political thinking, having forsaken the quest, is left with a mere intellectual pittance. By giving up, in principle, the very possibility of political philosophy, the modern political thinker highlights his own irremediable irrelevance. Political philosophy has, in fact, 'been replaced by ideology',[40] and ideology, Strauss needles his opponents, is 'a teaching not superior in truth and justice to any other among the numerable ideologies'.[41]

Nowhere is this bankruptcy so dramatically exposed as in 34 the widespread academic convention of replacing the study of political philosophy itself with accounts of the history of political thought.[42] This modern surrogate resigns itself to 'the expounding or the defence of a firmly held conviction or of an invigorating myth'.[43] So profoundly has this resignation taken root that 'the end result of modern political philosophy is the disintegration of the very idea of political philosophy. For most political scientists today, political philosophy is not more than ideology or myth.'[44]

Political philosophy has been reduced to ideology, and ide- 35 ology is no more than a pitiable rump of the truth. What had once been a 'humanising quest for the eternal order' has in our era 'become a weapon and hence an instrument'. When Julian Benda in his *La Trahison des Clercs* protested against the politicization of philosophy, it was the same misuse of the intellect that alarmed him. Unfortunately, Strauss cautions, Benda was part of the problem, not part of the solution.

> He committed the fatal mistake...of ignoring the essential difference between intellectuals and philosophers. In this he remained the dupe of the delusions he denounced. For the politicisation of philosophy consists precisely in this, that the difference between intellectuals and philosophers...becomes blurred and finally disappears.[45]

The same categorical confusion, Strauss contends, explains 36 the sociology of knowledge's miscarriage: it was never able to distinguish between intellectuals and philosophers. To the founders of the sociology of knowledge all those who trafficked in ideas were, indiscriminately, intellectuals.[46] In this, Strauss protests, the sociology of knowledge blundered profoundly. For 'it failed to consider the possibility' that 'philosophers form a class by themselves, or that what unites all genuine philosophers is more important than what unites a given philosopher with a particular group of non-philosophers'.[47] It failed, in short, to understand that philosophy is cognitively impenetrable by the likes of the sociology of knowledge.

37   In what way then is philosophy penetrable? Is it a law unto itself without interests or a human context? Is philosophy, in brief, approachable solely as philosophy? No, Strauss answers. Philosophers do have definable interests and a specific human context. To be sure, this is no retreat on Strauss's part. Quite the contrary; it is the baiting feint that precedes the full-scale attack. It is also one of the most original, unsettling and irascible contributions to the armoury of modernist arguments.

38   'The philosopher's dominating passion', Strauss begins, 'is the desire for truth'.[48] Other mundane interests hold no attraction for him. If he, for example, 'owing to the weakness of the flesh, becomes concerned with being recognized by others, he ceases to be a philosopher'.[49] The genuine philosopher 'has the greatest self-sufficiency which is humanly possible'.[50] Because truth transcends the competition for scarce resources, the philosopher is *essentially* foreign to political conflict: he has no interests to defend. He simply 'will not hurt anyone'.[51] Because he dismisses all—wealth, power, fame, even life itself—for the lofty ideal of knowledge, conventional categories of cognitive analysis are grossly inappropriate to his pursuits.

39   Yet the philosopher remains a *zoon politikon;* mundane entanglements force themselves upon him. He has no choice, therefore, but to 'leave the closed and charmed circle of the "initiated" if he intends to remain a philosopher. He must go out to the market place; the conflict with political men cannot be avoided'.[52] Although the philosopher desires no more than his island of contemplative serenity, the 'city' has a dismally consistent record of regarding him with suspicion and malice that regularly turn into repression and violence. The story of Socrates is *the* story of true philosophy. For the philosopher, then, political 'savvy' is a question of self-defence. He must engage in political activity to protect his single interest: making the world safe for philosophy. The selfish interest of the philosophers 'consists in being allowed to live the life of the blessed on the earth by devoting themselves to investigation of the most important subjects'.[53]

40   Because the philosopher is unwilling and (in practice) unable to rule himself, his primary political interest is in seeking a sympathetic patron who will grant his wish for freedom and security. This patron, Strauss writes with the battle-weariness of a veteran, is most definitely not the common people; it is rather the gentlemen or, more broadly, the urban patriciate.[54] Patrons may shield the philosopher from his natural enemies, but he needs to contribute to his own security as well. He re-

lies on the services of others so he must 'pay for them with services of his own if he does not want to be reproved as a thief or fraud'.[55] He must, Strauss insists, engage in 'philosophic politics'; that is,

> in satisfying the city that philosophers are not atheists, that they reverence what the city reverences, that they are not subversives, in short, that they are not irresponsible adventurers but good citizens and even the best of citizens. This is the defence of philosophy which was required always and everywhere, whatever the regime might have been.[56]

Appearing as sterling citizens requires, however, no little duplicity on the part of philosophers. The philosopher and the city are fundamentally hostile to one another. If he 'reverences what the city reverences,' it is only a shrewd tactic to make himself a *persona grata;* he reverences truth alone. He is, in fact, radically subversive because he accepts no authority save that of philosophy. This tension between the city and the philosopher is of unprecedented sharpness in modern times because the claims of philosophy are so widely denied, its programme so derisively dismissed. Philosophy, moreover, finds itself dangerously out of sympathy with the modern democratic consensus that reaches for its revolver at the merest suggestion that only a privileged few have access to the truth.[57]

How can the philosopher discharge his responsibilities to his compatriots while remaining loyal to the imperatives of philosophy? How to speak to the few and to the many at once? For Strauss, this dual loyalty represents the abiding dilemma of the philosophical enterprise. Philosophers confronting this vexing choice discovered immemorially that there was but one way to secure the blessings of both the city and of philosophy: 'to reveal the truth to some while leading others to salutary opinions'.[58] The *Vita Contemplativa* and the *Vita Activa* can coexist only through a prudential splitting of the personality, a philosophic version of 'rendering unto Caesar'. Strauss dubs it simply 'noble lying'.[59] Because philosophic writings are available to the many, the philosopher presents his teachings 'ironically', irony being for Strauss the 'dissimulation of the superior man—the dissimulation of wise thoughts'. 'If irony is essentially related to the fact that there is a natural order of rank among men, it follows that irony consists in speaking differently to different kinds of people.'[60]

When confronted with a particularly inhospitable environment, philosophy 'went underground' and 'accommodated itself in its explicit or exoteric teachings to the unfounded commands of rulers who believed they knew things which they did not know',[61] while preserving the truth for a 'small minority' of *cognoscente*. This two-tiered—exoteric and esoteric—character is the inevitable fate of philosophy in the public domain. As Strauss presents Farabi's doctrine:

> Society did not recognize philosophy or the right of philosophising. There was no harmony between philosophy and society.... The exoteric teaching was needed for the protection of philosophy. It was the armour in which philosophy had to appear. It was needed for political reasons.[62]

44   Little more is needed to draw a number of intriguing conclusions. First, if the trademark of true philosophy is to speak and be heard in two voices, the study of the great philosophers must always be a simultaneous exploration of what is meant and what is said. If our object is to reveal the hidden significance in the public text, the faintest nuances, the most obscure intimations, may well be of greater significance than what is actually written. A text's manifest meaning is no guarantee of its real meaning. Indeed, manifest meanings are suspect; they are often diversions to lead the common reader astray. The great bulk of Strauss's scholarly work on ancient, medieval and modern thought is incomprehensible unless it is understood in the light of this research programme. Even a short list of the thinkers to whom Strauss attributes an esoteric truth (and from whom this truth is teased in the most unconventional ways) would have to include Plato, Xenophon, Thucydides, Maimonides, Halevi, Farabi, Marsilius, Machiavelli, Spinoza, Locke and Rousseau.[63]

45   Second, and of particular interest to us, if a philosophic text is composed for two distinct audiences, what one hears bespeaks what one is. Those whose ears are attuned to the lofty register of the philosophical will not fail to distinguish its noble voice; for those who are philosophically tone deaf, only the exoteric is available. The true philosopher and the mere intellectual are categorically distinguished by their very reactions to a philosophic text.

46   To substantiate this point, Strauss introduces a telling distinction between 'interpretation' and 'explanation'.[64] Explanation is the staple of the intellectual, interpretation of the philosopher. Because it reduces all thought indiscriminately to the status of a (sociological, historical, economic, psychological) instrument, explanation is perfectly apposite to the intellectual, who is unable to conceive of any other role for cognitive activity. He explains because he cannot think. For

the philosopher, however, thought comes in at least two varieties: thought as instrument and thought as the lofty pursuit of truth. The former yields its paltry secrets to explanation, the latter is, *in essence*, unapproachable except as philosophy, although its form, its earthly embodiment, can be elucidated through interpretation.

The intellectual, believing that thought, generically, is iden- 47 tified with his own all-too-explainable musings, fails to

> make sufficient allowances for the deliberate adaption on the part of political philosophers of the past, of their views to the prejudices of their contemporaries. Superficial readers are apt to think that a political philosopher was under the spell of the historical situation in which he thought, when he was merely adapting the expression of his thought to that situation in order to be listened to at all.[65]

Intellectuals do not undersand that 'by proving that their political teaching as a whole is "historically conditioned", we do not at all prove that their political philosophy proper is "historically conditioned"'.[66] Ironically, all they succeed in proving is that they are intellectuals and not philosophers.

The sociology of knowledge is, therefore, the intellectual's 48 self-critique written into a formal system. By setting up 'explanation' as the exclusive mode of understanding, they deal themselves two fatal blows simultaneously: rendering their own explanatory mode vulnerable to the debunking explanations of others and revealing themselves as incompetent to judge the thought of those for whom truth is more than the cognitive will to power. Ironically, the philosopher's two-tiered presentation of truth is the consummate trap for the mere intellectual. It beckons him to reveal himself. It invites 'explanation'. Its anthropomorphic form calls out for anthropology, sociology and the other reductive disciplines. Sociological reduction is, in fact, the common and predictable response of the intellectual to the world of ideas. In short, the sociology of knowledge is self-incriminatory.

The intellectual's impulse to reduce ideas to epiphenomenal 49 status is no consequence of perversity or lack of magnanimity. Neither is it a matter of reasoned scepticism or no-nonsense historical analysis. These, conceivably, can be corrected by moral and intellectual tutoring. The intellectual is unable to think differently because the only liberating idea—the possibility of philosophy—is just what he is incapable of grasping. Like the bourgeois thinker in Marxist thought, Strauss's intellectual is a pitiful character for he can do no other. Moreover, this self-incriminating strategy vindicates Straussian interpretations of the philosophical masters against all his rivals. Because the master's esoteric meaning is open only to those who, as philosophers, know the need for and the art of esoteric formulation, those who disagree with Strauss are *prima facie* disqualified. To disagree is to concede one's non-philosophic character. As one commentator astutely observed: 'Strauss's interpretations enjoy an immunity not enjoyed by interpretations of Strauss'.[67]

50   Approaching the philosophers of the past sociologically is disqualified for yet another more basic reason. In a strange reversal of roles, Strauss castigates the sociologists of knowledge for the implicit absolutism of their approach. Beginning his argument with the shrewd disingenuousness of Socratic naiveté, he seemingly concedes the case to his adversaries: 'As most people today would readily admit, we have to judge an author according to the standards which prevailed in his age'.[68] Otherwise, we are certain to 'force' them 'into the Procrustean bed' of our own parochial assumptions.[69] What qualifies more fully as a parochial modern prejudice than the belief that all thought is relative to its historical environment? What more authentically reflects our own peculiar state of mind than the tendency to dismiss the truth-claims of past thinkers because of the alleged superiority of our own understanding? Historicism's underlying belief that it understands the thought of the past better than it understood itself—as the expression of, for example, a hidden interest or condition—is therefore egregiously unhistorical. It constitutes a systematic misunderstanding of the past based on the doctrinaire assumption that our thought is 'superior to the thought of the past'.[70] Historicism

> misses the meaning of other cultures because it interprets these through a conceptual scheme which originates in modern western society, which reflects that particular society and which fits at best only to that particular society.[71]

51   Of all the alternate ways of approaching the thought of the past only one can promise objectivity: understanding thinkers of the past as they understood themselves.

> If we abandon this goal we abandon the only practical criterion of objectivity in the history of thought.... For the seemingly infinite variety of ways in which a given teaching can be understood does not do away with the fact that the originator of the doctrine understood it in only one way, provided he was

not confused. The indefinitely large variety of equally legitimate interpretations of a doctrine of the past is due to conscious or unconscious attempts to understand its author better than he did himself. But there is only one way of understanding him as he understood himself.[72]

One scarcely needs to add that *he* understood his thought as true and not merely as the expression of an interest. It follows that to avoid anachronism we must take his thought as seriously as he did. Strauss has, in effect, manipulated the logic of relativism so as to force us to abandon it in the study of the masters. We are, in fact, duty-bound to study them neither as sociology nor as history but as serious aspirants to truth. Political philosophy becomes, therefore, not only possible but, strictly speaking, mandatory.

These virtuoso acrobatics give way at times to a contemp- 52 tuous Strauss who, locked in hand-to-hand combat, wields his weaponry with more venom and considerably less sophistication. A small sampling of these intellectualized maledictions cannot be avoided. Those who differed with him regarding the degree of Machiavelli's malevolence are tarred with their own brush. 'They misinterpret Machiavelli's judgement ... because they are pupils of Machiavelli.... They do not see the evil character of his thought because they are heirs to the Machiavellian tradition.'[73] Anyone who could benefit from Machiavelli 'must have been corrupted to some extent'[74] before his exposure to the Florentine's writings. Likewise Hobbes: he is widely respected because 'traditional morality has so far declined that his moral teaching now appears in a very favourable light'.[75] Finally, Strauss turns on his behaviourist colleagues in political science with the following lordly taunt:

> Only a great fool would call the new political science diabolical: it has no attributes peculiar to fallen angels. It is not even Machiavellian, for Machiavelli's teachings were graceful, subtle and colourful. Nor is it Neronian. Nevertheless one may say that it fiddles while Rome burns. It is excused by two facts: it does not know that it fiddles, and it does not know that Rome burns.[76]

What unifies all these attacks is that they do not attribute 53 simple error to an opponent. Nor do they confront an adversary's position at the level of substance or moral principle. It is an oblique, relativizing-incriminating argument that is relied upon to dispose of the opponent *together* with his position.

They uniformly charge that the truth is, essentially, unavailable to the likes of them. As opposed to the common and timeless *ad hominem* argument, Strauss's assaults disqualify his opponents at a far more basic level of consciousness. It is a global human pathology that keeps truth at bay. The obtuse and the mendacious are able, conceivably, to recognize that they do not know, the wicked may come to understand that sin has corrupted them. Those whom Strauss vilifies do not know, cannot know, and cannot know that they do not know.

54   Nowhere is modernist pathology more evident than with regard to the celebrated fact/value disjunction. It is, Strauss believes, the most unambiguous admission that transcendence—the philosophical vocation of perceiving the eternal values resident in the transient facts—is categorically denied. To inscribe it (in the style of Max Weber) on the portals of knowledge is only to elevate a symptom of cognitive disorder into a binding principle, a contemporary sickness into universal norm. More: every such distinction is an abject admission that the speaker is a cognitive cripple, that is, blind to reality's transcendent dimension and hence imprisoned in its arbitrary givenness.

55   But beyond its blindness to the possibility of philosophical transcendence, the distinction itself, even at its operational level, is patently indefensible. The values resident in the facts cannot be ignored even by those for whom philosophy is anathema. How, for example, can a study of art or religion be written without first distinguishing between art and trash, between religion and superstition?[77] What sort of 'facts' remain when, in discussing human civilization, criteria such as creativity, nobility, honesty, treachery, fraud and baseness are proscribed? Are the remaining facts recognizable as human conduct? For Strauss the answer is plain: facts and values are a palpable unity split only by those who aggressively disdain the very possibility of philosophy.

56   Indeed, they do not shrink from perverting the simple, manifest, commonsense reality available to us all so as to achieve their end of writing off philosophy as a hopeless pursuit. Who has ever experienced a human reality the factual components of which were segregated from its constituent values? Ironically, the 'emancipation' of social science from speculative pre-modern philosophy that was to guarantee access to the hard world of real facts succeeds only in mutilating that world. It creates a bicameral fantasy land that contravenes our most consensual understanding of experienced reality. This sin against common sense is, therefore, doubly culpable; it reveals itself as alien to the real world of thought and, simultaneously,

alien to the real world of practice. The perversity of this bi-furcated vision needs no more telling corroboration than the innocent way in which the social scientists' good sense over-comes their principles. They do not cease utilizing valuational categories in their 'value-free' analyses.[78]

Philosophy, by contrast, because it is grounded in the indi- 57 visible realm of common sense where fact and value are an integrated whole, is true to both thought and practice. Deriv-ing from the practical understanding of politics common to the citizen and statesman, it is able to elevate the fragmented and unwitting world of practice and opinion to the fully con-scious world of thought. If, therefore, the inevitable commerce between facts and values is the plague of all the contempo-rary social sciences—to be avoided, disguised or denied—for Strauss it is the essence of true thought. Perceiving the value in the fact is the very definition of philosophy.

Strauss's position belongs to a tradition of natural law 58 theorizing, which, although distinctly minor in twentieth-century philosophy, has had its distinguished champions (Erich Voegelin, Max Scheler, George Santayana, Jacques Mar-itain to name a few). Yet he rarely if ever adverts to those thinkers who broadly share his intellectual predilections. His characteristic posture is that of an isolated minority of one staving off the encroaching philosophical wasteland. If Strauss had many disciples, he had few allies. His success is, there-fore, starkly paradoxical. No contemporary political philoso-pher can claim as large or devoted a following and yet he never overcame his dubious standing in the intellectual community at large.

Many attribute the remarkable influence he wielded to the 59 personal model of the pure 'philosophical life' he presented as a teacher, but here again paradox intrudes. Although Strauss's spiritual passion moved his disciples deeply, the Strauss known outside his own circle is remarkable for very differ-ent qualities, for truculence and belligerence. This aggressive-ness was especially galling for those modernists at whom it was directed because it was crafted out of the very intellec-tual instruments they had themselves fashioned. In Strauss's own terms, the philosopher had descended into the 'city' and finding its denizens hostile to philosophy, had learned to speak their tongue, trade in their coin, do battle with their weapons; all this so as to vindicate philosophy and the philosophical life. In *argument,* no one wielded modernist weapons more skill-fully than he; in *truth,* no one was further from their assump-tions or ambience.

Notes

1. See, e.g., J. Schaar and S. Wolin, 'Review Essay on *Essays on the Scientific Study of Politics*', *American Political Science Review*, 57:1 (1963), 125–50; W. Berns, 'The achievement of Leo Strauss', *National Review* (7 Dec. 1973), p. 1347; A. Bloom, 'Leo Strauss, September 20, 1899—October 18, 1973, *Political Theory*, 2 (1974), 372–92; M. F. Burnyeat, 'Sphinx without a secret', *New York Review of Books*, XXXII:9 (1985), 30–6 and exchange of letters XXXII:15, 41–44 and XXXIII:7, 50–2; J. Cropsey (ed.), *Ancients and Moderns: Essays on the Tradition of Political Philosophy in Honor of Leo Strauss* (New York, Basic Books, 1964); W. Dannhauser, 'Leo Strauss: becoming naive again', *The American Scholar*, 44 (1974–75), 636–44; H. Jaffe, 'The achievement of Leo Strauss', *National Review* (7 Dec. 1973), p. 1355.

2. The modernist cognitive style is described and analysed in the following works: A. MacIntyre, *After Virtue* (Indiana, University of Notre Dame Press, 1981); P. Berger, B. Berger and H. Kellner, *The Homeless Mind, Modernization and Consciousness* (New York, Vintage, 1974); C. Lasch, *The Culture of Narcissism* (New York, Norton, 1979); R. Sennet, *The Fall of Public Man* (Cambridge, Cambridge University Press, 1977); P. Rieff, *The Triumph of the Therapeutic* (New York, Harper Torch Books, 1968); G. Remmling, *The Road to Suspicion* (New York, Appleton-Century-Crofts, 1967). See also the author's *The Grammar of Modern Ideology*, (London, Routledge, 1988), which deals with the confrontation between modernist relativism and the need for ideological certainty.

3. L. Strauss, *Natural Right and History* (Chicago, University of Chicago Press, 1953), p. 5.

4. Strauss, *What is Political Philosophy?* (New York, Free Press, 1959), p. 73.

5. Strauss, *Natural Right and History*, p. 40.

6. L. Strauss, 'Relativism', in H. Schoeck and J. Wiggens (eds), *Relativism and the Study of Man* (Princeton, Von Nostrand, 1969), pp. 35–41.

7. Strauss, *Natural Right and History*, p. 7.

8. Strauss, *Liberalism Ancient and Modern* (New York, Basic Books, 1968), p. 8.

9. Strauss, *What is Political Philosophy?* p. 57.

10. Strauss, *Natural Right and History*, pp. 18–19 and ff. See also L. Strauss, *Persecution and the Art of Writing* (Westport, Conn., Greenwood Press, 1975), pp. 110 and 157.

11. Strauss, *Natural Right and History*, pp. 124-25; see also pp. 2 and 10.

12. Strauss, *What is Political Philosophy?*, pp. 221–22.

13. Strauss, *Natural Right and History*, p. 100.

14. Ibid, p. 84.

15. Ibid, p. 86.

16. Strauss, *Liberalism Ancient and Modern*, p. 14.

17. Strauss, *Natural Right and History*, p. 12.

18. Strauss, *Liberalism Ancient and Modern*, p. 63.
19 Strauss, *Natural Right and History*, p. 24.
20. Strauss, *The Political Philosophy of Hobbes* (Chicago, University of Chicago Press, 1963), p. xv.
21. Strauss, *Liberalism Ancient and Modern*, p. 13; see also, *Natural Right and History*, p. 30; *Persecution and the Art of Writing*, p. 7; *On Tyranny* (London, Collier-Macmillan, 1963), p. 211; *What is Political Philosophy?*, pp. 11–12 and 39.
22. Strauss, *Natural Right and History*, pp. 124–25.
23. Strauss, *Persecution and the Art of Writing*, p. 17.
24. Strauss, *What is Political Philosophy?*, pp. 64 and 69.
25. Strauss, *What is Political Philosophy?*, p. 27; see also p. 78.
26. Strauss, *What is Political Philosophy?*, pp. 78–9.
27. Strauss, *The Political Philosophy of Hobbes*, p. 5.
28. Strauss, *The City and Man* (Chicago, Rand-McNally, 1964), p. 9
29. See, e.g., Strauss, *Liberalism Ancient and Modern*, p. viii.
30. Strauss, *Liberalism Ancient and Modern*, p. 20.
31. Strauss, *Liberalism Ancient and Modern*, p. 20.
32. Strauss, *Persecution and the Art of Writing*, p. 158.
33. Strauss, *Liberalism Ancient and Modern*, p. 63.
34. Strauss, *Natural Right and History*, pp. 5–6.
35. Strauss, *Natural Right and History*, pp. 294–323; *Liberalism Ancient and Modern*, p. viii.
36. Strauss, *Liberalism Ancient and Modern*, p. 212.
37. Strauss, *Natural Right and History*, pp. 35–80.
38. Strauss, *Natural Right and History*, pp. 47–8.
39. See, e.g., Strauss, *On Tyranny*, pp. 190–226; see also, A. Lieblich, 'Straussianism and ideology', in A. Parel (ed.), *Ideology, Philosophy and Politics* (Waterloo, Canada, Wilfred Laurier University Press, 1983), pp. 225–45.
40. Strauss, *The City and Man*, p. 2.
41. Strauss, *The City and Man*, pp. 6–7.
42. Strauss, *The City and Man*, pp. 7–8.
43. Strauss, *What is Political Philosophy?* p. 12.
44. Strauss, 'The crisis of political philosophy', in H. Spaeth (ed.), *The Predicaments of Modern Politics* (Detroit, University of Detroit, 1964), p. 41.
45. Strauss, *Natural Right and History*, p. 34.
46. Strauss, *Persecution and the Art of Writing*, p. 7.
47. Strauss, *Persecution and the Art of Writing*, p. 7.
48. Strauss, *On Tyranny*, p. 21.
49. Strauss, *On Tyranny*, p. 218.
50. Strauss, *On Tyranny*, p. 212.
51. Strauss, *On Tyranny*, p. 212.
52. Strauss, *On Tyranny*, p. 208.
53. Strauss, *Natural Right and History*, p. 143.
54. Strauss, *Natural Right and History*, p. 143; see also, *The City and Man*, p. 207, and *Liberalism Ancient and Modern*, p. 14.
55. Strauss, *On Tyranny*, p. 211.

56. Strauss, *On Tyranny*, p. 220.
57. See Strauss, *On Tyranny*, pp. 208–9, 217 and 226; *Liberalism Ancient and Modern*, pp. 19–20.
58. Strauss, *The City and Man*, p. 54.
59. Strauss, *Persecution and the Art of Writing*, p. 35.
60. Strauss, *The City and Man*, p. 51.
61. Strauss, *On Tyranny*, p. 226.
62. Strauss, *Persecution and the Art of Writing*, pp. 17–18. Farabi's comments are made in context of his study *Plato* (17) which is the second section of his *On the Purposes of Plato and Aristotle* [Strauss notes that the original was edited, annotated and translated into Latin by F. Rosenthal and R. Walzer as *Alfarabius De Platonis Philosophia* (London, 1943)].
63. See the following works of Strauss: for Plato, *The City and Man*, pp. 52–53; for Xenophone, *On Tyranny*, pp. 21–142; for Thucydides, *The City and Man*, pp. 143ff; for Maimonides, *Persecution and the Art of Writing*, pp. 38–94 and *Liberalism Ancient and Modern*, p. 142f; for Halevi, *Persecution and the Art of Writing*, pp. 95–141; for Farabi, *Persecution and the Art of Writing*, pp. 14–18; for Marsilius, *Liberalism Ancient and Modern*, pp. 185ff., especially p. 195; for Machiavelli, *Thoughts on Machiavelli* (Glencoe, Ill., Free Press, 1958), passim.; for Spinoza, *Persecution and the Art of Writing*, pp. 177ff. and *Spinoza's Critique of Religion* (New York, Schocken, 1965); for Locke, *Natural Law and History*, pp. 165ff.; for Rousseau, *Natural Law and History*, p. 260.
64. Strauss, *Persecution and the Art of Writing*, p. 143.
65. Strauss, *What is Political Philosophy?*, p. 63.
66. Strauss, *What is Political Philosophy?*, pp. 64–5.
67. Victor Gourevitch, 'Politics and philosophy', *Review of Metaphysics*, 22 (1968), 62–63.
68. Strauss, *Persecution and the Art of Writing*, p. 110.
69. Strauss, *Natural Right and History*, p. 56.
70. Strauss, *Persecution and the Art of Writing*, p. 158; see also, *On Tyranny*, p. 195 *Thoughts on Machiavelli*, p. 231.
71. Strauss, *What is Political Philosophy?*, p. 25.
72. Strauss, *What is Political Philosophy?*, pp. 67–68.
73. Strauss, *Thoughts on Machiavelli*, p. 12.
74. Strauss, *Thoughts on Machiavelli*, p. 28.
75. Strauss, *What is Political Philosophy?*, p. 171.
76. Strauss, *Liberalism Ancient and Modern*, p. 223.
77. Strauss, *Natural Right and History*, pp. 50ff.
78. Strauss, *Natural Right and History*, pp. 35–80; *Liberalism Ancient and Modern*, p. 215.

CHAPTER NINE
MARXISM

At the risk of belaboring the obvious, the reader would do well to recall at the very outset that Marxism—despite its general utility as a method of social analysis—is nevertheless a creed, a worldview, and not merely an approach to the study of politics. It does not rest content with the role of academic observer in the manner of the other approaches we have taken up. It mandates action, exhorts to political organization, and expressly denies that it is neutral as to political outcomes. While many of the other approaches have been accused of tacitly harboring values and ideological proclivities in violation of their proclamations of neutrality, Marxists freely admit to ethical commitments and understand their analysis as entailing specific action. Like the Straussians, but in the greatest ideological enmity to them, Marxists understand political analysis as too important a matter to be given over to political scientists.

For a doctrine that proclaims the inextricable unity of theory and practice, Marxist theory has lived a life well independent of Marxist practice. Cynics might even urge that Marxism as a theory seems to do best when it is furthest removed from Marxists in power. This surely has been the case for the past half-century, as Marxism in the Soviet Union has been transformed from a vital ideal into a starched and lifeless orthodoxy that is more adept at sloganeering and persecuting the nonconformist than at thinking creatively.

By contrast, in bourgeois Europe, a hundred Marxist flowers have bloomed. Indeed, Marxism has had few peers on the European intellectual scene for inventiveness and influence. On the continent especially, Marx has found himself in the embrace of some very odd non-Marxist bedfellows. He has been paired off with that archconservative Sigmund Freud in a "Freudo-Marxist" synthesis. He has been given an anxiety-ridden, French-accented existentialist reading. The structuralists and poststructuralists, the hermeneuticists and critical theorists all have claimed him for themselves. Even "Woodstock Marxism" (a strange American mutant with a strong postmaterialist streak) had its hour in the sun. Perhaps this was only the belated vengeance of Karl Marx himself: he had, after all, insistently contended that his ideas were suited for the advanced industrial states of Europe rather than for the underdeveloped nations of the East.

Marxism survived the heights of Soviet power during the cold war, and it will likely survive the dismantling of the Soviet empire and the debacle of Soviet ideology that we are now witnessing. Oddly, it has been said that Marxism may even emerge from the maelstrom invigorated and rejuvenated—more a pristine worldview than another ism. It will no longer need to carry about on its theoretical back the deformed and repulsive lessons of the Soviet experience. Arguably, Western Marxists will more easily disown and dissociate themselves from the bureaucratic authoritarianism with which they came to be identified, from the Marxists who gave Marxism a bad name.

The resilience of Marxism, its ability to survive the failure of its predictions, the perversion of its ideals, even the heinous crimes committed in its name, cannot be explained merely by the blind indoctrination of its adherents or by the totalitarian methods it has employed—although Marxism has always had both its zealous faction of "true believers" as well as its brutal Stalinist streak. Marxism's strength, especially as an academic, philosophical position, lies in its substantial power as an instrument of sociopolitical analysis and critique. Besides presenting a revolutionary doctrine and a blueprint for political reconstruction, Marx provided tools for understanding the dynamics of political conflict—tools that may well be the most viable part of his teaching. Marx's critiques of nineteenth-century liberalism, his dissection of the underlying realities of power, and his analysis of ideas and their relation to political hegemony (no less than the ideal he held out of a possible human future) represent permanent contributions to our intellectual heritage. Indeed, one need not be a card-carrying Marxist to profitably utilize the categories of Marxian analysis.

It has been regularly observed that, together with functionalism, Marxism is probably the most widely utilized method of political analysis in the contemporary social sciences. This juxtaposition of functionalism and Marxism as dominant approaches may not be sheer happenstance. Despite the chasm that divides the two approaches, there is a certain reverse symmetry or mirror-imaging that links these two methods of analysis. At some significant levels at least, their respective analyses bear witness to a single underlying logic that is, in each case, inverted or pursued in opposite directions. We would do well to explore this interesting parallel.

Probably the most fundamental interpretive question that faces the analyst of politics has to do with the nature of political conflict. No one, of course, would wish to deny that politics involves a continuous struggle of groups, interests, and ideologies for power. Nevertheless, the constitution and quality of this struggle, its essential causes and consequences, are the focus of profound controversy. To formulate the core issue in its simplest terms: is *conflict* or *consensus* the primary political reality? Does political conflict reflect the collision of nonnegotiable, antithetical, zero-sum interests that can be settled only by the coercive instruments of political power? Or does political conflict take place against the background of a more basic and shared loyalty to a common political community?

This essential question can be approached from a number of complementary perspectives. Are we to understand the conflicts endemic to human community as tending naturally to rend public order apart, or do they represent a necessary (perhaps even a healthy) struggle of interests and ideas that rests on the consensual unity of social life? Is the long-term survival of political communities secured through the power that coercively binds them together and without which there would be no basis for such union? Or is this social union maintained by natural bonds of solidarity, sociability, and fellowship that, while allowing for regulated conflict, are more basic than such conflict?

If the theorist of consensus must account interpretively for the omnipresence of conflict, the conflict theorist faces the opposite task: he needs to explain the undeniable existence of consensual elements in public life. For just as it would be impossible to deny the reality of political conflict, it would be no less audacious and improbable to deny the obvious fact that political communities of all kinds do manifest significant bonds of consensus and solidarity. There is no way of overlooking the importance of such unifying links as a common historical identity or cultural, linguistic, and religious solidarity or political nationalism. How then can these fraternal, bonding forces be accounted for by a point of view that understands human interests as mutually exclusive and human society as irremediably coercive?

While theorists of consensus are, of course, entirely willing to accept the existence of these consensual elements at face value, conflict theorists are compelled to account for phenomena that appear to fly in the face of their contentions. The answers they have tended to give parallel those of the consensus theorist in regard to conflict—only in reverse. If consensus theorists see conflict as secondary to the more basic bonds that integrate political communities, conflict theorists understand consensus as ancillary to the realities of conflict. Indeed, they understand these consensual elements as an essential part of the conflict itself. Those who are in the position of hegemony have every interest in stimulating the sense of sociopolitical solidarity to neutralize potentially injurious conflict and to disseminate the delusion that their control is in the general interest after all. This deceptive perception of unity mitigates what would otherwise be a bitter and threatening conflict, and in so doing it perpetuates the control of those already in power. Consensus no doubt exists, the conflict theorist contends, but its true source and significance become obvious only in the context of the struggle for political domination.

For the theorist of consensus, conflict plays a similar but inverted role. Without struggle and conflict, political communities would stagnate and ossify. They would lack the central mechanism that stimulates the rise of new elites, the renewal of institutions, the improvement of policy, and the elimination of the ineffective and obsolescent. Political conflict therefore has the positive function of preserving the unity of a society by keeping it on its collective toes, by pruning away those elements that, if left untended, might fester dangerously. In a word: just as the conflict theorist interprets consensus in terms of conflict, so the theorist of consensus interprets conflict in terms of consensus.

Marxists and functionalists represent the conflict and consensus theorists, respectively. Marxists understand class conflict as basic and implacable. Power is therefore a zero-sum commodity. Consensual sentiments, such as they are, merely cloud the nature of the struggle, diverting and disabling the otherwise revolutionary energies of the oppressed. Functionalists, by contrast, understand the divisions and differentiations that mark political communities as nonconspiratorial in nature. Social and political differentiation represent a necessary division of labor, particularly in the modern state. That one group possesses power does not necessarily mean that it is exploiting another for partisan advantage. Inequalities of power merely entail that specialized social functions (such as political leadership) must be discharged and that different groups are adept at discharging different social functions. Conflict, in the functionalist view, has a positive rejuvenating social role that serves the functioning of the political community as a whole.

The interpretive mirror-imaging should be clear. Manifest as well is the absolute centrality of this controversy in making sense of the political. But, acute readers are no doubt asking themselves, why should this important issue not be resolved by simple hands-on research? Isn't it an empirically adjudicable matter? Is there no way of measuring conflict and consensus to determine which is the more basic?

This question, as understandable as it is, misses the nature of interpretive as opposed to empirical questions. Even if such measurements could be made in a reasonably reliable and objective manner (a severe problem in its own right), we would be no closer to resolving the issue at hand. What stands between the sides to the controversy is not an empirical issue at all. Indeed, both sides may well be in perfect agreement as to the "brute facts" of conflict and consensus, their empirical presence in any given political reality. The essential point at which they part company is in regard to the interpretive evaluation of the facts, not the facts themselves. Like the half-empty, half-full glass, what we face here is a case of fixed facts with alternate interpretations. Is conflict to be understood in terms of consensus, or consensus in terms of conflict?

Are we, for example, to take at face value and without any further clarification a society that gives outward signs of being tranquil and fraternal? Does this outward appearance represent the true nature of that society's constitution? The Marxists, of course, perceive this ostensible placidity as obscuring deeper conflicts. Far from being an indication of the lack of conflict, they argue, the seeming solidarity we observe reflects the stunning victory of a ruling class over its potential class enemies. Its success in disarming these enemies is, in fact, so great that the latter accept the illusion of unity lock, stock and barrel. Despite their real interests, which should lead them to uncompromising opposition, they succumb to the ideological prevarications of the ruling class. Incongruously, they have come to believe that the chimerical bonds uniting them to their oppressors are greater than those that divide them.

The hard-headed empiricist will, no doubt, complain that he has been illegitimately short-changed. We can study the actual manifestations of consensus (and of conflict), he insists, regardless of their ultimate theoretical significance. Why waste energy on sterile issues of principle when the data available for us to gather is both ample and accessible? Do not the facts in themselves have value even without recourse to interpretive categories?

Possibly they do. But they are of distinctively limited value if their meaning and import remain unclear. As we repeatedly emphasized in the first two chapters, facts become meaningful only in the context of perspectives that lend them significance. Uninterpreted data lacking theoretical significance, like bricks randomly strewn on the ground, do not create a habitable structure of meaning. In the case of our placid, seemingly fraternal society, we might accumulate reams of observations confirming the existence of manifest consensus on all manner of subjects and yet be missing the kernel in the husk, the factors in the facts, the future lying dormant in the present. We might well be playing with statistical fool's gold, believing it to be the genuine article.

But the zealous empiricist, not to be silenced by such arguments, continues his assault. Even if interpretation is conceded to be necessary, are not the Marxist and functionalist contentions ever so near to being "nonfalsifiable" arguments, in the precise sense that Popper uses the term? Whatever the evidence, whether conflict or consensus empirically predominates, each of them remains immovably committed to his interpretive convictions. Both theories appear to be compatible with any and all evidence—they prohibit nothing. This is a serious charge, and it may well be justified. The "scientific" status of these interpretive contentions, at least in Popper's demanding sense, is in serious jeopardy.

It is doubtful that the Marxists, in response to this attack, will be greatly concerned with receiving Popper's scientific blessings. On the contrary, they will claim that limiting contentions about conflict and consensus to those that are falsifiable in Popper's special sense is tantamount to rendering them inert, shallow, and potentially misleading. The simple fact of consensus does not guarantee the underlying reality of consensus. Only a naively dogmatic empiricist would insist on such a question-begging conclusion. It is the meaning of the given that is at stake, not its brute givenness. And the real meaning of the given becomes available only when viewed through the broad lens of interpretation. If this signifies that elements of grand interpretive theories like Marxism are not falsifiable in the conventional experimental sense, so be it. This, however, is not a failing of the theory, they argue, but a consequence of the unique requirement in the social sciences for meaning over and

above the factually manifest. The real work of social scientific understanding, according to this position, begins only when all the laboratory
results are in.

This interpretive divide between Marxists and their opponents goes beyond the principled question of conflict or consensus. If, as the Marxists
claim, conflict is basic and irresolvable, then for every victor there must
be a vanquished. If there are only scarce resources to be had (whether in
terms of power, property, or prestige), then those who enjoy them do so
at the expense of those who do not. In more authentically Marxist words,
all political regimes are dictatorships; they rule *for* certain groups and *over*
certain groups. The state is the public instrument of organized power
utilized by those who rule against those who are ruled. Indeed, were
politics not about irresolvable conflicts of interest, the coercive power of
the state would be quite superfluous.

In most eras of history, say the Marxists, this class rule was relatively
direct and undisguised—even if it received all manner of justifications
through religious doctrines and traditional beliefs on morality and social
propriety. Liberal democracy, in this regard, is unique and unprecedented. In the guise of benign consensus, popular elections, and civil
rights, its use of less than overtly violent means, its ostensibly free market, it gives the *impression* of being different from its less sophisticated
predecessors. For Marxists, this impression belies the true reality. For
although the political instruments may be different, the ends are not.

Liberal democracy represents no less a class dictatorship than did the
rule of the lords over their serfs in the middle ages. In place of violence
and coercion, liberal democracy utilizes more subtle but no less effective means to entrench and ensure the rule of the privileged. Its weapons
of domination which are so routinely used as to become invisible, are
educational and ideological. It controls the flow of information, directs
the internalization of values we call socialization, trains for law-abiding
and obedient behavior, and coopts its potential class enemies with con-
sumerist inducements. This, the Marxist argues, represents a profound
hegemony over heart and soul, the creation of one-dimensional men
who do not normally require external coercion because they voluntarily
enslave themselves.

Whatever the repressive and mind-numbing devices utilized to obscure
the visibility of social conflict, the objective cleavages and contradictions
of liberal capitalism remain intact. In fact, were these cleavages not
clouded over by the machinery of domination, they would surely foment
all-out war between the ruling classes and the masses they dominate.
The oppressed are held in thrall, however, by the faulty perceptions
that the ruling classes have designed and instilled in their minds; they
suffer from what Marx called "false consciousness." Ordinarily, this self-
imposed obedience is sufficient for the purposes of effective control.

But it can occasionally happen that this dictatorship in silk gloves is
insufficient to control a surge of mutinous sentiment that threatens to

overwhelm the instruments of domination. When the seemingly benign and indulgent tactics of liberalism are seen for the repressive measures that they are, when economic crisis raises destitution and misery to new levels of intensity, when revolutionary forces emerge to endanger the system, capitalism can no longer rely on its soft-sell tactics. At these critical junctures, liberalism must expose its authentically repressive nature, its "mailed fist." It is driven to reveal the coercion and violence that (although hidden in the pretenses of consensus) were always the true nature of its class rule.

Many orthodox Marxists understand European fascism of the 1930s in this light. Faced by serious economic dislocations and a powerful challenge from the Left, liberalism deteriorated into a visible right-wing dictatorship that (whatever its irrational claptrap) was, in fact, a conscious last ditch effort to save capitalism from extinction. In its moment of authoritarian repression, liberalism's decorous veil fell away to reveal its genuinely brutal character. It should come as no surprise, Marxists observe, that members of the capitalist ruling classes were so often to be found among the supporters of fascism.

Normally, however, these draconic means of supporting class domination are unnecessary. Control over information and beliefs is both cheaper and more effective than overt violence. It is sufficient, in times of relative placidity, to present liberal capitalism in attractive ideological packaging and to control the social values that are publicly disseminated. In Marxist eyes, nothing qualifies more thoroughly as the ideological packaging of establishment values than the well-known liberal theory of pluralism.[1]

In the pluralist account of modern liberal democracy, no one group or elite has exclusive control over political power. There is no single ruling class, certainly no one class that dominates both the economic and political realms. Liberal democracies are composed of many elites that compete for power. These elites are distinct from one another in terms of the interests they pursue, the policies they favor, and the socioeconomic composition of their supporters.

Elites that fail to satisfy the expectations of their constituents will not long survive. Without the confidence of their respective interest-communities, failing elites will soon be replaced by others whose promise to perform effectively is more persuasive. For pluralists, the focus of this competitive struggle among the various elites is the ballot box. Although the "people" cannot practically rule by themselves, they do periodically determine electorally those who will be authorized to act in their name.

In this democratic struggle for power, so the pluralists argue, the state acts as arbiter. It regulates the contest without being part of it, preserves the rules of the game without having a stake in the game's outcome. Like an honest broker who facilitates the dealings of others, the state provides the impartial framework in which competing elites can pursue their objectives. The state with its vast apparatus, faithful to its role as umpire, repulses the advances of the many interests that would want to enlist its support for partisan ends.

Indeed, many of the input-output analyses (Chapters 3, 4 and 5 above) that Marxists identify with the ideology of liberalism, expressly reject the perception of the state as an independent, self-motivated, sectarian institution. In these accounts, the state navigates and steers rather than wielding power. It represents a conversion process that accurately and neutrally registers demands and supports without designing the outputs according to predetermined goals. The state regulates the political process; by no means does it control or direct it.

Needless to say, for Marxists this account of the modern liberal state is profoundly objectionable. It obscures the massive dominating power of the state and its institutions. It ignores the intimate relations between the ruling socioeconomic elites and the state. It clouds the essential unity of the ruling class regardless of tactical differences among its constituent branches. It makes light of the cleavages and contradictions that only the force of a coercive state can hold together—and much much more. Pluralism, the Marxist complains cynically, is precisely the kind of self-serving, ingratiating ideological portrait that we would expect the liberal state to draw of itself.

But are these two accounts of the modern liberal state our only available alternatives? Must we choose between the one version that understands the state as a conspiratorial instrument of class domination and the other that denies its active partisan nature? In the next chapter we take up a third and more recent approach that, in many ways, is intermediate between pluralism and Marxism. Some would prefer that we use the term corporatism to describe their research agenda. Others, from a somewhat different perspective, are partial to the popular slogan: "Bringing the state back in."

NOTE

1. Probably the most important formulations of the pluralist viewpoint are those of Robert Dahl. See especially his *Who Governs?* and *A Preface to Democratic Theory*.

SUGGESTIONS FOR FURTHER READING

Cardoso, F. H., and Faletto, E., *Dependency and Development in Latin America* (Berkeley, University of California Press, 1979).

Cohen, G. A., *Karl Marx's Theory of History: A Defence* (Oxford, Clarendon Press, 1978).

MacPherson, C. B., *Democratic Theory: Essays in Retrieval* (Oxford, Clarendon, 1973).

Miliband, R., *The State in Capitalist Society* (New York, Basic Books, 1969).

Mills, C. W., *The Power Elite* (New York, Oxford University Press, 1956).

Poulantzas, N. A., *Political Power and Social Classes* (London, Sheed and Warp, 1973).

John McMurtry

The State

1   Above the economic structure stands the state or, as Marx more precisely puts it, "the legal and political superstructure" ("the police, the army, the courts and bureaucracy," *RZ**, 193–94). This state or superstructure is the "official stratum" of society, which "arises upon" the economic structure as its sanctioned and coercive regulator.[1]

2   In general, what distinguishes the legal and political superstructure or state from the "underlying" economic structure to which it "corresponds" is that all its content is or has been consciously constructed by some form or other of recognized social authority.[2] On the other hand, the more fundamental content of the economic structure obtains "independently of the will of individuals" (*GID*, 357),[3] and is only "scientifically discoverable" (*CI*, 542). Marx maintains this general distinction in all his discussions of the legal-political superstructure and the economic base.

3   Clarifying this general distinction between the economic structure (E) and the legal-political superstructure (S) is a set of specific distinctions. These are:

    1. The relations S involves are in terms of formal *rights* and *obligations;* whereas the relations E involves are in terms of effective *powers* and *constraints* (*GID*, 80 and 352–59).
    2. S is the *de jure* representative of "the general interest"; whereas E is the *de facto* organization of particular material interests (*GID*, 45–46, 78).
    3. S's form is visible and institutional; whereas E's form is concealed and unacknowledged (*CII*, 791).

4   We can see, then, that the conventional criticism of Marx's distinction between economic substructure and legal-political superstructure is false. The distinction here, contrary to standard objections, is both precisely securable and substantial in character. The really contentious point here is not Marx's distinction *per se*, but the relationship that he supposes between the factors that he distinguishes. Why, the question is repeatedly put, is the economic order conceived as the "base" and the state its "superstructure"? Why does he conceive the former as primary, and the latter as secondary?

*See "Key to Abbreviations" on page 443.

From *The Structure of Marx's World-View* Princeton, N.J.: Princeton University Press, 1978, pp. 100–122. Reprinted by permission.

Marx suggests a number of mutually reenforcing answers to this query, which we can summarize by the following propositions:

1. *The legal and political superstructure arises in whole and in part only upon already existing antagonisms of material interest inherent in the production relations/economic structure* (which it "expresses" and "regulates") *and does not obtain independently of these economic antagonisms* (*PofP*, 151).[4] Thus, says Marx, the legal and political superstructure is the "official, active and conscious expression of the economic structure of society" (*YM*, 350) wherein (among other, secondary antagonisms) the material interest of the ruling class—to sustain its expropriation of the surplus labor of others—is systematically antagonistic to the material interest of the producer class from whom this surplus labor is expropriated. If, Marx holds, there were no such systematic antagonisms of material interest inherent in the economic order, as in the projected communist society, where there would be no private power to exploit society's forces of production, then there would be no legal and political superstructure required to preside over such divisions; just as, Marx contended, there was no state before such ruling-class ownership of the productive forces came into being.[5] Because the necessary material ground of the superstructure—antagonistic relations of production that it is historically constructed to meet—would no longer exist, it would "wither away." Insofar as the legal and political superstructure is thus dependent for its existence on the divisions of ownership in the economic system, it is derivative and the latter is primary. The two are related, in a phrase, as problem-raiser and problem-responder (thus Marx's term "reflex" for superstructure).

Marx's claim here of exhaustive dependency of the state or superstructure on antagonistic relations of production/economic structure does not, we might add, rule out a central planning and distributing agency for production in communist society. Such an agency is not a state or superstructure because it is wholly integral to the dynamic of needs and production. Distribution, for instance, is not dictated by ownership or juridical right, but by the principle of "to each according to his needs."[6]

2. Except in revolution (where the economic base is proximately altered by the operations of the legal and political superstructure), *any conflict between the requirements or laws of the class-patterned relations of production/economic structure*

and the requirements or laws of the legal and political superstructure is resolved in favor of the former. For example, the established civil rights of the superstructure will be suspended or ignored if their operation represents a threat to the ruling-class monopoly of productive forces, or to the "law of motion" of the economic base. The requirements of the latter take precedence over the requirements of the former in this, or any other, case of nonrevolutionary disjunction. In this sense too, then, the economic structure has primacy over the legal and political superstructure....

3. Since men cannot live on the content of the legal and political superstructure, whereas they can and do live on the productive-force content of the relations of production/economic structure, they act in accordance with the latter rather than the former:

> Material interests preponderate.... The Middle Ages could not live on Catholicism, nor the ancient world on politics. On the contrary, it is the mode in which they gained a livelihood that explains why here politics and there Catholicism played the chief part (*CI*, 82).

Insofar as men act in accordance with their relations to the material means of human life rather than their relations to the stuff of law and politics as such, the relations of production/economic structure are more "basic" than the legal and political superstructure. In this sense, which underlies sense (2), the former, again, has primacy.

6   To this point we have seen that Marx distinguishes the legal and political superstructure, or state, from the production relations/economic structure in a number of ways, and that on empirical grounds he regards it as a superstructure in its relationship to the latter.

7   The superstructure arises because, and only because, of antagonisms of material interest inherent in the economic base. It is a social mechanism for dealing with the problems of these antagonisms and would disappear or "wither away" with the removal of these latter in a communist society. We now ask, precisely how does the superstructure or state relate to the economic antagonisms it is "raised" to deal with? Marx's answer, reduced to formula, is this: *Except in revolutionary periods, the superstructure or state relates always to the problems engendered by the economic structure and its "laws of motion" so as to maintain these latter intact.*

That is, far from being the resolving mechanism of common 8 interest it is conventionally held to be, the state, for Marx, merely maintains the collective interests of the ruling class intact and, thereby, perpetuates the economic antagonisms it is raised to deal with by protecting their underlying structural cause from alteration or change. What it is claimed to be is thus an "upside-down" version of what it is. Thus, says Marx, the state is "a fraud." And thus, he says in defining its "real" as opposed to "pretended" function, "The bourgeois state is nothing but a mutual *insurance pact* of the bourgeois class both against its members taken individually and against the exploited class."[7]

There is a wide variety of ways in which the state is con- 9 ceived by Marx as protecting the ruling-class economic base and its inherent antagonisms of material interest. We can resolve his myriad descriptions and asides in this connection into the following set of propositions:

1. It *validates* some or all existing relations of production (powers) as legal property relations (rights) and, thereby, validates the ruling class's ownership monopoly and extraction of surplus value.

2. It *enforces* some or all existing relations of production by virtue of enforcing legal property relations that "express" the former, and again enforces the ruling class's monopolistic ownership and extraction of surplus value.

3. It *adjusts* whatever requires adjusting to perpetuate the ruling class's monopoly of ownership and extraction of surplus value; for example, in a capitalist social formation, by periodically regulating wages, imposing protective duties, forcing sale of labor power, funding capitalist ventures, waging imperialist wars, and persecuting dissidents.

4. It *adjudicates* individual and group disputes over proprietary claims, which disputes arise from the inherent antagonisms of the ruling-class economic order,[8] in a manner always consistent with the perpetuation of the latter.

5. It *misleads* some or all of the people of a society into acceptance of the ruling class's monopoly of ownership and extraction of surplus value by certain "mystifying" and "concealing" characteristics of its formally articulated content:

i. by its voluntaristic language, which masks economic compulsion by a vocabulary of personal "will" and "agreement" (that is, men do not personally "will" or "agree" to enter their various economic relations, as the voluntaristic language of legal and political contract pretends. On the contrary, they are generally "compelled" to enter such relations as a matter of practical necessity);

ii. by the "abstract" nature of its legal and political rights, which imply universal equality (capitalism) or mutuality (feudalism), while in fact permitting the opposite of these; that is, the abstract and equal right of all to private property in capitalist society permits in fact the virtual propertylessness of the vast majority (see *CI*, 583 ff.); while the universal mutuality of obligation in feudal society permits, in fact, the lord's extraction from the serf of surplus labor "without any compensation" (*CIII*, 790 ff.).

iii. by the community of interest or "illusory community" (*GID*, 45–46) it purports to represent, when a minority or ruling-class interest is in fact what it protects; that is, the modern state purports to be securing the "public interest," when in fact its law is merely "the will of the bourgeois class made into a law for all" (*CM*, 67), and its political mechanisms "merely the organized power of one class oppressing another" (see *CM*, 74).

10   As (i), (ii), and (iii) suggest, the legal and political superstructure has an important ideological dimension. That is why Marx describes it as "practico-idealist" in nature (*GID*, 85). However, because the ideological factor as a whole encloses considerably more area than that covered by (5), Marx generally extends separate treatment to it. . . .

11   Before proceeding further with our exposition of Marx's theory of the state, we attend to what has often been highlighted as a problem. That is, how can the superstructure be conceived of as an "expression" or "reflex" of the economic base, when it itself may have been a necessary condition of the latter's formation? For example, how can the capitalist legal and political superstructure be said to be an expression or reflex of capitalist economic structure when (as Marx himself indignantly affirms throughout his section on the "Primitive Accumulation" in *Capital*) "legal enactments" played a central role in forming this very economic base?

12   The answer is that the political and legal superstructure is related to the economic structure and its "laws of motion" in a different way *between* historical epochs (for example, the transition period from feudalism to capitalism) than it is *within* these epochs. In such transition periods, Marx holds, the productive forces have "outgrown" the economic structure and its laws, and thereby transformed the latter's historical status from a "form of social development" to a "fetter" on such development. In this situation, and only in this situation, the

state cannot both maintain the economic structure and its laws intact, and allow for the preservation and development of the productive forces. It is, on such occasions, confronted with what Marx called a "fundamental contradiction" in the mode of production. In this situation, and, again it must be stressed, only in this situation, the state operates as an agency for the qualitative alteration (as opposed to maintenance) of the economic order, in accordance with the requirements of productive-force development.[9]

But once this period of epochal transition is achieved, once 13 the economic order is so transformed that it is no longer a "fetter" on the productive forces, but a new "form of their development," then the superstructure is *ipso facto* deprived of the material grounds of its revolutionary potential, and reverts to its normal function of maintaining the economic base intact.

In summary, the legal and political superstructure operates 14 always as an "expression" or "reflex" of the economic infrastructure, except in periods of epochal transition, such as that between feudalism and capitalism or that between capitalism and socialism. Here, exceptionally, but in strict accordance with the "laws" of technological determinism, it is "seized" by a rising new class and used to alter the old economic order into "another, higher form" that conforms to society's current stage of productive force development. Once this revolution occurs, the rising new class becomes society's ruling class, with the state, again, as the mechanism whereby the underlying economic order is maintained intact.[10]

There is another *prima facie* paradox that arises out of Marx's 15 concept of the legal and political superstructure and its relationship to the economic base. The seeming paradox is this: how can the superstructure be held to be the mechanism for the ruling class to maintain its economic hegemony intact, when this same superstructure, as often noted by Marx, passes laws that seem to be explicitly against the present interests of ruling-class members? For example, English factory legislation limiting the working day of laborers to ten hours (a piece of legislation that earns considerable notice from Marx in *Capital*) compromised, on the face of it, the interests of factory owners. Because such legislation limited the time per day that the factory laborer could work for the owner's profit (so that economists such as Oxford's Nassau Senior claimed the "last hour"—the profit hour—was being eliminated), it seemed very much against at least some ruling-class members' economic interests. So how, when the bill was passed, could the superstructure still be held by Marx as the executor of ruling-class interests?

16   The first thing to be made clear here is that Marx claims only that the state superstructure maintains *collective* ruling-class interests intact. So it is perfectly consistent with this claim that this or that member or group of members have their particular interests derogated for the good of the class as a whole. In this case, the collective interests of the ruling class were served by, *inter alia*, the better preservation of the endangered "golden goose"—the labor force—which the bill in question secured. Only by understanding this collective sense of ruling-class interests can one understand Marx's concept of the state and its relationship to the economic base. To recite the famous remark in the *Communist Manifesto:* "The bourgeois state is nothing but a mutual insurance pact of the bourgeois class both taken against its members individually and against members of the exploited class."

17   However, Marx emphasizes in this case that not even the particular interests of a ruling-class sector (albeit a preeminent sector) were in fact compromised by this or any other form of factory legislation. Despite the ideological rhetoric of a number of industrial capitalists (such as earthenware manufacturers), press organs (such as *The Economist*), academic apologies (such as Oxford's Nassau Senior), and others who opposed such legislation as "impossible," what the latter's passage in fact meant (insofar as it was effectively worded and applied)[11] was merely the "intensification of labor" by, mainly, the improvement of machinery. Thus the economic position and surplus-value appropriation rate of even the particular interests of the industrial bourgeoisie were maintained intact. Indeed, Marx suggests such and similar legislation actually benefits the interests of this particular section of the ruling class, as well as the ruling class generally:

1. by requiring greater capital outlays for the improved machinery, and thereby "hastening on the decline of small masters, and the concentration of capital" (*CI*, 477); and

2. by "directly depreciating the value of labor power" (*CI*, 406), and thereby "setting free" laborers replaced by machinery to swell the "industrial reserve army" available to the ruling class, both for new ventures and for disciplining those already employed.

So what appears to be the derogation by the superstructure (that is, factory legislation) of the interests of a central ruling-class sector is here, in fact, the maintenance and, indeed, promotion of its interests. In this case, ruling-class interests are distributively as well as collectively secured by superstructural phenomenon. Such a course of affairs is typical, in Marx's view. Hence, even though a crucial distinction must be made between the collective and particular interests of the ruling class, with the former, as always, primary in the relationship between base and superstructure, both sorts of interest are, in Marx's view, typically held intact, despite appearances to the contrary.[12]

So far we have focused upon the way in which Marx conceives the state as reflecting ruling-class economic interests. Now we look at the way in which he conceives the state as indispensable to the maintenance of these ruling-class economic interests. Consider his metaphor of "reflex" here. A "reflex" not only reflects the anatomy of the organism out of which it arises, but it is also indispensable to the maintenance of this anatomy. (Marx, we note, not only conceives of the state superstructure as "reflex," but of the economic infrastructure as "anatomy.") Thus, though Marx regards the "reflex" mechanism of the state as depending for its very existence upon a ruling-class economic "anatomy," he considers the persistence, though not existence, of this "anatomy" as, in turn, requiring the "reflex" mechanism of the state to preserve it.   18

Leaving aside Marx's explanatory mode of "reflex" and "anatomy," we now identify the two general requirements of any stable ruling-class economic order, which Marx conceives the state to systematically fulfill: 19

1. social appearance of sanctity; and
2. collective agency of enforcement for ruling-class interests.

We have already treated these in finer detail above. What we are concerned to do here is to consider them briefly from the point of view of their necessity as defense mechanisms for the stability of the economic order, from which we will be in a better position to make sense of the central role Marx ascribes to the superstructural phenomenon of class struggle.   20

The first requirement provides the protection of "mask" to the economic base (a mask that ideology compounds). It constitutes for Marx the overall "illusory" quality of the legal-political superstructure, which in all societies of man's history conceals the true nature of its ruling-class economic system. Though he never directly says so, Marx generally implies this sanctification by the legal-political superstructure to be a re-   21 quired cover-up mechanism for the persistence of any ruling-class economic order, without which it would be exposed (in the long run, ruinously) for the systematic exploitation system it is. Though in considering this indispensable "veil" function of the superstructure we unavoidably introduce ideology into our ambit of inquiry, the mere official institutionalization of economic power by the state organization must be appreciated as itself a hallowing of that power. That is, the state's very nature as a ceremonialized bureaucratic system officering the whole of society accords the economic order it overlays the mystique of elevated, lawful status. This sanctification of the economic order by the state is, indeed, a fundamental, if unremarked, component of the routine of mystification Marx analyzes in "The Fetishism of Commodities" (*CI,* 71–83): the apparent magical autonomy of commodities deriving from the very nature of the state as a vast, consecrated order of ranks, regulations, offices, and protocols standing like the armies of Yahweh over the ownership and exchange of goods.[13] We have here, in other words, the phenomenology of Kafka in historical materialist form. Sanctified by the terrifying aspect of the state, the economic system grinds as if by the ordinance of the Lord, and its products shuttle and move in inexorable pattern as if ruled by His "invisible hand."

22   The second requirement, on the other hand, is a straightforward organizational requirement. The ruling-class economic structure requires more than the particular relations of ownership constituting it in order to survive intact. Some additional collective coordinator, adjudicator, adjuster of enforcement in the interests of the ruling class as a whole must exist—that is, a legal and political superstructure—or the economic order in question will be ill equipped to maintain its hold for long. In the first place, individual interests of the ruling class are not necessarily consistent with the interests of this class as a whole; therefore, some way of resolving possible conflicts between these particular interests must be established "on top of" the production relations/economic structure. The state or superstructure that thus arises is, in traditional terminology, the expression of a "Social Contract" among ruling-class members to be governed by a common representative of their interests as a whole in order to protect themselves from class-destructive internecine strife.

23   In the second place, individual economic powers of members of the ruling class are easier to resist or usurp than these powers enlarged in a collective form; therefore, some combination of these powers in the unified body of a superstructure is necessary to ensure the maximum security required to sus-

tain the systematically exploitative and antagonistic economic order beneath. The state might that is thereby raised is, to sustain the language of Social Contract theory, the "Leviathan" of the ruling class: the latter's combination of power into a single, sovereign body presiding over the economic system underneath as the unbrookable "organized power of one class for oppressing another" (*CM*, 74).

"Social appearance of sanctity" and "collective agency for enforcement of ruling-class interests" would seem, then, coincident requirements for the persistence of the ruling-class economic order. Otherwise put, they are the indispensable shields of any durable system of exploitation—holist "fraud" and "force," respectively. Of course, Marx believed that a non-class economic order would require no such superstructure or state, insofar as there would be no intrinsic antagonisms of material interest to mystify or enforce. But so long as the economic order is class-ruptured, an "active, conscious, and official expression" of this base contradiction, the state, must for Marx preside over the former to ensure the preservation of its ruling-class ownership pattern and "laws of motion" of surplus-labor extraction.[14]

It is only when this indispensability of the legal-political superstructure to the preservation of the ruling-class economic order is clearly comprehended that we can understand why Marx counts superstructural class struggle—and all class struggle for Marx is "political" or superstructural[15]—as so important in history: "The history of all hitherto existing society is the history of class struggle" (*CM*, 45). We can formulate Marx's argument here as follows:

1. The legal and political superstructure is the indispensable general protector of the ruling-class economic order.

2. Therefore, to maintain the ruling-class economic order, the legal and political superstructure must be under the control of the ruling class. Otherwise the former will be insecure to the extent that its essential mechanism of defense is insecure. Conversely, to alter the ruling-class economic order, the legal and political superstructure must be seized from the control of the ruling class. Otherwise the former will remain secure to the extent that its essential mechanism of defense is secure.

3. The only effective way either to keep or to seize control over the legal and political superstructure is through class-for-itself (that is, political) action. This class action necessarily involves some form or other of class struggle insofar as the existence of a class presupposes the existence of another class or classes with antagonistic material interests. Such class-for-

itself action—"class struggle"—is alone effective in keeping or seizing control of the protective superstructure, because it alone possesses the realized "general form" (great social group aware of itself, and committed to acting, as a great social group) and the material-interest content (common economic stake) together required to achieve disposition over state machinery. Without this realized general form, attempts to keep or seize control of the superstructure will be too particularistic to be socially effective. And without the content of common material interests, this general form, in turn, will be too "idealist" to endure through the pressures of unshared relations to the means of life. Political class action or class struggle is, thus, the key to control of the state or superstructure—demonstrably in the past; probably, therefore, in the future.

4. From (1), (2), and (3), class struggle must more or less certainly be considered as the sole effective agency for keeping or seizing control of the legal and political superstructure and thereby, since the latter is the necessary general protector of the economic order, the only mode of action whereby maintenance or change of the real "anatomy" or "form" of a society can be effected.

26   This underlying argument of Marx's theory of the state and class struggle is guided by several important supportive beliefs that it is crucial to identify. Assuming (1) to be true, for example, (2) as a whole is true only if one believes, further, that there is no other practicable way of altering the ruling-class economic order than by seizing its indispensable mechanism of defense, the state. Yet the ruling class itself, or its superstructural agents, or some combination of these, might evolve the state away from its historical function of ruling-class protection and into conformity with its long-pretended general interest function, with no such seizure "from beneath" required (a possibility in which social democrats believe). Or, again, the economic order might be altered by bypassing superstructural mediation altogether—with state repression at the same time effectively resisted and negated—through workers and others taking over, slowly or rapidly, the means of production directly (a possibility to which anarchists are committed). Or whatever. There are more ways than one to skin a cat, more ways than one to subvert the economic order than by seizing its superstructural armor from ruling-class control. But these alternative possibilities Marx must—and does—believe to be impracticable in inferring the latter part of (2) from (1). Then, even assuming all of (2) to be true—notwithstanding alternative possibilities like the above—(3) is true if and only if one

believes, still further, that great groups of men in society can-not be enduringly united on grounds (such as humanist) other than class relations of production or material interests. This sort of alternative Marx in one way or another certainly en-tertained, but—again—firmly rejected as lightheaded, is not downright reactionary.

However, despite his general *rigeur de ligne* here, there are 27 a few largely ignored hints in Marx's mature work that the schema we have set out above—reasoning from the indispens-ability of the superstructure as a general protector of the ruling-class economic order to the view that class struggle is the only mode of action whereby maintenance or change of the underlying "essence" of society is secured—is not quite so restrictive as is generally thought.

To begin with, the possibility of specific superstructural 28 agents not in fact protecting the ruling-class economic pattern, but being quite "free from partisanship," is not only allowed by Marx but described by him as having actually obtained, at the height of industrial capitalism (*CI*, 9).

Then again, he was well aware of the possibility that ruling- 29 class members (such as the young capitalist Robert Owen) could disengage from their present economic interests; and, indeed, he openly called for, in his Preface to *Capital*, their pro-moting through the superstructure the interests of the work-ing class: "Apart from higher motives, therefore, their own most important interests dictate to the classes that are for the nonce the ruling ones, the removal of all legally remov-able hindrances to the free development of the working class" (*CI*, 9).

Still again, he occasionally remarked on the possibility that 30 the class struggle need not be violent, and that power might change hands from the capitalists to the proletarians peace-fully: "We know of the allowances that we must make for the institutions, customs and traditions of the various countries: and we do not deny that there are countries such as America, England, and I would add Holland if I knew your institutions better, where the working people may achieve their goal by peaceful means" (*OB*, 494).

All these qualifications, however, are quite compatible with 31 Marx's line of thought as we have formulated it. He recognizes and applauds superstructural agents, such as the "courageous" factory inspector Leonard Horner, who honor the state's claim to be the protector of the interests of all. But men such as Horner, he holds, are the exeption, not the rule. He is impressed by the young millionaire Robert Owen's rising above economic interests to devote his life to industrial communes, but he observes that Owen remains élitist in his theory, and is not emulated, but vilified, by an increasingly defensive ruling class. He calls for "the classes that are for the nonce the ruling ones" to promote through the state the working class's "free development." But his appeal is not at all inconsistent with his line of thought, as it might first appear.[16] He emphasizes the possibility that "working people may achieve their goal by peaceful means," such as voting ruling-class representatives out of political office; but such possibility, so far as it effectively occurs or is alowed to occur, is still for him a "seizure" of the state from ruling-class hands, as it also is for them. In short, none of Marx's important qualifications here is inconsistent with his underlying argument. Rather, they disclose an openness and sophistication to his concept of the state that are not generally appreciated.

32   In summary, then, Marx conceives of the state as the indispensable "mask" and "weapon" protecting the ruling class's economic hegemony; holds that its existence as such requires its control by the ruling class to sustain this hegemony, and by some other class(es) to alter it; and maintains, in turn, that political class struggle is the only effective way of keeping or getting this control. This is, in brief, Marx's firm line on the legal and political superstructure and its disposition in all periods of history.

33   As we can readily discern, the importance granted to the superstructure in Marx's theory is very considerable. Indeed, he lays such great emphasis on it in his social philosophy (an inversion of Hegel's notion of the state as the bearer of the Universal) that one of the most moving criticisms of his position— exemplified by the anarchist Bakunin's opposition—is that he is an ultra-authoritarian, who betrays the working-class struggle in his German love for the state.[17] But whatever the merits of his position on the significance of the legal and political superstructure, we can see that—for all its dependence on the economic infrastructure—it is of central importance to Marx as a socio-historical factor. That it is normally in a "reflex" relationship with the economic "anatomy" underneath does not—as many have thought—render it somehow impotent or superfluous for him as a mechanism or phenomenon. On the contrary, the state is as vitally important for Marx in the ordinary life process of a society as defense mechanisms are for Freud in the ordinary life process of an individual. It is the historically constructed and visible hold whereby internal conflict is maintained in the grip of unseen (economic) structure: the

so-to-say conscious "ego-formation" of society overlaying, regulating, and repressing the hidden contradictions beneath, in the defense of established but unacknowledged interests and their enslaving pattern.

KEY TO ABBREVIATIONS

In each case, the first and last pages of the primary text (including author prefaces) are added in brackets to help the reader locate quotations in other editions. A star (*) indicates that the translator and/or editor is not given.

CI *Capital* (Volume I), Karl Marx. Trans. Samuel Moore and Edward Aveling, ed. Frederick Engels. Progress Publishers, Moscow, 1965 (7–774).

CII *Capital* (Volume II), Karl Marx, Trans. I. Lasker, ed. Frederick Engels. Progress Publishers, Moscow, 1967 (25–527).

CIII *Capital* (Volume III), Karl Marx, Ed. Frederick Engels. Progress Publishers, Moscow, 1954 (23–910).*

CM *Manifesto of the Communist Party.* Karl Marx and Frederick Engels. Trans. and ed. Frederick Engels and Samuel Moore. Foreign Languages Publishing House, Moscow, 1969 (11–91).

GID *The German Ideology*, Karl Marx and Frederick Engels. Trans. and ed. S. Ryazanskaya. Progress Publishers, Moscow, 1964 (21–596).

OB *On Britain*, Karl Marx and Frederick Engels. Lawrence and Wishart Ltd. London, 1962 (1–584).*

PofP *The Poverty of Philosophy*, Karl Marx. Ed. Frederick Engels. Progress Publishers, Moscow, 1966 (25–152).*

RZ *Articles from the Nene Rheinische Zeitung*, Karl Marx and Frederick Engels. Trans. S. Ryazanskaya, ed. B. Isaacs. Progress Publishers, Moscow, 1964 (21–596).

SC *Selected Correspondence*, Karl Marx and Frederick Engels. Foreign Languages Publishing House, Moscow, 1953 (25–571).*

YM *Writings of the Young Marx on Philosophy and Society.* Ed. L. D. Easton and K. H. Guddat. Doubleday, New York, 1967 (35–267).

Notes: (i) Unless otherwise stated, italics within excerpts from the above texts are added. (ii) All further references to the original German of these texts are from the *Marx-Engels-Werke* (Volumes 1–39): Dietz Verlag, Berlin, 1956–1968.

Notes

1. Sometimes Marx uses the term "superstructure" to refer to just legal and political institutions, and sometimes he uses it to apply more broadly to these as well as ideology and forms of social consciousness as a unitary whole. We use the term in the same permissive way, with the context rendering its precise referent evident.

2. Even the "gradual accretions" of law are consciously constructed, each accretion itself being the result of a process of formal deliberation, judgment, and codification. It is by virtue of being a conscious construction *on top of* the "hidden" mechanisms of the economic order that Marx uses the term *super*structure.

3. This favorite claim of Marx that relations of production obtain "independently of the will of individuals" is often wrongly interpreted as a denial of free will. Marx is, however, making no such metaphysical claim, but is merely stating the empirically incontrovertible truth that the economic order carries on independently of the will (as opposed to actions) of individuals (as opposed to groups). See *GID*, 357 ff.

4. Note here the similarity in principle to Locke's notion of the state as an "umpire" arising to resolve disputes over individual property. Like Marx, Locke (not to mention Hobbes and others) takes it as obvious that the erection of the state depends upon already existing antagonisms of interest. However, unlike Marx, these philosophers do not discern a ruling-class pattern to such antagonisms of interest, which for Marx renders the "umpire" or "Leviathan" of the state ultimately subordinate rather sovereign in its function.

5. Marx's theory of the genesis of the state seems superior to the Social Contract theory of Hobbes, Locke, and others inasmuch as the latter cannot explain how individuals first come to submit to this body, except by an as-if fiction of universal consent. Marx's theory, on the other hand, requires no such as-if posit. People's submission to the state is originally accomplished by organized force, whose function is to protect a ruling-class economic order (cf. the early Rousseau's less developed, but similar account in the *Discourse on the Origin of Inequality*).

6. Marx's theory of communist society must, however, be rigorously distinguished from the subsequent putative practice of it in "communist countries."

7. Note the telling satire of Social Contract theory informing Marx's declaration here (*Marx-Engels-Werke*, VII, 288).

8. What about proprietary disputes among productive workers themselves?

    i. These proprietary disputes constitute a small fraction of the proprietary disputes that the state adjudicates because productive workers' ownership is for the most part confined to ownership of personal labor-power, and because the costs of state adjudication are generally beyond productive workers' means to pay. Therefore, the domain of cases is minimal.

    ii. Where there are proprietary disputes among productive workers themselves, these derive from the inherent antagonisms of the ruling-class economic order.

9. These requirements of productive force development are what enable a new ruling class to supplant the old. The state does not cease to be a "class weapon" here. It changes from the "class weapon" of an old ruling class (such as feudal or capitalist), whose rule does not correspond to the technological requirements of the day, to the "class weapon" of a new ruling class (capitalist or proletarian, respectively), whose rule does correspond to the technological requirements of the day. Revolutionary political class struggle, then, is only the social medium whereby a necessary transfer of state power occurs in accordance with productive force requirements. It remains, thus, superstructural, even in its revolutionary function (a point that "Marxists" who fix only on class struggle have perilously, and we think world-historically, missed for a century).

10. Society's revolution from a capitalist to a socialist economic order is historically unique for Marx in that: i. the new ruling class is constituted of the "immense majority of society" (its productive workers), not, as in the past, "a small minority"; ii. its ruling-class order is only "transitional," not, as in the past, epochal; and iii. the legal and political superstructure that protects this rule of the productive workers does not remain, but, with the dissolution of society's "bourgeois remnants," withers away altogether. In short, with the full achievement of communal ownership of the forces of production, there are no classes and, thus, no state required to protect the ownership of one.

11. Marx frequently draws attention to the inadequate formulation and application of parliamentary legislation (e.g., *CI*, 479–80, 494–95), which ensures that little or nothing is, in fact, changed by such except official documents. This is one of the common duping features of the legal-political superstructure that occasions Marx's general description of the latter as "illusory."

12. This is not to say, certainly, that Marx is suggesting that legislation such as the ten-hour bill should have been opposed by the working class, or was even possible without their militant pressure for it. On the contrary, Marx's dialectical position here is that it is in precisely this sort of way that the seed of revolution is nourished within the bosom of the established order: what is good for the latter is also at the same time nurturing the agencies of its future destruction.

13. Consider here the standard inscription on American coinage: "In God We Trust."

14. It is also implied by Marx (e.g., *CI*, 15) that the *extent of the state's mechanisms of "fraud" and "force" increases in direct proportion to the extent of the struggle between the ruling and ruled classes:* so that, for example, the more proletarians organize as a class against capitalists as a class, the greater will be the state's mechanisms of "fraud" and "force." Thus, to apply this principle to

post-Marxian circumstances, to the extent that the struggle between proletarian and capitalist classes increases (for instance,
in prewar Germany) to just that extent will the state's mechanisms of "fraud" and "force" increase (prewar German fascism,
for instance); and, conversely, to the extent that such class struggle diminishes (such as in postwar Germany), to just that extent
will the state's mechanisms of "fraud" and "force" be reduced
(as in postwar German parliamentary democracy). Contrary then
to liberal-democratic theory, which sees fascism as an inexplicable aberration of the state's normal functions, Marxist theory, as
we have it, explains fascism as a paradigmatic exemplification
of these functions, obtaining in law-governed correspondence to
struggle between the proletariat and capitalist classes.

15. Thus Marx says such things as "the struggle of class against class
is a political [i.e., superstructural] struggle" (*PofP,* 150); and, more
elaborately:

> On the other hand, however, every movement in which the
> working class comes out as a class against the ruling classes
> and tries to coerce them by pressure from without is a po-
> litical movement. For instance, the attempts in a particular
> factory or even in a particular trade to force a shorter working
> day out of individual capitalists by strikes, etc., is a purely
> economic movement. On the other hand, the movement to
> force through an eight-hour, etc., law is a political movement.
> And in this way out of the separate economic movements of
> the workers there grows up everywhere a political movement,
> that is to say a movement of the class, with the object of en-
> forcing its interests in a general form, in a form possessing
> general, socially coercive force (*SC,* 328).

16. G. A. Cohen, in personal correspondence, makes the following
point here, worth citing *verbatim:*

> The *Capital,* p. 9 quote is not puzzling when we read the con-
> text which shows why it is in the interests of the ruling class
> to allow the working class to develop itself: it is because then,
> when the revolution comes, there'll be less chance they'll have
> their heads chopped off. If you're going to be displaced, better
> "humane" than "brutal" displacers. Here, interestingly, some-
> thing is in the interest of the people who are capitalists which
> is in no way in the interests of the survival of capitalism.
> Marx is saying that there is something in the interests of
> capitalists as individuals which they should consult against
> even their class interests, given the imminence of revolution.
> I don't want a deluge if it isn't going to be aprés moi.

17. Marx says, in a canonical text: "The movement of the proletariat is the self-conscious, independent movement of the immense majority, in the interest of the immense majority" (*CM*, 59–60). That is, the proletarian class struggle is a struggle of: i. the *immense majority* (i.e., all wage-dependent productive workers); ii. in a *self-conscious* way (i.e., comprehending itself as one class of such workers); iii. via an *independent* movement (i.e., not led by an external elite), and iv. for the *universal* interest, (i.e., the interest of all concerned). This is, it is clear, a radically democratic schema, not followed by Marx's most prominent successors, such as Lenin, who eschews at least principle (iii), and rarely acknowledged by his most outspoken critics, including Bakunin.

CHAPTER TEN

THE RETURN OF THE
STATE AND CORPORATISM

Despite their animosity for one another, Marxists and liberal pluralists share the tendency to view states and political institutions as subsidiary to other, more potent social forces. For neither of them is the actual machinery of government and administration the central focus of power. Both view the state as an arbitrator of struggles whose source lies elsewhere. Whereas Marxists view the outcome of this arbitration as a foregone conclusion—the ruling interests in society will inevitably get their way—liberal pluralists believe that there is no single ruling class and that there are no foregone conclusions in this competition. To understand this critical point, a short review of the conclusions reached in the previous chapter is necessary.

Terms like "the state" or "the state apparatus" are commonplace in Marxist literature. One can hardly read a Marxist essay without encountering statements such as "the state and its apparatus of control dominate the political process for the sake of the interests of the ruling class." The state, Marxists declare, is an active and biased participant in the struggle for hegemony. Because it is inevitably captured by the forces that control a political community's wealth, it acts to defend and advance partisan interests, to repress those forces that might threaten the ruling powers that be, to legitimate existing divisions of power, prerogative, and property.

Marxists have nothing but scorn for the liberal argument that the state is only an impartial arbiter for the various group interests. The notion that the state constitutes a high-minded clearing house for the efficient management and regulation of contending interests is dismissed by Marxists as so much perverse and self-serving bourgeois ideology. Much the same reaction can be expected for the idea that the state incarnates a "general will" transcending the particular concerns of different groups. What is deliberately being ignored in both of these ideological self-portraits is the marked determination with which the state pursues certain very predictable interests and the equal regularity with which it disdains others.

For all of their concentration on the state, however, Marxists do not recognize it as an independent source of initiative, policy, and action. In the end, their position is society-centered. The state reflects or expresses the dominant interests that prevail in society. It is an "executive committee" for ruling-class interests, a "superstructure" to other and more basic forces. To understand its role and functioning, it is imperative to look away from the state apparatus itself and toward those groups that wield it for their own purposes. Orthodox Marxists reject the proposition that the state qua state is an autonomous actor in the political process. Indeed, it is a cardinal element in their belief system that there cannot be—surely not for any significant stretch of time—a basic incongruity between those that control the socioeconomic level of public life and those that control the state.

If Marxists tend to view state activity as determined by the material base of civil society, they do, nevertheless, recognize the state as an active participant, indeed, a critical factor in the political struggle. Liberal pluralists, by contrast, tend to see matters quite differently. They have shown a marked reluctance to speak of the state as something distinct from the governmental process. Recall Easton's famous definition of the political, and the point becomes clear: it involves the authoritative allocation of resources. It makes no reference to the state—certainly not as an independent institution that allocates these resources according to an agenda it autonomously wills. Insofar as the state receives attention, it is as the arena in which the various interest groups contend for power within a single arbitrating framework. It is a fair bet that if, during the heyday of the behavioral revolution, anyone would have insisted on the self-standing and irreducible status of the state, he/she would have been accused of having committed a gross terminological mystification.

Government, of course, has its functions to discharge, but these are related more to steering, to converting inputs into outputs, to processing demands, and to allocating resources than to exercising its own prerogatives or being the autonomous source of political initiatives. To be sure, Easton did describe a category of inputs that he called "withinputs" (that is, inputs that originated from within the conversion process itself), but these were understood to be of secondary significance. Similarly, economic theorists of democracy, who tend to perceive of politics in terms of the market dynamics of supply and demand, have little room in their model for independent state intervention. The idea that the will of an autonomous state (1) shapes market forces, (2) is itself a party to the competition, (3) designs the context of market rivalries, and (4) acts even against the will of the participants to achieve certain policy goals is alien to their way of thinking.

This tendency to debunk conceptions of the state that claim to be more than a synonym for the process of government or the political system was an integral part of the behavioral revolution. In focusing on the dynamics of actual political behavior, states became reduced to the individuals and groups that comprised them. The commitment to "methodological individualism" made it difficult to relate to collective entities and empirically elusive constructions such as states. Perhaps most important of all, the study of the state as an independent entity was tainted by its association with the static formalities of the institutional-legal approach. And this was the very approach that behavioralism had set out to supplant.

The 1980s witnessed a major outpouring of research that, in a variety of ways, converged on a single broad front of agreement: "the explanatory centrality of states as potent and autonomous organizational actors."[1] Some have taken this transformation to be truly revolutionary. Skocpol, echoing the categories of Thomas Kuhn, writes that "a paradigmatic shift seems to be under way in the macroscopic social sciences, a shift that involves a fundamental rethinking of the role of states in relation to economies and societies."[2]

According to this old/new approach, the state is more than a dependent variable, more than a mere address for the aggregation and articulation of social interests. Although it is obviously the target of many demands, it is also the source of critical initiatives. A growing body of research indicates that political changes often originate from above, that is, through state-direction. Elites that are not recruited from the ruling classes and who reject their authority have embarked on ambitious programs of political reform. Not infrequently, the state's power is far more important in initiating change than the influence of parties or interest groups. In extreme cases, state power, responding not to aggregated inputs but heeding its own voice and political vision, has been used to unseat ruling classes, to initiate industrialization campaigns, and to embark on military adventures. The image of the state as a mechanism that processes demands originating elsewhere is therefore in need of substantial revision.

What particularly requires rethinking, the statists claim, are the prevalent tendencies to reduce politics, almost automatically, to political culture, political sociology, or political economy. Whether Marxist or liberal pluralist in inspiration, this tendency cannot withstand the scrutiny of recent research. Although it hardly requires repeating that viewing politics in terms of its cultural, social, and economic antecedents remains of undiminished importance, the statist approach is unwilling to accept these approaches as exhaustive. The state as a relatively autonomous political actor needs to be brought back in.

Nothing in this statist view is meant to return us to the days of the old legal-institutional approach with its state-centered formalisms. Neither is it meant to initiate a rush to construct grand theories of the state in the manner of Hegel. The state, as a wielder of sovereign power—not as a constitutional-legal entity or as a philosophical idea—is the focus of this approach. Its research agenda is directed to exploring the ways in which states as actors influence political outcomes.

But it is not only the state that appears to be making an intellectual comeback. Alongside the renewed concern with states as autonomous actors, there has arisen a broader and more diffuse return to taking institutions and political organizations seriously. To distinguish this approach from the old legal-institutional approach, March and Olson describe it as "the new institutionalism."[3] They characterize it as an attempt to blend "elements of the old institutionalism into the non-institutional styles of recent theories of politics." Although this groundswell of interest in the centrality of institutions remains "far from coherent or consistent," and although it often contains no more than "fragments of ideas," it has, they contend, insinuated its way into very substantial areas of political science research.

Like the statists, those returning to institutional analysis resist the tendency to reduce politics to economic forces and social contexts. Politics is not merely the aggregate consequence of individual behavior; it is far from exhausted by the calculation of self-interest. Nor are they entirely happy with a view of politics that begins and ends with the allocation of resources. These prevailing tendencies simplify and distort what is, in fact, a considerably more complex reality.

Institutions, they insist, are not simple mirrors to social forces. "Institutions seem to be neither neutral reflections of exogenous environmental forces nor neutral arenas for the performances of individuals driven by exogenous preferences and expectations."[4] In all of its variants, the "new institutionalism" attributes considerable significance to the role that institutions themselves play in shaping policy outputs.

> The bureaucratic agency, the legislative committee, and the appellate court are arenas for contending social forces, but they are also collections of standard operating procedures and structures that define and defend interests. They are political actors in their own right.[5]

Institutions often contain sufficient internal coherence to justify the claim that they, in themselves, "affect the flow of history." Possessing a standardized process of choice—in other words, an institutional decision-making process—affects the choice itself as well as its reception by society. Compromises accepted by a legislature, for example, "become endowed with separate meaning and force" not explicable in terms of the individual actors involved or the nature of the compromise achieved.

Preferences are not produced outside the process of political choice and then converted into authoritative outputs. It is more accurate to say that leaders perceive their policy alternatives in terms of the very administrative agencies through which decisions are made and implemented. In other words, the pursuit of alternatives necessarily takes place in an organized institutional context. Political objectives and meanings develop in the course of the political process itself rather than emerging in the socioeconomic context and then presenting themselves full-grown to the world of politics. Even the struggle for economic power and social standing—an arena that appears to be extra-political—has a bona fide institutional aspect. After all, holding office can easily alter the distribution of wealth, power, and access.

At a more philosophical level, viewing the organizations of government exclusively as agencies for allocation and regulation misses the very special significance that institutions possess in the construction of human meaning, human order, and human ends. We often clarify our sense of the human vocation, create and confirm our interpretations of life, and exercise our moral personalities as participants in the rituals of politics. The pleasures of political life are frequently in the process itself, in the odyssey of self-discovery and self-realization that it offers. Indeed, those who understand politics as entirely outcome-oriented—that is, as populated by rational actors directing their efforts toward the realization of specific interests—are likely to find themselves regularly bewildered by those who seem to care as much for the right to participate and for the ideas they defend as for the actual outcome.

Needless to say, this turn of the academic wheel of fortune and fashion has not been greeted with unanimous cheer. Gabriel Almond, the figure most associated with structure-functionalism in political science, has expressed serious reservations about the statist program.[6] First of all, Almond denies that the behavioral approaches of the 1960s are reductionist. Bringing the state in is entirely compatible with systems theory and structure-functionalism. Indeed, he claims that the role of the state receives ample treatment in the pre-statist literature. The concept of a political system that they advanced

> included the phenomena of the state—the legally empowered and legitimately coercive institutions—but it also included these new extralegal and paralegal institutions of political parties, interest groups, media of communication, as well as social institutions such as family, school, church and the like, insofar as they affected political processes.[7]

Beyond defending the record of systems analysis and structure-functionalism, Almond launches a spirited attack on the statists—one that is quite characteristic of the behavioral perspective. If the term "state" is to be meaningful and operational, it needs to be specified rigorously. States are a congeries of many distinct things. They comprise "bureaucracies, courts, armies, parliaments, parties, interest groups, media of communication and public opinion."[8] How then are we to weight these various constituent elements when we refer to state activity? What the state is depends on which measures we use to analyze it. In the end, therefore, either the term "state" will be "disaggregated," that is, broken down into its various components, or it will be rendered amorphous and obscure. Statists, Almond concludes, have urged the adoption of "ambiguous phraseology in the place of a hard-won tradition of operational rigor."[9]

Next of kin to the return-of-the-state movement are the corporatists. Both originated sometime in the late 1970s. Both corporatists and their statist allies accord the state an independence from class rule or interest-group politics. Like the statists, corporatists see their main theoretical opposition as coming from the pluralists and the Marxists. And, once again, like the statists, they do not regard their position as a radical abandonment of the pluralist and Marxist points of view. Rather, they understand their objective as the broadening, updating, and synthesizing of the approaches presented by their liberal and radical precursors.

If the return-of-the-state theorists focus on the state itself as a lever of change and initiative, the corporatists are more concerned with the relationship between the institutional organization of the state and the institutional organization of social and economic interests. They believe that both Marxists and pluralists overlook what has become the dominant mode of interface between these organizational conglomerates during the "late capitalist" era. If Marxists are too prone to reduce the state's actions to the advancement of dominant material interests, the pluralists are equally remiss in understanding the state as an arena for the processing of group interests. In truth, corporatists claim, the state and the bodies representing social interests in recent decades have become increasingly interdependent, an interlocking directorate. In other words, a process of incorporation has taken place in which the state and the major social and economic interest–related institutions act in concert with one another.

There is then a growing interpenetration between governmental authorities and organized interests in political decision making. Interest-group leaders are increasingly drawn into the machinery of government. They become part of the process through which policy is determined, a part of the *governmental* system and not merely a part of the *political* system. In other words, interest organizations become a partner to the state in directing public affairs. They no longer simply express interests; they become part of the process in which these interests are deliberated, formed, and implemented. As such, interest-group leaders not infrequently are prone to self-regulation; they tend to subordinate their own sectional interests to those of a perceived collective interest. Succinctly put, their independence from the state has become increasingly tenuous.

A number of factors have made for the obsolescence of the older (Marxist and pluralist) accounts. Growing concentration of economic power in large, near-oligopolistic firms and unions, growing interdependence of the economy's various components parts, the potential for large-scale damage in the event of technical or financial malfunction, etc., have made government intervention and regulation both indispensable and omnipresent. And yet the power possessed by those to be regulated is so great that state agencies are limited in their ability to enforce standards or policies to which their "clients" object profoundly. Without the cooperation of the regulated, it is unlikely that government policies will be successfully implemented. By the same token, these key interests are unable to capture the state for their purposes. What emerges is a process of corporate bargaining among the various groups. In this process, the state constitutes the arena in which the compacts are hammered out; it is, moreover, the coercive guarantor that these compacts will be adhered to.

While interest groups of secondary importance may retain their pluralist competitive character, corporatists contend that key interests tend to undergo the corporatizing process. Marxists would identify these key groups, of course, with the ruling economic class and dismiss other interests such as labor unions as subordinate and impotent. Pluralists, for their part, would be reluctant to admit that certain groups are overwhelmingly favored in the political process. They argue that capital and labor are "countervailing powers," that is, powers that compete freely and tend to balance each other in the governmental arena.

For the corporatists, these key interests neither balance one another competitively nor are they narrowly identifiable with a single, dominant, capital-based elite. Key interests tend to interlock; labor and capital, for example, tend to take joint responsibility for directing production. In the context of the state, policy issues are bargained to conclusions with which all three participants can accommodate themselves and for which all are prepared to take responsibility. What corporatists are attempting to describe, therefore, is a political system in which interests organize and relate to the state in a novel way, one that differs markedly from the standard conceptions of both capitalism and socialism.

Although there is nothing in either the corporatist or the statist position that is fatally irreconcilable with the liberal democratic ideal, neither can it be said that these views provide a particular cause for cheer. After all, the image of a massive interlocking directorate joining government, business, labor, the military, and so on, is uncomfortably close to views of a "power elite" that critics of liberal democracy voiced a generation ago. This critique, best known through its presentation in C. Wright Mills's *The Power Elite*, contends that the various elites controlling government, business, and the military (labor was seen as far less important) constitute a single dominating elite, members of which circulate easily between its various branches. This elite comprises a tightly knit complex of command positions that jointly control the public life of America. Very notably, Mills sees this power elite as irresponsible and self-centered, one that fails to represent the nation's real interests.

Part of this view, although surely not all of it, resurfaces in the corporatist/statist position. The ease of circulation and the concerted decision-making processes among the various elite groups are the most obvious points of convergence. Where the corporatists/statists differ from their power elite forebears is (1) in their estimation of the elite's independence from the popular base of government and (2) in the cohesiveness that binds the various elites into a single one. In Mills's view, the power elite is both a cohesive unit and a world apart; it is inbred and closed—primarily concerned with its own interests, prerogatives, and future.

From the corporatist/statist point of view, these conclusions do not necessarily follow. Decisions may be concerted and elites may circulate freely between command posts without entailing either oligarchic rule or a conspiratorial elite. The corporatist view merely asserts that, given the profound interdependence of the various elite groups in the modern liberal capitalist state, they tend to take joint responsibility for the policies they wish to implement. The various elites therefore are not simply different limbs belonging to the same dominating political body. They act together, because failing to do so would redound to everyone's injury and not necessarily because they form a cabal with sinister intentions. It may not be a New England town meeting, but it is still a far cry from a conspiratorial oligarchy.

NOTES

1. Theda Skocpol, "Bringing the State Back In," in Peter B. Evans, Dietrich Rueschemeyer, and Theda Skocpol, eds. *Bringing the State Back In* (Cambridge, Cambridge University Press, 1985), p. 6.

2. *Ibid.*, p. 7.

3. James G. March and Johan P. Olson, "The New Institutionalism: Organizational Factors in Political Life," *American Political Science Review*, 74 (1984), pp. 734–749.

4. *Ibid.*, p. 742.

5. *Ibid.*, p. 738.

6. "The Return to the State." *American Political Science Review*, Vol. 82, no. 3 (September 1988), p. 853.

7. *Ibid.*, p. 857.

8. *Ibid.*

9. *Ibid.*, p. 872. For a critique of Almond, see the comments of Nordlinger, Lowi, and Fabbrini in *ibid.*, pp. 875–901.

SUGGESTIONS FOR FURTHER READING

Almond, G. A., "The Return to the State," *American Political Science Review* 82, 3 (1988) pp. 853–874 and responses by Nordlinger, Lowi, and Fabbrini, pp. 874–901.

Berger, S., ed., *Organizing Interest in Western Europe: Pluralism, Corporatism and the Transformation of Politics* (Cambridge, Cambridge University Press, 1981).

Krasner, S., "Review Article: Approaches to the State: Alternative Conceptions and Historical Dynamics," *Comparative Politics* 16, 2 (1984) pp. 223–246.

Lehmbruch, G., and Schmitter, P. C., eds., *Patterns of Corporatist Policy Making* (Beverly Hills and London, Sage, 1982).

Nettl, J. P., "The State as Conceptual Variable," *World Politics* 20 (1968) pp. 559–592.

Winkler, J. T., "Corporatism," *European Journal of Sociology* 17 (1976) pp. 100–136.

Theda Skocpol

Bringing the State Back In: Strategies of Analysis in Current Research

A sudden upsurge of interest in "the state" has occurred in 1
comparative social science in the past decade. Whether as an
object of investigation or as something invoked to explain outcomes of interest, the state as an actor or an institution has
been highlighted in an extraordinary outpouring of studies by
scholars of diverse theoretical proclivities from all of the major
disciplines. The range of topics explored has been very wide.
Students of Latin America, Africa, and Asia have examined
the roles of states in instituting comprehensive political reforms, helping to shape national economic development, and
bargaining with multinational corporations.[1] Scholars interested in the advanced industrial democracies of Europe, North
America, and Japan have probed the involvements of states in
developing social programs and in managing domestic and
international economic problems.[2] Comparative-historical investigators have examined the formation of national states, the
disintegration and rebuilding of states in social revolutions,
and the impact of states on class formation, ethnic relations,
women's rights, and modes of social protest.[3] Economic historians and political economists have theorized about states
as institutors of property rights and as regulators and dis-
torters of markets.[4] And cultural anthropologists have explored
the special meanings and activities of "states" in non-Western
settings.[5]

No explicitly shared research agenda or general theory has 2
tied such diverse studies together. Yet I shall argue in this essay that many of them have implicitly converged on complementary arguments and strategies of analysis. The best way
to make the point is through an exploration of the issues addressed in a range of comparative and historical studies—
studies that have considered states as weighty actors and
probed how states affect political and social processes through
their policies and their patterned relationships with social
groups. First, however, it makes sense to underline the paradigmatic reorientation implied by the phrase "bringing the state
back in."[6]

From P. Evans, D. Rueschemeyer, and T. Skocpol, eds., *Bringing the State Back In*
(Cambridge, Cambridge University Press, 1985), pp. 3–37. Reprinted by permission.

3   *From Society-Centered Theories to a Renewed Interest in States.*
There can be no gainsaying that an intellectual sea change is
under way, because not long ago the dominant theories and research agendas of the social sciences rarely spoke of states. This
was true even—or perhaps one should say especially—when
politics and public policy making were at issue. Despite important exceptions, society-centered ways of explaining politics
and governmental activities were especially characteristic of
the pluralist and structure-functionalist perspectives predominant in political science and sociology in the United States during the 1950s and 1960s.[7] In these perspectives, the state was
considered to be an old-fashioned concept, associated with dry
and dusty legal-formalist studies of nationally particular constitutional principles. Alternative concepts were thought to be
more compatible with scientific, generalizing investigations.[8]
"Government" was viewed primarily as an arena within which
economic interest groups or normative social movements contended or allied with one another to shape the making of public
policy decisions. Those decisions were understood to be *allocations* of benefits among demanding groups. Research centered
on the societal "inputs" to government and on the distributive
effects of governmental "outputs." Government itself was not
taken very seriously as an independent actor, and in comparative research, variations in governmental organizations were
deemed less significant than the general "functions" shared by
the political systems of all societies.

4   As often happens in intellectual life, the pluralist and
structure-functionalist paradigms fostered inquiries that led
toward new concerns with phenomena they had originally
de-emphasized conceptually. When pluralists focused on the
determinants of particular public policy decisions, they often
found that governmental leaders took initiatives well beyond
the demands of social groups or electorates; or they found that
government agencies were the most prominent participants in
the making of particular public policy decisions. Within pluralist theoretical premises, there were but limited ways to accommodate such findings.[9] In the classic pluralist studies of
New Haven politics, Mayor Richard Lee's strong individual
initiatives for urban renewal were extensively documented but
not grounded in any overall state-centered analysis of the potential for certain kinds of mayors to make new uses of federal
funding.[10] In major works about "bureaucratic politics" such
as Graham Allison's *Essence of Decision* and Morton Halperin's
Bureaucratic Politics and Foreign Policy, government agencies
were treated individually, as if they were pure analogues

of the competing societal interest groups of classical plural-ism.[11] The structure and activities of the U.S. state as a whole receded from view and analysis in this approach.[12]

Like the pluralists, yet on a broader canvas, when structure- 5 functionalist students of comparative political development set out to "apply" their grand theories to Western European his-tory or to particular sets of non-Western polities, they often found poor fits between historical patterns and sequences and those posited by the original concepts and assumptions. "Po-litical development" (itself found to be an overly evolutionist conception) ended up having more to do with concrete inter-national and domestic struggles over state building than with any inherent general logic of socioeconomic "differentiation." Most telling in this regard were the historically oriented stud-ies encouraged or sponsored by the Social Science Research Council's Committee on Comparative Politics toward the end of its life span of 1954–1972.[13] In many ways, the ideas and findings about states to be reviewed here grew out of reactions set in motion by such confrontations of the committee's grand theories with case-study and comparative-historical evidence.

Especially among younger scholars, new ideas and find- 6 ings have also arisen from an alternative theoretical lineage. From the mid-1960s onward, critically minded "neo-Marxists" launched a lively series of debates about "the capitalist state." By now, there are conceptually ramified and empirically wide-ranging literatures dealing especially with the roles of states in the transition from feudalism to capitalism, with the socio-economic involvements of states in advanced industrial capi-talist democracies, and with the nature and role of states in dependent countries within the world capitalist economy.[14] Neo-Marxists have, above all, debated alternative understand-ings of the socioeconomic functions performed by the capital-ist state. Some see it as an instrument of class rule, others as an objective guarantor of production relations or economic accumulation, and still others as an arena for political class struggles.

Valuable concepts and questions have emerged from these 7 neo-Marxist debates, and many of the comparative and his-torical studies to be discussed here have drawn on them in defining researchable problems and hypotheses. Yet at the the-oretical level, virtually all neo-Marxist writers on the state have retained deeply embedded society-centered assumptions, not allowing themselves to doubt that, at base, states are in-herently shaped by classes or class struggles and function to preserve and expand modes of production.[15] Many possible forms of autonomous state action are thus ruled out by definitional fiat. Furthermore, neo-Marxist theorists have too often sought to generalize—often in extremely abstract ways—about features or functions shared by *all* states within a mode of production, a phase of capitalist accumulation, or a position in the world capitalist system. This makes it difficult to assign causal weight to variations in state structures and activities across nations and short time periods, thereby undercutting the usefulness of some neo-Marxist schemes for comparative research.[16]

8   So far the discussion has referred primarily to paradigms in American social science in the period since World War II; yet the reluctance of pluralists and structure-functionalists to speak of states, and the unwillingness even of critically minded neo-Marxist to grant true autonomy to states, resonate with proclivities present from the start in the modern social sciences. These sciences emerged along with the industrial and democratic revolutions of Western Europe in the eighteenth and nineteenth centuries. Their founding theorists quite understandably perceived the focus of societal dynamics—and of the social good—not in outmoded, superseded monarchical and aristocratic states, but in civil society, variously understood as "the market," "the industrial division of labor," or "class relations." Founding theorists as politically opposed as Herbert Spencer and Karl Marx (who now, not entirely inappropriately, lie just across a lane from one another in Highgate Cemetery, London) agreed that industrial capitalism was triumphing over the militarism and territorial rivalries of states. For both of these theorists, nineteenth-century British socioeconomic developments presaged the future for all countries and for the world as a whole.

9   As world history moved—via bloody world wars, colonial conquests, state-building revolutions, and nationalist anticolonial movements—from the Pax Britannica of the nineteenth century to the Pax Americana of the post–World War II period, the Western social sciences managed to keep their eyes largely averted from the explanatory centrality of states as potent and autonomous organizational actors.[17] It was not that such phenomena as political authoritarianism and totalitarianism were ignored, just that the preferred theoretical explanations were couched in terms of economic backwardness or the unfortunate persistence of non-Western "traditional" values. As long as capitalist and liberal Britain, and then capitalist and liberal America, could plausibly be seen as the unchallengeable "lead societies," the Western social sciences could manage the feat of downplaying the explanatory centrality of states in their major

theoretical paradigms—for these paradigms were riveted on understanding modernization, its causes and direction. And in Britain and America, the "most modern" countries, economic change seemed spontaneous and progressive, and the decisions of governmental legislative bodies appeared to be the basic stuff of politics.

As the period after World War II unfolded, various changes rendered society-centered views of social change and politics less credible. In the wake of the "Keynesian revolution" of the 1930s to the 1950s national macroeconomic management became the norm and public social expenditures burgeoned across all of the advanced industrial capitalist democracies, even in the United States. The dismantlement of colonial empires gave birth to dozens of "new nations," which before long revealed that they would not simply recapitulate Western liberal democratic patterns in their political organization or policy choices. Finally, and perhaps most importantly, by the mid-1970s, both Britain and the United States were unmistakably becoming hard-pressed in a world of more intense and uncertain international economic competition. It is probably not surprising that, at this juncture, it became fashionable to speak of states as actors and as society-shaping institutional structures.

Social scientists are now willing to offer state-centered explanations, not just of totalitarian countries and late industrializers, but of Britain and the United States themselves. Fittingly, some recent arguments stress ways in which state structures have distinctively shaped economic development and international economic policies in Britain and America and also ponder how the British and U.S. states might fetter or facilitate current efforts at national industrial regeneration.[18] In short, now that debates about large public sectors have taken political center stage in all of the capitalist democracies and now that Britain and the United States seem much more like particular state-societies in an uncertain, competitive, and interdependent world of many such entities, a paradigmatic shift seems to be under way in the macroscopic social sciences, a shift that involves a fundamental rethinking of the role of states in relation to economies and societies.

The Revival of a Continental European Perspective? In the nineteenth century, social theorists oriented to the realities of social change and politics on the European continent refused (even after industrialization was fully under way) to accept the de-emphasis of the state characteristic of those who centered their thinking on Britain. Even though they might positively value liberal ideals, Continental students of social life, especially Germans, insisted on the institutional reality of the state and its continuing impact on and within civil society. Now that comparative social scientists are again emphasizing the importance of states, it is perhaps not surprising that many researchers are relying anew—with various modifications and extensions, to be sure—on the basic understanding of "the state" passed down to contemporary scholarship through the widely known writings of such major German scholars as Max Weber and Otto Hintze.

13   Max Weber argued that states are compulsory associations claiming control over territories and the people within them.[19] Administrative, legal, extractive, and coercive organizations are the core of any state. These organizations are variably structured in different countries, and they may be embedded in some sort of constitutional-representative system of parliamentary decision making and electoral contests for key executive and legislative posts. Nevertheless, as Alfred Stepan nicely puts it in a formulation that captures the biting edge of the Weberian perspective:

> The state must be considered as more than the "government." It is the continuous administrative, legal, bureaucratic and coercive systems that attempt not only to structure relationships *between* civil society and public authority in a polity but also to structure many crucial relationships within civil society as well.[20]

In this perspective, the state certainly does not become everything. Other organizations and agents also pattern social relationships and politics, and the analyst must explore the state's structure and activities in relation to them. But this Weberian view of the state does require us to see it as much more than a mere arena in which social groups make demands and engage in political struggles or compromises.

14   What is more, as the work of Otto Hintze demonstrated, thinking of states as organizations controlling territories leads us away from basic features common to all polities and toward consideration of the various ways in which state structures and actions are conditioned by historically changing transnational contexts.[21] These contexts impinge on individual states through geopolitical relations of interstate domination and competition, through the international communication of ideals and models of public policy, and through world economic patterns of trade, division of productive activities, investment flows, and international finance. States necessarily stand at the

intersections between domestic sociopolitical orders and the transnational relations within which they must maneuver for survival and advantage in relation to other states. The modern state as we know it, and as Weber and Hintze conceptualized it, has always been, since its birth in European history, part of a system of competing and mutually involved states.

Although a refocusing of social scientific interests signifi- 15 cantly informed by the Weber–Hintze understanding of states may be upon us, the real work of theoretical reorientation is only beginning to be done. This work is understandably fraught with difficulties, because attempts are being made to think about and investigate state impacts against a background of deeply rooted theoretical proclivities that are stubbornly society-centered. Recent attempts by neo-Marxists and (what might be called) neopluralists to theorize in very general terms about "state autonomy" have not offered concepts or explanatory hypotheses rich enough to encompass the arguments and findings from various comparative-historical studies.[22]

Rather than dwell on the shortcomings of such general theo- 16 ries, however, the remainder of this essay will be devoted to an exploration of what some selected historical and comparative studies have to tell us about states in societal and transnational contexts. Two somewhat different, but equally important tendencies in current scholarship will claim our attention. First, we shall examine arguments about *state autonomy* and about the *capacities of states* as actors trying to realize policy goals. Then we shall explore arguments about the *impacts of states on the content and workings of politics*. The overall aim of this exercise is not to offer any new general theory of the state or of states and social structures. For the present, at least, no such thing may be desirable, and it would not in any event be feasible in the space of one essay. Rather, my hope is to present and illustrate a conceptual frame of reference, along with some middle-range issues and hypotheses that might inform future research on states and social structures across diverse topical problems and geocultural areas of the world.

The Autonomy and Capacity of States

States conceived as organizations claiming control over ter- 17 ritories and people may formulate and pursue goals that are not simply reflective of the demands or interests of social groups, classes, or society. This is what is usually meant by "state autonomy." Unless such independent goal formulation occurs, there is little need to talk about states as important actors. Pursuing matters further, one may then explore the "capacities" of states to implement official goals, especially over the actual or potential opposition of powerful social groups or in the face of recalcitrant socioeconomic circumstances. What are the determinants of state autonomy and state capacities? Let us sample the arguments of a range of recent studies that address these questions.

18   *States as Actors.* Several lines of reasoning have been used, singly or in combination, to account for why and how states formulate and pursue their own goals. The linkage of states into transnational structures and into international flows of communication may encourage leading state officials to pursue transformative strategies even in the face of indifference or resistance from politically weighty social forces. Similarly, the basic need of states to maintain control and order may spur state-initiated reforms (as well as simple repression). As for who, exactly, is more likely to act in such circumstances, it seems that organizationally coherent collectivities of state officials, especially collectivities of career officials relatively insulated from ties to currently dominant socioeconomic interests, are likely to launch distinctive new state strategies in times of crisis. Likewise, collectivities of officials may elaborate already established public policies in distinctive ways, acting relatively continuously over long stretches of time.

19   The extranational orientations of states, the challenges they may face in maintaining domestic order, and the organizational resources that collectivities of state officials may be able to draw on and deploy—all of these features of the state as viewed from a Weberian–Hintzean perspective can help to explain autonomous state action. In an especially clear-cut way, combinations of these factors figure in Alfred Stepan's and Ellen Kay Trimberger's explanations of what may be considered extreme instances of autonomous state action—historical situations in which strategic elites use military force to take control of an entire national state and then employ bureaucratic means to enforce reformist or revolutionary changes from above.

20   Stepan's book *The State and Society: Peru in Comparative Perspective* investigates attempts by state elites in Latin America to install "inclusionary" or "exclusionary" corporatist regimes.[23] A key element in Stepan's explanation of such episodes is the formation of a strategically located cadre of officials enjoying great organizational strength inside and through existing state organizations and also enjoying a unified sense of ideological purpose about the possibility and desirability of us-

ing state intervention to ensure political order and promote national economic development. For Brazil's "exclusionary" corporatist coup in 1964 and for Peru's "inclusionary" corporatist coup in 1968, Stepan stresses the prior socialization of what he calls "new military professionals." These were career military officers who, together, passed through training schools that taught techniques and ideas of national economic planning and counterinsurgency, along with more traditional military skills. Subsequently, such new military professionals installed corporatist regimes in response to perceived crises of political order and of national economic development. The military professionals used state power to stave off or deflect threats to national order from nondominant classes and groups. They also used state power to implement socioeconomic reforms or plans for further national industrialization, something they saw as a basic requisite for improved international standing in the modern world.

Ellen Kay Trimberger's *Revolution from Above* focuses on 21 a set of historical cases—Japan's Meiji restoration, Turkey's Ataturk revolution, Egypt's Nasser revolution, and Peru's 1968 coup—in which "dynamically autonomous" bureaucrats, including military officials, seized and reorganized state power. Then they used the state to destroy an existing dominant class, a landed upper class or aristocracy, and to reorient national economic development.[24] Like Stepan, Trimberger stresses the formation through prior career interests and socialization of a coherent official elite with a statist and nationalist ideological orientation. She also agrees with Stepan's emphasis on the elite's concern to contain any possible upheavals from below. Yet, perhaps because she is in fact explaining a more thoroughly transformative version of autonomous state action to reshape society, Trimberger places more stress than Stepan on the role of foreign threats to national autonomy as a precipitant of "revolution from above." And she highlights a structural variable that Stepan ignored: the relationship of the state elite to dominant economic classes. As Trimberger puts it, "A bureaucratic state apparatus, or a segment of it, can be said to be relatively autonomous when those who hold high civil and/or military posts satisfy two conditions: (1) they are not recruited from the dominant landed, commercial, or industrial classes; and (2) they do not form close personal and economic ties with those classes after their elevation to high office."[25] Trimberger also examines the state elite's relationship to dominant economic classes in order to predict the extensiveness of socioeconomic changes a state may attempt in response to "a crisis situation—when the existing social, political, and economic order is threatened by external forces and by upheaval from below."[26] State-initiated authoritarian *reforms* may occur when bureaucratic elites retain ties to existing dominant classes, as, for example, in Prussia in 1806–1814, Russia in the 1860s, and Brazil after 1964. But the more sweeping structural changes that Trimberger labels "revolution from above," including the actual dispossession of a dominant class, occur in crisis situations only when bureaucratic state elites are free of ties or alliances with dominant classes.[27] As should be apparent, Trimberger has given the neo-Marxist notion of the relative autonomy of the state new analytical power as a tool for predicting the possible sociopolitical consequences of *various* societal and historical configurations of state and class power.[28]

22   *State Autonomy in Constitutional Politics.*   Stepan and Trimberger deal in somewhat different, though overlapping, terms with extraordinary instances of state autonomy—instances in which nonconstitutionally ruling officials attempt to use the state as a whole to direct and restructure society and politics. Meanwhile, other scholars have teased out more circumscribed instances of state autonomy in the histories of public policy making in liberal democratic, constitutional, politics, such as Britain, Sweden, and the United States.[29] In different forms, the same basic analytical factors—the international orientations or states, their domestic order-keeping functions, and the organizational possibilities for official collectivities to formulate and pursue their own policies—also enter into these analyses.

23   Hugh Heclo's *Modern Social Politics in Britain and Sweden* provides an intricate comparative-historical account of the long-term development of unemployment insurance and policies of old-age assistance in these two nations.[30] Without being explicitly presented as such, Heclo's book is about autonomous state contributions to social policy making. But the autonomous state actions Heclo highlights are not all acts of coercion or domination; they are, instead, the intellectual activities of civil administrators engaged in diagnosing societal problems and framing policy alternatives to deal with them. As Heclo puts it:

> Governments not only "power" (or whatever the verb form of that approach might be); they also puzzle. Policy-making is a form of collective puzzlement on society's behalf: it entails both deciding and knowing. The process of making pension, unemployment, and superannuation policies has extended be-

yond deciding what "wants" to accommodate, to include problems of knowing who might want something, what is wanted,
what should be wanted, and how to turn even the most sweet-
tempered general agreement into concrete collective action.
This process is political, not because all policy is a by-product
of power and conflict but because some men have undertaken
to act in the name of others.[31]

According to Heclo's comparative history, civil service ad- 24
ministrators in both Britain and Sweden have consistently
made more important contributions to social policy development than political parties or interest groups. Socioeconomic
conditions, especially crises, have stimulated only sporadic demands from parties and interest groups, argues Heclo. It has
been civil servants drawing on "administrative resources of information, analysis, and expertise" who have framed the terms
of new policy elaborations as "corrective[s] less to social conditions as such and more to the perceived failings of previous
policy" in terms of "the government bureaucracy's own conception of what it has been doing."[32] Heclo's evidence also
reveals that the autonomous bureaucratic shaping of social
policy has been greater in Sweden than in Britain, for Sweden's premodern centralized bureaucratic state was, from the
start of industrialization and before the full liberalization and
democratization of national politics, in a position to take the
initiative in diagnosing social problems and proposing universalistic solutions for administering to them.

Heclo says much less than he might about the influences 25
shaping the timing and content of distinctive state initiatives.
He does, however, present evidence of the sensitivity of civil
administrators to the requisites of maintaining order in the
face of dislocations caused by industrial unemployment. He
also points to the constant awareness by administrators of foreign precedents and models of social policy. Above all, Heclo
demonstrates that collectivities of administrative officials can
have pervasive direct and indirect effects on the content and
development of major government policies. His work suggests
how to locate and analyze autonomous state contributions to
policy making, even within constitutional polities nominally
directed by legislatures and electoral parties.

Along these lines, it is worth looking briefly at two works 26
that argue for autonomous state contributions to public policy
making even in the United States, a polity in which virtually
all scholars agree that there is less structural basis for such
autonomy than in any other modern liberal capitalist regime.
The United States did *not* inherit a centralized bureaucratic

state from preindustrial and predemocratic times. Moreover, the dispersion of authority through the federal system, the division of sovereignty among branches of the national government, and the close symbiosis between segments of the federal administration and Congressional committees all help to ensure that state power in the twentieth-century United States is fragmented, dispersed, and everywhere permeated by organized societal interests. The national government, moreover, lacks such possible underpinnings of strong state power as a prestigious and status-conscious career civil service with predictable access to key executive posts; authoritative planning agencies; direct executive control over a national central bank; and public ownership of strategic parts of the economy. Given such characteristics of the U.S. government, the concept of state autonomy has not often been used by scholars to explain American policy developments.

27   Nevertheless, Stephen Krasner in his *Defending the National Interest* does use the concept to explain twentieth-century continuities in the formulation of U.S. foreign policy about issues of international investments in the production and marketing of raw materials.[33] A clever heuristic tactic lies behind Krasner's selection of this "issue area" for systematic historical investigation: It is an issue area located at the intersection of properly geopolitical state interests and the economic interests of (often) powerful private corporations. Thus, Krasner can ask whether the short-term push and pull of business interests shapes the definition of the U.S. "national interest" with respect to raw materials production abroad or whether an autonomous state interest is consistently at work. He finds the latter pattern and attributes it to actors in a special location within the otherwise weak, fragmented, and societally permeated U.S. government:

> For U.S. foreign policy the central state actors are the President and the Secretary of State and the most important institutions are the White House and the State Department. What distinguishes these roles and agencies is their high degree of insulation from specific societal pressures and a set of formal and informal obligations that charge them with furthering the nation's general interests.[34]

28   Unfortunately, Krasner does not expand on the concept of "insulated" parts of the state. In particular, he does not tell us whether various organizational features of state agencies make for greater or lesser insulation. Instead, Krasner primarily emphasizes the decree to which different parts of the fed-

eral executive are subject to Congressional influences.[35] And he cannot fully dispel the suspicion that the Presidency and the State Department may simply be subject to class-based rather than interest-based business influences.[36] Nevertheless, he does show that public policies on raw materials have been most likely to diverge from powerful corporate demands precisely when distinctively geopolitical issues of foreign military intervention and broad ideological conceptions of U.S. world hegemony have been involved. Thus, Krasner's study suggests that distinctive state-like contributions to U.S. policy making occur exactly in those instances and arenas where a Weberian–Hintzean perspective would insist that they should occur, no matter how unpropitious the overall governmental potential for autonomous state action. As J. P. Nettl once put it, "Whatever the state may or may not be internally,... there have... been few challenges to its sovereignty *and* its autonomy in 'foreign affairs.' "[37]

My own work with Kenneth Finegold on the origins of New Deal agricultural policies also suggests that autonomous state contributions to domestic policy making can occur within a "weak state." Such autonomous state contributions happen in specific policy areas at given historical moments, even if they are not generally discernible across all policy areas and even if they unintentionally help to create political forces that subsequently severely circumscribe further autonomous state action.[38] Finegold and I argue that, by the period after World War I, the U.S. Department of Agriculture was "an island of state strength in an ocean of weakness."[39] We attribute the formulation of New Deal agricultural interventions—policies that responded to a long-standing "agrarian crisis" but *not* simply in ways directly demanded by powerful farm interest groups— to the unique resources of administrative capacity, prior public planning, and practical governmental experience available to federal agricultural experts at the dawn of the New Deal. Our argument resembles Hugh Heclo's findings about innovative civil officials in Britain and Sweden. Essentially, we found a *part* of the early-twentieth-century U.S. national government that allowed official expertise to function in a restricted policy area in ways that were similar to the ways it functioned in Sweden, or in Britain between 1900 and 1920.

In addition, however, we trace the political fate of the New Deal's administrative interventions in agriculture. We show that, in the overall context of the U.S. state structure, this initially autonomous state intervention inadvertently strengthened a particular lobbying group, the American Farm Bureau Federation, and gave it the final increments of electoral and administrative leverage that it needed to "capture" preponderant influence over post-1936 federal agricultural policies. Subsequent state planning efforts, especially those that implied redistribution of economic, racial, or social-class power, were then circumscribed and destroyed by the established commercial farming interests championed by the Farm Bureau.

31   In short, "state autonomy" is not a fixed structural feature of any governmental system. It can come and go. This is true not only because crises may precipitate the formulation of official strategies and policies by elites or administrators who otherwise might not mobilize their own potentials for autonomous action. It is also true because the very *structural potentials* for autonomous state actions change over time, as the organizations of coercion and administration undergo transformations, both internally and in their relations to societal groups and to representative parts of government. Thus, although cross-national research can indicate in general terms whether a governmental system has "stronger" or "weaker" tendencies toward autonomous state action, the full potential of this concept can be realized only in truly historical studies that are sensitive to structural variations and conjunctural changes within given polities.

32   *Are State Actions "Rational"?* An additional set of comments must be made about the rationality of autonomous state actions. Often such actions are considered more capable of addressing "the capitalist *class* interest" or "society's general interests" or "the national interest" than are governmental decisions strongly influenced by the push and pull of demands from interest groups, voting blocs, or particular business enterprises.[40] In such perspectives, state officials are judged to be especially capable of formulating holistic and long-term strategies transcending partial, short-sighted demands from profit-seeking capitalists or narrowly self-interested social groups. But scholars skeptical about the notion of state autonomy often respond that state officials' own self-legitimating arguments, their claims to know and represent "general" or "national" interests, should not be taken at face value. State officials have no privileged claims to adequate knowledge of societal problems or solutions for them, argue the skeptics. Besides, their legitimating symbols may merely mask policies formulated to help particular interests or class fractions.

33   Surely such doubts about the superior rationality of state actions deserve respectful attention; yet we need not entirely dismiss the possibility that partially or fully autonomous state actions *may* be able to address problems and even find "solu-

tions" beyond the reach of societal actors and those parts of government closely constrained by them. Partly, the realization of such possibilities will depend on the availability and (even more problematically) the appropriate use of sound ideas about what the state can and should do to address societal problems. Partly, it will depend on the fit (or lack thereof) between the *scope* of an autonomous state organization's authority and the scale and depth of action appropriate for addressing a given kind of problem. Planning for coordinated systems of national transportation, for example, is unlikely to be achieved by state agencies with authority only over particular regions or kinds of transportation, no matter how knowledgeable and capable of autonomous official action those agencies may be. In sum, autonomous official initiatives can be stupid or misdirected, and autonomous initiatives may be fragmented and partial and work at cross-purposes to one another. Notwithstanding all of these possibilities, however, state actions may sometimes be coherent and appropriate.

Still, no matter how appropriate (for dealing with a given 34 kind of crisis or problem) autonomous state activity might be, it can never really be "disinterested" in any meaningful sense. This is true not only because all state actions necessarily benefit some social interests and disadvantage others (even without the social beneficiaries' having worked for or caused the state actions). More to the point, autonomous state actions will regularly take forms that attempt to reinforce the authority, political longevity, and social control of the state organizations whose incumbents generated the relevant policies or policy ideas. We can hypothesize that one (hidden or overt) feature of all autonomous state actions will be the reinforcement of the prerogatives of collectivities of state officials. Whether rational policies result may depend on how "rational" is defined and might even be largely accidental. The point is that policies different from those demanded by societal actors will be produced. The most basic research task for those interested in state autonomy surely is to explore why, when, and how such distinctive policies are fashioned by states. Then it will be possible to wonder about their rationality for dealing with the problems they address—and we will be able to explore this issue without making starry-eyed assumptions about the omniscience or disinterestedness of states.

Can States Achieve Their Goals? Some comparative-histori- 35 cal scholars not only have investigated the underpinnings of autonomous state actions, but have also tackled the still more challenging task of explaining the various *capacities* of states to implement their policies. Of course, the explanation of state capacities is closely connected to the explanation of autonomous goal formation by states, because state officials are most likely to try to do things that seem feasible with the means at hand. Nevertheless, not infrequently, states do pursue goals (whether their own or those pressed on them by powerful social groups) that are beyond their reach. Moreover, the implementation of state policies often leads to unintended as well as intended consequences, both when states attempt tasks they cannot complete and when the means they use produce unforeseen structural changes and sociopolitical reactions. Thus, the capacities of states to implement strategies and policies deserve close analysis in their own right. Here, I will not attempt any comprehensive survey of substantive findings in this important area of research. Instead, I shall simply indicate some promising ideas and approaches embodied in current investigations of state capacities.

36   A few basic things can be said about the general underpinnings of state capacities. Obviously, sheer sovereign integrity and the stable administrative-military control of a given territory are preconditions for any state's ability to implement policies.[41] Beyond this, loyal and skilled officials and plentiful financial resources are basic to state effectiveness in attaining all sorts of goals. It is not surprising that histories of state building zero in on exactly these universal sinews of state power.[42] Certain of these resources come to be rooted in institutional relationships that are slow to change and relatively impervious to short-term manipulations. For example, do state offices attract and retain career-oriented incumbents with a wide array of skills and keen motivation? The answer may well depend on historically evolved relationships among elite educational institutions, state organizations, and private enterprises that compete with the state for educated personnel. The best situation for the state may be a regular flow of elite university graduates, including many with sophisticated technical training, into official careers that are of such high status as to keep the most ambitious and successful from moving on to nonstate positions. But if this situation has not been historically established by the start of the industrial era, it is difficult to undo alternative patterns less favorable to the state.[43]

37   Factors determining a state's financial resources may be somewhat more manipulable over time, though not always. The amounts and forms of revenues and credit available to a state grow out of structurally conditioned, yet historically shifting political balances and bargains among states and between a state and social classes. Basic sets of facts to sort

out in any study of state capacities involve the sources and amounts of state revenues and the degree of flexibility possible in their collection and deployment. Domestic institutional arrangements and international situations set difficult to change limits within which state elites must maneuver to extract taxes and obtain credit: Does a state depend on export taxes (for example, from a scarce national resource or from products vulnerable to sudden world market fluctuations)?[44] Does a nonhegemonic state's geopolitical position allow it to reap the state-building benefits of military aid, or must it rely on international bankers or aid agencies that insist on favoring nonpublic investments and restrict the domestic political options of the borrower state?[45] What established authority does a state have to collect taxes, to borrow, or to invest in potentially profitable public enterprises? And how much "room" is there in the existing constitutional-political system to change patterns of revenue collection unfavorable to the state?

Finally, what authority and organizational means does a state have to deploy whatever financial resources it does enjoy? Are particular kinds of revenues rigidly "earmarked" for special uses that cannot easily be altered by official decision makers?[46] Can the state channel (and manipulate) flows of credit to particular enterprises and industrial sectors, or do established constitutional-political practices favor only aggregate categorical expenditures? All of these *sorts* of questions must be asked in any study of state capacities. The answers to them, taken together, provide the best general insight into the direct and indirect leverage a state is likely to have for realizing any goal it may pursue. A state's means of raising and deploying financial resources tell us more than could any other single factor about its existing (and immediately potential) capacities to create or strengthen state organizations, to employ personnel, to coopt political support, to subsidize economic enterprises, and to fund social programs.[47]

State Capacities to Pursue Specific Kinds of Policies. Basic questions about a state's territorial integrity, financial means, and staffing may be the place to start in any investigation of its capacities to realize goals; yet the most fruitful studies of state capacities tend to focus on particular policy areas. As Stephen Krasner puts it:

> There is no reason to assume *a priori* that the pattern of strengths and weaknesses will be the same for all policies. One state may be unable to alter the structure of its medical system but be able to construct an efficient transportation network,

while another can deal relatively easily with getting its citizens around but cannot get their illnesses cured.[48]

Those who study a comprehensive state-propelled strategy for change, such as a "revolution from above" or a major episode of bureaucratically sponsored reforms, may need to assess the overall capacity of a state to realize transformative goals across multiple spheres. Moreover, as Krasner points out, it may be useful to establish that "despite variations among issue areas within countries, there are modal differences in the power of the state among [for example] the advanced market-economy countries."[49] Nevertheless, such overall assessments are perhaps best built up from sectorally specific investigations, for one of the most important facts about the power of a state may be its *unevenness* across policy areas. And the most telling result, even of a far-reaching revolution or reform from above, may be the *disparate* transformations produced across sociopolitical sectors.

40   Thus, in a provocative article, "Constitutionalism, Class and the Limits of Choice in U.S. Foreign Policy," Ira Katznelson and Kenneth Prewitt show how U.S. policies toward Latin America have been partly conditioned by the uneven capacities of the American national government: strongly able to intervene abroad, yet lacking the domesstic planning capacities necessary "to direct the internal distribution of costs entailed by a less imperialist foreign policy."[50] To give another example, Alfred Stepan draws many of his most interesting conclusions about the contradictory and unintended results of Peru's episode of "inclusionary corporatism" from a careful analysis of the regime's uneven successes in restructuring the political involvements of various social groups and redirecting the course of economic development in various sectors.[51]

41   Many studies of the capacities of states to realize particular kinds of goals use the concept of "policy instrument" to refer to the relevant means that a state may have at its disposal. [52] Cross-national comparisons are necessary to determine the nature and range of institutional mechanisms that state officials may conceivably be able to bring to bear on a given set of issues. For example, Susan and Norman Fainstein compare the urban policies of northwest European nations with those of the United States. Accordingly, they are able to conclude that the U.S. national state lacks certain instruments for dealing with urban crises that are available to European states, instruments such as central planning agencies, state-controlled pools of investment capital, and directly administered national welfare programs.[53]

Analogously, Peter Katzenstein brings together a set of re- 42
lated studies of how six advanced industrial-capitalist countries manage the international trade, investment, and monetary involvements of their economies.[54] Katzenstein is able to
draw fairly clear distinctions between the strategies open to
states such as the Japanese and the French, which have policy instruments that enable them to apply policies at the level
of particular industrial sectors, and other states, such as the
British and U.S., which must rely on aggregate macroeconomic
manipulations of fiscal and monetary parameters. Once again,
as in the Fainstein study, it is the juxtaposition of different nations' approaches to a given policy area that allows relevant
policy instruments to be highlighted. Neither study, however,
treats such "instruments" as deliberate short-term creations of
state managers. Both studies move out toward macroscopic
explorations of the broad institutional patterns of divergent
national histories that explain why countries now have, or do
not have, policy instruments for dealing with particular problems or crises.

States in Relation to Socioeconomic Settings. Fully specified 43
studies of state capacities not only entail examinations of the
resources and instruments that states may have for dealing
with particular problems; they also necessarily look at more
than states as such. They examine states *in relation to* particular kinds of socioeconomic and political environments populated by actors with given interests and resources. One obvious use of a relational perspective is to investigate the power
of states over domestic or transnational nonstate actors and
structures, especially economically dominant ones. What capacities do states have to change the behavior or oppose the
demands of such actors or to transform recalcitrant structures?
Answers lie not only in features of states themselves, but also
in the balance of states' resources and situational advantages
compared with those of nonstate actors. This sort of relational
approach is used by Stephen Krasner in his exploration of the
efforts of U.S. policy makers to implement foreign raw materials policy in interactions with large corporations, whose preferences and established practices have frequently run counter
to the state's definition of the national interest.[55]

This is also the sort of approach used by Alfred Stepan to 44
analyze the successes and failures of Peruvian military leaders
in using state power to change the patterns of foreign capital
investments in their dependent country.[56] Stepan does a brilliant job of developing a consistent set of casual hypotheses to
explain the diverse outcomes across industrial sectors: sugar,

oil, and manufacturing. For each sector, he examines regime characteristics: degree of commitment to clear policy goals, technical capacities, monitoring abilities, state-controlled investment resources, and the state's international position. He also examines the characteristics of existing investments and markets as they impinge on the advantages that either Peru or foreign multinational corporations might hope to attain from any further investments. The entire argument is too complex to reproduce here, but its significance extends well beyond the foreign investment issue area and the Peruvian case. By taking a self-consciously relational approach to the balances of resources that states and multinational corporations may bring to bear in their partially symbiotic and partially conflictual dealings with one another, Stepan has provided an important model for further studies of state capacities in many policy areas.

45   Another, slightly different relational approach to the study of state capacities appears in Peter Katzenstein's *Between Power and Plenty*, where (as indicated earlier) the object of explanation is ultimately not state *power over* nonstate actors, but nations' strategies for managing "interdependence" within the world capitalist economy. One notion centrally invoked in the Katzenstein collection is that of a "policy network" embodying a patterned relationship between state and society. In Katzenstein's words:

> The actors in society and state influencing the definition of foreign economic policy objectives consist of the major interest groups and political action groups. The former represent the relations of production (including industry, finance, commerce, labor, and agriculture); the latter derive from the structure of political authority (primarily the state bureaucracy and political parties). The governing coalitions... in each of the advanced industrial states find their institutional expression in distinct policy networks which link the public and the private sector in the implementation of foreign policy.[57]

Katzenstein argues that the definition and implementation of foreign economic policies grow out of the nexus of state and society. Both state goals and the interests of powerful classes may influence national policy orientations. And the implementation of policies is shaped not only by the policy instruments available to the state, but also by the organized support it receives from key societal groups.

46   Thus, policy objectives such as industrial reorganization might be effectively implemented because a central state ad-

ministration controls credit and can intervene in industrial sectors. Yet it may be of equal importance that industries are organized into disciplined associations willing to cooperate with state officials. A complete analysis, in short, requires examination of the organization and interests of socioeconomic groups, and inquiries into the complementary as well as conflicting relationships of state and societal actors. This is the sort of approach consistently used by the contributors to *Power and Plenty* to explain the foreign economic objectives of the United States, Britain, Germany, Italy, France, and Japan. The approach is also used to analyze the capacities of these nations' policy networks to implement existing, or conceivable alternative, economic strategies.

The relational approaches of Stepan's *State and Society* and 47 Katzenstein's *Power and Plenty* drive home with special clarity some important points about all current research on states as actors and structures. Bringing the state back in to a central place in analyses of policy making and social change does require a break with some of the most encompassing social-determinist assumptions of pluralism, structure-functionalist developmentalism, and the various neo-Marxisms. But it does not mean that old theoretical emphases should simply be turned on their heads: Studies of states alone are not to be substituted for concerns with classes or groups; nor are purely state-determinist arguments to be fashioned in the place of society-centered explanations. The need to anaylze states in relation to socioeconomic and sociocultural contexts is convincingly demonstrated in the best current research on state capacities. And we are about to examine yet another cluster of studies in which a fully relational approach to states and societies is even more essential.

States and Patterns of Politics

The previous section focused on the state as a set of orga- 48 nizations through which collectivities of officials may be able to formulate and implement distinctive strategies or policies. When the state comes up in current social scientific discourse, non-Marxists, at least, are usually referring to it in this sense: as an *actor* whose independent efforts may need to be taken more seriously than heretofore in accounting for policy making and social change. But there is another way to think about the sociopolitical impact of the state, an alternative frame or reference not often articulated but perhaps even more important than the view of the state as an actor. This second approach might be called "Tocquevillian," because Alexis de Tocqueville applied it masterfully in his studies *The Old Regime and the French Revolution* and *Democracy in America*.[58] In this perspective, states matter not simply because of the goal-oriented activities of state officials. They matter because their organizational configurations, along with their overall patterns of activity, affect political culture, encourage some kinds of group formation and collective political actions (but not others), and make possible the raising of certain political issues (but not others).

49   To be sure, the "strengths" or "weaknesses" of states as sites of more or less independent and effective official actions constitute a key aspect of the organizational configurations and overall patterns of activity at issue in this perspective. This second approach is entirely complementary to the ideas we explored in the previous section, but here the investigator's modus operandi is not the same. When the effects of states are explored from the Tocquevillian point of view those effects are *not* traced by dissecting state strategies or policies and their possibilities for implementation. Instead, the investigator looks more macroscopically at the ways in which the structures and activities of states unintentionally influence the formation of groups and the political capacities, ideas, and demands of various sectors of society. Thus, much of Tocqueville's argument about the origins of the French Revolution dealt with the ways in which the French absolutist monarchy, through its institutional structure and policy practices, unintentionally undermined the prestige and political capacities of the aristocracy, provoked the peasantry and the urban Third Estate, and inspired the intelligentsia to launch abstract, rationalist broadsides against the status quo. Effects of the state permeated Tocqueville's argument, even though he said little about the activities and goals of the state officials themselves.

50   *Comparative Studies of State Structures and Politics in Industrial-Capitalist Democracies.* A good way to demonstrate the contemporary fruitfulness of such macroscopic explorations of the sociopolitical effects of states is to sketch some of the findings of comparative-historical scholars who have focused on differences among and within Western advanced industrial-capitalist nations. Analogous effects have been, or could be, found among other sets of countries—for example, among peripheral or "newly industrializing" capitalist nations or among the "state-socialist" countries—but the analytically relevant points would be similar. Thus, I shall confine myself to comparisons among the United States and some European

nations, drawing on a number of works to sketch ideas about how the structures and activities of states affect political culture, group formation and collective political action, and the issue agendas of politics.

In a highly unusual and path-breaking essay for its decade, 51 "The State as a Conceptual Variable," J.P. Nettl delineated a series of institutional and cultural differences in the "stateness" of the United States, Britain, and the continental European nations.[59] Some of his most telling contrasts referred to dimensions of political culture, that is, widely held ideas about the nature and locus of political power and notions about what can be attained in politics and how. In their essay entitled "Constitutionalism, Class, and the Limits of Choice in U.S. Foreign Policy," Ira Katznelson and Kenneth Prewitt apply and extend some of these ideas from Nettl.

Owing to the different historical paths their governmental 52 systems have traversed, argued Nettl, continental Europeans think of "sovereignty" as residing in centralized administrative institutions; Britons focus on political parties in Parliament; and U.S. citizens refuse to designate any concrete body as sovereign, but instead attribute sovereignty to the law and the Constitution. In Europe, according to Nettl, the administrative order is instantly recognizable as an area of autonomous action, and both supporters and opponents of the existing order orient themselves to working through it as the agent of the public good. But in the United States, as Katznelson and Prewitt nicely spell out:

> The Constitution does not establish...[an administratively centralized] state that in turn manages the affairs of society toward some clear conception of the public welfare; rather, it established a political economy in which the public welfare is the aggregate of private preferences.... The United States is a government of legislation and litigation.... Politics becomes the struggle to translate social and economic interests into law.... *The political culture defines political power as getting a law passed.*
>
> Dissatisfaction most frequently takes the form of trying to force a new and more favorable interpretation of the Constitution.... Never in this endless shuffling does the Constitution itself become the target. Rather, constitutional principles legitimate claims for a fair share of "the American way of life," and constitutional interpretations and reinterpretations are the means for forcing reallocations.[60]

In short, various sorts of states not only conduct decision- 53 making, coercive, and adjudicative activities in different ways, but also give rise to various conceptions of the meaning and methods of "politics" itself, conceptions that influence the behavior of all groups and classes in national societies.

54   The forms of collective action through which groups make political demands or through which political leaders seek to mobilize support are also partially shaped in relation to the structures and activities of states. This point has been richly established for Western countries by scholars dealing with causes and forms of social protest, with "corporatism" as governmentally institutionalized interest consultation, and with political parties as mediators between electorates and the conduct of state power.

55   Charles Tilly and his collaborators have investigated changing forms of violent and nonviolent collective protest in France and elsewhere in the West since the seventeenth century. In the process, they have pointed to many ways in which state structures, as well as the actions of state officials, affect the timing, the goals, and the forms of collective protest. Inexorable connections between war making and state making in early modern Europe meant, according to Tilly, that most "collective contention" in those days entailed attempts, especially by regional elites and local communities, to defend established rights against royal tax collectors and military recruiters.[61] Later, nationwide networks of middle- and working-class people in industrializing Britain created the innovative protest forms of the associational "social movement" through interactions with the parliamentary, legal, and selectively repressive practices of the British state.[62] Variations on social-movement "repertories" of collective action, always adapted to the structures and practices of given states, also spread across many other modern nations. Many additional examples of state effects on collective action could be given from Tilly's work. For many years, he has been a powerful proponent of bringing the state back in to the analysis of social protest, an area of political sociology that was previously dominated by social systems and social psychological approaches.[63]

56   If studies of collective action are a perennial staple in sociology, studies of interest groups have comparable standing in political science. Recently, as Suzanne Berger points out, students of Western European countries have ceased to view "interest groups as reflections of society." Instead, they find that "the timing and characteristics of state intervention" affect "not only organizational tactics and strategies" but "the content and definition of interest itself," with the result that each European nation, according to the historical sequence and forms of the state's social and economic interventions,

has a distinctive configuration of interests active in politics.[64] In addition, students of interest groups in Western Europe have vigorously debated the causes and dynamics of "corporatist" patterns, in which interest groups exclusively representing given functional socioeconomic interests attain public status and the right to authoritative participation in national policy making. Some scholars have directly stressed that state initiatives create corporatist forms. Others, more skeptical of such a strong state-centered view, nevertheless analyze the myriad ways in which particular state structures and policies foster or undermine corporatist group representation.[65]

Key points along these lines are driven home when the 57 United States is brought into the picture. In a provocative 1979 essay, Robert Salisbury asked, "Why No Corporatism in America?" and Graham K. Wilson followed up the query in 1982.[66] Both scholars agree that such basic (interrelated) features of the U.S. state structure as federalism, the importance of geographic units of representation, nonprogrammatic political parties, fragmented realism of administrative bureaucracy, and the importance of Congress and its specialized committees within the national government's system of divided sovereignty all encourage a proliferation of competing, narrowly specialized, and weakly disciplined interest groups. In short, little about the structure and operations of the American state renders corporatism politically feasible or credible, either for officials or for social groups. Even protest movements in the United States tend to follow issue-specialized and geographically fissiparous patterns. State structures, established interest groups, and oppositional groups all may mirror one another's forms of organization and scopes of purpose.

Along with interest groups, the most important and en- 58 during forms of collective political action in the industrial-capitalist democracies are electorally competing political parties. In a series of brilliant comparative-historical essays, Martin Shefter demonstrates how such parties have come to operate either through patronage or through programmatic appeals to organized voter blocs.[67] Shefter argues that this depended in large part on the forms of state power in existence when the democratic suffrage was established in various nations. In Germany, for example, absolutist monarchs had established centralized administrative bureaucracies long before the advent of democratic elections. Vote-getting political parties, when they came into existence, could not offer the "spoils of office" to followers, because there was an established coalition (of public officials tied to upper and middle classes oriented to using university education as a route to state careers) behind keeping public bureaucracies free of party control. Thus, German political parties were forced to use ideological, programmatic appeals, ranging from communist or socialist to anti-Semitic and fascist.[68] In contrast, Shefter shows how the territorial unevenness of pre-democratic central administration in Italy and the absence of an autonomous federal bureaucracy in nineteenth-century U.S. democracy allowed patronage-wielding political parties to colonize administrative arrangements in these countries, thereby determining that voters would be wooed with nonprogrammatic appeals, especially with patronage and other "distributive" allocations of publicly controlled resources.

59   The full scope of Shefter's work, which cannot be further summarized here, also covers Britain, France, and regional contrasts within the twentieth-century United States. With analytical consistency and vivid historical detail, Shefter shows the influence of evolving state administrative structures on the aims and organizational forms of the political parties that mediate between public offices, on the one hand, and socially rooted electorates, on the other. Unlike many students of voting and political parties, Shefter does not see parties merely as vehicles for expressing societal political preferences. He realizes that they are also organizations for claiming and using state authority, organizations that develop their own interests and persistent styles of work. Lines of determination run as much (or more) from state structures to party organizations to the content of electoral politics as they run from voter preferences to party platforms to state policies.

60   Structures of public administration and political party organizations, considered together, go a long way toward "selecting" the *kinds* of political issues that will come onto (or be kept off) a society's political agenda." In his book on policy making in relation to air pollution in U.S. municipal politics, Matthew Crenson develops this argument in a manner that has implications beyond his own study.[69] Boss-run, patronage-oriented urban machines, Crenson argues, prefer to highlight political issues that create *divisible* benefits or costs to be allocated differentially in discrete bargains for support from particular businesses or geographic sets of voters. Air pollution controls, however, generate indivisible *collective* benefits, so machine governments and patronage-oriented parties will try to avoid considering the air pollution issue. Entire political agendas, Crenson maintains, may be dominated by similar types of issues: either mostly "collective" or mostly "specific" distributional issues. This happens, in part, because the orga-

nizational needs of government and parties will call forth similar issues. It also happens because, once political consciousness and group mobilization are bent in one direction, people will tend to make further demands along the same lines. Once again, we see a dialectic between state and society, here influencing the basic issue content of politics, just as previously we have seen state–society interrelations at work in the shaping of political cultures and forms of collective action.

States and the Political Capacities of Social Classes. With so 61 many aspects of politics related to nationally variable state structures, it should come as no surprise that the "classness" of politics also varies in relation to states, for the degree to which (and the forms in which) class interests are organized into national politics depends very much on the prevailing political culture, forms of collective action, and the possibilities for raising and resolving broadly collective (societal or class) issues. Marxists may be right to argue that classes and class tensions are always present in industrial societies, but the political expression of class interests and conflicts is never automatic or econmically determined. It depends on the capacities classes have for achieving consciousness, organization, and representation. Directly or indirectly, the structures and activities of states profoundly condition such class capacities. Thus, the classical wisdom of Marxian political sociology must be turned, if not on its head, then certainly on its side.

Writing in direct critical dialogue with Marx, Pierre Birn- 62 baum argues that the contrasting ideologies and attitudes toward politics of the French and British working-class movements can be explained in state-centered terms.[70] According to Birnbaum, the centralized, bureaucratic French state, sharply differentiated from society, fostered anarchist or Marxist orientations and political militancy among French workers, whereas the centralized but less differentiated British "establishment" encouraged British workers and their leaders to favor parliamentary gradualism and private contractual wage bargaining.

Analogous arguments by Ira Katznelson in *City Trenches* and 63 by Martin Shefter in an essay entitled "Trades Unions and Political Machines: The Organization and Disorganization of the American Working Class in the Late Nineteenth Century" point to the specifically state-centered factors that account for the cross-nationally very low political capacity of the U.S. industrial working class.[71] Democratization (in the form of universal suffrage for white men) occurred in the United States right

at the start of capitalist industrialization. From the 1830s onward, electoral competition incorporated workers into a polity
run, not by a national bureaucracy or "establishment," but by
patronage-oriented political parties with strong roots in local
communities. In contrast to what happened in many European nations, unions and workers in the United States did not
have to ally themselves with political associations or parties
fighting for the suffrage in opposition to politically privileged
dominant classes and an autonomous administrative state.
Common meanings and organizations did not bridge work and
residence in America, and the early U.S. industrial working
class experienced "politics" as the affair of strictly local groups
organized on ethnic or racial lines by machine politicians.
Work-place struggles were eventually taken over by bread-and-
butter trade unions. "In this way," Katznelson concludes, "citizenship and its bases were given communal meaning separate
from work relations. The segmented pattern of class understandings in the United States...was caused principally by
features of the polity created by the operation of a federal constitutional system."[72]

64   State structures influence the capacities not only of subordinate but also of propertied classes. It is never enough simply to
posit that dominant groups have a "class interest" in maintaining sociopolitical order or in continuing a course of economic
development in ways congruent with their patterns of property ownership. Exactly how—even whether—order may be
maintained and economic accumulation continued depends in
significant part on existing state structures and the dominant-
class political capacities that those structures help to shape.
Thus, in my 1973 discussion of Barrington Moore's *Social
Origins of Dictatorship and Democracy*, I argued that the
"reformism" of key landed and bourgeois groups in nineteenth-
century Britain was not simply a product of class economic interests. It was also a function of the complexly balanced vested
political interests those groups had in decentralized forms of
administration and repression and in parliamentary forms of
political decision making.[73] Likewise, much of the argument in
my *States and Social Revolutions* about causes of revolutionary
transformations in certain agrarian states rests on a comparative analysis of the political capacities of landed upper classes
as these were shaped by the structures and activities of monarchical bureaucratic states.[74]

65   Again, the point under discussion can be brought home to the
United States. Along with U.S. industrial working class, Amer-

ican capitalists lack the political capacity to pursue classwide interests in national politics. This is one of the reasons invoked by Susan and Norman Fainstein to explain the incoherence and ineffectiveness of contemporary U.S. policy responses to urban crises, which northwest European nations have handled more effectively, to the benefit of dominant and subordinant classes alike.[75] Historically, America's relatively weak, decentralized, and fragmented state structure, combined with early democratization and the absence of a politically unified working class, has encouraged and allowed U.S. capitalists to splinter along narrow interest lines and to adopt an antistate, laissez faire ideology.[76] Arguably, American business groups have often benefited from this situation. Yet American business interests have been recurrently vulnerable to reformist state interventions that they could not strongly influence or limit, given their political disunity or (as at the height of the New Deal) their estrangement from interventionist governmental agencies or administrations.[77] And American business has always found it difficult to provide consistent support for national initiatives that might benefit the economy as a whole.

Obviously, industrial workers and capitalists do not exhaust the social groups that figure in the politics of industrial democracies. Studies of the effects of state structures and policies on group interests and capacities have also done much to explain, in historical and comparative terms, the political involvements of farmers and small businesses. In addition, important new work is now examining relationships between state formation and the growth of modern "professions," as well as related concerns about the deployment of "expert" knowledge in public policy making.[78] Yet without surveying these literatures as well, the basic argument of this section has been sufficiently illustrated.

Politics in all of its dimensions is grounded not only in "society" or in "the economy" or in a "culture"—if any or all of these are considered separately from the organizational arrangements and activities of states. The meanings of public life and the collective forms through which groups become aware of political goals and work to attain them arise, not from societies alone, but at the meeting points of states and societies. Consequently, the formation, let alone the political capacities, of such apparently purely socioeconomic phenomena as interest groups and classes depends in significant measure on the structures and activities of the very states the social actors, in turn, seek to influence.

Conclusion

68   This essay has ranged widely—although, inevitably, selectively—over current research on states as actors and as institutional structures with effects in politics. Two alternative though
complementary, analytical strategies have been discussed for
bringing the state back in to a prominent place in comparative
and historical studies of social change, politics, and policy
making. On the one hand, states may be viewed as organizations through which official collectivities may pursue distinctive
goals, realizing them more or less effectively given the available
state resources in relation to social settings. On the other hand,
states may be viewed more macroscopically as configurations
of organization and action that influence the meanings and
methods of politics for all groups and classes in society.

69   Given the intellectual and historical trends surveyed in the
introduction to this essay, there can now be little question
whether states are to be taken seriously in social scientific explanations of a wide range of phenomena of long-standing interest. There remain, however, many theoretical and practical
issues about how states and their effects are to be investigated.
My programmatic conclusion is straightforward: Rather than
become embroiled in a series of abstruse and abstract conceptual debates, let us proceed along the lines of the analytical
strategies sketched here. With their help, we can carry through
further comparative and historical investigations to develop
middle-range generalizations about the roles of states in revolutions and reforms, about the social and economic policies
pursued by states, and about the effects of states on political
conflicts and agendas.

70   A new theoretical understanding of states in relation to social
structures will likely emerge as such programs of comparative-
historical research are carried forward. But this new understanding will almost certainly not resemble the grand systems
theories of the structure–functionalists or neo-Marxists. As we
bring the state back in to its proper central place in explanations of social change and politics, we shall be forced to respect the inherent historicity of sociopolitical structures, and
we shall necessarily attend to the inescapable intertwinings
of national-level developments with changing world historical
contexts. We do not need a new or refurbished grand theory of
"The State." Rather, we need solidly grounded and analytically
sharp understandings of the causal regularities that underlie
the histories of states, social structures, and transnational relations in the modern world.

Notes

This chapter is a revision of "Bringing the State Back In: False Leads and Promising Starts in Current Theories and Research," originally prepared for a Social Science Research Council conference entitled "States and Social Structures: Research Implications of Current Theories," held at Seven Springs Center, Mt. Kisco, New York, February 25–27, 1982. I benefited greatly from conference discussions. Subsequently, reactions from Pierre Birnbaum, David Easton, Harry Eckstein, Kenneth Finegold, and Eric Nordlinger also helped me to plan revisions of the conference paper, as did access to prepublication copies of Stephen Krasner's "Review Article: Approaches to the State: Alternative Conceptions and Historical Dynamics," *Comparative Politics* 16 (2) (January 1984), 223–46 and Roger Benjamin and Raymond Duvall's "The Capitalist State in Context," forthcoming in *The Democratic State*, ed. R. Benjamin and S. Elkin (Lawrence: University of Kansas Press, 1985). Most of all, I am intellectually indebted to discussions and exchanges of memos with all of my fellow members of the 1982–83 Social Science Research Council Committee on States and Social Structures: Peter Evans, Albert Hirschman, Peter Katzenstein, Ira Katznelson, Stephen Krasner, Dietrich Rueschemeyer, and Charles Tilly.

1. Important examples include Alice Amsden, "Taiwan's Economic History: A Case of Etatism and a Challenge to Dependency Theory," *Modern China* 5 (1979): 341–80; Pranab Bardhan, "The State, Classes and Economic Growth in India," 1982–83 Radhakrishnan Memorial Lectures, All Souls College, Oxford; Douglas Bennett and Kenneth Sharpe, "Agenda Setting and Bargaining Power: The Mexican State versus Transnational Automobile Corporations," *World Politics* 32 (1979): 57–89; Peter B. Evans, *Dependent Development: The Alliance of Multinational, State, and Local Capital in Brazil* (Princeton, N.J.: Princeton University Press, 1979); Nora Hamilton, *The Limits of State Autonomy: Post-Revolutionary Mexico* (Princeton, N.J.: Princeton University Press, 1982); Steven Langdon, *Multinational Corporations in the Political Economy of Kenya* (London: Macmillan, 1981); Hyun-chin Lim, "Dependent Development in the World System: The Case of South Korea, 1963–1979" (Ph.D. diss., Harvard University, 1982); Richard Sklar,*Corporate Power in an African State: The Political Impact of Multinational Mining Companies in Zambia* (Berkeley: University of California Press, 1975); Alfred Stepan, *The State and Society: Peru in Comparative Perspective* (Princeton, N.J.: Princeton University Press, 1978); and Ellen Kay Trimberger, *Revolution from Above: Military Bureaucrats and Development in Japan, Turkey, Egypt and Peru* (New Brunswick, N.J.: Transaction Books, 1978).
2. Important examples include Douglas Ashford, *British Dogmatism and French Pragmatism: Central-Local Policymaking in the Modern Welfare State* (London: Allen & Unwin, 1983); Pierre Birnbaum, *The Heights of Power: An Essay on the Power Elite in France*, trans.

Arthur Goldhammer (Chicago: University of Chicago Press, 1982); David Cameron, "The Expansion of the Public Economy: A Comparative Analysis," *American Political Science Review* 72 (1978): 1243–61; Kenneth Dyson and Stephen Wilks, eds., *Industrial Crisis: A Comparative Study of the State and Industry* (New York: St. Martin's Press, 1983); Peter Hall, "Policy Innovation and the Structure of the State: The Politics—Administration Nexus in France and Britain," *Annals of the American Academy of Political and Social Science* 466 (1983): 43–59; Peter A. Hall, "Patterns of Economic Policy among the European States: An Organizational Approach," in *The State in Capitalist Europe*, ed. Stephen Bornstein, David Held, and Joel Krieger (London: Allen & Unwin, forthcoming); Hugh Heclo, *Modern Social Politics in Britain and Sweden* (New Haven, Conn.: Yale University Press, 1974); Chalmers Johnson, *MITI and the Japanese Miracle: The Growth of Industrial Policy, 1925–1975* (Stanford, Calif.: Stanford University Press, 1982); Peter Katzenstein, ed., *Between Power and Plenty: Foreign Economic Policies of Advanced Industrial States* (Madison: University of Wisconsin Press, 1978); Steven Kelman, *Regulating America, Regulating Sweden: A Comparative Study of Occupational Health and Safety Policy* (Cambridge, Mass.: MIT Press, 1981); Stephen D. Krasner, *Defending the National Interest: Raw Materials Investments and U.S. Foreign Policy* (Princeton, N.J.: Princeton University Press, 1978); Theodore J. Lowi, "Public Policy and Bureaucracy in the United States and France," in *Comparing Public Policies: New Concepts and Methods*, ed. Douglas E. Ashford, vol. 4 of *Sage Yearbooks in Politics and Public Policy* (Beverly Hills, Calif.: Sage, 1978), pp. 177–96; Leo Panitch, ed., *The Canadian State Political Economy and Political Power* (Toronto: University of Toronto Press, 1977); Theda Skocpol and John Ikenberry, "The Political Formation of the American Welfare State in Historical and Comparative Perspective," *Comparative Social Research* 6 (1983): 87–148; S. Tolliday and J. Zeitlin, eds., *Shop Floor Bargaining and the State: Historical and Comparative Perspectives* (Cambridge and New York: Cambridge University Press, 1984); and John Zysman, *Political Strategies for Industrial Order: State, Market and Industry in France* (Berkeley: University of California Press, 1977).

3. Important examples include Michael Adas, "From Avoidance to Confrontation: Peasant Protest in Pre-Colonial and Colonial Southeast Asia," *Comparative Studies in Society and History* 23 (1981): 217–47; Betrand Badie and Pierre Birnbaum, *The Sociology of the State*, trans. Arthur Goldhammer (Chicago: University of Chicago Press, 1983); Pierre Birnbaum, "States, Ideologies, and Collective Action in Western Europe," *Social Science Journal* 32 (1980): 671–86; Jose Murilo de Carvalho, "Political Elites and State Building: The Case of Nineteenth-Century Brazil," *Comparative States in Society and History* 24 (1981): 378–99; Mounira Charrad, "Women and the State: A Comparative Study of Politics, Law, and the Family in Tunisia, Algeria, and Morocco" (Ph.D. diss., Harvard University, 1980); Daniel Chirot, *Social Change in a Peripheral Society: The Cre-*

ation of a Balkan Colony (New York: Academic Press, 1976); Stanley B. Greenberg, *Race and State in Capitalist Development* (New Haven, Conn.: Yale University Press, 1980); Michael Hechter, *Internal Colonialism: The Celtic Fringe in British National Development, 1536–1966* (Berkeley: University of California Press, 1975); Ira Katznelson, *City Trenches: Urban Politics and the Patterning of Class in the United States* (New York: Pantheon Books, 1981); Joel S. Migdal, *Peasants, Politics, and Revolution: Pressures toward Political and Social Change in the Third World* (Princeton, N.J.: Princeton University Press, 1974); Gianfranco Poggi, *The Development of the Modern State: A Sociological Introduction* (Stanford, Calif.: Stanford University Press, 1978); Joseph Rothschild, *Ethnopolitics: A Conceptual Framework* (New York: Columbia University Press, 1981); Theda Skocpol, *States and Social Revolutions: A Comparative Analysis of France, Russia, and China* (Cambridge and New York: Cambridge University Press, 1979); Stephen Skowronek, *Building a New American State: The Expansion of National Administrative Capacities, 1877–1920* (Cambridge and New York: Cambridge University Press, 1982); Ezra N. Suleiman, *Politics, Power, and Bureaucracy in France: The Administrative Elite* (Princeton, N.J.: Princeton University Press, 1974); Charles Tilly, ed. *The Formation of National States in Western Europe*, Studies in Political Development no.8 (Princeton, N.J.: Princeton University Press, 1975); and Charles Tilly, *The Contentious French* (Cambridge: Harvard University Press, forthcoming).

4. See especially Douglass C. North, "A Framework for Analyzing the State in Economic History," *Explorations in Economic History* 16 (1979): 249–59; Douglass C. North, *Structure and Change in Economic History* (New York: Norton, 1981); and Robert H. Bates, *Markets and States in Tropical Africa: The Political Basis of Agricultural Policies* (Berkeley: University of California Press, 1981).

5. See especially Clifford Geertz, *Negara: The Theatre State in Nineteenth-Century Bali* (Princeton, N.J.: University Press, 1980).

6. Sociologists may recognize that the title of this chapter echoes the title of George C. Homans's 1964 presidential address to the American Sociological Association, "Bringing Men Back In." Of course, the subject matters are completely different, but there is an affinity of aspiration for explanations built on propositions about the activities of concrete groups. This stands in contrast to the application of analytical conceptual abstractions characteristic of certain structure-functionalist or neo-Marxist "theories."

7. Among the most important exceptions were Samuel Huntington's path-breaking state-centered book, *Political Order and Changing Societies* (New Haven, Conn.: Yale University Press, 1968); Morris Janowitz's many explorations of state–society relationships in *The Military in the Political Department of New Nations* (Chicago: University of Chicago Press, 1964), and *Social Control of the Welfare State* (Chicago: University of Chicago Press, 1976); and James Q. Wilson's conceptually acute probings in *Political Organizations* (New York: Basic Books, 1973). In his many works in political so-

ciology, Seymour Martin Lipset has always remained sensitive to the effects of various institutional structures of government representation. In addition, Reinhard Bendix consistently developed a state-centered Weberian approach to political regimes as a critical counterpoint to structure-functionalist developmentalism, and S.N. Eisenstadt and Stein Rokkan elaborated creative syntheses of functionalist and Weberian modes of comparative political analysis.

8. For clear paradigmatic statements, see Gabriel Almond, "A Developmental Approach to Political Systems," *World Politics* 16 (1965); 183–214; Gabriel Almond and James S. Coleman, eds., *The Politics of Developing Areas* (Princeton, N.J.: Princeton University Press, 1960); Gabriel Almond and G. Bingham Powell, Jr., *Comparative Politics: A Developmental Approach* (Boston: Little, Brown, 1966); David Easton, "An Approach to the Analysis of Political Systems," *World Politics* 9 (1957): 383–400; and David B. Truman, *The Governmental Process* (New York: Knopf, 1951).

9. Eric A. Nordlinger's *On the Autonomy of the Democratic State* (Cambridge: Harvard University Press, 1981) has stretched pluralist premises to their conceptual limits in order to encompass the possibility of autonomous actions by elected politicians or administrative officials. Tellingly, Nordlinger defines "state autonomy" purely in terms of the conscious preferences of public officials, who are said to be acting autonomously as long as they are not deliberately giving in to demands by societal actors. By insisting that public officials have wants and politically relevant resources, just as voters, economic elites, and organized interest groups do, Nordlinger simply gives officials the same dignity that all actors have in the fluid "political process" posited by pluralism. State autonomy, Nordlinger in effect says, is simply the creative exercise of political leadership. No matter what the organization or capacities of the state, any public official at any time is, by definition, in a position to do this. In my view, the value of Nordlinger's book lies, not in this rather insipid general conclusion, but in the researchable hypotheses about variations in state autonomy that one might derive from some of the typologies it offers.

10. See Robert Dahl, *Who Governs?* (New Haven, Conn.: Yale University Press, 1961); Raymond E. Wolfinger, *The Politics of Progress* (Englewood Cliffs, N.J.: Prentice-Hall, 1974); and Nelson W. Polsby, *Community Power and Political Theory* (New Haven, Conn.: Yale University Press, 1961). In thinking about the missing analytical elements in these studies, I have benefited from Geoffrey Fougere's critical discussion in "The Structure of Government and the Organization of Politics: A Polity Centered Approach" (Department of Sociology, Harvard University, September 1978).

11. Graham Allison, *Essence of Decision: Explaining the Cuban Missile Crisis* (Boston: Little, Brown, 1971); and Morton S. Halperin, *Bureaucratic Politics and Foreign Policy* (Washington, D.C.: The Brookings Institution, 1971).

12. I have benefited from Stephen Krasner's discussion of the bureaucratic politics perspective in *Defending the National Interest*, p. 27. Krasner's own book shows the difference it makes to take a more macroscopic, historical, and state-centered approach.
13. See Leonard Binder, James S. Coleman, Joseph La Palombara, Lucian W. Pye, Sidney Verba, and Myron Weiner, *Crises and Sequences in Political Development*, Studies in Political Development no. 7 (Princeton, N.J.: Princeton University Press, 1971); Gabriel Almond, Scott C. Flanagan, and Robert J. Mundt, *Crisis, Choice, and Change: Historical Studies of Political Development* (Boston: Little, Brown, 1973); Tilly, ed., *Formation of National States*; and Raymond Grew, ed., *Crisis of Political Development in Europe and the United States*, Studies in Political Development no. 9 (Princeton N.J.: Princeton University Press, 1978). The Tilly and Grew volumes openly criticize the theoretical ideas advocated by the Committee on Comparative Politics that sponsored these projects, and Tilly calls for the kind of approach now embodied in the mission of the Committee on States and Social Structures.
14. A sampling of the most important neo-Marxist works includes Perry Anderson, *Passages from Antiquity to Feudalism* (London: New Left Books, 1974); and *Lineages of the Absolute State* (London: New Left Books, 1974); Gösta Esping-Anderson, Roger Friedland, and Erik Olin Wright, "Modes of Class Struggles and the Capitalist State," *Kapitalistate*, no. 4–5 (1976): 186–220; John Holloway and Simon Picciotto, eds., *State and Capital: A Marxist Debate* (London: Arnold 1978); Ralph Miliband, *The State in Capitalist Society* (New York: Basic Books 1969); Nicos Poulantzas, *Political Power and Social Classes*, trans. Timothy O'Hagen (London: New Left Books, 1973); Claus Offe, "Structural Problems of the Capitalist State," *German Political Studies* 1 (1974): 31–57; Göran Therborn, *What Does the Ruling Class Do When It Rules?* (London: New Left Books, 1978); and Immanuel Wallerstein, *The Modern World System*, vols. 1 and 2 (New York: Academic Press, 1974, 1980).

Some excellent overviews of the neo-Marxist debates are those of Martin Carnoy, *The State and Political Theory* (Princeton, N.J.: Princeton University Press, 1984); David A. Gold, Clarence Y. H. Lo, and Erik Olin Wright, "Recent Developments in Marxist Theories of the Capitalist State," *Monthly Review* 27 (1975), no. 5: 29–43; no. 6: 36–51; Bob Jessop, "Recent Theories of the Capitalist State," *Cambridge Journal of Economics* 1 (1977): 353–73; Bob Jessop, *The Capitalist State: Marxist Theories and Methods* (New York: New York University Press, 1982); and Ralph Miliband, *Marxism and Politics* (Oxford: Oxford University Press, 1977).
15. Of all those engaged in the neo-Marxist debates, Fred Block goes the farthest toward treating states as truly autonomous actors. See his "The Ruling Class Does Not Rule: Notes on the Marxist Theory of the State," *Socialist Revolution* (1977): 6–28; and "Beyond Relative Autonomy," in the *Socialist Register 1980*, ed. Ralph Miliband and John Saville (London: Merlin Press, 1980),

pp. 227–42. For congruent positions, see also Trimberger, *Revolution from Above*, as well as my own *States and Social Revolutions* (Cambridge and New York: Cambridge University Press, 1979) and "Political Response to Capitalist Crisis: Neo-Marxist Theories of the State and the Case of the New Deal," *Politics and Society* 10 (1980): 155–201. Block and I are jointly criticized for overemphasizing state autonomy in Carnoy, *State and Political Theory*, chap 8; and Block, Trimberger, and I are all critically discussed in Ralph Miliband, "State Power and Class Interests," *New Left Review*, no. 138 (1983): 57–68.

16. The scope of many neo-Marxist propositions about states makes them more applicable/testable in comparisons *across* modes of production, rather than across nations within capitalism. Therborn, in *Ruling Class*, is one of the few theorists to attempt such cross-mode comparisons, however.

17. I do not mean to imply pure continuity. Around the World Wars and during the 1930s depression, when both British and U.S. hegemony faltered, there were bursts of more state-centered theorizing, including such works as Harold Lasswell's "The Garrison State," *American Journal of Sociology* 46 (1941): 455–68; and Karl Polanyi's *The Great Transformation* (Boston: Beacon Press, 1957; originally 1944).

18. For some suggestive treatments, see Stephen D. Krasner, "United States Commercial and Monetary Policy: Unraveling the Parodox of External Strength and Internal Weakness," in *Between Power and Plenty*, ed. Katzenstein, pp. 51–87; Stephen Blank, "Britain: The Politics of Foreign Economic Policy, the Domestic Economy, and the Problems of Pluralistic Stagnation," in *Between Power and Plenty*, ed. Katzenstein, pp. 89–138; Andrew Martin, "Political Constraints on Economic Strategies in Advanced Industrial Societies," *Comparative Political Studies* 10 (1977): 323–54; Paul M. Sacks, "State Structure and the Asymmetrical Society: An Approach to Public Policy in Britain," *Comparative Politics* 12 (1980): 349–76; and Dyson and Wilks, eds., *Industrial Crisis*.

19. For Max Weber's principal writings on states, see *Economy and Society*, ed. Guenther Roth and Claus Wittich (New York: Bedminster Press, 1968; originally 1922), vol. 2, chap. 9; vol. 3, chaps. 10–13.

20. Stepan, *State and Society*, p. xii.

21. See *The Historical Essays of Otto Hintze*, ed. Felix Gilbert (New York: Oxford University Press, 1975; originally 1897–1932).

22. For discussion of the most important neopluralist theory of state autonomy, see note 9. The works by Poulantzas and Offe cited in note 14 represent important neo-Marxist theories of state autonomy. Poulantzas's approach is ultimately very frustrating because he simply posits the "relative autonomy of the capitalist state" as a necessary feature of the capitalist mode of production as such. Poulantzas insists that the state is "relatively autonomous" regardless of varying empirical ties between state organizations

and the capitalist class, and at the same time he posits that the state must invariably function to stabilize the capitalist system as a whole.

23. Stepan, *State and Society*, chaps. 3 and 4. See also Alfred Stepan, "The New Professionalism of Internal Welfare and Military Role Expansion," in *Authoritarian Brazil*, ed. A. Stepan (New Haven, Conn.: Yale University Press, 1973), pp. 47–65.

24. Trimberger, *Revolution from Above*.

25. Ibid., p. 4.

26. Ibid., p. 5.

27. Thus, in commenting on Stepan's work, Trimberger argues that he could have explained the repressive and "exclusionary" nature of the Brazilian coup (in contrast to Peru's "inclusionary" reforms, which included mass political mobilization and expropriation of hacienda landlords) by focusing on the Brazilian military's ties to Brazilian and multinational capitalists. In fact, Stepan does report ("The New Professionalism," p. 54) that Brazilian military professionals received their training alongside elite civilians, including industrialists, bankers, and commercial elites, who also attended the Superior War College of Brazil in the period before 1964.

28. Trimberger's work thus speaks to the problems with Nicos Poulantzas's theory discussed in note 22.

29. For France; there is an especially rich literature on state autonomy, its consequences, and its limits. I am deliberately leaving it aside here, because France is such an obvious case for the application of ideas about state autonomy. See the works, however, by Birnbaum, Hall, Suleiman, and Zysman cited in notes 2 and 3, along with Stephen Cohen, *Modern Capitalist Planning: The French Experience* (Berkeley: University of California Press, 1976); and Richard F. Kuisel, *Capitalism and the State in Modern France: Renovation and Economic Management in the Twentieth Century* (Cambridge and New York: Cambridge University Press, 1981).

30. Heclo, *Modern Social Politics*.

31. Ibid., p. 305.

32. Ibid., pp. 305–6, 303.

33. Krasner, *Defending the National Interest*.

34. Ibid., p. 11.

35. See also Krasner, "United States Commercial and Monetary Policy, pp. 51–87.

36. Thus, Krasner has the most difficulty in distinguishing his argument for "state autonomy" from the structural Marxist perspective according to which the state acts for the class interests of capital as a whole. His solution, to stress "nonrational" ideological objectives of state policy as evidence against the class-interest argument, does not strike me as being very convincing. Could an imperialist ideology not be evidence of class consciousness as well as of state purpose: One might stress, instead, the perceived geopolitical "interests" at work in U.S. interventions

abroad. "Free-world" justifications for such interventions are not obviously irrational, given certain understandings of U.S. geopolitical interests.

37. J.P. Nettl, "The State as a Conceptual Variable," *World Politics* 20 (1968), 563–64.

38. Kenneth Finegold and Theda Skocpol, "Capitalists, Farmers, and Workers in the New Deal—The Ironies of Government Intervention" (Paper presented at the annual meeting of the American Political Science Association, Washington, D.C., August 31, 1980). Part of this paper was subsequently published as Theda Skocpol and Kenneth Finegold, "State Capacity and Economic Intervention in the Early New Deal," *Political Science Quarterly* 97 (1982): 255–78.

39. Skocpol and Finegold, "State Capacity," p. 271.

40. In contrasting ways, both Krasner's *Defending the National Interest* and Poulantzas's *Political Power and Social Classes* exemplify this point.

41. Or perhaps one should say that any state or state-building movement preoccupied with sheer administrative–military control will, at best, only be able (as well as likely) to implement policies connected to that overriding goal. This principle is a good guide to understanding many of the social changes that accompany state-building struggles during revolutionary interregnums.

42. See Tilly, ed., *Formation of National States*: Michael Mann, "State and Society, 1130–1815: An Analysis of English State Finances," *Political Power and Social Theory* (Greenwich, Conn.: JAI Press, 1980), vol. 1, pp. 165–208; and Stephen Skowronek, *Building a New American State: The Expansion of National Administrative Capacities* (Cambridge and New York: Cambridge University Press, 1982).

43. See Bernard Silberman's important comparative-historical work on alternative modes of state bureaucratization in relation to processes of professionalization: "State Bureaucratization: A Comparative Analysis" (Department of Political Science, The University of Chicago, 1982).

44. Windfall revenues from international oil sales, for example, can render states *both* more autonomous from societal controls and, because social roots and political pacts are weak, more vulnerable in moments of crisis. I argue along these lines in "Rentier State and Shi'a Islam in the Iranian Revolution," *Theory and Society* 11 (1982): 265–83. The Joint Committee on the Near and Middle East of the American Council of Learned Societies and the Social Science Research Council currently has a project entitled "Social Change in Arab Oil-Producing Societies" that is investigating the impact of oil revenues on state-society relationships.

45. See Robert E. Wood. "Foreign Aid and the Capitalist State in Underdeveloped Countries," *Politics and Society* 10 (1) (1980): 1–34. Wood's essay primarily documents and discusses the anti-state-building effects of most foreign aid, but it also notes that "the 'overdeveloped' military institutions fostered by aid can pro-

vide a springboard for statist experimentation unintended by aid donors" (p. 34). Taiwan and South Korea would both seem to be good examples of this.

46. See John A. Dunn, Jr., "The Importance of Being Earmarked: Transport Policy and Highway Finance in Great Britain and the United States," *Comparative Studies in Society and History* 20 (1) (1978): 29–53.

47. For "classic" statements on the social analysis of state finances, see especially Lorenz von Stein, "On Taxation," and Rudolf Gold-scheid, "A Sociological Approach to Problems of Public Finance," both in *Classics in the Theory of Public Finance*, ed. Richard A. Musgrave and Alan T. Peacock (New York: Macmillan, 1958), pp. 202–13 and 28–36, respectively.

48. Krasner, *Defending the National Interest*, p. 58.

49. Ibid.

50. Ira Katznelson and Kenneth Prewitt, "Constitutionalism, Class, and the Limits of Choice in U.S. Foreign Policy," in *Capitalism and the State in U.S.–Latin American Relations*, ed. Richard Fagen (Stanford, Calif.: Stanford University Press, 1979), p. 38.

51. Stepan, *State and Society*, chaps. 5–8.

52. This concept is discussed by Peter Katzenstein in *Between Power and Plenty*, pp. 16, 297–98.

53. Susan S. and Norman I. Fainstein, "National Policy and Urban Development," *Social Problems* 26 (1978): 125–46; see especially pp. 140–41.

54. Katzenstein, ed., *Between Power and Plenty*.

55. Krasner, *Defending the National Interest*, especially parts 2 and 3.

56. Stepan, *State and Society*, chap. 7.

57. Katzenstein, ed., *Between Power and Plenty*, p. 19.

58. I am indebted to Jeff Weintraub for pointing out the affinities of this second approach to Tocqueville's political sociology.

59. Nettl, "The State as a Conceptual Variable," pp. 559–92. A recent work pursuing related issues is Kenneth Dyson's *The State Tradition in Western Europe: A Study of an Idea and Institution* (New York: Oxford University Press, 1980).

60. Ira Katznelson and Kenneth Prewitt, "Limits of Choice," in *Capitalism and the State*, ed. Fagen, pp. 31–33.

61. Charles Tilly, *As Sociology Meets History* (New York: Academic Press, 1981), pp. 109–44.

62. Ibid., pp. 145–78.

63. For an overview of Tilly's approach to collective action in critical response to earlier sociological approaches, see *From Mobilization to Revolution* (Reading, Mass.: Addison-Wesley, 1978).

64. Suzanne Berger, "Interest Groups and the Governability of European Society," *Items* (Newsletter of the Social Science Research Council) 35 (1981): 66–67.

65. See Suzanne Berger, ed., *Organizing Interests in Western Europe: Pluralism, Corporatism, and the Transformation of Politics* (Cambridge and New York: Cambridge University Press, 1981); Philippe C. Schmitter and Gerhard Lehmbruch, eds., *Trends to-*

ward Corporatist Intermediation, vol. 1 of *Contemporary Political Sociology* (Beverly Hills, Calif.: Sage, 1979), and Gerhard Lehmbruch and Philippe C. Schmitter. eds., *Patterns of Corporatist Policy-Making*, vol. 7 of *Modern Politics Series* (Beverly Hills, Calif.: Sage, 1982).

66. Robert H. Salisbury, "Why No Corporatism in America?" in *Corporatist Intermediation*, ed. Schmitter and Lehmbruch, pp. 213–30; and Graham K. Wilson, "Why Is There No Corporatism in the United States?," in *Corporatist Policy-Making*, ed. Lehmbruch and Schmitter, pp. 219–36.

67. See Martin Shefter's "Party and Patronage: Germany, England, and Italy," *Politics and Society* 7 (1977): 403–51; "Party, Bureaucracy, and Political Change in the United States," in *The Development of Political Parties: Patterns of Evolution and Decay*, ed. Louis Maisel and Joseph Cooper, vol. 4 of *Sage Electoral Studies Yearbook* (Beverly Hills, Calif.: Sage, 1979), pp. 211–65, and "Regional Receptivity to Reform: The Legacy of the Progressive Era," *Political Science Quarterly* 98 (1983): 459–83.

68. In fact, Shefter shows ("Party and Patronage," p. 428) that parties in the Weimar Republic that might have preferred to use patronage appeals to garner peasant votes were prodded into ideological appeals because bureaucratic autonomy was so great. Thus, they resorted to anti-Semitic and nationalist "ideas" to appeal to the peasantry, a class that is often supposed to be inherently oriented to patronage appeals.

69. Matthew Crenson, *The Un-Politics of Air Pollution: A Study of Non-Decisionmaking in the Cities* (Baltimore, Md.: Johns Hopkins University Press, 1971), especially chaps. 5 and 6.

70. Pierre Birnbaum, "States, Ideologies and Collective Action in Western Europe," *International Social Science Journal* 32 (1980): 671–86.

71. Katznelson, *City Trenches*; and Martin Shefter, "Trades Unions and Political Machines: The Organization and Disorganization of the American Working Class in the Late Nineteenth Century," forthcoming in *Working Class Formation: Nineteenth Century Patterns in Western Europe and the United States*, ed. Ira Katznelson and Aristide Zolberg (Princeton, N.J.: Princeton University Press).

72. Katznelson and Prewitt, "Limits of Choice," p. 30.

73. Theda Skocpol, "A Critical Review of Barrington Moore's Social Origins of Dictatorship and Democracy," *Politics and Society* 4 (1973): 1–34.

74. Skocpol, *States and Social Revolutions*.

75. Fainstein and Fainstein, "National Policy and Urban Development."

76. Ibid., pp. 39–40; and David Vogel, "Why Businessmen Distrust Their State: The Political Consciousness of American Corporate Executives," *British Journal of Political Science* 8 (1978): 45–78.

77. See David Vogel, "The New Social Regulation in Historical and Comparative Perspective," in *Regulation in Perspective*, ed.

Thomas McGraw (Cambridge: Harvard University Press, 1981), pp. 155–85.

78. See Gerald L. Geison, ed., *Professions and the French State, 1700–1900* (Philadelphia: University of Pennsylvania Press, 1984); Arnold J. Heidenheimer, "Professions, the State, and the Polic(e)y Connection: How Concepts and Terms Evolved over Time and across Language Boundaries" (Paper presented at a panel, Professions, Public Policy and the State, Twelfth World Congress, International Political Science Association, Rio de Janeiro, Brazil, August 12, 1982); Terry Johnson, "The State and the Professions: Peculiarities of the British," in *Social Class and the Division of Labour*, ed. Anthony Giddens and Gavin Mackenzie (Cambridge and New York: Cambridge University Press, 1982), pp. 186–20; Dietrich Rueschemeyer, *Lawyers and Their Society: A Comparative Study of the Legal Profession in Germany and the United States* (Cambridge: Harvard University Press, 1973); Dietrich Rueschemeyer, "Professional Autonomy and the Social Control of Expertise," in *The Sociology of the Professions*, ed. R. Dingwall and P. Lewis (London: Macmillan, 1983); Bernard Silberman, "State Bureaucratization"; and Deborah A. Stone, *The Limits to Professional Power: National Health Care in the Federal Republic of Germany* (Chicago: University of Chicago Press, 1980).

Alan Cawson

Corporatism and Political Theory

Introduction

1   In the last fifteen years the concept of corporatism has made a dramatic impact on the field of political studies. It not only revitalised the topic of interest group studies, which had been in the doldrums after some energetic theory building by American scholars in the late 1950s, but also has had a significant impact on a much wider area. Scholars have used the notion of corporatism[1] to explore politics in countries as far apart geographically and politically as Brazil and Britain, the Soviet Union and the United States, Australia and Rumania.[2] Political studies are perhaps no more prone than other branches of knowledge to fads and fashions, but it is certainly true that 'corporatism', like 'pluralism', 'Marxism', 'democracy', and so on, has been used rather loosely to refer to somewhat different things.

2   The attention given to corporatism in the last ten years has been remarkable, and if nothing else indicates the dissatisfaction of scholars with the conceptual tools available to make sense of what they observe around them.[3] Although it may be premature it is worth beginning this essay on the theory of corporatism by asking what it was that it was seeking to replace. Is it possible to identify a dominant orthodoxy or paradigm that outlived its usefulness, so that we may speak of a theoretical shift and define exactly what it is that has shifted? I think that even at this early stage it is possible to do this, even though the conclusions must remain tentative.

Competing Paradigms

3   Many writers on corporatism follow Schmitter's early lead in identifying pluralism as the orthodoxy or paradigm that is being challenged. As one might expect from writing with a polemical as well as a serious analytical purpose, the lines of battle are sometimes confused, and the strength of the enemy misrepresented for the purposes of propaganda. Recent counter-attacks have accused corporatists of erecting a straw man, and of claiming as their own parts of the territory belonging to the opposition. Corporatists contend that pluralists fail

From *Corporatism and Political Theory* (Oxford, Basil Blackwell, 1986), pp. 1–21.

to understand existing political processes; pluralists contend that corporatists fail to understand pluralism, and in particular its capacity for adjustment to comprehend new developments, without, many of them say, the need for a new theory or a new term.

Pluralism has been under attack before, from a number of 4 directions. In the early 1960s a broadside was mounted against the pluralist idea of power as goal-directed action observable in decisions, with the claim that non-decisions and institutional routines filter out many demands before they can be acted upon, or even put. The pluralist approach celebrated the observable democratic tip of a very undemocratic iceberg. As the skirmishes proceeded, it became clear that the issues were not really fundamental disagreements about the nature of social science, such as were to surface later, but ideological disagreements between 'orthodox' and 'radical' positions. Pluralism proved its elasticity as a theoretical approach by simply absorbing the idea of non-decisions into its category of decisions: the first decision on the public agenda is what decisions should be on the agenda, and this is studied using the same methods as are applied to the study of all other decisions. One of the reasons why such an elegant and disarming solution was possible was that pluralist concepts relied exclusively on observable phenomena and this made research easier. The research output of the rival 'neo-elitist' school was tiny and largely forgettable.

A much more important battle was fought over the concepts, 5 forms and method of political inquiry, and in particular over the relationship between politics and economics. Pluralist theory sits comfortably within the separate discipline of political science because it contends that the economic and the political are not only distinct spheres of behaviour but they also require separate theoretical treatment. Marxism, drawing its strength from its holistic and integrating approach, with allies in several disciplines, challenged not only the central conclusion of pluralism, that power in capitalist societies was dispersed, but also the basic tools used to reach this conclusion. Furthermore it contested the process by which such tools are fashioned. Its central claim was the unity of political economy under the decisive influence of the productive forces of the economy. The separation of political interests in a political sphere, to be studied by political science, was seen as a very minor part of the mystifying process of bourgeois ideology whereby liberal democracy concealed from view the process of class exploitation.

6   Now this would not do by itself as a challenge to pluralism
because politics was so scantily developed in Marx's attempt
to unravel the mechanisms of capitalism. Before the attack
could be mounted the conceptual armoury had to be crafted,
and this was done by developing a theory of the state which
showed how what appeared as politics, in the actions of governments, in the law, and in the public sphere generally, was
determined by underlying relations of production. This work
was done in the late 1960s and early 1970s, by rereading Marx
to elaborate the idea of structures (economic, political and ideological) and present the view that humans acted as agents of
these structures. A structural interpretation of politics built
on these foundations emphasised the role of the state in or-
ganising the domination of workers by capitalists. The fact
that capitalists themselves acted at arm's length from the state
(celebrated by pluralists), and that labour parties could form
governments and improve the material condition of workers
(confirmation to pluralists of the responsiveness of the state
to multiple interests), was grist to the structuralist mill. The
first allowed the state the freedom to get on with the job of
safeguarding the supremacy of the capitalist class as a whole
free from day-to-day interference from sections of it; the second helped to deceive workers that their interests lay within
capitalism rather than in its overthrow.

7   The weapons were fashioned, however, in theoretical terms
of such laboured opaqueness that few of the protagonists were
ever entirely certain that their guns were loaded and fewer
still got to fire them at an enemy. Crucial terms in the argument, such as 'the last instance' (which was supposed to
retain the decisive effects of the economic) and 'relative autonomy' (which was supposed to free the state to act in a predetermined fashion) were notoriously difficult to specify, and
there was always the underlying unease amongst the troops
that if humans really were bearers of underlying structures,
having no freewill of their own, then any changes in politics,
or even in the debates they were engaged in, would be simply a
matter of hanging around waiting for the right 'contingencies'
or 'conjunctural' conditions. It is not easy to maintain morale
on that basis.

8   Pluralists reacted to such onslaughts with blank incompre-
hension. Why bother to take part in the battle when your opponents were slugging it out with each other and you could walk
through the hail of bullets with no apparent ill effects? Why not
smile complacently when one protagonist (Poulantzas) tells
another (Miliband), who has tried to refute pluralist theories
by assembling counter-evidence consistent with Marxist ideas

about the way in which the state works in the capitalists' interests, that he should not fight on ground contaminated by such poisons as empiricism? Why not congratulate yourself when one of the foremost interpreters of Poulantzas in English scatters throughout his book on *The Capitalist State* a formidable list of no less than nineteen theoretical sins, from reductionism and essentialism to formalism, theoreticism and, of course, empiricism,[4] and then concludes with a chapter which sets out a position which, according to another Marxist, is indistinguishable from orthodox political science (Offe, 1983), forcing one of those exercises in self-criticism for which Marxists are justly famous (Jessop, 1983).

The Need for a New Approach

I hope to show in this book that pluralists should not take 9 comfort from the failure of Marxism to get its act together. Critical theory, whether Marxist or not, has a tradition of introspection and self-consciousness of which pluralists would do well to take at least a small dose. If the pluralist house is in order, then how can the attractions of neo-elitism, neo-Marxism, and now neo-corporatism to a wide range of students of politics be explained? I want to argue that pluralism was once capable of understanding the diversity of political phenomena within capitalist societies, that changes in those phenomena force a reconsideration of pluralism as an explanatory and interpretive account, and that the weight of evidence and theoretical critique point to the need for a new paradigm, not necessarily to supplant pluralism but certainly to supplement it and force the recognition of the need to reduce the scope of its applicability.

The danger of this argument is that it might fail to capture 10 the diversity and richness of pluralism itself; that in seeking to specify what is pluralism, and by antithesis, what is corporatism, a false conception might arise. It is not an easy task to specify what pluralism is, and to separate its explanatory purposes from its political ones. Pluralist theory claims to be an accurate description of interest politics and of the workings of liberal democratic political systems. It also makes the claim (sometimes overtly, sometimes not) that pluralism is morally superior to alternative forms of political systems, such as fascism or communism. I will not deal with the second claim in any detail in what follows, but will concentrate on whether we can use pluralist versions of key political concepts to construct explanations of how political processes work. But the book as a whole is not a critique of pluralism, rather it is an exploration of corporatism and a (perhaps) premature assessment of its potential as the basis for a reconstruction of political theory. In the rest of this introductory chapter, I shall, however, try to make explicit the different theoretical perspectives of pluralism, Marxism and corporatism. I want to illustrate how difficult this task is in practice by contrasting two quotations, the first by a writer who identifies himself as a 'pluralist'; the second by someone who accepts the label of 'Marxist'.

> The institutionalisation of the interdependence between the public authorities and the interest groups may, in certain spheres, develop to the extent of the partial and informal 'incorporation' of groups into the machinery of government. The degree of involvement by interest-group leaders in public decision-making and policy implementation, their willingness to subordinate their sectional interest to what they accept as the public interest, may be such that they cease to be genuinely independent of the state. Such an arrangement has great advantages for the state, as it does not need to create an unwieldy bureaucracy to achieve the mobilisation of support for public policies but can operate in a functionally decentralised fashion. However, only those groups that have something to offer the state are candidates for such virtual 'incorporation'. Those that are simply making demands upon it, the pure pressure groups, are persona non grata. (Hayward, 1979, p. 37)

> In an advanced industrial economy, interest organisations have the power to interfere with public policy making in highly dysfunctional ways; hence the need to 'keep them out'. At the same time, however, such representative organizations are absolutely indispensable for public policy, because they have a monopoly of information relevant for public policy and, most important, a substantial measure of control over their respective constituencies. Therefore they must be made integral components of the mechanisms through which public policy is formulated. (Offe, 1981, p. 131)

11   Now it seems to me that these two statements about the relationship of interest groups to the state have much more in common with each other than either does with its 'home' paradigm. And more important still, their nature is so distinctive that they fit much more easily within an emergent paradigm of corporatism.

A Dualist Strategy

Offe, incidentally, is more conscious of this problem than 12
Hayward, and argues for a 'dual or combined explanation that
relies exclusively neither on the social class nor on the pluralist group paradigm' (p. 139), but Hayward too completes his
essay by quoting an ideal-typical description of corporatism
and saying that it is premature to pass judgement on it (p.
39). In Hayward's view society is becoming decreasingly pluralistic but it is too early to jettison the pluralist paradigm
because it is descriptively less distorted than the alternatives.
But there is, I believe, in Offe's suggestion the possibility of an
even less distorted paradigm, which is explored in the following pages. It is that by modifying Marxist theory to respecify
the role of the state and the nature of interest organisation,
we can explain some of the political processes concerned with
production in capitalist society, and that by modifying pluralism and restricting its scope we can explain those other
processes concerned with consumption. The tension between
corporatist politics and pluralist politics can then be used to
explain the conflicts and cleavages in contemporary capitalist
systems. This 'dual politics' thesis is set out in the final chapter
of the book, and its implications for democracy are discussed.

The Differences Explored

I will aim to bring out the differences between pluralism, 13
Marxism and corporatism by starting out with a brief survey of the concepts, basic to any political theory, of interests,
groups and organisations, power and decisions, government
and the state, according to how they are seen from these perspectives. I will try to bring out the essential differences without, I hope, doing them too much injustice. It will be evident
from this exercise that the corporatist perspective is something
of a synthesis of those aspects of pluralist and Marxist theory
which I think should be retained and elaborated. One objection to this procedure will be that it ignores the irreconcilable
methodological and epistemological differences between pluralism and Marxism, and rejects a priori an incompatibility
which arises from the philosophically distinct conceptions of
human nature which underlie them.

I will not deal with this objection here, because if we take 14
that as the starting point then the project is stalled at the outset and knowledge remains in ideologically separated domains

policed at the frontiers by eager thought policemen. I will also not deal directly with the concepts of structure and agency because the whole work is addressed to the relationship between the two. Agency assumes the capacity to act differently; how differently can only be explored through an understanding of structure, and in particular what I see as structural constraints. These constraints are in turn best seen as enduring residues of actions; they can be transformed by action but at a cost in terms of resources like energy and money. Only an extreme pluralist sees no constraints; only an extreme Marxist sees no agency. The heartland of the debate lies between these extremes, and mapping that terrain is a task to which this book is addressed.

15   *Interests.*   One major disagreement between pluralists and Marxists concerns the attribution of interests to actors, and whether a person may not be conscious of what his or her interests are. *Pluralists* suggest that interests are the preferences expressed by people, and that the only way of finding out what a person's interest is is by asking. If a person believes a policy to be in his or her interests, then we have to take that statement as evidence of that person's interests, even though we may suspect the person to be mistaken. Some pluralists concede that wants may differ from interests, in the sense, for example that I might want a cigarette even though I know it to be against my interests (in remaining healthy), but here also the conception of interest is subjective, and the possibility that I might have an interest of which I am not aware is discounted.

16   The advantage of such a formula is that it is simple to apply in empirical research through the use of questionnaire surveys and interviews. Respondents may be asked whether, for example, they support a particular policy, and their positive answers are taken as standing for an interest in that policy being enacted. The more intensely people hold an interest, the more likely are they to join an association and participate in politics. Conversely, the less people participate in politics, the less interested they are judged to be in the issues involved. There are several objections to such a way of imputing interest. One is that it assumes that people determine their interests freely, with free access to information, so that they cannot be wrong. Alternative conceptions of interest have generally relied on some concept of 'objective' interest, which is discoverable through research, or argued for theoretically. It is then the difference between the alleged objective interest, and the revealed preference, which has to be explained, often in terms of the effects of ideology leading to false consciousness. A fur-

ther objection, discussed below, is that this approach assumes that statements about the interests of groups are statements about the individual preferences of group members, and refuses to accept that the interest of the group may be distinct from that of its members in the way that wholes can be said to be more than the sum of their parts.

Marxists share two basic views which contrast strongly with 17 those of the pluralists. The first is that interests are formed in a class-divided society, and the relations of production which are the basis of class formation are also fundamental to how interests are both shaped and perceived. Class interests are considered to be much more important in politics than any other kind of interest. This view contains the important point that interests are formed through social relationships, and do not exist prior to those relationships. The pluralists, by contrast, are interested in the relationships between expressed preferences and political action. They are interested in whether participation is related to interests; whether power can be observed through the resolution of conflicts of interest and so on. They do not from the beginning suggest that particular kinds of interests give rise to groups which are always powerful, because they argue that such questions can only be determined empirically, and they believe that the weight of evidence refutes the claim that particular elites or classes are in permanent positions of power.

For Marxists this question is crucial because it opens up 18 the possibility of transforming people's interests through class struggle. Their second basic view stems from this: the capitalist system of class exploitation is not in the objective interests of the working class. But the working class in advanced capitalist countries has shown few signs of wanting to get rid of the system. The difference between their objective interest and manifest preferences is then explained in terms of the effects of ideology, leading to a false consciousness of their real interests. The public ideology of capitalist societies is couched in terms of citizenship and formal equality which denies the existence of class divisions. Thus there exists the crucial political task of procuring a revolution in the name of the objective interests of that class, which may or may not include as part of its project the prior task of convincing the working class that its interest is in revolution, i.e. bringing subjective preferences and objective interests into line.

Corporatists study interest organisations and concentrate on 19 the issue of how organisational interests may be conceived, and how they may differ from individual interests. Many of these organisations are class ones, but their interests are not assumed to be captured by any concept of objective class interest, or assumed to be aggregate of the interests of members. The contention is that the process of organisation can shape people's interests: like Marxists they emphasise social relations as formative of interests, but the key social relations in late capitalism are held to be within and between organisations, rather than at the level of relations of production and class formation. If trade unions show no revolutionary consciousness it is not because of the distorting effects of ideology (summed up in Lenin's view of 'labourism') but because of the organisational requirements involved in both defending members' interests and defining them. The focus is not on the individual, or on the class structure, but on the process of collective action.

20   *Groups.*   For *pluralists* groups are extremely important in the political process. Individuals sharing an interest which is affected by governmental action, or which requires action from governments, form political groups which seek to make claims and demands upon government. In extreme versions of pluralism it is argued that all political phenomena are explainable in terms of a group process, but most pluralists subscribe to partial theories of groups which explain their activities within democratic and governmental processes. Groups make their claims by exerting influence through the marshalling of political resources, such as membership (which carries weight with politicians because of the potential votes involved), information (which governments need to make policies; the more specialised the information the more valuable it is); and sanctions (non-cooperation and in the case of trade unions, the strike). An impressive range of empirical studies of groups in action has charted these processes in detail, and has demonstrated great inequalities in the power of different groups. Some are consulted at every turn, have instant access to senior bureaucrats and ministers, get their way more often than not; others are weak and dependent upon petitioning, street protests, lobbying members of parliament and so on. I will deal below with the question of how pluralist theory accounts for such differences in the power of groups; here I want briefly to discuss the nature of the group process.

21   Underlying most pluralist conceptions is a view of politics as a system, with government at its centre. Groups are part of the political system, but not part of the governmental system. They develop within a society with specialised political institutions for government, and those which become 'pressure groups' or 'interest groups' enter the political system because they make demands upon government. Political parties

are sometimes seen as a special form of pressure group which has an interest in forming a government; other groups make claims on government but do not want to become government.

Interest groups are now widely seen as an integral part of 22 the democratic process within liberal democracies, and help to make elected governments more responsive to individuals in society. The strength of public interest in a particular issue can be gauged by the proliferation and impact of competing groups. If groups are 'successful' they secure favourable public policies; the more they are successful the more power is attributed to them. Because pluralists relate action to individual interests, it is assumed that the lack of activity on an issue is a reliable guide to the strength of public feeling. If people are disgruntled by the actions of government, they will form a group to protest or seek redress. Inactivity is taken as an indication of consent to government policies. Groups are useful because they can deal with single issues, and influence policy in a much more specialised way than electoral processes, which bundle issues together. Governments need groups because they reinforce democracy and extend the availability of information.

One of the effects of the seemingly intractable economic 23 problems now facing governments has been that this benign view has given way in recent years to a pessimistic one, in which excessive demands made by groups, and extravagant bids by parties for votes, are seen to lead to 'overload' and 'ungovernability'. I do not propose to discuss this view here, but it is worth emphasising that it shares with the benign view the location of government as the target for group activity, and the process of exerting, or attempting to exert influence, as the key one. Policy implementation takes place though the law and through bureaucracies, and again groups may attempt to influence the processes of administration.

To sum up: the basis of the pluralist position is that groups 24 form in society, some are interest groups which make demands on government and seek policies in furtherance of their members' interests, and the most powerful groups are the ones whose policy preferences regularly prevail.

Most *Marxists* do not give much attention to groups as such, 25 or spend much time discussing exactly how class interests are organised, although many do recognise different fractions of capital and the distinct interests of diverse sections of the working class. Discrepancies in the power of organisations are explained in terms of the class interests that underlie them. The power of capital is given by the economic structure and reinforced by the state; the weakness of working class organisations is a mirror image of the power of capital, but within a general analysis of working-class subordination, variations in power are related to the degree of class consciousness which in turn is argued to affect the strength of class organisations.

26   Groups as such are not significant in the analysis of power structure and political conflict because they are argued to reflect other more crucial political forces. Moreover the sheer number and variety of interest groups is argued by Marxists to act, like elections, as a smokescreen concealing class domination. The invitation to participate in politics through pressure groups is seen as a largely, if not wholly symbolic gesture, which is encouraged by the capitalist class because it diverts attention away from the real relations of power.

27   Trade unions are analysed in terms quite different from those used to describe pressure groups, because of the role they are argued to be capable of playing in developing a socialist consciousness, but not by themselves: they need the prodding of a socialist party to overcome their sectional outlook and inherent tendency to work within rather than against the capitalist system. But it is their class character and political role which marks out trade unions as different from other interest organisations in the Marxist approach, not any special features of their organisational form. The organisational forms of capital are rarely studied by Marxists, partly because most of their attention is devoted to the working class and the state, and partly because Marxist theory provides a structural rather than an organisational explanation of the power of capital. The relative weakness of many employers and trade associations compared to many trade unions is explained in terms of the greater dependence of labour on organisation compared to the structural advantages conferred upon capital.

28   The main distinctiveness of the *corporatist* approach to interest groups lies in the view that organisation is both constrained by and shapes the nature of the interests concerned. The crucial distinction is between functional interests, or work-related interests, and other kinds. According to corporatist theory groups can, and do, form around political preferences, but these processes are far less significant for politics and power relationships than groups which form around socio-economic functions within complex industrialised societies. The early history of groups which represent functionally defined interests may well be of voluntary association and competitive interaction, but as the competitive market economy gives way to oligopolistic interdependence, and the intervention of the state in the economy widens and deepens, such groups undergo a substantive change in their character. They no longer

merely reflect or represent interests, but are part of the process of forming them. Moreover (as will be discussed below) they take part in bargaining public policies with state agencies, and reach agreements of a binding character which involve the leadership of corporatist groups disciplining and controlling their members.

The most important groups which become 'corporatised' in 29 this sense are class organisations of capital and labour, which perform different functions in the division of labour. Unlike Marxists, who ascribe a governing character only to organisations of capital, corporatist writers recognise that trade unions in many advanced capitalist countries have also become an important part of the process of government. Few corporatists, perhaps, would argue that trade unions have become *as* powerful as capitalist organisations, because they, like the Marxists, recognise the structural asymmetry of the two interests in the process of production, but there is no assumption in corporatist theory that trade unions are *always* junior partners. Their power varies from country to country, and from time to time in the same country, according to such factors as the state of the economy, the nature of the legal system, the characteristics of collective bargaining, and their professionalism and organisational competence.

Not all groups in capitalist societies are corporatised 30 groups; there remains a (numerically) substantial sphere of competitive pluralist groups. But where public policies concerning economic issues are concerned, where key interests are located in the process of economic production, corporatist theory suggests that the power of pluralist groups is sharply circumscribed. Where issues involve no relevant functional constituency, for example in moral and ethical issues, corporatist arrangements which act to insulate key groups from competitive pressures are inappropriate. But the distinction between corporate and competitive groups, between corporatist and pluralist spheres of interest group politics, is not a distinction between material and non-material issues. By asking questions about the nature of collective action itself, as well as the nature of the interest involved, corporatist theory suggests that in addition to interests formed around moral issues, the economic interests of small producers, who are effectively subordinate to the market, and of individual and small consumers are not organised in corporatist groups. The observations will be developed much further in chapter 2.

Power. *Pluralists* argue that power can be defined as the ca- 31 pacity of one actor to achieve his ends against resistance by others. It is not itself a property of actors, but exists and can be observed in the relationships between actors, especially in decisions where the outcomes of power relationships are 'registered'. Pluralists argue that there is a wide variety of resources which can be used as the basis for exercising power, and that these resources are widely dispersed in capitalist democracies. The most widely dispersed of all is the vote, so that those parties and leaders who seek votes are obliged to make their policy offerings attractive to voters. Pluralists recognise that those who actually participate in decisions and exert power are few in number, but their power is restricted in two ways: by the necessity of seeking re-election, and because of the limited scope of their power. Scope is limited because of the way in which public tasks are divided into different bureaucratic organisations which compete with each other for funds from the state budget. An elite at the head of one department or agency has its power restricted by the functions of the agency, and by the interdependence between one agency and another.

32   Thus although there is inequality in the distribution of political resources, it does not add up to a permanent structure of inequality throughout society because groups without one kind of resource can offset their disadvantage by mobilising other kinds of resources. Thus the economically weak can use the ballot box; political power does not follow economic power but can be used to offset it. In broad terms, pluralists would argue that the working class have enjoyed the advantages of political power, through social democratic government, in that political parties have attracted their votes by pursuing policies that are in the interests of the working class. Electoral competition is seen as a crucial mechanism which operates to prevent the accumulation of political power by those who already hold economic power.

33   For *Marxists* political power reflects economic power, and the key to the analysis of the distribution of power in society is the pattern of the relations of production. Ownership of the means of production confers massive advantages in terms of power, because however they are elected, and whatever they promise, political elites have to make concessions to the interests of the economically dominant class. This is because capitalist societies are structurally dependent upon economic production, and those processes are controlled by capitalists. It is this fact which accounts for the ability of the capitalist class to maintain its dominant position, whatever the political complexion of the government in power. Labour or social democratic governments may make real concessions to working class interests, but there is a clear line across which they

will not move. That line comprises the control of capital over the means of production; not only private property rights in the ownership of capital but also in its disposal. The right to work is conditional on the state of the economy insofar as it does not infringe the rights of capital. Marxists argue that in practice in capitalist society the right to work is subordinated to the right to manage: where they conflict capitalist society has to concede the right to manage.

For Marxists, then, the dispersal of power in capitalist so- 34 ciety is always contingent and restricted to issues where the essential property rights of capital are not threatened. The appearance of power might be pluralistic; the reality is otherwise, and indeed the discrepancy between appearance and reality is a powerful weapon in the hands of the capitalist class for it conceals the underlying non-negotiable basis on which the power of capital is based.

Corporatists would argue that everything in capitalist soci- 35 ety is in principle open to negotiation, even the basis of capital itself. They argue that policies such as economic plans and investment strategies, where they are linked to incomes and social policies and negotiated in a tripartite manner between representatives of capital, labour and the state, do represent an infringement of the rights of capital, but also represent an infringement of the autonomy of labour. Whilst in some countries in certain periods they are prepared to argue that labour has achieved some kind of parity of power with capital, they do not argue that this is evidence of the dispersal of power in capitalist society.

On the contrary, corporatist theory points to inequality and 36 hierarchy in the distribution of power as does Marxist theory, but departs from Marxism in attributing such inequality to class structure and the differential power of capital and labour. Corporatists identify organisation and the mobilisation of bias involved in organisation as the most important phenomenon of power. Organisations achieve power by a process of social closure whereby they attain the status of monopoly representative of a particular category of functional interest. It is the nature of the interest, and the monopoly position gained through closure of the political market place, which accounts for inequalities of power. Class interest is an extremely important basis for social closure, but it is not the only one. Professional groups may achieve a high degree of power through such means, although corporatists would join with pluralists in stressing the restricted scope of their power. What prevents small businessmen or consumer groups from exercising a degree of power comparable to large corporations and producer groups is the inability to enforce closure around their interests. Small business is vulnerable to the pressure of the market; consumers are vulnerable to the power of producers.

37   Working class organisations deserve special attention in this argument because of the presumption within Marxism that they are always junior partners when they became involved in tripartite policy negotiations. Trade unions comprise two basic types: craft unions, where organisation is aimed at protecting the market power of particular skills; and industrial unions, where workers in a specific industry combine to protect and advance their common interests. Industrial unions have been identified by Marxists as potentially more useful to a socialist movement, because they more closely identify with a common class rather than with particular skills. Corporatist theory has gained from such insights into the nature of union organisation and the representation of class interests by positing a relationship between the ability of the trade union movement to represent broad encompassing class interests and its ability to secure and enforce bargains in negotiations with capitalist organisations. It is not that one causes the other, but that both cause each other. The more tangible the benefits obtained from corporatist negotiation, the more the organisation is able to represent its members effectively. Conversely the more effectively it is able to represent its members, the more trade union organisations are able to bargain better terms for their members. Corporatism is under certain conditions a 'virtuous circle' in which the foregoing of maximum immediate wage increases leads to higher long-term wages and conditions for workers. But so far little is certain about how such circles can turn vicious as well, with the failure of corporatist bargains undermining the organisational capacity of the partners, and hence the possibility of further bargains.

38   What is evident from the above is that corporatist theory does not accept the pluralist or Marxist propositions that power is a 'zero-sum' concept in which for one group to increase its power necessarily implies a reduction in the power of other groups. Both pluralism and Marxism use relational concepts of power, but with the assumption of a fixed stock of power resources. For the latter working class power can only increase if the power of capital is curbed. For pluralists power is a kind of vacuum in which the accretion of it by one group calls for the corresponding countervailing accretion of it by an opponent, and thus the limitation of the power of the first group.

39   The problem with these views, which occasionally surfaces in some Marxist writing, is that power is not simply relational

but also creational. Power, for organisations as well as for individuals, is control over self as much as control over others. The positive use of power, to create conditions under which control of self is enhanced, need not involve a loss of power to or by other groups. But it does seem to require certain organisational and political conditions, and these are the subject of discussion in subsequent chapters.

The State. *Pluralists* manage to do without a theory of the 40 state as such because their political theory of party government and group pressure has no room for one. If 'the state' means anything at all to pluralists, it is as a synonym for 'government' or 'civil service', or it represents the public side of the distinction between public and private. If we were able to accept the pluralist theory of government without too many reservations, then we would not need a theory of the state. But it is the manifest inability of pluralist theory to account for the growth and role of public authority which justifies the development of state theory.[5]

It is, however, possible to say something about the implicit 41 theory of the state in pluralism. The basic point is that the public and the private sphere are considered to be separate. Pluralists see groups as the legitimate expression of interests in society, but government as the guardian of the public interest, with the party system and parliament the means for giving expression to that interest. The freedom for private interests to organise is considered to be an important restraint on the power of the public sphere; the competitive political marketplace of countervailing powers is argued to act as a restraint upon the groups themselves. The role of government is to respond to legitimate claims and adjudicate between them through public policies. The key features of the state in pluralist theory is that it is neutral with respect to interests in society, and responsive to them.

Recently some pluralists have argued that groups make too 42 many claims—the private sphere expects too much of the public sphere—and if there is indeed a crisis of public authority in contemporary democracies it is a crisis induced, in a sense, by there being too much democracy. The public sphere has expanded because of the increased demands made of it; and because group activities call up countervailing powers, the proliferation of pressure groups has led to a paralysis of government. But many pluralists recognise that governments cannot do without interest groups both as a source of information for policy making and as a litmus test of public opinion. For some, group proliferation and policy stagnation is the price

that democracies must pay; others argue that some way must
be found to reduce the burden on the state by restricting the
access to government and the influence of pressure groups.

43   *Marxists* have challenged the view of the neutral state at its
root by claiming that the state is part of the fabric of capitalist
society rather than external to it. They differ in the extent to
which they see the state as an instrument of class domination
or as a mechanism for ensuring the unity of the capitalist class,
but what they have in common is more important; namely
that the state is a capitalist state and that its role within the
society is a consequence of the class nature of that society. For
many Marxists the state does not have its own interests; it is
to be seen as a battleground upon which the interests of rival
classes are fought out and its policies register the state of class
struggle. But it is not an equal struggle because for the working
class the terrain is always enemy terrain: all matches have to
be played away from home. For other Marxists the state exists
as a system of power with its own power base distinct from
class, and in chapter 3 below I discuss recent views that policy
can be interpreted as a partnership between state power and
class power.

44   State theory within neo-Marxism has also emphasised the
functions which the state performs vis-à-vis economy and society, and has traced the shift from a laissez-faire state which
performed the minimum necessary for capitalism to work, to
an interventionist state which intervenes directly in the processes of capital accumulation to compensate for failures in the
market. Such views emphasise the differences between competitive and monopoly capitalism: in the latter phase market
failures can be socially and politically disruptive so that state
intervention is necessary to avoid a spiral into crisis and decay.
The Marxist concept of contradiction has been employed to
portray these functional necessities as inherently crisis-ridden:
for example, in that the more the state intervenes to bolster the
legitimacy of the system through measures such as social welfare provision, the more it drains the resources of the private
sector and inhibits the process of capital accumulation. Such
views are strikingly similar to the arguments about pluralist
decay and 'overload' cited above, although they tend to explain
the source of instability in the economic system rather than in
the political demands of interest groups.

45   Whereas pluralists stress the neutrality and responsiveness
of the state, Marxists point to its class character and its active interventionism. Most Marxists would argue that the state
is a structure which is bound together by an essential unity,
not necessarily of purpose but certainly of function, in safe-

guarding capitalist interests. Only the public face of the state is neutral, but in crisis conditions the class character of its interventions is revealed.

There is, however, considerable confusion as to what 'the 46 state' actually is. Pluralists overcome this problem by refusing to use the concept except as a simple substitute term for government. Marxist structural theory often sees it as a mechanism for perpetuating class domination, but if the state does not have power of its own, but is an arena for class struggle, then it does not make sense to speak of the state 'acting'. In chapter 3 I will discuss a view of the state as a system of power and argue that action takes place within that system, constrained both by the state system itself and by the relation of the state system to the economy and the power of organised interests.

For *corporatist* theory, the concept and the theory of the state 47 presents a problem which has yet to be adequately resolved. Much corporatist writing uses the term as a synonym for government, as when the three parties involved in tripartite policy bargaining are identified as business, labour and the state. This usage does, however, differ substantially from pluralism in that government is not seen as simply reactive and responsive, but makes use of interest groups in formulating and implementing policy. Moreover governments deliberately restrict access to policy-making to certain groups on which a 'public status' is conferred. This 'corporatism for the strong and pluralism for the weak' is an important modern form of divide and rule. It implies also that, unlike in pluralist theory, governments cannot be neutral with respect to organised interests, although the bias in government cannot be understood simply as a class bias.

It is here that the confusions in corporatist theory are appar- 48 ent. Corporatism represents a fusion of the processes of interest representation and policy implementation into a reciprocal relationship between the state and organised interests. But whilst a great deal of attention has been paid to examining the interest organisations themselves, and the conditions under which they can intermediate between the state and their memberships, very little attention has been given to the organisation of the state itself. Corporatist theory shares some of its account of state interventionism with Marxism: the transformation of the competitive capitalist economy into a monopoly form which cannot by itself reproduce the conditions of its existence. Moreover corporatism stresses the growing interpenetration of public and private spheres, which is illustrated in the difficulty of saying unambiguously whether certain kinds of institutions are public or private. This is evident not only from the proliferation of quasi-governmental bodies, but also from the dependence of much of the private sector on state support.

49   Clearly the argument that policy is determined and implemented in negotiation between the state and interest organisations presupposes that state agencies exercise power in their own right, which means that the state system must be to a greater or lesser extent autonomous. If it lacks autonomy and is 'colonised' by private interests, then there is no corporatism. Conversely, if the state is completely autonomous and independent, and interest organisations in society are subordinate to state agencies in each sphere of public policy-making, then there is no corporatism. In the following chapter I discuss the concentration and development of oligopoly amongst interest organisations which is a precondition of the development of corporatism, and in chapter 3 I present some preliminary remarks concerning the nature of the state system and its distinctive power base. The existing literature on corporatism does not, however, permit more than a tentative discussion of state theory.

50   This is evident from the inconclusive accounts of state power and, more especially, on the ambiguity concerning the issue of whether the state system embraces distinctive interests. One possible argument would be that interests of the state comprise the aggregate of individual interests of those who work within it, i.e. the professional interests of civil servants. These civil servants form a bureaucratic caste, with definite privileges and an interest in protecting and expanding them. Another answer would be to point to the state as the only structure in society which is based on a general interest; so much so that it might better be viewed as above society, embodying some transcendental essence. The power of the state then derives from a widespread acceptance of such a view. A third argument would point to the power exercised by the state as a special kind of bureaucracy able to monopolise the legitimate use of force in a given territory; the state has a distinct power base because it is the only institution able to deploy this particular resource.

Conclusion

51   The arguments developed in this book are not intended to settle these issues. Indeed one question that is raised is whether a single general theory of the state is at all possible or desir-

able. If we are interested in comparing different societies with comparable economic systems and levels of development, then a general theory of 'the capitalist state' will obscure the important differences that we would wish to reveal. Even if we were to accept that capitalist states were instruments of the dominant capitalist class in each country, say France and Britain, it might still tell us very little of what we want to know about the two countries. Why does the capitalist class in France apparently permit a major role for its instrument in reconstructing, rationalising and nationalising private industry, when in Britain the capitalist class appears to resent encroachment on its managerial autonomy? Capitalist false consciousness? On the other hand, if we are interested in the broad sweep of history such apparently profound differences might appear much less significant and the idea of a 'capitalist state' in contradistinction to a 'feudal state' or an 'absolutist state' might be tenable.

It largely depends on what our explanatory purpose is; in other words, what is the scope of the phenomena that we are interested in examining? A state theory which is appropriate for explaining the differences in industrial policy in present-day Britain and France might not be at all useful for comparing the different ways in which policies are made within the same country; for example, for examining the differences between health policy and industrial policy. In the latter case the way in which the state system itself is organised, and the nature of affected interests, may be crucial variables which would only be obscured by a more general theory. 52

What then is the frame of reference for corporatist theory? As I see it there are two main contributions that corporatism can make. The first is in comparing capitalist democracies at the level of whole systems, allowing for and exploring different patterns of relationships between state systems and organised interests. At one extreme might be a case where a strong state confronts weakly organised interests (France); at the other might be a case where a weak state confronts powerful interest organisations (Britain). In between these cases lies the heartland of what in chapter 5 I call 'macro-corporatism': where (for different historical reasons that can be illuminated by corporatist analysis) the balance of power between the state system and major encompassing interest organisations is more even, and public policies reflect the outcome of negotiations between what are often called 'social partners'. Corporatist observers might differ somewhat in the way that they rank order such cases, but all would include Austria, Sweden, the Netherlands and West Germany on their lists. 53

54   The second contribution concerns the comparative analysis
      of public policy-making rather than nation-states. Here cor-
      poratist theorists are interested in the relationships between
      state agencies and interest organisations in particular pol-
      icy fields, what I call in this book 'meso-corporatism'. Even
      in cases of weak macro-corporatism, like Britain, France and
      Canada, particular policy areas are often highly insulated from
      competitive group pressures and subject to joint determina-
      tion and implementation. For specific and very interesting
      reasons, it appears that agricultural policy is almost always
      determined through corporatist negotiation, and in other pol-
      icy areas strong professional groups appear as negotiating
      partners with state agencies. It seems clear that the type of
      policy and the nature of relevant interests to a large extent
      determine the incidence of meso-corporatism, but as will be
      evident from the discussion in chapter 6, a great deal of re-
      search needs to be done to explain how these processes work.

55   These two different but related research agendas demand
      rather different theoretical approaches, but what they have in
      common is a focus on organisation as the crucial social pro-
      cess which transforms the relationship between interests and
      politics. Corporatist theory makes no prior assumption that
      particular interests, either class, sectoral or professional, are
      basic, and nor does it assume that organisations are all species
      of the same genus. Organisation is the process which links the
      structural categories of interest to politics, but in doing so im-
      portant biases are introduced. All interests do not have the
      same potential for organisation: when some interests are or-
      ganised into politics others are organised out of politics. Large
      capitalist firms can exert power over the market; others are
      subordinate to the market. In the same way some interest or-
      ganisations can exert power over the political market; others
      are subordinate to it. It is the task of corporatist theory to il-
      luminate these processes, to explain both the appearances and
      the underlying constraints, and to provide a critical appraisal
      of their effects. In this way it can make a contribution to the
      enduring questions of politics: who gets what, when, how and
      why?

Notes

1. Many authors prefix corporatism with expressions such as 'neo',
   'liberal', 'societal', 'modern' etc. to emphasise the differences from
   pre-war ideas of the corporate state. Except where necessary to
   distinguish differences within recent concepts, I have preferred to
   use the unqualified term throughout this book, but only to refer to
   modern usage.

2. See Cawson and Ballard (1984) for a bibliography of works published in English, where references to these applications, amongst many others, can be found.

3. Schmitter's truly seminal article, 'Still the century of corporatism?' (1974) remains the most widely quoted single study. A rapid search for the *Social Sciences Citation Index* reveals 58 citations in the years 1981 and 1982 alone.

4. The full list is economism, essentialism, reductionism, politicism, idealism, eclecticism, instrumentalism, historicism, subjectivism, functionalism, structuralism, formalism, reformism, epiphenomenonalism, determinism, logocentrism, empiricism, subsumptionism, and voluntarism.

5. It is interesting that the two countries in which the pluralist tradition in politics is the strongest, Britain and the United States, are those where the concept of the state in common parlance is almost non-existent. For Americans, 'the state' means one of the fifty states in the Union; for the British its means nothing apart from country, nation, or less frequently, government. Of the many possible explanations for this, to my mind the best candidate is the common law tradition in Britain and the United States, which has impeded the development of a formal system of public law.

CHAPTER ELEVEN

EPILOGUE

If it is true that theories of politics reflect the changing world of politics, it would seem that we are in for some major transformations in our approaches to the study of public life. Probably more political systems have changed in the late 1980s and early 1990s than in any comparable period since World War II—if not since 1848. Communism as a world force has spent itself; what began as the great "wave of the future" in 1917 ended some seven decades later as a shipwreck to be abandoned with all Godspeed. Its ideas were swept away—in the words that Trotsky had used to describe the future of liberal capitalism—into the dustbin of history.

Just as soon as the jackboot of Soviet repression was lifted, a veritable hothouse of prohibited ideas and aspirations luxuriated. Nationalist, religious, and bourgeois sentiments flourished like mushrooms after the rain. Perhaps most remarkable of all, it became clear that even after seventy odd years of unprecedented totalitarian control, the deepest strata of popular loyalties had not been substantially touched.

It is not unlikely that we will soon view the Communist Empire as we now do the Austro-Hungarian Empire (the more audacious would say the Holy Roman Empire). But the collapse of communism and of the Soviet Empire marks not only the historical fiasco of ideas associated with centralized authoritarian communism; it represents no less the triumph of the pluralist-democratic ideal. Whatever one's ideological predilections, it is difficult to deny a simple truth: given their choice, the overwhelming majority of individuals belonging to what we broadly refer to as Western civilization prefer regimes that are sympathetic to private enterprise, political pluralism, and human rights. Moreover, it seems to be clearly established that free market economics is the greatest engine for the creation of wealth and technological advancement that human history has yet to create.

Some took these truths as the cue for positively apocalyptic pronouncements. Not only had the pluralist-democratic ideal triumphed against all its erstwhile rivals; what was involved was nothing less than an "end of history." The great ideological and practical struggle between forms of sociopolitical life that had rocked the West for generations had come to a happy end. Western style democracy was to be the true wave of the future.

Others were not so sure. Free enterprise was creating an underclass whose last word had yet to be heard, a physical environment that was being fouled, perhaps irremediably, and a mindless consumerism whose long-range effect on civic ideals was difficult to calculate. Pluralism, as we saw in the chapter on corporatism, was being challenged by sober scholars who pointed to a growing incorporation of power at the top. Moreover, it appeared that non-Western nations were not yet aware of history's termination. Democracy in the Third World did not seem to be striking deep roots, even with the passage of time. Religious fundamentalism was rife, the business of making war was flourishing, and, distressingly, much of the world's most critical natural resources lay under the feet of ruthless local potentates, some of whom were set on a direct collision course with the West.

Whatever the final verdict on the "end of history" debate, the great contemporary transformations in thought and practice are of potentially critical significance for the study of politics. It is not unreasonable to contend that they will be for the political scientists of the 90s what the Vietnam war was for the generation of the 60s. As the decisive consciousness-shaping events of the time, they promise to provide both the inspiration for approaches that are presently in the offing and the standards by which they will be judged. Could it be that we face a new burst of creative activity comparable to the one that marked the 50s and 60s, a major redirection and rethinking of the terms, models, concepts, and methods by which the world of politics is studied?

No contemporary approach, whether new or renewed, can avoid coming to terms with the prodigious changes that have recently overtaken both the international order and the general ideological climate. No approach can avoid dealing with the surge of democratic sentiment and the victory of democratic systems in many parts of the world. For that matter, the remarkable tenacity of "primordial" identifications, both national and religious, will require thoughtful treatment by any approach that aspires to intellectual respectability. Similarly, no approach can avoid earnestly addressing the belligerent confrontation between the "First" and the "Third" World that, doubtless, will remain a central axis of our concerns for a long time to come. Approaches that fail to confront at least a significant part of these challenges convincingly will likely find themselves where the old-fashioned legal-institutional approach finds itself today: as a quaint and hoary footnote in the discipline's history.

Nor can the discipline avoid soberly examining its own record in anticipating these crucial historic events. It cannot be said, in all candor, that this record is particularly impressive. The performance of the professionals and experts in predicting and accounting for the collapse of the Communist regimes in Eastern Europe, the unification of Germany, Tienanmen, and the war in the Persian Gulf has, on the whole, not been better than that of journalists, barbers, or soothsayers.

Does this mean that political science is somehow mortally compromised? Do honesty and humility require that we, in the future, forswear the role of pundits and make it clear to those who would cast us in this role that they have misunderstood our professional capacities? Does it perhaps mean that the old behavioral dream of a predictive political science in the image of the natural sciences needs to be laid to a well-deserved rest? Maybe what needs to be concluded is simply that the divide between description, understanding, and analysis on the one hand, and prediction on the other has not significantly narrowed since the day that John Burgess received his epochal telegram.

Some have contended that the rational choice model of political science has been seriously battered by recent occurrences. In failing to account for the primordial loyalties that fuel conflict and underlie so many deep political identifications, it lacks, they surmise, the capacity to treat real political events and actors meaningfully. Others see the incipient swell of a new wave of democratic theorizing that will incorporate the variegated experience of Eastern Europe, Spain, Portugal, and the Third World states. Still others look for a resurgence of theories of modernization sensitive to the tension-ridden relations between the "developed" and the "undeveloped" regions. It has been suggested that new classificatory schemes of political systems will be necessary to accommodate much that is new to the politics of the 90s and to replace much that appears to be on the way to obsolescence, such as the indiscriminate label *totalitarian*. A new luster may well return to psychopolitical studies of individual leaders (such as Gorbachev, Havel, and Saddam Hussein); after all, it would seem perverse in the light of recent events to discount the importance of the "individual in history."

But having failed to forecast weighty political events, it is unlikely that we will have more success in forecasting the future shape of the discipline designed to study them. Still, we may be forgiven our impatient curiosity. Many of these incipient ideas and approaches are, after all, in motion already, within arm's length, vaguely familiar, perhaps even easily accessible. Nor is it impossible that their future developers, articulators, and champions are counted among those who read these very lines.

INDEX